The Unstable Ground:
Corporate Social Policy
in a Dynamic Society

The Unstable Ground: Corporate Social Policy in a Dynamic Society

S. PRAKASH SETHI, Editor

Symposium sponsored by the National Affiliation
of Concerned Business Students (NACBS)
and
Schools of Business Administration,
University of California, Berkeley

 Melville Publishing Company
Los Angeles

Copyright © 1974, by John Wiley & Sons, Inc.

Published by **Melville Publishing Company,**
a Division of John Wiley & Sons, Inc.

Library of Congress Cataloging in Publication Data:
Main entry under title:

The Unstable ground.

  (Melville series on management, accounting, and
information systems)
  "Symposium sponsored by the National Affiliation of
Concerned Business Students (NACBS) and Schools of Business Administration, University of California, Berkeley"
and held Nov. 1972.
    1. Industry—Social aspects—United States—Con-
resses. 2. Corporations—United States—Congresses.
3. Industry and state—United States—Congresses.
4. Consumer Protection—United States—Congresses.
I. Sethi, S. Prakash, ed. II. National Affiliation
of Concerned Business Students. III. California.
Univeristy. Schools of Business Administration.
IV. California. University. Graduate School of
Business Administration.

HD60.5.U5U57   301.5'1   73-18300
ISBN 0–471–77685–8

Printed in the United States of America

10 9 8 7 6 5 4 3 2 1

And the Lord said, "Behold, they are one people, and they have all one language; and this is only the beginning of what they will do; and nothing that they propose to do will now be impossible for them. Come, let us go down, and there confuse their language, that they may not understand one another's speech." ... Therefore its name was called Babel, because there the Lord confused the language of all the earth. ...

—Genesis 11:6–9

Foreword

●●

Several years ago a West Coast business leader and I were discussing the problems facing our society and the responsibility that business has for helping to solve them. He told me that far too many businessmen "don't even know it's raining." Since then I have had occasion to talk with a number of corporate executives from different parts of the country about what has come to be called "corporate responsibility." My perception is that more and more business leaders are beginning seriously to consider the new pressures and manifest problems which are analyzed in this volume.

The essays gathered here and the symposium that produced them are signs of a growing awareness of the need for a new corporate social policy. In a unique blend of theoretical ideas and practical applications, many critical issues and groups are discussed—environment, ecology, consumerism, discrimination, the minority groups, the church, the activists and public interest law firms, the problem of measuring corporate performance, the nature and direction of organizational changes. The contributors represent a cross section of leading academicians, prominent businessmen, and articulate spokesmen of various interest groups. Hopefully, some of their ideas will suggest concrete action and lead to effective corporate reform.

Put quite simply, the difficult question inherent in the challenge of corporate responsibility is: How far should business go in helping to resolve the problems of our society? Once that question is answered the dialogue can center—as many of the essays in this book do—upon the methodology of corporate reform.

In my own book, *The Second American Revolution*, I suggested that there are, broadly speaking, two answers to the question of "how far." The first and more limited answer is that corporations should do only that for which they are clearly and directly responsible and for which they feel competent.

For example, business should take all reasonable steps in internal management to make working conditions congruent with human needs. The development of the human potential of employees should be stressed. In relating to consumers, business should make sure that all its products are safe, nonpolluting, and fairly advertised. And every business should live up to the spirit—not just the letter—of government regulations and laws in such areas as fair employment and environmental protection.

If every company lived up to these standards, our situation would be vastly improved. And yet it is a minimal view of corporate responsibility for it rests on the beliefs of many businessmen that they are not competent to deal with many of our vexing social problems.

But the hard reality is that no one sector of our society is competent to deal with these problems—not business, not government, not labor, not the nonprofit organizations. The only answer is that all sectors must become involved, each in its own distinctive way, but in full and collaborative relationship with the others.

Involvement of this nature is the second level of corporate responsibility —full and dedicated participation with others in seeking answers to our problems and an improved quality of life for all our citizens.

I certainly am not suggesting that businessmen can neglect business by going overboard in a new zeal for working on social issues. But I do not believe there is any real danger of this. Businessmen are not likely to forget their basic obligation to maintain healthy and viable companies. Moreover, I suspect that a company which is competent in the business field can also be competent in the social field, if only the understanding and commitment to become involved exist.

In my book I suggest several of the ways that the higher level of corporate responsibility can be manifested. Still other ways are discussed in some of the essays in this volume. But in the first instance, concrete action depends on a basic will and spirit on the part of businessmen, the determination to look beyond the daily and pressing demands of business to the broader issues which must concern us all.

As difficult as this new stance will be, I do not believe there is any real alternative for business leaders. For, as the editor of this volume says in his introductory chapter, "It is a fallacy that business can prosper—or, indeed, even exist—without regard to broader social concerns."

Our society now has an urgent need for the creativity and organizational skill that have been the hallmarks of American business in the past. American managerial genius must adjust rapidly to the new values emerging in our society. Our problems have become so difficult and the currents of change so sweeping that business leaders cannot afford to hesitate or falter in the face of the challenge.

Certainly we cannot look to business for all the answers to our social problems, as we looked to government in the past decade. This would be a mistake. Nor do I mean to suggest that a more enlightened view of corporate responsibility would by itself produce a new age of national prosperity and pride. But significant changes have small beginnings. And now is a time for beginnings.

I have come to believe in recent years that we are in the midst of a revolution in our society second in importance only to the first American Revolution two hundred years ago. It is a humanistic revolution, a gradual revolution, and it is the dynamics of this revolution that demands a new social awareness on the part of all of us, including American business.

In 1976 the nation will observe the two hundredth anniversary of the signing of the Declaration of Independence. Then in 1989 we will commemorate the launching of the Republic. I think of this 13-year period as a Bicentennial Era, a 13-year span in which the nation has an unparalleled opportunity to reaffirm its faith in traditional values and, at the same time, accept the challenge of the future. The Bicentennial Era is a time for all elements of our society—including most certainly the business community—to become actively involved in overcoming our social problems, setting goals for the future and working together to accomplish them.

Recently I had a very interesting conversation with the chairman of one of the largest industrial corporations in the United States. We were discussing corporate responsibility, and the subject of the Bicentennial came up. "If we don't take advantage of this opportunity to become involved," he said, "we'll never have a better one."

John D. Rockefeller, 3rd

Preface

●●●

It is perhaps rhetorical to say that the sixties have been the most turbulent years in the history of American society. Each generation tends to exaggerate its own experience in relation to the experiences of earlier generations, and the present generation is no exception. While we must wait for history to render a verdict, it is almost certain that this period will be marked as one of the turning points in the evolution of American society, and the effects of changes initiated in this decade are likely to be felt for many more decades.

Some significant features of the sixties have been the disenchantment by almost every segment of society with one or more of its social institutions; the questioning by large numbers of the American people—especially youth —of the underlying premises of many of our economic, social, and political institutions; the unwillingness of socially disenfranchised groups to accept the status quo; and the ever-increasing gulf between the myth and the reality of socioeconomic and political justice. None of these pressures can be dismissed as just temporary aberrations in a dynamic society that is basically stable and that deals equitably with its members.

All the changes demanded are not equally necessary or desirable, nor are the groups demanding them always altruistic. Although we may indict established institutions for resisting legitimate demands for improvement and for being sluggish in the responses to social pressures, we must also condemn some of those most vociferous in demanding changes for using destructive and self-serving methods, and for pressing for goals impossible to attain.

Another trend of the sixties, which is only now beginning to assert itself, is the resurgence of the old American tradition of self-reliance—a willingness to make sacrifices and work for desired changes in the social system, rather than expect others, usually the government, to do it. Thus, we witness the creation of many groups of citizens who volunteer to spend their time, energies, and resources to correct a wrong or prevent an abuse. The groups and causes vary in size and longevity. They range from local groups formed to stop the use of nonreturnable bottles or to prevent housing developments on coastlines, to groups such as Common Cause and Nader's Raiders, whose activities have national purpose. These groups have a high mortality rate, since it is difficult to sustain momentum once a cause is temporarily won or the intensity of the issue has subsided. However, a significant number of these groups have survived their infancy and are likely to be around for a long time to pursue their activities with visible social impact.

One such group is the National Affiliation of Concerned Business Students (NACBS). Founded in 1971 by graduate business students from ten of the leading colleges and universities in the nation, it has since been incorporated as a nonprofit educational organization. The main objectives of NACBS are to promote research and discussion about the roles of the corporation and the individual businessman in society. NACBS believes that the survival of the corporation and the health of the whole society depend significantly on the responsiveness and the responsibility of American business. American business must find ways to mobilize its resources, along with other parts of society, to solve the problems of poverty, racism, environmental pollution, and injustice of all kinds.

Originally a student organization, NACBS has expanded its constituency to include business school faculties and businessmen. The organization's board of directors reflects this broadened constituency and is composed of two faculty members, Professors Ivar E. Berg, Jr. (Columbia University) and S. Prakash Sethi (University of California, Berkeley); two students, Messrs. Charles Byer (Wharton) and Michael Safdiah (New York University); and three young businessmen, Clair W. Sater (Syntex Corporation), Richard Steffens (Hewlett-Packard), and Carl Fields, Jr. (First National City Bank of New York). There is also an advisory board of 30 persons representing different kinds of business activities. NACBS is, above all, the outcome of the efforts of Kirk Hanson, its executive director, who nursed it through its formative period and, with the assistance of friends and well-wishers, made it into a viable organization whose activities command attention from its various constituencies and whose seriousness of purpose and independence in pursuing its objectives are recognized by both supporters and critics.

NACBS receives its operational funds from annual contributions from corporations, which do not exercise any control over its activities and programs. At present, the following 34 corporations sponsor NACBS:

Aetna Life and Casualty
American Can Co.
Arthur Andersen & Co.
Atlantic Richfield Co.
Bendix Corporation
Borden, Inc.
CNA Financial Corporation
CPC International, Inc.
Chase Manhattan Bank
Chrysler Corporation
Cummins Engine Co.
The Dow Chemical Co.
Equitable Life Assurance Society
    of the United States
Exxon Corporation
Ford Motor Co.
General Electric Co.
General Mills, Inc.
General Motors Corporation

John Hancock Mutual Life
    Insurance Co.
Honeywell, Inc.
Kaiser Affiliated Co.
3M Corporation
McGraw-Hill, Inc.
Mead Corporation
Montgomery Ward & Co.
Newsweek, Inc.
J. C. Penney Co.
PepsiCo, Inc.
Prudential Insurance Co.
    of America
Quaker Oats Co.
Sperry Rand Corporation
Standard Oil (California) Co.
Standard Oil (Indiana) Co.
Syntex, Inc.

NACBS has also received funds from various foundations and individuals to support special projects.

One of NACBS's most ambitious projects was to sponsor a symposium entitled "Corporate Social Policy in a Dynamic Society," held at the University of California, Berkeley, in November 1972. The symposium's objective was to bring together scholars, researchers, business leaders, government administrators, and students from representative business schools who were concerned with the role of business in solving pressing contemporary social problems. The program emphasized thoughtful and constructive reflection on problems and practical solutions, and tried to avoid inflammatory and discord-producing rhetoric. The extent to which we have succeeded in achieving this objective is for the reader to decide. This volume is the edited version of selected papers that were presented at the symposium.

Kirk Hanson and Karen Arenson, director and associate director, respectively, of the NACBS, assisted me in preparing the program for the symposium. The topics selected and the depth of their treatment reflect my own biases, and so I must take sole responsibility for any shortcomings in the coverage of subject areas.

I am grateful to the Schools of Business Administration, University of California, Berkeley, which cosponsored the symposium and generously furnished faculty time and personnel for logistical support.

The Rockefeller Foundation provided funds to cover a substantial portion of the cost of the symposium. A grant from Ford Foundation made possible the attendance of some of the student representatives and faculty at the symposium. Their contributions are gratefully acknowledged.

I am thankful to a great many people for helping with the conference. Too numerous to mention by name are the many hardworking and helpful program chairmen and panel discussants. I would also like to acknowledge the efforts of the Committee for Corporate Social Responsibility (CCR) at the Stanford Business School, and Charles Plosser, Alan Oberrotman, Hamid Etemad, Mrs. Ann Kauth, Deborah Nichols, and Cornell Cooper.

A number of people contributed their time and energies in the preparation of the manuscript. For some, it was a labor of love. For typing, my thanks are due to Mrs. Wendy Quinones, Mrs. Ellen McGibbon, Mrs. Betty Kendall, Mrs. Helen Way, Mrs. Virginia Douglas, and for copyediting, to Mrs. Nancy Blumenstock. Except for Mrs. Quinones, they are on the staff of the Institute of Business and Economic Research, University of California, Berkeley. Both the Institute and its director, Professor Joseph W. Garbarino, have my gratitude for their assistance.

Berkeley, California   *S. Prakash Sethi*

Contents

●●●

INTRODUCTION
Corporate Social Policy in a Dynamic Society: The Options Available to Business

●●●

● S. PRAKASH SETHI

Schools of Business Administration
University of California, Berkeley

An institution's role in a dynamic society must constantly evolve in order for the institution to adapt itself to the changing needs and expectations of the society. Business, being a social institution, is no exception. The social concern about the impact of business—and its dominant institution, the corporation—on various segments of society is not new. But the intensity of recent debate about its proper role and the magnitude of the changes called for are certainly unprecedented. While extremist rhetoric has often drowned the voice of reason, there exists a genuine and widespread concern about the need for basic reforms. The question being raised is not how the corporation can be made more socially responsible, but what the role of the corporation should be in a society.

It is a fallacy that business can prosper—or, indeed, even exist—without regard to broader social concerns. Nor will the dominant social concerns always be economic ones. The separation of economic enterprise from the larger social and political purposes of natural life is impossible when there is no space for separation. In the narrowness of the experiential space, the

1

very act of survival calls for interaction and interdependence leading to cross-pollination of value systems.

The twentieth-century corporation has replaced the church as the dominant social institution in the lives of citizens of the industrialized nations. Like the white man's religions of a bygone era, the white man's economic institutions cast a long shadow on the rest of the world. The trend toward bigger and more powerful concentration of economic resources in fewer institutions is likely to persist in the foreseeable future. The new situation is here to stay. However, the forms of these economic instruments and the degrees of external control exercised upon them will depend to a large extent on the willingness and ability of today's corporations to adapt to tomorrow's social needs. The corporation will have increasingly greater influence on the people's lives. But, regardless of its dominance, it is living on borrowed time if it does not relate to changing social needs and expectations and instead insists on imposing upon society a value system and *raison d'etre* that is largely irrelevant.

Until now, the American corporation has not had to experience reformation. It is used to waves of high praise and condemnation, but reformation in its self-understanding has not occurred. Free enterprise, to most people, has been what business wanted it to be. Its character and interpretation, therefore, have changed from time to time only when it suited the needs and exigencies of business rather than the needs of the times and the people Thus, while federal subsidies for Lockheed and Penn Central, oil depletion allowances, and import quotas are justified as bolstering the free enterprise system in a changed economy (and are therefore good), the fixing of minimum standards of pollution control, safeguards for consumers from shoddy products and deceptive advertising, and the forcing of large corporations to disclose to the public more information about their affairs are condemned as hampering free enterprise (and are therefore bad).

This one-sided definition of free enterprise is not acceptable, however, to a large portion of society. With the ever-increasing interdependence between business and society and the all-pervasive nature of large corporations, business must become the business of the many if it is to be a socially viable institution and retain its current form and substance.

The social dominance of corporations has not been without a price. In a dynamic and changing society, the dominant institution invariably receives all the blame and criticism for whatever is wrong in that society, while the credit for what is right in that society will either be ignored or given only grudgingly. Such is clearly the case with business corporations today.

As Schumpeter recently pointed out, the rise of the intellectual elite and its freedom to question and criticize the system can only survive in an environment that is nurtured by a system in which individual freedom reigns supreme. Similarly, today's American youth grow up with the stereotype of an unexciting and callously selfish corporation, and are often unaware of, and unwilling to hear about the many positive contributions that business makes.

An institution that is near enough to the larger community to have a measure of its confidence and that is far enough away to have something novel to say is in a better position to present its viewpoint effectively to society. Conversely, businessmen may be listened to primarily for their cleverness and dexterity in reasserting the platitudes that hold the culture together. But as far as their having something important to say is concerned, expectations are low. This cozy and taken-for-granted relationship to culture helps to explain a general lack of imagination in business pronouncements.

What are the alternatives open to business? It seems to me we can pursue one of three courses of action. The first approach is to ignore the existence of the problem altogether, assuming that it will eventually take care of itself. Call it business *of the few*.

The second approach involves taking action to restore to business its former privileges and prerogatives. It is an aggressive approach to win back the ground it once occupied. Call it business *for the few*.

The third approach seeks a redefinition of the role of business and an accommodation with other groups and institutions in society. Call it business *of the many* and business *for the many*.

Those who maintain that survival can be insured merely by ignoring the problem of postponing the issue are not likely to have many followers, and their position is quickly dismissed by the larger community. The counterattacking position that seeks to hold onto previously occupied ground represents some danger and must be taken seriously. The arguments of this group have the comfort of familiarity, and they appeal to superficial logic. They provide a safe haven for those who would stand to lose in the new order of things. They offer a criterion and rationale within which failure can be explained away and defeat can be justified. Their position is not much different from that of a marketing manager who would willingly accept a loss of $10 million in sales because of alleged competitive conditions in the market, but who would hesitate to spend $50,000 on marketing research because of a tight budget.

There is yet another reason why this position must be taken seriously. The insecurities induced by change often produce erratic action. Although doomed, the unpredictability of such an erratic action may cause serious damage to the social fabric. The solution lies in taking into account the human mind's natural fear of change and in making the change process smooth and gradual so that it does not bring about an overall collapse of the total system.

Broadening the base of business—both in responsibility and accountability—calls for a recognition of the existence of a community of interests in a society. It calls for a federalism of interests, in which all social elements are asked to converse and cooperate—not negotiate and concede—with others. It permits the development and growth of different viewpoints, aimed at achieving a common goal—a better society for all. Critics of this approach might rightly point out that it means killing off some of the vitalities that proved useful for this nation's young and growing economy. However, not to do so would be to sanctify the means and abandon the goals. There is still no disputing the nation's philosophical goals. Perhaps what is needed is a different kind of fervor, a different kind of passion, and a different kind of process to achieve these goals.

I am clearly not in favor of revolutionary change agents, revolutionary change methods, or even revolutionary changes. History is replete with examples of revolutions that failed—not because the cause was unjustified, but because the revolutionaries had no workable alternative to offer.

Today's radical cries for the destruction of the system, while the reactionary cries for a reversal to the pure, free-enterprise system. Yet neither is willing to pay the price for a reversal of the trend. As Robert Shnayerson, Editor-in-Chief of *Harper's*, once said: "Man depends on institutions . . . it is one thing to lambaste temporary leaders and policies; it is another to uproot society's vital structures. Sick institutions need help, not revolution, which, although popular, leads only to chaos and tyranny."

Should the views of the forward-looking businessman prevail in broadening the base of corporate power and accountability, a new environment will be created where ideas and actions will be freely exchanged. There would then be less hiding behind the legal prerogatives of large corporations and less concern for self-advertisement and protecting the good name of business. Above all, business as an institution will be scaled down to a humanistic level and will provide the necessary relief to both the businessman and his opponents, as well as operating room within which to maneuver and make mistakes in the spirit of give and take.

PART I

Differing Perspectives on the Social Involvement of Business

●●

When our rewards go to people for thinking alike, it is no surprise that we become frightened at those who take exception to the current consensus.
—William O. Douglas, Justice,
United States Supreme Court*

The positive connotation associated with the term "social responsibility" of business has led to its being coopted by groups of such different leanings and outlooks that it has come to mean all things to all people.[1] Language so debased becomes meaningless and simply breeds contempt. It confuses instead of enlightens; it obfuscates instead of clarifies; and it provides escape from fulfilling obligations instead of calling for an accounting.

As a social institution, business is a part of the society and, therefore, has always been involved in society's activities and problems either through its actions or inactions. The controversy is over the nature of the activities that business could and should legitimately be involved with. Authors such as Milton Friedman and Henry Manne have consistently

---

*All the epigraphs used in the Part opening texts of the book have been taken from *Life Before Death in the Corporate State* by Nicholas Johnson, published by the Committee on the Barbara Weinstock Lectures, University of California, Berkeley, 1971.

[1] For a discussion of the uses and abuses of the term, see Dow Votaw, "Genius Becomes Rare," in *The Corporate Dilemma: Traditional Values versus Contemporary Problems*, by Dow Votaw and S. Prakash Sethi (Englewood Cliffs, N.J.: Prentice-Hall, 1973), pp. 11–45.

6

maintained that the social responsibility of business **is** business and that business can best perform its social role by doing what it knows best— produce and distribute goods, desired by society as determined in the marketplace, in the most efficient manner and for the profit of its owners.[2] However, in its extreme form, it is rare to find many adherents of this view, even among businessmen. The reasons for the lack of followers for this idea are many and varied and are rooted in the changes that have occurred in the last few decades in the economic system and industrial structure, the emergence of large corporations, the deterioration of the physical environment and, above all, the changes in society's expectations. The last change, especially, has led to a fundamental reexamination of the proper roles of various social institutions, including business institutions.[3]

Business in general and large corporations in particular were aware of the changing social expectations. To some extent business has always contributed to social causes to improve the quality of life and its own operational environment. However, during the 1960's, the urban crisis, the violence, the social unrest, the problems of minority groups, and the alienation of youth lent a new urgency to the need for doing something different as well as something more. Business reacted to these challenges partly out of a sincere desire to participate in the solution of social problems and partly as a defensive gesture to forestall more government regulation and more demands from various "extremist" groups. Business leaders and large corporations formed organizations such as the Alliance for Businessmen, New Detroit Committee, Rochester Jobs, Inc., to involve business in social issues. Before too long everybody joined the bandwagon.

Unfortunately, the euphoria did not last long. There was a large gap between the rhetoric and reality of corporate social responsibility. A great deal of so-called corporate activities turned out to be no more than public relations puffery. Moreover, the publicly perceived socially responsive activities were overshadowed by the sheer magnitude of certain corporate activities that were considered by large segments of the public to be socially irresponsible manifestations of corporate arrogance and disregard for society's needs and concerns. Notable among these were GM's investigation of Ralph Nader, Dow Chemical's manufacture of

[2]Milton Friedman, *Capitalism and Freedom* (Chicago: University of Chicago Press, 1962); Henry G. Manne and Henry C. Wallich, *The Modern Corporation and Social Responsibility* (Washington, D.C.: American Enterprise Institute for Public Policy Research, 1972).

[3]Votaw and Sethi, *The Corporate Dilemma.*

napalm, Eastman Kodak's confrontation with a local black group and the church on the hiring of blacks, and IT&T's pressuring of newsmen in its abortive attempt to acquire the American Broadcasting Company.[4]

However, the most important reason, I believe, has been that the problems have not responded to businessmen's ministrations and have not yielded to "quickie" solutions. The problems are too complex; solutions will be slow and gradual in coming. By and large, businessmen have been either unwilling or unable to devote the time and resources required to effect such solutions. The promise was too big while the performance was too small, with the result that even the affected groups were not prepared for the slowness of change, thus leading to disappointment, further aggravation, and pressure on the government through political processes to effect changes in corporate behavior.

The result has been a change in emphasis and direction by all parties concerned. There is some disillusionment among the businessmen. The aura of Don Quixote has gone from the activities of business in social involvement. Thoughtful businessmen have refrained from making wild claims about their capacity for action and self-laudatory statements about their activities. Furthermore, a large part of what was termed "social injustice" and its correction therefore fell within the realm of socially responsive activities has since been institutionalized either through government statutes or by business as a norm for their operations.

However, the pressure on business to modify its behavior has not diminished but has intensified over a wider area of activity. More and more business actions are coming under scrutiny by public agencies, private groups, and even by businessmen themselves. The magnitude of business-society conflicts remains unaltered, and there is a continuous need for all concerned—businessmen, public officials, private groups, and educators—to study and analyze the situation with a view toward seeking effective and harmonious ways of solving these conflicts and harnessing the energies of business in attacking the problems that beset our society.

Dow Votaw's article from an educator's viewpoint is organized around the idea that "the ultimate goal is corporate social reform, but the immediate goal is the reform of higher education." Votaw addresses himself to the latter, with specific attention to the role of business schools in providing basic, innovative education for manager trainees as well as continuing education for managers.

---

[4]S. Prakash Sethi, *Up Against the Corporate Wall: Modern Corporations and Social Issues of the Seventies*, 2d ed. (Englewood Cliffs, N.J.: Prentice-Hall, 1974).

To the criticisms of business school education made by Professor Dean Berry of the European Institute of Business Administration at Fontainebleau in 1972, Votaw makes the following points:

(1) On the issue of teaching versus experience, Votaw makes recommendations based on the notion that higher education should serve as a means of communication between society and the corporation.

(2) Berry sees management education as undermined by the lure of academic respectability; Votaw counters that there should be increased academic involvement combined with more prominent social responsibility leadership by business school faculties.

(3) Lastly, Votaw advocates that business schools "relate the challenging issues of society to business" as a corrective for the diminished repute of business in America (which Berry cited).

T. F. Bradshaw, writing from the viewpoint of an executive, begins and ends his article with reference to what he calls "the Friedman doctrine of corporate responsibility," which is "to make a profit." Bradshaw states his personal conviction that the Friedman doctrine does not adequately meet legitimate social concerns. He couples this view with examples of the many difficulties encountered by the corporations that have taken reform initiative.

The crux of the issue, for Bradshaw, is that corporations and the people who manage them are held accountable by rules that are primarily, although not exclusively, fiscal in nature: return on investment, earnings per share, and growth. He recommends that the basic thrust of efforts by informed businessmen should be to change the rules, **i.e.,** the evaluative standards and policies by which corporations operate. New evaluative standards should account specifically for social costs, such as pollution control, and experienced businessmen should use their special competencies to promote changes in the rules.

Mary Gardiner Jones uses a detailed case history of flammable cellular foam products to show the gaps in institutional responsibility for the development and enforcement of product safety standards. Hers is the regulator's view, and she argues that the "initial, primary" responsibility lies with industry because industry is the sole possessor of full information at the product development stage. Industry has the most direct access to the distribution channels that are a means of disseminating information about proper uses. And only the manufacturers can assess the adequacy of existing standards for new products.

The most basic problem is to develop mechanisms of accountability within both industry and government, Jones asserts. She suggests that industry responsibility for premarket testing of product safety be lodged with a single individual who can be held directly accountable. As a means of compelling government to take an active role in meeting statutory responsibilities, Jones urges that specific governmental agencies be cited in all relevant statutes.

In his discussion of the role of corporations from an activist's viewpoint, Philip W. Moore offers definitions of "corporate responsibility" and "corporate activism" that lead to consideration of the components, such as shareholders and consumers, that legitimize the corporation's functions as an economic and social institution. He reviews the ways in which each of these components can bring its interests to bear and concludes that the existing procedures for this are inadequate. What is needed, he says, is a new constitution of corporate government, one that defines the internal process and the external environment within which corporations must work.

Moore suggests that we develop new systems by which corporations are held directly accountable to the groups affected by corporate decisions. He specifically advocates shifting accountability away from management and from government, on the grounds that the various components must share in decision making if they are to have a "real role in the overall corporate function."

Jerrold M. Grochow points out that the 20–30 age group encompasses the special interest groups of shareholders, managers, and consumers. The distinctive feature of the younger age group is that it shares high levels of expectation about corporate honesty and the rights of shareholders as owners to participate in establishing corporate policies.

Grochow considers the nature of corporate social reform, with its particular relevance for young managers, and states that new, broader definitions of efficiency are required to assess corporate impact on human and environmental concerns. Profits no longer suffice as a gauge of the differential effects of corporate social reform. New processes are needed for the complex balancing of interests, and it is here that young managers, utilizing analytical and research tools, have a role.

SELECTED BIBLIOGRAPHY

The reader who is interested in pursuing further study and research on the topics included in this section may find these references useful. References marked with an asterisk (*) are especially recommended for an overall view and for authoritative viewpoints on different perspectives of the issues covered.

*Adam, John, Jr. "Put Profit in Its Place." *Harvard Business Review*, March-April 1973, pp. 150–160.

*Andrews, Kenneth R. "Can the Best Corporations Be Made Moral?" *Harvard Business Review*, May-June 1973, pp. 57–64.

Aron, Raymond. "Student Rebellion: Vision of the Future or Echo from the Past?" *Poltical Science Quarterly* 84, no. 2 (June 1969): 289–310.

*Athos, A. "Is the Corporation Next to Fall?" *Harvard Business Review*, January-February 1970, pp. 49–61.

*Avner, C. "Evolution of the Corporation as a Social Institution." *Commercial Law Journal* 75, no. 8 (August 1970): 241–247.

Barnett, Rosalind C., and Tagiuri, Renato. "What Young People Think About Managers." *Harvard Business Review*, May-June 1973, pp. 106–118.

Bartimole, Roldo. "Keeping the Lid On: Corporate Responsibility in Cleveland." *Business and Society Review/Innovation*, Spring 1973, pp. 96–103.

Bell, Daniel. "The Corporation and Society in the 1970's." *The Public Interest*, Summer 1971, pp. 5–32.

*_____. *The Coming of Post-Industrial Society*. New York: Basic Books, 1973.

*Blumberg, Phillip I. "Corporate Responsibility and the Social Crisis." *Boston University Law Review* 50, no. 2 (Spring 1970): 157–210.

*_____. "The Politicalization of the Corporation." *The Business Lawyer*, July 1971, pp. 1551–1587.

Bowen, Howard. *Social Responsibilities of the Businessman*. New York: Harper & Row, 1963.

Bradley, Gene E. "What Businessmen Need to Know About the Student Left." *Harvard Business Review*, September-October 1968, pp. 49–60.

Brady, Robert A. *Business as a System of Power*. New York: Columbia University Press, 1951.

Brayman, Harold. *Corporate Management in a World of Politics*. New York: McGraw-Hill Book Co., 1967.

*Burck, Gilbert. "The Hazards of Corporate Responsibility." *Fortune*, June 1973, p. 114.

Carr, Albert Z. "Is Business Bluffing Ethical?" *Harvard Business Review*, January-February 1968, pp. 143–153.

_____. "Can an Executive Afford a Conscience?" *Harvard Business Review*, July-August 1970, pp. 58–64.

*Cheit, Earl F., ed. *The Business Establishment*. New York: John Wiley & Sons, 1964.

*Committee for Economic Development. *Social Responsibilities of Business Corporations*. New York: Committee for Economic Development, June 1971.

Coppock, R.; Dierkes, M.; Snowball, H.; Thomas, J. "Social Pressure and Business Actions." Paper presented to the Seminar on Corporate Social Accounts, Battelle Seattle Research Center, November 10–11, 1972.

Council on Economic Priorities. "Minding the Corporate Conscience: The 1972 Movement for Corporate Responsibility." *Economic Priorities Report*, March-April 1972.

_____. "Minding the Corporate Conscience 1973." *Economic Priorities Report*, January-February-March 1973.

Dahl, R. "Alternative Ways of Controlling Corporate Power." Address given at the Nader Conference on Corporate Accountability, Washington, D.C., Fall 1971.

Director, Steven, and Doctors, Samuel. "Do Business School Students Really Care About Social Responsibility?" *Business And Society Review/Innovation,* Spring 1973, pp. 91–95.

Domhoff, G. William. *Who Rules America?* Englewood Cliffs, N.J.: Prentice-Hall, 1967.

Drucker, Peter. "The Concept of the Corporation." *Business and Society Review/Innovation,* Fall 1972, pp. 12–17.

Epstein, Edwin M. *The Corporation in American Politics.* Englewood Cliffs, N.J.: Prentice-Hall, 1969.

Finn, David. *The Corporate Oligarch.* New York: Simon & Schuster, 1969.

*Friedman, Milton. *Capitalism and Freedom.* Chicago: University of Chicago Press, 1962.

Friedmann, Wolfgang G. "Corporate Power, Government by Private Groups, and the Law." *Columbia Law Review,* 1957, pp. 155–186.

*Green, Mark J.; Moore, Beverley C., Jr.; and Wasserstein, Bruce. *The Closed Enterprise System.* New York: Grossman, 1972.

Green, Mark J. *See also* Nader, Ralph.

Grether, E. T. "Business Responsibility Toward the Market." *California Management Review,* Fall 1969, pp. 33–42.

Hazard, Leland. "Business Must Put Up." *Harvard Business Review,* January-February 1968, pp. 2–13.

Hobbing, Enno. "Business Must Explain Itself." *Business and Society Review/Innovation,* Fall 1972, pp. 85–86.

Hook, Sydney, ed. *Human Values and Economic Policy.* New York: New York University Press, 1967.

*Jacoby, Neil H. *Corporate Power and Responsibility.* New York: Macmillan Co., 1973.

Jessup, John K., and Kristol, Irving. "On 'Capitalism' and the 'Free Society'." *The Public Interest,* Winter 1971, pp. 101–105.

Leavitt, Harold. "The Corporation President Is a Berkeley Student." *Harvard Business Review,* November-December 1967, pp. 152–157.

*Lundborg, Louis B. Testimony as Chairman of the Board, Bank of America NT&SA before the Senate Committee on Foreign Relations, Washington, D.C., April 15, 1970. San Francisco; Bank of America.

Magnuson, W. F., and Carper, J. *The Dark Side of the Marketplace.* Englewood Cliffs, N.J.: Prentice-Hall, 1968.

Manne, Henry G. "The Myth of Corporate Responsibility—Or Will the Real Ralph Nader Please Stand Up?" *The Business Lawyer* 26 (1970): 533–539.

*Manne, Henry G., and Wallich, Henry C. *The Modern Corporation and Social Responsibility.* Washington, D.C.: American Enterprise Institute for Public Policy Research, 1972.

Mason, Edward, ed. *The Corporation in Modern Society.* Cambridge: Harvard University Press, 1959.

Mayer, Lawrance A. "A Large Question About Large Corporations." *Fortune,* May 1972, p. 185.

McCall, David B. "Profit: Spur for Solving Social Ills." *Harvard Business Review,* May-June 1973, pp. 46–56.

Miller, Arthur S. "Corporate Gigantism and 'Technological Imperatives'." *Journal of Public Law* 18 (1969): 256–310.

Mintz, Morton, and Cohen, Jerry S. *America, Inc.* New York: Dial Press, 1971.

Monsen, R. Joseph. "The Unrecognized Social Revolution: The Rise of the New Business Elite in America." *California Management Review* 14, no. 2 (Winter 1971): 13–17.

Moss, Frank E. *Initiatives in Corporate Responsibility.* Washington, D.C.: Government Printing Office, 1973.

*Nader, Ralph, and Green, Mark J., eds. *Corporate Power in America.* New York: Grossman, 1973.

Reuschling, Thomas L. "The Business Institution—A Redefinition of Social Role." *Business and Society Review/Innovation*, Fall 1968, pp. 28–32.

*Rockefeller, John D. III. *The Second American Revolutions Some Personal Observations.* New York: Harper & Row, 1973.

Rockefeller, Rodman C. "Turn Public Problems to Private Account." *Harvard Business Review*, January-February 1971, pp. 131–138.

*Schelling, Thomas C. "On the Ecology of Micromotives." *The Public Interest*, Fall 1971, pp. 59–98.

*Schwartz, Donald E. "Towards New Corporate Goals: Co-Existence With Society." *The Georgetown Law Journal*, October 1971, pp. 57–109.

*Sethi, S. Prakash. *Business Corporations and the Black Man: An Analysis of Social Conflict, the Kodak-Fight Controversy.* Scranton, Pa.: Chandler Publishing Co., 1970.

*_____. *Up Against the Corporate Wall: Modern Corporations and Social Issues of the Seventies.* Englewood Cliffs, N.J.: 2d ed. Prentice-Hall, 1974.

_____. *See also* Votaw, Dow.

Spencer, Hollister. "The Dangers of Social Responsibility—Another Perspective." *The Conference Board Record*, November 1972, pp. 54–57.

*Votaw, Dow, and Sethi, S. Prakash. *The Corporate Dilemma: Traditional Values versus Contemporary Problems.* Englewood Cliffs, N.J.: Prentice-Hall, 1973.

Walton, Clarence C., ed. *Business and Social Progress.* New York: Praeger, 1970.

*Ways, Max. "Business Needs To Do a Better Job of Explaining." *Fortune*, September 1972, p. 85.

White House Conference on the Industrial World Ahead. *A Look at Business in 1990.* Washington, D.C.: Government Printing Office, 1972.

Corporate Social Reform: An Educator's Viewpoint

●●

● DOW VOTAW

Schools of Business Administration
University of California, Berkeley

More than 20 years of viewing the issue of corporate social reform are not easily condensed into a short paper. A vast array of possible topics and questions must be reduced to a manageable few, and even the avenues of approach to the subject must be ruthlessly winnowed. One's temptation to wax philosophical or abstract, anecdotal or prophetic, critical, or eulogistic, must be kept under control. However, one must try to extract from the chaff a single, dominant theme: a preoccupation with specific recommendations for action. Such a preoccupation is long overdue. Ignored in most discussions of corporate social responsibility and conspicuously absent in academic sermonizing about the subject are any particulars even remotely associated with actual conduct. This state of affairs should not come as a surprise. Specific recommendations are not as easy to produce as moralistic pronouncements and, furthermore, require one to take a stand and even to stick one's neck out.

Most of the problems associated with prescription can be minimized or even eliminated by simply writing an Rx for aspirin and bed rest, but, for several reasons, I do not want to take that easy way out. In the first place, it has been done many times before, without any measurable contribution to knowledge. More important, my attempt to use that old escape under present circumstances might lead to a serious misunderstanding, because I intend to prescribe, not for corporations, but for collegiate schools of management and business administration. The ultimate goal is corporate social reform, but the immediate goal is the reform of higher education. I do not find it comfortable to begin with specific recommendations for action. Before prescription, one needs diagnosis; before diagnosis, a case history, together with symptoms and laboratory tests.

The issue of corporate social reform has many facets. My primary concern is with the need to improve the ability of the corporation to respond to social change and to new social challenges and expectations, or, to put it somewhat differently, to improve the ability of the corporation to perform the broader role being thrust upon it by society. This perception of the issue helps considerably to narrow the field, but not enough. I would like to concentrate my attention on the mechanisms through which the corporation gets its signals from society, the means by which social change, challenge, and expectation are communicated to the corporation. There has been a lot of discussion in recent years about one aspect of this issue, namely, the need to improve corporate sensitivity to changes in society. My emphasis, while encompassing this aspect, is more concerned with improving a specific means of communication as a step toward improved sensitivity.

Communication Mechanisms Between Corporations and Society

Before identifying the subject means of communication, let us review briefly and generally the existing mechanisms by which intelligence moves from society to the decision centers of the corporation. Economic information is conveyed by means of the market system. Although not without defects, it is fast, efficient, and accurate, as far as the transmission of economic information is concerned, but can be misleading and dangerous if relied on to convey other than that which is strictly economic. We have learned at great cost in recent years that the market often conveys precisely the worst kind of information concerning the corporation's social, political, and ecological environment. It has been a hard lesson to learn, but we finally seem to be learning it: the market is a narrow, one-dimensional information system, and economics is too narrow a base from which to approach most of society's problems.

There are other mechanisms through which social, political, and ecological, as well as economic, information can be transmitted. Theoretically, at least, the shareholders' meeting is a means of communication between society and the corporation and a means by which other than economic information can be conveyed. But a half century of controversy has only convinced us that the shareholders' meeting has, in most instances, been a very ineffective source of information to the corporation and means of communication for society. Rarely heard and little heeded, the shareholder's voice, even on the infrequent occasions when there was only one voice, has not played a major role.

An important and heavily relied upon mechanism that conveys information from all across the social spectrum is the force of law. Many corporate spokesmen view this as the only means by which noneconomic information can be conveyed and the only way in which the doctrine of social responsibility can be given substance. The defect in this view is made all too apparent when the managers who espouse it then oppose, with every means at their command, any attempts by society to employ it. The force of law, as a method of conveying social information to the corporation, will always be important, but, by itself, is insufficient. Furthermore, it is often very slow, frequently overreactive, and is always subject to deviant and unrepresentative pressures.

Disruption has long been in use as a way of transmitting messages from society to the corporation. Strikes, boycotts, sit-ins, violence, and demonstrations, although once used largely in an economic context, have recently been used to convey other kinds of social information, sometimes with considerable impact. However, it must be said that information transmitted in this fashion is usually distorted, blurred by static and emotion, and just plain inaccurate. A highly structured, technologically interdependent society such as ours cannot afford to rely to any great extent on disruption as a means of communication.

Much has been written in the past decade or so about new machinery by which the world outside the corporation may be heard inside. Some developments are already taking place. Despite the confusion and uncertainty surrounding the roles of the new kinds of outside directors on many boards and the prevailing view that most of these steps are window dressing, they may still be the forerunners of new information machinery. Neither these new structures nor the improvement of old mechanisms are likely to make very much difference, however, unless another, and so far unmentioned, means of communication begins to operate more effectively. *In the long run, the only way in which genuine corporate social reform can occur is for the thinking of managers to be changed.* Some of society's messages are being transmitted on a new wave length, which many managers are not tuned to receive. Obviously, formal education is not the only means by which the thinking of managers can be changed, but it is one of the most important instrumentalities for bringing about that end. It is usually slow in taking effect, but can, I think, be made a lot faster. This, then, is the starting point for an educator's view of corporate social reform.

At this point, let me shift from my earlier medical metaphor to a biblical metaphor and take as my text the Apocalypse and the Revelations, not of Saint John, but of Professor Dean Berry, head of INSEAD, the European Institute of Business Administration at Fontainebleau, according to *The Economist* of August 12, 1972. Under a headline "Business Schools—Goodbye, America," the following appears:

> Most European business schools set up in the 1960's were a direct attempt to imitate the Americans. The argument was that American business was successful because it had good managers, and it had good managers because it had business schools. In a set of papers just published by the Organization for Economic Cooperation and Development, Professor Dean Berry . . . makes another slashing attack on this fading philosophy. He argues that management education in elite American schools is dying, and that European schools could be heading for the graveyard within five years, if they are not careful. Europe, he says, has drawn all the wrong lessons from the early success of the schools like Harvard. Business schools do not produce businessmen; they can only teach the language and style of business, and cannot substitute for experience. . . . American management education is dying because it is being sucked into academic respectability. This is because the American dream is fading, and youth no longer holds business in such respect.

I believe that the above statment is wrong on several accounts, but especially in the casual allegations and in the premises underlying its conclusions. Let us take a look at some of its propositions.

> Business schools do not produce businessmen; they can only teach the language and style of business, and cannot substitute for experience.

It is not entirely clear what is being said. If we should substitute "law" for "business" in these statements, we would come up with: Law schools do not produce lawyers; they can only teach the language and style of law, and cannot substitute for experience. This seems on one level to be a kind of truism and on no level to be an argument that law schools are dying or that they should be. It would appear that Berry does not take into account that, in an important respect, the task of educating managers differs from that of educating other professionals and semiprofessionals. When a student receives his degree from a school of law, medicine, architecture, engineering, or accountancy, he is usually regarded by the community, and by himself, as a lawyer, doctor, architect, engineer, or accountant, even though he may have certain examinations or other formal qualifying procedures to satisfy before he begins his practice.

On the other hand, it has been observed that the student of management neither regards himself nor is regarded by the community as a manager on his graduation. Often, an extended period of elementary managing, or even of doing something else, lies ahead of him before he begins to use many of the managing skills he has learned in a college or university curriculum. It may be five, ten, or more years before he reaches a level of responsibility comparable with what the young lawyer or doctor may achieve soon after graduation. One explanation for this paradox is the extremely hierarchical character of the large public and private organizations where most young managers begin their careers, in contrast with the direct and immediate confrontation the young lawyer or doctor may have with the demands of his profession. Observable tendencies away from the hierarchical and toward more horizontal types of organization may shorten, but not eliminate, the young manager's hiatus.

Whether entirely correct or not, the observation with regard to the time lag of the management graduate does make a point: the schools of management are not training today's managers, but tomorrow's. One realizes, with no small amount of dismay, that many of the top managers of the period from 1985 to 2010 are now enrolled in our schools of management. Today's MBA student will only be 50 years old in the year 2000. I do not mean to suggest that the young business graduate will have no influence or responsibility until the turn of the century. The young are the major carriers today of the seeds of profound and rapid social change and, as such, will have their impacts much sooner than did I or my compatriots. Thirty years ago it was easier to train managers. The future looked, and usually turned out to be, pretty much like the past and present. Not very many basic social values and assumptions were under assault, unlike today when everything seems to be up for grabs. The policy of growth is being challenged; material gains no longer equal a better life; the work ethic seems to be in the process of being replaced by a voluptuary system; and even madness is seen as a new form of truth.

In the light of these observations, what course of action is suggested for the schools of management? Berry's premises would seem to dictate the abandonment of substance for language and style, when it is actually language and style that appear to be undergoing the most rapid change. I recommend three courses of action:

(1) Greater emphasis on continuing education. The schools of management should probably shift more of their resources to "executive programs" and to other formats whereby managers can return periodically for training and for an exchange of ideas, particularly in

matters concerning social change. Obviously, these efforts will not be effective unless the schools have something to offer returning managers. It would seem that the most important thing they must offer is the very thing that they are not providing at present and have not provided in the past, namely: help in interpreting social change to the managers and in finding new values, goals, and guiding principles. Perhaps students should be discouraged from entering graduate management programs until they have had several years of experience.

(2) New and better ways of disseminating ideas and information from university centers to managers. The emphasis should be on higher education as a means of communication between society and the corporation. The goal should be to speed up what is usually a slow process. Frequent workshops and symposia are possible techniques and probably should be established on some sort of routine basis. Educational television channels could be used to much better effect than has been the case so far. Awareness of the process and its goals on the part of all those involved will be necessary if these means of communication are to do what they are supposed to do.

(3) It would probably be beneficial if we took Alvin Toffler's advice and devoted the same kind of attention to the study of the future that we now devote to the present and past.

American management education is dying because it is being sucked into academic respectability.

Here we have a symptom mistaken for the disease, something which can be a very serious error indeed. Treating a patient for a rash when what he has is an allergy to penicillin can produce unfortunate results. On the contrary, management education is not being sucked fast or far enough into academic responsibility.

If there is anything new at all in the doctrine of social responsibility, the impetus for it has come from the managers or elsewhere, but not from the schools of management. This is not necessarily because managers were aware of what they are doing, but because they were seeking help from the schools and from society and, in so seeking, stimulated the doctrine. One need not be astonished at how fast Milton Friedman's views on social responsibility have faded or at how widely and rapidly corporations have accepted the new doctrine. Managers, it seems, have suspected for a long time that they were not just economic automatons mindlessly following the rules of the "free market" or of profit maximization or taking orders from shareholders. They have realized that in situations characterized by market power, their decisions required making choices from among a number of alternatives and taking into account social, political, and ecological factors as well as economic ones. Consciously and unconsciously, managers have been seeking new values, goals, and guiding principles to help them in making these choices. Managers have not very often known what was happening to them and have frequently resisted what was in conflict with their training and conventional learning, but one of the major threads of the new doctrine of social responsibility must, nonetheless, be the search for new guiding principles.

Most managers have not articulated or even understood the process, but they have been seeking something that most schools of management have failed to give them, but which they must have if they are to respond properly to the rapid and profound changes taking place in their setting. Unlike the elite law and medical schools, schools of management have usually been followers, not leaders or innovators. They have not interpreted the social scientists, humanists, or even the physical and life scientists—and new developments in those disciplines—to managers. They have let the managers go it alone and then criticized when the results were not perfect. Academics tend to regard business in much the same way the church did during the early middle ages; as being wholly outside their value system. Saint Thomas Aquinas and the Schoolmen learned and pointed out the folly of this view in the thirteenth century. As a result, trade and commerce were brought within the medieval value system. Some schools of management regard themselves as being outside the academic value system, while others seem to isolate themselves inside the academic value system, leaving business outside, to the great loss of all concerned. All of this emphasizes my point that meaningful corporate reform will have to be preceded or accompanied by reform in higher education for management.

Berry's premise that a decline in management education has been caused by its being sucked into academic respectability would seem to require a course of action based upon the withdrawal of management education from its present association with colleges and universities, the replacement of faculty with academic credentials by a staff of experienced managers, and the perpetuation of schools of management as imitators and followers. Somehow, these steps do not seem well calculated to restore management education to life, revive the American dream, or recreate a favorable business image in the eyes of the young. Certainly, they do not appear to accomplish what is needed most—to communicate society's expectations and standards to the corporation, help managers field new norms and guiding principles, and aid corporations to respond appropriately to new challenges.

A more promising approach, recommended by the circumstances, would include the following:

(1) More academic responsibility, not less. Only in this fashion can the schools of management play a constructive role in interpreting social change to the corporation and help to discover and identify new values and guiding principles. More respectability should also help to improve the repute of both business and business education.

(2) More time and attention to the overriding issue of the corporation's role in society. Instead of relegating this issue to afterthought or academic fad, it should occupy center stage and become a part of all traditional functional fields. It is hard to believe, but nonetheless true, that many schools of management around the country still give no attention whatever to the relationship between the corporation and the wider society.

(3) The schools of management should assume roles of leadership and innovation in their profession, rather than continuing to be its recording secretaries.

This is because the American dream is fading, and youth no longer holds business in such respect.

The attitude of youth toward business is an important issue, and Berry's observations about it are probably accurate. His prescription, however, is undoubtedly wrong. It is a shortage of academic respectability, not too much of it, that disaffects the youth. It is the lack of concern for the really challenging issues in society, not the opposite, that turns students away from business and the business curriculum. Alfred North Whitehead, in his famous address to the American Association of Collegiate Schools of Business in 1927, said: "The only justification for a university is that it preserves the connection between knowledge and the zest of life. . . . The main function [of a business school] is to produce men [and women] with a greater zest for business." Most schools of management are not now achieving that end, and it seems unlikely that it can be achieved if one starts from Berry's premises, or from Milton Friedman's. The image Friedman creates of the manager as the "servant," "agent," or "employee" of the "stockholder-owner" in order to "make as much money as possible," describes a singularly unzestful career, and not just for the young. Zest for life derives from challenge, and the most challenging issues in society today are not to be found in a business career if we exclude business from academic respectability, from its links with the humanities and social sciences, and from all goals and values except the economic.

If we are to have a new corporate response to society's challenges, we must also have a new response from higher education. We should be as interested in education *about* business and management as we are in education *for* business and management. Schools of management have an obligation to their students to stay at the forefront of knowledge and an obligation to the community as a whole to be the leaders, not the followers, in matters having to do with management training; norms and standards of management behavior; awareness of social trends and forces; changing values, attitudes, and ideologies; and innovations in organization and management techniques. If we remain in the passive role or the follower's role and hand onto our students only that which is already being done in the business world, or that which was being done the last time we looked, we have failed on every count. This is not to stay that we should be unaware of what is now going on, or that we should look only to the future and ignore the present and the past. It is to say that the schools are more than just channels for the transmission of conventional learning or current history. If the schools can adjust their goals to include these matters, if they can begin to relate the challenging issues of society to business, if they can help to communicate to the great corporations the new expectations that society has for them, and if they can help the corporations to respond appropriately to these new demands, there should be no shortage of zest in a business career.

It would be a shame if the schools of management failed: to help managers find the new goals, values, and guiding principles needed for making choices; to interpret social change to the corporation and the corporation to society; to provide their students with a zest for business or to encourage managers to "think greatly on their functions" (another Whitehead admonition); or to open doors to new perceptions, new philosophies, and new ways in which managers can see themselves and their roles in society. The schools of management should help to make it possible for managers to encounter new ways to think of themselves. Near the end of C. West Churchman's book, *The Design of Inquiring Systems,* for example, he writes as follows:

> . . . we have learned that some steps in the direction of developing natural inquiring systems could be taken if men and women in their various activities could come to see in what ways these activities could be construed as inquiry. For example, the manager of a corporation normally thinks of himself as the administrator or policy maker. He is not accustomed to thinking that what he does is to inquire, that his various actions might be construed not as maximizing profits, but as discovering something about how a particular organization behaves in a certain type of environment when certain things happen to it. He

might be aghast at the notion that each decision on his part could be construed as an "experiment" because to experiment with the funds of the corporation might seem irresponsible. But if he had a broader insight into the nature of inquiry, he might come to see that this description is indeed appropriate; each action on his part is an attempt not only to improve the financial status of the corporation, but also to increase the understanding of the way in which the corporation behaves and ought to behave.

Schools of management should provide the forum, the opportunity, and the encouragement for managers to consider new perceptions of their roles, such as this one, and not just through enrolled students, but constantly.

That this has not already been done is not entirely the fault of educators. As H. I. Romnes of American Telephone and Telegraph said at a Conference Board Symposium in New York last year:

> For too long, I feel, businessmen have been disposed to regard educators as merely spectators of society, overly given to moralistic judgments, while unburdened by the necessity of facing the consequences of moral decisions. But it would take an uncommonly stubborn businessman to deny that educators today, in their confortations with the young, are developing an experience of an aspect of the real world that we in business can hardly claim to know very much about yet. What is more, there is hardly a business of any size today that does not turn to the world of education to help in the development of its human resources, and for insights about the future directions of the world around us.

I suspect that there is a great deal more about which business would like to turn to the schools of management for help—if we saw ourselves less as spectators and more as leaders, innovators, and interpreters.

Education is one of society's major instrumentalities for communicating with the corporation, and schools of management are important parts of that instrumentality. They are sources of help, advice, innovation, and solace, as well as mechanisms for bringing about change. If management is ever to be regarded as a profession on a level comparable with some of the more established ones, the schools of management will have to begin to realize some of their potential as leaders of that profession. The social reform of management education must accompany the social reform of the corporation.

Corporate Social Reform: An Executive's Viewpoint

● T. F. BRADSHAW

President
Atlantic Richfield Company

Corporate social responsibility is an amorphous, complex, and controversial matter. I will be talking more about the limits of social responsibility, because it must be obvious that corporations can not cure all social ills and, indeed, in many areas should not even try. Corporations are special-purpose economic institutions, and part of my thesis will be that they depart from that purpose at their own peril. This nation is richly endowed with many and varied institutions. Social change is, I believe, accomplished through these many institutions and not through any one.

This diversity is the source of this country's strength and its ability to respond to the need for social change. This means that universities have large roles to play in bringing about social change, as do political parties, governmental units, concerned citizens' groups, environmental organizations, and corporations. Although each may be dealing with the same problem or social goal, each has its own area of competence and departs from that area of competence as its own peril.

I suppose I should define what I mean by social goals so that we can start off with an area of disagreement. My personal list contains these:

—Clean air and water. The human animal lives on these natural resources and can compromise only so far.

—Health. The health of a nation's people is surely a greater asset than its mines or its forests.

—Environment. All people need an environment that is not degrading.

24

This includes what we live in, what we look at, what we work in, what we travel in—everything around us.

—Self-fulfillment. Every individual has a basic need to reaffirm that he is a human being—that each day he has used his unique gifts of judgment, humor, and sympathy.

—Meaningful leisure. Modern technology is making more leisure time available to greater numbers of people at all income levels. How people spend their leisure in our new society will determine the quality of that society.

—Dignified old age. Of all segments of our society, the elderly may be the most neglected because their needs are the least understood.

This is a very personalized list, as you can see. Yours may be quite different, but you and I are together if our goals rest on the basic assumption that the end objective is the realization of the dignity and worth of the individual. Quite obviously, no single corporation can achieve all of these goals, nor can all companies taken together—nor should they try.

What Are the Limits to Corporate Intervention?

One limit to corporate intervention has been defined by Milton Friedman. The Friedman doctrine of corporate responsibility, boldly stated, is "make a profit." By the way, he also decries businessmen wasting their time by making speeches on social responsibility. In his book, *Capitalism and Freedom*, Friedman says,

> There is one and only one social responsibility of business—to use its resources and engage in activities to increase its profits so long as its stays within the rules of the game, which is to say, engages in free and open competition without deception of fraud.[1]

Another point of view is put forth by the attractive and articulate woman who heads up the Council on Economic Priorities. At a party in Washington, she said to me, "We have changed the rules, and you are still playing the same old game."

Well, if the game has been changed, no one has let us know about it. My company is still judged by its return on investment, its earnings per share, and its growth track record. The price of failure to obey this rule is extremely high: the corporation can go out of existence; people can be let out

[1] Milton Friedman, *Capitalism and Freedom* (Chicago: University of Chicago Press, 1962). p. 133.

of work. There can be unemployment, even among presidents. So Friedman is right—as far as he goes.

But, of course, he doesn't go far enough. Friedman overlooks two things: First, the businessman does not exist solely in a world of cold, gray economics; he also exists in a real world where people's needs go far beyond their economic needs. He is a man before he is a businessman. He has pressures on him from within himself to become a part of the whole social pattern and to accomplish more than making a profit. He also has pressures on him from without because, as a business man, he is a part of the power structure. As a part of that power structure, he must direct his portion of that power to accomplish some of the broader aims of the society in which he lives.

Second, Friedman overlooks the fact that the rules have been changing and are going to change at an explosive rate in the future. We may yet reach that state in which a businessman is judged by the social goals he accomplishes, as well as the profits he makes. We are not yet there.

How then can the businessman operate to fulfill himself as a whole man and not just as an economic man? In two ways: First, he can, and must, operate within the present rules, and within those rules, he can accomplish a considerable amount of social advancement. Second, he can become an aggressive force for changing the rules. This, after all, is still primarily a business-oriented society—not a military society, or a truly political society. Therefore, the businessman has a very large responsibility for helping to change the rules.

I would like to discuss with you the two roles the businessman can play in bringing about social change—making meaningful changes within the rules and then changing the rules.

Working Within the Rules

There are some things that the businessman does because he has to—the law tells him that he must. He pays taxes—many billions of dollars—generally half of his before-taxes profit, plus property taxes, excise taxes, and so on. He also pays billions of dollars into the social security fund.

You may want to wash out all of this because these business dollars contribute to social progress by force of law, and I don't want to waste your time talking about yesterday's social revolutions. On the other hand, in order to stay in business, we must fulfill these responsibilities. At the very least, these obligations provide the businessman with an interest in the government's progress toward social reforms.

Another area we don't usually think of is collective bargaining—another great social reform, a revolution in its time, and now a conservative way of life. Many people think of collective bargaining as being merely wage negotiations. It is that, of course, but it has become and must be a contract for employment, hospitalization, medical care, retirement benefits, and conditions of work. Therefore, it becomes a contract in the social arena.

Collective bargaining can be an extremely important agent for the spread of social doctrine. Which is the force for forward motion: Is it the union or management? Many people readily accept the idea that it is the union. I don't accept that at all. I think it is a very poor management indeed that does not come to the bargaining table with a vision as to what social progress should result in the longer run from a new social contract.

I think we sometimes tend to overlook the role of corporate contributions in achieving social change. It was not very long ago that corporate management did not have legal sanction to channel shareholders' money to various institutions. Today, corporate contributions are about $1 billion a year. Some people believe this is too small, and I am among them. If we are to have a healthy mixed economy with both public and private education and public and private medical facilities, much more will be needed. Here, however, working within the rules means watching carefully that we do not get out of line with the companies with which we compete. Perhaps a rule change is called for.

Another area of social concern is minority employment. Here the law sets levels of minimum achievement. How far beyond them should a corporation go and how does the corporation translate statistical goals into people goals—changing peoples' attitudes?

Let me use my own company's management as an example. We were awakened by the Watts riots. What did we do about it? First, we brought together in groups our management people from all over the country. We had our management people meet with a group of militant blacks, who told it like it was.

Secondly, we made a management commitment. We explained the policy to our people up and down the line and told them that we were going to see that it worked. Our new policy was that if two equally capable people applied for a job and one was black and the other was white, we would hire the black.

Next, to oversee this problem, we appointed a vice-president who had been with the company for many years and who, as a matter of fact, headed our industrial relations division. We took him from his job and made him Director of Minority Affairs.

Finally, we followed up to ensure progress. I still get a report on my desk every quarter indicating the minority balance in all parts of the company. When I see that an area is lagging, I do something about it. Our results, I think, are excellent. We are slightly above the ten-percent minority employment level—and we are continuing to add to the number of minority members in upper management positions. We now employ about 30,000 people.

It was an extremely difficult thing to achieve this kind of a minority balance in a highly technical company in a short period of time. Although we are still not satisfied with the results, we think we are on our way.

Up to now I have been dealing with things either required by the rules or readily accepted within the context of the rules. There is another stage of corporate social responsibility—starting experimental programs within the company that I hope will spread outside of it. They can be compared to dropping a pebble in a pool, with the ripples moving outward in ever-widening circles.

As an example, we became intrigued by the problem of retrieving hard-core dropouts from society. In Philadelphia, we conducted an experiment that cost as much as we might spend on an expensive oil well. That is a lot of money. In addition, the program required a tremendous effort by many people within the company. We also hired experts from the outside.

We recruited really hard-core people—people with prison records, people who had never worked, people whose parents had never worked. We wanted to see whether there was some combination of education, attitude, training, and work experience that might unlock the door that made these people social prisoners. We wanted to see whether they could become service station operators or refinery employees.

I would like to report that this experiment achieved great success, but I can't. In business terms, it failed. We spent about $10,000 per person, and very, very few were retrieved. But is a social experiment ever a failure? We think we gained experience from this experiment which will enable us to make the next one more fruitful. Perhaps someone else will drill a good well on the basis of information from our dry hole.

Another example of experimentation in the joint public and private sector is the Street Academy Program, which is designed to salvage Harlem's dropouts. Each street front academy is financed by a corporation, and our corporation has sponsored one for a number of years. In six years, some 300 of the street academy graduates have entered college. Are these successful? Even if the cost balance does not indicate success, the effort must be considered worthwhile if the Board of Education of New York City gains knowledge about what it is doing wrong and what the street academies are doing right.

Still another example is neighborhood rehabilitation. Smith, Kline & French International Company has done a splendid job of dropping a pebble in the pool by rehabilitating the neighborhood surrounding its

Philadelphia headquarters. Its program includes the conversion of some 70 abandoned houses into 200 very liveable apartments, and their rents are very low. The concept originated with an executive of Smith, Kline & French who became aware of the problem because he was taking an active role in local government—serving as a member of the City Planning Commission. This effort was succesful because it sparked similar programs in the neighborhood and has taught the Planning Commission a great deal, too.

What are the conclusions to be drawn from these examples of companies working within the rules to achieve social goals?

First, the effort must be within competitive tolerance. You disobey Friedman's law at your own risk. We can stand a dry hole in Philadelphia on a hard-core program, but a small company couldn't. Even a large corporation must be cautious. It can afford only so many dry holes.

Second, programs within or outside a company must have total top management commitment. Lower echelon managers can initiate good programs, and, I hope they will. But if they go off on their own, they run too great a risk. Similarly, middle management must support corporate efforts. Whatever the origin of the program, total commitment is necessary.

Third, those efforts that are within a company, such as minority employment, must be judged as total programs. We are either successful in what we do about integrating minorities within our company, or we are unsuccessful.

Fourth, the outside efforts, the experimental programs can only be successful if they lead to further action by other organizations within our society, whether business, government, or any other kind or organization. The problems are too large to be handled by any one corporation or any group of companies. Corportaions cannot solve all social ills. But corporations are a major institution in our industrial society and they have, in my opinion, very large responsibilities: (1) to operate to a full extent within the rules and, (2) to create as many experimental situations as possible so that new approaches can be picked up and become a part of our social pattern.

Changing the Rules

Now let us turn from operating within the rules to changing the rules. Some of you may have read a book by J. M. Clark called *The Social Control of Business.*[2] In this book Clark points out that the products of business have never borne full costs. I think we know this When consumers buy

[2]John M. Clark, *Social Control of Business* (New York: McGraw-Hill Book Co., 1939).

coal, they have not been charged for the costs of the uglification of the land caused by strip mining. When they buy electricity, they have not been charged for the sulphur dioxide in the air created by the generating plants. Business has never been charged for the costs of air and water pollution. These social costs have never been included in the costs of products.

Another social cost is the cost of rehabilitation of men who are made obsolete in a fast-moving, fast-changing society. This problem is with us today and will be with us tomorrow in spades. A man's career will be a very short one indeed unless means of rehabilitating and retraining are developed so that he can have the opportunity to go on to another career. In the future, a man may have three careers in the course of his natural life, whereas years ago one career would have sufficed.

Social costs can be built into prices and, therefore, into the structure only by changing the rules. This is the biggest challenge to business management—how to change the rules so that corporations can play a full role in helping the American people realize their full potential in a new society.

Should the businessman become a prime mover in changing the rules? Either the businessman will lead in the arena of social change or somebody else will. The businessman who stays out will have no one to blame but himself if the solutions offered are not workable.

How Can the Businessman Bring About Change?

I have three rules:

Rule (1):   He should stick to his own competencies. Now I just made a rough list of what I think are mine. I know quite a lot about pollution; I know how oil products pollute the air and water. I know quite a bit about training programs. We have a highly trained, highly technical organization. We train people all the time. We train them to change because our business changes enormously. I know a lot about transportation systems. A great many of the dollars collected by our company are dependent on the sale of fuel for transportation, whether they are cars, trucks, or buses, or even the fuel that creates electric transportation. I know something about economic security, for I have lived either with having it or not having it most of my life. I know a lot about employment, and I know what unemployment does to people. I know a lot about pensions because this is part of the economic security matter. Those are what I think are my competencies. So, rule number one; stick to your competencies.

Rule (2): Within those competencies, become a prime mover for change at the rule-making level, whether it is in national government, regional areas, or states.

Rule (3): Don't fight to preserve the status quo, because there are plenty of others who will do that for you. Fight for constructive changes that will apply to all companies in your industry. In my area of competencies, this would mean that I should fight for the stiffest pollution control laws that are technically and economically feasible. I know something about this. All too often businessmen appear at hearings in a totally defensive posture—"You can't do this to us." Businessmen must take a new attitude. It is a matter of appearing at the hearing and saying, "You must do this to us. This is what it will cost, what is technically feasible and this is what the result will be in the water or in the air."

I should work to create government and business training programs for displaced persons. We are running out of time on this one. There is a great deal to be done, and I and other businessmen should be leading in this area because I believe we know more about it.

I should work for total transportation systems at the expense of the automobile, and I do. New York City is choking itself to death with the automobile. What is needed in New York City and in many other cities is a full, rounded transportation system, and we need very stiff regulations on the use of automobiles within city limits. The Highway Trust Fund should be used for total transportation systems.

I should be working for pensions, and I am. A recent Senate committee investigation of pensions indicates that one out of seven working Americans will not receive the pension to which he thinks he is entitled. I don't know how accurate these figures are, but the argument is right because of the length of time that is required for vesting and because pensions are not portable.

Now these may seem to be very simple beginnings for a revolutionary. But I think that if we are to arrive at the stage of society where business institutions are judged by their attainment of social goals as well as profit goals—if social costs are to be included on the debit side of the ledger—then we must advance step by step. There can be no grandiose plan for leaping over history.

Now I have one last rule: Obey Friedman's law and make a profit. That will create jobs, and that is the most revolutionary concept there is.

Corporate Social Reform: A Regulator's Viewpoint

●●●

● MARY GARDINER JONES
Commissioner
Federal Trade Commission

Perhaps this article should have been subtitled "The Regulator's Dilemma." An even more appropriate title would be "The Public Welfare: Whose Responsibility?" Much has been made of the failures of governmental regulatory agencies to serve the public welfare: you hear a lot about their ineptitude, the interminable delays in their procedings, and their lack of drive and imagination.[1] More recently, however, the failures of corporations to respond to public needs have emerged as a subject of public comment.[2]

To highlight the problems confronting both industry and government in discharging their roles in serving consumer needs, I am presenting a brief case history of the introduction and promotion of a relatively new class of products generally called cellular or foamed plastics. The problems that this case history illuminates do not involve the responsibility, if any, of corporations for such social and community problems as racial discrimination, racial and technological unemployment, teeming ghettos, inadequate and unequal educational opportunities and the like, much as these can

---

[1]See, e.g., Henry G. Manne, "The Myth of Corporate Responsibility, or, Will the Real Ralph Nader Stand Up?" Business Lawyer (November 1970), p. 533.

[2]Several excellent symposia illustrate the types of heat and occasional light typically generated by discussions of this topic, e.g., Business Lawyer, November 1970 and November 1971; and Daniel DeLucca, ed., Business in a Changing Social Order (Philadelphia, Penn.: Council on Business Ethics, St. Joseph's College, 1965).

affect the long-range interests of corporate citizens in a flourishing and healthy society. Nor does it involve the equally difficult moral and ethical problems of corporate responsibility for the spillover effects of products on pollution, manufacture or war materials, or investment of corporate funds in unpopular countries.

Instead, I am dealing with the responsibility of the corporation for the public welfare as the public is affected by the production, promotion, and sale of the products that the corporation has developed on its own initiative for the express purpose of furthering its business and in the hope of adding to its profitability. An integral part of my discussion concerns the responsibility and power of government to protect the public when such products pose special hazards to their users that cannot be easily detected or guarded against.

The facts on which this case history is based are largely from available public reports, court records, newspapers, magazines, press releases, and conversations with knowledgeable people. Its message will be different for each of us. I hope, however, that these facts will enable us to reach some agreement on a definition of the problem and, perhaps, even on the responsibility that each of us should bear for finding a solution to it.

About ten years ago, a new class of products began to appear commercially in substantial amounts in the market place. Its generic name is cellular or foamed plastics; the specific types are polyurethanes, polystyrenes, polyvinyl chlorides, polethelenes, polypropylenes, polyesters, phenolics, and thermoplastic and thermosetting products. These products are chemicals produced by mixing a variety of resins, polymers, and other chemical agents in various combinations so that they can be sprayed into preformed shapes or onto fabric molds. Current home and office uses are in roof and wall insulation, furniture, bedding, and seat cushions, and the industry sees the greatest growth for their cellular foam products in the home furnishings and construction fields. Virtually every month, a new use for these materials is announced.

The industry comprises a relatively small number of chemical companies who produce the two basic ingredients for the foam. Intermediate processors, known as compounders and formulators, produce foam components for particular types of end products. It appears that most of the companies that produce the basic ingredients are also intermediate processors. Finally, there are many thousands of companies, known as applicators, who apply the finished products.

Industry advertisements directed to intermediate processors and end users proclaim the architectural achievements that have been made possible by these foams during the past "decade of progress." "New foam homes" ads appearing in *American Home* describe them "as sturdy as concrete, as sculpturally free as the homeowner and architect dare to be." The new manufacturing systems for machine tooling foams for furniture design are glowingly advertised as permitting the "utmost in styling' and "the widest styles of furniture in the least amount of time." Industry ads emphasize the economies of these products to homeowners with claims that foam insulation cuts labor time drastically, saves money, and "slashes heating and cooling bills." Foam is also increasingly advertised for its superior uses for wall accessories, drawers, and decorating furniture because of its "high impact resistance, high gloss, and high styling." Lightness and consequent lower material requirements because of its faster molding cycles and less expensive tooling are other promotional claims for foams.

However, foams have one additional characteristic that is not mentioned by the industry in any of their promotional materials: under certain conditions foams can be explosively flammable. They react violently in a fire, giving off an extraordinary intensity of flames, heat, and dense, toxic smoke. While these materials will not ignite casually, once they do catch fire they burn with a speed and intensity that can destroy a large structure in a matter of minutes.

In Kahoka, Missouri, in 1969, a fire broke out in the basement of a private home in which the interior walls had been coated with one of these foam components and left in an exposed condition. The foam-insulating material was labeled by the manufacturer as "nonburning and self-extinguishing." The fire caused the death of two small children and the total destruction of the house.[3]

In November 1970, 145 teenagers were killed in St. Laurent-du-Pont, France, by a fire that broke out in a dance hall whose walls had been lavishly sprayed with foam in order to give the appearance of a "white grotto or cave."[4]

On August 26, 1970, a fire involving foamed plastic seats alone completely gutted a just-completed, unoccupied wing of the BOAC terminal at Kennedy International Airport. The fire consumed, at breakneck speed, 600 seats along a 330-foot length.[5]

Thus, the fire-hazard potential in these products is by no means theoretical. It is real—and lethal. Yet, there is still virtually no public effort being made, as far as I know, to promote a widespread understanding of the general flammability hazards that lurk in these products or to take specific steps

[3]*Childress* v. *Cook Paint & Varnish Co.,* Case No. 11,077, Cir. Ct., Schuyler County, Mo., October 6, 1971.

[4]*Paris Match,* no. 1123, November 14, 1970.

[5]J. C. Abbott (Fire Protection Manager, BOAC), "Fires Involving Upholstery Materials," NFPA *Fire Journal,* July 1971, pp. 88–90.

in their construction or use to eliminate or minimize their flammability characteristics.

Indeed, despite the many fires involving these products, industry continues to promote them as self-extinguishing. The ASTM (American Society for Testing and Materials) standard, which provides the justification for this claim, remains in effect, and industry, as far as I know, has made no effort to promote the development of a new set of standards or codes as guidelines for the proper use of foams.

The cost to the nation from fires of all causes is substantial. Although the nation spends $2.7 billion a year on fire protection, the value of property loss in 1971 was $2.8 billion, an increase of $215 million over 1970. More than 12,000 men, women, and children have been killed by fire in *each* of the past six years, a death rate which is twice that of Canada, four times that of Great Britain, and six and one-half times that of Japan. Public interest in preventing this human loss and reducing this waste of resources is obvious and needs no belaboring.

Fire prevention and the establishment of standards of flammability have never been regarded in this country as the responsibility of individual manufacturers. Instead, responsibility has been shared among industry-oriented, private, standards-making bodies; federal agencies with specific authority over certain types of flammability problems; state and local building code authorities; and various fire-prevention organizations.

In the case of foams, industry took no initial responsibility of any kind, either to identify the flammability characteristics of these products or to provide customers and the general public with instructions to ensure their safe use. Indeed, in its promotional literature, repeated by its salesmen, industry has consistently heralded these new products as self-extinguishing and, for an appreciable period of time, has described them as "nonburning." These representations appear in technical bulletins put out by various manufacturers as late as 1972, at least three years after their lethal flammability potential was tragically displayed and two years after industry's own surveys revealed the inadequacy of the ASTM and UL (Underwriter's Laboratory) tests on which these self-extinguishing claims were based.[6]

---

[6]In 1969, the cellular foam industry requested Underwriter's Laboratory to conduct a study of the flammability of these products. The first part of the study, which has been made public, documented two major facts: (1) plastic foam fires differ from fires involving conventional materials in their high speed of flame spread, great heat intensity, and production of large quantities of black smoke, thus making manual fire fighting more difficult; and (2) foam fires occurring in real buildings behave in a manner quite different from those projected in the laboratory tests, which form the basis for the ASTM and UL standards and which are generally relied upon by most building codes.

Despite the fact that existing flammability standards for construction materials are recognized as wholly inadequate, neither the American National Standards Institute, The American Society for Testing and Materials, nor Underwriter's Laboratory have formulated new standards or publicized the inapplicability of existing standards to these new products.

Some fire insurance companies have recently demonstrated concern about these materials, and a few articles are beginning to appear in insurance trade journals discussing the flammability problems inherent in foams. Whether these companies have also taken steps to regulate the use of foams in buildings that they insure is not known.

The only private organization concerned to any substantial extent with the flammability characteristics of cellular foams is the National Fire Protection Association (NFPA), which is a data collection agency on fires and their causes or circumstances. NFPA is currently preparing a pamphlet, the first of its kind, on plastics in building construction, to provide some guidance in the field of people such as building-code inspectors and fire-insurance evaluators who are responsible for evaluting plastic materials in buildings.

This is the record of industry and nongovernmental agencies over the past ten years, while data on the lethal potential of foams have been accumulating.

The record of government agencies has not been demonstrably different. To my knowledge, state and local building codes, of which I understand there are about four major ones in the country, continue to rely on the ASTM and UL standards for measuring acceptable flammability characteristics of construction materials used in commercial buildings. Moreover, these codes relate only to commercial buildings and not to private residences or to interior furnishings. I know of no steps being taken to develop flammability standards applicable to home construction.

While both the U.S. Department of Commerce and the U.S. Department of Health, Education and Welfare (HEW) have been assigned special responsibility to develop and administer flammability standards for certain types of products, neither department, to my knowledge, has taken any action within their respective jurisdiction to regulate or measure the flammability properties of these new foam materials.[7] Nor has this problem been the subject of any special study or concern by either of the two com-

---

[7]HEW and Commerce are charged with primary responsibility for administering two basic statutes governing flammability: the Hazardous Substance Act and the Flammable Fabrics Act. Both acts are designed to protect the public against unusual or unacceptable flammability hazards of various products.

missions recently created by Congress to make special studies of the problems of product safety and of fire prevention and control.[8]

It is my understanding that, shortly after the Apollo fire, the National Science Foundation (NSF) was asked by the Department of Defense (DOD) and the National Aeronautics and Space Administration (NASA) to study and report on flammability problems associated with polymer materials.[9] NSF is only now putting together a committee to carry out this charge. I am informed that the special flammability characteristics of foams and the inadequacy of ASTM standards has been brought to the attention of the President's Special Consumer Advisor, but I know of no effort being made by that office to publicize the problem and warn consumers of these hazards or to see to it that appropriate government agencies act to develop safeguards in the manufacture and use of these products.

The attitude of both government and industry toward the general problem of product safety and the particular problem of flammability of cellular foams is typified by statements recently made by spokesmen of these two groups. In a recent speech to the Association of Home Appliance Manufacturers meeting in Chicago, Richard O. Simpson, the Acting Assistant Secretary of Commerce for Science and Technology, who is directly responsible for product and safety matters, including flammability problems, stated his conviction that product safety "is a shared responsibility—shared by the manufacturer, the government, and the consumers." While urging industry to take the lead in developing safety standards and ensuring the safety of the products they manufacture and sell, he went on to point out that "almost half of those injured in household accidents assumed for themselves *the primary responsibility* for causing the accidents" (emphasis added) and observed that consumers must be aware of their responsibilities, recognize the risks in daily living, and be receptive to information about products, including their safety features. To Simpson the role of government and

---

[8]The National Product Safety Commission was authorized by Public Law 90–146 and commenced its work on March 27, 1968. Its final report, forwarded to the President and Congress on June 30, 1970, contained no mention of these products or of their special flammability characteristics. The National Commission on Fire Prevention and Control (due to expire in July 1973) is apparently aware of the problem but has not devoted any special attention or priority to it.

[9]The formal charge to NSF was to initiate a broad survey of fire suppressant polymeric materials for use in aeronautical and space vehicles; to identify needs and opportunities; to assess state of the art in nonflammable polymers (including available materials, production, costs, data requirements, methods of testing, and toxcity); and to describe a comprehensive program of R&D to upgrade the technology and accelerate application where advantages would accrue in performance and economy.

industry lies essentially in providing "safety information, education, and persuasion as *the single most important step* to take to reduce accidents, injuries involving products" (emphasis added). Other steps urged for industry to take included the development of safety standards for a broad spectrum of products, a recognition by top management of the importance of these standards formulation efforts, and improved cost benefit and risk benefit analyses to assist producers, distributors, and consumers in improving product safety standards.

The attitude of industry evinces a similar lack of urgency and ambiguity about the steps that should be taken to ensure product safety. Thus, although the plastics industry is beginning to make cautious public reference to the existence of a problem with plastic foams and the need for care in product design, at the same time it is cautioning its members against "preoccupation with the flammability problem at the expense of the diligent pursuit of solutions for the several other problems it faces.[10]

A similarily ambiguous attitude was taken by the chairman of the Plastic Industries Committee, responsible for investigating the flammable characteristics of cellular foams. In announcing the first findings of these studies (that plastic foams behave very differently in simulated laboratory fires than they do in "real fires"), the chairman was careful to emphasize that the tests were not designed to prove anything specific about plastics. Instead, he said, they were designed to provide building-code authorities with more information than standard tests provided and to lead to increased safety in the use of all building materials. He specifically denied that any evidence existed to justify limitations on plastics more severe than those on other combustible products, such as wood![11]

These ambiguous statements about the responsibility for product safety and the particular fire hazard of cellular foams are in sharp contrast with the findings of the Missouri judge who presided over the damage suit brought by the Childress family for the deaths of their children and the destruction of their home as a result of a foam fire. After listening to the testimony, the judge had no lingering doubts about the inherent flammability of these products or about industry's irresponsibility in relying on the patently inadequate ASTM flammability standards:

> The evidence conclusively established the unconscionable irresponsibility of defendant in marketing for home use an explosively flammable product as "non-

[10]*U.S. Foamed Plastic Markets & Directory, 1970–71* (Stanford, Conn.: Technomic Publishing Co., 1971), p. 44.

[11]Public release of the Society of the Plastics Industry, New York City, September 16, 1970.

burning and self-extinguishing," on the basis of a test, not explained to the buyers that was so patently inept and inadequate that any layman would be bound to regard it as better calculated to conceal than reveal the deadly properties of the substance. And the result was what *anyone* should have foreseen; the house burned "with explosive intensity," and the children with it. What excuse can there be for such callous indifference to responsibility so grave? The only one put forward here, viewed charitably, is bumbling ineptitude. Defendant employed an independent laboratory to test the product and, in spite of the use for which it was specifically designed and the dangers naturally to be anticipated from that use, made no effort to analyze the farcical nature of the test or to take any precaution against the tragedy it invited. I think that conduct amounts to constructive malice; certainly it is a most abrasive form of aggravation—which by the dictionary's definition at least, is not dependent on malice, either actual or constructive.[12]

Essentially these are the facts that my staff presented to the Federal Trade Commission in 1972. You can now understand why I suggested that a regulator's dilemma was a more accurate description of our problems with corporate responsibility than merely a point of view.

The question that these facts posed for the FTC was what role, if any, it could or should play in attempting to find a solution to the problem of responsibility. On whom should the primary responsibility be imposed in the introduction of a new product that has special flammability characteristics to ensure that these products are not unduly hazardous and are properly used?

The FTC is in no sense an expert on flammability or on fire prevention and control, and it has no authority or expertise to formulate standards of flammability. It also does not have direct authority to prevent unsafe products from reaching the market nor can it regulate the degrees of hazards that products may pose to those who use them or are exposed to them.[13]

The FTC's powers, with respect to product safety, are grounded in its jurisdiction to prohibit unfair or deceptive acts or practices. Traditionally, the FTC's involvement with hazardous products has been limited to banning affirmative misrepresentations about the safety of products or, where appropriate, requiring product hazards to be affirmatively disclosed.

But in my opinion, Assistant Commerce Secretary Simpson notwith-

---

[12]*Childress* v. *Cook Paint & Varnish Co.*

[13]While the FTC shares responsibility for the enforcement of the Flammable Fabrics Act with Commerce, it has no independent power to identify products requiring flammability standards nor any authority to set standards or modify their content if they appear inadequate. It simply enforces whatever standards the Department of Commerce determines are necessary.

standing, informing consumers of possible hazards can never be regarded as providing enough protection to consumers when the hazards being warned against can involve loss of life and/or substantial property losses. Warnings of hazards are notoriously difficult to phrase in such a way that even those consumers who appreciate the warning have in effect anything more than one option—to accept the risk or to refrain from purchasing. Consumers should never be confronted with such alternatives. They cannot be expected to, and should not be asked to, make the necessary trade-offs between the extra risks that use of these products may entail and the various advantages of cost, design, and ease of installation that these products are said to have. I am also convinced that society cannot regard loss of life or property as an acceptable price for consumer carelessness or inattentiveness to the warning or for their failure to understand or appreciate the significance of the warning. Moreover, since the hazard here can fall on a much wider group of people than those whose inattentiveness or carelessness is the cause of a catastrophe, it is obvious that society cannot rely solely on warnings about hazards when wholly innocent citizens may have to pay the price for the failure of other citizens to heed the warning.

While warnings and full disclosures about hazards are important, they cannot be looked to, in my judgment, as the sole regulatory action. Thus, while the FTC must act in the face of deception or unfairness, it still can be said to have only a peripheral role in addressing the basic hazards of these products for their users.

It would seem that, of all the federal agencies concerned with the public welfare, the Department of Commerce has the clearest role to play. It has specific authority to promote the formulation of all types of standards, and in the flammability field it can formulate such standards for certain uses of plastic foams. Yet Commerce has taken no public steps to date to establish such standards to guard against the special foams.[14]

Even if the data are not yet sufficiently available or analyzed to permit new standards to be immediately formulated, certainly the Department of Commerce is in a position to convene a conference of representatives from the plastic foam industry, the fire insurance industry, the principal standards organizations, as well as fire marshalls and state or local building-code

---

[14]While the department's National Bureau of Standards has developed flammable standards for mattresses and is working on similar standards for upholstered furniture, these standards are designed solely from the point of view of a cigarette as the source of ignition. Thus, the explosive burning properties of interior furnishings, such as mattresses or furniture, made from or containing cellular foams that might be started by a wastepaper basket fire are outside their chosen frame of reference.

administrators to explore the dimensions of the problem and to provide leadership for the necessary steps to minimize the flammability hazards of foams. Moreover, some interim information on the adequacy or inadequacy of the current flammability standards and fire protection techniques should be disseminated to the construction industry, the architectural schools, fire marshalls, and likely end users to that the can take whatever action appears to be necessary to guard against the risks involved.

With no such action by Commerce or HEW[15] as well as the, thus far, low-key role played by the National Commission on Fire Prevention and Control, the FTC has had to come to grips with the question of what role it should play. Should the FTC assume from the failure of these two agencies to act that the flammability problems posed by foams are more apparent than real? Or should it take the position that, irrespective of the hazards, it was not designed by Congress as the primary agency to deal with flammability hazards and that, therefore, it would be inappropriate for it to move into this area on the basis of a generalized jurisdiction to prevent unfair and deceptive acts or practices?

I do not believe, nor does the Commission, that responsibility for consumer protection can be so neatly segmented or arbitrarily carried out. I am convinced that responsibility is a trust that must be lived up to whenever it is engaged and however narrow the power is to discharge it. Fortunately, the entire Commission shared this view and accordingly took action.

On October 3, 1972, the Commission announced that it had directed its staff to investigate the possible existence of fire hazards associated with the marketing and use of certain plastic products in the construction and furnishing of building and homes. The staff was also directed to look into the question of "whether the flammability standards used by the plastics industry with regard to such products may be misleading insofar as end use fire environment is concerned."

As far as I am aware, the Commission is the only federal agency to date that is actively involved in investigating the facts about cellular foams and exploring what action, if any, should be taken to protect the public.

It is my hope that, as a result of the Commission's action, industry may be stimulated to develop a program to deal with the new flammability

---

[15]HEW's Bureau of Product Safety, which administers the Hazardous Substance Act, takes the position that the act only applies to products used by "consumers" and not to intermediate products used commercially, such as in residential or office building construction. To my knowledge, HEW has taken no action under this act to regulate the flammability of cellular foam products, even when used in the home.

hazards posed by these products. But does the fact that government can and ultimately must act in order to promote the public safety relieve the business community from any concomitant responsibility for the safety of products which they develop and put on the market? I think the answer is clearly in the negative.

There are some who would argue that it is because government does assume the ultimate responsibility for product safety that industry does not take a more active role in ensuring the safety of its products. I cannot accept such a proposition, the logical implication of which is that, if government abandoned all responsibility, industry would take up the slack. There is no evidence to support this, and I do not believe the public should be subjected to the consequences in the event the proposition proved false for even one industry member.

It is of course true that the flammability characteristics of foams and the best protective techniques to deal with them will slowly become known as fire experts gain more experience with this kind of fire. However, the emergence of this knowledge will be only after the fact—painful lessons learned after tragic fires, at the expense of human life and suffering and needless destruction of property. This to me is also an unacceptable way of dealing with the hazards posed by these products. The time lag before the competitive system would react to drive the unsafe product off the market is too long to rely on this type of long-term solution to protect the public. What forces than can be looked to to provide this protection?

I am convinced that industry must assume the primary initial responsibility for the protection of the public from product hazards. It seems clear, in this case, for example, that only the manufacturers of these products are in the position of full knowledge of the peculiar flammability propensities of foams, and of having this knowledge well in advance of the appearance of foams in the marketplace. No new product emerges without careful pre-market testing for performance, likely uses, and market acceptance. When, as here, the products are technologically new and require new techniques of manufacture or installation, it is only the manufacturers who are in a position to disseminate the required information about how to use these products to the actual consumers.

Who but the manufacturers of these products are in a better position to make certain that the myriad foam applicator companies know and use the appropriate quality of these foams for insulation purposes and that they do not use the cheapest types of these materials without appreciating that they require fireproofing or protection materials? Who but the manufacturers can make certain that the architects and construction companies are sufficiently familiar with the properties of these products to enable them to gear their designs to the proper use and care of these products? Who but the manufacturers can disseminate the necessary information to the thousands of plumbers and local handymen who do interior household repairs about the fire hazards in the use of blowtorches on walls insulated with cellular foam materials? Certainly, the manufacturers should have sufficient interest in maintaining the good will of their customers and in the long-term consumer acceptance of these products to make sure that the products are not rejected because of tragic fires and losses of life and property associated with their use.

The manufacturers of the cellular foam products did in fact prepare detailed technical bulletins on the special construction properties of these new products for the industrial middlemen who would use the products as raw materials, the architectural schools whose knowledge of the new materials could provide an important source of market demand and acceptance, the construction companies who might use the new materials, and the ultimate consumers who, like the architectural schools, could be a source of market demand. Unfortunately, these manufacturers chose to remain silent on the one, crucially important characteristic of cellular foams, which concerned their safe use by the myriad of processors and end users. In my view, this omission represents highly irresponsible conduct on their part.

I would even go further in delineating responsible conduct on the part of manufacturers who are introducing new, unknown products that involve this kind of latent, invisible, and largely unexpected hazard. In this case, one of the likely, larger users of these products is the home-improvement industry, which is easy to enter and highly competitive, and of which some segments use door-to-door high-pressure, and sometimes highly deceptive, sales techniques. Given the known characteristics of this distribution channel, it seems to me that manufacturers have a special duty to ensure the responsible use of their products by these distributors. Careful selection of distributors through some type of franchise system and control over distributors who seek financial aid from them are some of the avenues open to them to make sure that safeguards necessary in the application of these materials are rigorously followed.

Finally, it seems clear that only the manufacturers of these products are in a position to know the extent to which the existing flammability standards are applicable to these new materials. Surely, then, it is not unfair to inquire whether manufacturers of such products do not also have a minimum obligation to make sure that the standards organizations and building-code inspectors are aware of the special flammability characteristics of these materials so that they can evaluate the applicability of their various flammability ratings to these new materials. I would go further and suggest that it is the manufacturers who should take the initiative to see to it that adequate flammability standards are formulated, even on an interim basis, in order to ensure the safe use of these products.

In sum, while I do not believe that responsibility for the protection of the public against serious product hazards is the exclusive province of industry, I also do not believe that they can totally ignore the problem. Industry must take the first essential steps of exploring the dimensions of any hazards inhering in products they produce and of making public the basic information bearing on their safe use.

I also believe that government has an equally clear duty to see to it that products in the marketplace are safe or are being used with maximum precautions. Yet, achieving public accountability is at least as difficult as ensuring corporate accountability. The Department of Commerce's inaction while at the same time knowing about the flammability hazards of these products, the slowness of the NSF to implement its charge to study the problem and recommend solutions, and the lack of priority accorded to the problem by the National Commission on Fire Prevention and Control, all clearly document the difficulties of any exclusive reliance on the public sector for the protection of the public from product hazards.

Thus, the real problem which confronts us lies not so much in allocating some general areas of responsibility between the private and public sector, but rather in creating mechanisms for both private and public accountability which ensure that each sector will in fact discharge its assigned responsibilities.

The first question in ensuring industry accountability is whether industry can come forward with its own proposals to provide this assurance or whether government must devise some system to enforce such accountability. There is no doubt that government has tools that could be invoked for this purpose. At one extreme, government could impose civil or criminal sanctions for injuries caused by product hazards that could have been foreseen and that were not disclosed. Or government could require that for each new product offering (in certain product categories) industry file a statement—comparable to an environmental impact statement—outlining the product hazards that may inhere in its use.

My own feeling is that the essential problem of product safety will never be completely solved until industry accepts its primary responsibility and develops its own procedures to assure its own accountability in carrying out this responsibility. I am convinced that industry—and, therefore, business school students—must come forward with their own proposals to assure society that product safety is regarded and accepted by every manufacturer as a primary initial responsibility of industry. Industry should develop internal procedures for premarket testing of the safety of its products, and this responsibility should rest on a single individual who can be held accountable in the event of serious public injury caused by company products that were not guarded against or disclosed to the company before the new product went on the market. In short, I am convinced that it is time for corporations to treat the public's safety as an important and separate consideration in the marketability of a product, on a par with the product's likely acceptability, profitability, and contribution to the growth of the company.

By the same token, we must ask ourselves whether we can devise a similar system to ensure that regulators will discharge their responsibilities for protecting the public welfare.

One solution to the lack of forthright action by government may come from the diffusion of responsibility for product safety among diverse agencies. The current legislation to establish a single product safety agency to be responsible for product safety may provide an important solution to this problem. Congress recently passed and sent to the President the Consumer Products Safety Act, which establishes a five-member commission to protect the public against the risk of unreasonable hazards from consumer products and to establish safety standards for such products. The current diversity of jurisdiction over flammability problems, now spread through several agencies, will be transferred to the new commission. Moreover, consumers are given the express right to petition the agency for action and to bring suit in the event the agency fails to carry out its statutory mandate.

Similarly, the proposal to create a consumer advocate office within the federal establishment provides another important avenue to hold government accountable to the public for its action or inaction. Finally, the citizen's right to intervene in government proceedings or to sue to compel government attentiveness to its statutory responsibilities constitutes another important weapon to force responsible government action. I am convinced that all of these channels for compelling governmental accountability to its statutory responsibilities should be expressly and affirmatively provided as an integral part of all statutes conferring product safety responsibilities on government agencies.

This case history reveals how badly the public's interest is served when neither the public nor the private sector appreciates clearly just what its role should be and hence fails to take adequate action. Public safety must be the initial responsibility of the business which produces the product creating the hazard, as well as the responsibility of government, in order to ensure that all adequate safeguards are being taken. The problem is an urgent one. I have suggested a few possible lines of approach. None of these may be practical or adequate, but perhaps they will serve to stimulate my readers to identify feasible and practical lines of attack to ensure that new products with high-risk potential will not be offered on the market before adequate safeguards against their hazards have been developed and put into effect. It will then be up to the public sector to make sure that the safeguards are adequate and the risks reduced to the absolute minimum.

Corporate Social Reform: An Activist's Viewpoint

●●

● PHILIP W. MOORE

Executive Director
Project on Corporate Responsibility,
Washington, D.C.

My task in this article, as I see it, is to develop a theme of corporate responsibility from the activist perspective. It is a bit of a misnomer to ascribe the label "corporate activist" to groups such as the Project on Corporate Responsibility, while using other labels to describe other movements, such as "consumer," "antiwar," "environmental," "feminist," "black," and so on. The fact is that the people involved in all of these movements are corporate activists.

Ralph Nader is described as a consumer advocate, but in truth he is a corporate activist, and a good one at that. When the antiwar movement tries to stop Dow's manufacture of napalm and when Clergy and Laity Concerned try to stop Honeywell's manufacture of antipersonnel weapons, they are corporate activists trying to stop the war. When Jesse Jackson demands that A&P increase its minority hiring, he, too, is a corporate activist.

Any woman who demands better advertising policies, better jobs, equal pay for equal work, or daycare centers is a corporate activist. And so it is with the environmental movement whose concerns about clean air, clean water, restoration and preservation of land and other natural resources are inevitably directed at the corporation. A community organizer is a corporate activist whenever community concerns are directed at the corporation or whenever bad corporate policies are issues around which communities are organized. Saul Alinsky was, and his successors are, corporate activists. And, certainly, labor leaders, labor organizers, and union members are corporate activists by definition. Cesar Chavez is a great Chicano leader, a great organizer of farm workers, and a great corporate activist.

Finally, there is the biggest movement of all. This is the movement which is an amalgam of all other movements, and it defies labeling or categorizing. It is a new movement; it has just begun, but it will have the biggest impact on all of our lives. This is the movement to humanize our institutions—all of them. This is the movement "to green" America; this is the movement to assert control over the forces that affect all of us, day to day. It is the source of going back to the land. It is the source of the Lordstown strikes, and it underlies the malaise and the subtle tension that affects all of our institutions. As of these energies coalesce into an identifiable movement, this movement, too, will have its biggest impact on the corporation.

In fact, I think it is fair to say that every important social and political movement in this country must at some point focus on the corporate institution. And the reason is simple. Corporations are powerful; they are where the action is; it's corporate products that pollute or don't work; it's corporate jobs that are not available to blacks or women. Corporations use an impersonal language with terms like efficiency, profit, and mass production that belie a lack of human concerns. Corporate leaders are visible and privileged; they earn lots of money; they don't suffer from dirty air or crowded living conditions or traffic jams. They don't fight wars or get discriminated against. In fact, they seem to enjoy the benefits of corporate life without suffering any of the consequences which are so often a by-product of their own business practices. For whatever reason, the corporation is simply extremely powerful and may well be the most powerful single institution in this country. For any social change to be effective, the corporation has to be committed to that change. All the good laws, the good cases, the good ideas, and the good people are never felt by the beneficiaries of all that goodness until the corporations are committed to implementing those good things.

Perhaps I have belabored the point, but it requires emphasis and repetition. For the tendency to label the corporate movement as something different from other movements is a fundamental misunderstanding of the meaning of corporate responsibility. Corporate responsibility means the responsibility that the corporate institution has to all activist concerns, and potentially everybody is an activist. Corporate activism in turn means all those concerns that are influenced by, determined by, caused by, or solved by corporate conduct. And this is true across the entire spectrum of social action, whether we are talking of war and corporations, the environment and corporations, minorities and corporations, jobs and corporations, consumers and corporations, or people and corporations. Whatever the substantive concern of a person or group, the actions of that person or group will inevitably require that the corporation respond to those concerns. And groups like ours are trying to give voice to those concerns—a permanent voice—not because there is anything inherently good about a better board structure or more disclosures, but because those changes in structure and process are a precondition to giving the concerns of citizen activists greater access to corporate power.

Lest you worry about access to corporate power, remember that activism is simply an expression of public concern. The role of activists is to set forth options for society. Activism requires forceful and articulate presentations of these options for the public. Only those activist options which generate major popular support will ever have any impact. That is the check on activism. Where would Ralph Nader be if his auto safety options did not strike a responsive popular concern? Where would Martin Luther King have been if the Montgomery bus boycott hadn't presented an option for millions of blacks in this country? Or Cesar Chavez or George McGovern?

And the opposite side proves the same point. If Martin Luther King hadn't supported that bus boycott, if Nader hadn't written that book, if Chavez hadn't started that grape boycott, then the public would have been the loser because they wouldn't have been presented the option. Oh yes, leadership has a way of emerging to articulate public concerns, but when and where, in a particular period, this happens—or how it happens—is the role of activists.

For those of you who are concerned that activists do not reflect public need, remember, by definition, activism that doesn't have public support will never succeed. You will never hear that voice in the darkness, and you don't even have to concern yourself with that activism. For those of you who worry that activists are privileged elites, the beneficiaries of society, remember this: It is an unfortunate fact of this country that in order to make a forceful and articulate presentation of public options, one must have a reasonable degree of security from the adverse consequences of forceful actions, and one must have a reasonable degree of skills and talents in order to present articulate options. The fact is that activism is a luxury in this country involving risk-taking that few people are able, or willing, to afford.

And what about us, the so-called corporate activists? If there is a corporate activism that is separable from any other social activism, it has something to do with a felt need to assert control over the forces that affect our lives. One such force is the corporation. Our role is to present options as forcefully and as articulately as we are able. We know that the specific options will not be adopted, but we also know that the options point to the direction of changes. It's still early yet, hard to tell if the public supports any of the directions that we've presented. And time will tell. If there is no popular support for these options—if these options don't reflect public concerns—we will all blend away like so much sand on the beach. But if the public does pick up these options, and I think there is sufficient evidence to show that it will, the corporation will have no choice. It will change or be changed.

And the changes will invite activism. It will build activism into its processes—As it must—for activism will not go away. The war may end; we may solve the problem of racism in this country; we may clean up the environment and abolish poverty; but there will be new concerns and new problems and new activities. That is why our institutions must be capable of absorbing all of the dynamics of our society. And when they do we will have a totally different institution. It will not look the same as it looks now, we may even call it by a different name, but that corporate institution will be our partner, not our adversary.

You may argue that it is not the function of a corporation to determine national priorities. That, you say, is the function of government. Nor do corporations start or end wars, and I suppose you could argue that it is not the function of the corporation to solve society's problems of racism or the environment. Rather, those are problems resolved by people and their governments, and the corporations simply follow the government mandate, like all citizens.

I think in the last analysis we would all agree that the corporation does not have an external social obligation that is very different from any other charitable activity. The corporation does not have a "social" responsibility to society and it is true that we would not want corporate leaders, especially current ones, determining social policy for people. But while all that is true, the corporation does have a function that is defined, or should be, by society. And that function is economic. That function is to keep the economy moving: to provide jobs and income, and to deliver goods and services to the nation at the cheapest possible total costs. But what is forgotten in this neat little equation is that the economic function has a tremendous impact on society, a social impact, if you will. And if society determines that the economic function previously delegated to corporations is no longer serving society, then society has the right and obligation to reexamine that function and, if necessary, to revoke the delegation of authority and redefine the function.

I believe that that is what is going on right now in this country. Our society is reexamining the function of the corporation, and asking the question: Is the primary economic function of the corporation as it exists today serving the overall objectives of society? And if activists, are reexamining this function, then it is completely nonsensical to keep referring to old, outmoded, and mythical functions that society is in the process of revoking as justification for corporate irresponsibility. Rather, we should address ourselves to the question of whether the corporation is serving its function and whether its function can be better served.

In theory the legitimacy of any social institution is determined by the extent to which its various components recognize its function and accept the way in which the function is being carried out. In theory, corporate legitimacy is bestowed by the shareholders as owners, the consumers through the marketplace, workers through the unions (with some market components), and the public through its government. When theory is set off against practice, none of the functions are being served by the constituents of the corporations, and thus the corporation has been shorn of its legitimacy.

In theory, shareholders are the owners of the corporation, and as owners, they elect directors who determine policy for the corporation and hire managers to implement the policies. In theory, managers are accountable to the shareholders through duly elected boards of directors. But the reality is quite the opposite. In fact, corporate managers control the boards of directors. They nominate the boards, and, through control of the proxy machinery, they elect them. In fact, directors are accountable to the managers, and the shareholders are simply a rubber stamp. This is obvious and, I think, undisputed.

In theory, consumers give legitimacy to the corporation through the marketplace. Consumers determine the need for the product, the price, the supply, and the quality of the product. But that is not the reality anymore. The major corporations are either too big or too remote from the consumer to allow any meaningful consumer sovereignty. The requirements of planning and the technology of communication mean that corporations will try to predetermine the success of their products with huge advertising campaigns. GM plans its products some ten years in advance of when they will enter the marketplace. Moreover, through these advertising campaigns corporations contrive demands for products that the public simply doesn't need and that may have damaging secondary consequences. How many people, for example, need electric pencil sharpeners, which increase the demand for power in this country? Basic industry, like the steel industry, is so removed from the ultimate consumer that there are few ways that the consumer can directly influence steel companies.

In theory, the public asserts control through government. Legislation proscribes or prescribes certain kinds of corporate activity, and the courts enforce those mandates. But, in fact, several key elements of this form of public legitimacy have broken down. One is the disproportionate power that corporations have to influence the elections of officials, as well as the course of legislation. McGovern's fund-raising theme is a simple example. He needed one million people to contribute $25 each, while Nixon needed 25 people to contribute $1 million each. The second is the way that corporations can fight full implementation of previously watered-down legislation. Corporations can spend years fighting off the filing of an antitrust complaint, much less its prosecution. Corporations can outspend, in tax-deductible money, the U.S. attorney's office that is trying to enforce a federal environmental law. Another reason is that corporations are able to build in fines and other penalties as part of the cost of doing business. This is particularly true of social ordinances. The corporations will simply pay the $200 daily fine rather than spend the money to fight the case or stop pollution. And, finally, corporations have a disproportionate influence on public attitudes through advertising and public relations efforts.

The last element of legitimacy is the employee. In my view this is the one area in which the theory and reality coincide. Unions, through collective bargaining, accept management prerogatives; they accept the concept of management control of corporations, and work simply to control corporate decisions on the bread-and-butter union issues. So, for better or worse, legitimacy continues with union employees, But with the increase of the Lordstown-type strikes, union members are less and less accepting management control in certain areas. For example, management has always been able to determine production rates or plant locations, even though these decisions have a huge impact on the lives of union members. But, with these strikes and with increasing union demands both here and abroad for greater labor control of traditional management decisions, union members are no longer conceding production rates, safety, and other decisions to managers. Just as the unions were the last constituency of corporations to be recognized, they will be the last constituency to challenge corporate legitimacy, but they will, and we see signs of it already. So much for the Declaration of Independence, now let's move on to the Constitution.

The impact of this erosion of legitimacy means that there is no effective way for the public or other constituents of the corporation to build its concerns into corporate decision making. The public can't use laws or elections; the shareholders can't use shareholder actions; consumers can't use the marketplace; and workers, if they are to use union mechanism, will have to challenge areas of management prerogatives, thus breaking down traditional notions of collective bargaining. Given this picture, it is virtually impossible under the current structure for any constitutent to influence corporate policy on any issue.

If you really think about what it takes to get this country or its institutions to do anything about a problem, you will realize how inhibiting just the immensity of the task is. Shareholders exercising the traditionally accepted right of nominating directors would have to spend a million dollars to try to elect a director, and the odds against him are so great that it wouldn't be worth the effort. Imagine what it's like for a person or groups of people to try to stop the war; to try to stop corporate pollution; to insure rights and a fair chance for minority groups, and for a consumer to buy only nonpolluting products. If you think about that in real terms, not just in theory, it is obvious why the thrust of any change must be in terms of structure—the way the corporations run. People have got to have access to decision making to express their concerns and to influence policies that affect their lives.

Let me put it in concrete terms. Let's go back to the civil rights movement—the movement on which we have the longest modern perspective. We can date its modern beginning in 1954 with the Surpreme Court opinion on school integration. The late 1950's saw the attempts to integrate southern schools and the passage of the first civil rights bills. Then came the demonstrations against wrong being perpetrated—Rosa Parks was too tired to stand up—and Martin Luther King organized the Montgomery bus boycotts. There were the Birmingham bombings and the sit-ins. In 1963, Martin Luther King gave his "I have a dream" speech in the Capitol, and anyone who didn't know that we had a racial problem then was either blind or racist, or both. The courts had intervened by then and were beginning to protect the civil rights workers. In 1964 came the Mississippi Summer Project and the passage of the civil rights bill. The year 1965 saw the pas sage of the voting rights bills. We were getting legislative responses to the problem of racism.

The corporation was still not involved. In fact, we were still assuming this was a southern problem. But then the riots broke out in city after city— the long hot summers. Only then did we begin to get some economic response. Money poured into the ghettos; we got poverty programs and the Equal Employment Opportunities Commission (EEOC). Corporations invested in Bedford-Stuyvesant and began to hire and promote blacks. By 1970, affirmative action programs were required; at least a commitment to the programs was required.

I point to the civil rights movement as an example of the problem of responsiveness. The corporate response to the problem—which it had been aware of since 1954—was triggered by urban riots. We have to ask ourselves, why does it take so long? Why do corporations get into it so late with such a long lag time and so reluctantly? But it is not unique to the civil rights movement.

In 1951, GM knew, as did the rest of the auto industry, that automobiles cause pollution. Hagen-Smit proved that in Los Angeles. But it wasn't until 1970, and over the vigorous opposition of industry, that Congress passed a law requiring that cars be pollution-free five years later. Assuming the industry stays on schedule, there is a lag time of 24 years. We have to ask ourselves, why? If the corporation knew it in 1951, why did it have to wait for huge public demonstrations and a costly delay to commit itself to the solution? And it's true with auto safety or migrant workers. Why is it that corporations who know that migrant working and living conditions are inhuman still don't respond to the problem?

What is particularly vexing about the question is that corporate leaders are not evil people. They don't intend to dirty the air or exploit other people. Rather, it has to do with the criteria by which corporate decisions are made and the people to whom corporate decision makers are accountable.

The fact is that if a corporation is not accountable to the people affected by corporate practices, the corporation, like any other institution, will simply not respond. There is no incentive; there is no requirement; there is no reason for a corporation to respond to people to whom they are not accountable. This is particularly true where criteria for making decisions, such as profit, create an incentive to disregard the harm incurred by people to whom corporations are not accountable. Why should a corporation making a profit in South Africa try to stop apartheid when the people who suffer from apartheid have no way of holding that corporation accountable for their harm? It was only when the American public raised questions about American corporations in South Africa that American corporations begin to respond to apartheid. Why should the corporation respond to the problem of black people before the public holds the corporation accountable? Why should a corporation respond to the problem of pollution before there is such an outcry that the public, despite the odds against them, finally holds it accountable? The incentive is to withhold information from the public in order to delay public awareness and therefore public accountability. Why should a corporation try to cure a defect in its product when the people that suffer the harm can't even hold them accountable—in this case, the consumers? Even if a consumer can afford a lawyer, file the lawsuit, get the evidence, and withstand being tied up in court for years, the corporation will settle out of court, without even admitting liability to that consumer. Then, another consumer has to go through the whole process all over again.

Regardless of how good or well-intentioned corporate decision makers are and regardless of the general ethic of fairness, the lack of any meaningful corporate accountability to virtually everybody in society creates an incentive for the corporation to disregard the harm that its business may bring to society. Responsiveness will come under the current structure only after the expenditure of millions of dollars and people-hours in organizing huge public campaigns to get legislation to stop the practice—and then only in a watered-down version.

What is required is a shift of accountability from management to the people affected by corporate decisions. We need a system of corporate governance by which affected people control decisions. We need a system in which the shareholder can hold the directors accountable for their decisions—in fact, not just in theory. We need a system by which union members can strike or in other ways hold corporate decision makers accountable for their concerns. But, most of all, we need a system by which the public, and affected segments of the public, can require the corporation to account to them directly, not through the government—it is too slow.

What we need is a whole new constitution of corporate government. We need a constitution that defines the internal process by which corporations work and the external environment within which corporations work. We need a constitution much like our own—not one that solves problems, but that sets forth the processes by which problems are solved. The constitution could be done in a lot of ways.. It could do it by public ownership. Or perhaps a voting rights act allowing public election of directors; perhaps complete access to courts and remedies; certainly it means complete public disclosure of data.

In essence, the corporate constitution would open up the corporation to activism. It would create a system of access in which the antiwar activist, the black activist, the environmental activist, and the consumer activist could press their demands on the corporation.

Each of the reforms I would consider increase the access of public concerns to corporate decision making. The new structure is dynamic, there is no question about that. But that is what is required in a dynamic and changing society. The ease of insulated corporate decision making that has existed in the past is already forever gone. The only question left is, what will replace the old model?

For starters, we have to stop talking about myths as if they are real. We have to stop talking about shareholder democracy when there is none. We have to stop talking about the marketplace when there is none. We have to stop talking about public responsibilities when there are none. We have to look at the corporation as it is. And we have to analyze it in terms of the function it is supposed to serve for society. Then we have to decide if its function is being served and whether the components of that function, each of the different groups that are involved, have any real role in the overall corporate function.

If the shareholders have no function, then we have to decide whether we want to reinvest them with function or do away with the myth of the function. If the consumers have little power, then we have to decide whether to increase their power through the old marketplace or seek some other model. And so it is with employees and the general public. It is not a complex analysis, nor should it be plagued by ideology. It simply requires honesty—an admission of things as they are, and an acceptance by corporate leaders today that the individual power they enjoyed in the past will be substituted by a collective power in the future, in which the various components of decision making will share the decision-making responsibilities in proportion to their function or interest.

None of these reforms will make the activist go away. Indeed, it is just the opposite. Changes in these directions will open up the corporation to activist concerns. It will encourage activists. And the corporation will be better able to implement the changes called for by the activists.

Nor will these reforms set forth solutions to problems. Rather, the reforms will put the solutions in the hands of the people affected by the problems. And that is as it should be. In closing, I would like to quote from Jack London in 1899:

> Some there are among us who wish we had a haven-descended aristocracy of brains at least, who could take these things out of the people's hands, out of your hands and mine, and make them and keep them right. I do not feel thus.
>
> It is better that the people should suffer, with the remedy in their own hands, than that they should be protected by some power not of themselves.

Corporate Social Reform: A Young Person's Viewpoint

●●

● JERROLD M. GROCHOW

Management Consultant
American Management Systems, Inc.
Arlington, Va.

The viewpoint of a particular group in society regarding any controversial topic is usually composed of widely divergent ideas. When the "group" in question is one composed of students and young people in general, this problem is further compounded by the constant flux of attitudes, positions, and roles that they occupy. For this reason, it is useful to attempt to look at underlying principles: the basic set of values based on their individual and collective life experience which today's youth bring to bear in viewing their world. In fact, the viewpoint of a young person about corporate social reform can best be illuminated by analyzing the various roles that young people find themselves in in terms of the values that they hold.

My remarks should not be viewed as those of either a radical or an idealist, but rather as those of a representative of a segment of the current younger generation, a segment characterized by having a college education, a comfortable economic background, and a desire to improve, by evolution, the world in which we all live. While this may at first appear to be a rather small group, it is not. Between 25 and 50 percent of the 20–30 years age group can be characterized this way. Yankelovich has called this group "forerunners" because it seems to manifest views that often emerge in the population at large at a later time. A sufficient number of attitude studies exist to verify this general conclusion, and the reader is referred to them for the statistical evidence.[1] It is to these people, as well as to the young assembly line workers and the unemployed ghetto youth, that this article is dedicated, to these young people who look at corporate America with hope, and with fear.

To begin with, it is appropriate to state as a basic premise that corporate social reform is not an option, but a requirement. Further, it can be stated that society's ability to plan for and execute reforms is viewed as being not as great as it should or can be. The individual feels lost in a society dominated by bigness. It is this bigness that has made society what it is today, yet it is this bigness that is hampering progressive reform. This view of society often leads to overreaction in terms of proposed corporate reformation. But, it is clear that young people and many of their elders as well are willing, in ever-increasing degrees, to accept the fact that free enterprise does not mean giving corporations free rein; that the "corporate citizen" has as much, if not a greater, responsibility to the society within which it thrives as the human citizen; and that change in this direction may be harder on some than on others, but is a necessity for the continuance of a thriving society.

These statements may have a familiar ring, a ring that is hard to hear over the riots, the bombing of buildings, and with even more difficulty, through the current "apathy of youth," which the newspapers so delight in reporting. But these aspects of the current youth scene are on the fringes—the radical's answer to social problems and the dropout's nonanswer. The concerned voices, however, exist—perhaps 20 percent of my contemporaries, but that is a far greater number than were echoing such rational but different sentiments five years ago. And, of course, the growth rate of a trend rather than the absolute magnitude is what is really important for the future.

We will continue to read about the "apathy of youth"; we will continue to read, as was recently stated in the investment letter of a large brokerage firm, that, "People as a whole don't care about broad social issues." But we will also continue to see—as many people in industry have already noted—a continuing increase in the numbers of young people asking new questions of prospective employers, asking more questions of the producers of products, asking different questions as shareholders, and asking difficult questions as members of the public at large.

These are the roles in which today's youth will interact with the cor-

[1]Such studies have been published by Daniel Yankelovich and Associates, the JDR III Fund, Potomac Associates, Opinion Research Corporation, and the *National Review*, among others.

porate society: as consumers, as employees (or potential employees), as shareholders (or potential shareholders), and certainly as members of the public at large, the electorate. This interaction with corporations in each of these phases of a person's life is a fact of today's society. It is, therefore, of the utmost importance that corporate reform not be just another series of maneuverings carried out in closed boardrooms, but a *process* in which people, in all of their positions and roles, take part, and which takes place in the open, in candor, and with the realization that we must all work together in order to achieve our goals.

To a young employee, corporate social reform means being able to look at the company as a whole—at its good points and its bad points—without fear of retribution. In some cases, it may mean an "open-door" policy to the president's office; in others it may mean standing on a picket line or organizing a boycott of the company's products. The employee has a joint responsibility in this area: he must have an awareness of the consequences of various actions, both to himself and to the corporation. A recent book by staff members of the *Washington Monthly* details a number of horror stories of corporate punishment of reform-minded employees.[2] The newspapers similarly tell us of the consequences to the company of employee class action suits (for example, the recent AT&T sex discrimination case),[3] of product boycotts, etc., in a number of cases involving very large sums of money. An employee must be sure not only of his or her cause but of having exhausted traditional lines of communication before resorting to more drastic action. But, in any case, it is important for corporate management to understand the motivations and actions of its younger employees. That is a part of corporate social reform.

To a young consumer, corporate social reform means corporate leadership in product labeling, truthful advertising, and reliable products. It means not having to read about lawsuits brought by government agencies against supposedly consumer-oriented corporations.[4] It means not having to wonder what motivates a manager to hide the defect in his product or what principles he must be applying when he does so. For the consumer, it means trying to acknowledge the rules of corporate competition but not

[2]Charles Peters and Taylor Branch, *Blowing the Whistle: Dissent in the Public Interest* (New York: Praeger, 1972).

[3]"Job Bias at Bell Charged by Panel," *New York Times,* December 2, 1971, p. 1; "AT&T to Grant 15,000 Back Pay in Job Inequities," *ibid.,* January 19, 1973, p. 1; and "AT&T Bias Settlement Confuses and Angers Workers," *ibid.,* January 20, 1973.

[4]"Ad Man Burned Over Baker's Bow to FTC," *Business Week,* July 10, 1971, p. 25; "FTC's Pro-Consumer Stance Spurs Hostility," *New York Times,* May 30, 1972, p. 53; and "Car Makers Give FTC Data to Back Advertising," *ibid.,* October 14, 1972.

tolerating attempts to thwart its mechanisms by deception, concealment, or collusion. The establishment of a corporate ethic regarding the relationship of the consumer to the corporation is a part of corporate social reform.

To a young shareholder, corporate social reform means the end of management efforts to stop shareholder groups asking for equal time on important issues of policy. It means not adhering to the argument that the only people who should own stock in a company are those who agree with management. It means being open to the fact that the shareholders are indeed the *owners* and may have very legitimate reasons for their interest in various corporate policies. Such enlightened attitudes on the part of corporate management are part of corporate social reform.

To a young member of society-at-large, corporate social reform means not having to wonder about the behind-the-scenes deals of big corporations with big government for the betterment of big business at the expense of society. It means an understanding of the role of corporations in society as the producers of goods and services—not as the legislators of policy or the judges of laws. It means reaffirming the need for the corporate entity while simultaneously defining its limits. In this regard, a total social review of corporations and their relationship to other segments of society is needed. And this review will certainly be a part of corporate social reform.

It might be argued that there are a number of viewpoints that have been omitted in this short review of youth's roles in society. There is one in particular, however, which is especially relevant to this volume, sponsored as it is by the National Affiliation of Concerned Business Students. And that is, of course, the view of a young manager—and I am one who counts himself as someday falling within this category. What does corporate social reform look like from the corporate side of the fence? It is here, perhaps, where all the issues that have been spoken of and those that have been alluded to come together: for it is here that we truly have a chance to influence the things of which we speak. It is as managers that we must be able to synthesize our principles, our values, and our understanding of problems, to work for the improvement of the corporation of which we are a part.

And it is here where the most difficult questions of all can be found. How are we to implement changes of the order of magnitude that has perhaps been implied without destroying the system in the process? What methods are we to use, what tools are at our disposal, how do we grapple with the complex social issues, with their evaluation and measurement? How can we accomplish the tasks that we have set for ourselves?

It must be admitted that there are no complete answers to these questions. The methodologies of social scientists are inexact at best, wrong at worst. The corporate planner, much as any other person trying to predict the future, must deal with uncertanties and unknowns—both in data and in assumptions about the "states of nature." Although our abilities to deal with these areas are limited, what is more astounding is that many major projects throughout our society do not even use the planning tools already available. In haste to arrive at quick results, (or, often, quick profits), projects with possible impact on thousands of people, acres of our habitat, and who knows what psychological and sociological effects are begun by corporations and legislatures alike—all with the espoused purpose of solving this or that problem, but few with any real assurance of doing positive good.

It might be assumed at this point that a halt in all material forms of progress is being advocated. This is certainly not the case. On the other hand, certain types of "efficiencies" may have to be sacrificed for other types of "benefits" (recall that different segments of society will be affected by social reform in different ways). Processes whose profits are currently based on very narrow definitions of efficiency will make way for new processes more efficient in terms of total impact—environmental and human as well as traditional ones. (At lot can be learned in this area from techniques such as "systems analysis," pioneered in the Pentagon.) It is not clear what re-definitions must be made in order for our total social concern to be incorporated into the incentives of those in the corporate sphere. Time and effort on the part of researchers, managers, and students are needed to arrive at some of these answers before it is too late—before we have taken an irreversible step without knowing where our foot will land.

The viewpoints represented above have not been formed in a vacuum. As well as discussions with hundreds of contemporaries in many different spheres, I have talked with over 200 businessmen (and they were mostly *men*) in several contexts about the social responsibilities of corporations. Research of the literature on values and value systems of youth, as well as results of surveys in these areas, have provided valuable background. All these experiences have been important in refining one young person's viewpoint of corporate social reform. That viewpoint is a combination of demands, of hopes, of suggestions, and of desperate pleas. It can perhaps be summed up in the phrase, "making the corporate person humane."

It is something that is intensely personal, yet commonly shared with many others in today's youth generation and with those both older and younger. It is a viewpoint more encompassing than that of a specific role, yet more narrow than any: corporate social reform represents the best possibilities for the future. And that future is the same, whether one is a worker on the assembly line, a ghetto youth looking for a job, a student in college, or a newly hired M.B.A. already in the heart of corporate America.

It is common to be frightened of the challenges ahead, but a character-istic of most youth is also a hopefulness that we can profit by each other's experiences and learn from each other's ideas. And that should be the tone heard through this statement of youth's viewpoint: business people, stu-dents, and researchers willing to listen to each other and analyze and evalu-ate with all of their powers working toward basic goals that are commonly held.

The viewpoint of *this* young person is, "let's get on with it."

PART II

Corporate Social Audit: Definition and Measurement of Socially Responsive Behavior

●●

There is a new value system emerging in this country, starting with the youth but not limited to them. It is becoming one of the new facts of life for the rest of us to deal with. It challenges basic assumptions that we not only have taken for granted, but have virtually dominated our national life for most of our lives. When Calvin Coolidge in 1925 said, "The business of America is business," a thoughtful people nodded "Why yes—that's right." Today's young people are saying, "That's not enough." Some are going further and saying, "Business is ruining America. Business is destroying our natural resources—polluting our air and our water—and why? To produce garbage—things we don't need—and must throw away to keep the economy going. It's a garbage economy, and we don't need it."

The people who talk that way are not all hippies and not all young. An increasing number of older people are raising questions like that; and a few of them have been doing it for a long time.

—Louis B. Lundborg, Chairman of the Board,
Bank of America

Inherent in the question of corporate social responsibility is the development of a criterion, other than the one currently applicable, for the evaluation of the corporation's role in society. Corporations, like all other social institutions, operate in society under an explicit or implied social contract whereby an institution agrees to perform certain socially relevant and desirable functions and in return receives certain rewards.

However, before a new criterion is developed for evaluating the role of business in society or providing business with new guidelines for oper-

63

ating in a socially acceptable manner, three conditions must be fulfilled:

(1) Definition: What is socially responsible behavior?
(2) Measurement: How can it be measured?
(3) Accountability: To whom should the corporation be responsible?[1]

These are not simple conditions, and parts of them clearly lie in the political arena. Corporate social audit is aimed at providing answers to the second condition. It is intended to provide greater structure and meaning to the term "corporate social responsibility." The three conditions are, of course, interrelated. One cannot measure what one cannot define. Conversely, the definition question will be greatly influenced by what components are measurable, while the question of accountability is likely to become clearer by satisfying the other two conditions.

"The purpose of social audit at the micro level, therefore, is to help break down all or a large part of the broad-term, social responsibiilty of business into definable components and to develop scales that can measure these components."[2] The task is admittedly quite difficult, and current attempts at social audit are at the exploratory stage. Two broad lines of investigation are being pursued. One approach may be termed "Maximum Capability Utilization and Best Effort." The other may be termed "Reaction to Perceived Reality." The former is aimed at "allowing management maximum discretion in selecting those projects that will make the best use of the firm's capabilities in delivering desired and socially relevant outputs at the least cost. This approach is internally oriented, deliberately planned for the long term, and is relatively independent of current public fads."[3] The latter approach argues that there is really no criterion to determine what is socially responsible behavior and how much of it would be acceptable to the general public or to various interest groups. Consequently, social responsibility is whatever public expectations are, and a firm would do well to satisfy those expectations to the maximum extent possible. Thus, it is not the "real" social needs, however well defined, that are important; it is the "perceived" needs. Of course, there is no reason why these two approaches cannot be judiciously combined to develop effective corporate strategies.

---

[1] S. Prakash Sethi, "Corporate Social Audit—An Emerging Trend in Measuring Corporate Social Performance," in *The Corporate Dilemma: Traditional Values Versus Contemporary Problems,* by Dow Votaw and S. Prakash Sethi (Englewood Cliffs, N.J.: Prentice-Hall, 1973), pp. 214–231.

[2] *Ibid.,* p. 219.

[3] *Ibid.,* p. 223.

The article by Shocker and Sethi presents a methodology by which corporations can measure public responses to alternative sets of actions—each set including both costs and benefits to the public—that a corporation might pursue. Bauer and Gray suggest how a firm might go about developing a social audit for its activities. They argue that the approach to developing a social audit must differ for different companies, at least initially, and that firms would do well to move slowly in this area by building on their experiences and learning from their mistakes. Butcher presents a case study of how the Bank of America went about developing a system of social audit and what lessons, if any, can be learned from that experience.

The reader is thus briefly exposed to the current state of the art in the hope that he will find it of interest as a starting point in his own work and pursue it further in the light of his own experiences and needs.

SELECTED BIBLIOGRAPHY

*Abt Associates, Inc. "1971 Annual Report and Social Audit." Cambridge: 1972.

*American Institute of Certified Public Accountants. "Social Measurement." Proceedings of a symposium held in Charleston, S.C., April 5, 1972.

Bank of America. "Social Problems and the Bank of America." A fact sheet, May 1972.

Bauer, Raymond A., ed. *Social Indicators.* Cambridge: M.I.T. Press, 1966.

*Bauer, Raymond A. and Fenn, Dan H., Jr. *The Corporate Social Audit.* New York: Russell Sage Foundation, 1972.

*_____, and _____. "What *Is* a Corporate Social Audit?" *Harvard Business Review,* January-February 1973.

Charnes, A.; Cooper, W. W.; and Kozmetsky, G. "Measuring, Monitoring and Modeling Quality of Life." *Management Science,* June 1973, pp. 1172–1188.

Corson, John J. "The Great What-Is-It: The 'Social Audit'." *Nation's Business,* July 1972, pp. 54–56.

Drobny, Neil L. "Social Accounting in Environmental Planning." Paper presented at the Seminar on Corporate Social Accounts, Battelle Seattle Research Center, November 10–11, 1972, p. 13.

Elliott-Jones, M. F. "Matrix Methods in Corporate Social Accounting: Some Extensions of Input-Output Economics." Paper presented at the Seminar on Corporate Social Accounts, Battelle Seattle Research Center, November 10–11, 1972, p. 11.

Flanagan, John C. "Inputs to Corporate Social Accounts Gained From Intensive Longitudinal Studies of Individuals' Quality of Life." Paper presented at the Seminar on Corporate Social Accounts, Battelle Seattle Research Center, November 10–11, 1972.

Juster, F. Thomas. "A Framework for the Measurement of Economic and Social Performance." Prepared for Conference on Measurement of Economic and Social Performance, November 4–6, 1971, p. 73.

*Especially recommended for an overall view and for authoritative viewpoints on different perspectives of the issues covered.

Lamson, Robert W. "Corporate Accounting for Environmental Effects." Prepared for the Seminar on Corporate Social Accounts, Battelle Seattle Research Center, November 10–11, 1972, p. 19.

Lawler, Edward E. "Quality of Working Life and Social Accounts." Prepared for Seminar on Corporate Social Accounts, Battelle Seattle Research Center, November 10–11, 1972.

*Linowes, David F. "Measuring Social Programs in Business: A Social Audit Proposal for Immediate Implementation." Paper presented at the 24th Annual Meeting of the American Accounting Association, Southeast Region, Louisiana State University, Baton Rouge, April 28, 1972.

*Linowes, David F. "Let's Get on with the Social Audit: A Specific Proposal." *Business and Society Review/Innovation*, Winter 1972–1973, pp. 39–49.

Mobley, Sybil C. "The Challenges of Socio-Economic Accounting." *Accounting Review* 45, no. 4 (October 1970): 762–768.

*Moskowitz, Milton. "The Social Audit: Redemption Through Mathematics." *Business and Society* 5, no. 20 (October 31, 1972): 1–4.

*Sethi, S. Prakash. "Getting a Handle on the Social Audit." *Business and Society Review/Innovation*, Winter 1972–1973, pp. 31–38.

_____.*See also* Votaw, Dow.

*Sheldon, Eleanor, and Moore, Wilbert E., eds. *Indicators of Social Change*. New York: Russell Sage Foundation, 1968.

Steiner, George A. "Should Business Adopt the Social Audit?" *The Conference Board Record*, May 1972.

U.S., Congress, Senate, Committee on Congress, Consumer Subcommittee. *Initiatives in Corporate Responsibility*. Washington, D.C.: Government Printing Office, 1973.

*Votaw, Dow and Sethi, S. Prakash. *The Corporate Dilemma: Traditional Values versus Contemporary Problems*. Englewood Cliffs, N.J.: Prentice-Hall, 1973.

*Wiener, Anthony J. "Some Qualitative Changes in Expectations of Corporate Performance." Presented for discussion at the Seminar on Corporate Social Accounts, Battelle Seattle Research Center, November 10–11, 1972.

Yankelovich, Daniel, Inc. "Corporate Priorities: A Continuing Study of the New Demands on Business". Brochure describing firm's services. Stanford, Conn.: 1972, p. 24.

An Approach to Incorporating Social Preferences in Developing Corporate Action Strategies

●●●

● ALLAN D. SHOCKER
Graduate School of Business
University of Pittsburgh

● S. PRAKASH SETHI
Schools of Business Administration
University of California, Berkeley

Any social institution—and business is no exception—operates in society via a social contract, expressed or implied, whereby its survival and growth are based on:

(1) the delivery of some socially desirable ends to society in general, and
(2) the distribution of economic, social, or political benefits to groups from which it derives its power.

In a dynamic society, neither the sources of institutional power nor the needs for its services are permanent. Therefore, an institution must constantly meet the twin tests of legitimacy and relevance by demonstrating that society requires its services and that the groups benefiting from its rewards have society's approval.

67

In classical economic theory business institutions amply meet both these tests in the very process of surviving and being successful. In a market economy, in which the demand for and supply of various products and services are individually and freely determined, this theory argues that a business that successfully satisfies a market demand is indeed delivering a social good, and the investors, who benefit from the success of this business, are indeed being rewarded legitimately and fairly. This hypothesis, however, is not completely tenable, because the underlying assumptions of traditional economic theory are no longer totally valid.

Although business continues to justify its legitimacy and relevance to society on the basis of traditional criteria, many social groups are expressing dissatisfaction with business performance in meeting changing social needs and expectations. This dissatisfaction, whether based on valid information or not, is widespread and persistent.[1]

Why Does Business Need a New Approach to Understanding Social Preferences?

There are two sets of interrelated considerations that may account for the current gap between social expectations of business and business claims of performance. The first set deals with the assumption of maximizing profits to insure maximum production of socially desirable goods. In this case, although the rewards are clearly established, the assertion of the delivery of socially desirable goods is questionable at best and not clearly demonstrable at worst. Any number of circumstances could make the assumption of automatism untenable. These might include: imperfect working of the market mechanism, changing social needs and expectations, and the ability of business to resist those changes, including the resulting operational readjustments and rewards, through its control of or influence on economic resources and legal and political processes.

The dilemma of business becomes apparent by relaxing the assumption of automatism between business rewards and delivery of socially desirable goods. Many spokesmen of the business world state that they are in the business of producing profits and not goods and that if society wants business to produce a goods mixture that does not maximize profit in the long run, it should "now be paid for doing so deliberately."[2] The distinction be-

---

[1]"America's Growing Anti-Business Mood," *Business Week*, June 17, 1972, pp. 100–103.

[2]William G. Capitman, "Alternate Empirical Approaches to Corporate Social Responsibility," presented to the Institute of Management Sciences, 19th Annual Meeting, Houston, April 1972, p. 8.

tween what "social goods business automatically produces, and which it ought to be paid for as a result of deliberation"[3] is not clear or easily determinable.

The second set of considerations has to do with the measures by which institutional performance and rewards are reported. The current method of reporting these factors simply reflects a firm's ability to exploit its external environment. To the extent that a firm's profit does not proportionately reflect the external economies exploited by it or the diseconomies created by it, profits cannot be a true measure of a firm's "reward" for delivering socially desirable goods.

Corporations have gradually come to recognize most of the criticisms of their activities and their effect on society's institutions in general and individual citizens in particular. However, recognition of the problem does not by any means lead to its automatic resolution. Various groups have clamored for corporations to become "socially responsible," and there is nary a corporation that is unwilling to embrace this term. However, the trouble starts immediately when one asks: What constitutes socially responsible behavior? How should it be measured and compared between various corporations in terms of their willingness and ability to perform? To whom should the corporations be responsible? Or, in other words, what constitutes society, if different social groups make conflicting claims on a corporation's resources?

The term "corporate social responsibility" is subject to multiple interpretations, but implies consideration by the corporation of the interests of groups other than those with direct economic ties to the firm. An ever-growing number of individuals, groups, and institutions are endeavoring to monitor corporate actions and inactions for indications of socially responsible behavior and to develop strategies for exerting pressure on corporations to change their behavior in a manner that is more in accord with the expectations of one or more of these groups.[4]

This paper is based on the following assumptions:

(1) Regardless of our preferences, society is going to measure the corporation's performance according to some preconceived notions of

[3]*Ibid.*, p. 8.

[4]Examples of some of these groups are: Council on Economic Priorities, New York; the Nader groups, such as Campaign GM and Project on Corporate Responsibility; and Interfaith Committee on Social Responsibility in Investment, National Council of Churches, New York. However, the approach of this paper envisions a broader set of groups, including those with both direct and indirect interests in the affairs of the corporation, *e.g.*, employees, shareholders, legislative bodies, regulatory agencies, and media editors.

good behavior. These notions will constantly change in our dynamic society.

(2) Because the corporation is a social institution, it must alter its behavior from time to time to conform more closely to changing social expectations.

(3) A pluralistic and democratically organized society is comprised of different groups. Each of these groups has its own goals and, hence, its own criteria for evaluating a corporation's behavior. Invariably, these criteria are broad and general, and their application encompasses a high degree of subjectivity. Moreover, such criteria are often poorly communicated to the organization and frequently conflict in the guidance they provide for corporate action.

(4) It is generally true that the corporation only imperfectly understands the consequences of inadequate response—the set of forces that will be set in motion if the corporation fails to live up to the expectations of various groups. Notwithstanding the inadequacy and imperfection with which it is understood, the process of Action → Evaluation → Pressure → Reaction is a continuously occurring fact of life, and the corporation would be foolhardy to ignore an opportunity to understand it better. A firm's failure to achieve this understanding may cause its actions to lead it into unforeseen and often undesired ends.

Therefore, in order to adapt to a changing external environment, the best strategy for the corporation is to develop a systematic mechanism by which to measure the preferences of various groups for corporate actions and the relative strengths of these groups to affect corporate welfare. This information should be incorporated into its decision-making strategies so that it maximizes social satisfaction, sustains incentives for its stockholders to continue investing in it, and mobilizes its resources efficently so that its traditional constitutent groups, *e.g.*, employees, creditors, suppliers, and buyers, are satisfied with its performance.

Thus, the purposes of this paper are threefold:

(1) To demonstrate a method by which a firm may measure and monitor, on a continuing basis, the priorities that different groups and individuals place on a *prespecified* set of social goals.

(2) To develop the means by which the firm may combine the differing viewpoints of these groups into a *single* set of priorities as a usable guide for decision making.

(3) To suggest how this framework might be extended in developing suitable responses to these external pressures.

Monitoring External Group Priorities

The methodology for monitoring external group priorities includes: (1) identification of "reference groups" or individuals, whose priorities are to be monitored; (2) specification of those criteria or dimensions potentially important to those groups and capable of being affected by the organization; (3) construction of a number of "social action profiles," designed to represent different combinations and levels of these dimensions; (4) determination of group preferences among alternative profiles and satisfaction (or dissatisfaction) with the level of social good represented by each profile; and (5) analysis of these preference judgments to determine priorities for the different social dimensions implied by the groups' preference judgments and analysis of satisfactions to determine the level of "social good" acceptable to the groups. Let us consider these steps in greater detail.

1. Identification of Reference Groups

The first and most crucial step is the identification of those groups and key individuals in them whose judgments have importance for the firm. These individuals will be asked to serve as respondents during later data collection. The task of identifying such individuals and their groups is not easy. Some of the groups may be established and well known to the firm—shareholders, employees and their unions, legislators, editors, and columnists. But, at any time, others may be in the process of evolving. An evolving interest group is seldom stable and may have little permanent leadership. Moreover, various groups may have different capacities to "harm" a firm's long- or short-run interests, and their survival and growth may, to some extent, be bolstered or thwarted by the recognition gained from a firm's response to their preferences. In addition, some of these groups and their interests may be so diametrically opposed that a firm would invariably alienate one group if it chose to accept the preferences of another.

Nevertheless, a firm must make a start in identifying these groups and, as further experience is gained, must continuously redefine them. An example of one approach is that used by General Electric (1972). The company was interested in finding out the nature and extent of the "major demands" that are likely to be made on business corporations in the 1970's. As a part of this study, the company identified 13 "constituencies-pressure groups," for the purpose of assessing their "influence-effectiveness" on corporate actions. The groups included, among others, consumers, shareholders, unions, academic critics, and "moralists." Effectiveness was defined as the ability to affect legislation, legal actions, public opinion, and employee action. Although the groups were broadly defined, subjective judgments of their importance to the firm could be used to guide the firm in making further refinements.

2. Dimension Specifications

The next step is to identify and develop scales for those socioeconomic dimensions that influence a firm's decisions and are at the same time meaningful to various respondents. These dimensions are ones for which the firm is interested in obtaining group priorities. Examples of such dimensions may be the number of hard-core trainees hired, support for community cultural activities, maximum pollution emission standards, increase in wages and fringe benefits for employees, and comprehensiveness of consumer services and protections to be offered. They may also include qualitative attributes, such as the degree of beautification of community and surrounding areas or the protection of employee rights of free speech, providing appropriate scales of measurement can be developed. What dimensions are included and how they are scaled will, of course, depend strongly on the nature of the company situation and the groups and individuals whose opinions are being sought. Social costs as well as benefits should be included in these scales.

3. Construction of Social Action Profiles

Once the set of potentially important dimensions has been specified and scaled, the firm must develop a large number of "social action profiles" in terms of them. A social action profile is a representation of different levels on each of the dimensions for which a firm is seeking to measure reference group priorities. These profiles could, but need not, represent the social or economic consequences of any specific actions that the firm might contemplate. We can argue that any major action that a firm takes will have social consequences. The construction of a plant, for instance, potentially affects minority hiring, pollution, worker safety, community beauty, traffic congestion, zoning restrictions, etc. We presume that such actions or fictitious counterparts could be represented on prespecified scales in terms of these effects. It is important to understand that these profiles need not be developed to correspond to real events. Their purpose is merely to serve as stimuli to which key individuals in the different reference groups can react. (As we will note later, an ability to translate contemplated actions into their social consequences in this way will greatly extend the usefulness of this approach.) Consequently, profiles can be created arbitrarily, provided an attempt is made to keep them realistic and comparable with each other. Realism requires that each profile be believable to the key individuals who will be asked to evaluate it, *i.e.*, the individual must believe that the firm could accomplish the depicted combinations of levels of social benefit and cost in the time frame specified. Comparability requires that all profiles be premised on approximately the same level of the firm's resources, so that they appear to be true *alternatives, eg.*, a situation in which one dominates another on all dimensions should be avoided. If an action of the firm does not affect a particular dimension, this should be indicated by, say, a zero level of that dimension.

4. Obtaining Preferences Among Alternative Profiles

Some or all of the social action profiles are presented to a number of respondents from each reference group in order to obtain their preferences. One way of collecting such data is to ask each respondent to state a preference for one profile when the profiles are presented to him in pairs, *i.e.*, state which of two social outcomes he would prefer. Furthermore, each respondent could be asked to indicate whether each profile is acceptable to him, *i.e.*, meets his minimal criteria for acceptable social performance by the firm.

A respondent is *not* asked explicitly to evaluate each social dimension. Rather, he is asked to react to different *combinations* of these dimensions and to select the combination in each pair that represents a higher level of social responsibility to him. Since all this information about the alternative is contained in the profile given the respondent, his preferences among profiles are presumably based upon some processing of this information. If the profiles have been well constructed, they present different degrees of attractiveness to him. Some may represent high levels of accomplishment on dimensions of low priority for him and low levels of accomplishment on dimensions of high priority. Others may represent moderate levels of accomplishment on some high-priority dimensions, coupled with low levels of accomplishment on others. By analyzing an individual's choices among entire profiles, when he is forced to trade off different dimensions, it is possible to infer the relative importance of these dimensions.

5. Analyze Each Group's Preferences

The approach used to analyze a group's preferences among profiles to determine its priorities for the underlying social dimensions is similar to one that has had increasing application in the marketing field as a means of understanding and predicting consumer choices among alternative products (Bass, Pessemier, and Lehmann 1971; Green and Carmone 1970; Pessemier *et al.* 1971). As already intimated, this approach affords a means by which the trade-offs that are a normal part of any complex decision can be analyzed to infer the relative importance of each underlying dimension, provided the dimensions that characterize the choice objects (the social action profiles) are known.

A group's "utility" for any profile is conceptualized as a weighted combination of the attributes of that profile. Preferred alternatives are those with higher utilities. This type of model is known as a compensatory decision model. Two mathematical forms for such a utility function have appeared in the literature. The simplest model supposes that utility is merely the sum of the weighted attributes of the stimulus profile. If

y_{jp} = a measure of the jth profile on the pth social dimension (p = 1,2,...,t)

w_p = a measure of the importance (priority) attached to the pth dimension by the individual (group)

u_j = a measure of the utility of the jth profile for the individual (group)

then

$$u_j = \sum_{p=1}^{t} w_p y_{jp} \quad \text{or} \quad u_j = f\left(\sum_{p=1}^{t} w_p y_{jp} \right) \tag{1}$$

An alternative, more general model assumes that the group possesses some goal or criterion value for each social dimension. Let

x_p = a measure of the group's goal or criterion value for the pth dimension

Then, utility for a profile is inversely related to the sum of the weighted distances between the criterion level for each dimension and the actual level of the profit on that dimension. If

d_j = a weighted measure of the distance between the jth profile and the criterion, for example

$$= \left[\sum_{p=1}^{t} (x_p - y_{jp})^2 w_p \right]^{1/2} \quad \text{(the Euclidean distance)}$$

then one such example might be

$$u_j = a/d_j \tag{2}$$

in which

$$a = 1 \sum_{j=1}^{n} (1/d_j)$$

= a constant for any prespecified set of n profiles. The effect of this constant is to standardize a group's utilities so they sum to unity

Under this second model, the "closer" a profile is to the criterion, the more it will be preferred (the higher its utility). Analytical procedures exist for estimating the parameters w_p for the first model (1) and both the w_p and x_p in the second model (2). (See Srinivasan and Shocker 1972a and 1973 for discussions.) If the social dimensions are such that a group will always prefer more (or less) of every dimension when that dimension alone is considered, then a model similar to (1) is appropriate. For instance, it may be reasonable to argue that individuals will always prefer less pollution to more, more modern facilities to fewer, and more civil justice to less. However, if there is a position on some dimension beyond which preferences will decrease, e.g., an individual may think more minority hiring is advantageous only to a certain point, beyond which he would think it increasingly disadvantageous, then a model similar to (2) is appropriate.

We have talked of a group utility function but have collected individual data. A group function has meaning only if members of a group are regarded as relatively homogeneous in terms of their decision processes. Data can be readily combined that is obtained from the many individuals comprising such a group, to estimate a single set of priorities representing the group, because these data are ordinal. There are far fewer conceptual problems in combining ordinal judgments, such as paired comparison preferences between profiles, than cardinal ones. We do not have to ask whether one individual psychologically means the same thing as another when he assigns a particular value to his utility for a profile, because we do not require him to estimate such utility.

When the mathematical form of the group utility function has been specified and its parameters estimated, the group's utility for any prespecified profile is calculable. Since the various profiles have been classified by individuals at step (4) as connoting either acceptable or unacceptable social performance by the firm, the utility values for these profiles are usable in defining a region of acceptability. The boundary of this region can only be specified approximately, as individual judgments may prove inconsistent.

If the degree of inconsistency is acceptably small, this may be taken as evidence of the validity of these procedures.

Some Methodological Issues

The basic purpose of our approach is to improve communication between the firm and the varied groups that constitute its environment. Consequently, the development and implementation of the approach must be relevant for such groups. In making these procedures operational, the researcher must draw upon respondents from these groups for guidance whenever possible. Later, replications of the methodology (follow-up studies) may be less dependent on such guidance.

In developing a set of social dimensions, the problem is not so much one of generating alternatives as it is of finding those that are of critical and continuing importance to one or more of the groups. Fortunately, a study of cognitive processes has shown that individuals consider relatively few attributes of objects in making evaluations of them (Miller 1956). The firm may need to embark on preliminary testing, using a process that attempts to generate large numbers of plausible dimensions, and, by systematically relating them to some preference criterion, reduce their number. Various approaches to this task are identified in Shocker and Srinivasan (1972). The dimensions used need to be carefully defined so that each attribute of a profile conveys new information to respondents, *i.e.*, the overlap in the information communicated by different dimensions should be minimal.

Another set of issues concerns the scaling of dimensions underlying the profiles. An assumption underlying our approach is that measurement of individuals' preferences among profiles is predictive of how such individuals will react to corporate actions that "match" the profiles (Stefflre 1968). Before implementing this approach, the prudent firm should investigate alternative ways of constructing profiles. Stefflre's work (1971) provides some guidance in this task; he has stressed the importance of understanding the vocabulary that respondents use to describe the stimuli of interest (the social consequences of corporate actions) and basing descriptions of such stimuli (the profiles) on this vocabulary.

We have noted that profiles should be both realistic and comparable, since the results are dependent on the seriousness with which respondents take their task and on the trade-offs they must make between different attributes of such profiles. The number of profiles constructed for use in data collection should be large enough to insure that the estimation of the attributes' weights is reliable, yet small enough so that the task of making the paired comparisons does not become fatiguing. Generally, there should be three to four times as many profiles as underlying dimensions. This is yet another reason for attempting to find small numbers of conceptually distinct underlying dimensions. If there are ten dimensions, some 35 profiles are needed. This number of profiles would require almost 600 paired comparisons—a rather formidable task for a single respondent. If it is reasonable to regard respondents from a given reference group as having approximately the same decision function, we can spread out the task of making paired comparison preferences over all the respondents by using overlapping samples from the set of possible pairs of profiles. We have found in our own research that 50 to 75 paired comparisons per respondent is a reasonable expectation (Srinivasan and Shocker 1972b). Therefore, if four replications of each paired comparison are desired, a sample of some 35 to 50 respondents is required from each group. These numbers appear feasible.

Discussion

Our approach will lead to estimation of a group's priorities for the socioeconomic dimensions underlying the social action profiles. Moreover, through this procedure, the firm is able to order different profiles in terms of a measure of utility to respondents and to determine which profiles (combinations of the social dimensions) represent acceptable social performance to the group. The firm is now in a position to utilize this information in its internal decision making.

To date, the most serious attempt at measuring public expectations of corporate behavior has been that developed by Daniel Yankelovich, Inc. (1972). This approach consists of a continuing study of the degree and valence of public attitudes in four major areas of business-public conflict: corporate growth versus the physical environment, corporate efficiency versus consumer protection, traditional versus new rewards for work, and new versus old corporate relationships with government and society. These four broad areas are subdivided into 30 types of demands. Data are collected through 2700 interviews of representatives of nine major governmental and public groups. Although Yankelovich has not detailed his methodology, it appears that respondents are asked explicitly to consider each demand together with some of the trade-offs (other demands or other values they hold) that may be required to satisfy the demand, and then rank the importance of each demand to them. Data are tabulated by different respondent groups and by demographic and socioeconomic variables.

Although the objectives of the Yankelovich approach and those advocated in this paper appear similar, there are substantial differences in methodology. Yankelovich has respondents react to each social dimension independently and assign explicit measures of importance to it. Our approach has respondents react to particular *combinations* of dimensions and *infers* the relative importance of each. The advantage of our approach lies in the fact that weights for each dimension are estimated *simultaneously* rather than sequentially and by implicit rather than explicit consideration of the trade-offs between different *levels* of the different dimensions (implied by preferences for different profiles). We argue that our method of obtaining data from respondents is potentially more valid because respondents are asked to react to stimuli (profiles) in a manner that more nearly approaches their occurrence in reality (people normally react to objects or actions representing combinations of dimensions). People see a chair, not its height, weight, or color, separately. Our approach has the disadvantage, relative to Yankelovich's construction, that fewer dimensions can probably be considered.

Further, Yankelovich has the problem of comparing priorities (and trade-offs) of different individuals in order to aggregate them for determining group (or public) priorities and comparing these across time. There are conceptual problems in summing or averaging ranks or arbitrarily scaled values according to individuals. Different individuals may psychologically mean different things by their judgments, and adding these together can be likened to adding apples and oranges. Paired comparisons, on the other hand, are more legitimately comparable. Measures of group priorities can be obtained, *not* by measuring individual priorities and averaging them, but by deducing a single set of priorities maximally consistent with the total group's individual paired comparison judgments. This permits extension of our methodology to the measurement of a single set of priorities maximally consistent with the totality of paired comparison judgments obtained from all respondents (taken from all groups together) in order to provide a single guide to the firm's behavior.

Finally, we note that in the Yankelovich study data are collected through large numbers of personal interviews, making the cost of data collection considerable. Consequently, the costs of these studies are borne by many corporate clients and the collected data shared. Our approach would permit data collection to be carried out at a much lower expense (because data can be collected through questionnaires) so that it is feasible to expect a single firm to be able to support the study. The importance of this is that the firm can collect data more adequately related to its specific situation and needs. If the firm is identified to respondents, they need not react to social issues in general, but to actions as they might be implemented by that firm. The usefulness of the resulting information in making predictions about a group's reactions to actions of the firm should consequently be greater.

Some Plausible Extensions of the Approach

We have indicated an approach that is capable of being extended to the analysis of the priorities of individuals, groups, or larger collections of groups through the aggregation of pairwise preference judgments among prespecified "social action profiles" and have tried to argue for its basic validity. The approach can be extended to facilitate managerial decision making in a number of other useful ways. Such extensions will generally require additional research before they can be used.

This approach to the measurement of priorities has been facilitated by the ability—even desirability—of generating social action profiles arbitrarily. The need for relatively large numbers of such profiles and the desirability of constructing them to encompass a diverse set of values of the social dimensions (for purposes of increasing the reliability of the priority estimates) makes the lack of dependence of the methodology on actual events a benefit. It may even prove economically infeasible to develop large numbers of valid representations of real or contemplated actions abstractly in terms of their social consequences. To the extent, however, that the firm is able to develop suitable representations for a limited number of such actions, it can use this model to predict a group's utility for those actions. We noted earlier that, if the firm has collected data from each group regarding the acceptability (or lack of same) of each social action profile, it can use these data to define an acceptability region for the group in terms of this utility scale. Consequently, the group's utility function may be used to predict whether any contemplated action of the firm falls into the acceptability region for the group studied and, indeed, how acceptable it is to that group. These predicted utility values can be used to rank competing action alternatives and so enable decision makers to consider different group preferences in choosing among them.

In using this approach over a period of time, the firm should not only seek to measure different groups' utilities for its actions, but also the behaviors of those groups as they affect the firm. Such behaviors may range from no action, letter-writing, and speeches to demonstrations, boycotts, legal actions, and legislation. The firm may seek to investigate the relation between a group's appraisals of the firm's behavior (as measured by its "utilities" for actions the firm has taken) and the group's own behavior. Perhaps, also, some measure of a group's attitude toward the firm could be related to its evaluation of the firm's actions. This kind of relation is useful to study, both because of its importance in validating our approach and its relevance to creating within the firm an improved understanding of the ways in which the firm's behavior leads to reactions within the environment.

REFERENCES

Bass, Frank M.; Pessemier, Edgar A.; and Lehmann, Donald R. "An Experimental Study of Relationships Between Attitudes, Brand Preference, and Choice." Lafayette, Ind.: Krannert Graduate School of Industrial Administration, Purdue University, 1971.

General Electric Corporation. "Social Pressures on Business: A Systematic Analysis for Corporate Priorities." A presentation to the Board of Directors, August 3, 1972.

Green, Paul E., and Carmone, Frank J. *Multidimensional Scaling and Related Techniques in Marketing Analysis.* Boston: Allyn & Bacon, 1970.

Kristy, N. F. "Criteria of Occupational Success Among Post Office Counter Clerks." Ph.D. dissertation, University of London, England, 1952.

Miller, George A. "The Magic Number Seven, Plus or Minus Two: Some Limits on Our Capacity for Processing Information." *Psychological Review* 63 (1956): 81–97.

Pessemier, Edgar A.; Burger, Philip; Teach, Richard; and Tigert, Douglas. "Using Laboratory Brand Preference Scales To Predict Consumer Brand Purchases." *Management Science* 17 (February 1971): 371–385.

Shocker, Allan D., and Srinivasan, V. "A Consumer-based Methodology for the Identification of New Product Ideas." Pittsburgh: Graduate School of Business, University of Pittsburgh, 1972.

_____, and _____. "Estimating Weights of Multiple Attributes in a Composite Criterion Using Pairwise Judgments." Rochester, N.Y.: Graduate School of Management, University of Rochester, 1972.

Srinivasan, V., and Shocker, Allan D. "Linear Programming Techniques for Multidimensional Analysis of Preferences." Rochester, N.Y.: Graduate School of Management, University of Rochester. *Psychometrika,* September 1973.

Stefflre, Volney.   "Market Structure Studies: New Products for Old Markets and New Markets (Foreign) for Old Products." In *Applications of the Sciences in Marketing* by Frank Bass, Charles King, and Edgar A. Pessemier. New York: John Wiley & Sons, 1968.

_____.   *New Products and New Enterprises: A Report on an Experiment in Applied Social Science,* Irvine: University of California, March 31, 1971.

Yankelovich, Daniel, Inc. *Corporate Priorities: A Continuing Study of the New Demands on Business.* A brochure describing firm's services. Stamford, Conn.: 1972.

The Corporate Social Audit: Getting on the Learning Curve

● RAYMOND A. BAUER

Graduate School of Business Administration
Harvard University

Within the past year or year and a half the idea of a corporate social audit has indeed caught on. From my own perspective, in the fall of 1971 I knew of about a half dozen companies that were trying it. By the beginning of 1972, the number had jumped to a dozen. Now it must be at least several dozen. Virtually every large corporation I know of is trying or thinking of trying a social audit or something like it.

Of the growth of the literature, I am more confident. When Dan Fenn and I combed the literature in the fall of 1971, we found two, perhaps three, and if you stretched your definition, perhaps four concrete proposals about what a social audit should be. In the past few months I have read a half dozen brand new unpublished manuscripts and have seen several more in print.

The concept of a corporate audit gives promise of the development of a key institution in facilitating the evolving role of the corporation. It is now trite to observe that the corporation is under pressure to do things that it did not do in the past. And the pressure is of a new kind, coming from activists who have learned how to mobilize public and political pressure in new ways. All of these pressures and demands on the corporation are an

81

integral part of our broad attempt to turn our institutions and priorities around so that our society will perform better in serving human needs.

There can be no doubt that I am enthusiastic about the broad goals of this social turnabout that we are attempting. Almost a decade ago, I got several colleagues together to start working on a book which came out in 1967 under the title *Social Indicators.*[1] The major thesis of that book is that there are important defects in the measures that we have for keeping score on the performance of our society. The measures are biased toward understanding economic performance, and weak in helping us to understand the human meaning of what is going on. I am gratified that this notion has caught hold well beyond anything expected.

This does not by any means mean I approve of everything that is being done in that name. I fear some of it may be witless and stupid. I have long been aware of the difference between intending good and doing good. Nothing frightens me more than well-intended simplistic persons. If we quarrel with their judgment, we seem to be speaking against virtue.

I say this with full awareness of the possibility—nay, the probability, that the corporation may indeed be asked to do things that it cannot and should not do. In another context I would willingly take off my shoes and settle in for a long bull session on that topic. In this context, however, I prefer to stand relatively neutral. Without having a fixed position on what the role of the firm should be, I do recognize the existence of strong pressures on the firm to change, and an acceptance of these pressures, with varying degrees of reluctance, by a considerable portion of the business community.

To be specific, I would not on this occassion like to enter into debate with the Friedmanesque position that the social responsibility of the corporation is to earn profits—period. I would only urge that those who preach this position have the human decency to provide their converts with a survival kit.

Perhaps I should state the basis on which I make my pontifications. Dan Fenn and I have published with the Russell Sage Foundation a monograph on this subject.[2] This is primarily an analytic essay on what forms the audit might take, and the problems likely to be associated with the various forms. I also have been wandering around interviewing people about what they are up to. I have shared the fruits of these wanderings with other participants in this conference, such as Dan Fenn, Bernard Butcher of the Bank of America, and Dan Gray and Gary Marple of Arthur D. Little, Inc.,

[1]Raymond A. Bauer, ed., *Social Indicators* (Cambridge: M.I.T. Press, 1966).

[2]Raymond A. Bauer and Dan H. Fenn, Jr., *The Corporate Social Audit* (New York: Russell Sage Foundation, 1972).

all of whom have also been doing a certain amount of wandering. I have also served as a consultant for several audit attempts, and have given unpaid and unsoliciated advice to others. And, I have been reading. It is on the basis of this that I will pontificate on how things are going.

I have personally seen perhaps a dozen successful modest efforts to assess corporate social performance in the past couple of years. They might be called partial audits, or something like that. It is interesting that almost all of these efforts were carried out by persons who at the time had never heard the term "social audit." Unencumbered by any fixed notion of what a social audit is, they just did something useful.

Of all of the couple of dozen social audits attempted specifically in that name in the past two years, only two seem to have been brought to completion as yet. One is that at Arthur D. Little. Another is the audit of Abt Associates. As those of you who are familiar with this latter audit know, it is quite different in concept from what most people are doing. Abt converts social pluses and minuses of his firm into dollar forms in a social balance sheet. There is another difference, however, that you should keep in mind—in fact, two differences. The first is that the spearhead of the Abt audit was the president of the firm, Clark Abt himself. The second difference is that Abt Associates is a considerably smaller firm than most for which an audit might be relevant.

I can give you the following consolation; if you are trying a corporate social audit, you are doing about par for the course if: The idea of an audit came from somebody at the very top, and you don't know exactly what was on his mind, nor do you have the access to him to check whether or not the two of you are thinking alike or could learn to think alike. Your budget and manpower are too small for the job. The job itself is too big. Some of your most important executives are doubtful about the whole idea. Some of your most important executives have or are going to have their toes stepped on. You are involved in theological debates about what to include in the audit. The audit has ground to a halt or been put on the back burner one or more times. And, all of these things fall outside of the intrinsic difficulties of deciding what the audit is or should be and the technical problems of doing it.

I had not anticipated the organizational problems of doing a social audit. The idea usually starts originally with someone's idea that it would in some way be a good thing to do, with little notion of exactly why or how it should be done, or what resources are needed for doing it. In most instances it is in some way political. It may mean an increase in power of someone inside the firm. It means that the performance of executives is going to be judged. And, even when executives are not worried about themselves, some are anxious about what it will reveal to the public about the firm. While it may not be possible to solve all organizational problems, the anxieties of executives should at least be attended to or the audit will not get off the ground.

Another key problem I have noticed is the failure to draw the distinction between what a social audit might be eventually, and what can reasonably be done. Some persons have the aspiration of developing a "model social audit" that can be adopted by others. Frankly, I like these people too much to encourage them in this attempt.

I will grant one exception to this. If you buy Clark Abt's model for yourself, then such a model exists. However, this is a particular concept about which I have reservations for most firms at this time, which will come out as I talk.

Clark Abt and I have discussed our differences privately, and on one occasion, at his gracious invitation, publicly. I only hope that we can be explicit enough and clear enough about our reasons for disagreement that this will be fruitful. After all the years that Clark and I have known each other, it was inevitable that we should eventually find just one thing on which we were not in perfect agreement. All I resent about the present disagreement is that it makes me seem stuffy, cautious, conservative, lacking in vision, and perhaps a bit old. This hurts.

There is certainly no reason for our not *thinking* about what one or more model social audits might be at this time. In fact, in the monograph Dan Fenn and I did, we do a lot of speculating on this theme. I think this speculation is useful because it is instructive for understanding the choices and compromises we will have to make as we learn to do such audits.

But, to attempt to *do* such a model social audit at this time would mean an arbitrary choice of the purpose of the audit—a matter on which there is by no means consensus. It would also mean the solution of a considerable number of technical problems that I think are far from solution. It would also mean taking on a workload that is excessive at this stage of *beginning* to learn. As a matter of fact, it would mean asking management for a commitment of resources and patience that I just can't believe in. In fact, I am convinced that the surest way of doing nothing at this time is to set our aspirations too high.

Let me take up the points I have made so dogmatically in a little more detail.

In our Russell Sage Foundation monograph, Dan Fenn and I identify a variety of motives for doing a social audit. There is the broad dichotomy between auditing for reporting to the public and auditing for internal decision making. Auditing for these two purposes is likely to demand slightly different forms of data and different standards of reporting. Internal decision making, at this stage, can benefit from relatively imprecise data and informed judgments with which the public would not be satisfied. And, certain forms of data, such as the true costs of social programs, would be valuable for internal decision making, and probably of little interest to the public. In fact, the reporting of such true costs might be regarded with suspicion as a form of inflation of the corporation's social contribution.

Regarding auditing for internal decision making, we identified at least four motives, which persons may have an varying mixtures. They are: satisfying the corporate conscience, staying out of trouble, solving social problems, and improving the financial wisdom of social programs. Since then I have encountered a fifth motive, which may in the end prove most important of all. That is auditing the performance of units within the firm for purposes of enforcing social policies. Each of these motives poses different informational requirements. The easiest requirements to meet are those that satisfy the corporate social conscience. However, since this is idiosyncratic to the values, aspirations, and resources of the individual corporation and its officers, it is most difficult to imagine what a transferable "model" might be for this motive.

Each of the other motives, if carried to its logical extension, has informational requirements that now, and perhaps forever, are unattainable in ideal form. For example, staying out of trouble would require assessing corporate performance against the expectations of all one's relevant constituencies. This would ideally demand continuing political and social intelligence, along with appraisal of all the firm's relevant actions. This can be very costly indeed.

Auditing for purposes of solving social problems would demand definition and analysis of such problems, matching them to the firm's capabilities, and a performance assessment of the firm's actions—ideally. However, a true performance assessment, an assessment of the actual consequences of a firm's actions, is in itself probably intractable in many instances. One will have to learn what approximate compromises are possible and acceptable.

Auditing for the purpose of improving the financial wisdom of a firm's programs could embrace all of the above, plus an estimate of the true costs of what a firm is doing, combined with the integration of such information with the firm's conduct of its regular business. As an overall goal, I frankly think that this objective is pie in the sky. There may be limited instances in which this is possible. For example, one might be able to assess the impact of the firm's social performance on its ability to recruit desirable new executive material.

Let me dwell a little on this point. I find that there are many who hope that the social audit will be found to be a way to justify social expenditures in terms of their contributions to profits. I do not doubt that one can find individual benefits that the firm derives from its socially responsive activities. But don't kid yourself. I have very recently been going through one of my favorite sports, reading the literature in cognitive psychology. All of our models of decision making view a central part of that process as that of making trade-offs. We all value many things. And any choice of action is likely to favor one or more of the things we value over other things we value. If we act rationally, we will, by definition, act in such a way that we achieve the optimum mixture of good things, sacrificing some of them in order to achieve more of another. But, the study of the way man's brain actually works shows unequivocally that our mind is extremely adroit at avoiding the conflict that such trade-offs engender. One of our favorite devices is to argue that *in the long run* two apparently conflicting good things are not actually in conflict. I suspect something like this is going on with the expectation that the social audit will show how doing social good will contribute to profitability.

Auditing to enforce social policy within the firm can be quite feasible by concentrating on a limited number of key issues, such as minority and female employment policies, employee safety, and pollution. Records of performance on such issues generally exist. The key problems that will remain are several. Should the measures of performance be bolstered by a diagnostic process audit that will help to understand the performance? Should the costs of such programs be part of the audit? Many companies feel that airing the costs at this point will give the divisions and departments ammunition for justifying unsatisfactory performance. If costs are included, should they be out-of-pocket costs or total costs? How is total cost measured? What are the norms by which performance is judged? And finally, should performance on social issues become part of the measurement system by which executives are evaluated?

Cutting across all of the complications I have mentioned is the distinction between the social impact of a corporation and the company's social programs. By "social impact" I mean the impact of everything that the firm does. In some industries, it can be argued that social programs are mere cosmetics with respect to the impact of the firms in that industry. Yet, the auditing of a firm's social impact by virtue of its regular business is quite a different order of task than that of assessing the firm's social programs. I would argue that, at this stage, to attempt both across the board is more than should be attempted.

The key trick is to identify some definable domain of things to be audited that is doable and has some reasonable rationale. There are several ways of doing this that come readily to mind. One might be to concentrate solely on explicit social programs that are not part of the regular business. The disadvantage of this formulation, I have learned as a result of friendly criticism, is that it excludes some obvious candidates—pollution and minority and female employment. Another would be to confine the audit to all nonproduct impacts of the business' activities. Thus, an automobile manufacturer, under this rubric, would be concerned with stationary pollution from its manufacturing activities, but not with pollution caused by the automobiles it manufactures. This may not be a tenable formula for some firms, particularly those dealing with consumer goods. A third rationale might be to limit study to those issues that the company's constituents think are important. A fourth would be to concentrate on those issues that managements are most concerned with.

The choice of a rationale for keeping the audit to manageable size should, of course, be tailored to the situation of the particular firm.

In short, my position is the following: I think there is definitely a point in speculating about what we hope the social audit should eventually be. I do not think that this is a good idea, however, if it leads us to set unrealistic aspirations for ourselves at this stage. What we need to do is to set ourselves a task of which we are capable, one that by itself is worth doing, and one that will furnish a base from which we can progress. We need to learn how to get on the learning curve.

Having said that we should get on the learning curve, I probably should be more specific about what has to be learned, which in turn requires some specification of what we already know, namely, what is the state of the art?

Unfortunately much that has to be learned apropos the social audit conforms only loosely to what we ordinarily denote with the phrase "state of the art." These subjects include: deciding what territory a given audit will cover; how to organize an auditing team and keep the audit rolling; how to conduct an audit to minimize organizational resistance and eventually gain organizational support; deciding what criteria of adequate performance to use; etc. Individual firms have done a good deal of this sort of learning. At the moment this learning is transferable only in the most general sense. I have tried to do some of that with this paper by at least alerting prospective auditors to the problems they are likely to encounter. Perhaps the cases we are gathering will prove instructive. Regrettably, this type of organizational learning is very complicated, and the sharing of the learning can expose one to embarrassment. The most valuable learning experiences are apt to be traumatic. Most organizations do not want to wash their dirty linen in public, even if the name of the laundry is disguised. If we turn to more specific aspects of the audit itself I can be more concrete.

After a decision has been made about what territory a given audit will cover, the next step is to make an inventory of what the firm is doing in the various categories. This task will be highly variable, depending on the issues covered and the size and structure of the firm, as well as how diligent the central office and other parts of the firm have been in maintaining records of the relevant activities. Sometimes it will require diligent sleuthing. One of the devices that has been used in a questionnaire survey to operating units asking them what they are doing. For practical purposes, all firms with which I have had contact have been dependent on what could be assembled from records and what reporting units tell them. I am aware of only one instance when a firm has sent a corporate team out to audit what its operating units was doing, and this was done only to help the operating units evaluate their own performance. The results were not reported back to corporate officers and copies of the resulting reports were not even kept at corporate headquarters.

Clearly, eventually, corporate staff will have to develop the capability and acceptance of auditing what the operating units are doing. A press report indicates that Sears Roebuck and Company is going to try this idea. Perhaps we can learn from them.

Once an inventory of activities has been made, it may be desirable to assess the costs of these activities. A simple assessment of out-of-pocket costs should not be difficult except for the dependency on operating unit for such data on their activities. Assessment of true costs, on the other hand, is a different matter. Bascially the accounting profession understands this problem, but very little effort has been made about assigning true costs to the sort of activities that would go into a social audit. Several firms have tried this task with varying success. I know of two firms that are reorganizing their accounting programs so that they can assess true costs routinely. However, there has been virtually no experience in comparing alternative procedures and conventions, a matter that must be pursued in view of the fact that the ascertaining of true costs of even regular business activities involves many arbitrary decisions. My colleagues Neil Churchill and John Shank are working on this problem together with a major accounting firm.

To determine how well the firm is doing involves a measure of performance and the selection of a norm against which to judge that performance. For some problems, performance measures are readily available. Minority and female employment are the most obvious examples. Almost every firm has employment records. Corporate giving is another matter if willing to use level and direction of effort as a measure of performance. To find out how much good the giving did, however, the task is probably hopeless. Techniques are available for measuring pollution control performance. If employee satisfaction is an audit concern, there are well-established survey techniques and a good deal of experience in measuring performance. However, as we spell out in *The Corporate Social Audit*, the measure of ultimate performance for many activities may never prove possible. What may be required is a process audit, to which I will return shortly.

The matter of location and selection of norms is again a hodgepodge about which little can be said in a short space of time. Again, for minority and female employment, data are available by industry, but these demand adjustment for the composition of the local population. Furthermore, they may show how well a firm is doing relative to similar firms, but they do not answer the question of how much is enough. The choice of norms for judging antipollution performance is tricky. Local standards vary enough so that the norm of compliance with the law may be a rubber yardstick. The Council on Economic Priorities suggests that use of the best available technology as a criterion is the only nonrubber yardstick, but this may be too stringent a measure for some people's taste. The Conference Board has assembled some norms on corporate giving. But, for topics such as relations with minority suppliers, participation in urban development, conduct of business in foreign countries, and a whole host of other activities, there are no assembled norms I know of. It is possible to look around for a variety of other firms and see what they are doing before deciding what standards to apply.

One way out of the dilemma of not being able to assess the performance of many programs and the absence of norms is what my colleague Neil Churchill has dubbed a "process audit." This involves determining just what a firm is doing in a given area in considerable detail and assembling intermediate levels of performance (*e.g.*, number of people affected, attitudes toward a program, etc.). Even when there is a measure of performance, a process audit can help in understanding what might be required to improve that performance. So far the notion of a process audit as part of the social audit is pretty much untried, although some are being designed. Models may be found in the various evaluations the Government Accounting Office has made of federal programs. Another relevant experience is that of the accounting profession with management audits.

The value of process audits, if we can develop them effectively, is that they would enable us to bypass questions of ultimate performance and norms by which to judge activities by substituting a judgment about the magnitude and quality of effort. If the *magnitude and quality* of effort are as good as can reasonably be expected, then performance is by definition adequate. The difficulty of process audits is that they may require a high degree of detail for the public to have confidence that the audit has an adequate basis.

At this stage, each company will be pretty much on its own in starting up an audit. There is very little literature to guide businesses in many of the choices they will have to make and the things they will have to do. For some things they will have in house expertise and there are a few people around who have accumulated some experience. At Harvard we have already gathered a few cases that may be instructive.

The development of a useful body of literature is likely to be difficult because of the variety of tasks in the audit and the myriad of circumstances that must be taken into consideration.

Methodology: One Approach to the Corporate Social Audit

● DANIEL H. GRAY
Senior Staff Consultant
Arthur D. Little, Inc., Boston

When I compare my thoughts of a year ago on the subject of corporate social responsibility with my thoughts today, I am stuck by how perishable one's ideas are on this part of the learning curve. My present thoughts are rather jumbled; no matter which way I try to structure them, there are always some awkward ones left over.

One thought does seem quite compelling to me, though it may be repudiated in time. It is the conviction that now is not the time in the history of the invention of the social audit to concentrate on numerical measurement. The pressures on us to be quantitative are strong—including the pressure we put on ourselves. Quantification is such a clear avenue to respectability that we are tempted to force our way along it. Our primitive knowledge may seem more elegant when expressed in numbers than it does in ordinary language, but we are not apt to deceive many people very long with a forced facade of quantification. The danger is that we may waste valuable time deceiving ourselves.

On this occasion I will speak as though I knew my own mind, and as though I knew what was right and what was wrong—not because I do, but because it may provoke helpful rebuttal. The way I see things is highly conditioned by the role in which I am cast. In some societies I would be

91

known as a running dog, or as a lackey of some kind, but in this society I am what is called a management consultant. That conditions my approach to the social audit. As consultants my colleagues and I have pondered and rejected several approaches to the problem of helping business firms (and other kinds of organizations) to adapt themselves to the rising demand for new kinds of corporate social responsibility.

One thing we have decided not to be is a common scold. This is what a great many people in the field of social responsibility are. Like Rex Harrison singing, "Why can't a woman be more like a man?", they ask, "Why doesn't business come closer to my values and standards?" The common scold technique attempts, through moral and ethical pressure, to coerce businessmen toward actions that they are supposedly too irresponsible to take on their own. This is not an approach that will take a consultant very far with his client. So instead of asking how a business can be made more socially responsible, we ask our clients who, if not they, will take the initiative in deciding how these new social demands are going to be met. Do they want to be actors or spectators? If they cannot be persuaded to meet some of these demands in timely and socially acceptable ways, other institutions—existing or yet to be invented—will have to do so. We pose the problem in terms of a capable organization trying to meet some newly formulated needs and to preserve its initiative. It works better than preaching and scolding.

We have also decided not to pose as social responsibility scientists. This means resisting the temptation to hide all the uncertainty and ambiguity and indeterminateness of the situation behind words and numbers that sound as though they were precise. It means not pretending to know exactly what is meant by "the quality of life" and "nature's balance" and "social responsibility." It means acknowledging the existence of confusion and complexity. It means remembering that behind all the fancy, auto-intoxicating terms like "equation," "matrix," "profile," "vector," "coefficient," "function," and "quotient" lie a lot of fragmentary, elusive, tentative, disjointed insights and intuitive groping. Before dressing up a social responsibility proposition in pseudo-scientific garb, try to see how it looks in simple prose. Simple notions in humble form help keep one's expectations more realistic.

A third role we have examined and rejected is that of the "stretch accountant." Because conventional accounting has been so useful to business, it is only natural to try to stretch it to cover social costs and benefits. Like many others, we have gone down that road; unlike some others, we have decided that it is a blind alley. We have concluded that traditional corporate accounting is a derivative of, and is coterminous with, the theory of a market economy. As such, it is concerned with transactions. Yet the social problems that disturb us most lie outside the realm of transactions. To some extent, they have become problems because they had to be excluded for our theory of a market economy to achieve closure. Accounting has the same kind of closure. It owes its rigor to what it excludes. To try to stretch it to measure all social costs and benefits is to violate its very foundations. Isn't it ironic that a theory that has encouraged us to neglect "externalities" is now embarrassed by its inability to measure "external" distress? It looks to us as though it is not "stretching" but innovation that is required if we are to have social accounting. Accounting has renovated itself in the past—most recently in the areas of national-income accounting and management accounting—and must now do so again.

Fundamental innovation will require that we give up the idea that simple profit maximization and transactions proliferation are by themselves adequate proxies for social welfare. This means that social accounting will require some ideological change. We are ready for such change—if only we knew what to substitute for what displeases us. People almost always hang onto things that they don't like and know to be inadequate, if something better isn't yet in sight. ("Better the devil we know. . . .") Market theory, our present guide to social welfare, excludes whatever lies outside the realm of transactions. These exclusions are increasingly the center of our concerns, giving us the feeling that we (and our accountants) are the victims of premature closure. Breaking closure and then re-creating it around a bigger universe is tough work—especially if the smaller universe has been the scene of great accomplishments. But that's what social accounting and the search for the social audit are all about.

If "stretch accountants" want to find sophisticated measurements to deal with external costs and benefits that lie outside the realm of transactions, they will find them only by inventing new kinds of accounting. Such invention will not be possible until there is a new theory from which it can be derived. The way theory controls measurement is interestingly exhibited in the history of thinking about insanity. We used to define insanity as possession by demons, and later on as retribution for sins. When we switched from demonology to the notion that insanity is evidence of a sinful life, measurement turned to an inventory of naughty deeds. (Cf. Mr. Linowes' social audit[1] as an inventory of good deeds.) Subsequently, meas-

---

[1]David Linowes, "Measuring Social Programs in Business: A Social Audit Proposal for Immediate Implementation," paper presented at the 24th Annual Meeting of the American Accounting Association, Southeast Region, Louisiana State University, Baton Rouge, April 28, 1972.

urement shifted again—to the calibration of skull contours, to the recording of brain waves, to the analysis of the birth trauma, to the anatomy of melancholy, and now to computerized documentation of faulty molecular structures of acids and proteins. Each new measurement thrust was triggered by a new theory about what we now call "mental health." What should be measured in a "social audit"? We won't know until we have new theories. Meanwhile, we live with a theory that is getting us into deeper trouble because of its built-in measurement limitations. As consultants interested in this work, we realize, therefore, that we need to get inside the theoretical thinking of our clients. This is not all that easy, since most businessmen feel a loss of effectiveness when they start questioning assumptions and talking about theories. They don't particularly like having their theories or their ideological thinking made the subject of explicit analysis or debate.

So scold, if you like; or mutter pseudo-scientific incantations; or stretch and strain at conventional accounting; we have decided to get theoretical. By "theoretical" we don't mean academic or withdrawn. Our patron saint, at this stage of trying to help invent the social audit, is John Wayne—not because we admire the Wayne ideology, but because John Wayne knows how to cope. He doesn't stop a runaway stagecoach by standing in front of it and denouncing its irresponsibility. He gets on a horse and moves at about the same speed in about the same direction as the thing he wishes to control, until it's a fairly easy matter to jump over and bring the thing under control. That is the kind of method we need, if we are going to try to get inside the business mind and influence the thinking that goes on there.

We've grown accoustomed to hearing very stringent, often impossibly perfectionist demands from businessmen when they describe the kind of social accounting they require if they are to take on new social responsibilities. These exacting demands are a device for holding the problem at bay. Actually, business is full of quick-and-dirty, arbitrary, and inconclusive measurements. Consider the average study about whether a company headquarters should be moved to Connecticut; it has none of the elegance demanded of a social audit. Consider how a typical advertising budget gets renewed: Having spent so many dollars on media messages, having achieved such-and-such a Nielsen rating, and having moved the share-of-market indicator up so many points, the Board is ready to renew or expand the budget for next year. This is not a very meticulous measurement approach to a significant decision, but it is considered adequate. Why, then, the demand for dazzlingly sophisticated technical measurement when it comes to a social responsibility budget? The answer is that the advertising budget gets by relatively easily because it is accepted as being within the domain of a profit-seeking enterprise, and the social responsibility budget faces impossible demands because it is generally still perceived as lying outside of that domain. The message we get from this is not that business is irresponsible, but that we need to prove, in however limited a demonstration project, that their are "areas of convergence" in which what is important to business as such is also important to business as a social institution with social obligations and needs.

Enough of these convergencies or coincidences can be found to keep you very busy, even though you can't assure yourself that any one of them will by itself lead to a master solution of the whole problem. Nevertheless, each one is apt to change the nature of the game, opening up new possibilities and providing fresh learning. If you want to look for convergences, where can you find them? Let me give two examples of vehicles that can serve both the business strategy and the social strategy of an organization. One company we've worked with found that its business future depended significantly on its developing a mass market presence. It had always dealt with a few very well-to-do- customers, but now faced the necessity of dealing with a large number of less well-to-do customers. If it failed to achieve this, it would be in serious competitive difficulties. It operates in and is tied to a city that is going downhill very rapidly, with one neighborhood after another slipping into decay and deterioration. So the social need to help arrest urban disintegration, and the business need to create a mass market, were inescapably tied together, in the sense that they required a common strategy. Not noblesse oblige but stark necessity required that these two problems be addressed together. This set the stage for business investment in an action-research prototype project that would test (1) some plausible propositions about community economic development and (2) some experimental techniques for combining the efforts of various interested parties. In the process of defining the remedial propositions to be tested, we found ourselves thinking of new patterns of measurement. Our client developed a social accounting concept which discriminates between "fighting chance" neighborhoods and those too far gone to be retrieved by a reasonable scale of effort. This new piece of accounting measures such things as how many businesses have entered and exited, how many windows are broken in a city block, how many people in the area register to vote, how many go to church, how many have lived in the same place for more than a year, and a number of other quantifiable and less-quantifiable things. This is how theories of causation and remedy yield new criteria and new measuring techniques when tested in an R&D approach.

Investment in action research on a low-profile, modest-budget basis is the way we try to climb the learning curve. We take a bite of reality and it bites back at us in one of these situations. We change our theory a bit, and get a new indication of what to try to do and to measure. This is real-time experimentation, which requires that we be explicit about our economic and social theories concerning the cause of distress and the remedy of distress. There are formidable problems of scale, and there are uncontrolled variables which put an end to any pretense of being purely scientific, even though we try hard to be as objective and as careful and as scrupulous as we can. The only purely scientific social accountant would have to be dictator of the community, assigning the obedient variables their proper roles. Social change in a democracy is much less tidy and much more of an iterative process.

A second example of an "area of convergence" that permits the testing of a plausible hypothesis, can be found inside many companies in which the business problem of sluggish productivity coincides with the social problem of upward mobility for blacks and women. There is a whole body of theory in organizational behavior and organizational development, that offers believable and testable propositions bearing directly on the alienation and immobility of minority people and the motivation and productivity of workers. These propositions can be converted into action-research projects by marking out in an organization a vertical corridor reaching from a manager to a superintendent to a supervisor to a chain of workers, down to an entry level job. This corridor is then managed and monitored in new ways, to test in real time the validity of propositions about how the mode of training and the mode of supervision can have, at one and the same time, a good effect on the traditional balance sheet and a good effect on the vertical mobility of women and blacks in that organization. You find yourself designing new measuring devices such as a "climate index," an "alienation index," a "system cost" for achieving promotions, and a "productivity profile"—taking care not to be seduced by that fancy terminology. You become an educated groper and a voracious learner with a slowly accumulating residue of knowledge deposited by perishable propositions. Although measurement is the ultimate purpose, it is not the immediate concern. The first concern at this state is to find convergence, in order to establish in the minds of business persons that eventually it is profitable to apply the managerial and organizational capabilities of business to a whole set of new social demands that somebody must meet. Businesses are concerned about the deterioration of the business milieu, the decline in their prestige, and the possible loss of initiative in these matters. They do not want to be mere spectators at the defintion of their own social responsibilities.

What we are now trying to help our clients do in response to new social demands is to incorporate these demands into their business objectives.

Business has been through this many times before. Business has, through the centuries, taken on more and more obligations, sometimes enterpreneurially, sometimes by prescription and law. Since corporations are competent engines of change, with great resources of energy, skill, and imagination, they are among the reasonable nominees for the role of solving urgent social problems—especially if government is bogged down to the point of paralysis in the morass of institutionalized bureaucracy spawned by the last great wave of social change in America. Without arguing for *carte blanche* for business leaders, we are trying to get them to see the benefits in a more socially responsive pursuit of profits.

They will act faster and more effectively if they perceive the convergence of their business needs and society's needs, and if they have a calculus that can reckon with more variables than their current theory of accounting can embrace.

The Program Management Approach to the Corporate Social Audit

●●●

- BERNARD L. BUTCHER
  Assistant Vice-President
  Bank of America

John Corson, Chairman of Fry Consultants, recently published an article entitled "The Social Audit: The Great What Is It?"[1] That phrase pretty well sums up the general public image of this subject. It is also a fair summary of the confusion in the ranks of those currently playing the social audit game.

For widely varying reasons, a number of companies, consultants, and academics have embarked on the development of what they consider to be a "corporate social audit." Interest in these developments has spread widely, and several people—including David Rockefeller—have gone so far as to predict that social audit information will be required to supplement financial statements within the next five years.

The result of this aroused interest has been an explosion of "learned essays" on the subject and a series of hastily arranged conferences attended by corporate officers who want to find out what all the noise is about. Most people leave these conferences shaking their heads and still mumbling versions of John Corson's "What Is It?" question.

The purpose of this paper is to bring a little order to the subject, to ex-

[1]*Nation's Business*, July 1972, pp. 54–56.

plain in some detail one concept of the social audit, and to place that concept in its proper perspective. The paper is divided into four sections:

(1) a review of several different actual approaches, as opposed to theoretical expositions, that have so far been used in the social audit;
(2) a contrast of these efforts with the "program management" approach;
(3) a brief history of the Bank of America's activity in this field; and
(4) an analysis of the strengths and limitations of the "program management" approach.

Alternative Definitions

The major social audit projects that have been undertaken so far can be grouped into three general categories: the *social indicator* approach, the *constituent impact* approach, and the *corporate rating* approach.

Social Indicator Approach

The idea that corporate social performance can be somehow quantified springs from an older effort by many social scientists to develop some sort of overall quality-of-life index. This index would show ups and downs in the social health of the nation—just as the national income accounts reflect economic health—and would be based on a system of statistical social indicators.

Incidentally, a bill was recently passed the Senate—sponsored by Senator Walter I. Mondale (D-Minn)—calling for the creation of a "Council of Social Advisers" similar to the President's Council of Economic Advisers. Unfortunately, the lack of adequate social statistics means that the social advisers will be working without the hard data like what is available to the economic advisers. The danger is that this council will become a highly political body—existing only to pass blessings on social programs proposed by the President.

Outgrowths of the overall social indicator movement are efforts by departments such as Housing and Urban Development, Health, Education and Welfare, and the General Accounting Office to quantify the impact of social programs such as job training, low-cost housing, daycare centers, etc. These efforts to pin down and return on the taxpayers' investment in federal social programs have met with only limited success so far.

Two banks are now attempting to apply the social indicator concept to corporate community involvement. Last year's annual report of the First National Bank of Minneapolis identified ten aspects of the quality of life in the Twin Cities—job opportunities, health, transportation, etc.—and the bank is now presumably attempting to develop measurements for each one, which will enable it to channel its resources for maximum effectiveness.

In a separate effort, a New York bank has engaged an outside consultant and formed a top-level committee on the social audit. This bank plans to experiment in two economically stagnant areas of New York City, in which it has branches. It will direct a number of special loan and other programs into these areas to reinforce government efforts. The results will be monitored by measuring changes in branch performance as well as selected community social indicators.

Both the New York and Minneapolis experiments suffer from two very severe limitations. The first is the reliability of the social indicators themselves: Does an increase in the number of high school graduates going to college *really* indicate higher quality education? Does an increase in home ownership *really* indicate better housing? This type of basic question has been troubling social scientists for years.

The second limitation is that it will be next to impossible for these banks to determine what impact their individual programs have had on changes observed in the community. There are so many variables at work in any community that the input of one company will more than likely to be highly obscured.

Constituent Impact Approach

A second approach to the social audit has been an attempt to set out, in the traditional balance sheet form, all of the many interrelationships between a company and its various constituencies—employees, customers, suppliers, the immediate community, and the general public.

The 1971 Annual Report of Abt Associates, a consulting firm in Cambridge, Massachusetts, contains a social income statement that lists the social costs and benefits of the company's operation as they relate to each constituent group. Such things as fringe benefits and a daycare center are listed as social benefits to the company's employees while "overtime worked but not paid" is listed as a social cost to that constituent group. Environmental improvements and local taxes are listed as community benefits, while the value of local services consumed is termed a social cost to the community.

While Abt Associates is actively trying to peddle this approach to other companies, it does not appear to have much value as a decision-making tool. The traditional financial statement format is somewhat contrived, and the cost of gathering this type of information for a larger, more complex organization would probably be prohibitive.

One aspect of the constituent impact approach holds real potential for development as an effective management tool. This is the research being conducted, principally at Michigan University's Institute for Social Research, into the concept of human resources accounting. Part of this research has been translated into practical application by the R. G. Barry Corporation of Columbus, Ohio. In three successive annual reports, Barry has been presenting separate financial statements in which the value of its human resources is included like any other asset. Salary and training costs are viewed as investments with expected long-range return rather than as controllable expenses. Barry feels that this concept has done much to improve labor-management relations, reduce turnover, and upgrade productivity.

Corporate Rating Approach

This is an attempt, largely by groups and individuals outside the corporate structure, to determine which companies are responding well to social and environmental demands and which are acting in an irresponsible manner. The move toward corporate social ratings has been motivated largely by universities, foundations, church groups, and certain mutual funds that wish to maintain portfolios of "socially responsible" stocks.

Each of these groups is working to establish its own criteria of evaluation. Most current ratings are highly subjective, relying on some general composite image of the corporation and its industry. Questions like what to measure, how to measure, how to weight the diverse aspects of social performance, and how to rate companies across industry lines are still largely unresolved.

The most scientific work in this field is being done by the Council on Economic Priorities in New York. The council has done several highly regarded and well-publicized industry studies, for example, pulp and paper and electric utilities, which rank companies according to their pollution control efforts. No attempt is made to factor in other items, such as employment practices, to arrive at an overall social rating.

Corporations should keep a close eye on any consensus criteria developed for the evaluation of social performance. However, this is essentially an external approach with little direct application to management decision making.

Social Program Management

The efforts of the Bank of America contrast with the social indicator approach, the constituent impact approach, and the corporate rating approach in two important ways:

—First, we have concentrated our efforts on measuring only those activities in which we are involved largely for social reasons. The social impact of our mainstream banking activity is considered to be beyond quantification at this point.

—Second, we have been attempting to develop an internal management information system that will allow us to better evaluate and administer our special socially oriented programs. The implications of this system for external reporting have been of secondary importance.

We have concentrated on what might be called the "program management" approach to the social audit. The objectives of this approach have been to develop a system that will: (1) reflect an approximation of the costs of our social programs; (2) evaluate the effectiveness of these programs; and (3) allow us to budget intelligently and improve our social return on investment.

History of Project

Two developments led directly to our involvement in the social audit. In February 1971, President Clausen of the Bank of America gave a widely publicized speech entitled "Toward an Arithmetic of Quality" in which he encouraged the development of an overall national quality-of-life measurement as well as a measure of corporate social involvement.[2]

A few months prior to President Clausen's speech, the bank had organized an "Ad Hoc Committee on Social Priorities," which recommended, among other things, that a social activities inventory be taken and that a cost estimate and social budget be developed. The public relations department prepared the inventory, which is now periodically updated, and the controller's department made a cost analysis of these programs for the year 1970.

This cost estimate is highly subjective, both in terms of the items included and excluded and in the interpretation of opportunity and out-of-pocket cost. For this reason, the information developed has never been used for decision-making purposes, and a similar analysis was not made for 1971. Even so, the compilation of an inventory of activities has been a valuable exercise, and we have been among the leaders in developing a methodology for estimating the costs of social programs.

---

[2]A. W. Clausen, President of Bank of America, before the Conference Board, Sixth Annual Financial Conference, New York, February 18, 1971.

We recognized at that time that cost estimates alone could do more harm than good. Without a corresponding estimate of benefits, things like special loan programs would be portrayed as straight expense items rather than as investments with expected long-range return both to the bank and to society. The natural reaction of management would probably be to minimize these expenses rather than to become further involved.

With this in mind, an experiment was organized this summer utilizing three M.B.A. students and one bank man. The object was to pin down costs and to explore the possibility of quantifying the benefits associated with four of our social programs. Each individual audited a separate program and attempted to find a methodological common denominator, which could be applied across the board to other special programs. The four programs were selected for analysis because they have some elements of cost to the bank—either directly or in terms of sacrificed income—and we hope they generate some benefits in return:

(1) the New Opportunity Home Loan Program—reduced home loan terms to low-income borrowers;
(2) the Small Business Administration-Minority Enterprise Program—liberalized terms for minority entrepreneurs;
(3) the "Banking on People" Program—our National Alliance of Businessmen hard-core hiring and upgrading effort; and
(4) the Student Loan Program.

Even though some direct benefits can be quantified, such as the reduced turnover of "Banking on People" graduates, we realized early in the summer that it would be nearly impossible to quantify the long-range impact of our social programs on the bank and on the broader community. Even though we should expect minority business development or hard-core employment programs to improve the "bankability" as well as the general well-being of minority communities, we can find no way at this time of quantifying "return on investment" for explicitly social programs.

We therefore lowered our sights from an attempt to quantify explicitly long-term benefits to an analysis of the degree to which our social programs are meeting their stated objectives. In other words, we are no longer attempting to measure the impact of these programs, only to determine if program objectives are being met.

For example, if the SBA-minority enterprise program is designed to produce X-number of successful minority businesses, how well is it meeting that objective? If the student loan program is designed to allow more young people to go to college and to increase our retention of college graduate customers, how well are we meeting those objectives?

The four program evaluations have been submitted and are now in the process of being analyzed. Each one contains three basic elements :

(1) Historical perspective. This section analyzes the actual reasons for our entry into a particular social program and explores the original objectives of the program. Generally speaking, corporate social programs are entered into for a myriad of reasons, many of which have little to do with a positive, rational policy of social involvement. This type of analysis should help us to formulate realistic objectives for existing programs and more rationally evaluate future possibilities.

(2) Cost analysis. This section attempts to add up the direct costs, allocated costs, and sacrificed income associated with each program. Many thorny problems must be dealt with here. For example, we know our rate of return on student loans—but what rate do we compare this with to determine sacrificed income? Once a methodolgy is developed here, we should be able to compile this data on a regular basis and budget our expenditures more intelligently.

(3) Benefit analysis. As stated above, there are few elements of social benefits that can be quantified in dollar terms—similar to the cost side of the ledger. In most cases, surveys have been designed to determine from those affected by our programs whether or not our objectives are being met. If these surveys are administered periodically, we should be able to improve both the social and economic efficiency of our programs.

The next logical step will be for us to expand this type of analysis to other socially motivated programs and to refine at least the cost and benefit analyses so that they can be administered on a regular basis. The result of this process could be a yearly budgeting system for nontraditional programs in which direct costs and sacrificed income are related back to budget estimates, and program performance is periodically evaluated against pre-established objectives.

Evaluation

The program management type of social audit just described has several advantages from the viewpoint of the corporation. Since most large companies have now placed someone in charge of the general social policy area, this exercise should give that individual some feel for the nature of the beast he is wrestling with.

The approach translates squishy social programs into the comparatively rational, cost-benefit terminology familiar to businessmen. And it should allow management to incorporate social considerations—and dollar commitments—into its overall planning and budgeting process.

So the program management approach appears to be both feasible and valuable. However, this type of audit has several major limitations which must be kept clearly in mind:

—First, this approach will not be very useful for external reporting purposes. Even if the many assumptions that must be made in the cost section are fully accepted, there exist no standards against which to judge whether too much or too little has been invested in social programs. And information in the program evaluation and benefits sections is intended primarily for management.

—Second, the approach concentrates attention on about one percent of corporate activities, namely, those nontraditional items that contain some element of expense and are classified as "socially oriented." Clearly, any corporation must be primarily concerned with the other 99 percent. Public interest criticism of business has been focused mainly at mainstream activities—not special programs. And this is the area in which business has its greatest social impact.

In the banking industry, for example, critics are not merely urging that we adopt a few more special loan programs. Rather, they want a rethinking of our political involvements. They want to make sure that the best interests of underdeveloped countries are fully considered in our international operations. They are concerned that our general lending policies reflect a certain social awareness and that our loan practices are clearly in the best interests of the average consumer.

They want our services to be advertised and presented honestly and openly. And they are urging that *all* employees be given the opportunity for self-fulfillment and personal involvement. This is the "99 percent" that apparently cannot be quantified in a social audit.

—The *third* limitation is that the program management approach is of little value in the selection of priorities—it tends to evaluate individual social programs in a vacuum. The process does not include an estimate of the needs and demands of the communities we serve, weighted by the particular capabilities and limitations of the individual business.

Performance is related only to the objectives of that particular program. Relatively little information is generated about the impact of these programs on any particular social problem. By focusing on programs rather than problems, the possibility of concentrating a broad range of capabilities on a single problem area might be overlooked.

The selection of priorities in the social policy field must be a key item of management concern. Although a rational *process* can be developed that will lead to the selection of priority areas of concern, the essential decisions and choices will remain subjective. The program management audit will be of little value unless corporate policies and programs are logical extension of well-conceived social priorities.

Conclusions

Notwithstanding these limitations, the conclusion is reached that the development of a program management type of social audit is a worthwhile endeavor—one that will provide corporate management with a valuable tool in the murky social policy area. The costs associated with designing the system and gathering the data should not be underestimated. But socially oriented programs will be of growing importance on the corporate scene, and these programs should be monitored at least as closely as our traditional activities.

We must be careful, however, to keep the methodology and data developed in their proper perspective. If we concentrate too heavily on budgeting and evaluating special programs, we run the risk of failing to concern ourselves with the bigger, but essentially subjective, issues of priority selection and overall corporate social impact. We hope that we do not lose sight of potential opportunities for dealing positively with areas of social concern within the framework of our normal business operations.

PART III
Legal Approaches to Corporate Structural Reform

●●

An important thing to understand about any institution or social system, whether it is a nation or a city, a corporation or a Federal agency: it doesn't move unless you give it a solid push. Not a mild push—a solid jolt.
—John W. Gardner, *Common Cause*

There is a large body of literature testifying to the fact that managements of large corporations are self-perpetuating oligarchies, responsible to no one but themselves. It is a legal fiction that management works for the stockholders and that, in reality, stockholders are largely at the mercy of management, their only option being to sell their stock in a company when they do not approve of its activities. Furthermore, it is contended that, given the complex nature of today's business and the nature and dispersion of stock ownership, the typical stockholder is neither capable of understanding nor interested in the affairs of the company in which he owns stock.

Under these circumstances, the question of legitimacy for corporate management becomes important and worthy of serious discussion. Modern corporations are repositories of vast economic resources and their actions affect the lives of millions of people. In a real sense, they are private governments operating under legal constraints that may be substantially irrelevant.

In this section, three distinguished legal scholars review and comment on a number of widely discussed proposals for legal approaches to corporate structural reform, with a view to evaluating their strengths and weaknesses in affecting the changes in corporate behavior that they espouse.

Phillip Blumberg is concerned with corporate reform by changing the

107

composition of the board of directors with the inclusion of special interest or public directors. Blumberg maintains that special interest representation implies a change in the allocation of power within the corporation if the groups represented are effectively represented and the corporation's accountability is increased Blumberg also looks into the question of public interest and government directors who are not associated with any particular group.

To evaluate the effectiveness of various types of outside directors and the types of organizational structures under which they might serve on the corporate board, Blumberg looks at the experiences of West Germany, Sweden, Yugoslavia, the United Kingdom, and Latin America. After discussing the limitations to and possibilities of applying these approaches in the U.S., Blumberg concludes that at present there is insufficient interest in trade unions, government, and legal, business, and political circles in changing the method of selection and composition of corporate boards. Unless this interest intensifies, the discussion remains academic for the near future. However, he warns that mere change in the composition of corporate boards will not necessarily solve our problems, and any reform in this direction must be accompanied by reforms in other areas of corporate activity.

Melvin Eisenberg starts with three propositions: that in large corporations management has significant discretionary power; that management's interests in preserving its own security and advancing its own prestige frequently come in conflict with objective decision-making criteria; and that management is typically unskilled in dealing with the social implications of business decisions. For these reasons and on political grounds, the excessive concentration of power in the hands of a small number of individuals is to be avoided. He critically examines two approaches to attacking the problem: participation by corporate client groups, i.e., employees, suppliers, customers, and shareholders.

For a multitude of reasons, Eisenberg finds that the inclusion of client groups is not likely to be very effective in broadening management's accountability. In addition to possible conflicts of interest, it is not certain whether these representatives would necessarily act in the public interest, thereby making management more efficient (from society's viewpoint). He also rejects the possibility of making the "average shareholder" more active in the management of the corporation. He takes note of the increasing ownership of corporate stocks by institutional investors, such as banks, insurance companies, pension funds, and mutual funds. He concludes that corporate control can be realized more effectively if we analyze voting membership in terms of shareholdings rather than shareholders. He also foresees a trend in which institutions will begin to take more interest in corporate management, thereby reducing management's discretionary powers. Since institutional investors represent a more diversified group of interests and people, it is likely that their outlook will be more broadly based and socially more desirable.

Donald Schwartz develops and discusses a proposal for federal chartering of corporations. He suggests that federal incorporation must be looked at as an integral, albeit a small, part of the larger fabric of economic policy. In suggesting reform of corporate law, he aligns himself with the constituency that views it primarily as a constraint on management's power within the prevailing economic system. Schwartz briefly traces the history of efforts at federal chartering and notes that the current impetus has come largely from public-interest-oriented activists who seek to make corporations more socially responsive. After carefully discussing the arguments in favor of federal chartering, he evaluates other alternatives, short of the major overhaul of existing corporate laws envisaged in federal chartering, toward accomplishing the objective of the reformers. Schwartz discusses at length the various methods by which existing state and federal laws may be amended to improve them and concludes that this approach is feasible and could be effective.

Schwartz notes that a wide variety of proposals are currently being lumped under the term "federal chartering," for instance, those made by shareholders' groups and Nader's Raiders. Clearly, federal chartering means totally different things to different groups. Schwartz proposes a model for federal chartering aimed at correcting the two major problems in the present system—lack of accountability and lack of varied input.

Among the proposals made by Schwartz are the following:

(1) Federal chartering should be limited to large corporations with significance outside of their immediate vicinity, perhaps corporations with $10 million in assets and 300 holders of its securities. This would include all companies listed on the **Fortune** list of the 1000 largest companies.

(2) The federal chartering proposal should provide specific guarantees and increased disclosure of information in the areas of corporate records and reports, directors and management, shareholders, and organic or fundamental changes.

SELECTED BIBLIOGRAPHY

*"Application of the Sherman Act to Attempts To Influence Government Action." *Harvard Law Review* 81, no. 4 (February 1968): 847–858.

Areeda, Phillip E. "Antitrust Laws and Public Utility Regulation." *The Bell Journal of Economics and Management Science*, Spring 1972, pp. 42–57.

"Arthur Goldberg on Public Directors: A Business and Society Review Interview." *Business and Society Review/Innovation*, Spring 1973, pp. 35–39.

Blumberg, Phillip I. "The Politicalization of the Corporation." *The Business Lawyer*, July 1971, pp. 1551–1587.

Bork, Robert H. "The Supreme Court vs. Corporate Efficiency." *Fortune* 76 (August 1967): 92.

*Cheit, Earl F., ed. *The Business Establishment*. New York: John Wiley & Sons, 1964.

Dahl, R. "Alternative Ways of Controlling Corporate Power." Address given at the Nader Conference on Corporate Accountability, Washington, D.C., Fall 1971.

Daniel, Coldwell, III. "The Regulation of Private Enterprises as Public Utilities." *Social Research*, Summer 1967, pp. 347–354.

*Dodd, E. M., Jr. "Statutory Developments in Business Corporation Law." *Harvard Law Review* 50 (1936): 27–59.

*Eisenberg, Melvin Aron. "The Legal Roles of Shareholder and Management in Modern Corporate Decision-Making." *California Law Review*, January 1969, pp. 1–60.

*————. "Access to the Corporate Proxy Machinery." *Harvard Law Review* 83 (May 1970) : 1489–1526.

*————. "Megasubsidiaries: The Effect of Corporate Structure on Corporate Control." *Harvard Law Review* 84 (May 1971) : 1577–1619.

Epstein, Edwin M. *Corporations, Contributions, and Political Campaigns: Federal Regulation in Perspective*. Berkeley, Calif.: Institute of Governmental Studies, May 1968.

————. "The Historical Enigma of Corporate Legitimacy." *California Law Review* 60 (November 1972): 1701–1717.

*Folk, Ernest L. "Recent Developments in Corporation Statutes." *Journal of Legal Education* 20 (1968): 511–522.

Friedmann, Wolfgang G. "Corporate Power, Government by Private Groups, and the Law," *Columbia Law Review* 57 (February 1957): 155–186.

Heilbroner, Robert L. "Rhetoric and Reality in the Struggle Between Business and the State." *Social Research* 35.3. (Fall 1968): 401–425.

*Jennings, Richard W. "The Role of The States in Corporation Regulation and Investor Protection." *Law and Contemporary Problems* 23 (Spring 1958): 193–230.

McKie, James W. "Regulation and the Free Market: The Probelm of Boundaries." *The Bell Journal of Economics and Management Science*, Spring 1970, pp. 6–26.

*Nader, Ralph. "The Case for Federal Incorporation." Address given at the Nader Conference on Corporate Accountability, Washington, D.C., Fall 1971.

Nader, Ralph, and Green, Mark J., eds. *Corporate Power in America*. New York: Grossman, 1973.

*Noll, Roger G. *Reforming Regulation: An Evaluation of the Ash Council Proposals*. Washington, D.C.: Brookings Institution, 1971.

*Especially recommended for an overall view and for authoritative viewpoints on different perspectives of the issues covered.

Park, John Nelson. "Freedom, Value and the Law: Three Paradoxes." *Ethics*, October 1951, pp. 44–47.

*Posner, Richard A. "National Monopoly and Its Regulation." *Stanford Law Review* 21 (February 1969): 548–643.

Posner, Richard A. "Antitrust Policy and the Consumer Movement." *Antitrust Bulletin*, (Summer 1970), pp. 361–366.

*President's Advisory Council on Executive Organization. *A New Regulatory Framework: Report on Selected Independent Regulatory Agencies.* Washington, D.C.: Government Printing Office, January, 1971.

*Ratner, D. L. "The Government of Business Corporations: Critical Reflections on the Rule of 'One Share, One Vote'." *Cornell Law Review* 56 (November 1970): 1–56.

*Ruml, B. *Corporate Management as a Locus of Power in Social Meaning of Legal Concepts No. 3: The Powers and Duties of Corporate Management.* 1950.

Scheibla, Shirley. "Gentleman's Agreement? Government Is Making Business Its Unwilling Partner in Bias." *Barron's*, December 23, 1968, pp. 9–17.

*Schwartz, Donald E. "The Public-Interest Proxy Contest: Reflections on Campaign GM." *Michigan Law Review* 69 (January 1971): 421–538.

Taylor, John F. A. "Is the Corporation Above the Law?" *Harvard Business Review*, March-April 1965, pp. 119–130.

The Conference Board. *Competition, Efficiency and Antitrust.* 8th Conference on Antitrust Issues in Today's Economy. New York: The Conference Board, 1969.

*U.S., Congress, Senate, Committee on the Judiciary. *Federal Licensing of Corporations: Hearings on S. 10 and S. 3072.* 75th Cong., 1st sess.

Reflections on Proposals for Corporate Reform Through Change in the Composition of the Board of Directors: "Special Interest" or "Public" Directors

●●

● PHILLIP I. BLUMBERG
School of Law
Boston University

This paper is concerned with proposals for corporate reform through change in the composition of the board of directors by the inclusion of "special interest" or "public" directors. Such proposals have become an increasingly frequent topic for intellectual inquiry in the United States and have been the subject of shareholder proposals in a number of so-called public interest proxy contests.

Factors Contributing to Such Proposals

The proposals for broadening the composition of the board of directors reflect a series of factors:

112

(1) *Corporate power.* Recognition of the large public corporation as a political and social institution of paramount dimensions in a society in crisis. Recognition of the power and role of the major corporation in American society inevitably leads to evaluation and review of its structure for governance.

(2) *The social and environmental crisis.* We are living in a world undergoing profound and accelerating change, change in attitudes and values, and in institutions. Further, the intensity of the social and environmental crisis, the struggle for racial and social justice, the concern with the physical impact of industrial technology on the quality of life and on life itself inevitably leads to a reexamination of previously accepted institutions and relationships. The large corporation as a major influence in the society is, along with society, swept up in the process for change.

Similarly, the acceptance of the as yet poorly defined concept of corporate social responsibility has given rise to a reconsideration of the basic objectives of the corporation, including its structure, especially board structure.

(3) *Lack of accountability.* Management of the large public corporation lacks accountability. Although there is still argument to the contrary,[1] it is difficult not to conclude that with the separation of ownership and control resulting from the widespread distribution of shares, shareholders in the large corporation, generally speaking, no longer have an effective independent voice in the selection of the board or in other matters submitted for their consideration. Except in unusual cases, board members have become a self-perpetuating group, accountable only to themselves or perhaps to the chief executive officer who was responsible for their selection (who himself is accountable to no one). Further, management's ability to rule unchallenged by take-over threats from outsiders may rest on its continued ability to achieve minimally acceptable earnings per share.[2] In the typical case, however, management lacks accountability.

(4) *Lack of legitimacy.* The corporation is no longer an enterprise that significantly involves only its owner-managers. It affects wide segments of the society. "Private" has become "public." In contrast, the social and economic groups whose lives and fortunes are profoundly

---

[1] See, *e.g.*, Melvin Eisenberg, "The Legal Roles of Shareholders and Management in Modern Corporate Decisionmaking," *California Law Review* 57, no. 1 (1969): 33–53.

[2] See Henry Manne, "The Myth of Corporate Responsibility—Or Will the Real Ralph Nader Please Stand Up?," *Business Lawyer* 26 (1970) : 533, 535.

affected by the corporation have no role in its direction. Regulation through government in specified areas of conduct is regarded by some as only a limited and inadequate response. Such reform groups want the affected social and economic groups to participate in corporate decision making. They demand changes in the board because it is unrepresentative. Even if the board were not self-perpetuating and the stockholders possessed power of selection in realistic terms, the problem of legitimacy of a board of directors reflecting solely stockholder interests would remain.[3] The problem of accountability might be resolved, but the issue of legitimacy would still remain.

(5) *Rejection of the concept of managerialism.* This conviction that the interests of vitally affected groups are not receiving adequate consideration in the corporate decision-making process represents a rejection of the concept of managerialism. This is the concept that the board of directors acts as a trustee not solely for stockholders but for employees, consumers, the community, and other groups as well, and that the function of the board is to mediate among the legitimate claims of these conflicting groups. However, this view has little support in reality. Further, it runs directly contrary to the established legal principle that the board of directors owes single-minded loyalty to the advancement of the interests of stockholders.[4]

Purposes to Be Achieved by Reform of the Board of Directors

The different reform proposals currently in vogue have a fundamental common objective. They seek to transform the large corporation into a public institution, in which the public or the groups affected by the corporation participate in a meaningful manner in the corporation decision-

---

[3]See Abram Chayes, "The Modern Corporation and the Rule of Law," in *The Corporation in Modern Society*, ed. Edward Mason (New York: Atheneum, 1966), pp. 25, 40–41; Bayless Manning, book review, *Yale Law Journal* 67 (1958): 1477, 1490–1491.

[4]*E.g., Parke* v. *Daily News Ltd.* (1962), Ch. 927, 963; and *Dodge* v. *Ford Motor Co.*, 204 Mich. 459, 170 N.W. 668 (1919): "A business corporation is organized and carried on primarily for the benefit of the stockholders. The powers of the directors are to be employed for that end." See Harry Henn, *Law of Corporations*, 2d ed. (St. Paul: West Publishing Co., 1970), p. 475; and L. C. B. Gower, *Principles of Modern Company Law*, 3d ed. (London: Stevens, 1969), p. 522. (Gower regards the traditional view as "increasingly anachronistic.")

making process. These reform proposals may be divided into two different classes: the efforts to broaden the perspectives of the board and more sweeping proposals for change in the very structure of the board through the addition of special interest or public representatives.

Broadening the perspectives of the board. One approach is to strengthen the board by the addition of members from different backgrounds and experience who can provide a fresh look at the problem. This may be termed the "window-out" aspect. A related objective is to provide additional public disclosure, to achieve a ventilation of the decision-making process, to reduce the secrecy of the inner corporate circle, and to improve channels of communication. This may be termed the "window-in" aspect.[5]

Board representation for interest groups or the public. A more far-reaching proposal is to achieve the transformation of the corporation into a public institution through representation on the board of the special interests affected by the corporation or of public or government representatives. The essence of special interest representation is that the representatives reflect the interests of the group selecting them, rather than the interests of the institution in whose governance they are participating. However, it is not clear to whom such a representative would be accountable when an organized constituency does not exist. This is an effort to achieve political or economic influence for an economic or social class. Thus, insofar as employee representation is concerned, it is an attempt to strengthen union power or create industrial democracy or social justice, as well as economic justice, for employees.[6] It is part of an effort to achieve greater employee individual fulfillment and job satisfaction through employee participation in decision making on all levels. Board representation is only as aspect of the larger movement for greater employee participation.

---

[5]See Peter Vanderwicken, "Change Invades the Board Room," *Fortune*, May 1957, p. 156.

[6]See Paul Blumberg, *Industrial Democracy* (London: Constable, 1968); H. Clegg, *Industrial Democracy and Nationalization* (Oxford: Blackwell, 1951); H. Clegg, *A New Approach to Industrial Democracy* (Oxford: Blackwell, 1963); F. Emery and E. Thorsrud, *Form and Content in Industrial Democracy* (London: Tavistock Publications, 1969, distributed in U.S. by Barnes & Noble); P. Van Gorkum, *Industrial Democracy in the Netherlands—A Seminar* (1969); I. Adizes, *Industrial Democracy: Yugoslav Style* (1971); Irish Management Institute, *Industrial Democracy—A Symposium* (1969). The discussion in this paper on employee representation follows my presentation, "The Constituencies of the Corporation—New Direction for Employees," before the American Bar Association National Institute's conference on Corporations Under Attack—Response to New Challenges, New York City, October 27, 1972. See Phillip Blumberg, book review, *Texas Law Review* 50 (1972): 598.

Broadening the Perspectives of the Board

The most popular of the current reform proposals is the growing movement to strengthen the board through the addition of individuals who can bring fresh perspectives and values to board deliberation. This includes such groups as blacks, women, nonbusinessmen, and young people.

(1) Blacks. Approximately 70 major American corporations have recently elected blacks to their boards of directors. Black members on the board of directors are becoming a part of the accepted pattern of American corporate life.[7]

(2) Women. At the present time, approximately 20 major American corporations have women directors. The recent action of General Motors in adding a woman to its board will no doubt accelerate this process.

(3) Nonbusiness persons. Corporations such as Dayton-Hudson Corporation and First Pennsylvania Company have added nonbusiness persons to their boards because they brought a new perspective not previously represented in the board deliberations.[8]

(4) Foreign nationals. A fourth category is the addition of foreign nationals to the boards of American corporations conducting significant parts of their business abroad. This process is in its early stages, but there are increasing signs of recognition that the boards of American multinational corporations should include persons of non-American origin in order to function more effectively.[9]

These are attempts to strengthen the board by broadening its perspectives through the addition of new inputs in the decision-making process.

The selection of such new directors by the board itself has certain obvious strengths and weaknesses. The selection by the board assures the new member of a harmonious reception and a full inclusion in the deliberations of the board. Conversely, without independence and firmness by the individuals in question, the board action has limited significance. Further, putting aside the basic question of whether the board as a whole really has a decisive impact on corporate policy or whether it is a prisoner of the corporate bureaucracy or technostructure, it is obvious that the addition of an isolated black or woman director or two is not likely to change the alloca-

[7]*Wall Street Journal,* October 5, 1972, p. 1, col. 6.

[8]See Dayton-Hudson Corporation, *Quarterly Report,* 1971 (inside front cover); *New York Times,* January 24, 1972, p. 59, col. 2.

[9]See *Business Week,* August 19, 1972, p. 60.

tion of power within the corporation. Although at present it may be just a symbolic gesture, it will have considerable significance of its own because of its influence on public attitudes.

At the same time, it represents an effort of profound significance to give recognition to the aspirations of deprived groups for a fuller participation in the decision-making process. It simultaneously symbolizes the dedication of the board to nondiscriminatory principles in the operation of the enterprise.

Special Interest Representation

Special interest representation has more profound objectives than simply broadening the perspectives of the board. It seeks to change the allocation of power within the corporation, to assure affected groups of participation in the decisions that involve them and achieve accountability and legitimacy for the corporation.

There have been recent public interest shareholder proxy proposals for many types of special interest representatives: employees, consumers, women, minority groups, dealers, suppliers, environmentalists, persons experienced in conversion from military to nonmilitary production, public interest advocates, and even investment bankers.[10] Many of these are clearly intended solely as symbolic gestures, or are justified in terms of broadening board perspectives, without, at least for the moment, undertaking a campaign for a reallocation of corporate power. In any event, they have attracted limited support thus far.[11]

[10]*E.g.*, American Telephone & Telegraph Company, "Notice of Meeting and Proxy Statement," April 22, 1971, pp. 12–13; *ibid.*, April 19, 1972, pp. 13–15; Chrysler Corporation, "Notice of Meeting and Proxy Statement," March 3, 1972, p. 25; Ford Motor Company, "Notice of Annual Meeting and Proxy Statement," April 7, 1972, pp. 20–21; General Motors Corporation, "Notice of Annual Meeting and Proxy Statement," April 6, 1970, pp. 19–20; *ibid.*, April 5, 1971, pp. 34–37; Honeywell, Inc., "Notice of Meeting and Proxy Statement," April 2, 1971, p. 8; Jewel Companies, Inc., "Notice of Annual Meeting and Proxy Statement," May 15, 1972, pp. 10–11; Northern States Power Company, "Notice of Meeting and Proxy Statement," May 10, 1972, pp. 8–9.

[11]The Northern States Power proposal to add two "public interest advocates" received 9.13 percent of the votes cast; the Chrysler proposal to add "women and representatives of employee organizations, consumers, and minority groups" received 4.91 percent, and the identical American Telephone & Telegraph proposal received 3.80 percent. The remaining proposals received less than 3 percent of the votes. Council on Economic Priorities, *Economic Priorities Report*, July-August 1972, pp. 49–50.

Employee directors. The proposal for employee representatives on the board of directors is unquestionably the most serious of the proposals for special interest representation. It is based on the belief that of all the groups affected by the corporation, it is the employees upon whom the corporation has the most important impact.[12] The employees are therefore entitled to participate in corporate decision making, including representation at the board level.

The proposal is reenforced by the German experience, in which industry has prospered notwithstanding two decades of employee representation on boards, and the increasing acceptance in Europe generally of the principle of employee representation.

The crucial aspect about the proposals for employee representation on an American board of directors is that they do not reflect any serious objective of the American trade union movement or of workers generally. The proposals are being advanced without grass-roots support.

Consumer, supplier, or dealer directors. There is no experience available to assist in determining the significance of proposals for consumer, supplier or dealer directors. There is little or no support for these proposals; they are purely theoretical or symbolic. Further, there are serious mechanical problems in determining the constituency: Who is entitled to vote? How are votes allocated? What is the distinction between major and incidental purchasers or suppliers? What is the distinction between individuals and corporate purchasers or suppliers? What are the procedures for notice to the persons affected, for the conduct of a contested campaign, for the election itself?[13]

The desirability of adding consumer directors to the board receives little support from the history of the consumer-owned enterprises in the country, such as the mutual insurance companies owned by policyholders or the mutual savings banks owned by depositors.[14] These consumer-owned com-

---

[12]Gower, *Principles of Modern Company Law*, pp. 10-11: "Insofar as there is any true association in the modern public company it is between management and workers rather than between the shareholders inter se or between them and management . . . the employees are members of the company for which they work to a far greater extent than are the shareholders whom the law persists in regarding as its proprietors."

[13]See Eisenberg, "Legal Roles of Shareholders," pp. 16-21; Robert Dahl, "Citizens of the Corporation," *New York Times*, March 17, 1971 ,p. 45, col. 5; and John Flynn, "Corporate Democracy—Who Needs It?," *New York Times*, March 17, 1971, p. 22 (address to Conference on Corporate Accountability, October 30, 1971).

[14]See John Hetherington, "Fact v. Fiction: Who Owns Mutual Insurance Companies," *Wisconsin Law Review*, 1969, p. 1068; and Gary Kreider, "Who Owns the Mutuals? Proposals for Reform of Membership Rights in Mutual Insurance and Banking Companies," *University of Cincinnati Law Review* 41 (1972): 275.

panies invariably involve self-perpetuating boards and have not demonstrated a discernible degree of concern for consumers that differs from the attitudes of their stockholder-owned competitors. If possible, there is even less degree of accountability because of the absence of the stock market as a measure of performance and the takeover bid as a possible discipline.

Environmentalists as directors. It is hard to take seriously proposals for environmentalists, economic conversion experts, investment bankers, etc., as directors, except as symbolic or quixotic gestures.

Stockholders as special interest directors. Another special interest group that has not been the subject of such proposals paradoxically appears to be the only group that may realistically hope to achieve such recognition in the foreseeable future. These are the stockholders themselves. As pointed out, although the stockholders elect the board as a matter of form, it is apparent that this is fiction. Through control of the corporate proxy solicitation machinery, the board in fact selects itself and obtains its election from passive stockholders who, as a practical matter, are unable to act independently or effectively. The board may, therefore, be fairly said to represent itself, not the stockholders.

Financial institutions—mutual funds, investment trusts, bank trust departments, pension and welfare funds—have substantial concentrated holdings in many public corporations. Looking at the holdings of mutual funds alone, one finds that a high percentage of shares of a limited number of major companies is held by the fund.

According to a New York Stock Exchange study, 28.3 percent of the equity shares of listed corporations are held by pension funds and financial institutions; the total exceeds 40 percent with the inclusion of nonbank trusts, foreign institutions, investment partnerships, and unregistered mutual funds.[15] These institutions would possess the power, if they were prepared to act in concert, to express the traditional powers of owners and elect their representatives to the board.

The potential power clearly exists, but as the Institutional Investor Study Report of the Securities & Exchange Commission concluded, is as yet unexercised.[16] Nor is there any indication that such institutions are now, or in

[15]New York Stock Exchange, *1972 Fact Book* (New York: New York Stock Exchange), p. 50. During 1971, institutions were responsible for 68.2 percent of the dollar volume of all trading on the New York Stock Exchange, excluding members' trading for their own accounts (p. 53).

[16]U.S., Congress, House, 92d Cong. ,1st sess., 1971, H. Doc. 92–64, pt. 8: 124–125; and *ibid.*, pt. 5: 2749–2770.

the future will be, ready to act in concert.[17] Recognition that exercise of management control over portfolio companies has little advantage and serious disadvantage will most likely mean that such potential power will rarely if ever be exercised through concerted action of the financial institutions. Designation of directors on the boards of portfolio companies would not only limit the flexibility of funds in disposing of their shares but would make them highly vulnerable to public criticism for interlocking directorates and to increased regulatory controls. Such concern with the possibility of governmental controls has obviously increased with the critical Patman subcommittee report on the shareholdings of banks and trust companies in their fiduciary capacities.[18]

A more likely possibility is pressure by funds for the election of prominent public figures to the board, not to represent the funds as such but to represent public stockholders generally. If such a development were to occur, it could constitute a form of special interest representation for shareholders. The objectives of such shareholder directors presumably would be generally congruent with the objectives of the incumbent management, except perhaps in the area of executive compensation. Such directors, not dependent on management favor for their selection, could function as genuinely independent directors, and a measure of accountability could be achieved.

The question, however, is whether such a form of shareholder representation deals with the fundamental problem. It may restore a measure of accountability and introduce public influence into the private institution. It restores legitimacy, however, only by being prepared to accept the shareholder in the large American corporation as a person entitled to the traditional perquisites of ownership, notwithstanding his basic relationship as a temporary investor or supplier of capital. It clearly does not provide any

---

[17]One of the isolated cases in which institutional investors have acted in concert to protect their positions as shareholders is *Unied Funds, Inc.* v. *Carter Products, Inc.*, Common Clearing House, Fed. Sec. L. Rep., para. 91, 288 (Baltimore Md. City Cir Ct. 1963) (injunctive relief obtained against proposed issuance of nonvoting common stock that probably would have resulted in delisting from the New York Stock Exchange). Institutional investors have also played some roles in connection with transfers of control. U.S., Congress, House, 1971, H. Doc. 92-64, pt. 8: 125–127; and *ibid.*, pt. 5: 2771–2843. See in general, R. Barber, *The American Corporation* (New York: E. P. Dutton, 1970), pp. 53–67; and "Why the Big Traders Worry Industry," *Business Week*, July 25, 1970, pp. 53–61.

[18]U.S., Congress, House, Committee on Banking and Currency, Subcommittee on Domestic Finances, 90th Cong., 1st sess., staff report, *Commercial Banks and Their Trust Activities: Emerging Influence on the American Economy* (Washington, D.C.: Government Printing Office, 1968).

recognition for the other interests in society who are vitally affected by the corporation and who play no role in the decision-making process.

Public or Professional Directors

Still another approach to the problem is the addition of public or professional directors to the board, suggested by Justice Douglas 30 years ago as a method of protecting public investors. Robert Townsend has recently revived the proposal, changed its orientation by charging the public directors with a quasi-trusteeship to represent not only public investors but the community at large, and added supporting features for funding and staff assistance.[19]

A basic problem with the public or professional director is the question of selection. Who is the appointing authority? If it is the board that does the appointing, the public director becomes simply a variation of the efforts of a board to broaden its perspectives by including individuals with different values among its membership and hardly represents a fundamental change in board compositiion. So long as the public or professional director is without a constituency or appointing agency with public influence, the extent of change of corporate objectives will not be major.

The New York Stock Exchange has successfully pressed for the election of at least two outside directors[20] to the boards of listed corporations. Even if the Exchange were to go further and require as a condition to listing that listed corporations elect to their boards persons selected from a panel nominated by the Exchange or some other independent agency, it might further implement the pressure for outside directors and Justice Douglas' objective of further protecting investors. It would hardly satisfy reformers intent on achieving power within the corporation, or those nonshareholder groups presently unrepresented on whom the conduct of corporate affairs has such a profound impact.

In any event, it is clear that the effectiveness of outside or public or professional directors will be severely limited so long as they are part time, not well compensated, and are not assisted by an independent staff.

---

[19]Robert Townsend, "The Ups and Downs of Working Life," *Center Magazine*, January-February, 1972, pp. 27, 34–36; and *New York Times*, November 1, 1971, p. 34, col. 2.

[20]New York Stock Exchange, *The Corporate Director and the Investing Public* (New York: New York Stock Exchange), (1965), p. 7.

Government Directors

The remaining alternative for structural reform is the addition of government directors to represent the public interest. This hardly seems a satisfactory solution. The thought of a government representative in every board room stirs little enthusiasm. Lack of confidence in the appointing authority, lack of confidence in the type of individual likely to be selected, and concern for further increase in centralized governmental power obviously contribute to such lack of enthusiasm. The appointees of President Nixon, for example, are hardly likely to be regarded as allies of social reform groups in their efforts to change the direction of corporate policy.

The limited experience in the United States with government-appointed directors in the Union Pacific Railroad, the Illinois Central Railroad, and the Prudential Life Insurance Company, gives little confidence that such representatives will help produce decisions that better reflect the public interest. Although the experience with government directors in such newer ventures as Communications Satellite Corporation is still limited, there is no indication thus far that it will provide a meaningful redirection of corporate affairs with greater social sensitivity.

Nor does the European experience with government directors provide support for the proposal. Neither the British experience over two decades with government directors on the boards of nationalized companies, nor the French experience in similar circumstances, has proved particularly effective.[21] A greater degree of public accountability and sensitivity to the needs of the community at large does not appear to have been attained.

The European Experience with Employee Representation

Support for employee representation on the board, or the more sweeping reform of employee ownership and management of industry, arises from the extensive European experience.

German codetermination. The major support for the concept of special interest directors arises from the German experience with co-determination, or employee directors on the supervisory board (*Aufsichtsrat*), the

[21]See Gower, *Principles of Modern Company Law*, p. 60: "The [English] public corporation solves the problems of the realtion between shareholders and managers by abolishing the former, but this does not solve the problem of controlling the managers"; and Wolfgang Friedmann and J. Garner, *Government Enterprise* (New York: Columbia University Press, 1970), pp. 113, 315.

upper board in the two-tiered German board structure. This upper board elects the members of the managing board (*Vorstand*) and supervises and inspects, but does not manage. The managing board is the executive arm of the corporation, combining both the direction of day-to-day operations and policymaking. In steel, coal, and iron firms with 1000 employees or more, with full codetermination, employee representation is restricted to one-third of the supervisory board.[22]

The German model of the dual board with one-third labor representation on the upper board has been adopted in the proposed statute for a European Company (*Societas Europaea*) in the European Economic Community.[23] The French Law of June 18, 1966, similarly requires the representation of two nonvoting labor directors on the boards of public corporations (*sociétés anonymes*).[24]

The results of the German experience are mixed. In steel, iron, and coal, where labor representation includes one-half of the supervisory board as well as a veto power over the designation of the labor director on the managing board, full codetermination seems to have provided labor with an effective share of power, has apparently contributed to reduced labor strife, and generally has worked satisfactorily. In other industries, where labor representation is restricted to one-third membership on the supervisory board, or partial codetermination, labor representation generally has been regarded as not particularly meaningful. Power in fact has not been shared.

[22]Law of May 21, 1951, 1 BGBl. 347; Law of October 14, 1952, 1 BGBl. 681; Law of August 7, 1956, BGBl. 707, as amended; Law of July 15, 1957, 1 BGBl. 714. For a general review of the German experience, see C. de Houghton, ed., *The Company: Law, Structure, and Reform in Eleven Countries* (London: Allen and Unwin, 1970), pp. 213–221; M. Fogarty, *Company and Corporation—One Law?* (London: Geoffrey Chapman, 1965); A. Shuchman, *Codetermination: Labor's Middle Way in Germany* (Washington, D.C.: Public Affairs Press, 1957); H. Spiro, *The Politics of Codetermination* (Cambridge: Harvard University Press, 1958); Frame, "Worker Participation with Particular Reference to Codetermination in the Federal Republic of Germany," *Victoria University Law Review* 5 (1970): 417; and Detlev Vagts, "Reforming the 'Modern' Corporation: Perspectives from the German," *Harvard Law Review* 80 (1966): 23.

[23]Commission of the European Communities, *Proposed Statute for the European Company*, Art. 137(1), Supp. to Bull. 8–1970 of the European Communities. See P. Sanders, "The European Company on Its Way," *Common Market Law Review* 8 (1971): 29; and P. Storm, "A New Impulse Towards a European Company," *Business Lawyer* 26 (1971): 1443.

[24]The works council (*comité d'enterprise*) of a *société anonyme* may appoint two of its members, who are to be present in a nonvoting advisory capacity at all meetings of *conseil d'administration* (in corporations using the single-board system) or the *conseil de surveillance* or upper board (in corporations using the dual-board system). Law No. 66–427 of June 18, 1966. See Common Clearing House, Common Market Report, *European Stock Corporation*, ed. P. Sanders (1969).

Often, labor representation has not been taken seriously and has served as a source of sinecures for old faithful trade union officials, with management control essentially unimpaired.[25]

Yugoslav worker self-management. The Yugoslav experience with worker-owned industry has attracted worldwide attention. As a unique blend of socially owned enterprise operated both for profit under market conditions and for the benefit (after payment of capital charges) of the workers employed in the enterprise, the Yugoslav model is most interesting. Control is in the hands of the plant workers and the local communes, with the League of Communists playing a significant role behind the scences. The shift of the locus power from the federal government to the plant and the local community reflects the strong centrifugal forces in Yugoslavia that make decentralization politically desirable, in light of the divisive influences separating the Serbs, Croats, Slovenes, Macedonians, Montenegrins, and other ethnic groups in the nation. The development has been associated with problems of capital formation and a high level of inflation, which apparently reflect, at least in part, worker pressure for short-term profit maximization. Paradoxically, concern with short-term objectives may be greater in worker self-managed Yugoslav industry than in the United States where management has been increasingly inclined to be concerned with the long-term view.[26]

Whatever the intellectual interest in this experiment, it is hardly a realistic alternative. Even Professor Dahl, one of its leading American proponents, concedes the unlikeliness of American labor support for the program. He visualizes its possible adoption in the United States as a result of middle-class pressure.[27] It may be noted that presently there is not the slightest indication of any support for this visionary conclusion.

Sweden. Sweden is moving in the direction of employee representation on the board. A number of companies, including Volvo, have experi-

[25]See Fogarty, *Company and Corporation—One Law?*, pp. 120–121, 126–128; and D. Granick, *The European Executive* (Garden City, N.Y.: Doubleday & Co., 1962), p. 220.

[26]For a general review of the Yugoslav experience, see Adizes, *Industrial Democracy*, p. 7; M. Broekmayer, *Yugoslav Workers' Self-Management* (Ridel, 1970); de Houghton, *The Company*, pp. 320–336; J. Kolaja, *Workers' Councils: The Yugoslav Experience* (New York: Praeger, 1966); G. Macesich, *Yugoslavia: The Theory and Practice of Development Planning* (Charlottesville: University Press of Virginia, 1964); S. Pejovich, *The Market-Planned Economy of Yugoslavia* (Minneapolis: University of Minnesota Press, 1966); and J. Vanek, *The Participatory Economy* (Ithaca: Cornell University Press, 1971).

[27]Robert Dahl, *After the Revolution?* (New Haven: Yale University Press, 1970), pp. 134–136.

mented with the voluntary designation of employee directors as part of a campaign to deal with job dissatisfaction.[28] The 1971 Conference of the Confederation of Swedish Trade Unions demanded the designation of two employee representatives on all boards.[29] Swedish Premier Olaf Palme is pressing for the mandatory appointment of employee and government directors to the boards of all companies with more than 100 employees.[30]

Conflicting European trade union attitudes. An illuminating aspect of the European experience is the mixed nature of trade union reaction to proposals for employee representation on the board.

The English unions in the past traditionally opposed such representation. As C. A. R. Crosland puts it, English union attitudes have displayed "not merely apathy but a barely concealed hostility."[31] They have regarded board representation as involving a confusion in roles and impairing their ability to challenge management. The union has been perceived as the opposition and therefore by definition would not participate in the exercise of board power.[32]

In recent years, British union attitudes have tended to change. Before the Donovan Commission, some union representatives argued for voluntary participation on the boards of nonnationalized industries. A minority of the commission agreed, but the commission report regarded such a movement as unwise and premature.[33]

In sharp contrast, the German unions have regarded board membership as an objective of high priority. It has replaced socialism as the objective of the trade union movement.[34] At the present time, German unions are pressing for the extension of full codetermination or one-half representation on

---

[28]*Business International* 18 (May 28, 1971): 175.

[29]See T. Lidbon, "Industrial Democracy in Sweden," *Free Labor World*, November 1971, p. 14; and *Business Europe* 11 (September 24, 1971): 310.

[30]See *New York Times*, November 12, 1972, p. 28, col. 1.

[31]C. A. R. Crosland, *The Conservative Enemy; A Programme of Radical Reform for 1960s* (New York: Schocken Books, 1962), p. 218.

[32]See Fabian Society, "The Future of Public Ownership," Tract No. 344, 1963, p. 21; and Puckey, *The Board Room* (London: Hutchinson, 1969), pp. 96–97: "I have yet to hear a senior [English] union official give wholehearted support to worker representation on boards in the private sector."

[33]See Gower, *Principles of Modern Company Law*, p. 63, n. 53; and Friedmann and Garner, *Government Enterprise*, p. 39.

[34]Spiro, *Politics of Codetermination*, pp. 5, 35–36, 39–41.

the boards of all German corporations, rather than solely in iron, coal, and steel.[35]

The Confederation of Swedish Trade Unions has taken a middle ground. It has endorsed mandatory employee representation on boards, while emphasizing that the confederation would maintain its independence of action.[36]

Latin America. In his recent review of Latin American enterprise, Professor Bayitch reports the establishment of codetermination in nationalized industries in four countries. After observing that nationalization represented a reaction to foreign ownership rather than a movement for social reform, he notes that there has been provision for substantial employee representation on the boards of nationalized Latin American industries, including electric utilities in Argentina, tin in Boliva, copper in Chile, and oil and railways in Mexico. The Peruvian industrial reform law also provides for employee membership on boards.[37]

Problems Presented by Reform Proposals Generally

The proposals for special interest representation on a board presents serious problems.

Limitations on the applicability of the European experience. There is a complete lack of United States experience. All we can do is speculate how solutions attempted in cultures abroad might function at home. It is evident that experiments in industrial organization abroad may provide some insight and understanding in appraising possible change in American industrial organization to deal with the known problems of the existing order. This does not mean that European models may be expected to function in the same manner in the vastly different climate in the United States. The European experience reflects German solutions to German needs and Yugoslav solutions to Yugoslav needs. To lift these solutions from their

[35]Friedrich, "German Co-Determination: Parity Is the Goal," *Columbia Journal of World Business*, January-February 1970, p. 49; de Houghton, *The Company*, pp. 220-221, 361-368, 370.

[36]See A. Geijer, "Industrial Democracy in the Seventies," *Free Labor World*, April 1971, p. 15.

[37]S. A. Bayitch, "Empresa in Latin American Law: Recent Developments," *Lawyer of the Americas* 4 (1972): 399, 429-433; J. Abramowitz, V. Koven, and A. Valdez, "The Peruvian General Law of Industries," *Harvard International Law Journal* 12 (1971): 312; *New York Times*, October 5, 1972, p. 16, col. 1; and *Wall Street Journal*, August 4, 1972, p. 6, col. 4.

political, economic, historical, and cultural setting and transport them to the United States is of dubious validity.

Conflict of Interest. To whom would the special interest owe primary loyalty? Under traditional corporation law, the director owes undivided loyalty to the corporation and to the shareholders; further, such loyalty runs to all shareholders and not merely to those who elected him.[38] Would not the special interest director designated to represent the interests of the group responsible for his designation be confronted with a fundamental conflict of interest?

British nationalized industries have sought to avoid this problem by requiring primary loyalty to the corporation. Labor directors added to the boards of nationalized firms have been required to resign all formal affiliation with the trade union movement. The labor directors come to the board as persons with a trade union perspective, but not as representatives of the trade union movement.[39] The same pattern has occurred in Norway.[40]

If, however, the special interest director comes not merely as a person with a labor perspective but as a representative, the problem of conflict seems inevitable so long as there is no corresponding change in the objectives of the enterprise.

This would be the result if isolated special interest representatives were added to the boards of American corporations as presently constituted. On the other hand, if the concept of special interest representation were accompanied by a broadening of the objectives of the corporation and the advancement of shareholder interests were no longer the primary goal, the premise of undivided loyalty to shareholders would disappear. The question would then arise whether the loyalty of the special interest director to the interest group which designated him was inconsistent with the new objectives set for the enterprise.

---

[38] *E.g., Parke* v. *Daily News Ltd.* (1962), Ch. 927, 963; and *Dodge* v. *Ford Motor Co.*, 204 Mich. 459, 170 N.W. 668 (1919): "A business corporation is organized and carried on primarily for the benefit of the stockholders. The powers of the directors are to be employed for that end." See Henn, *Law of Corporations*, p. 475; and Gower, *Principles of Modern Company Law*, p. 522. (Gower regards the traditional view as "increasingly anachronistic.")

[39] See Friedmann and Garner, *Government Enterprise*, p. 39; A. Sturmthal, *Workers Councils* (Cambridge: Harvard University Press, 1964), pp. 56–57; W. Robson, *Nationalized Industry and Public Ownership* (Toronto: University of Toronto Press, 1960), p. 217; and M. Fogarty, *A Companies Act 1970?* Political and Economic Planning No. 500, October 1967, p. 75.

[40] See Emery and Thorsrud, *Form and Content*, p. 73.

Thus, it would appear than in the end, special interest representation accompanied by a restatement of the goals of the corporation would require the fashioning of new fiduciary standards for directors to reflect the changed composition of the board and the revised objectives of the corporation. Such standards would almost inevitably involve the realization that, except in most unusual circumstances, special interest representatives would place loyalty to the group which designated them and which they represent above all other loyalties, whether to the enterprise as a whole, the community, or the nation.

The board would then function essentially as a political institution. There is a serious question whether such a board could effectively function in the face of the pressures on the individual board members to advance the interests of the groups which they represent. Thus, in France, the tripartite structure of nationalized corporations with government, employee, and consumer directors has been strongly criticized as resulting in a constant tug of war between the different representatives and interests instead of providing a balanced administration in the public interest.

Effectiveness of the special interest director. Without regard to the troubling question of loyalties, the imposition of a minority number of special interest directors on an unwilling board may accomplish little. The hostility of the majority of the board may remove much of the significance of the development. If decisions are made in caucus prior to the board meeting, which is then reduced to an empty formality; if there is an inadequate flow of information; or if there is limited cooperation from management, the special interest director will not be able to function effectively. This is illustrated by the German experience with partial codetermination. Minority representation has built-in limitations. Mr. Townsend's proposal that the public director receive corporate funds to support an independent staff of his own would provide a partial answer. There is still a serious question of whether or not support from the board as a whole is essential for the effective functioning of any director.

Adequacy of representation. A fundamental problem of special interest representation is the difficulty of assuring adequate representation of all groups on the board. Even if such a difficult objective were somehow achieved with recognition for all interests in appropriate degrees, the further problem arises of whether a board so selected could in fact manage. The board would have become a microcosm of the community. Disputes would appear inevitable, and the ability to resolve them doubtful. Further, board decisions would involve shifting alliances between the constituent groups, "log-rolling" in which groups exchange support for reciprocal advancement of their respective proposals, and lead to a condition aptly described as "gangsterism" by Beardsley Ruml decades ago.[41] The board becomes the battleground for competing interests.

Problems Presented by Proposals for Employee Representation

Notwithstanding its increasing acceptance abroad, proopsals for employee representation present serious problems.

Lack of trade union support. The fundamental difficulty is that the proposal, at least at the present time, is a theoretical solution to problems of American industrial organization advanced by intellectuals lacking affiliation with the persons whose interests they seek to advance.

American unions and workers are generally not interested in the proposal for board representation. Further, as Professor Robert Dahl points out, ". . . workers and trade unions may be the greatest barriers at present to any profound reconstruction of economic enterprise in this country."[42] Until such attitudes change, consideration of the advantages and problems involved in such a proposal should be regarded as an educational exercise, not without interest and not without possible usefulness, but completely separated from political realities.

To the extent that the proposal for employee representation is intended as a method of increasing union power, it may fairly be asked whether such representation is required to enable the major unions to deal in equal terms with the major industries, whether such representation would advance the interests of any group other than the workers directly affected, and whether employee directors are any more likely than other directors to be concerned with the impact of the corporation's operations on the consumer, the community, the environment, or indeed, other workers generally.

Illusory nature of the proposal. A serious question is the extent to which the board of directors actually determines corporate policy and supervises the management of the enterprise and the extent to which the board is the

[41]B. Ruml, "Corporate Management as a Locus of Power in Social Meaning of Legal Concepts No. 3: The Powers and Duties of Corporate Management," 1950 ,p. 234.

[42]Robert Dahl, "Power to the Workers?" *New York Review of Books*, November 19, 1970, pp. 20, 22.

prisoner of senior management or the chief executive officer.[43] Dramatic developments such as the Penn Central debacle illustrate the limitations on the exercise of corporate sovereignty by the board.[44] If the corporate bureaucracy or technostructure ultimately exercises corporate power, board representation may be much less meaningful than anticipated. Although the problem of management control over the board by its power of designation is not present in employee representation, numerous difficulties—control over the availability of information, the problem of identifying and understanding the fundamental problems facing the enterprise, the problem of part-time directors endeavoring to supervise full-time corporate management—still remain.

Impairment of Board operations. It may well be questioned whether the advantages of employee representation outweigh the disharmony and lack of unity that it may bring to the board. Conflict on the board makes effective functioning difficult. It constitutes a serious distraction from consideration of corporate problems. It makes participation on the board a thoroughly unpleasant experience. When such conflicts have arisen among competing stockholder groups, independent directors have often demonstrated an unwillingness to be "in the middle" and have frequently resigned. The board must pull together or it cannot govern effectively.

Reform Proposals and Changes in Board Structure

From the foregoing discussion, it is apparent that some of the problems presented by proposals for special interest representation on the board of directors arise because of the unitary board system with which we are familiar. The question arises whether a change in the structure of the board may sidestep some of these problems.

The dual board model. It is perhaps no accident that codetermination has arisen in Germany and been adopted in the European Company Draft Statute as part of a corporate structure that features a dual board. Under the German system, faithfully followed in the European Company Draft Statute, employees are represented only on the upper or supervisory board. The supervisory board has important, but limited, functions. It does not manage; it does not set policy; it is not concerned with day-to-day opera-

---

[43]See Myles Mace, *Directors: Myth and Reality* (Cambridge: Harvard Business School, 1971), pp. 125–127.

[44]See Rush Loving, Jr. "Penn Central Bankruptcy Express," *Fortune*, August 1970, p. 104.

tions. Its major roles are two-fold. It elects the members of the lower, or managing board. It receives reports from the managing board and supervises. The managing board, which conducts the business of the corporation, does not include employee representatives.

The insulation of the employee directors from the conduct of the business and the determination of business policy significantly reduces the problems of lack of harmony or unity that would arise in the unitary American or English board. Further, as a political matter, it evidently makes the introduction of employee representation more acceptable to management and shareholders.

Incipient moves in the United States toward the dual board structure. There do not appear to have been any formal efforts to introduce the dual board structure into the United States. Nevertheless, some movement in this direction has occurred on the practical level. A number of major corporations have sought to reorganize senior management through the creation of a collegium of officials at the highest level. Thus, organization of the office of the chairman or the office of the president, which includes not only the officer in question but a limited number of directors, working full time and without other duties or titles, may fairly be regarded as the establishment of a new dual structure, not without some resemblance to the German managing board. Such a system is already in effect in a number of major American corporations.

Perhaps, the growing influence of executive committees points in the same direction. In those cases in which there is an active executive committee meeting monthly or more frequently and a relatively inactive board meeting quarterly confining its action to ratification of the acts of the executive committee, a functional change of significance has taken place. In such cases, as well, there is a resemblance to the dual board system.

One should not make too much of the development of the office of the chairman or the office of the president. It is still in the early stages, and its ultimate significance is not clear. One cannot, however, dismiss the possibility that it might in time lead in practice to some variation of the dual board system.

Prospects for Acceptance of Reform

There is no indication at the present time that radical change in the American corporate structure to embrace employee or other special interest representation in the senior councils of the corporation (whether in a single or dual board system) is apt to become a serious possibility in the near future. Until the proposal for employee representation is adopted and vigorously pursued by American trade unions, it is purely an academic suggestion. Further, there is the inescapable fact that American trade unions do not represent American employees as a whole. Out of a total labor force of 83 million, only 20 million are union members.[45]

Nevertheless, there are powerful factors at work at fundamental levels which in time could make the possibility of employee representation, in particular, a challenging reality. Accordingly, the possibility of such a development cannot be dismissed.

Changing attitudes of employees. It is clear that the fundamental relation of the employee to the employer is undergoing change. The attitudes of employees toward work are a matter of increasing concern. Job alienation, increased absenteeism, increased labor turnover, declining productivity, resistance to dull and repetitive work assignments, weak morale, hostility toward the production line, are familiar features of the current scene and have made business aware of the importance of increasing job satisfaction.[46] Lordstown is today a part of the vocabulary.

Human fulfillment through paticipation in decision making has been recognized as one of the most effective methods of dealing with the problem of worker alienation. Enfranchisement and involvement in job organization, work allocation, and production have become established techniques for labor participation. The pressures that make for such participation at the grass-roots level may conceivably over the long pull make for representation on the board level as well.

Added to this underlying dissatisfaction with work is the growing phenomenon of employee dissent. The emergence of underground employee newspapers that are highly critical of employer policies, leafletting on company premises and boycotts by employees protesting company attitudes, the phenomenon of "whistle blowing" or unauthorized disclosure of company conduct deemed socially undesirable all illustrate the current ferment. Employer-employee relationships are obviously being affected by the profound and accelerating change in society itself. The magnitude of the degree of change in values, in attitudes, in so-called consciousness may conceivably create a social and political climate in which employee representa-

---

[45]U.S., Department of Commerce, *Statistical Abstract of the United States* (1971), p. 234
[46]*Business Week*, September 9, 1972, pp. 79, 108 (special issue on productivity); *ibid.*, March 4, 1972, p. 69; *Wall Street Journal*, August 21, 1972, p. 1, col. 6; and *ibid.*, September 12, 1972, p. 12, col. 3.

tion on the board—entirely visionary at the present time—may become a realistic possibility in the future.

The foregoing factors will undoubtedly strengthen a movement toward greater job participation and employer-employee interaction on the grassroots level. Such a movement may well mean greater employee participation in the decision-making process on the lower levels of management. This may in turn lead ultimately to pressure for employee representation on the board level. However, a number of students of worker participation have concluded that board representation may be distinctly less useful and less important in achieving the values that flow from worker participation than opportunities on the plant level.[47]

Federal incorporation. The development of interest in federal incorporation of major corporations may create the stage for consideration of employee representation on the board. The increasing abdication by the various states of control over the internal conduct of corporate affairs and increased concern with the role of the large corporation in society make enactment of a federal incorporation statute within the next 15 years a realistic possibility.[48]

The open question is the substantive content of any such statute. That is quite another question, and one for which we have little glimpse of what may be expected. It is clear, however, that consideration of such a fundamental departure as a federal incorporation statute would inevitably involve a basic review of possible areas of corporate reform. Consideration of employee representation on the board, or for public or government directors would find priority places on any such agenda.

Impact of the European experience. A third fundamental factor is the strength of the movement for employee directors outside of the United States. The world is increasingly becoming smaller and the experiences of other nations increasingly significant at home. The widespread European acceptance of employee representation of the board will unmistakably have impact on American business attitudes.

In addition, the multinational experience of many large American corporations has profound implications. Firsthand experience with the reality

---

[47]See Blumberg, *Industrial Democracy*, pp. 2–3; Emery and Thorsrud, *Form and Content*, p. 10.

[48]But cf. Senator Hart's statement, released February 3, 1972. Senator Hart (D-Mich) favors federal incorporation and informed a Georgetown Law Center seminar in February 1972 that "my most optimistic guess is that we might get six votes right now in the whole Senate."

of employee representation can only increase understanding of the proposal and reduce resistance to it. Business that operates its foreign subsidiaries successfully notwithstanding employees on the foreign subsidiaires' boards cannot contend as successfully that such representation produces unworkable results.

Conclusion

Special interest representation in general and employee representation in particular are presently no more than topics for academic discussion in the United States. Nevertheless, there are deep-seated underlying forces that could conceivably make proposals of this nature, particularly for employee representation, a matter of realistic concern in the future.[49]

[49]See Andrew Shonfield, "Business in the Twenty-First Century," *Daedalus*, Winter 1969, pp. 202–203.

Voting Membership in Publicly Held Corporations*

● MELVIN A. EISENBERG
Boalt Hall
School of Law
University of California, Berkeley

I begin with three theses, which I will not attempt to prove:

(1) In large corporations, management typically has a significant amount of discretion about the allocation and management of corporate resources, and an ability to perpetuate itself in office even when it is allocating and managing such resources inefficiently.

(2) Management's interest in preserving its own security and advancing its own prestige frequently comes in conflict with objective decision-making criteria. Furthermore, management is typically unskilled in dealing with social implications of business decisions. Therefore, it cannot be presumed that management will invariably or even consistently exercise its discretion in order to utilize corporate assets in the most efficient manner—whether efficiency is measured strictly in terms of return on investment or also includes social costs.

(3) For these reasons, and also on the political ground that excessive concentration of power in the hands of a small number of individuals is to be avoided if possible, it is desirable to limit management's discretion in allocating and managing corporate resources.

While a number of techniques can be utilized to serve this purpose, the

*Copyright 1973 by Melvin Aron Eisenberg.

one that I will focus on its direct participation by members of the organization, but by persons other than managament. More specifically, I will focus on whether such participation is likely to be efficacious in the case of (a) corporate client-groups: employees, suppliers, and customers (including in the latter category distributors, dealers, and consumers); and (b) shareholders.

Client-Groups

A leading exponent of direct participation by client-groups is Professor Abram Chayes, who puts the case as follows:

> Of all those standing in relation to the large corporation, the shareholder is least subject to its power. . . . Shareholder democracy, so-called, is misconceived because the shareholders are not the governed of the corporation whose consent must be sought. . . . Their interests are protected if financial information is made available, fraud and over-reaching are prevented, and a market is maintained in which their shares may be sold. A priori, there is no reason for them to have any voice, direct or representational, in . . . prices, wages, and investment. They are no more affected than non-shareholder neighbors by these decisions. . . .
>
> A concept of the corporation which draws the boundary of "membership" thus narrowly [*i.e.*, restricts it to shareholders] is seriously inadequate . . . because the line between those who are "inside" and those who are "outside" the corporation is the line between those whom we recognize as entitled to a regularized share in its processes of decision and those who are not.
>
> A more spacious conception of "membership," and one closer to the facts of corporate life, would include all those having a relation of sufficient intimacy with the corporation or subject to its power in a sufficiently specialized way. Their rightful share in decisions on the exercise of corporate power would be exercised through an institutional arrangement appropriately designed to represent the interests of a constituency of members having a significant common relation to the corporation and its power.[1]

In evaluating this approach, it is important to keep in mind that many client-groups have had some sort of institutionalized relationship with the corporation, but that these relationships have usually been built on the

---

[1]Chayes, "The Modern Corporation and the Rule of Law," in *The Corporation in Modern Society*, ed. E. Mason (1959). Cf. R. Eells, *The Government of Corporations*, (1962), pp. 79–85, 206; Dion, "Property and Authority in Business Enterprise," *University of Detroit Law Journal* 38 (1961): 600; Manning, "The Shareholder's Appraisal Remedy: An Essay for Frank Coker," *Yale Law Journal* 72 (1962): 223, 239.

models of negotiation or litigation, rather than on the model of direct participation in decision making through voting. In dealing with the interests of a given client-group, it is therefore necessary to separate the questions of (1) whether it is desirable to augment by law the client-group's power *vis-a-vis* the corporation; and (2) if so, whether such power should be augmented by increasing the client-group's power of negotiation (as under the National Labor Relations Act) by conferring upon it new substantive rights which can then be enforced, if necessary, through litigation or litigationlike processes (as under the Automobile Dealers' Day-In-Court Act or certain of the antitrust laws);[2] or by giving it direct voting participation in corporate decisions. Those who wish to augment the power of client-groups frequently fail to make clear whether they are merely suggesting that the traditional kinds of institutional relationships be strengthened or extended, or are advocating that the relationships between client-group and corporation move beyond the traditional models based on negotiation and litigation into a new model of direct participation. The latter approach is usually implicit, however, surfacing both in phrases such as "a regularized share in [the corporation's] processes of decision," and in the general tone of such proposals, which usually indicates that the author contemplates some radically new institutional relationship. But the failure to be explicit creates substantial problems in evaluation, because the idea of direct participation by client-groups, like eugenics, is grand in principle but susceptible to meaningful discussion only at the level of execution. If we postpone for a moment the position of labor and consider suppliers and customers, a number of difficulties immediately present themselves at that level:

(1) Suppliers and customers do not have the skills required to make corporate decisions—at least, not *qua* suppliers and customers. The skills needed to be a leather merchant are not necessarily those needed to decide the business or structural problems faced by shoe manufacturers, nor are such skills acquired with the purchase of one or more pairs of shoes.

(2) Lurking in the background of such proposals is the idea that all suppliers and customers are small. Of course, if that were true, giant corporations would be neither suppliers nor customers. Since they are both, the question must be answered, are *all* customers and purchasers to have a voice in corporate affairs, or only small ones? If the

[2] See, *e.g.*, Clayton Act, secs. 4–5, 15 U.S.C. 15–16 (1964); Automobile Dealers' Day in Court Act, 15 U.S.C. 1221–1225 (1964). See generally. S. Macauley, *Law and the Balance of Power* (1966).

latter is the case, the proposal seems romantic to a fault. But if the former is the case, does that not mean that GM will have a vote in Greyhound, by virtue of being a supplier, and in U.S. Steel, by virtue of being a customer? If so, a disease worse than the cure is hard to imagine, since instead of limiting the power of giant corporations, this proposal would extend it even further and thoroughly cartelize American business in the process.

(3) Closely related to the last problem, there appears to be no feasible way, other than by dollar volume, to allocate votes among the members of such groups.

(4) The interests of suppliers and customers in large part conflict with those of the corporation. The primary objective, although not necessarily the sole objective, of a business corporation must be to turn a profit. If a corporation takes in less than it pays out, it must soon be liquidated. If it merely attains equilibrium it will not long survive, because without profits or the prospect of profits neither internal nor external funds will be available when, as will inevitably occur, new funds are needed to adapt the corporation's business to changes in technology or the structure of the market. But suppliers and customers do not share this primary objective. Perhaps they recognize some vague long-range interest in assuring that the enterprise with which they deal survives, but this will seldom affect their short-range here-and-now calculations. If suppliers and customers are nevertheless to be given a voice in corporate decision making, will it really be necessary to take a vote? How long does it take to figure out how leather dealers will vote on a shoe manufacturer's merger with a producer of Corfam? Is it not perfectly clear that such a dealer would apply one test to resolve every decision he is called upon to make: whether the decision will result in larger or smaller purchases of leather from him at higher or lower prices?; and that customers will apply a comparable test? Is there any possibility that this is desirable? We must conclude, with Beardsley Ruml, that

> A scheme of representation of these interests [in the corporation] would be a travesty on democratic procedures. It would result in business political gangsterism that would destroy the efficiency of business management. It would inject, into circles requiring the most intimate confidence, individuals whose reliability was uncertain and whose motives and ambitions . . . would be injurious to the true welfare of [those] who have an interest in the success of the business.[3]

[3]Ruml, "Corporate Management as a Locus of Power," *Chi-Kent Law Review* 29 (1951): 228, 242–243.

Turning to labor, many of the same problems exist, although perhaps in less severe degree. There is the lack of skill—working in a shoe factory or being head of a machinist's union does not equip one to deal with decisions on either materials or mergers; there is the implicit though questionable[4] assumption that labor is invariably weak and the corporation invariably strong; there is the conflict of interest—although employees may have the survival of the enterprise somewhat more in mind than customers and suppliers, their short-run interests will often severely conflict with the long-run interests of the enterprise, as in the case of technological advance.

Labor can, however, be differentiated from suppliers and customers in at least one important way: There is readily at hand a principle for allocating labor's votes—one per employee. Indeed, in Germany labor has been given a formal role in corporate decision making. German corporate law parcels out the functions performed by our board of directors between the supervisory board, a policy-making body, and the board of managers, an executive body.[5] Under the so-called codetermination principle, German law provides for labor representation on the supervisory board of most large corporations and on the board of managers of large coal, iron, and steel-producing corporations.[6] Clearly, then, labor participation in corporate decision making is mechanically feasible. But granted its feasibility, is it desirable in the American context? After a study of codetermination and its applicability to American problems, Professor Detlev Vagts concluded that it was not:

> One must first of all reckon with the fact that both American management and organized labor would oppose the move. . . .
> . . . America has a long tradition of collective bargaining fostered by law which has admitted the unions to a voice in questions of policy and administration. Management must talk and bargain with union representatives about topics on which in Germany codetermination has the most effect. . . . In this way the unions have a voice in making decisions without the operational responsibilities that inhere in the German approach. This already highly developed institution could hardly exist side-by-side with codetermination. Most American commentators find a system in which management and labor bargain as representatives

[4]Cf. Winter, "Collective Bargaining and Competition: The Application of Antitrust Standards to Union Activity," *Yale Law Journal* 73 (1963): 14.

[5]Steefel and von Falkenhausen, "The New German Stock Corporation Law," *Cornell Law Review* 52 (1967): 518, 526–536; Vagts, "Reforming the 'Modern' Corporation: Perspectives from the German," *Harvard Law Review* 80 (1966): 23, 50–53.

[6]Steefel and von Falkenhausen, "New German Stock Corporation Law," pp. 537–539; Vagts, "Reforming the 'Modern' Corporation," pp. 64–78. See generally, W. Blumenthal, *Codetermination in the German Steel Industry* (1956); H. Spiro, *The Politics of German Codetermination* (1958).

of conflicting interests less likely to produce pressures and conflicts within individual roles and see a major reconstruction of the labor relations structure on the German model as undesirable.

It should also be remembered that years of collective bargaining emphasis here have produced a union leadership very different from that of Germany. . . . It is doubtful that the collaboration involved in codetermination would run as smoothly in many American unions as it has in Germany. In short, codetermination is a complex institution. Its adoption involves a great deal more than having some labor representatives sitting on corporation boards of directors. It would involve a substantial rearrangement of our industrial relations picture, even assuming that it were considered desirable to enhance labor's power in this fashion.[7]

On a more general level, it is open to serious question whether the idea of codetermination—direct voting participation by any client-group, whether labor, suppliers, or customers—is not out of step with the fundamental nature of American institutions. Codetermination is a harmonizing and objectivizing principle; its basic premise is that persons with divergent objectives and training can work in tandem and make decisions in an objective way, even when self-interest may be involved. In contrast, American institutions are generally premised on the deliberate exploitation of divergence and conflict to achieve socially desirable ends. Thus, it may be doubted whether the codetermination principle is congenial to the American temperament, and therefore whether it would work here even if mechanically feasible. In the American framework, at least, the interests of client-groups, and certainly the interests of the public, might be better protected by institutions that take account of the fact that the relationship between an enterprise and its client-groups encompasses both collaborative

[7]Vagts, "Reforming the 'Modern' Corporation," pp. 76–78. Similarly, Blumenthal concluded: "It is clear that codetermination is a peculiarly German phenomenon which developed only because of a particular historical and environmental setting. Perhaps it provided a means of overcoming the traditional intransigence of many German employers in their dealings with workers. In view of past history of resort to legislation rather than to free agreement in German labor relations, codetermination may have been a good means of accomplishing for German labor what American workers, for example, have long since achieved by other means. American labor has won similar benefits without having to shoulder the onerous responsibilities of company management. The strains and stresses which such a dual responsibility imposes on the union could not be contained in the United States as they were in Germany. Few American labor leaders could expect to be supported by their members under similar circumstances. Above all, the incentive to institute codetermination is lacking, for it accomplishes nothing that cannot be gained under free collective bargaining." Blumenthal, *Codetermination in German Steel Industry*, p. 114.

and conflicting purposes; in other words, by institutions modeled on the processes of negotiation and litigation.[8]

Shareholders

Most of the considerations applicable to client-groups are not applicable to shareholders. There is an obvious way to allocate votes—by shares; and the shareholders' interest (*qua* shareholders) coincides with that of the corporation. It is commonly argued, however, that two other factors serve to make shareholder voting meaningless—lack of skill and lack of interest. The two arguments are interrelated, in that they both flow from the assumption that "the average shareholder" owns but a trifling amount of stock. But this assumption, *even if true*, is itself virtually meaningless, since it is based on the fallacious premise that the expectations and interest of "the average shareholder" are of great economic or legal significance. This premise is deceptive because corporate economics and corporate law are not bottomed on the democratic principle of one-man-one-vote, but on the proprietary principle of one-share-one-vote. What counts is not shareholders, but shareholdings. An inquiry into the expectations of the average shareholder will therefore be of little more than sociological relevance unless there is a true People's Capitalism, in which shareholders and shareholdings correlate closely. But the opposite is the case: The shareholdings of the average shareholder are negligible, *and if all the shareholdings of all the average shareholders are aggregated, the result is still negligible*, because, as is widely recognized (except by stock-exchange publicists), the ownership of stock is very highly concentrated. Thus, in *Effects of Taxation—Investments by Individuals*, Butters, Thompson, and Bollinger estimate that as of 1949 approximately 4,500,000 spending units owned marketable stock.[9] Of these, 50,000–100,000, or 1–2 percent, owned approximately 65 percent of the total marketable stock, by value, held by individuals; another 950,000 units owned approximately 30 percent of all such stock; and the remaining 3,500,000 units owned approximately 5 percent.[10] From a different perspective, a Federal Reserve survey estimated

[8]For examples of such institutions, see Macauley, *Law and Balance of Power.*

[9]Defined as stock open to investment by the public—that is, listed on an exchange or readily sold over the counter. J. Butters; L. Thompson; and L. Bollinger, *Effects of Taxation: Investments by Individuals* (1953), pp. 373, 402, 499.

[10]*Ibid.*, pp. 373–389. For a comparable analysis, see U.S., Congress, Senate, Committee on Banking and Currency, *Factors Affecting the Hock Market*, 84th Cong., 2d sess., 1955, p. 90.

that as of 1962, 41 percent of publicly held stock owned by individuals, by value of equity, was held by spending units whose total wealth was $500,-000 or more, and 65 percent was held by spending units whose total wealth was $200,000 or more, while only 4 percent was held by units whose total wealth was less than $25,000, and only 11 percent was held by units whose total wealth was less than $50.000.[11] Other studies have reached comparable conclusions. Thus, a survey of 2932 publicly held corporations, conducted under the auspices of the Brookings Institution and the New York Stock Exchange, showed that as of 1951, 2.1 percent of the shareholdings of common stock in the surveyed corporations accounted for over half of the total value of all such stock, while two-thirds of such holdings accounted for only 10 percent of such stock by number and 13 percent by value.[12]

Turning from the perspective of shareholders to that of corporations, a 1967 study found that in approximately 150 of the *Fortune* 500, a single individual or members of a single family held 10 percent or more of the stock. Since another 20 or so privately owned corporations would have been included in the *Fortune* 500 that year if they had published their financial results,[13] this study shows that approximately one-third of the 520 *largest* industrials have individually or family-owned blocks of at least 10 percent outstanding. Undoubtedly this percentage would be much higher if ten-percent blocks owned by groups of business associates, or by other corporations, had also been included in the study.

Furthermore, even a ten-percent figure is too high for purposes of measuring shareholder expectation. The ten-percent figure is commonly used as the size of shareholding that gives *control* of publicly held corporations.[14] Although it may be too low for that purpose, it seems much higher than the minimum size shareholding that would give rise to an interest in major corporate decisions.[15] At least in the publicly held corporation, a

[11]D. Projector and G. Weiss, "Survey of Financial Characteristics of Consumers," 1966, p. 136.

[12]L. Kimmel, "Share Ownership in the United States," 1952, pp. 41–43. *See also* Victor Perlo, "'People's Capitalism' and Stock Ownership," *American Economic Review* 48 (1958): 333, 337–341.

[13]Vagts, "Reforming the 'Modern' Corporation," p. 32. Cf. Folk, "Recent Developments in Corporation Statutes," *Journal of Legal Education* 20 (1968): 511, 519.

[14]Cf. Larner, "Ownership and Control in the 200 Largest Nonfinancial Corporations, 1929 and 1963," *American Economic Review* 56 (1966): 777, 779; Sheehan, "Proprietors in the World of Big Business," *Fortune*, June 15, 1967, p. 178. See, generally, Enstam and Kamen, "Control and the Institutional Investor, *Business Law* 22 (1968): 289, 315.

[15]U.S., Securities and Exchange Commission, *Public Policy Implications of Investment Company Growth*, 89th Cong., 2d sess., 1966, H. Rept. 2337, p. 308 (cited as SEC Mutual Fund Study).

figure of one percent would seem more appropriate.[16] Notice that these figures cover the very largest of our corporations; it is only to be expected that shareholding concentration becomes even greater as corporate size and total number of shareholders become smaller. This is confirmed by the results of a comprehensive study, conducted by the SEC Special Study, of over-the-counter corporations in which the broker-dealer community had shown interest during the last three months of 1961. This survey showed that in about half or more of each category of sampled corporations with less than 1000 shareholders, the 10 largest record shareholders held 50 percent or more of the stock; in more than half the sampled corporations with 1000–1999 shareholders, the 10 largest record shareholders held at least 40 percent of the stock; in about half or more of the sampled corporations with 2000–2999 or 3000–4999 shareholders, the 10 largest record shareholders held at least 30 percent of the stock; in almost 30 percent of the sampled corporations with 5000 shareholders, the 10 largest record shareholders held over 30 percent of the stock; and in about 40 percent of such corporations, the 10 largest record shareholders held almost 20 percent of the stock.[17]

[16]Wharton School of Finance and Commerce, *A Study of Mutual Funds*, 87th Cong., 2d sess., 1962, H. Rept. 2274, pp. 26, 412, n. 19 (cited as Wharton Study). *See also* SEC Mutual Fund Study, p. 308.

[17]U.S., Securities and Exchange Commission, Report of the Special Study *of Securities Market of SEC*, pt. 3, 88th Cong., 1st sess., 1963, H. Doc. 95, p. 30. Listed and foreign issues were excluded from the sample.

Similarly, Victor Perlo studied the 1954 reports of public utility and railroad corporations required to report to regulatory agencies on their largest record shareholders, and found that the 20 largest record common stockholders in the three largest railroads, at that time the Pennsylvania, New York Central, and Southern Pacific, held 19.2, 42.6, and 15.3 percent, respectively, of the common stock; that the ten largest record common stockholders in the three largest power companies, PG&E, Con. Ed., and Commonwealth Ed., held 10.0, 8.9, and 7.7 percent of the outstanding common stock, respectievly; and that the figures for smaller railroads and power companies were comparable. (The three largest communications utilities were AT&T, General Telephone, and Western Union. The 20 largest record common stockholders of AT&T and Western Union owned 4.2 and 24.1 percent of such stock, respectively, but figures for General Telephone were not available.) Perlo, " 'People's Capitalism' and Stock Ownership," pp. 340–341.

Of course, some record shareholdings may represent a large number of small individual shareholdings held in the name of one broker, but New York Stock Exchange calculations as of 1965 showed that the total amount of publicly held stock held in the name of brokers and dealers was only 7.5 percent by number of shares and 7.1 percent by market value, some of which was undoubtedly owned by the brokers and dealers themselves. See New York Stock Exchange, "Methodology and Sample Design of 1965 Census of Shareowners," 1965, Tables III, IV. Similarly, some record shareholders may represent various personal trust funds held in the name of a single bank nominee, but in such cases the holdings for which the bank is trustee are likely to be voted together.

Given these figures, it may very well be true that the majority of share-holders—shareholders taken as a lot—care a little about corporate decisions. Why should they, when their stakes amount to five or ten percent of all marketable stock? The question is, what are the interests and expectations of that relatively small number of stockholders who hold the balance? Is it not likely that many of these major holders will own substantial blocks in particular corporations—substantial either in percentage or absolute dollar terms—and will either be skilled investors or be under the guidance of investment professionals? Is it not likely, in other words, that even if "the average shareholder" is not highly interested in major corporate decisions or highly skilled in evaluating them, those shareholders who own the bulk of shares held by individuals will consider such decisions with both care and skill?

Furthermore, "the average shareholder" becomes even less economically and legally relevant when we expand the inquiry to include institutional investors.[18] The importance of such investors as shareholders has increased substantially over a long period of time for two reasons: Such institutions have been growing faster than the economy as a whole,[19] and they have been investing an increasing proportion of their assets in stock, particularly stock in publicly held corporations.[20] The New York Stock Exchange estimates that as of 1971, financial institutions other than bank trust departments and foreign institutions held 28.3 percent of all stock listed on the Exchange by market value—up from 12.7 percent as recently as 1949.[21] Including bank trust departments and foreign institutions, financial institutions probably held over 40 percent of all such stock.[22]

With tottal holdings this large, institutional holdings in given corpora-

[18]See Henderson, "Institutional Investors in the Equity Market," in *Conference on Securities Regulation*, ed. R. Mundheim (1965), p. 136 (cited as Duke Conference on Securities Regulation). The major types of nonprofit institutions with important endowment funds are foundations, universities, and hospitals. Another category of institutional investor is the bank or investment counselor acting as administrator of an investment account.

[19]New York Stock Exchange, *Institutional Shareownership* (New York: New York Stock Exchange, 1964), pp. 7–8, 11–13 (cited as Institutional Shareownership).

[20]See Institutional Shareownership, pp. 8, 13–14; Loss, Securities Regulation 17, 2d ed. 1961, Supp. 1962 at 1, n. 56; Henderson, "Institutional Investors," p. 139. Cf. Hoenemayer, "The Life Insurance Company as an Institutional Investor," in Duke Conference on Securities Regulation, p. 191, Sheehan, "Life Insurance's Almighty Leap into Equities," *Fortune*, October 1968, p. 162.

[21]New York Stock Exchange, *1968 Fact Book* (New York: New York Stock Exchange, 1968), p. 42.

[22]*Ibid.*

tions must also be substantial. Although little information on such holdings is available,[23] the following data on holdings by investment companies provide a striking picture of the probable magnitude of such holdings:

(1) According to figures compiled by Vickers Associates on the "Favorite Fifty" stocks (by dollar holdings) held by investment companies as of September 1966, such companies owned 5–10 percent of IBM, Xerox, Gulf Oil, Minnesota Mining & Manufacturing, Mobil Oil, General Telephone, International Nickel, Royal Dutch, Westinghouse, Merck, Goodyear, Union Oil, RCA, Litton, and Texas Utilities Co.; 10–15 percent of Avon, Continental Oil, Southern Co., Florida Power & Light, Boeing, Gillette, and Sinclair Oil; 15–20 percent of IT&T, CBS, Texas Instruments, United Air Lines, Amerada Petroleum, Anaconda, Pan American, Atlantic Richfield, Magnavox, Louisiana Land & Exploration, and Reynolds Metals; 20–25 percent of Polaroid, Burroughs, Lockheed, and TWA; 26.2 percent of Delta Air Lines; and 41.2 percent of Northwest Airlines.[24]

(2) Many investment companies are grouped into complexes by virtue of being under the management of a common investment advisor. (Ten such complexes accounted for 55 percent of all mutual fund assets as of June 30, 1966.)[25] The Wharton School's Study of Mutual Funds reported that as of 1958, mutual fund complexes owned 1503 holdings of one percent or larger. About half of these holdings were 2 percent or larger, 183 were 5 percent or larger, and 62 were 8 percent or larger. In each case, this was about twice the size of the comparable figure for 1952, only six years earlier.[26]

(3) Looking at this question from the perspective of the portfolio corporations, the Wharton study found that as of 1958, mutual fund company holdings of one percent or more accounted for five percent or more of the outstanding voting stock of 297 corporations, and ten percent or more of the outstanding voting stock of 77 corporations. These figures (which were almost three times as large as comparable 1952 figures) undoubtedly would have been larger if all mutual fund holdings, rather than only holdings of one percent or more, had been aggregated.[27]

---

[23]Cf. Louis, "The Mutual Funds Have the Votes," *Fortune*, May 1967, pp. 150–151; R. Mundheim, "Foreward," *Law and Contemporary Problems* 29 (1964): 647, 651.

[24]"Favorite Fifty," *Barron's*, November 28, 1966, p. 5.

[25]SEC Mutual Fund Study, pp. 247–249.

[26]Wharton Study, pp. 406–407, 408 (Table VII–4).

[27]*Ibid.*, p. 412 (Table VII–6).

(4) The Wharton study also reported on the holdings of particular complexes, in particular portfolio corporations. For example, the Axe-Houghton complex was found to own 5 holdings of 20 percent or more of a portfolio corporation's outstanding voting stock, 3 holdings of 10–20 percent, and 4 holdings of 5–10 percent; the National Securities Series had 113 holdings of 1 percent or more, 18 of which were of 5 percent or more; IDS had at least 195 holdings of 1 percent or more, 30 of which were 5–10 percent; and MIT had 146 holdings of 1 percent or more, 4 of which were 5–10 percent.[28]

The most striking aspect of these figures is this: As large as they are, they represent only investment company holdings, and of the total New York Stock Exchange shares (by market value) held by all institutional investors, investment companies hold less than 20 percent.[29]

The role of the institutional investor as a shareholder has been the subject of much debate in recent years. Most of the debate has centered on whether such investors owe some obligation to other shareholders in their portfolio corporations to oversee management and attempt to change management when such a change seems necessary.[30] Generally speaking, the

---

[28]*Ibid.*, pp. 405, 409–410. Similarly, according to *Fortune*, as of December 1966, the Fidelity complex owned 5–9.9 percent of Admiral; American Commercial Lines; Beaunit; Bucyrus Erie; Burroughs; Carborundum; Central Aguirre Sugar; Chicago, Milwaukee, St. Paul & Pacific Railroad; Crowell-Collier & MacMillan; Foltrol; General Instrument; General Precision Equipment; Ludlow; Mack Trucks; Maust Coal & Coke; MGM; Newport News Shipbuilding; Northwest Airlines; Pennzoil; Raytheon; Sanders Associates; Transcontinental Bus System; and Vornado; and 10–19.9 percent of Chicago & North Western R.R.; Pabst Brewing; Stanley Warner; and Copperweld Steel; and the Dreyfus Fund held at least 17 holdings representing 5 percent or more of a portfolio company's outstanding common stock. Louis, "Mutual Funds Have Votes," pp. 151, 205.

[29]See New York Stock Exchange, *1968 Fact Book*. This calculation is based on total estimated institutional holdings, including those of bank trust departments.

[30]See, *e.g.*, D. Baum and N. Stiles, *The Silent Partners* (1965), p. 149 and *passim*; SEC Mutual Fund Study, pp. 307–311; Wharton Study, pp. 24–27, 399–428; "Symposium—Mutual Funds as Investors of Large Pools of Money," *University of Pennsylvania Law Review* 115 (1967): 669, 673–682.

This debate has focused on only one type of institutional investor, the mutual fund. However, most of the elements that have emerged from the debate are equally applicable to other institutional investors. See Henderson, "Institutional Investors," pp. 136–137. One major difference relates to bank trust funds, since unlike other institutional investors, a bank must often consult with third persons before making an investment decision. See Buek, "Trust Companies and Banks as Institutional Investors," in Duke Conference on Securities Regulation, pp. 147, 148–149.

institutional investors take the position that their primary obligation lies to their own beneficiaries (using this term in its broadest sense to include shareholders in investment companies), not to their fellow shareholders in portfolio companies; that their staffs have neither the time nor the skill to oversee management; and that a company that requires a management change will normally be an unsound investment, so that the institutional investor should switch out as quickly as possible rather than stay in and try to accomplish the change.[31]

Some of these arguments appear overstated. There must be cases in which a corporation's assets outshine its management, and thus, in which an insti-tutional investor would do better by trying to change management than by switching.[32] It seems likely that there have been additional, unstated, reasons for backing management, including obedience to the mores of the financial community;[33] a desire to stay on good terms with management in order to promote a free flow of inside information;[34] and, in the case of certain institutions, particularly banks, a desire to obtain or retain the business that management gives the institution in its other capacities. Nevertheless, the position that the primary duty of a financial institution is to protect the interests of its own beneficiaries, and that such institutions are in any event not equipped to oversee management, seems essentially sound.[35]

However, other types of corporate changes (other, that is, than changes in management) involve much different considerations. While the staffs of financial institutions may not have the skills to oversee ordinary business decisions, there is a class of decisions on what might be called structural matters (*e.g.*, mergers, partial liquidations, major acquisitions), which tend

---

[31]See, *e.g.*, Wharton Study, pp. 418–419; Brown, "Institutional Investor as Shareholder," in Duke Conference on Securities Regulation, pp. 207, 210–212, 217–219, 223–224; Buek, "Trust Companies as Institutional Investors," pp. 675–682. Another argument is that selling shares itself constitutes a sanction against management. Cf. Manne, "Current Views on the 'Modern Corporation'," *University of Detroit Law Journal* 38 (1961): 559, 572, n. 35.

[32]Cf. Wharton Study, pp. 26–27; Louis, "Mutual Votes Have Votes," p. 205.

[33]Cf. Brown, "The Investor as Shareholder," p. 217 ("positive action [against management] . . . is never pleasant . . ."); Manning, "Book Review," *Yale Law Journal* 67 (1958): 1477, 1486.

[34]See Wharton Study, pp. 418–419.

[35]As the Wharton Study concluded: "Since the prime responsibility of the management of a mutual fund is the supervision of an investment portfolio, substantial diversion of effort from this activity, or retention of a holding in a company whose management has proved a disappointment, would be difficult to justify in terms of the purported function of this institution." *Ibid.*, p. 26.

to involve precisely the kind of investment analysis at which such staffs are expert—probably more expert than management. (In fact, when structural decisions are being considered, management will frequently consult a financial institution, such as an investment banker, for advice.) Furthermore, a decision to reject a proposed structural change is perfectly consistent with a decision to retain an investment. Indeed, the proposed change may be rejected just because the portfolio corporation is sounder as it stands than it would be if the proposed structural change were made. Finally, although an institutional investor may have no obligation to its fellow shareholders to retain a bad investment, it does have a clear obligation to its own beneficiaries to make sound decisions in connection with the investments it holds. Therefore, unless an institutional investor is prepared to sell every time a structural change is proposed, it is under a fiduciary obligation to use its best judgment in voting on the matter. And this merely reinforces what should be its own self-interest, that is, to maximize its investment performance.

It is therefore to be expected that institutional investors would take a careful interest in structural changes, if not in changes in management, and the available data indicate that this in fact is what occurs. The Wharton study found that proxies raising more-than-routine issues, or issues involving poilcy questions, did in fact tend to get careful scrutiny.[36] A statement

---

[36]"Particularly among the very large companies, fairly elaborate routines have been sometimes developed whereby proxy requests are automatically turned over to industry specialists, who initially examine each proxy statement. Where the agenda involves issues calling for more careful consideration, the industry specialist usually prepares a memorandum on the issues, along with his recommendations, which are then taken up by an officer or committee of officers. This is roughly the procedure followed by MIT, Investors Diversified Services, Keystone Custodian Funds, and National Securities & Research Corp.

"A more common procedure is one in which proxy solicitations are referred to an officer delegated to handle them, who refers them where deemed necessary to the research staff of the company. Solicitations received by Dividend Shares, e.g., are scrutinized by [the officer in charge of portfolio administration] before being approved for execution. In cases where further study appears indicated, the appropriate industry specialist of the investment adviser is requested to investigate and report his findings. Where basic policy questions are involved, the matter is discussed with the investment committee of the company." *Ibid.*, p. 418.

This is not to say that all mutual funds handle proxies this way, but the larger funds, which apparently do, account for more than half of total mutual fund assets. Getting down to specifics, the Wharton Study found that:

"Open-end companies have shown a greater willingness to oppose portfolio company managements on matters affecting the voting, preemption, and income rights of shareholders. . . . The Wellington Fund has voted regularly against proposals to eliminate preemptive rights of shareholders. . . . MIT, National Securities Series, and others, have

by the president of one of the largest mutual fund complexes makes the same point:

> Proper exercise of the voting rights on stocks held in the investment portfolios of institutions is a matter of trust and responsibility for the managers. In many respects, it is equal to their responsibilities for the careful selection and supervision of investment holdings. . . .
>
> Unfortunately, there has in the past been some tendency for institutional investors to consider proxy statements and proxies received from portfolio companies in a more or less routine manner. This attitude has changed substantially in recent years as the size of holdings by institutional investors has grown. Even so, it seems important to emphasize the responsibility which each institutional investor has for the proper evaluation of matters submitted for stockholder decision. It seems obvious, but it must be emphasized, that proxy statements and proxies are to be secured in all instances by institutional investors, and each of them must be reviewed carefully by a knowledgeable person in the light of the effect of the issues involved on the status of and prospect for the investment before action to be taken is decided upon. In my opinion, the procedure for processing and voting proxies followed by each institutional investor should have no aspect of the rubber stamp and should permit no built-in bias toward voting in favor of all proposals by corporate management.
>
> I also stress the need for careful consideration of all proxy material by institutional investors because matters included in proxy statements are of the type in which such investors are likely to have the greatest expertise.[37]

The basic attitude-shaping elements of institutions other than mutual funds would seem essentially the same.[38] That such institutions do not invariably back management proposals is indicated by the following data, assembled from various sources, showing the number of times trust departments of particular banks voted against management in given years:

voted on several different occasions against changes in the voting rights of common stockholders, reduced preemptive rights, increases in common stock issues, the issuance of convertible bonds or preference shares, and similar matters. . . .

"Although the smaller open-end companies report few discussions of prospective mergers with portfolio companies, they are of frequent occurrence among the companies (or control groups) with assets in excess of $150 million. One of the very large companies reports that: 'In cases where the fund is a large holder (and this is the usual case) companies almost invariably submit merger proposals for informal consideration prior to the formal making of the proposal'." *Ibid.*, pp. 419–420, 426.

[37]Brown, "Institutional Investor as Shareholder," pp. 214–215; Louis, "Mutual Funds Have Votes," p. 150; Enstam and Kamen, p. 300. Cf. R. Baker and W. Cary, *Corporations —Cases and Materials*, 3d ed. (1959), p. 881, n. 1; R. Mundheim, "The British Experience: Institutions as Shareholders," *The Institutional Investor*, January 1968, p. 36.

[38]Cf. Henderson, "Institutional Investors," pp. 136–137.

Bank	Year	Votes against management proposals
Bankers Trust	1966	3
Irving Trust	1966	5
Chase Manhattan	1966	8
Chemical	1966	10
First National City	1966	7
Morgan Guaranty	1966	0
Security National	1966	0
United States Trust Co.	1963	35
United States Trust Co.	1962	50

Similarly, the SEC's Institutional Investor Study reported 584 votes against management by 215 large institutional investors during the period of January 1, 1967 to September 30, 1969, including 351 such votes by bank trust departments.

The tendency to exercise an independent judgment on structural changes seems likely to increase with the passage of time. Psychologically, the predisposition to vote in management's favor seems to be breaking down. On several occasions in the last few years, mutual funds have gone so far as to vote for insurgent slates of directors. The decision in *SEC* v. *Texas Gulf Sulphur Company*, the radiations of that decision, and the *Merrill Lynch* and *Investors Management* cases are likely to cut deeply into the flow of inside information from management to institutional investors, thereby eroding the economic basis for that predisposition. Finally, as institutional investors soak up an ever-larger proportion of total stock, they will come under increasing pressure to maximize performance by cultivating the investments they have, rather than by switching into new ones.[39] This was well put by David Rockefeller, Chairman and Chief Executive Officer of the Chase Manhattan Bank:

> I might . . . draw your attention to one important change in savings that *is* occurring: namely, the tendency for personal savings to flow more and more through institutions—through insurance companies, pension funds, mutual funds and the like—rather than through individual savings accounts. During the Sixties, corporations will find themselves dealing increasingly with these sophisticated investors. Moreover, I suspect that such investors will become more de-

[39]See Sobieski, "In Support of Cumulative Voting," *Business Law* 15 (1960): 316, 321; "Big-block Buyers May Speak Up," *Business Week*, November 26, 1966, pp. 139, 140.

manding of management as time moves on—that as holdings expand, institutions, as well as individuals, will feel obliged to take more active interest in seeing that corporations do indeed have good managements. This will be true especially if their holdings become so large that they cannot readily or quickly liquidate their investments, as is now their practice when they become dissatisfied with the management of a corporation in which they hold shares.[40]

The short of the matter is that presently one-third of the stock in corporations listed on the New York Stock Exchange is held by highly sophisticated investors with a growing interest in structural changes other than changes in management; that the proportion of such stock held by such investors will soon reach 40–50 percent; and that much of the balance of the stock of such corporations seems to be held by wealthy individual shareholders with very substantial shareholdings, who may be assumed to be either themselves sophisticated investors or guided by professionals in their investment decisions. Only a small fraction of stock, even in publicly held corporations, appears to be under the direct ownership of unsophisticated investors with tiny holdings. "The average shareholder," who holds center stage in the theories of so many commentators, appears to be only an extra in the real corporate world. When the issue is analyzed in terms of shareholdings rather than shareholders, the concept of shareholders' voting membership in the corporate institution is seen as both valuable and fully realistic.

[40]Address before the Special Conference for Financial Executives of the American Management Association, quoted in Baum and Stiles, *Silent Partners*, p. 80.

The Federal Chartering of Corporations: A Modest Proposal

●●●

● DONALD E. SCHWARTZ
Law Center
Georgetown University

Federal chartering is not a new idea. Its origins date back to the constitutional conventions. Bills were before the Congress in the early part of this century and hearings were held in the Senate in 1937 and 1938. What impels the current reconsideration of this remedy? Who supports it?

Proposals for a federal corporation law have emerged from recent criticism of our economic policy as a possible device for restructuring large corporations. Discussion of this idea has ranged from consumer groups to the platform writers of the Democratic party.[1] This paper intends to add to that discusison by furnishing some background and by proposing suggested contours for such a law. Whether such a reform makes sense can perhaps be judged better in the light of this discussion. Therefore, as well as submitting the proposal, I will try to raise some questions about the wisdom of proceeding in this direction.

Corporation law reform is only a small part of the larger fabric of economic policy. The wisdom of federal incorporation can only be evaluated as a part of that larger fabric. Does this reform make sense in terms of the

---

[1]See, generally, Ralph Nader, "The Case for Federal Incorporation," address given at the Nader Conference on Corporate Accountability, Washington, D.C., Fall 1971.

overall goals for economic policy? What is "sensible economic policy"? No doubt there is confusion about economic policy that includes disagreement among the proponents of federal chartering. Some proponents favor this kind of law reform as a means of redistributing wealth and reallocating economic priorities. Some would like economic policy to reflect centralized planning rather than market forces. Others favor federal chartering as a means of unleashing market forces, in some cases to strengthen management while in others to constrain. Most observers, I believe, have come to desire some greater degree of regulation through corporation law, more of a constraint on management's power, while desiring that such reform come with (more or less) our prevailing economic system. This is the liberal constituency that has favored antitrust enforcement and government regulation of business and now has varying degrees of suspicion of that regulation. This is the group that must support federal chartering if it is to stand any chance of adoption.

It is with this latter group that I align myself. The questions I shall raise, then, address themselves to whether federal incorporation makes sense in terms of an economic policy that declares that one of the goals of economic policy is the attainment of some degree of distributive justice. I am assuming "sensible policy" to allow, and at times to compel, government action to promote the aims of liberty and justice for all. Sensible policy, in these terms, dictates that society attack those problems, such as pollution and discrimination, that have fueled the corporate responsibility drive. Further, this notion of sensible policy mistrusts great concentrations of private power and, indeed, of any power that is basically unaccountable to the persons affected.[2]

Arguments for Federal Chartering

The main support comes from those who have most vocally criticized the social performance of business. Foremost, clearly, is Ralph Nader, but he is not alone.[3] These reformers argue that the public interest has been ad-

[2]In an editorial entitled, "The Corporate State," the *New York Times* commented: "The crucial task facing the United States and other democratic societies is to find workable answers between the extremes—to limit concentrations of corporate power without undermining the efficiency of business; to permit the market to allocate resources to achieve socially desirable purposes in response to the democratically exercised choices of society." *New York Times*, July 4, 1972, p. 16.

[3]In October 1971, Nader sponsored a Conference on Corporate Law in Washington, D.C., devoted entirely to the subject of federal chartering of corporations (referred to as Nader Conference).

versely affected by corporate conduct necessitating new corrective methods. A secondary theme is sounded by those who seek to advance shareholder interests through the enlargement of the democratic process within the corporation, and here the spokesman is Lewis Gilbert, just as he was in 1937.[4] However, it is the social critics who have brought the issue to the fore and who place it in the democratic platform.

Criticism from the reformers is directed at the great concentration of power in the hands of relatively few corporations. That concentration of power is of itself something to fear, but, in addition, it is claimed that corporate conduct specifically has worked against the public interest in such areas as pollution, minority opportunity, the war, product safety, and generally, in meeting our society's needs. This is not to suggest that there is a sinister antipublic-interest bias within the corporation. A more sophisticated analysis might conclude that there is an absence of forces within the corporation or within the economy to work against the adverse public impact that results from the furthering of management's goals for the corporation. Competition is alleged to be insufficient to constrain the exercise of management's great private power or to direct it toward better goals. Government regulation, it is charged, has failed to protect the public largely because the regulatory bodies have served the private interests that they were supposed to regulate. Worse, government regulation, to a large degree, has strengthened the power of the large corporations. Critics from the Left and and Right have vied with each other in recent years to see who could keep the greater score on government regulation which was once a panacea proposed by the left.[5]

Where does this leave the unguarded public interest? It seems to place a greater emphasis on people's ability to help themselves. Nader sees this help coming from an army of what he calls public citizens, that is, people who devote all or substantially all of their time, like young lawyers working in public interest law firms. An enlarged role for these public citizens to constrain the power of large corporations envisions their functioning as private attorneys general, acting to enforce the public interest and bringing about the imposition of restraints or sanction that government agencies, either out of timidity or complicity, will not seek.

Self-help also envisions public citizens playing a role within the corporation. However, reformers contend that people can scarcely do this under

---

[4]U.S., Congress, Senate, Subcommittee of Committee on the Judiciary, *Federal Licensing of Corporations: Hearings on S. 10 and S. 3072*, 75th Cong., 1st Sess., 1937, p. 326.

[5]Simon Lazarus, "Halfway up from Liberalism: A Critical Look at the Regulatory State as a Response to Corporate Power," address given at Nader Conference.

some of the existing economic and legal ground rules, and they urge changing those rules. This means more explicit and easily enforceable rules against large corporate size, and mandatory disclosure of significantly more information to permit self-protection. The tools for self-help must include remedies and sanctions that address themselves to the real people who make the artificial person (the corporation) act, and not just to the fictional buffer. And, finally, new methods are necessary for deciding how the artificial person will exercise its power.

The reformers contend that state corporation laws under which corporations have been chartered are a main impediment to proper ground rules and the functioning of public citizens. State law fosters corporate secrecy and protects individuals from being held personally accountable for the conduct of the corporation, which is really the conduct of individuals. This is not because of the doctrine of limited liability, which protects shareholders and is properly acknowledged to be essential for the amassing of sufficient capital to fuel the economy, but rather because of the consequences of the doctrine of *persona ficta* under which all corporate deeds are performed.[6] This provides a degree of insulation to the corporate management from the consequences of misuse of corporate power, and generates an unfortunate complacency in the minds of the flesh-and-blood persons who make the corporation act, which, in effect, makes the exercise of power unaccountable. Only positive legislation can alter this condition.

State corporation law is premised on perceiving the shareholders as the ultimate interest group within the corporation. In seeming to give shareholders power, and making them the only body to whom corporate managers are even formally accountable, the law casts doubt on the legitimacy of concern about corporate performance by all nonshareholders, and of all criteria of performance save profit.[7] The law, having thus ousted nonshareholder interests from corporate councils, the separation of ownership of the corporation from its management then proceeds to oust even the shareholder interest from any actual control and thereby renders management, in effect, unaccountable to anybody.[8] It is at this point that Mr. Gilbert and the other friends of small shareholders register their protest.

The thrust of these arguments is that whatever other changes in the law

[6]*Dartmouth College* v. *Woodward*, 4 Wheat. 629 (1819).

[7]Thus, Professor Friedman is able to claim, with considerable support, that the only responsibility is to increase profits. Friedman, "The Social Responsibility of Business Is to Increase Its Profits," *New York Times*, September 13, 1970, sec. 6 (magazine), p. 32.

[8]A. Berle and G. Means, *The Modern Corporation and Private Property*, rev. ed., (New York: Harcourt Brace Jovanonch, 1969).

are needed, one must also revamp the statutory charter under which corporations are created. This necessarily means the creation of a federal chartering law to replace the existing system of state incorporation.[9]

Improvement in the Existing Laws as an Alternative to Federal Chartering

The premises on which these arguments rest must be closely examined before any proposals are made to change the law. Moreover, since such an alternative would involve a considerable upheaval of a system that has functioned for a long time, one should first explore less tumultuous ways of dealing with these problems. In other words, can we achieve the desired reforms without upsetting the federal balance to this degree?

Those who doubt federal chartering but who agree that there are problems with the present system may argue that the shortcomings can be dealt with by reforming state law, or by correcting the problems one by one through the present federal regulatory agencies. Both of these suggestions have serious problems. First, consider reform of state law. It is axiomatic that state corporation laws have been designed to appeal to the private interests of corporate managers, who are, after all, the individuals who make the decision of where to incorporate. The history of state incorporation, at least since about 1875, has been increasingly to "liberalize" corporation laws from the standpoint of those who wield corporate power.[10] Such laws do not regulate corporate conduct.

Professor Ernest L. Folk, III, the principal draftsman of the Delaware corporate law revision of 1967, has explicitly described how and why this process works. He writes:

Understanding the realities of corporate law revisions requires us to identify and assess a major fiction. Committees undertaking to rewrite corporation statutes usually believe, with varying degrees of devoutness, that they are pursuing an ideal of fairly and equitably balancing the varied and sometimes con-

---

[9]The clean-sweep approach did not originate with today's reformers. The same view has been sounded by at least one libertarian economist. H. Simon, *Economic Policy for a Free Society*, 58 (1948).

[10]E. M. Dodd, Jr., "Statutory Developments in Business Corporation Law," *Harvard Law Review* 50 (1936): 27; Rutledge, "Significant Trends in Modern Incorporation Statutes," Washington University Law Quarterly 22 (1937): 305; "Comment, Law for Sale: A Study of the Delaware Corporation Law of 1967," *University of Pennsylvania Law Review* 117 (1969): 861; Nader, "The Case for Federal Incorporation"; *Louis K. Liggett Co. v. Lee*, 288 U.S. 517 (dissent by Brandeis, J.) (1933); Ballantine, *Corporations*, rev. ed. (1946), p. 37.

flicting interests of the constituents of any corporation. In a large corporation, these constituents include management (which subdivides into the varying interests of the directors, both outside and inside), the officers, and others, the shareholders (which may subdivide into possibly conflicting groups), the creditors, employees, and the general public.

This is a fiction. Corporation law revision committees are not organized to work that way; they are not expected to do so; they do not do so and the final product reflects no such approach; clearly, the Delaware statute does not represent a balancing of interest. The excellent and able committee consisted chiefly of pro-management corporation attorneys, with a divided minority representing the specialized interests of the Secretary of State office and of the derivative suit plaintiff. The majority was strengthened by two representatives of the service companies. Presumably, an acknowledged goal of balancing interests would dictate that no particular segment of the corporate community should command a majority, either singly or in coalition; but would require representatives of other potentially affected interests. Although this would not range from John Birch Society member to Haight-Ashbury hippy, it would be a wider spectrum than that represented in the Delaware development, or, for that matter, in other corporation law revisions. Indeed, I find that the Delaware committee embraced a greater variety of interests than counter-part groups in other states. Thus, the inevitable structure of the groups charged with the revision belies the notion that interests are being balanced, for usually the only interest represented is management.[11]

Moreover, chartermongering is an inevitable result of a federal system that permits a corporation to adopt as its legal domicile a state with which it has no physical connection and then to conduct business everywhere it chooses. While this might not have appeared to have been a problem in the early stages of economic development when large corporations were very rare, it emerges as the main problem once economic power passes into the hands of about 500 enormous corporations.[12] The result is what Nader has described as a version of Gresham's Law, with the bad law driving out the good.[13]

---

[11]E. L. Folk III, "Some Reflections of a Corporation Law Draftsman," Conn. J.B. 42 (1968): 409, 411–412.

[12]For a description of chartermongering, see Jennings, "The Role of the States in Corporation Regulation and Investor Protection," *Law and Contemporary Problems* 23 (1958): 193, 194.

[13]Nader, "The Case for Federal Incorporation." An excellent example is furnished by the comment of the sponsor of the proposed new Michigan corporation law. He describes the bill as a bipartisan effort "with the primary purpose of providing a unified, simple code that would, in the words of some, 'out-Delaware Delaware'." Downs, "Michigan To Have a New Corporation Code?" *Wayne Law Review* 18 (1972): 913.

There is also a strong argument against correcting the problems by merely expanding the present regulatory system. Federal regulation generally has tended not to be successful. There is a tendency for the regulated to gain control of the watchdog. Indeed the prophecy of Attorney General Olney regarding the Interstate Commerce Commission (ICC) has too often been fulfilled.[14]

Furthermore, federal regulation, no matter how extensive, must still follow state court law to determine the nature of the corporation and to define such terms as "business judgment." Existing law has the effect of relieving corporate managers from serious threat to liability. A system of federal corporations drawing on a new model could depart from existing decisions.

Some reformers would add yet another argument against merely improving existing regulation. The thrust of their objective is to constrain the economic muscle possessed by large corporations, which enables them to exercise a comprehensive economic-social-political power. Muscle and power usually go together, and neither the market nor government regulation have been able to do much about the exercise of power so long as the muscle remains. The reformers ultimately desire to relocate the power more within individual hands, since they believe that shifting the power to government hands is no shift at all. The objective, therefore, is to reduce the size of corporations and government regulations alike and strengthen the position of individual private citizens who will act directly—not through institutions—against corporate abuse.

Even those who share the reformers' concerns must have serious questions at this point. The power possessed by large corporations grew out of their amassing of great wealth, and measures that retaliate against this success might seriously threaten future growth of the economy. How much growth is desirable in future years has become a hotly debated subject, as has its corollary question—should we adopt policies that redistribute what we have? Moreover, efforts to reallocate economic muscle and power will affect institutions in our society beyond the corporation, and, indeed, will have a profound affect on all aspects of our society, not just its economy.

One result of arming and arousing public interest lawyers as enforcers

---

[14]In 1892, Richard S. Olney, the Attorney General under President Grover Cleveland, told the President of the Burlington Railroad that the Interstate Commerce Commission "can be of great use to the railroads. It satisfies the popular clamor for a government supervision of railroads, at the same time that supervision is almost entirely minimal. The part of wisdom is not to destroy the Commission, but to utilize it." Cited by Representative Richard L. Ottinger (D-NY) in testimony before the Subcommittee on Transporation and Aeronautics of the Committee on Interstate and Foreign Commerce, House of Representatives, November 17, 1969, 91st Cong. 1st sess., p. 320.

of the public interest would be to judicialize many of the conflicts within our society that at present are dealt with in other ways. Negotiation with regulators and the marketplace are two alternative methods. Sometimes we choose to accept a degree of abuse because the remedy for eliminating th abuse would entail too little benefit at too great a cost. These mechanisms might break down if the courts are thrust into all controversies, with a consequent malfunctioning of the entire economic system. This result might prompt a reaction from the legislature to protect, and perhaps, overprotect, the economic process. I think it is very important to grasp the full dimensions of the proposed reforms in order for them to be properly evaluated.

Thus, the spirit of the new zeal for federal incorporation is reflected in a search for new models of corporate structure and economic structure. The comments by Professors Lynn and Dahl made at the Nader Conference provide one view of the scope of a federal chartering law and the dimensions of its possible impact. For example, Professor John J. Flynn, of Utah Law School, affirmed that "any discussion of a federal corporation law must first consider whether the basic concept of a corporation is any longer realistic, necessary or justifiable as the receptacle of society's resources for organizing economic activity. Should these aggregations of a society's wealth, the productive resources of many nations, and the livelihood of thousands of people be clothed with a legal personality entitled to perpetual life with an infinite power to accumulate wealth, managed by a board of directors that does not direct and owned by shareholders who do not own?"[15] He also suggested that a federal law should define its work force as the new constituency of the corporation, conceding the effect of this proposal to be revolutionary and having a broad impact on many fields of law and economics.[16]

Professor Robert Dahl, a Yale political scientist, directed attention to considering what a federal chartering statute should seek to achieve with respect to forms of ownership and management.[17] Starting with the premise that the corporation should be thought of as a political system, he indicated his preference for control by corporate employees along the lines that corporations are structured in Yugoslavia.[18]

---

[15]J. J. Flynn, "Corporate Democracy—Who Needs It?", address at Nader Conference, p. 14.

[16]*Ibid.*, at 25–26.

[17]R. Dahl, "Alternative Ways of Controlling Corporate Power," address at Nader Conference.

[18]See J. T. Kolaja, *Workers Councils: The Yugoslav Experience* (New York: Praeger, 1966). The sweep and scope of that proposal can be appreciated perhaps from this insight by

Protection of Shareholders' Rights

As mentioned earlier, the other force in the drive for federal incorporation has been the protection of shareholders' rights. This is a lesser issue, I believe, because the main protection for shareholders will come from an unmanipulated marketplace and from vigilant courts enforcing the fiduciary duties of management. Of course, the adoption of federal securities legislation went very far toward protection of shareholders' rights. In fact, these laws have probably gone much further in protecting shareholders' rights than anyone would have conceived at the time of their adoption. These laws have gone from merely requiring disclosure to investors and prohibiting fraud toward providing substantive protection for the rights of shareholders by imposing, in fact if not in form, a federal fiduciary standard. Through an interpretation of the Securities and Exchange Commission's (SEC's) Rule 10b–5 the courts have created a federal common law of corporations to advance shareholders' rights.[19] The significance of this development has been that the federal courts have vindicated and protected the rights of shareholders from abusive management practices. To a large extent this has been necessitated because state corporation law has, in the main, abandoned its efforts to regulate corporations in the interests of shareholders.[20]

All this would seem to further indicate that there would be a minimal need for a federal corporation law for the protection of the shareholders. The reforms proposed by Mr. Gilbert include such things as the requirement of mandatory cumulative voting, the abolition of staggered boards of directors, a requirement of annual meetings, prohibitions of voting trusts and nonvoting stock, and the requirement that a transcript of the annual

Elisabeth Mann Borgese: ". . . self-management is a process that moves on a different plane from that of ownership. Self-management, in fact, articulates relations among people much more than relations between people and things. Therefore, what is important is not that the workers should own resources or the means of production, but that nobody else should own them and thereby be placed in a position of hiring and firing and otherwise directing and manipulating the workers. Its self-management need not be based on workers' ownership. It certainly excludes the possibility of ownership by others. The Yugoslav concept of social ownership in fact is a negative concept. It is the negation of ownership." Borgese, "The Promise of Self-Management," *The Center Magazine*, May-June 1972, pp. 54, 57.

[19]A. Fleischer, Jr., "Federal Corporation Law: An Assessment," *Harvard Law Review* 78 (1965): 1146; *Superintendent of Insurance* v. *Bankers Life and Casualty Co.*, 92, S. Ct. 165 (1971).

[20]Folk, "Recent Developments in Corporations Statutes, *Journal of Education* 20 (1968): 511, 515.

meeting be maintained and made available. No amount of such tinkering can possibly alter the fact that the small shareholder will remain in a minority position subject to the power of the management and the board of directors and that the working of shareholder democracy cannot correct any imbalance of power.[21]

Yet, while all this is true, there remains something to be said for Mr. Gilbert's concern for federal incorporation. What Mr. Gilbert has demonstrated from the outset has been the enormous power possessed by management, often by management with a very small shareholder interest. Cumulative voting is not likely seriously to diminish the power of corporate management, but in some cases at least, it might result in putting a watchdog or a heretical voice on the board of directors. At least, management thinks it is enough of a threat to prevent its adoption whenever possible. Delaware, the pacesetter in this respect, has long made cumulative voting optional,[22] which is a way of eliminating it in the case of the large corporation. This has been Mr. Gilbert's main cause over the years. He is probably right in thinking that cumulative voting can be saved in the large corporation only through federal incorporation. Evidence of this is the proposed revision of the Michigan Corporation Law, which would eliminate the mandatory cumulative voting presently required in that state.[23]

The legitimacy of Mr. Gilbert's concerns may also be illustrated by an amendment to the Delaware Corporation Law in 1969 that allows a corporation to eliminate an annual meeting with the consent in writing of a majority of its shareholders, rather than all of the shareholders as previously required.[24] No rule of the SEC requires the holding of an annual meeting, although New York Stock Exchange policy does. However, Fuqua Corporation, a company whose shares are listed on the New York Stock Exchange, in a widely publicized gesture, amended its bylaws in 1972 to eliminate the requirement of an annual meeting as permitted under Delaware law.[25] This amendment will not be effective unless the New York Stock

---

[21]Manning, "Book Review," *Yale Law Journal* 67 (1958): 1477.

[22]Sec. 214, Delaware General Corporation Law.

[23]Moscow, "Aspects of Shareholders' Rights," *Wayne Law Review* 18 (1972): 1003, 1006. Ironically, at the last two annual meetings of General Motors Corporation, Mr. Gilbert has proposed that the corporation reincorporate in Michigan. GM management recognized that the purpose was to gain the effect of mandatory cumulative voting and opposed the resolution. GM proxy statement, April 5, 1971, p. 26. In 1972, management noted that even this purpose would not be obtained if the law revision was enacted. GM statement, April 13, 1972, p. 40.

[24]Sec. 228, Delaware General Corporation Law.

[25]*New York Times*, April 23, 1972, sec. 3, p. 1.

Exchange consents and the Exchange has indicated that it will take the matter under advisement.[26] Clearly, no issue would more raise the hackles of Mr. Gilbert and his friends than the elimination of the annual meeting, and in my opinion, rightfully so. If enough states imitate Delaware in this respect, and if enough corporations apply pressure, the annual meeting will disappear. Michigan, in its proposed revision, promises to become the second state that allows the elimination of the annual meeting.[27]

What Kind of Federal Incorporation Law?

Obviously Mr. Nader and Mr. Gilbert, each desiring the adoption of a federal incorporation law, are not thinking of the same kind of law. Many of Mr. Gilbert's reforms would be acceptable to Mr. Nader, principally because they would not interfere with his goals, but the reverse is not true. This calls for the need to translate much of the discussion of federal incorporation into consideration of specific proposals. For the most part the catchwords "federal incorporation" and "federal chartering" have been about as illuminating as the slogan, "Make love—not war." Until we know with whom and against whom, we really don't know if we are in favor of it.

The following discussion of concrete suggestions for a federal law chartering corporations is not exhaustive. Rather, it aims merely to mention some specific proposals that are designed to correct the two major problems in the present system—lack of accountabiilty and lack of varied input. The model here proposed may be considered conservative because it assumes a system of competing private enterprises with minimal governmental regulation of corporate decision making. It also adopts much of the prevailing corporate structure.

The first question which must be answered in our scheme of federal incorporation is, who is covered? The purpose of this statute is to control those corporations that have a significant impact outside of their immediate vicinity. For purposes of federal securities law, Professor Loss proposes a special federal status for companies that have $1 million in assets and 300 holders of its securities.[28] I think this would include too large a number of corporations. The aim of the statute is to impose some new ground rules for companies that have a significant public impact, and not just those that

[26]*New York Times*, April 20, 1972, sec. 3 (letter from Lee D. Arning, Senior Vice-president, New York Stock Exchange).

[27]Moscow, "Aspects of Shareholders' Rights," pp. 10011–10014.

[28]American Law Institute, Federal Securities Code, sec. 401 (Tentative Draft No. 1, 1972).

affect their investors. By the same token the group affected by the New York Stock Exchange figure of $14 million in assets and 3000 shareholders seems too small.[29] A more appropriate threshold is $10 million in assets and 300 holders of its securities. This would include all companies listed on the *Fortune* 1000 list with a sufficient number of security holders.[30] It should be noted that in connection with selecting this number, a decision is made to maintain the present system of regulation by the SEC and the Federal Trade Commission (FTC), although it assumes the creation of a new corporations commission. But the federal incorporation law, as here envisioned, cannot take over all of the regulatory functions.

The substance of the federal statute would contain major changes in four sections: those dealing with corporate records and reports, directors and management, shareholders, and organic or fundamental changes.

Corporate Records and Reports

The changes in this section are intended to render the corporation (and management) more accountable to a larger constituency. Putting more information in the hands of the public will increase the effectiveness of the private attorneys general as well as help to make those who run corporations more aware of their public role. This same information, turned over to other federal agencies, will aid in the enforcement of coexisting laws.

The disclosures should be made in the annual report sent to the shareholders and filed with the federal incorporation agency. This would ensure the wide circulation of the information that this section requires to be effective. Essential to effective disclosure provisions is a flexibility to implement new reporting requirements as legislation increases corporate responsibilities and as a need for broader disclosure becomes evident. To provide such flexibility, the commission should be given the authority to enact rules and regulations governing both the form and substance of the report.

Shareholders should know who has a substantial interest in the corporation. All interest above five percent should be reported, and for the very large companies (over $50 million) one percent interests. In view of the expanding role of the investment manager and institutional holdings, both actual voting control and beneficial interests should be disclosed.

Disclosure might also include a report on employment of minority groups, steps undertaken to equalize opportunity, and efforts that have

---

[29]New York Stock Exchange, Inc., Company Manual, sec. B1, at B-3 (1971).
[30]*Fortune*, June 1972, p. 120.

been taken to help unprepared minority group members become eligible for employment. Data on air, water, and waste pollution should be reported, both summarily to measure compliance with applicable laws and quantitatively to indicate the nature and amount of emissions from the company's operations. In keeping with the spirit of disclosure, companies should also be required to report any variation or modification in the legal standards because of special circumstances. Other subjects of disclosure should include workers' safety and injuries allegedly stemming from the company's products, whether or not liability resulted.

This report would impose no undue hardship because the required information is no more than that already gathered in the operation of a well-run company. Responsibility for the report and the accuracy of its representations would lie with the board. This obligation would be buttressed by the logical presumption that the board has knowledge of the matters contained in the report.

Directors and Management

This section is designed to make those who run corporations more accountable and to increase the diversity of influences on the board. The problem with the present system of corporation law is more than unaccountability. Large American corporations tend to suffer from a lack of diverse input at top management levels. Often, the officers and board members of these companies are so inbred that they resemble the emperors of ancient Rome. And like the emperors they can develop an insanity that evidences itself in a belief in their own divinity. These directors believe that divergent points of view come from quarters occupied by the enemy.

Many supporters of federal incorporation have suggested a politicalization of the board.[31] Some, like Professor Dahl, claim that the major corporations are already political systems, but not functioning properly. Even those who do not share that view ponder how we can introduce new voices into corporate decisions.[32] Obviously, both of these views reject the notion that the marketplace—the invisible hand—takes care of the problem. However, the most difficult problems just begin with the assumption that there is a need to change the management structure. Proposals ranging from

---

[31]P. I. Blumberg, "The Politicalization of the Corporation," *Busines Lawyer* 26 (1971): 1551, affords a good description.

[32]John L. Bunting; Jan Deutsch; Leon E. Hickman; and A. F. Conrad, "The Corporate Machinery for Hearing and Heeding New Votes," *Business Lawyer* 27 (1971): 195.

Yugoslavian self-determination,[33] to German codetermination,[34] to placing designated constituencies on the board,[35] to one man, one vote,[36] and many more, all contain the danger that either they are elaborate schemes that amount to little substance, or that they endanger the ability of the corporation to fulfill any economic mission. The plain fact may be that no device for the politicalization of the corporation can succeed within our existing economic framework. A fact not so plain, but I believe equally valid, is that the essence of our economic framework is essential to the maintenance of our political system. Therefore, I believe only modest changes are possible.

A related question that the framers of federal chartering must face concerns the role of the employee under the statute. The law could give employees management participation, but what this would do to the existing pattern of labor relations, worked out over long years of struggle, is problematical. It is unlikely that labor spokesman would favor any significant change. In other words, labor leaders would probably regard collective bargaining as more important to the rights of workers than a role in the management of the corporation. Further, a role in management might create a conflict of interests regarded as intolerable.

Two changes in existing corporate laws may serve to make directors more accountable. Corporate directorships should be made a nearly full-time job. This would tend to increase the familiarity that each director has with his company's business. The number of boards that any one individual can sit on should be limited to a number consistent with this new emphasis. Perhaps companies should salary directors and require more frequent board meetings.

The board would also become more accountable if directors were given greater personal liability not indemnifiable by the corporation.[37] A federal incorporation statute might extend traditional responsibility and place management under a duty to supervise its employees' conduct in order to prevent corporate violations of the law. Such responsibility should not render directors, executive officers, or management personnel strictly liable; a due diligence defense should be available.

---

[33]See Kolaja, *Workers Councils: The Yugoslav Experience.*

[34]D. F. Vagts, "Reforming the 'Modern' Corporation: Perspective from the German," *Harvard Law Review*, 80 (1966): 23, 64.

[35]D. E. Schwartz, "Towards New Corporate Goals: Co-Existence with Society," *Georgia Law Journal* 60 (1971): 57, 60.

[36]D. L. Ratner, "The Government of Business Corporations: Critical Reflections on the Rule of 'One Share, One Vote'," *Cornell Law Review* 56 (1970): 1.

[37]H. Henn, *Law of Corporations*, 2d ed. (1970), p. 429.

Increasing the variety of inputs into the decision-making process of the corporation can be accomplished by two further changes in existing corporate law. First, more varied people should be put on the board. This can be facilitated by requiring cumulative voting, eliminating staggered terms for board members, and taking the proxy machinery away from management. The strength of cumulative voting in putting a minority interest on the board of directors can be borne witness to by the fact that Campaign GM was not far from being able to elect a board member with the amount of proxies it accumulated.[38] Some public interest groups have amassed sufficient proxies to have done this. Staggered terms should be eliminated because they are incompatible with cumulative voting.

Consistent with the addition of minority representation on the board should be provisions in the statute for these minority members to have resources available for their use. In order for them to perform their job, they should be able to hire counsel and other staff, and be able to check on management.

Another way to increase input is by creating a public policy committee. This is suggested only as one possible device to make the board more cognizant of its public impact. In order to be effective, the committee should be composed of no more than two-thirds management representatives and should be required to hold public meetings and to publish reports. General Motors has a committee composed of outside directors. Its effectiveness, however, cannot be judged since it neither holds open meetings nor makes public reports. Associated with the idea of a public policy committee is the suggestion for a corporate social audit.[39] This has received some attention lately; however, much work remains to be done before it has developed to a point where it could be legislated.

Shareholders

This section should be redesigned to give the "corporation's owners" more influence over policy. Of primary interest is taking exclusive control of the proxy machinery away from management, as urged by Professor Eisenberg in his 1970 *Harvard Law Review* article. The proxy machinery should be restructured to: (1) allow easier access by more stockholders and (2) to allow stockholders to vote on important issues.

---

[38]See generally, Schwartz, "The Public-Interest Proxy Contest: Reflections on Campaign GM," *Michigan Law Review* 69 (1971): 419.

[39]David Rockefeller, "Social Audit," *New York Times*, May 1, 1972, p. 33. See *Business Week*, September 23, 1972, p. 88, describing the Bauer-Fenn effort.

Any shareholder who can substantiate a minimum amount of support should be allowed to have his proposal printed on management's proxy. The allowable subject matter of such proposals should include any significant subject affecting corporate policy. The details and procedures for the implementation of this suggestion could be established by the regulatory agency.

The stockholders should be allowed to "vote" on major proposals as well as for nominees for the board of directors, instead of merely authorizing a proxy. This could be accomplished by having nominations for the board in March and an election through the mail in May. The ballot could also contain a proxy authorization to deal with those items that were not on the agenda for the annual meeting in March. This suggestion would tend to put some minority interests on the board, while the present system merely perpetuates management by allowing it to solicit proxies and then "vote" them at the meeting in its own interest.

Organic or Fundamental Changes

A federal incorporation statute should contain a requirement of regulatory approval for mergers and sales. Experience has shown that when the standard for affecting shareholders' rights is one of fairness, the courts allow enormous liberty to management. Moreover, disclosure may be of dubious significance in protecting the shareholders' interest. The California approach is worthy of consideration.[40] Further, in preventing unreasonably large concentrations of power, advance notice is necessary in order to formulate a reasoned and consistent policy.

Conclusion

It is not this paper's intention to propose a specific federal incorporation law. Rather, it attempts to give the background of present discussion in this area and to add to that discussion by providing concrete illustrations. These suggestions are only a fragile skeleton of the full measure that should be thought through.

[40]California Corporations Code, sec. 25009 (West 1955).

PART IV

Government Regulation of Business

●●

We are approaching the condition of King Oedipus of Thebes. Thebes was a tribal society, and when the King set about investigating the responsibility for misery and disorder, he found out *he* was the criminal.

—Marshall McLuhan

Every increase in the complexity and size of the U.S. economic system has been followed by a parallel increase in the type and magnitude of government regulation of economic activity, either to correct some real or alleged weaknesses of the system or to channel its resources toward socially desirable ends. "There ought to be a law against it" is not an idle cry when it comes to the regulation of business. Nevertheless, one can hardly find a well-informed observer who is satisfied with the current state of regulation. The reasons for dissatisfaction range across the entire spectrum, from too little to too much regulation.[1]

This part discusses various facets of the regulatory process—its strong and weak points—and, if some form of regulation is necessary and desirable, how it should be developed and enforced so that the desired social ends are accomplished without thwarting initiative in the marketplace and sapping its dynamism. The authors do not emphasize so much what has happened, but rather, given the current state of affairs, what the best courses of action are for the future.

Leo Pellerzi notes that a corporation, at common law, is only a legal fiction and that before the Sherman and Clayton acts the "legal definition of corporate responsibility was simply a device to separate corporations from responsibility." However, today corporate officers can go to jail for

[1]For different viewpoints on government regulation, the readers may wish to see Bernstein 1955, Cary 1967, Cox et al. 1969, Friendly 1962, Green and Moore 1972, Kohlmeier 1970, MacAvoy 1970, McKie 1970, Posner 1969, and Wilson 1971. For complete citations, see selected bibliography at the end of this part introduction.

169

antitrust violations. Pellerzi focuses on federal regulation of business operations and says that at least two assumptions are involved: (1) that there is an overriding national policy to have a free competitive system, and (2) the system cannot serve the total needs of society without some form of federal regulation.

The federal regulation of business, primarily against the abuses of economic concentration, started with the concept of federal agencies. These agencies, by the acts of Congress and the courts, have a quasi-judicial power as well as a regulatory power to promote and regulate the welfare of those who are being regulated. However, Pellerzi indicates that in about 1000 cases over which he presided as an administrative law judge, the term "public interest" never meant anything of substance to him "beyond the materially related interests of the parties" that were before him. He extends the matter by noting that in many pervasive hearings across the country the definition and actual components of public interest are "after-the-fact rationalization[s] of the completed process," and he immediately questions: "How do you get someone into a particular proceeding who wants to present 'public interest' in a dimension beyond the specific interests of the parties in the hearing?" In such circumstances, despite the fact that there is a doctrine of inter-vention by a party interest, parties try to limit the hearings and not let anyone come in and muddy things up.

Regarding the adequacy of the regulatory job of agencies, Pellerzi questions the first assumption, whether there exists a national policy of protecting a free and competitive system, and whether this should be used as a guideline for regulatory agencies. He indicates that agencies are functioning with little or no knowledge of what is happening in the industry that they are regulating, and with their limited exposure to public interest (in the true sense, not as described above), the agencies are not able to function properly. However the courts have started redefining cer-tain components of public interest and have directed agencies to observe the new definitions. Pellerzi proposes that Congress take a much more active role in specifying national policy and related social responsibility matters to prevent judgments on the basis of fairness doctrine.

In Louis M. Kohlmeier, Jr.'s review of regulatory agencies, many of the criticisms regarding their inadequate functioning are examined, as well as the proposals for their improved functioning. In rather great detail he treats the topics of reforms and reform accomplishments. Then he ob-serves that they did too little, too late; in some instances only because of the court's directions after extensive public complaints. He notes that the agencies were created years ago to respond to specific economic or social causes of the day and eventually to bring about some changes that Congress believed would not be brought about by the forces of free competition. Thus, Congress equipped them with enough power so that they not only could regulate the industries under their charge but also protect them from competition both from within and without. Under such a mandate, Kohlmeier thinks, the agencies are inherently incapable of defending today's public interest. He speculates on the sources of inadequacies by addressing such topics as whether independence is a source of weakness, or whether ambiguous mandates have stopped the agencies from functioning well. Kohlmeier concludes that the problems of the agencies today are too large and too burdensome, and there are reasons to believe that agencies are not serving the public interest of consumers, the private interest of their regulated industry, or the interest of the government itself.

In his article, Dan H. Fenn, Jr. refutes the "capture theory," which says that federal agencies operate by responding to the greatest pressure. He cites the 1963 work of Raymond Bauer and draws upon personal experience, including membership on the Tariff Commission under President Johnson, to show that agency membership is heterogeneous and that individual characteristics and ambitions are a significant variable in differential responses to a complex operating environment.[2] Each agency member, says Fenn, has the dual responsibilities of making decisions on specific cases and of determining what function he thinks his agency should play. The latter involves internal efforts, such as mobilizing votes and securing orientation on policy issues, and external, intragovernmental maneuvers through Congress, the White House, and the federal bureaucracy. Case histories are given to illustrate these points. Fenn concludes with two suggestions to his initial query of how federal regulatory agencies can be made "repositories of public interest." Shorter terms for commissioners and greater presidential attention to selection would improve the agencies' responsiveness to current public interest, he thinks.

Of all interest groups, the general public has the least access to the workings of federal regulatory agencies, says Robert N. Katz. Katz's examination of the appointment procedure shows that the public has no channels comparable to those that exist for presidential consideration of nominations from industry or Congress. Katz identifies a secondary stage of influence by correlating types of decisions with the predilections for which members of various agencies have been selected. Additionally, he

[2]Raymond A. Bauer; Ithiel Poole; and Lewis Dexter, *American Business and Public Policy* (New York: Atherton Press, 1963).

points to agencies' frequency of interactions with special interest groups, disguised as a consultative relationship, versus infrequent, random interactions with the "public interest." Industry access has serious consequences for the use of agency time as well, says Katz. Detailed case histories are used to support his contention that the functioning of agencies is severely hampered by business attempts to reduce competition through the regulatory process.

For these shortcomings and abuses Katz recommends: (1) a procedure to prevent the use of commissions to reduce competition; (2) a four-step procedure to compel the public counsel to intervene in cases involving the public interest, and to be responsible for notifying the public and facilitating its participation; (3) limited life commissions, which would be responsible for justifying their own continuation; (4) full publicity in adequate time to all affected parties; this includes such practicalities as the mailing of requisite documents to applicants rather than requiring perusal in a Washington, D.C. office, which is currently standard procedure. Adoption of these points might help to restore the public interest to the work of regulatory agencies, Katz concludes.

SELECTED BIBLIOGRAPHY

*American Bar Association. "Report of the ABA Commission to Study the Federal Trade Commission." Chicago: 1969.

*"Application of the Sherman Act to Attempts To Influence Government Action." *Harvard Law Review* 81, no. 4 (February 1968): 847–858.

Areeda, Phillip E. "Antitrust Laws and Public Utility Regulation." *The Bell Journal of Economics and Management Science*, Spring 1972, pp. 42–57.

Baur, Raymond A.; Poole, Ithiel; and Dexter, Lewis. *American Business and Public Policy*. New York: Atherton Press, 1963.

*Bernstein, Marver. *Regulating Business by Independent Commission*. Princeton, N.J.: Princeton University Press, 1955.

Blumberg, Phillip I. "Selected Materials on Corporate Social Responsibility." *The Business Lawyer*, July 1972, pp. 1275–1299.

*Borod, R. S. "Lobbying for the Public Interest—Federal Tax Policy and Administration." *New York University Law Review* 42, no. 6 (December 1967): 1087–1117.

Brozen, Y. "Rule by Markets and Rule by Men." *The Freeman*, September 1967, pp. 515–527.

*Cary, William L. *Politics and the Regulatory Agencies*. New York: McGraw-Hill Book Co., 1967.

Cater, Douglass. *Power in Washington: A Critical Look at Today's Struggle To Govern in the Nation's Capital*. New York: Random House, 1964.

*Especially recommended for an overall view and for authoritative viewpoints on different perspectives of the issues covered.

*Cheit, Earl F., ed. *The Business Establishment*. New York: John Wiley & Sons, 1964.

Cherington, Paul W., and Gillen, Ralph L. "The Company Representative in Washington." *Harvard Business Review*, May-June 1961, pp. 109–115.

Cohen, Dorothy. "The Federal Trade Commission and the Regulation of Advertising in the Consumer Interest." *Journal of Marketing* 33, no. 1 (January 1969): 40–44.

Cooper, G. "Tax Treatment of Business Grassroots Lobbying: Defining and Attaining the Public Policy Objectives." *Columbia Law Review* 68, no. 5 (May 1968): 801–859.

Corson, John J. "More Government in Business." *Harvard Business Review*, May-June 1961, 81–88.

*Cox, Edward F.; Fellmeth, Robert C.; and Schulz, John E. *The Nader Report on the FTC*. New York: Richard W. Baron Publishing Co., 1969.

Crandall, Robert W. "FCC Regulation, Monopsony, and Network Television Program Costs." *The Bell Journal of Economics and Management Science*, Fall 1972, pp. 483–508.

Domhoff, G. William. *Who Rules America?* Englewood Cliffs, N.J.: Prentice-Hall, 1967.

*Epstein, Edwin M. *The Corporation in American Politics*. Englewood Cliffs, N.J.: Prentice-Hall, 1969.

*Fellmeth, Robert C. *The Interstate Commerce Omission*. New York: Grossman, 1970.

_____. *See also* Cox, Edward F., et al.

Fenn, Dan H., Jr. "The Case of Latent Lobby." *Harvard Business Review*, January-February 1967, pp. 22–29.

Finn, David. *The Corporate Oligarch*. New York: Simon & Schuster, 1969.

*Friendly, Henry J. *The Federal Administrative Agencies: The Need for Better Definition of Standards*. Cambridge: Harvard University Press, 1962.

*Green, Mark J.; Moore, Beverely C., Jr.; and Wasserstein, Bruce. *The Closed Enterprise System*. New York: Grossman, 1972.

Green, Mark J. *See also* Nader, Ralph.

Heilbroner, Robert L. "Rhetoric and Reality in the Struggle Between Business and the State." *Social Research* 35.3 (Fall 1968): 401–425.

Holton, Richard H. "Business and Government." *Daedalus* 98 (Winter 1969): 41–59.

Hutchinson, G. Scott. "Reactions to the Latent Lobby." *Harvard Business Review*, July-August 1967, pp. 166–168.

Keelr, Theodore E. "Airline Regulation and Market Performance." *The Bell Journal of Economics and Management Science*, Fall 1972, pp. 399–424.

Key, V. O., Jr. *Politics, Parties and Pressure Groups*. 5th ed. New York: Thomas Y. Crowell Co., 1967.

*Kohlmeier, Louis M., Jr. *The Regulators: Watchdog Agencies and the Public Interest*. New York: Harper & Row, 1969.

Larson, John A., ed. *The Regulated Businessman: Business and Government*. New York: Holt, Rinehart & Winston, 1966.

Levitt, Theodore. "The Johnson Treatment." *Harvard Business Review*, January-February 1967, pp. 114–128.

*Liebhafsky, H. H. *American Government and Business*. New York: John Wiley & Sons, 1971.

*MacAvoy, Paul W. "The Effectiveness of the Federal Power Commission." *The Bell Journal of Economics and Management*, Fall 1970, pp. 271–303.

_____. "The Formal Work Product of the Federal Power Commissioners." *Bell Journal of Economics and Management Science,* Spring 1971, pp. 379–395.

Marcus, Sumner. "New Weapons Against Bigness." *Harvard Business Review*, January-February 1965, pp. 100–108.

*McConnell, Grant. *Private Power and American Democracy*. New York: Alfred A. Knopf, 1966.

————. "The Spirit of Private Government." *American Political Science Review*, September 1968, pp. 754–770.

*McKie, James W. "Regulation and the Free Market: The Problem of Boundaries." *The Bell Journal of Economics and Management Science*, Spring 1970, pp. 6–26.

Miliband, Ralph. *The State in a Capitalist Society*. London: Weidenfeld and Nicolson, 1969.

Mueller, Dr. Willard F. "The Rising Economic Concentration in America: Reciprocity, Conglomeration, and the New American 'Zaibatsu' System." *Antitrust Law and Economics Review*; Part 1, Spring 1971, pp. 15–50; Part 2, Summer 1971, pp. 91–104.

*Nader, Ralph, and Green, Mark J., eds. *Corporate Power in America*. New York: Grossman, 1973.

*Noll, Roger G. *Reforming Regulation: An Evaluation of the Ash Council Proposals*. Washington, D.C.: Brookings Institution, 1971.

————. "The Behavior of Regulatory Agencies." *Review of Social Economy*, pp. 15–19, March 1971.

Nonet, Philippe. *Administrative Justice: Advocacy and Change in a Government Agency*. New York: Russell Sage Foundation, 1969.

*President's Advisory Council on Executive Organization. *A New Regulatory Framework: Report on Selected Independent Regulatory Agencies*. Washington, D.C.: Government Printing Office, January 1971.

*Posner, Richard A. "National Monopoly and Its Regulation." *Stanford Law Review* 21 (February 1969): 548–643.

"Public Disclosure of Lobbyists' Activities." *Fordham Law Review* 38 (March 1970): 524.

Richardson, M. E. "Lobbying and Public Relations—Sensitive, Suspect or Worse?" *Antitrust Bulletin* 10, no. 4 (July-August 1965): 507–518.

*Scheibla, Shirley. "Gentleman's Agreement? Government Is Making Business Its Unwilling Partner in Bias." *Barron's*, December 23, 1968. pp. 9–17.

The Conference Board. *Competition, Efficiency and Antitrust, Eigth Conference on Anti-
The Conference Board. *Competition, Efficiency and Antitrust, Eight Conference on Antitrust Issues in Today's Economy*. New York: The Conference Board, 1969.

*Turner, James S. *The Chemical Feast: Report on the Food and Drug Administration*. New York: Grossman, 1970.

*Wilson, James Q. "The Dead Hand of Regulation." *The Public Interest*, Fall 1971, pp. 39–58.

A Conceptual View
of the Regulatory Process

●●●

● LEO M. PELLERZI
Assistant Attorney General
U.S. Department of Justice

My focus in this article is on federal regulation of the business corporation. Starting with the corporation, I will discuss the matrix and the dynamics of "regulation."

First, at common law a corporation is a legal fiction; there is no such thing in reality except the artificial person recognized in law. For a great number of years, of course, the legal definition of corporate responsibility was simply a device to separate corporations from responsibility. The Clayton and Sherman acts basically changed that, and today corporate officers can go to jail for violation of antitrust laws.

If we look at the development of the corporation as a social institution, there is a great deal of truth in Peter Drucker's concept of the corporation as the new social order. Corporations are pervasive in the United States: In 1800 there were 300 of the limited type of business corporation, and today there are over 2500 of them listed on the two major stock exchanges plus many thousands not so listed. In 1800 the U.S. had a population of 5.3 million people, and today there are six to seven times that many corporate stockholders alone. The part of corporate enterprise that is under comprehensive governmental regulation today produces approximately ten percent of the GNP.

It is important to realize that I am talking only, or at least primarily, about business corporations. My outlook would be different if I were dis-

cussing municipal corporations, ecclesiastical corporations, or eleemosy-
nary (nonprofit) corporations.

My focus is on federal regulation of the business corporation. Laws concerning this regulation are increasingly being revised and clarified. It is
also important to note the legal dynamic that bears upon regulation. Let us
make two assumptions: (1) that it is an overriding national policy to have
a competitive free-enterprise system; and (2) that this system will not serve
the total needs of our society without some form of regulation. Historically,
these propositions have the support of experience. Regulation of corporations was started in this country primarily to deal with the abuses of economic concentration. Two models are the Federal Trade Commission,
which Dan Fenn describes very well in this volume, and the Interstate Commerce Commission, the grandfather of the independent regulatory agencies.

The primary legal attributes of an independent regulatory agency are
that it exercises legislative power pursuant to a delegation that, under our
constitutional system, requires a standard; and that it exercises quasi-judicial power essential to the decision-making process that underlies regulation. It is enlightening to look back and note that the independent regulatory agency was initially vested with essentially a legislative function and
found its origins in the same historical period as the Sherman and Clayton
acts. Here Congress was saying to the executive branch: In order to maintain this overriding national policy of a free-enterprise system, a free-com-
petitive system, we are authorizing you to invoke the power of the judiciary
to act as a referee in the game of free competition for profit. So the two
tracks started out in the same era and were substantially aimed at the same
problem—abuses of the concentration of economic power.

However, there were some significant accretions, such as the Transportation Act of 1920, whereby the Interstate Commerce Commission (ICC) was
given the responsibility to wet-nurse the surface transportation industry.
The ICC was given minimum-rate power, and it was not only to regulate
but to look after the welfare of this industry. It was given, in effect, promotional responsibility. There is also a promotional clause in the Civil Aviation Act; I recall that when I was General Counsel of the Civil Service
Commission, President Johnson put out an executive order on ethics, and
I found some practices in the Civil Aeronautics Board (CAB) that I did not
think were too appropriate. They involved trips by members of the CAB
on what were called inaugural-route promotional flights. These were promotional flights—some may be called on a flying saturnalia—and they
usually involved some rather nice place like Mexico City or Rio. When I
inquired into this, the CAB replied that this was part of its activities to

to promote civil aviation and referred to the promotional clause in the Civil Aviation Act. There had been some controversy over this before, and the Comptroller General had written an opinion about it. As far as I am aware, that is perhaps the most significant use to which that provision of the law has been put.

Regulators and the Welfare of Those Who Are Being Regulated

I think in all cases of combined promotional and regulatory authority, the record of these commissions to look after the welfare of the regulated industry is dismal, to stay the least. The method of operation of the independent commission is such that it is incapable, in my judgment, of dealing with the problem, under current economic and political conditions. So this is essentially a development in which Congress gave up a little bit of its authority to independent technical bodies to regulate and promote industries, and it also gave them a standard, which the courts eventually found to be adequate, and that was: Go forth and regulate in the public interest for the public convenience and necessity. This standard was called by one distinguished congressman a "glittering abstraction." If the regulatory bureaucracy is infected with any one virus that affects its ability to cope with the public-interest issues inherent in the activities under regulation, it was spawned by the standard of policy abstractions, which provides no motivation and no guidance to it or its staffs, *i.e.*, a policy vacuum.

Who Represents the "Public Interest"?

In the approximately 1000 cases that I presided over in almost ten years as an administrative law judge, the "public interest" never meant anything of substance to me beyond the materially related interests of the parties that were before me. Among the parties, all represented by lawyers, were the principal motor carriers, all the class-one rail carriers in the United States, and most of the 500 largest corporations. Somewhere in that representation there should have been a discernable public interest looking at this thing called "corporate social responsibility." But it was never represented as such, and to the extent that there are open, pervasive hearings across the country, dealing with these large regulatory issues and involving hundreds of witnesses plus thousands of pages of testimony, the effect is to obscure much of the problem. Unfortunately, defining the components that go to make up the public interest in a highly complex regulatory matter is really an after-the-fact rationalization of the completed process. Therefore, against the policy abstractions, what has actually occurred is not the use of the legislative authority to maximum advantage, but, rather, the over-judicialization of the process. The basic nature of the regulatory process has been *ad hoc* adjudication or balancing of the interests of the litigants to the particular proceeding.

How do you get someone into a particular proceeding who wants to represent "the public interest" in a dimension beyond the specific interests of the parties in the hearing? There are, of course, the common law or legislated doctrines of intervention by a party in interest. With them, the primary parties to a proceeding have the right to be heard about whether or not this group or this individual or this representative is entitled to come into their hearing and muddy it up. When you are trying to determine whether or not the phone rates should be lower or whether or not a corporate acquisition should take place, the injection of a representative who argues in favor of concepts or policies that are "in the public interest" is not welcomed by anyone connected with the process. Indeed, such intervenors often are made to appear as meddlesome soothsayers who have little at stake. For the regulatory agency, this presents a dilemma, because, first, it is not prepared to cope with such intervention in the sense that the real issues are decided by reference to the particular economic interests of the parties in chief. Second, the question of what degree of interest or collateral interest or public interest or extra-party interest the agency recognizes enlarges the size and scope of hearings that are already large and open enough. Under the existing regulatory scheme, public-interest representation means the battle for the right to intervene in a hearing; the right to have that intervention funded by the agency or by the government; the right to appeal to the courts as an aggrieved party for review of an order of a regulatory commission; and the right to have the representation on appeal paid for in certain cases.

Real and Alleged Failures
of the Regulatory Agencies

Most of the litanies of the failures of the regulatory agencies are overstated, but there are grains of truth in just about all of them, which apply with varying degrees of validity and accuracy to different agencies. The Ash Commission dealth with this quite extensively, but from the focus that the agencies are not responsive to executive policy, although I don't know where that notion really came from. Presumably, the executive branch is better qualified to determine what is in the public interest than the agencies, Congress, or the courts. Bear in mind that when this all started it was primarily a legislative power that was being exercised. In his article, which appears later in this part of the book, Fenn notes that the original concept of independent regulatory commissions was that they are not responsible to the President and, if they are not responsible to the President, they do not necessarily have to be responsible for his policies or accountable to him, and they are not. Members of these commissions are appointed for definite terms and, subject to good behavior, they can serve for that time whether the President likes the way they comb their hair or not.

One criticism of regulatory agencies, which on its surface seems to be valid, is that they do not function in tune with national policy goals. I remember reading the reports of two different commissions on national policy goals, and I still don't know whether we have any real national policy goals or not, at least goals established by the executive branch of the government. Therefore, I feel that this criticism is valid, but it is because of the problem inherent in establishing national goals and not any problems in pursuing them once they are indentified.

There is, however, what I regard as an inherent national-policy goal pertaining to economic regulation, and that is that we maintain a free-enterprise, competitive, economic system. There are, to be sure, those things that Congress has specified as a goal or as a standard for industry generally or for the conduct of public affairs or to protect the general health and welfare, but they do not seem to have the pervasive lasting qualities necessary to national goals. We have listened to complaints about the consensual form of decision making for many years. I feel that this form of decision making contributes to the fictional separation from responsibility that the early corporations had. The commissioners individually weren't responsible; the commission acted, but you couldn't find out who voted for what or how. So eventually what was a bad symptom became diagnosed as a disease.

However, I believe the consensual form of decision making is probably a strength that can be demonstrated by a great many cases. The thing that needs curing is a procedural matter. All that is needed is a public recording of how each commissioner voted on each case. There is strength in diversity and more balance; if you have five members on a commission, there are sure to be some who are concerned with the public interest. I think that eleven commissioners are too many, and I think also that the Ash Commission's recommendation for a single administrator misses the mark.

Defining National Policy Goals

I discussed earlier the difficulties of defining national-policy goals for the guidance of the regulatory agencies, but it is not difficult to see that, in many cases, agencies function with little or no knowledge of what is happening in the industry that they are charged with regulating and little or no knowledge of the effects of other federal agencies or programs on that industry. For example, the ICC has been administering the federal highway program for nearly 100 years in almost total ignorance of the economic and social impact of the superhighways—an impact that is greater than any other federal program in the last three decades except for the nuclear weapons program. Nor has the ICC been able to deal with the most important consequence of the federal highway program—the tremendous expansion of the manufacture and use of private automobiles.

The courts have started to define certain components within the abstraction of the concept of public interest and have directed various agencies to consider a specific component as one of their responsibilities. For example, the Federal Trade Commission was ordered by the courts to regulate cigarette advertising on the basis of its public interest responsibility and not on any fairness doctrine.

It is obvious that Congress must also take a much more active part in specifying national policy goals so that the forces of free, competitive enterprise can begin to achieve progress toward these goals. Congress must reassert its authority and responsibility as the branch of government most responsive to the people—and hence to the public interest—as it has done in the Environmental Protection Act.

I do not mean to underestimate the dangers of economic overconcentration, both to our competitive-enterprise system and to our basic charter of liberties, but we are not now dealing effectively with this problem by using the classic regulatory agency. Regulatory agencies can begin to function in the public interest only when all three branches of the United States government supply them with clear-cut mandates to accomplish national goals.

Effective Regulation
in the Public Interest

●●●

● LOUIS M. KOHLMEIER, JR.

Washington, D.C., Correspondent
Wall Street Journal

When I contemplate this matter of the regulators and their successes and failures in serving the public interest, my mind is drawn to the words of Emma Lazarus that are inscribed at the Statue of Liberty in New York harbor:

> Give me your tired, your poor,
> Your huddled masses yearning to breathe free,
> The wretched refuse of your teeming shore,
> Send these, the homeless, tempest-tossed, to me:
> I lift my lamp beside the golden door.

Inasmuch as the United States these days is concerned much more with population control than with attracting new immigrants to our shores, perhaps the inscription could be declared surplus federal property and the Statue of Liberty moved to Washington and rebuilt on the Constitution Avenue Mall midway between the Interstate Commerce Commission (ICC) and the Federal Trade Commission (FTC), where it would serve to inspire all the regulators. I would not describe the regulatory agencies as wretched refuse. But they have been criticized and maligned almost since the first of them, the ICC, was created 85 years ago, and I suspect that the volumes of accumulated criticism of the agencies weigh more than the similarly serious studies of the presidency, the Congress, or the Supreme Court.

Under all this weight, the agencies quite naturally are tired and poor.

181

They are homeless within government and tempest-tossed outside of it. They still are yearning to breathe free of interfering presidents, congresses, and industry lobbyists. And they still have not found that golden door to which well-meaning reformers have been lifting their lamp for years and years. One almost is drawn to the conclusion that something prophetic eluded us in the fact that the ICC was born the same year Emma Lazarus died.

Federal Regulatory Agencies

The Populists, who created the mold when the ICC was born in 1887, thought they had invented the perfect instrument of public administration in the structurally independent, politically bipartisan, multimember regulatory commission. The agencies were to be above partisan politics and beyond the reach of both politicians and vested interests. In splendid isolation, they were to be free to address themselves to complex economic and social problems, guided only by the wisdom of expert knowledge and experience in their respective fields of endeavor. The Supreme Court described the intended function of the agencies very well when it said they were created by Congress "with the avowed purpose of lodging functions in a body specifically competent to deal with them by reason of information, experience and careful study of the business and economic conditions of the industry affected."[1]

The great body of criticism of the agencies has been built by traditionalists—by latter-day Populists, up to and including Ralph Nader and his still-growing tribe of Nader's Raiders—who still believe that the independent regulatory commissions are capable of performing in the public interest. They insist that there is nothing wrong with regulation that cannot be cured by men of good will. The specific cures that have been and still are recommended depend to some degree on the predilections of the specific reformers. By and large, the legal community has sought to make the procedures of the agencies more like those of courts and thus presumably to make them more fair. Various economists have criticized the agencies for their failure to make bolder use of their rule-making powers and thus their failure to engage enthusiastically in economic planning. Some politicians have criticized the agencies for listening to other politicians. And some other reformers have been critical simply because many of the regulators appointed by various presidents have not had full faith and trust in the

[1]*Federal Trade Commission* v. *R. F. Keppel and Bros. Inc.*, 291 U.S. 304, 314 (1934).

regulatory statutes, and probably lacked the ability to regulate well even if they possessed the faith.

The point is that all of the traditional criticism of the agencies and the efforts to reform them have shared a belief in the system of independent, bipartisan, multimember commissions. The reformers insist that the regulators would perform in the public interest if only better men and women manned the agencies, if the agencies were more fair and more efficient (conflicting objectives in themselves), or if some other tinkering could be accomplished.

In my opinion, the Naders of the world are wrong, the flaws in the regulatory process are fatal, and the time has come to admit that the independent regulatory agencies never have been and never will be permanent, trustworthy repositories of the public interest as that term was defined by the Populists and is defined now by liberal reformers. I concur with the opinion recently expressed in a Brookings Institution study that evaluated the regulatory reform proposals of the 1970 Ash Commission, the group of traditionalists that attempted to tinker with the agencies. The Brookings study said, "The problem of regulation run much deeper than the Ash report implies, perhaps reaching to the heart of the democratic process itself."[2]

Reforms in Regulatory Agencies

I do not contend that all regulation at all times in all agencies has failed to serve the public interest. For example, there was a time in history, many years ago, when the ICC kept railroads' rates low, as Congress intended. To take another and more recent example, it seems to me that the National Labor Relations Board (NLRB) has been reasonably true to its mandate, through Republican as well as Democratic administrations, which is to ensure employees of the right to organize and bargain collectively with their employers. Unions do not and should not always get their way at the NLRB, but the ever-flowing river of employer appeals from NLRB decisions would seem to be evidence enough that the board by and large has remained true to its mandate.

After a dozen years in Washington, I also do not believe that regulators are venal men and women who can be bought by regulated industries. A few regulators have accepted vicuna coats and assorted other gifts, either

[2]Roger G. Noll, *Reforming Regulation: An Evaluation of the Ash Council Proposals* (Washington, D.C.: Brookings Institution, 1971), p. 2.

from industry lobbyists or from the lobbyists' political allies in Congress or the White House. But I do not find convincing evidence that the public interest has been compromised simply because a few regulators have accepted gifts or even because many more regulators have been wined and dined by industry executives and lobbyists. It seems to me that bureaucrats are no less and no more honest, trustworthy, and efficient than similarly situated men and women at other very large institutions, such as General Motors or a large university.

Nor do I agree with the liberals who wrap all their criticisms of the regulators together and swing hard with the allegation that regulation has failed to serve the public interest because the regulators have been captured by the regulated. This charge seems to be enjoying a new popularity these days, as in an article titled "The Nixon Formula for Crippling Regulators," which appeared recently in *The Progressive*.[3] I think history supports the generalization that the affected industry almost invariably has fought against the initial enactment by Congress of new regulatory programs, and I am certain that after a regulatory agency has been in existence for some years its industry constituency is its strongest supporter. But to draw from this the conclusion simply that the regulators have been captured by the regulated is of no real help. The allegation tends to ignore industry dynamics, political realities, and the strange place in which the weary regulators find themselves today.

Finally, I must include in this list of demurrers a willing acknowledgment that the traditionalist reformers have scored some points over the years. Regulation undoubtedly is more uniformly fair among the agencies because of the Administrative Procedure Act of 1946, which was peculiarly the legal profession's contribution to reform. Maybe there is hope even that some public good will flow from the Freedom of Information Act, an amendment to the 1946 law that President Johnson signed into law on July 4, 1966. Some have hope even for the institutionalized tinkering, which became possible in 1964 with the creation of the Administrative Conference of the United States as a permanent body. Admittedly, there have been other reforms, or at least changes. Most would agree, I think, that President Nixon named better men to the FTC because of the criticisms of it that were voiced late in the Johnson administration by Ralph Nader and early in the Nixon administration by an American Bar Association committee. The FTC nowadays unquestionably is enforcing laws against false advertising with vastly greater effectiveness than prior to these criticisms. And history is repeating itself; industry is complaining bitterly

[3]October 1972, pp. 31–35.

and President Nixon is expected by many to replace his better men with what might be called "strict constructionists."[4]

The reform forces in recent years have made two additional advances that, although tentative, offer additional hope for the future of regulation in the public interest. First, the antitrust division of the Department of Justice has been taking a more active role as a party to specific cases and as a court intervenor in issues before a number of agencies, including the ICC, the Civil Aeronautics Board (CAB), and the Securities and Exchange Commission (SEC). The antitrust division, for instance, has opposed some railroad and airline merger proposals on the ground that they are not in the public interest because they are unnecessarily anticompetitive. The antitrusters also have argued before the SEC that the New York Stock Exchange should be required to open its "private club" trading facilities to pension funds and other institutional investors.

The second of these tentative advances consists of various court decisions requiring some of the regulatory agencies to allow certain public interest groups some sort of participation in particular pending cases. The best evidence of this new crack in the regulators' doors probably is the flood of challenges that have been filed at the FCC to applications of radio and television stations for renewal of their licenses.

In sum, I respect the reformers for their accomplishments, but I fear they are too little and too late. Court orders requiring the regulatory agencies to listen to public-interest groups, such as those representing a television station's audience, do not by any means require the regulators to adopt the views of the public-interest groups. Indeed, there is no substantial reason for believing that the challenged station owners really are in danger of losing their licenses. Similarly, the antitrust division's arguments and interventions are no guarantee whatsoever that the antitrusters' view of the public interest will be adopted by the regulators. To the contrary, the Supreme Court has declined, wisely it would seem, to enter this ticket; the Court generally has upheld the regulators and thrown out the antitrusters, not explicitly because the antitrusters are wrong but because Congress entrusted such matters to the expertise of the regulatory agencies.[5]

The Power and Capability of Regulatory Agencies

I earlier noted my agreement with the suggestion in the Brookings Institution study that the problems of regulation may reach the heart of the

[4]*Ibid.*, p. 33.

[5]See, *e.g.*, *Seaboard Air Line Railroad Co.* v. *U.S.*, 382 U.S. 154 (1965).

democratic process itself. I would suggest further that perhaps these public agencies are inherently incapable of regulating in the public interest, as they are now constituted within our form of government.

It has been said often enough that the agencies combine the three functions—legislative, executive, and judicial—that are divided among the three constitutional branches of the federal government. The agencies make rules that have the force of law; they are prosecutors as well as planners; and they sit in judgment on the cases they bring. This concentration of all three kinds of powers has bothered some constitutional purists, but the powers would not seem to pose a public danger because they are distributed thorugh many agencies and each is small when compared with an executive branch department, such as Health, Education and Welfare, or Justice. This is not to say that the agencies are not powerful; they are uniquely powerful in our form of government. But the power of each is confined to a particular sphere, and Congress divided spheres such as transportation among three regulatory agencies. (The three are the ICC, the CAB, and the Federal Maritime Commission, although the total number of federal offices that have transportation functions, including those in the executive branch with some regulatory powers, is more than a dozen.)

The independent exercise of all three kinds of power poses a certain dilemma, however. The U.S. Constitution provides certain checks and balances that are intended to assure the independence of the executive, the legislative, and the judicial branches, one from another. In constitutional theory, the regulatory agencies are extensions of Congress' assigned power to regulate commerce and are arms of Congress. Congress could have accomplished many regulatory purposes through legislation but chose not to do so, mostly perhaps because political considerations mitigated against such drastic legislation.[6] Instead, in most instances, Congress created an agency and, frequently in vague and even contradictory terms, directed the agency to solve a pressing economic or social issue of the day.[7]

Thus, the regulators were launched on stormy, uncharted seas with very little in the way of foul-weather gear. Congress provided them with no sure means of protecting their independence and is unlikely to do so. It gave them specified terms of office, usually five or seven years, but has never seriously considered giving regulators the lifetime tenure that the Founding Fathers deemed a necessary protection for federal judges. The only readily apparent alternative would be to allow regulators to run for office

[6]See Henry J. Friendly, *The Federal Administrative Agencies: The Need for Better Definition of Standards* (Cambridge: Harvard University Press, 1962), pp. 141–175.
[7]*Ibid.*, p. 10.

and thereby acquire the protection that is afforded by an elective constituency, but Congress also has not seriously entertained this alternative.

Thus, the regulators are functionally independent and powerful, yet they are almost defenseless when their independence is challenged. It seems to me that history bears out the conclusions that the regulatory agencies have set their courses independently, without direct or indirect communication with publicly constituted authority. The public interest that the regulators are supposed to act for is too diverse and unorganized a force to make itself heard. Congress by and large ignores the agencies and presidents take the attitude that, since the regulators owe them nothing, they will utilize the agencies for political patronage appointments and little more.

The regulators thus are left with the only constituency available to them, and indeed the only protection that may be available: the regulated. Even at that, it probably is true that the regulators do not get untoward amounts of help or hindrance from the regulated on board policy matters. Rather, the storms inevitably hit hardest when the regulators decide specific cases to which real price tags are attached. For example, when the FCC threatens to deny renewal of a television station license worth $20 million or more to its holder, the regulated typically do not run straight to the regulators. They run to Congress and, if possible, to the White House; the poor and weary regulators are left to muse over the public interest. Worse, Congress may enact legislation to prevent the regulators from doing what they intended or to undo what the regulators have done: such legislation was threatened to prevent the FCC from engaging in any wholesale denial of radio- and television-station licenses, and legislation was enacted to foreclose the FTC from requiring cigarette manufacturers to advertise a stern warning that smoking can cause cancer. Worse still, regulators who persist in defying presidents and Congress know from history that they will not be reappointed.

Congresses and presidents have inflicted other, perhaps more serious, indignities on the regulators. With and without the help of industry lobbyists, regulatory laws have been enacted that require the regulators to promote as well as to regulate an industry. Thus, many of the laws are ambiguous as well as vague. The Atomic Energy Commission and the CAB, for example, were directed to promote as well as regulate, and they were created before there was a real atomic energy industry or a commercial aviation industry. On the other hand, Congress clearly had the welfare of the railroad industry in mind when it told the ICC to promote railroads in 1940.

To make matters worse, congresses and presidents have created new programs and agencies that conflict with the existing mandates of regulatory agencies. The prime example, of course, is the Highway Trust Fund, under which the urban and rural portions of the interestate highway system have been financed. The motor vehicle traffic that the new system spawned has made it difficult or impossible for the ICC to fulfill its mandate to promote and regulate the nation's railroads. And, to complicate matters further, Congress for many years subsidized the airlines and the regulated merchant shipping industry, and the lawmakers to this day are a long way from providing equal treatment to railroads and urban mass transit.

Still another complication is worthy of note. Occasionally, when Congress has failed to act, the Supreme Court abandoned caution and marched into the thicket, with consequences no less disastrous. The Court in 1954 ordered the Federal Power Commission to regulate natural gas producers' prices, which until then had been regulated by the forces of competition. It seems to me that coincidence alone does not explain the fact that after 1954 exploratory discoveries of new natural gas sources in this country declined, and today the nation faces the possibility of severe gas shortages, even though there is ample gas in the ground.

One additional dilemma of regulation by a multiplicity of independent agencies is worthy of note. Reformers often charge the agencies with being slow to react or with failing entirely to react to technological and social change. The charge has some validity, but I wonder whether these agencies, as they are presently constituted, are institutionally capable of reacting in the public interest. For example, the NLRB was created in 1935 to secure labor's right to organize and bargain and, in my opinion, it has remained reasonably true to its mandate. But in the years since 1935, organized labor has grown very powerful, and when Senator McGovern during the recent election campaign merely suggested that labor's power now bears a certain likeness to industry power, George Meany reacted with a wrath worthy of any big industrialist. The point is that times have changed and in theory the NLRB should address itself to the new balance of power and the possibility that labor also is capable of abusing the public interest. But the NLRB has not and very probably never will.

The conclusion suggested is that independent regulatory agencies tend to be static and inflexible. They were created, some of them many years ago, to respond to quite specific economic or social crises of the day, and it is important to recognize also that they were created to bring about some change or development that Congress in its wisdom believed would not or could not be brought about by the forces of free competition. It should not be surprising then that the regulators' bag of tools is loaded with protectionist, anticompetitive devices. Protectionism is indigenous to their trade. When the FCC drew up the master plan for television in this country, it chose a plan that restricted the number of commercial stations more than technological considerations required, and the nation presumably will be burdened forevermore with that essentially protectionist master plan.[8] The SEC, effective as it has been in ridding the stock market of manipulators, always has been and still is quite protective of the dominant "private club" position of the New York Stock Exchange. The CAB has never allowed a new trunkline to enter the commercial aviation business since the board was created in 1938. The CAB's answers to the airline industry's financial ills never seem to go beyond more mergers and higher fares, no matter how many empty seats there are on ever bigger aircraft. And the ICC is almost as protective in approving railroad mergers, ruling against the entry of new competitors into the trucking business, and approving rate increases for both railroads and trucks. The ICC, of course, forced the bankrupt New York, New Haven & Hartford Railroad on the old Pennsylvania and New York Central railroads before it would approve the merger of the Pennsy with the Central, and then the entire structure collapsed. The ICC is not responsible for highway competition, and maybe the Penn Central would have collapsed anyway. But the dreary experience seems not to have dimmed the ICC's enthusiasm for mergers, quite possibly because it knows no alternatives.

Conclusions

I have painted a dreadfully pessimistic picture, but I hope I have suggested the reasons why, in my opinion, the problems of the independent regulatory agencies are substantially more serious than acknowledged by the Ash Commission and the long line of traditionalist reformers who preceded the Ash Commission. Whatever the chances of reform might have been in the past, there is reason to believe that the problems of the agencies today are too large and too burdensome. In brief, there is reason to conclude that the agencies are not serving the public interests of consumers, the private interests of regulated industries, or the interests of government itself. And, meanwhile, public aspirations for economic stability and security have been rising.

In a sense, Congress seems ready to throw up its hands at the mess for

---

[8]See Louis M. Kohlmeier, Jr., *The Regulators: Watchdog Agencies and the Public Interest* (New York: Harper & Row, 1969), pp. 203–228.

which it is so largely responsible and at the aspirations that go above and beyond public regulation of selected vital industries, including transportation, communications, energy, and finance. It was back in 1946 that Congress passed the Employment Act, conferring on the president responsibility for full employment and full purchasing power, and it was last year that President Nixon with the approval and encouragement of a Democratic congress instituted wage and price controls. This congressional abdication may seem unrelated to the independent regulatory commissions, but it is not unrelated. The regulators' propensity for approval of price increases already has drawn the attention of Mr. Nixon's price controllers. More important, however, is the fact that the White House increasingly, if unofficially, is intruding in regulatory agency affairs. President Nixon has asked for legislation that would strip the old ICC of some of its powers over transportation rates and substitute the regulation of free competition. It is significant that in this Mr. Nixon is repeating a request first made of Congress by President Kennedy. Presidential power, whether Republican or Democratic, it would seem, cannot abide the burden of ICC regulation. Congress has not yet acted, but predictably it will act. Republican Senator John Tower of Texas and Senator Mike Mansfield, the Democratic majority leader, believe the ICC should be abolished outright. In such a combination there must be success, probably not in abolishing the ICC but in trimming its power substantially.

I certainly do not pretend to know where all of this will lead. Broadly, the President slowly but surely is accumulating authority commensurate with his responsibility to assure the public interest in the economic sphere of American life. Some of the powers of the independent regulatory agencies may not impinge on presidential prerogative. Others will, and yet Congress may well strip agencies of most of their powers without abolishing agencies. Rarely does Congress admit to its mistakes. Beyond all that, there would seem to be the long-term question of whether the President can indeed straighten out the mess of regulatory dilemmas and contradictions. What does seem certain is that the president, Republican or Democratic, is going to try, and in this new concentration of power, we may yet face a constitutional dilemma far larger than those I have written about.

Dilemmas for
the Regulator

●●

● DAN H. FENN, JR.

Graduate School of Business Administration
Harvard University

How can regulatory agencies be the repository of the public interest? By and large, the public assumes that they are not today, an assumption often made intuitively without criteria, measurement, or testing. Some people believe that these agencies have failed because they have been captured by big business. Some businessmen, on the other hand, assert that they have been captured by the politicians, the consumerists, or the bird-and-bunny people. Some observe that the laws are poorly drafted or that many agencies are mandated to promote the industry without statutory provision for the consumer. Some say it is because the commissioners are so often lawyers, not economists, or perhaps that they are bad or poor economists. So the explanations may vary, but the judgment is the same.

If regulatory agencies are indeed failing to protect the public interest and if we want to improve them, we need to start by understanding why they perform as they do. It would also help if we could reach some kind of agreement either on what the "public interest" is or, at least, on the most appropriate and credible mechanism by which that determination could be made at a given time. I am constantly intrigued, incidentally, by the tenacity with which we cling to a kind of Platonic vision of the public interest despite the way the public policy-making process works. To hear ourselves talk, one would think that there is some pristine and whole object called "good public policy" sitting out there that is constantly being nicked,

191

warped, shattered, and generally ruined by the attacks of "special interests." Actually, of course, public policy emerges as the end-product of a process in which a variety of interests take their whacks. It is more like a showman created by a gang of kids building here and altering there until it satisfies than it is a preexisting work of art marred by the destructive hands of clumsy and irreverent barbarians. But all this is beyond the scope of this paper.

Reexamining Myths About Regulatory Agencies

I want to try to make a contribution to this effort by looking at the agency from one particular perspective: that of the regulator himself. In so doing, I am encouraged by the blockbuster impact caused by Raymond Bauer and his colleagues, Ithiel Poole and Lewis Dexter, when they took a similar (though far more rigorously formulated) approach to legislative bodies.[1]

Along with the simple explanation of regulation, we were also brought up on the idea that "legislators and legislatures always respond to the direction of the greatest pressure." Thus, the way to get something done in a legislative setting, we were told, is to put the pressure on a majority of representatives. It is interesting, incidentally, that no one ever explained to us exactly what "pressure" was (though we had vague notions about broads, booze, and bucks); no one even spelled out why response to pressure was "bad" in a representative form of government if it resulted in a vote in accord with the majority of a member's constituents (even though we might not agree with the decision); and no one thought to question the portrait of the legislator that inevitably flowed from the model, which made him look more like one of Robert Frost's birches than a human being.

Bauer and his colleagues decided that this time-honored "analysis" deserved a hard look and, with characteristic wisdom, they determined that the appropriate perspective from which to observe the process was that of the legislator himself. This took them into the system in a unique way and the results we all well know: some have said it revolutionized the teaching of political science. At the very least, it has vastly broadened and deepened our understanding of how a legislature really functions.

Bauer et al. found that one man's "heavy pressure" went unnoticed by his neighbor who was receiving the same phone calls and letters; that one

[1]Raymond A. Bauer; Ithiel Poole; and Lewis Dexter, *American Business and Public Policy* (New York: Atherton Press, 1963).

woman's "key issue" was a routine matter to her colleague; that the legislator himself plays a much more dynamic role in the system than the "birchtree" model would indicate; and, above all, that there are real people in the operation whose personalities, aspirations, and views of their jobs vary enormously, so that the process turns out to be far more complex, intriguing, and messy than we had been taught in high school. That, of course, any skilled lobbyist or articulate legislator could have told us long ago if we had asked him and then listened with open minds and ears.

I welcome what I see as a developing trend to apply the same kind of scrutiny to our traditional views of regulatory agencies and how they operate. Thus, my larger purpose, beyond simply describing the dilemmas of a regulator as I see them, is to contribute to and stimulate a reexamination of the shibboleths about regulation that we were taught in our youth and that we glibly perpetuate—notably the "capture theory," which holds that regulators are subservient to the industries for which they are responsible.

An extremely important point needs to be made at this point—so important, in fact, that it deserves an article of its own. We are extremely casual in our definition of "regulation," forcing together under that umbrella term a host of different agencies and different functions. We are *never* going to unscramble the question of why regulation operates as it does until we stop looking at agencies and start looking, separately, at the *functions* that such agencies perform. They set rates, grant licenses, suggest legislation, settle disputes, find facts and make reports, draw up industry rules, promote an industry, bring complaints, interpret vague laws, and provide expert advice to the President and Congress. In this article I am consciously generalizing across agencies, because the perspective I am taking here permits it, but no comprehensive analysis can be made of the regulatory process until we look at it by activity instead of as a whole.

Selection of Regulators

The place to start in a look at the regulator is: How did he get there? We all know, of course, that he is nominated (and appointed) by the President by and with the consent of the Senate. But how does the President happen to nominate him in the first place?

There are two determinants of the type of person who ends up as a regulator: the method of selection and the criteria for selection.

Broadly speaking, presidents have gone in one of two directions in their methods of selection. The first, which has been irreverently called "BOG-SAT" (Bunch of Guys Sitting Around a Table), is not commonly characterized by an active recruiting effort, at least at the White House level. Rather, it draws on a reservoir of names that may or may not be related to a particular job, which come in from Congress, the national committees, industry, consumer groups, other office holders, White House staff members, friends of the administration outside the government, or the potential office holder himself. The staff's function here is to winnow, to select from the pile those who, for one reason or another, they deem the most appropriate to suggest to the President.

President Kennedy took a different approach to filling the roughly 300 top posts that were under his direct control. For the first time, he established a continuing talent-search office as part of the White House staff whose task was to identify upcoming vacancies in departments and agencies, talk to a variety of people about the sort of person who should be recruited to fill the post, and then telephone a network of men and women around the nation to collect names of possible appointees. After a careful check on the suggestions, the recruiters were ready to offer the President a list of people and some specific recommendations.

Theoretically, at least, this system should enable a president to put his special stamp on the regulatory agencies, to pick men and women who share his attitude on the role and function of such agencies. Actually, as we shall see in a moment, even a systematic approach like this one is subject to so many vagaries in practice that the static level in the system is high.

What about the criteria for nomination? Although they tend to be imprecise and undefined, seldom going beyond a phrase like "our kind of guy," they have real content nonetheless. At the beginning of his administration, Dwight Eisenhower appointed several men to head agencies in whose programs they did not believe, such as T. Coleman Andrews at the Internal Revenue Service and Congressman Albert Cole at the Housing and Home Finance Administration. Sounds strange, but given his initial commitment to minimal government, it makes sense: Who would be more likely to cut an agency down to the barest essentials than someone who did not believe in its program?

President Kennedy's version of "our kind of guy" for the regulatory agencies was a person who was bright, young, aggressive, innovative, and activist, consumer-oriented, willing to make mistakes, knowledgeable about how to make things happen, and skilled in dealing in a political environment. President Johnson, on the other hand, was more inclined toward the judicial, the umpire, the low-key regulator.

Presumably, then, with a more systematic approach to the recruitment and selection of regulatory commissioners and a penchant for activist, consumer-oriented appointees, the Kennedy regulators should all have looked and sounded like Newton Minow, conforming to the President's concept of what was in the public interest. But, of course, they did not. I can recall at least five who were considerably less than bright; at least three, including a chairman, who were primarily interested in keeping everything as calm and quiet as possible both inside and outside the agency; perhaps five whose devotion to the consumer was so slight as to be undiscernable; maybe eight who showed no evidence of having had a new idea in the past quarter century. (Obviously some people are showing up in several of these unhappy categories.)

Why did it turn out this way? Recently I went through about 25 regulatory appointments where I felt I knew pretty well what had happened. I separated them into different piles: those where the quality of the man was the major reason for his appointment; congressional "musts" (and we had only about 30 of those in the course of a year, many of whom did not end up in presidentially appointed posts); appointments made to solve a personnel problem in another agency; those where there were some personal ties of friendship or association with White House staff (in some cases, friendships that developed during a campaign); and those who fell into a minority group. Granting some overlaps, including one man who clearly fell in two groupings, I found that 11 were in the "quality" file, five in the "congressional must" group, seven in the "personal friendship" box, two "personnel problems" elsewhere, and two minority appointees.

Incidentally, I have not mentioned "pressure from industry." That omission is not inadvertent; most direct suggestions from business came to the White House during the Kennedy years via Congress, and it was simply one factor in the complex equation that went into each nomination, sometimes a positive and sometimes a negative. Interestingly enough, the most direct, persistent, orchestrated, obviously organized, and manipulated intervention we ever had on an appointment was from the educational fraternity on the selection of a commissioner of education.

What conclusion can we draw from all this? An important one, to my mind. Given the fact that the road to appointment as a regulatory commissioner is such an uncertain one, that men and women were selected for very different reasons and by different criteria, even within the framework of one administration never mind over the course of several, it is hazardous indeed to generalize about these people. I know one commissioner who wanted to be a judge, one to be a senator, one to reshape his agency, one to stay on until he retired, one to become a public figure, one to help the consumer, one to have a nice, quiet, prestigious job. They had different aspirations, different reasons for being there, different views of the job, different friends and associations, different career goals and paths. Consequently, they faced different dilemmas and, like Bauer's legislators, felt different pressures, and grave doubt is thrown on the simplistic "capture theory" unless it is broadened to embrace a variety of constituencies.

So much for the process of appointment: What does a regulator find when he sits down in his new office?

The Regulator's Dilemmas

In the first place, the regulator cannot help but be struck by the enormous advantages of his position. He is an independent operator in an independent agency. He has a term appointment; he cannot be removed unless he is caught with his arm in the cookie jar up to the elbow. His vote is his own; no one can tell him how to cast it. People can talk to him, urge him, argue with him, but no one can order him to say aye or nay. This is, indeed, an extraordinary privilege for a public officer in the executive branch, and a vital distinction for the observer to bear in mind. If a person "succumbs to pressure," to use the common idiom, it is his choice; it is because he sees that as the appropriate thing for him to do under the circumstances. But it is his choice and no one else's. The Secretary of Commerce can be ordered by the President to make decisions against the exportation of walnut logs even contrary to his better judgment, but the President has no way of enforcing an order to the FCC commissioner to vote for X applicant for a TV channel in preference to Y.

Concomitantly, his voice is his own. If he wants to make a speech for or against a policy or write a decision, no one can tell him not to do so. He can make his choices on whatever basis he wishes, and can explain that statement however he wants to and he is protected. He is blessed with the governmental version of academic freedom. The fact that commissioners often do not exercise that freedom does not mean they do not have it.

All this does not mean that the commission is free of an entangling series of dilemmas. The first and most important of these is the question: What kind of a commissioner do I want to be?

Let me now list some of the subquestions under that key one:

(1) Do I want to play an essentially judicial role here, judging cases evenhandedly as they come before me, or do I want to be an advocate for the consumer, for the businessman, for the political interests of the administration, or for the prevailing congressional opinion?

(2) Do I want to operate on a case-by-case basis, like a judge, or do I want to hew closer to the original conception of the regulatory agency as

a policy-making body somewhere between the Congress and the President?

(3) Do I want to be an "inside commissioner," trying to persuade my colleagues and win some votes for what I think is right by negotiating with them and accreting support? Or do I want to follow the lead of men like Commissioner Nicholas Johnson who says that he decided within his first three weeks on the FCC that this course was hopeless (and perhaps temperamentally unattractive), so he went "outside" and made his pitch to public opinion?

(4) Do I want to accept a managerial responsibility in the large sense of that term, working to shape this agency along lines that I think are appropriate, or do I want simply to let it run by itself and concern myself exclusively with cases as they come up?

(5) Do I want to be an activist, an innovator, or do I want to maintain the status quo?

Different men and women will answer such questions differently, depending on their personal aspirations, their concept of their job, their future plans, and the administration that they serve.

The issues posed here break into two parts: the commissioner as a substantive decision maker and the commissioner as a top executive of a federal agency.

To start with the first category, a certain number of cases will virtually decide themselves. I remember a dumping decision we had on the Tariff Commission. A petitioner came in and declared that he was being injured by peat moss coming into the United States from Canada at unfairly cheap prices. So the Treasury Department went to work and found that the prices were, in fact, unfair. They then sent the matter to the commission, which conducted an expensive extensive investigation and discovered that none of the Canadian peat moss was coming anywhere near the area where the complainant was selling his goods. So there was no way he could have been injured.

But a number of other cases and questions with which a commissioner is faced will be tough to decide, and the sheer facts will not provide him with the answer. How, for example, do you determine which of five competing applicants should be given a permit to operate a TV station, assuming they are all decent, out of jail, and financially competent?

At this point, the dilemmas rise up around the office. For example: What does the law say? What should the law say? What does the law mean? What did Congress intend? What is fair? What makes sense? What can I conscientiously defend? What will my colleagues, the press, the courts, my staff, the industry, and Ralph Nader think and say? What will the people who practice before us—who I see all the time at this part or that reception—what will they think of me? What will officials in other agencies say? What will the professors writing in law reviews or business journals say? What will the National Association of Concerned Business Students think?

Different commissioners will be troubled by a different mix of these questions. My erstwhile colleague on the Tariff Commission, Dr. James W. Culliton, former Dean of the Notre Dame Business School, might tend to be interested in the professors and deans and aggressively disinterested in the people in the industry or the Tariff Commission bar. Commissioner Nicholas Johnson might be interested in what the industry says and what his colleagues think in a reverse kind of way: if they did not roast him, he'd feel he had failed! One chairman I can recall, who was once a staff man on the Hill, would not care very much about the NACBS, but he would surely be interested in congressional reaction. Another former colleague of mine was highly concerned with how the other commissioners, particularly the chairman, felt about the matter and especially sensitive to the interests of a certain industry in the district he had once represented in Congress.

So, like Bauer's legislators, different commissioners feel and respond to different dilemmas and pressures.

I suggested that a commissioner has, potentially, two kinds of responsibilities: deciding specific cases, and managing the agency with which he is associated. By "managing," I am not talking about counting paper clips and drawing organization charts; I am talking about determining what function he thinks his agency should play, what direction it should take, and what resources it needs to get there. It means assembling those resources and either persuading the existing staff of his objective or bringing people on board to support him.

A man like Caspar Weinberger or Miles Kirkpatrick at the FTC or Joseph Swidler at the Federal Power Commission, who really wants to change his agency and head it off in a new direction with a new purpose and style is faced with a whole series of dilemmas that the status quo commissioner does not even realize exists.

To illustrate, let me focus on the Tariff Commission, where I once served as vice-chairman. I recognize that the commission is not, strictly speaking, a regulatory agency, but it does have many of the same formal characteristics. The commissioners are presidential appointees; they have relatively long terms; they are the administrative heads of their agencies; they have some quasi-judicial powers; they are in an independent agency, not totally beholden either to Congress or to the President.

The chairman, when I was appointed, believed that the commission should be quiet and unobtrusive. He liked to refer to it as a fire department, with its staff wrapping hoses and keeping the equipment in good repair against the day when the alarm would ring, when someone would knock on the door with a case to be considered. He might, some of us thought, have added that the first effort in such an event would be to persuade the petitioner to try some other firehouse down the street. By and large, his view of the commission and the commission's view of itself was just that.

Some of us felt that the agency should have a far loftier and more active cast. In our view, we should be equipped to handle cases, but we should view such work as the least of our functions. We realized that the commission had originally been established by Woodrow Wilson in 1916 as a kind of in-house Rand Corporation to make fundamental studies and investigations of foreign trade policy and provide the Congress and the President with policy guidance. As a matter of fact, the whole concept of reciprocal trade negotiations came from just such a study. This function, we felt, was highly important and worth the time and attention of public servants.

But there were problems. Several of our colleagues, including the chairman, were actively opposed to our whole vision of the agency; others were disinterested in our view but tilted against it. So dilemma number one: How do you accrue the necessary votes to push through some broad studies, a personnel recruiting and training program to support such studies, and a stiff reporting system to keep track of them?

Second: How do you move a staff that has been selected for, trained to, and accustomed to one kind of commission to support another vision of the agency? Where is the line between causing such trauma that rebellion breaks out and moving more slowly than you need to? What are the key programs and policies that you need to change and which are peripheral? When do you persuade, when do you lean, and when do you order?

Third: How do you enlist or at least neutralize Congress, the Budget Bureau, and the White House in your efforts? In our case, we found the chairman adamant about a management survey, which we felt could be used to open up a number of issues, so we went to a friend in the Budget Bureau and persuaded him to turn the heat on the commission to take a look at its management structures and procedures. At a later stage, however, I suspect we were outpoliticked by some staff members who went to the Hill and enlisted some congressmen in an effort to get the chairman to block a key part of our reform program.

In our case, what headway we did make was greatly aided by the bitterness of the feud between some of our colleagues and the chairman. This kind of internecine warfare was known in the commission: one man had thrown an ashtray at the chairman during a commission meeting. Lest you think that bitter personal antagonism between members of regulatory commissions are restricted to the Tariff Commission, I would urge a look at the FCC, the FPC, the FTC, and the FMC at various moments in their recent histories.

At any rate, these people disliked the chairman far more than they liked or agreed with us, and therefore, at least as I was able to understand what was going on, they supported our position on some issues just to needle him.

There is, of course, room in all this for industry intervention. The fact that we did not have any may have been a function of many things. I can easily see a business group—or a consumer group for that matter—getting wind of some changes being worked in a regulatory agency, say in terms of staff appointments and responsibilities, and going to key congressmen to try and stop it. Whether or not they succeed would depend, of course, on the degree of interest of the congressman and the kind of people on the commission at the time. I should suppose if they were—or a majority of them were—industry-oriented, calls from Congressman Don Riegel and Senator William Proxmire would cut relatively little ice. But the point is that there are many forces other than industry holding these agencies in place and there is nothing inherent in them that automatically gives industry an open hand.

Let me make mention here of another source of potential intervention and that is the President or the presidency. One aspect of the capture theory holds that industry impinges on the President who, in turn, impacts on the commissioner through his power of reappointment. I hope that my earlier remarks have indicated that this might or might not be effective depending on the commissioner being approached. Some would be deeply affronted and be led to look eagerly for chances to vote against such a president's wishes; others would brush it aside because they planned to retire shortly anyway; still others would accede; and a fourth group who either did not want or did not need another term would ignore the suggestions being made.

But whatever the theoretical possibilities are, how to respond to White House intervention is not a dilemma that commissioners now have to face. It is true, of course, that a president telegraphs his general line of thought by the appointments he makes, by the questions his budget examiners ask, by structural changes he may seek, or new legislation he sends to the Hill. At the Kennedy Library[2] there is a transcript of a panel discussion between Newton Minow, Joseph Swidler, William Tucker, Alan Boyd, and William

[2]John F. Kennedy Library, Waltham, Mass.

Cary about the regulatory agencies during the Kennedy administration. It is not so startling that these men were never called on individual cases; the fire that was lit under Sherman Adams during the Eisenhower years truly singed the pants of presidential aides even unto the present day. But it is interesting to note that most of these men had virtually no contact with the White House, never mind the President, on any kind of question, even including whether or not they were doing a good job. But they felt those judgments all the same through a kind of osmosis: offhand remarks at press conferences, comments on the role of the regulatory agency in a speech, suggested changes in legislation like Clay Whitehead's recent proposals on news commentary, overheard or reported comments of White House staffers. And, in a larger sense, if they were doing some moving and shaking they felt they were in step because moving and shaking was going on all over the town.

During my tenure on the Tariff Commission, which was mostly during Lyndon Johnson's presidency, I can recall only twice—both during the brief period when I was acting chairman—that there was any White House intervention whatsoever. In one instance, some of our staff people were going to the Hill to testify on a controversial agreement with Canada. A White House aide called me and suggested they should be "briefed" by the White House before they went. I told him that was all right with me, but reminded him that the first question the committee would ask was, "Have you heard from the White House on this?" since they are so jealous of the independence of these agencies. And I told him further that I would not tell them to lie; they would have to disclose the nature of the contacts. Under the circumstances, he decided it was best to withdraw the offer.

The second time was a very minor matter; we were requested to launch a certain investigation on our own motion instead of waiting for the President to ask us to do so. Since we agreed it was a project that should go forward and would eventually be undertaken anyway, we saw no problem in responding positively to the request.

Conclusions

I cannot know at this point what the reader's impression may be. I hope, however, that he has a sense of some confusion. If so, I have succeeded in getting across my own state of mind. How do you explain the behavior of regulatory agencies? What kind of a model can you construct that takes account of the variety of kinds of people who are commissioners and the different routes that have brought them to their positions? How can you include the variety of mixes of dilemmas that they face? How can you factor in the impact of the personal feuds or staff intransigence or congressional relationships? One astute observer recently said that if you want to understand the behavior of a particular regulatory agency, especially in its toughest and most important decisions, you have to start by looking at the people who are commissioners. You are going to find, he said, very different results depending on who happens to be there at the moment.

While I agree with him, that does not help me draw any generalizations about the behavior of regulatory agencies over a period of time, or the regulatory process in the United States in general. I recall the famous old story about Grayson Kirk, one-time president of Columbia University, at this point. After a speech, a pleasant old gentleman came up to him and thanked him profusely: "You know, Dr. Kirk, I was confused about that topic when I came in here tonight. Now that I have heard you, I am still confused—only at a higher level."

If my comments have served to muddy the image of how regulatory agencies function, of how the process works, my mission will have been accomplished. The recognition of messiness may be the beginning of understanding, albeit complicating the task of the academic model-builders who reject such considerations because they invalidate their artistic designs.

Way back at the start of this paper, I mentioned the topic of this section: How can the regulatory agency be the repository of the public interest? I have not, in fact, forgotten that question.

In our society, elections are the principal mechanism we have for determining what the public interest, in a large sense, is at any given time. If we feel we want to promote the interests of industry, we elect a president and an administration that seem to tend in that direction. If we think it is time to give the consumer a break, we choose a Teddy Roosevelt or a Woodrow Wilson.

The difficulty, as I see it, is that the regulatory agency does not very rapidly or very satisfactorily follow that lead. The reason lies partly in the term system and partly in the extraordinary carelessness with which commissioners are selected. In my view, then, it follows that shorter terms for commissioners and more presidential attention to the kind of people he names offer a real opportunity to attune these agencies to the public interest as it is, rather crudely, defined by the society at that moment.

I do not mean by this statement that procedural and structural refrains are irrelevant and unnecessary. I do mean to say that there is nothing in the regulatory agency as such that makes it inevitably and automatically passive or active, consumer-oriented or business-oriented, broad-gauged or tunnel-visioned, though there are various forces that tend to nudge it into a business-oriented, passive stance unless someone consciously pushes it into another posture. In sum, therefore, we can neither understand the behavior of a regulatory agency nor shape it more to our concept of the public interest unless we understand the people at the head of it and involve ourselves vigorously in their selection.

Business Impact on Regulatory Agencies

●●

● ROBERT N. KATZ

Schools of Business Administration
University of California, Berkeley

A discussion of the ways in which independent regulatory agencies may become the repository of the public interest assumes two things: that such
agencies have not or are not serving as guardians of the public interest, and
that "public interest" can be defined. There have been many articulate
critics of the regulatory agencies, and the outcries are not new.[1] Assuming
that such presumptions are well-founded, it is indeed worthwhile to consider what can be done to insure that the public interest is manifest in actions of the independent regulatory commissions. A number of proposals
have been set forth. The Ash Commission recommended a single administrator.[2] Richard Posner, writing in the *Stanford Law Review*, advocated
abolishing the agencies and replacing them with strict and broad enforcement of the antitrust laws. Devoutly as solutions may be desired, it is unlikely that reform will come easily or will last long. It was only after Ralph
Nader's scathing report on the Federal Trade Commission and an in-depth
study by the American Bar Association (by a committee chaired by Miles

---

[1]Marver Bernstein, *Regulating Business by Independent Commission* (Princeton, N.J.:
Princeton University Press, 1955); Henry M. Trebing, "What's Wrong with Commission
Regulation?" *Public Utilities Fortnightly* 65, no. 10 (May 12, 1960); and Robert C. Fell-
meth, *The Interstate Commerce Omission* (New York: Grossman, 1970).

[2]President's Advisory Council on Executive Organization, *A New Regulatory Framework*,
Washington, D.C.: Government Printing Office, January 1971.

Kirkpatrick, late chairman of the FTC) that the FTC was reorganized to be hopefully more responsive to consumer needs, interests, and protection.[3] History of lack of reform despite pleas for reform verifies that reform is slow in coming. There are many reasons for this, among which are that the special interests who have coopted some agencies do not desire reform, that congressional inertia precludes reform, and that congressmen will not easily give up patronage opportunities.

What, then, can be done to enhance the effectiveness of the regulatory agencies? To answer this question, it is necessary to analyze the activities of the business community with respect to the regulatory commissions, the magnitude of matters dealt with by the commissions, and the manner of operation of the commissions.

Selection of Commissioners

The regulatory commissions deal with the granting of operating rights for transportation and communication routes and channels, construction of pipelines and power facilities, and the raising of large sums of money. With respect to the granting of rights to operate television stations or transportation routes, there is no doubt that the properties involved and the decisions rendered have tremendous economic, political, and social consequences that are often far greater than those involved in matters before the federal courts. Yet, as a number of observers have noted, commissioners are appointed with little fanfare.[4] Ordinarily, the consideration of a presidential nominee by a senate committee receives no widespread announcement, there is no solicitation of views from the public, and nomination hearings attract little attention. Louis Kohlmeier points out that it is rare indeed when a president's nominee is not confirmed by the Senate; in fact, no nominee has been rejected in some 23 years. Kohlmeier also points out that the President first clears his nominee with the industry to be regulated. Actually, industry's role in commissioner selection is even greater.[5]

There is an erroneous belief that the courts always deal with matters of greater magnitude than the regulatory agencies. There is the additional

---

[3]Edward F. Cox; Robert C. Fellmeth; and John E. Schulz, *The Nader Report on the FTC* (New York: Richard W. Baron Publishing Co., 1969).

[4]Louis M. Kohlmeier, Jr., *The Regulators: Watchdog Agencies and the Public Interest* (New York: Harper & Row, 1969). *See also* Morton Mintz and Jerry S. Cohen, *America, Inc.* (New York: Dial Press, 1971), p. 33.

[5]Kohlmeier, *The Regulators.*

fact that federal judges receive lifetime appointments. (It has been argued that commissioners should receive lifetime tenure as well, since this would remove their compulsion to compromise principles to insure their reappointment.) Perhaps because individual commissioners are only one among several to vote on any given single issue, there has been less concern with the manner of appointment of members of the independent regulatory commissions. Commissioners are appointed by the President for a specific term, subject to the advice and consent of the Senate. I have been unable to find any instance, in recent years at least, in which a presidential nominee to an independent regulatory commission was rejected by the congressional committee that clears the name before submission to the floor or by the Senate. This is not true with respect to cabinet posts or judges.

However, it would seem to be more appropriate that there be closer scrutiny of appointees to the commission than of cabinet members, for the latter serve at the pleasure of the President and are really advisers to the President. They perform in a ministerial or executive capacity, whereas commissioners are called upon to act as judges arbitrating disputes and rights of parties, which have long-lasting effects. The late Senator Bartlett of Alaska did question at length proposed appointees to the Federal Maritime Commission, but, notwithstanding his concern over their lack of expertise in maritime matters, he did not stand in the way of the presidential appointments to that commission. When the President considers an individual for an appointment to his cabinet, he makes what apparently is an exhaustive study to find the man who most suits his needs and will serve his interests best. When a nominee is chosen by a president for appointment to the federal bench, again an exhaustive study is conducted. Frequently the bar association of a particular judicial district or jurisdiction will submit names for consideration. The Department of Justice does some screening. The Federal Bar Association Committee on the Court of Claims makes its comments on potential judges for the Court of Claims. This again illustrates the depth of study involved in appointment to the federal judiciary.

Industry Influence on Commissioner Selection

Appointment to an independent regulatory commission is a far different matter. The President receives recommendations from the industry involved on all potential appointees; in most instances, these result in the elimination of controversial names. The industry involved, however, actually has a far greater role in nominee selection than the veto power, because it exerts efforts to insure that appointees favorable to that industry are appointed. How, then, does a president consider the public interest in selecting a nominee? The President does not hear from individual consumers of power when he is filling a vacancy on the Federal Power Commission. When the Federal Communications Commission has an opening, the President neither hears from nor solicits the opinions of television listeners. In fact, in many instances, the President is not greatly concerned with selecting an appointee at that level. Rumor has it that it was a foregone conclusion in 1966 that the next appointee to the Federal Martime Commission would come from the State of Maryland because President Johnson had supposedly promised that position to a designee of Congressman Edward Garmatz, Chairman of the House Merchant Marine and Fisheries Committee. In other words, although the appointee may have been extremely well-qualified, such qualification was incidental as a reason for his appointment. Apparently, the commitment to Congressman Garmatz was the first and foremost reason for his selection.

With respect to other appointments, the interests to be regulated frequently exert considerable effort in urging the appointment of some one who would be receptive and responsive to their needs and desires. For example, when there is an opening on the Tariff Commission, the Nationwide Committee for Import/Export Policy, a group of high tariff-protectionist interests, actively promotes the appointment of one who is receptive to its needs. For example, it was no coincidence that a member of the Tariff Commission was previously associated with the law firm of Oscar Chapman, council to the sugar industry, an industry quite concerned with tariff policy. Speaking of the Tariff Commission, it is interesting to note that, when a president has a particular interest in or concern with a certain area, the calibre of his appointees to a commission is high. For example, President Kennedy was deeply concerned with trade and tariff policy, and, as a result, his appointments to the Tariff Commission were individuals of considerable competence who displayed frequent concern with the public interest.

Congressional Influence on Commissioner Selection

Key congressmen and key senators have what may be termed a vested interest in seats on the various commissions and influence the president's appointments as a matter of patronage. Thus, it is unlikely that any commissions will be dissolved or their duties and authorities substantially altered.

Congressmen are very jealous of opportunities to exercise political patronage and the opportunity to designate a commissioner is not one that congressmen or senators would give up lightly.

It has been pointed out that the Federal Trade Commission was, for many years, the resting place for Tennesseians who wanted to be in Washington, because the late Senator Estes Kefauver had a tremendous impact on the workings and activities of the Federal Trade Commission.[6] When a good friend of Senator Dirksen's was up for reappointment to one of the commissions, his failure to be reappointed and his successor were not announced until after the President had found another place for him so that Senator Dirksen would not be too unhappy. That individual went from the Federal Martime Commission to a place where he was less busy, namely, the Subversive Activities Control Board. Again, this gives one some inkling of the regard that the President had for the work of that commission and the issues involved in comparison to those of the Subversive Activities Control Board. Shortly after that, President Johnson appointed the husband of one of his secretaries to the Subversive Activities Control Board; people don't get excited over appointments to that board.

Industry Influence on Agency Processes

It should be obvious that, once special interests have had an impact on the appointment of commissioners, they have the advantage over a general "public interest," because individuals who are sympathetic to or responsive to those special interests constitute a goodly portion of the commission. This obviously would have considerable influence upon the general direction that a commission will take, if it is oriented toward a broad, general direction and does not approach problems on a piecemeal, case by case, or crisis basis. Even in the latter situation, the probable outcome of a specific matter has a degree of predictability, given the outlook and previous propensities of certain commissioners.

Special interests also have a considerable impact on the staff of the commissions, an impact that far outweighs that of consumer interests. This impact is not necessarily sinister or nefarious; it results from the frequent and ongoing interaction with members of the staff of the various commissions. While it cannot be inferred from this that the staff derogates the public interest by frequent contact with industry representatives, it can be inferred that they are, at least, more familiar with the positions espoused by

[6]Cox; Fellmeth; and Schulz, *Nader Report on the FTC.*

special interest representatives and are more accessible to them on an informal basis. For example, in the transportation industry there are bar associations that regularly bring industry practitioners together with various commission attorneys.

Assuming absolute impartiality on the part of the commission, there is still less frequent contact with those rare practitioners who represent "the public interest." This will continue to be so until there is a more formalized representation of the public interest, either by a Department of Consumer Affairs or by the development of well-heeled consumer interest groups. It is only natural that, if a pending policy matter is causing concern to a staff member, he or she will discuss the matter with special interest representatives in whom they have great confidence and for whom they have respect. There is thus some sharing of expertise, but at the same time there is a definite input by a special interest.

Business also influences the regulatory process by using it to try to reduce competition. The Supreme Court recently held that it is unlawful for parties to combine to harass and deter others from access to agencies and courts, in a case that involved allegations that certain highway carriers conspired to institute proceedings to resist and defect applications by other carriers seeking to acquire transfer or register operating rights.[7] The transportation industry is notable for this type of activity. In 1965 a trucker in Nebraska caused much chagrin for the railroads and the Interstate Commerce Commission when he filed a rate for the transportation of yak fat.[8] As the trucker anticipated, the railroads objected to the rate, and the ICC commenced its usual proceedings before realizing that a prank was involved. This exercise serves to illustrate that competitors, as a standard practice, routinely object to applications filed by other competitors.

Many people believe that the problems encountered by Tucker in the 1940's in seeking to produce and market an automobile were prompted and initiated by competing automobile producers who threw in Tucker's way all available roadblocks from the regulatory commissions.[9] In September 1968, a steamship carrier sought to preclude a competitor from picking up emergency cargo, under a contract with UNICEF destined for shipment to Biafra, on the ground that the competitor had not published a tariff with the Federal Maritime Commission 30 days in advance of the effective date. The FMC granted special permission to the carrying carrier to publish its tariff with the 30-day notice, and the unsuccessful bidder objected to the

[7]*California Motor Trans. Co.* v. *Truckers Unlimited*, 92 Sup Ct 609 (1972).
[8]ICC Docket M–19432 (1965).
[9]See "Tucker Torpedoed" *Newsweek*, June 20, 1949, p. 69.

commission's waiver of its rules. In this case, the court recognized that the rules of the commission were properly and prudently waived; adherence to the rules would have lessened competition without offsetting redeeming factors.[10] These examples illustrate the ways in which companies try to use the regulatory processes to force out competitors.

That the activities of the regulatory agencies often redound to the benefit of vested industry interests would appear to be borne out by the fact that many FTC trade regulation rules were issued without challenge to the FTC rule-making authority. It was only in 1971 that such authority was challenged.[11]

It appears that this challenge was so late in coming because that case was the first in which the toes of vested industry interests were stepped on. Until that time, the rules issued by the FTC served to protect industry members from marauders and shady competitors. The rules on the posting of octane ratings on gasoline pumps required a change in conduct of all industry members, including the dominant companies in the industry.

Other examples abound. Competitors complain to the Federal Trade Commission alleging improper acts of their competitors. Those that are justified of course enhance protection of the public interest; however, there are some instances in which the complaint is submitted for the sole purpose of harassing a competitor. Based on personal experience and observation, I would conclude that the staff of the FTC does a reasonably good job of screening out the cases without merit; unfortunately this takes staff time that could better be devoted to other matters and involves the time and expense of an industry member in supplying information to the staff.

Actions to Protect the Public Interest

What, then, can affirmatively be done to insure that the public interest is represented in commission decisions? First, in every matter before the commission, the commission should require a statement from the Office of the Public Counsel or Hearing Counsel that the initiation of the complaint or proceeding was not for the purpose of eliminating or harassing a competitor unless there is also present the possibility of redeeming public interest.

---

[10]*Worldwide Carriers, Ltd.* v. *Fed. Maritime Comm. & Hansa Line*, No. 68 Civ. U.S.D.C., S.D.N.Y. (1968).

[11]*National Petroleum Refiners Association et al.* v. *Federal Trade Commission*, U.S. Dist. Ct., District of Columbia Action 1180–1271 (now pending on appeal before the U.S. Ct. of Appeals, D.C.).

Second, in every case the commission should require a statement from the Office of Public Counsel on whether or not the case presents an issue involving the public interest. This has been done informally by some commissions and by some individual commissioners. All too often, however, it is discretionary as to whether or not the public counsel intervenes in a complaint in which adversary interests are represented. If the public interest is involved, it should be the duty of the Office of Public Counsel or Hearing Counsel to do the following:

(1) Notify other potentially interested government agencies so that they can appear and present statement.
(2) Notify the industries and consumers or consumer groups involved.
(3) Coordinate the participants of broad public segments in hearings. A recent decision held that the commission must consider the arguments and positions of sectors of the public; for example, appearances before the FCC are not limited to competitors for a license.
(4) Inform the commission of the total length of time that the matter should require for prosecution and insure that the time schedule is adhered to.

Third, rather than establish or reorganize commissions for indeterminate periods of time, Congress should grant such commissions a specific lifetime. At the end of this "life," the burden should be on the commission to establish justification for its continuation. This would give consumer-interest groups an opportunity to question and challenge the manner in which a given commission has served the public interest. Commissioners should be appointed for the life of that commission, because tenure would relieve commissioners from the pressures indicated earlier. The late Senator Paul Douglas, among others, noted that it is the first wave of a commission staff that regulates most effectively in the public interet and without subservience to special interests. This commitment diminishes with successive waves, unless there is a major shakeup and reorganization of the commission, which rarely happens now. As mentioned, it was only after the study of the FTC by the American Bar Association and the appointment of Casper Weinberger and Miles Kirkpatrick (chairmen firmly committed to revitalizing an agency that had been accused of bordering on the moribund) that a substantial change in direction took place. A built-in expiration date could make a needed revitalization much easier to bring about. This is neither a new nor novel suggestion; a number of political scientists have made this or similar recommendations in times past.[12] Unfortunately,

[12]References in n. 1; *see also* Paul Douglas, *Ethics in Government* (Cambridge: Harvard University Press, 1952).

because of the political problems discussed earlier, these suggestions have not met with any great success.

Most importantly, all commissions should insure that all their activities are thoroughly and fully publicized so that all parties affected by their actions are informed before the fact. When commissions testify before Congress, the testimony frequently reflects input to the staff from the industry involved. The consumer is ordinarily unaware of the preparation of such testimony and, if aware of the hearings, does not now have the opportunity to funnel input to the congressional committee through the regulatory commission. Therefore, a daily report of the activities of commission staff should be filed with the secretary of the commissions for public perusal. There is no reason why information should not be readily available to a consumer-interest group or a reportorial watchdog when a staff member of the FTC meets with an assistant attorney general of the Justice Department to discuss the subpoena of documents, or when a member of industry meets with a staff member of the FTC to discuss packaging and labeling criteria. If a staff member decides to drop a complaint, the members of a commission may not be fully aware of the potential complaint or of its lack of prosecution. Thus, not only is there lack of information available to a consumer, but I have also observed lack of information on matters reaching the commission.

It is further interesting to note that in early January 1973 the FTC was sued by two nonprofit organizations challenging their settling of complaints and alleging that their consent order procedure does not allow adequate public participation. The complaint argued that the commission should revise its rules to provide public notice when negotiations are begun, permit intervention and participation by the public in negotiations, permit public comments on proposed settlements before commission votes are taken, and, finally, require the commission to issue statements of reasons why it accepted such consent orders.[13] While such actions certainly are a step in the right direction, these rules would still not make available for public scrutiny the vast area in which staff members decide to refrain from issuing or seeking a complaint after a visit from members of a special-interest group.

Special interests have ways of insuring that they are kept abreast of the daily activities of the comimssions. For example, an investment house retains a Washington law firm to keep it informed of the actions of the Interstate Commerce Commission that will affect stock values to certain companies. The individual consumer cannot afford a similar luxury.

---

[13]*S.O.U.P., Inc., S.A.V.E., Center for Auto Safety* and *A.S.H.* v. *Federal Trade Commission*, U.S. Dist. C., Washington, D.C.

The manner in which activities of the commissions are publicized also leaves much to be desired in this day and time. For example, the Interstate Commerce Commission publishes in the *Federal Register* receipt of applications for approval of agreements and indicates that,

> The complete application may be inspected at the Office of the Commission in Washington, D.C.
>
> Any interested person desiring to protest and participate in this proceeding shall notify the Commission in writing within 20 days from the date of publication of this notice in the *Federal Register*. As provided by the general rules of practice of the Commission, persons other than applicants should fully disclose their interests, and the position they intend to take with respect to the application. Otherwise, the Commission, in its discretion, may proceed to investigate and determine the matters without public hearing.

The National Archives of the United States has somewhat eased the problem by enlarging the print of the *Federal Register* to make the copy more readable. This, however, does not provide for any wider dissemination. Some people felt that passage of the Freedom of Information Act (4 U.S.C. 552) in 1967 would make available to the public records and information that would insure the public's right to examine records for public-interest protection. Ralph Nader's investigators frequently cited difficulty in obtaining public records, notwithstanding the provisions of the referenced act. One may readily question how many interested parties are aware of pending hearings and have an opportunity to notify the commission of their interests. Furthermore, how many of those people had the opportunity to examine the application at the office of the commission? Shouldn't the commission make available by mail copies of the application, with costs being borne by the applicant? The Environmental Protection Agency, instead of providing interested parties 20 days, is more generous and provides 30 days for interested persons to submit comments regarding proposals for exemptions from the act. For example, all of 30 days was afforded to submit comments on the exemption of xylene from the requirements so that it could be used in pesticide formulas. Other issues of the *Federal Register* indicate that the Federal Power Commission afforded potential protestors to the abandonment of utility service only 17 days to file objections. The commission did note that, if a petition for leave to intervene was filed or if the commission felt a formal hearing was required, it would give such notice. In practically every instance, the petitions and documents were available for inspection at the office of the commission, but with such a vast amount of material being disseminated through the Government Printing Office, why can't the nature of applications and complaints be disseminated also without requiring interested parties to go to the commission to study the documents?

Conclusions

In summary, a limited lifetime for agencies and the burden for justifying their renewal could eliminate commission and special-interest entrenchment, which can continue long after the need for the agency has expired. Insuring that commissions are not used to affect anticompetitive actions would insure that the public interest is represented and would prevent commissions from bogging down in matters that Congress never intended them to adjudicate. Finally, regular full and open disclosure of staff activities would be not only enlightening to the commissioners themselves in some cases, but also a means of insuring that the public (consumer) interest had the same opportunity for representation to the staff as the special interest. If the foregoing measures are pursued, it is possible that the regulatory agency will again speak for the public interest.

PART V

Organizational Imperatives and Corporate Social Responsibility

●●

He responds, as I've explained, only to stimuli affecting his corporation. That's the thing, you see. He has totally identified with his corporation. I'm sure if you talk to him about his corporation, he'll hear and understand you and might even talk to you. Otherwise he has no sensory faculties at all.

—Dr. Klune in Paddy Chayefsky's play, *The Latent Heterosexual*

One of the more difficult problems facing large corporations has to do with making changes in their organizational structures and operating procedures that will make their organizations and their junior and middle-level managers meet the stated objectives of top management by being more sensitive and responsive to their external environment.

As Ackerman points out, in its efforts to reconcile the needs of social responsiveness with company profit objectives, the U.S. corporation is confronted with two sets of problems:[1]

(1) The organizational innovations that enable the corporation to cope with growing competition and product diversity and to adopt technological and economic changes may inhibit effective responses to social concerns.

(2) The need or desire to absorb a growing array of social demands into the operation, which affect product design and marketing policy to name just two, may reduce the corporation's effectiveness as a producer of goods or services.

The major problems in resolving these conflicts are: the different

[1]Robert W. Ackerman "How Companies Respond to Social Demands," *Harvard Business Review*, July-August 1973, p. 89.

215

natures of the two types of decisions, the point of decision making and the impact of a decision on various parties, the type of information needed to make different types of decisions, the attributes of executives most suitable to make these decisions, and the different incentives requird to motivate them.[2]

Modern corporations are geared to make rational decisions related to the efficient and profitable production of goods and services. If a new problem such as job training for the hard-core unemployed is presented to the corporation as a cost function, it can be handled in a conventional manner within the system, but a decision on the social dimensions of such a problem falls outside the conventional decision-making structure and can only be handled on an **ad hoc** basis with the attendant high risk of disastrous results.

By training and temperament, corporate management is magnificently skilled in dealing with the conventional types of problems relating to its busniess objectives. The external environment (parameters) of these problems are well-defined and constant, or slow to change. The only variables are internal, and with these managment already has experience and familiarity. However, the validity of management's evaluation of a problem depends almost entirely on its assumption of an unchanging external environment; change in the external environment also alters the nature of the problem and makes a previously satisfactory solution ineffective. Job training, for instance, is an example of a problem encountered by the corporation in dealing with social demands.

Although on the surface these new problems appear similar to those previously faced by management, they are not susceptible to solution by management's old methods of decision making because of the changes in management's environment—changes in social values, motivation, attitudes toward business, and social norms of distributive justice. The changes in society's needs and expectations have led to different interpretations of similar phenomena.

Management is also solution-oriented as well as problem-oriented. It becomes frustrated when solutions do not fall into **a priori** patterns. It may spend five years testing a new product before it goes out into the marketplace, but it expects social problems to be solved quickly. When

---

[2]The subsequent discussion in this section is primarily based on S. Prakash Sethi and Dow Votaw, "How Should We Develop a New Corporate Response?" in *The Corporate Dilemma: Traditional Values versus Contemporary Problems,* Votaw and Sethi (Englewood Cliffs, N.J.: Prentice-Hall, 1973), pp. 204–209.

they cannot be solved quickly, management gives them up as beyond the scope and competence of business and passes the buck to government.

The second dimension of corporate management's inadequate responses to today's social problems stems from the nature of decisions that management, both at the policy level and at the operational level, is traditionally accustomed to make. Decision making at any level is closely related to a number of factors: the nature of the reward system, the availability of information, the validity of previous experience, training in analyzing information, individual perceptual biases, the fear of failure, and the knowledge of the costs of uncertainty. Even when top management makes a policy decision on a social issue, the implementation of this policy on the operational level of management is frequently inadequate and ineffective. It is difficult, if not impossible, to alter basic beliefs and methods acquired over long years of experience by management edict alone.

Management decisions are of two types: routine and innovative. Routine decisions are aimed at solving recurrent problems, and the outcome of these decisions is predictable in the sense that an extensive set of rules and procedures has already been set up to cover a finite number of situations. Situations calling for routine decisions have these characteristics: adequate information is available; a tested mechanism exists to collect such information; the decision maker is trained to understand and apply the information to the situation; and the dimensions of a decision can be predefined.

However, innovative decisions deal with situations that are one of a kind, that occur irregularly, and whose scope and effect cannot be predetermined or predicted. Decisions involving corporate contacts with minority groups or other social pressure groups are basically of the innovative type and are likely to continue to be so for some time. The causes of the problems have not been eliminated, the issues have not yet crystallized, and the group alignments are not stable.

Thus, the decision maker trained in making routine types of decisions has great difficulty in making an innovative decision. The information available is not complete, and it is not easy to determine the relevance of this information. His past experience is of little value because he is dealing with a new set of variables. He has only a limited understanding of the importance of the issues to himself or to his company, and his ability to comprehend and use new information is limited because of his place in the organizational hierarchy and the lack of time available for him to learn new methods of evaluating this information.

Faced with so many known factors, he is necessarily cautious. His perception is selective, and he tends to select only the types of information with which he is already familiar, thereby sacrificing the very information which may be crucial for the new decision. When forced to use information of unknown prior reliability, he tries to put it into old and familiar molds or "frames of reference" which make the information usable. The effect of decisions so arrived at is not hard to visualize. Decisions, which at another time or place might have been correct ones, suddenly turn sour on the executive, take on a new dimension unforeseen by him, and have their effect transcend his limited horizon. . . .

If corporations are to achieve any measure of success in dealing with changing social environment, they must develop new organizational blueprints. It is to their own advantage to initiate experimentation with new procedures in corporate structure and behavior, or it will be thrust upon them by outside elements. To disregard external pressures is to provoke the kind of general public regulation for which our public institutions are ill prepared and whose side effects may be worse than the restraints for which regulation was originally intended.[3]

The articles in this section address themselves to various facets of this problem.

Neil H. Jacoby develops a general theory of the social role of the corporation, taking into account public opinion and political factors, which have been largely ignored by previous models of corporate behavior. He argues that social problems are largely the result of the gap between rising expectations and a more slowly responding reality, and that this gap also functions in the public view of business corporations and their activities. Public expectations of business are exaggerated, however, and business should educate the public to its real and limited capabilities in social areas. Jacoby postulates a new theory to justify an ideal level of social involvement by corporations. He believes that rapidly growing political influence on business behavior—consumer pressure, for example—is extremely important in explaining the corporation's current behavior, and unites social involvement with long-run maximization of profits. Government policies, too, can be valuable inducements to socially desirable actions by corporations, and governmental regulation is necessary to trigger certain forms of behavior, such as massive industrial antipollution programs. He recommends several voluntary internal changes that corporations could make to become more responsive to new demands in ways that serve their own enlightened self-interest.

Ian H. Wilson believes that business must internalize methods to cope with the pace, complexity, and pervasiveness of change in society, if it is

[3]*Ibid.*, pp. 207–208.

to develop a responsive, operational corporate social policy that will truly integrate social responsibility and business needs. The strategic planning process is the logical place to begin reform because in the face of accelerating social change such planning must expand its time horizons, because social expectations of business are also accelerating, and because questions of social responsibility are now central to planning and performance. He argues that the typical two-input model of planning should be expanded to include not only economic and technological inputs, but also social and political inputs, and illustrates this with a lengthy description of the planning framework developed at General Electric. This new framework includes all of the major social expectations by which the corporation's performance will be judged, and a systematic means of assigning corporate priorities to changing social pressures. The process of priority assignment is also extensively illustrated. Wilson warns that the adoption of his proposals does not guarantee the development of an adequate social policy, but he stresses that if social responsibility factors are ever to have anything like equal consideration with traditional business needs they must be integrated into the highest levels of corporate planning.

Phillip T. Drotning discusses the evolution of early corporate efforts at socially responsible actions, from extensions of traditional public or community relations programs to more sophisticated approaches that seek to make social responsibility profitable. He sees changes in business attitudes toward government regulation and toward the traditional input of social data to make corporate decisions. In this vein, he argues that there is growing recognition among corporate executives that, to be effective, social policies must be implemented with the same management tools used to indicate serious concern and enforce performance in other, more traditional areas. In any conflict between management's stated social goals and financial goals, performance parity can only be assured by equalizing penalties and rewards, especially since the implementation of social goals often involves traumatic changes in principles on which corporation members have operated throughout their productive lives. The fact that this kind of implementation program has not been generally adopted by business, Drotning believes, indicates that for the most part, rhetoric notwithstanding, business is still concentrating on its traditional short-term profit goals. He does believe, however, that programs such as equal employment opportunity and minority purchasing can be highly successful when entered into wholeheartedly, and offers American Oil Company's programs as examples of what a corporation can do in social terms at little or no cost and perhaps even for a profit to itself.

John Paluszek describes the results of a study of seven companies who made organizational commitments to social responsibility. Much of what he describes underlines Drotning's previous remarks about the necessity for enforcing any commitment that is to show results. Paluszek's report covers such areas as staffing, budgeting, social accounting, communications, and data, all of which were handled differently by the different companies involved, but which were nonetheless central to any successful commitment.

Rebecca A. Gould and Eugene J. Kelley examine two of the possible methods of adaptation to changing social demands: symbolic adaptation such as rhetoric, and establishment of **ad hoc** study committees, and certain types of organizational change; and behavior adaptation, which is the actual implementation of social policies through corporate programs, cooperative industry programs, and individual contributions. They also discuss methods by which these changes may be communicated to the public. These methods are weak, however, and these weaknesses must be identified and eliminated by any firm attempting to design an adequate social communications program. Some of these weaknesses are: the attitude of the corporation sending the social messages, mistrust on the part of those receiving the messages, lack of integration in reporting corporate adaptations, and lack of objectivity in reporting. The paper then describes a communications model designed to minimize these weaknesses. The model depends on three basic guidelines by which the authors believe a firm may achieve successful communication with its changing environment: an integrated total social-performance report, objectivity in reporting, and honesty on the part of the firm making the report.

George P. Hinckley and James E. Post attack the problem of business's relationship to other social institutions. The concept of performance, they feel, is central to this relationship and to defining its dimensions. The distinction between performance in the social arena and in the more narrow economic arena is a useful starting point for the examination of the corporation's relationship with other social institutions, and the authors describe these two types of performance. They also note the various types of stimuli that can provoke organizational activity toward a desired end, be that end economic or social performance. The question of who is to be the final judge of performance, of business's legitimacy in society, is touched upon briefly, and the authors suggest that there is a fundamental difference between the view that businessmen have of their charter in society and the view of that charter that many segments of society are beginning to adopt. This dichotomy, they stress, makes imperative the development of a comprehensive and systematic method of analyzing the corporation's performance.

John W. Collins and Chris G. Ganotis report the results of a survey of managers on their attitudes toward corporate social responsibility. They argue that the gap between stated corporate social policy and its actual implementation may be partly attributed to an attitudinal gap between those who formulate the policy and those who must implement it. A knowledge of employee attitudes could help to determine the best ends and/or methods for policy implementation, or the need to influence employee attitudes for successful implementation. Their findings show: (1) a sense of futility among junior and middle-level managers about their ability to affect corporate social policy; (2) an unexpected lack among young managers of "corporate liberalism" and a low level of perception of the need for corporate involvement in social issues; (3) no ideological barriers to corporate social involvement; (4) strong feeling against government intervention in such involvement; (5) strong preference that associated costs should be borne by consumers and stockholders rather than employers; and (6) a wide gap between positive managerial attitudes toward pollution control and negative attitudes toward providing greater job opportunities for minorities and women. The authors point out that, although this study is of consequence primarily to the firm that commissioned it, it nevertheless provides a foundation for an area in which further inquiry is needed.

SELECTED BIBLIOGRAPHY

Abt, Clark C. "Managing the Socially Responsible Corporation: New Accounting Tools." Garret Lecture delivered at the *Columbia University Graduate School of Business*, January 1973.

*Ackerman, Robert W. "How Companies Respond to Social Demands." *Harvard Business Review*, July-August 1973, pp. 88–98.

*Alberts, David S., and Davis, Johnson Marshall. "Decision-making Criteria for Environmental Protection and Control." Paper written for the 12th American Meeting of the Institute of Management Sciences, Deroit, September 29-October 1971.

*Alexander, Tom. "The Social Engineers Retreat Under Fire." *Fortune*, October 1972, p. 132.

Armstrong, Robert W. "Why Management Won't Talk." *Public Relations Journal*, November 1970, pp. 6–8.

*Especially recommended for an overall view and for authoritative viewpoints on different perspectives of the issues covered.

*Baldwin, William. "The Motives of Managers, Environmental Restraints, and the Theory of Managerial Enterprise." *Quarterly Journal of Economics*, May 1964, pp. 238-256.

*Bauer, Raymond A., and Greyser, Stephen E. "The Dialogue that Never Happens." *Harvard Business Review*, November-December 1967, pp. 2-12, 186-190.

*Bradt, William R. *Organizing for Effective Public Affairs: How Companies Structure the Corporate Unit*. Studies in Public Affairs No. 5. New York: The Conference Board, 1969.

*Chamberlain, Neil W. *Business and Environment: The Firm in Time and Place*. New York: McGraw-Hill Book Co., 1968.

_____. *The Place of Business in America's Future*. New York: Basic Books, 1973.

Carr, Albert Z. "Is Business Bluffing Ethical?" *Harvard Business Review*, January-February 1968, pp. 143-153.

_____. "Can an Executive Afford a Conscience?" *Harvard Business Review*, July-August 1970, pp. 58-64.

*Drotning, Philip. "Why Nobody Takes Corporate Social Responsibility Seriously." *Business and Society Review/Innovation*, Fall 1972, pp. 68-72.

Drucker, Peter. *Technology, Management and Society*. New York: Harper & Row, 1970.

*Fenn, Dan H., Jr. "Executives as Community Volunteers." *Harvard Business Review*, March-April 1971, pp. 4-16, 156-157.

Hanrahan, George D. "Why Social Programs Fail." *Economic and Business Bulletin*, Spring-Summer 1972, pp. 51-59.

Hobbing, Enno. "Business Must Explain Itself." *Business and Society Review*, Fall 1972, pp. 85-86.

*Jacoby, Neil H. *Corporate Power and Responsibility*. New York: MacMillan Co., 1973.

_____. "Organization for Environmental Management—National and Transnational." *Management Science*, June 1973, pp. 1138-1150.

Janger, Allen R., and Shaeffer, Ruth G. *Managing Programs for the Disadvantaged*. New York: The Conference Board, 1970.

Jennings, Eugene E. *The Executive in Crisis*. New York: McGraw-Hill Book Co., 1965.

Jessup, John K., and Kristol, Irving. "On 'Capitalism' and the 'Free Society'." *The Public Interest*, Winter 1971, pp. 101-105.

Kefalas, Asterios G. "The Management of Environmental Information: A Machine for Adapting a System to Its Environment." Presented at the 12th American Meeting of the Institute of Management Sciences, Detroit, September 29-October 2, 1971.

Lewin, Kurt. *Resolving Social Conflicts*. New York: Harper & Row, 1948.

Leavitt, Harold. "The Corporation President Is a Berkeley Student." *Harvard Business Review*, November-December 1967, pp. 152-157.

Mace, Myles. *Directors: Myth and Reality*. Cambridge: Harvard Business School, 1971.

Mayer, Lawrence A. "A Large Question About Large Corporations." *Fortune*, May 1972, p. 185.

Miller, Arthur S. "Corporate Gigantism and 'Technological Imperatives'." *Journal of Public Law* 18 (1969): 256-310.

Myers, M. Scott. "The Human Factor in Management Systems." *California Management Review* 14, no. 1 (Fall 1971): 5-10.

Myers, S. C. "A Simple Model of Firm Behavior Under Regulation and Uncertainty." *The Bell Journal of Econmics and Management Science*, Spring 1973, pp. 304-315.

*Narver, John C. "Rational Management Responses to External Effects." *Academy of Management Journal*, March 1971, pp. 99–115.

*Paluszek, John. *Organizing for Corporate Social Responsibility*. Special Study No. 51. New York: Presidents' Association, American Management Association, 1973.

Peters, Lynn H. *Management and Society*. Belmont, Calif.: Dickenson Publishing Co., 1968.

*Sethi, S. Prakash. *Business Corporations and the Black Man: An Analysis of Social Conflict, the Kodak-Fight Controversy*. Scranton, Pa.: Chandler, 1970.

_____. *Up Against the Corporate Wall: Modern Corporations and Social Issues of the Seventies*. 2d ed. Englewood Cliffs, N.J.: Prentice-Hall, 1974.

_____. *See also* Votaw, Dow, Fall 1969, and 1973.

The Conference Board. *Business Amid Urban Crisis: Private-Sector Approaches to City Problems*. Studies in Public Affairs No. 3. New York: The Conference Board, 1968.

_____. *Corporate Organization for Pollution Control*. New York: The Conference Board, 1970.

Vanderwicken, Peter. "Change Invades the Board Room." *Fortune*, May 1957, p. 156.

*Votaw, Dow, and Sethi, S. Prakash. "Do We Need a New Corporate Response to a Changing Social Environment?" *California Management Review* 7, no. 1 (Fall 1969): 3–32.

_____. *The Corporate Dilemma: Traditional Values versus Contemporary Problems*. Englewood Cliffs, N.J.: Prentice-Hall, 1973.

*Walton, Clarence C. *Ethos and the Executive*. Englewood Cliffs, N.J.: Prentice-Hall, 1969.

The Corporation as Social Activist*

● NEIL H. JACOBY

Graduate School of Business Administration
University of California, Los Angeles

Social assessment of the corporation has led me to analyze the issues of corporate concentration and fragmentation, of corporate political involvement and detachment, and of autocracy and democracy in corporate government. My analysis revealed shortcomings in current corporate and government behavior in each of these areas—and I propose reforms. This article appraises three critical social responsibilities of the corporation: helping to solve social problems, improving the environment, and supplying military hardware to the government.

The social responsibilities of the business corporation have been a central topic of public discussion in recent years. But what is the meaning of "corporate social responsibility"? The public, it appears, has endowed it with a very broad meaning. Thus, when consumers raise their voices in protest against unsafe, faulty, or misrepresented products; when employees

*From *Corporate Power and Responsibility* © 1973. The Trustees of Columbia University in the City of New York (New York: MacMillan Co., 1973). My underlying thesis was originally developed for a conference, "The Corporation and the Quality of Life," held at the Center for the Study of Democratic Institutions, September 27-October 1, 1971, and was presented under the title, "The Business Corporation in Social Service: Problem Solver for Government." This article also draws on my "What is a Social Problem?" *Center Magazine* 4, no. 4 (1971), and my article entitled, "Capitalism and Contemporary Social Problems," *Sloan Management Review* 12, no. 2 (1971).

complain of routinized jobs, bureaucratic paralysis, or inhumane working environments; when governmental officials investigate the putative misbehavior of military hardware makers, drug vendors, or conglomerates; when protests emanate from university campuses over the failure of corporations to eliminate poverty, hard-core uenmployment, racial discrimination, crime, and urban decay; when stockholders demand that their companies leave South Africa, boycott Angola, or appoint women, blacks, and youths to their boards of directors—all are complaining in one way or another that business is not discharging its social responsibilities.

Such broadside criticism of corporate behavior is to be expected in an age of high public expectations and widespread skepticism, when all institutions are under attack. From one point of view, it flatters corporate enterprise. The very success of the American business system in expanding production and elevating living standards has led the public to believe that the corporate system possesses unused capabilities to achieve other social goals.

Paradoxically, it is the public belief in corporate capabilities, rather than the loss of confidence in them, that inspires criticism. Chairman James M. Roche of General Motors was wrong when he accused corporate critics of threatening our free economic system.[1] The truth is the contrary: having lost faith in government, the trade union, the church, and the university to bring mankind to Utopia, many critics have turned to the profit-seeking corporation. It becomes very important, therefore, to understand the limitations as well as the possibilities of corporate action in the social field.

I present here a general theory of the social role of the business corporation, a theory that takes public opinion and political factors into account. This theory will help to justify what I believe is the ideal level of corporate social involvement and will reconcile such involvement with the principle of optimizing the long-run interests of the shareowners. Implicit in the theory are also the guidelines and policies that enterprises should adopt in responding to the public demand for social action. First, however, it is necessary to examine the nature of social problems.

Social Problems as Expectation-Reality Gaps

I propose that the designation of some social condition as a "social problem" derives from a gap between a society's expectations about that condition and the present realities—from a disparity between what is and what

---

[1]*Wall Street Journal*, November 15, 1970.

people believe should be.[2] Such a designation is basically a subjective rather than an objective phenomenon. The importance of a social problem is therefore as much determined by public expectations as it is by real conditions. Thus, poverty is perceived to be a serious social problem in the United States when 11 percent of the population have incomes below the official "poverty" level. Twenty-five years ago the problem of poverty was perceived to be less serious, although 27 percent of the people then lived under the same poverty line! The explanation of the paradox is that public expectations of eliminating poverty outraced realities. Other social problems like housing, crime, malnutrition, health, drugs, and racial discrimination are amenable to the same analysis.

The primary cause in enlarging social problems in the United States during the postwar era has been rising public expectations, rather than a failure of real conditions to improve. The quality of life has risen dramatically in many ways since World War II.[3] Yet public sensitivity to what is viewed as social failings has become sharper than ever. This is so because American society is "wound up" and structured to enlarge expectation-reality gaps; the political and intellectual communities and the mass media all function as "gap enlargers" by elevating expectations and by depreciating social achievements.

Of course, for each social situation that is viewed as a problem there is an optimal gap between expectations and realities. Such a gap performs a useful function—public demands should be higher than current realities to provide incentive for improvement. When a gap becomes extremely large, however, and expectations of change are elevated to unattainable heights, it becomes dysfunctional and leads to public disillusionment, frustration, and, in extreme cases, to violence and other antisocial behavior.

There are also optimal rates of change in public expectations and in real social conditions. Thus, the rate of improvement in, say, the nation's housing stock, is dependent on the rate of increase in the real GNP and on the priority given to housing by national economic policies. This real increase is constrained within rather narrow bounds—a four or five percent gain each year. But there is no resource constraint on public expectations of additional housing, which may soar almost as high as the human imagination can take them. Ideally, the rate of change in public expectations would parallel the rate of change in objective possibilities for improvement; as

[2]See Neil H. Jacoby, "What is a Social Problem?" *Center Magazine* 4, no. 4 (1971), for a full statement of the concept.

[3]See Panel on Social Indicators, *Toward a Social Report, A Report to the President* (Washington, D.C.: Department of Health, Education and Welfare, 1969).

mentioned above, expectations should be slightly ahead. It follows that political leaders should try to mold public expectations within constructive limits while they are working to improve real social conditions.

The "social tension" of a society might be defined as the sum of the expectation-reality gaps of all the social problems within the range of public consciousness. Because the number of problems that the people of a nation can cope with effectively at any time is limited by their stock of wisdom and energy as well as by available economic resources, national leaders and the mass media may, by dramatizing one social deficiency after another, stimulate public expectations so powerfully that multiple social "crises" are created in the public's mind. This process went on under the Johnson administration in the 1960's. By 1968, public frustration, *i.e.*, social tension, had reached a dangerous level in the United States. The people demanded immediate social improvements that were far beyond the capability of the society to deliver. Violence and radical activism mounted to a peak.

Three elements of an ideal social policy can thus be identified: maintain for each social problem a functional gap between expectations and realities; achieve a rate of change in expectations that is proportional to real possibilities for improvement in each social condition; and work to limit the social conditions actively in the public consciousness to that number for which available resources permit significant real gains.[4] These conditions should be established, of course, through the democratic processes of public discussion and representative government.

The expectation-reality gap concept may be used to clarify public perception of the social role of the large business corporation. Public opinion polls make clear that Americans hold high expectations of the role that business should play in bettering our society, but believe that the realities of business performance have fallen short of their expectations.[5] Indeed, two-thirds of the people believe that business corporations should spend some of their profits for social purposes.

The question then arises: To what extent are public expectations of the social performance of business appropriate and functional and to what extent exaggerated and dysfunctional? The public rightly expects from busi-

---

[4]President Nixon made this point in his State of the Union message to Congress in January 1971.

[5]See the results of a study made during 1970 by Opinion Research Corporation, cited in *Social Responsibilities of Business Corporations* (New York: Committee for Economic Development, 1971), pp. 14–15. Founded in 1942, CED is an influential organization of the top executives of 200 leading American corporations and universities. It studies important public issues and publishes statements on national policy.

ness a higher level of socially responsible performance than it has displayed in such problems as air pollution or automobile safety. On the other hand, the public has exaggerated the technical, financial, and managerial capabilities of business corporations, by themselves, to alleviate poverty, hardcore unemployment, poor education, or urban slums. The public tends to forget that profit-seeking business needs profit motivations to become active and that, in these areas, only government can create them. As Chairman C. B. McCoy of E. I. du Pont de Nemours & Co. observed recently, the call for business social responsibility has validity, but businessmen should educate the public to the fact that corporation executives are not urban planners or policy makers and cannot solve social ills.[6]

Political and Economic Interactions in the Social System

To understand the social role of business, American society must be visualized as an open and dynamic system in which the political and economic subsystems interact. Figure 1 depicts the basic elements of this system. The primary flow of influence runs from changes in public values, via the political process, to changes in governmental allocations of public resources and in public regulation of the private sector; and then, via the market process, to changes in the relative quantities and prices of business products.

For example, the rising value placed by Americans on clean air led to the enactment of federal and state standards limiting pollutant emissions from automobiles. Manufacturers thereupon modified their cars to meet these standards, recovering their higher costs in higher prices. Essentially, they internalized in the purchase price of automobiles the external costs of air pollution, which had formerly been thrust upon the public. Because no one manufacturer could afford to internalize these costs due to the competitive disadvantage he would suffer, government had to enact standards applicable to all automobile makers. In resolving many social problems, governmental legislation is essential to trigger socially desired business action. Until government acts to create a market for clean air, pure water, slum-free cities, or employment of the disadvantaged, the profit-seeking corporation's involvement cannot be extensive. Criticism of business for lack of social conscience is pointless if government fails to provide incentives to business.

Yet the corporation is not a mere reactor to changes in public values and

[6]Address to the Business Council, May 7, 1971.

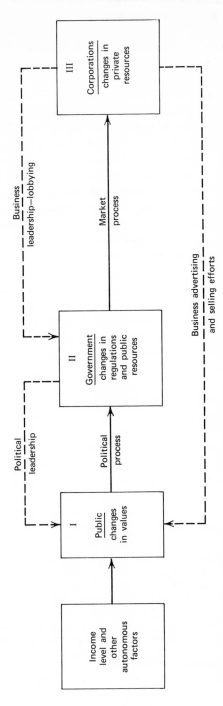

FIGURE 1. Dynamic relationships among public values, governmental regulations, and corporate resource allocations: ————, primary flow of influence; ------, secondary flow of influence.

governmental regulation.[7] As figure 1 indicates, it is also a secondary source of influence *on* public values and legislation. Corporate advertising and selling efforts help to shape public values, but they are also responses to demands created by those values. Corporate lobbying influences the nature of the public regulation of the private sector. Similarly, political leaders not only respond to changes in public values, but they also mobilize and amplify changes.

If the political and economic subsystems of American society are to interact in the public interest, it is desirable that the business community facilitate rather than obstruct the political and market changes called for by shifts in public values. Often in the past business has been obstructive, as is illustrated by the initial opposition of American automobile manufacturers to automobile safety and antipollution regulation. But businessmen have a wide scope for initiative in helping government design policies that will facilitate business responses to social demands. Only if the public understands the interaction between the profit-seeking corporation and government will its expectations of corporate social action be realizable. On the other hand, exaggerated public expectations that corporations will quickly resolve all of the nation's social problems can lead to frustration, resentment, and punitive action that could hinder social progress.

Social Responsibility in Three Models of the Business Enterprise

Want of an adequate theory of the ideal behavior of the large business corporation lies at the heart of current confusion over the social role of business. The basic difficulty is not so much ignorance of corporate social involvement, but rather the lack of an adequate criterion by which it should be judged. A theory of ideal corporate behavior is required that has operational validity in the real world.

[7]The primary processes of value formation in American society occur in the home, the school, the church, and in the political system of the state. It is here that each person acquires and assigns priorities to his values. Only after values have been so ordered does the business corporation enter the scene as a satisfier of the value-based wants of the public. However, it would be naive to assert that the corporation has not come to play a significant role in the formation of individual and social values. After all, half of the work force spends half of its waking hours within the business corporation. And all of us spend many of our nonworking hours surrounded by the products and services of corporate enterprise, which circumscribe our choices and shape the quality of our day-to-day existence. Clearly, the corporation is, to some extent, a creator of values as well as a responder to them.

Many theories have been advanced about the motivation and the behavior of business enterprises, each differing from the others in its emphasis on particular psychological or economic factors.[8] Without too great a loss, we may focus our attention on the two main theories of enterprise behavior. The theories, which have succeeded each other historically, are the "classical market model" and the "managerial model." After examining the notion of social responsibility in each of these models, I will propose a third theory, the "social environment model," which I hope, avoids the faults of its predecessors and provides a rational explanation of corporate social action that is consistent with the motive of profit optimization. Positions on major issues of corporate behavior in the three models are set forth in Table 1.

TABLE 1. Characteristics of Three Models of Behavior of the Business Enterprise

	Classical Market Model	Managerial Model	Social Environment Model
Nature of the Economy	Perfectly competitive	Monopolistic-oligopolistic	Effectively competitive
Levels of Profits	Normal	Supernormal	Normal
Enterprise Goal	Short-run profit maximization	Security and growth of business volume	Long-run profit maximization
Locus of Decision-Making power	Entrepreneurs	Managers	Stockholders—Board of Directors
Nature of Competition	Price	Price; product variation; and selling costs	Multi-vectored dynamic process
External Constraints on Enterprise Behavior	Markets	Markets	Markets, public opinion, and political pressures
Determinants of Social Activity	None	Social and charitable propensities of managers	Long-run profit maximization

[8] For a discussion of these theories, see Richard M. Cyert and James F. March, *Behavioral Theory of the Firm* (Englewood Cliffs, N.J.: Prentice-Hall, 1963); J. G. March and H. A. Simon, *Organizations* (New York: John Wiley & Sons, 1958); and William Baumol, *Business Behavior, Values and Growth*, 2d ed. (New York: Harcourt, Brace and World, 1967).

The Classical Market Model

This model of enterprise behavior was formulated by members of the classical school of British economic theory, which began with Adam Smith and developed mainly through the writings of David Ricardo, John Stuart Mill, and Alfred Marshall. The classical vision of the motive and mode of operation of the enterprise was, of course, based on observation and interpretation of the industrial structures and processes that characterized late eighteenth-century and nineteenth-century Britain. That economy was composed of relatively small enterprises, managed by owner-founders or their family heirs, which produced relatively simple products. The classical school held that, except for "natural" monopolies and illegal conspiracies among competitors, large numbers of independent firms tended to make for "atomistic" market structures and for perfect competition. The entrepreneur, in the acquisition of productive factors and in the sale of his products, reacted to information coming to him from markets. Because products and methods of distribution were simple, competition was conducted almost wholly on the basis of price. The limited resources of the enterprise made it necessary for the entrepreneur to maximize his profits in the short run.

Classical theory gave a convincing explanation of the way in which, under perfect competition, the effort of the entrepreneur to maximize his profits concurrently served the interests of society. Competition compelled each firm to produce with maximum efficiency and at lowest cost, and to offer its products to the public at prices that covered costs plus profits just sufficient to keep it in business and to drive inefficient firms out of the market. As Adam Smith put it, the entrepreneur will be "led by an invisible hand to promote . . . the interests of society more effectually than when he really intends to promote it."

The classical market model did not contemplate involvement by the firm in the solution of social problems, in the sense that we now understand it. Guided by the rule of profit maximization, the enterprise was considered to have discharged its responsibilities to society by efficiently meeting market demands for its products. Such, essentially, was the view of business social responsibility up through the initial decades of the twentieth century.

The Managerial Model

During the 1930's economists became aware of the widening gap between the classical market model of enterprise and the then current nature of corporate business. The catastrophe of the Great Depression precipitated a critical examination of all economic institutions, including the business corporation. In their *The Modern Corporation and Private Property*, Berle and Means first analyzed the implications of the widespread separation of ownership from the management of large business corporations.[9] They concluded that this institutional change had altered the goals of enterprise and had lodged decision-making powers firmly in the hands of hired managers responsible to directors and stockholders only in very limited ways. Later, Chamberlin and Robinson further challenged the classical theory of competition by observing that it failed to take into account the phenomena of product variation, advertising, and selling costs.[10] Regrettably, they did not present these factors as new dimensions of competition—which they truly were—but as evidences that monopoly power was pervasive. During the 1930's, there was also much concern about the increasing size of corporations and the concentration of output. The studies and final report of the Temporary National Economic Committee, made during 1939–1941, emphasized these trends and expressed doubts about the adequacy of competition.[11]

Building on these criticisms and analyses, a number of economists developed, during the 1940's and 1950's, a new view of American enterprise that may appropriately be called the managerial model because it emphasizes the central role of professional managers.[12] Managerialists see the giant corporation as the dominant actor in the economy. Because in many industries output is concentrated in a few great companies, the economy is seen to be permeated with oligopoly. Competition being muted, profits are abnormally high. Professional managers hold the reins of power. They are effectively free from control, either by the unorganized stockholders or by boards of directors whose composition they control through the proxy machinery. Hence, the corporation is no longer operated to optimize profits for stockholders. Its goal is to maximize the satisfactions of its managers, who seek security, power, and prestige for themselves through the growth of the firm. An alternative concept, espoused by some managerialists, is that the corporate executive is essentially a trustee, concerned with an equitable

---

[9]Adolph Berle and Gardiner Means (New York: MacMillan Co., 1932).

[10]Edward S. Chamberlin, *Theory of Monopolistic Competition* (Cambridge: Harvard University Press, 1938); and Joan Robinson, *The Ecoonmics of Imperfect Competition* (London: Macmillan & Co., 1938).

[11]See especially *Final Report of the Temporary National Economic Committee* (Washington, D.C.: Government Printing Office, 1941).

[12]See, *e.g.*, Clarence Walton, *Corporate Social Responsibilities* (Belmont, Calif.: Wadsworth Publishing Co., 1967) and its extensive footnote citations. Galbraith has carried the managerial concept to an extreme in his *The New Industrial State* (Boston: Houghton Mifflin Co., 1967).

division of corporate gains among owners, workers, suppliers, and customers.[13] In either case, the behavior of the firm is largely determined by the discretionary power of management and is only loosely constrained by competition.

Clearly, a considerable involvement of the business corporation in social activities is possible under the managerial model. Once profit optimization is removed as the criterion of good managerial behavior, many reasons can be found for spending corporate funds for social purposes. Managers have a wide authority to allocate corporate resources for different purposes and frequently have ample monopoly or oligopoly profits to spend on social amelioration and philanthropy. Under this model a company's social involvement is limited only by the humanitarian propensities of its management.

The Social Environment Model

Historical processes have a perverse habit of overturning popular doctrines. Just as the market model of enterprise behavior gave way to the managerial model, so the managerial model is now being challenged for its inability to depict and explain current realities. We have already seen that large corporations in the highly concentrated industries stubbornly refuse to behave like monopolists or oligopolists. They continually innovate and bring new products into the market. Their profit rates, far from being abnormally high, have been lower than those of medium-sized companies during recent years. Indeed, competition has expanded along new dimensions and involves many variables in addition to price.

With the massive institutionalization of shareownership, the rise of stockholder organizations, and the gearing of executive compensation to the profitability of companies through bonuses and stock options, the notion that managers behave contrary to the interests of the shareowners has become obsolete in its application to most companies.[14] Shareowners are reasserting their role as the ultimate arbiters of corporate policy. In this

---

[13]See, e.g., Edward S. Mason, ed., *The Corporation in Modern Society* (Cambridge: Harvard University Press, 1959); and Ralph Cordiner, *New Frontiers for Professional Managers* (New York: McGraw-Hill Book Co., 1956).

[14]See, e.g., Robert J. Larner, *Management Control and the Large Corporation* (Cambridge: Dunellen Publishing Co., 1970), who concludes, "although control is separated from ownership in most of America's large corporations, the effects on the profit orientation of firms and on stockholders' welfare have been minor" (p. 66). Wilbur G. Lewellen, *The Ownership Income of Management* (New York: National Bureau of Economic Research, 1971) also produces convincing evidence that professional managers of large corporations share with stockholders the goal of profit maximization (pp. 11–12).

new situation, the philanthropic behavior of business corporations has tended to demonstrate a penurious adherence to corporate self-interest.

The inadequacies of the managerial model make it necessary to adopt a new model that more adequately explains enterprise behavior in contemporary society, especially its social involvement. As Kuhn has observed, a model is never abandoned because of its refutation by facts, however damaging, but because it is replaced by another model.[15] I propose, therefore, a new theory of enterprise behavior, which I call the social environment model because its central tenet is that the enterpries reacts to the total social environment and not merely to markets. I offer this social environment model as explanatory of actual corporate behavior, as a basis for predictions of corporate social action, and as suggestive of the norms a profit-seeking enterprise *should* follow in relation to social problems.

The most novel and important characteristic of the social environment model is the explicit recognition that corporate behavior responds to political forces, public opinion, and governmental pressures. Whereas both classical and managerial theory ignored the impact of political forces, the social environment theory analyzes corporate behavior as a response to both market and nonmarket forces because both affect the firm's costs, revenues, and profits.[16] It has been the pressures of public opinion, the demands of stockholders, the urgings and threats of legislatures and bureaucrats, and the proddings of such enthusiastic ombudsmen as Ralph Nader—all nonmarket forces—that have induced large companies to allocate resources to social purposes. Whether their motives were defensive or offensive, corporations made these allocations basically to enhance their profits in the long run, perhaps also to defend existing profits against erosion. Large size and greater financial security enable the contemporary corporation to act with reference to a more distant horizon than the relatively small firm of the nineteenth century was able to contemplate (see Table 1).

The Rise of Political Influence
on Enterprise Behavior

The swift rise of political influence on business behavior, of which the burgeoning consumerism movement, for example, is one cause, is an im-

---

[15]Thomas S. Kuhn, *The Structure of Scientific Revolutions* (Chicago: University of Chicago Press, 1962).

[16]There is a widening perception of the fact that both the classical and the managerial theories provide too constructive a framework for understanding enterprise behavior, and that the viability of the firm depends on its adaptability to is total environment. See, *e.g.*, William R. King, "Systems Analysis at the Public-Private Marketing Frontier," *Journal of Marketing* 33 (January 1969): 84–89.

portant but little-noted phenomenon of our times. It has been discussed by Hirschman in connection with his distinction between "voice" and "exit" as alternative reactions of people to what they consider to be deficient business performance.[17] If a company were deficient in performance, the standard reaction assumed by classical theory was the exit or withdrawal from market dealings with the firm. The alternative, which is increasingly used, is to voice one's protest to the management in terms ranging from grumbling to violence; today, both exert influence on the firm's behavior.

Ignored by economic theory, "voice" has been dealt with in political theory under the rubric of "interest articulation." It can play either an exclusive or a complementary role to "exit" in disciplining corporate behavior. Voice is the only remedy available to dissatisfied customers in a situation in which they cannot exit because the products of all firms in an industry have the same deficiency, *e.g.*, bumpers on the automobiles of all makers collapse with an impact that occurs at more than three miles per hour! In many instances, voice may be the more powerful instrument because it aims to change an objectionable condition rather than simply to escape from it. Used intelligently, it is a healthy development in American society to which corporate managers must adjust.

People may employ voice not only to express dissatisfaction with products on the market, but also to condemn corporate failure to develop and offer improved products. An example would be the failure of an automobile manufacturer to make a safer vehicle. Rather than boycott the present products of the company—a market reaction—the public might put strong pressures on the company to install safety devices—a political reaction. If compliance is cheaper than combating such pressures, the company will comply, thus optimizing profits while improving the product.

The political pressures on an enterprise are transformed into market pressures when government enacts laws or regulations compelling all firms in an industry to behave in the socially desired manner. For example, strong public pressures to reduce emissions of pollutants from vehicles led to the passage of the Federal Air Quality Standards Act. All automobile makers were then obliged to produce cars meeting the standards. The new law expressed a social consensus that relieved the dissatisfactions of the public and that transformed political pressure into market pressure.[18]

[17]Albert O. Hirschman, *Exit, Voice, and Loyalty* (Cambridge: Harvard University Press, 1970).

[18]Daniel Bell contends that this trend will be strong. See his "The Year 2000—The Trajectory of an Idea," *Daedalus*, Summer 1967, pp. 639-651.

Corporate Social Action and Self-Interest

The great virtue of the social environment model is that it reconciles the principle of enlightened self-interest with corporate concern for social responsibility. Although intelligent corporate executives have long reponded to nonmarket influences, such responses have not found a place in the accepted theory of the firm. Received theory does not take into account the rise in political pressures exerted on enterprises by stockholders, consumers, ecology, civil rights, and other interest groups.

Rational enterprise managers judge the yield of outlays for social purposes by their long-run effect on profits. They measure the return on the "investment" in each social program. Each social outlay is tested by a cost-benefit analysis. Among the benefits may be a reduction in the costs of defending the firm's actions before the legislative or executive agencies of government, an avoidance of onerous governmental regulations, or a reduction in property damage at the hands of activists. Social pressures generate costs, the amount of which can be minimized by appropriate corporate outlays. When viewed in the perspective of my model, there is no conflict between profit maximization and corporate social activity. The popular notions that a company that pursues profit must eschew a social role or that social involvement means a sacrifice of profit are unfounded.[19] On the contrary, the contemporary corporation must become socially involved in order to maximize its profits.

No firm can afford to ignore public attitudes and expectations. Thus Dow Chemical could not be oblivious to the adverse effects on its recruitment of college graduates of widespread student protests of its sale of napalm to the Department of Defense. Nor could General Motors ignore the possibility that congressional hearings on automobile safety, sparked by Ralph Nader's *Unsafe at Any Speed*,[20] would lead to punitive legislation costly to the company. On the other hand, charitable gifts may cultivate

---

[19]This error is frequently made; *e.g.*, President B. R. Dorsey of Gulf Oil Company told his shareholders at their annual meeting in 1971 that "maximum financial gain must now . . . move into second place, wherever it conflicts with the well-being of society." Many stockholders replied indignantly, "Not with my money!" "The Outlook," *Wall Street Journal*, March 22, 1971, p. 1. In their article, "Do We Need a New Corporate Response to a Changing Social Environment?" Dow Votaw and S. Prakash Sethi strangely assert that the "old" concepts of profit maximizing and responsibility to shareholders are "outmoded"! (*California Management Review* 7, no. 1 [Fall 1969]: 3–32).

[20]Ralph Nader, *Unsafe at Any Speed: The Designed-in Dangers of the American Automobile*, rev. ed. (New York: Grossman, 1972).

good will and generate larger sales from an approving public. Neighbor rehabilitation can pay off in enhanced business volume or higher property values. Hiring the disadvantaged may enable a company to escape new taxes, repressive governmental regulation, or disruption of business by dissidents.

It is often said that big companies should "legitimize" their great economic and political power by assuming larger social responsibilities. But neither is the premise correct that big companies have such power, and if it were, nor would the alleged conclusion follow that it should mimic the government. I have already shown that the economic power of even the largest enterprises is closely constrained by market competition and governmental regulation, and that their political power is more than balanced by that of other interest groups in society. Should the power of any enterprise become inordinate, the remedy is to curb that power—not to accept it and then ask the firm to become socially responsible in using it! The more important point, however, is that the corporation should and does engage in social ameliorative activity because it serves its enlightened self-interest and not because it is powerful. Enterprises must balance an equation of social presssure with social action, not an equation of power and responsibility. The firm's social involvement should be based on political and economic grounds.

The social environment theory is congruent with a basic principle advocated by the Committee for Economic Development. It is in the enlightened self-interest of the corporation to devote resources to improving the environment in which it operates, because it "is dependent upon the good will of a society which can sustain or impair its existence through public pressures on government."[21]

In a provocative statement Friedman has written that it would undermine the very foundation of a competitive economy if corporate managements generally abandoned the rule of making as much money for their stockholders as possible.[22] Unfortunately, Friedman failed to add that social involvement is consistent with self-interest and that corporate managers need a sophisticated understanding of business-social relations in order to operate on that principle. Those economists and businessmen who assert that the purpose of business is business and not social do-gooding are as much in error as the radicals of the New Left who would compel business to concentrate on social improvement.

[21]Committee for Economic Development, *Social Responsibilities*, p. 27.

[22]Milton Friedman, *Capitalism and Freedom* (Chicago: University of Chicago Press, 1962), p. 133.

The Rationale for Corporate Giving

Because contributions for charitable and educational purposes were the earliest form of corporate social action, their pattern enables us to test the validity of our theory. Corporate giving was stimulated by federal legislation in 1935 authorizing companies to deduct from taxable income up to five percent on account of such gifts. It was further enhanced by the decision of the court in the A. P. Smith case of 1953 that such gifts were desirable even though a corporate management could not show that they produced any direct benefit to the donor company.[23]

Managerial theory clearly suggests that, as companies grow larger, gifts will comprise a rising fraction of corporate income. Because monopoly profits are alleged to rise with growing size, corporate managers presumably will seek to gain still greater power and status in society through corporate gifts. Giant corporations would be expected to donate larger fractions of their pretax incomes to social causes than smaller companies because they tend to operate in concentrated industries in which monopoly power and profit rates are alleged to be the highest.

Yet the facts are inconvenient to managerial theory. Big corporations have donated *smaller* fractions of their pretax income than have small companies, probably because the owner-managements of small firms do not have to answer to outside stockholders.[24] Corporate donations in the aggregate have accounted for under one percent of pretax income—less than one-fifth the amount of allowable deductions. The percentage of pretax income donated has *not* risen during the past 20 years. Most significantly, the predominant fraction of all corporate gifts is made to schools, hospitals, welfare and civic agencies, of communities in which the donor firms operate facilities and from which they derive rather specific benefits. Evidently, American business corporations have tended to follow the principle of enlightened self-interest rather than that of pure philanthropy in making contributions. The social environment theory provides a better explanation of corporate behavior than does managerial theory. It is likely that

---

[23]*A. P. Smith Manufacturing Co.* v. *Barlow et al.*, 13 N.J. 145, 98 A. 2d 551 (1953). For a full history of this subject, see Morrell Heald, *The Social Responsibilities of Business: Company and Community, 1900–1960* (Cleveland: Case Western Reserve University Press, 1970).

[24]A survey of 1000 corporations revealed that the major companies donated about 0.66 percent of pretax incomes in 1968, compared to 1 to 3 percent for small concerns. See Committee for Economic Development, *Social Responsibilities*, p. 41.

donations of officers' time and of equipment and supplies conform to much the same pattern as monetary gifts.[25]

The percentages of gifts from pretax income by corporations in different industries throw light on the factors that determine the level of community involvement by business. The range of philanthropic effort was great. Banks and printing and publishing firms were the most liberal contributors, followed by apparel makers, motion-picture exhibitors, department stores, and other retailing and service industries. At the low end of the giving spectrum are oil and gas-drilling companies, electronic communications firms, and public utilities (see Table 2).

Taking the percentage of pretax income donated by firms in each industry as an index of its social involvement, corporate giving is generally in proportion to the extent of local public contacts that generate social pressures. Thus, the profitability of a commercial bank is heavily dependent on the character of its neighborhood and the good will and confidence of the local population. A bank is therefore likely to be active in community matters. The profits of an oil-producing firm are far less affected by such factors. (Public utility firms were low because the regulatory agencies have discouraged contributions.)

While gifts have been the means by which corporations have alleviated some of the social pressures of the communities in which they operate facilities, changes in products or in production processes have been the means by which they have responded to national pressures brought by the public. Thus, while the automobile and petroleum industries stood at the bottom of all industries in the ratio of gifts to net income, they have expended vast sums in rebuilding refineries and automobile engines in order to reduce air pollution.

The degree of social involvement by a corporation appears to be determined by the size of the public's expectation-reality gap in regard to its performance, and, most important of all, the strength of the incentives to social action provided by government.

Public Policies to Trigger Corporate Social Action

Although political pressures can induce social action by business corporations, the most efficient instruments for expanding their social roles are (1)

---

[25]For a full discussion of the development of corporate gifts to education in the United States, see Kenneth G. Patrick and Richard Eells, *Education and the Business Dollar* (New York: MacMillan Co., 1969).

TABLE 2.   Percentages of Pretax Net Income of U.S. Business Corporations Donated to Charitable Organizations, by Industry, 1966–1967.

	Percentage of Pretax Income Donated
Banking, printing, and publishing	2.1
Apparel and leather goods manufacturing	2.0
Motion-picture exhibition, department stores, mail-order, retailing, furniture manufacturing, laundries, beauty shops, photographers, personal service firms	1.6
Chemical manufacturing, photographic manufacturing, scientific equipment makers, watchmakers, textile manufacturing	1.4
Specialty retailing, stone, clay, and glass manufacturing, wholesaling	1.3
Construction contracting, food manufacturing, hotels and motels, rubber and plastic manufacturing	1.2
Advertising agencies, janitorial services, lumber, paper manufacturers, stock and commodity brokers, transportation equipment manufacturers other than automobiles	1.1
Electrical equipment makers, metal and steel fabricators	1.0
Farming and fishing, investment companies, insurance companies, oil refining, real estate firms	0.9
Consumer financing, machinery manufacturers, mining companies	0.8
Automobile repair shops, tobacco manufacturing, railroads, airplanes, shipping companies	0.7
Electric, gas, and sewer utilities	0.6
Telephone, and radio and television broadcasting	0.4
Automobile and truck manufacturing, automobile parts makers	0.3
Oil- and gas-drilling companies	0.1

(From study of C. W. Shever and Company, New York, based on data from the 1966 and 1967 tax returns of 939,846 companies in 42 industries, compiled by the U.S. Internal Revenue Service, and reported in the Wall Street Journal, January 11, 1971.)

government contracts and incentives to produce desired social goods and services, (2) the establishment of environmental or other standards to which all enterprises must conform, and (3) the imposition of penalties on those who damage the public interest. The optimum instrument, or combination of instruments, will vary with the particular social problem on which corporate action is sought.

Such incentives as rent subsidies, governmental leases, low-interest-rate mortgage loans, and accelerated depreciation have proved effective in expanding the supply of low- and middle-income housing. Governmental condemnation, clearance, and assembly of land tracts for sale to redevelopers have facilitated urban renewal programs. Contracts for training the hard-core unemployed have been used to good advantage. In reducing air and water pollution, federal or state standards limiting the emission of pollution have been very important. Fines or penalties charged per unit of pollutants emitted, such as the proposed federal tax per pound of sulfur emissions, are further methods of internalizing pollution reduction costs, of making prices reflect full costs. Governmental subsidies, loans, credit guarantees, and tax benefits can also be employed in environmental improvement.

Two points need emphasis: (1) Government legislation or regulation is necessary to trigger corporate social action. Governmental regulation of all firms in an industry is superior to private political pressure applied only to some firms in that industry, because it can bring about uniform adjustments. To no small degree, criticisms of business derive from a failure to comprehend these truths. The tardiness of the political system in reaching consensus and embodying it in laws and regulations has, more often than not, created crises and led to excessive voice. Business has been wrongly blamed for many faults in American life, but it has been rightly criticized for not facilitating their correction. (2) Business will only actualize its full potential for improving the quality of life if government creates markets for the social goods that business can supply.

Corporate Policies to Respond to Social Needs

To assure timely responses to the new demands occasioned by changes in social values, corporations should revamp both their policies and organizations. Many far-sighted companies have already done so. Specific measures of this kind include the following:

(1) Develop "social sensors" to identify and measure changes in public values, attitudes, and expectations that bear upon the company's performance. They must go beyond traditional market-research programs that are focused on consumers' attitudes toward the company's products, and should embrace public opinion polls and surveys on a wide range of subjects.

(2) Develop feedback processes within the company to evaluate and act on the information acquired. Some corporations meet this requirement with a staff department of public affairs reporting to the president or board chairman. To assure consideration of these inputs at the highest policy level, it is also desirable to create a standing committee on public affairs of the board of directors. Directors with special knowledge and interests in social problems should be appointed to this committee.

(3) Establish channels of communication with social groups. Two-way channels of communication should be established with consumers, employees, students, and leaders of political, labor, religious, and educational institutions, as well as with the mass media. These channels should be used regularly as sources of intelligence about attitudes and values, and as instruments to transmit information about the company's goals, activities, and accomplishments.

(4) Create a "social account." A systematic record should be kept of all company outlays made to improve the quality of life. They will include not only monetary contributions to social agencies, but also the value of employee time and of equipment and supplies loaned or donated for public purposes, the amount of capital and operating expenses incurred to abate pollution, to train hard-core unemployed, or to help resolve other social problems.

(5) Make an annual "social audit." Such an audit made under the direction of the committee on public affairs of the board of directors, would measure the company's progress toward the social goals it has set for itself. These could include employing minorities and women, meeting pollution standards, improving working conditions, conducting training programs, conserving resources, enhancing communties, or other goals.[26] Although it would be premature to publish such audits until goals are defined and programs to achieve them are developed, ultimately they should be published. As David Rockefeller has said, "Because of the growing pressure for greater corporate accountability, I can foresee the day when, in addition to the annual financial statements certified by independent accounts, corporations may be required to publish a 'social audit,' similarly certified."[27]

[26]See *Indicators of Social Change*, edited by Eleanor Sheldon and Wilbert E. Moore (New York: Russell Sage Foundation, 1968).

[27]David Rockefeller, address to the Advertising Council reported in *Los Angeles Times*, January 3, 1971.

The behavior of the business corporation is being ever more strongly influenced by political forces. Increasingly, corporate executives are required to measure, react to, and help shape the public attitudes that surround them. The American corporation must be responsive to these forces, while continuing to meet market demands in ways that serve its enlightened self-interest.[28]

[28]George A. Steiner reached a similar conclusion, but through a somewhat different argument. See his *Business and Society* (New York: Random House, 1971), p. 164.

Reforming the Strategic Planning Process: Integration of Social Responsibility and Business Needs

●●

● IAN H. WILSON

Consultant
Business Environment and Planning
General Electric Company

One of the prime organizational imperatives for the development of a responsive, operational "corporate social policy" must be reform of the strategic planning process. Indeed, one may argue that this reform is *the* essential prerequisite to making that true integration of social responsibility and business needs without which a social policy is all too liable to turn into an empty public relations gesture.

Obviously, there are other important reasons for reforming the business planning process in most companies, and there are other aspects of reform than those included here. However, I will focus on those reasons and those aspects that are most directly related to my focal theme, *i.e.*, corporate social responsibility. What is included in this paper must not, therefore, be construed as the total picture of strategic planning, reformed or otherwise.

245

My reasons for focusing on the strategic planning process are:

(1) The pace, complexity, and pervasiveness of change dictate some important shifts in business planning. Because change is so rapid, planning must be more far-seeing, operating with a more distant time horizon than previously, *i.e.*, it must focus on strategy, not on tactics. Because change is multidimensional and complex, planning must consider a broader set of inputs than previously. Because of the uncertanties caused by change, planning must be better prepared to deal with alternative futures, *i.e.*, contingency planning must be more detailed and explicit.

(2) The concept of corporate social responsibility is being broadened and deepened. Up until recently it was defined almost exclusively in quantitative, material terms, *i.e.*, improving the material standard of living for the majority, with lesser degrees of emphasis on certain peripheral areas of corporate performance, such as educational and cultural support and community activities. Now, however, the corporation's social charter is being redefined to include a range of qualitative expectations concerning the scope and objectives of a company's business, its style of operations, its governance, and its support for social objectives.

(3) Questions of social responsibility are no longer peripheral, but central to decisions about corporate planning and performance. This is not to say that the corporation has, or should, become a nonprofit charitable institution. Indeed, to argue—pro or con—in those terms would be to misconstrue the new social charter as being merely an extension of the old, peripheral do-good concept. Rather, this proposition asserts that social responsibility and business needs are now so intertwined that they cannot logically be separated; both factors must be weighed, simultaneously, at the primary level of corporate planning, *i.e.*, the formulation of strategies and the process of resource allocation. Or to put the matter another way: Virtually all business decisions are now infused with social significance, and matters of social responsibility are now of such importance and concern to management that they must be handled in a businesslike manner. If, as has been said, social responsibility is too important to be left to the PR staff, it is equally true that strategic business decisions are too important (to the corporation) to be made without reference to the potential impact of changing social conditions.

The Need for a
"Four-sided Framework"

Although the fact that social responsibility is now central to corporate decisions may seem apparent, virtually all that passes for long-range planning today still ignores or minimizes this vital ingredient. Typically, corporate planning is based on only two sets of inputs—economic and technological. Thus, economic forecasting will supply, at the macroeconomic level, projections of future GNP, consumption and investment expenditures, productivity, inflation, and so on, while marketing research will focus more sharply on analyses of the relative attractiveness of mature, developing, and potential markets. Technological forecasting is expected to supply as planning inputs predictions about state-of-the-art developments in new products, new systems, and new materials; forecasts of completion dates for the company's development projects; and assessments of competitors' technical competence, domestically and worldwide.

These two inputs, supplemented by financial forecasts (which are, after all, also economic forecasts at the microeconomic level), have been presumed to give us all the hard data necessary for planning purposes. For the rest, great reliance has been placed on the assumption of "other things being equal." Yet, if businessmen have learned one thing from the tumultuous 1970's, it surely should be that other things have an uncomfortable habit of *not* being equal. An otherwise soundly conceived plan based on these two sets of conventional inputs can be very vulnerable to attack on its open flanks—the social and political—for it is there that the tumult and the change has perhaps been greatest from a business point of view.

Both business logic and changing public expectations would seem to suggest that strategic plans should be formulated only within a framework of four major parameters—social, political, economic, and technological. (In fact, even this is a simplistic model, and we have elaborated on it in our planning system at General Electric.) On the one hand, business planning has always been concerned with the assessment of risk: If there are now new dimensions to risk, it is a matter of elementary prudence to introduce a new element to the forecasting process. On the other hand, if public expectations of corporate performance are now broader and more sophisticated, strategic planning should establish a broader set of performance criteria and goals, and seek more sophisticated data on the two new parameters (social and political) that, I suggest, must be added to the planning framework.

Rather than further elaborate the theory, let me illustrate it by what we are trying to do in this regard at General Electric. We have made it a requirement that the first step in the planning process should be the development of a long-term environmental forecast, and that this forecast should make explicit the environmental assumptions upon which all corporate strategies—marketing, manpower, technological, financial, and social (as this symposium is using the term)—are based.

In developing this required long-term forecast for our planning cycle, we produced nine separate views of aspects of the future business environment—tunnel visions of the future—dealing with probable developments in nine distinct spheres: international, defense, social, political, legal, economic, technological, manpower, and financial. In each of these segments, we tried to: (1) give a brief historical review (1960–1970) as a jumping-off point for our analysis of the future; (2) analyze the major future forces for change—a benchmark forecast for 1970–1980; (3) identify the potential discontinuities, events that might have low probability but high significance for General Electric; and (4) raise the first-order questions and policy implications suggested by these forecasts.

These were, by definition, segmented views of the future; as such, they would have been quite inadequate for planning in a world and society in which the interrelatedness of trends and institutions is a distinctive characteristic. To pull together the separate forecasts in the nine segments and to blend quantitative and qualitative data, we used cross-impact analyses and scenarios as integrative mechanisms.

From the hundreds of specific trends and events identified in the nine environmental segments, we identified the 75 or so that had the highest combined weighting of probability and importance. (Some events that were quite probable had little significance for General Electric, while others of low probability would have critical importance should they occur.) A cross-impact analysis examined these 75 trends-events, asking: If event A occurs, what will be the impact on the other 74? Will the probability of their occurrence increase? Decrease? Remain the same? In effect, this process enabled us to build sets of "domino chains," with one event triggering another, and then to construct a small number of consistent configurations of the future.

It is essential to deal with alternative futures, rather than to rely on a single, simplistic set of environmental assumptions. The use of multiple scenarios, of the type developed by Herman Kahn, is a good technique for presenting such alternatives and for integrating the hard data of technological, economic, and financial forecasting with the soft data of social and political analyses. In the end we developed four alternative scenarios, and, as a commentary on the uncertainty of the future, we rated even our benchmark (or most probable) forecast no better than a 50-percent probability.

There are many advantages, it seems to me, in commencing the strategic planning process with an environmental analysis such as this. In terms of defining corporate social policy, the utility of this analysis lies in:

(1) Making explicit all the environmental assumptions on which corporate planning and policy making should be based.
(2) Integrating the social factors and the business factors into the planning framework.
(3) Confronting future corporate problems as a system of interrelated issues and pressures, *i.e.*, seeing them as a piece, rather than piecemeal, with all their attendant complexities and trade-offs.
(4) Identifying the spectrum of probable future constraints and opportunities for corporate performance.
(5) Providing an opportunity, early in the planning cycle, for determining needed corporate responses to changing conditions.

Social responsibility is, I believe, best defined in terms of "social responsiveness," that is, in the ability of the corporation to respond constructively and opportunely to changing social needs and expectations.

Broadening the Concept
(and Evaluation) of "Strategy"

Social needs and expectations can be for new goods and services, in either the public or the private domain, or they can be for new styles of corporate performance and policy. Together, they form a total package of expectations; together, they constitute the charter according to which society expects the corporation to perform. The interlocking nature of these expectations is the fundamental reason why the planning framework must be enlarged to include new inputs and new perceptions of the future. It is also the reason why we need to conceive of strategy in broader terms.

It is not merely that we must have a more distant time horizon for our strategy, though that is undoubtedly true. To try to insure that our short-term actions do not lead us ultimately into traps or blind alleys, we need to speculate about the future ten years hence at least. More fundamentally, however, we must rid ourselves of the dangerous notion that strategy applies only to the economic and technological aspects of a business.

In our approach to strategy, we currently suffer from the same sort of limitation that afflicts our planning framework. We are prepared, that is, to acknowledge the necessity for strategy as it applies to investment, technology, production, and marketing. For the other aspects of a business, we seem content to rely on tactics and improvisation. However, if I am anywhere near being right about the pace and nature of the change in public expectations of corporate performance, such an approach—or lack of an approach—is almost precisely designed to maximize the amount of *reaction* in corporate policy making, and minimize the number of corporate initiatives; to maximize the constraints and added costs on the business, and minimize the opportunities for creating new markets, utilizing new resources, winning new vitality, and new public acceptance.

In General Electric we have defined strategy as "that activity which specifies for a business a course of action that is designed to achieve desired long-term objectives in the light of all major external and internal factors, present and future." In such a definition there is no restriction on the scope of objectives and courses of action, limiting them only to, say, financial goals, technological objectives, and marketing strategies. It implies, indeed encourages, the notion that we need strategies for the totality of a business, including, importantly, strategies for manpower development, for labor-management relations, for organization development, for business-government relations, for community action programs, and for dealing with the developing issues of corporate governance.

This broader definition of strategy is underscored when one considers that the first element of strategy must be a definition of "mission." The mission of a business determines its long-term goals and objectives: it at once raises questions about the scope and nature of a company's activities, about the style of its operations, and about the proper mix of objectives. Add to this the fact that an important end result of strategic planning is the allocation of corporate resources, and it becomes even clearer that all matters of strategic importance to the corporation, and the strategic planning process must therefore be made to embrace them all.

There is a third and final enlargement of scope that is needed to reform the strategic planning process, and that is the criteria used for strategy evaluation. In assessing the relative merits of alternative strategies, we are used to considering their impact on corporate growth, market position, return on investment, cash flow, and earnings per share. However, in view of what I have termed the new dimensions to risk, we need to add to these criteria an assessment of each strategy's social responsiveness, political viability, and employment attractiveness.

To understand the significance of these new criteria, consider some of the questions that might be asked under each of these headings:

Social responsiveness:

—To what extent will the strategy increase the company's ability to contribute toward the attainment of national goals and the serving of "social needs" markets?

—Will the strategy increase or decrease involvement in products and manufacturing facilities that are inherently more polluting?

—What impact will the strategy have on the company's "social legitimacy," *i.e.*, its recognition and public acceptance as a major social asset?

Political viability:

—Will prospective expansion of government regulations and controls tend to raise the level of risk and so impair the attractiveness of the strategy?

—Will the strategy raise or lower the level of exposure to antitrust action?

—How will the policies and programs needed to implement the strategy affect the acceptability of corporate objectives to government leaders?

Employment attractiveness:

—Will the strategy tend to enhance the company's public and campus image as a good place to work?

—Will the strategy tend to enhance the company's ability to attract needed talents and skills?

—Will the challenge and excitement of the corporate mission and objectives tend to increase employee morale and therefore the level of commitment and productivity?

If society is going to evaluate corporate performance against a broader set of criteria, it surely makes good business sense for management to ward off future problems—or to seize anticipated opportunities—by building these criteria into its own strategy evaluation process. The fact that there are no simple, quantifiable answers to such questions certainly complicates the task: however, it in no way diminishes the need for it.

Social Pressures and Corporate Priorities

In a pluralistic society such as ours, it is predictable that the criteria by which corporate performance is judged at any one time will be many and varied. The social pressures on the corporation will also shift over time. In the face of such variety and shifting, it is essential that there should be located in the strategic planning process some systematic means of assigning corporate priorities to these pressures. Almot certainly the demands that are made on the corporation at any one time will exceed its ability to respond equally and effectively to all; it is doubtful if the corporation can ever be all things to all people. Furthermore, there is a legitimate question to be raised about the social ranking of these demands: Not every demand is equally valid or pressed with equal vigor.

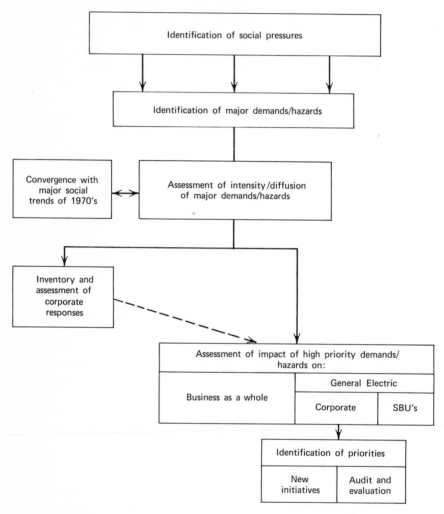

FIGURE 1.   Social pressures on business: a systematic analysis for corporate priorities.

In an effort to meet this need for priority-analysis, we are experimenting with a systematic screening and analysis procedure, whose main elements are shown in figure 1. Essentially, this is an attempt to supply a rational, systematic, and (as nearly as possible) objective evaluation of social pressures, with a view to determining priorities for corporate response in the development of strategy or the determination of policy.

The first step in the process is building up an inventory of social pressures as expressed in the major complaints made about corporate performance. At this stage we have aimed to be as comprehensive and inclusive as possible, preferring not to omit any, and have grouped the pressures into eight principal categories: marketing-financial; production operations; employee relations-working conditions; governance; communications; community and government relations; defense production; and international operations.

Next comes the identification of the major demands and hazards associated with these complaints. In this context, "demands" are defined as the range of solutions advocated to remedy the defect that is complained about, e.g., federal chartering to curb market power or stringent emissions standards to control pollution. "Hazards," on the other hand, are the adverse consequences that might flow from inadequate corporate response to some of these demands: A good example would be the progressive alienation of employees and lowered productivity that would flow from failure to meet demands for meaningful, significant work assignments. At this stage of our research the total number of identified demands and hazards is on the order of a hundred.

The third step is a two-phase screening process that is performed on each one of these demands and hazards. In an effort to arrive at their relative social validity and ranking, we have assessed each one in terms of:

—Its "convergence" with the major social trends of the 1970's. To what extent are 13 major trends[1] likely to accelerate or impede the realization of each demand or hazard? The impact of each trend on each demand is assigned a numerical score from one to ten, either positive or negative depending on whether the impact is accelerating or impeding.

---

[1]The major trends are: increasing affluence, rising level of education, proliferating technology, emergence of postindustrial society (services economy), growing interdependence of institutions (including business-government partnerships), increasing emphasis on individualism, growing pluralism (groups, organizations) and diversity of life styles, the "equity revolution", growing emphasis on quality of life (ecology, culture, education, Maslow's levels four and five), redefinition of work-leasure patterns, continued increase in foreign competition, growing and changing role of government, and continued urbanization.

An aggregate convergence score is then computed for each demand-hazard.

—The intensity-diffusion of pressure behind it. To what extent are 14 major constituencies/pressure groups[2] of the corporation likely to press for this demand? Each demand is ranked four, three, two, or one, according to whether it might be included in the top, second, third, or bottom quartile of each group's demands and interests. An aggregate intensity-diffusion score is then computed for each demand.

This third step makes it possible to plot each demand on a scoring sheet using the aggregate scores for convergence and intensity-diffusion. It may appear that we have become obsessed with quantification, but we recognize that this numerical scoring is only a means to the end. The important point is not the precise score assigned to each demand, but its final position in relation to the median score on both axes. In other words, our purpose is to identify and focus on those demands that fall in the high-high quadrant of the chart, scoring high on convergence with major trends and intensity-diffusion of pressure.

The fourth and fifth steps are then performed only on these high priority demands. (This is not to say that we can wholly ignore demands falling in the other three quadrants, only that they would, on current assessment, appear to have a lower order of social validity and ranking.) These two assessment steps deal with:

—The impact of these demands on the business community as a whole and on General Electric at both the corporate level and on the strategic business units, which are the operating components of the company.
—An inventory and evaluation of corporate responses to date to these demands.

So far the impact analysis has been done only on a rudimentary basis, assessing the high priority demands on a low- to high-impact scale. The evaluation of corporate responses is in process and is, in a sense, a never-ending task.

The outcome of this whole process should be at least an approximation to a set of corporate priorities on social pressure that should be factored into strategic planning and decision making. Based on the evaluation of corporate responses to date, it should also be possible to differentiate between those areas in which new initiatives are clearly called for and those

---

[2]The major costituencies are: consumer groups, shareowners, government, unions, blue-collar workers, managers and professional workers, small businesses, minorities, women, college youth, environmental groups, Populists, academic critics, and "moralists."

in which the main need is continuing audit and evaluation of existing responses.

Conclusion

In these remarks about some needed changes in the strategic planning process, my focus has been on changes needed to reflect social factors more adequately in decision making and on methodology, process, and system. Nothing that I have proposed will guarantee the development of a corporate social policy that all or most would consider adequate to the times: it will, however, make it more likely. There are a multitude of organizational imperatives to be faced if we are to prepare ourselves adequately to meet changing social needs. The reforms suggested here deal with only one of the facets of organizational complexity. They are quite necessary, though not sufficient, prerequisites.

The basic fact remains: If social responsibility factors and traditional business needs are ever to be considered on anything like an equal footing, they must be integrated at the stage of corporate planning that determines strategies, policies, and resource allocation.

Organizing the Company
for Social Action

●●●

● PHILLIP T. DROTNING
Director of Urban Affairs
Standard Oil Company (Indiana)

Since the mid-sixties, when the flames of Detroit and Newark and Watts became the hotfoot that stimulated increased corporate social concern, the larger corporations have undergone a gradual evolution of corporate social strategy. Corporate management in many companies has moved from the ignorance and desperation of 1965 and 1966, through a period of frustration and confusion, into a posture that is beginning to make sense as far as the future of American business and the nation are concerned.

Daniel Yankelovich has commented that it was probably unfortunate that corporate concern with its social responsibility began with the urban crisis.[1] He notes that out of their early experience with the urban problem businessmen formed a series of judgments:

> First, they came to regard the demands of the public sector as a moral issue of what business *ought* to do to be a good citizen rather than as a practical issue of what business had to do to survive and prosper in our society.
>
> Secondly, business executives, with some notable exceptions, came to regard activities with a social responsibility label as marginal to the day-to-day operations of the business.
>
> And third, they came to regard the question of what and how much to do as largely optional.

[1]Daniel Yankelovich, in an address commissioned by the National Association of Manufacturers, New York City, December 1971.

256

These conclusions are incorrect on all three counts. The claims of the public sector are practical as well as moral. They have everything to do with the day-to-day operations of any company. . . . Above all, the decision of whether or not to heed the demands of the public sector is becoming less optional all the time. The demands of the public sector are rapidly becoming translated into binding legislation by government, a precondition for winning the goodwill of the public, and an investment consideration by some institutional investors.

Two more elements of management judgment that dominated early corporate efforts in the social arena should be added. First, the problems were perceived as largely urban and racial. Second, they were often perceived as a public relations problem to which the response was largely rhetorical.

As a consequence of these attitudes, the initial efforts of most companies were simply an extension or adaptation of the traditional corporate community relations role. The only difference was that corporations discovered some new communities to relate to—communities in which the faces were black or brown, the language often Spanish, and some of the names quite colorful, like Broken Arrow or Running Deer.

Most corporate efforts were directed toward establishing communications with these minority communities, innovating highly visible public relations programs to give people hope that we were on the threshold of significant social change, and doling out money in support of new community organizations that sprang up in every corner of the urban ghetto.

What the corporations did then was to seek ways to spend money, but not too much, on social responsibility, largely in the hope that this action, combined with liberal doses of executive social rhetoric, would keep public criticism at a minimum.

Out of this experience, more sophisticated approaches to social responsibility have arisen. The senior executives of many major corporations have begun to identify a number of requirements for valid and effective corporate social involvement. They recognize that truly significant corporate involvement in social problem solving will require that management discover ways to make social responsibility profitable. The task of management, at all levels, is not to find ways to spend money on social responsibility, but to search for ways to make money through socially responsible behavior. Furthermore, it has become clear that many companies have failed in their efforts to become socially involved because their chief executives, in their haste, have overlooked the basic role of the corporation in a competitive, free-market economy.

A business organization is not, nor can it ever be, a nonprofit philanthropic organization. Yet, some chief executives have verbalized on public platforms social objectives for their companies that would, if implemented, lead to economic disaster for their shareholders. These rhetorical exercises, although they may have had some transitory public relations value, have led to false and unrealized expectations on the part of the public, and frustration and confusion within the corporate organization.

It should be instructive, in this context, that the most vocal critics of embryonic corporate social efforts—both conservative and liberal—appear to be in agreement on the primary corporate role: effective performance of its economic function within a competitive, capitalistic, free-market economic system.

In the performance of this function, the corporation allocates resources to the needs on which society places the highest value, provides jobs and income, supports through taxes the social programs of government, and through philanthropy the social programs and services that they want and need. The only significant dispute among critics centers around such issues as whether our competitive form of capitalism is really competitive, whether this traditional mission could not be conducted in more socially responsible ways, and whether, within the profit framework, there is not also room for some forms of social investment by the corporation that can be justified by enlightened self-interest or long-range economic concerns.

There is movement among some executives to renounce the historic knee-jerk opposition of business to all forms of government control and regulation, per se. Surfacing among some corporate leaders is a determination to evaluate proposed legislation and regulation on its merits rather than reject *all* government intervention in business activity. Some executives have even begun to urge that business advocate legislation that will, in effect, create what John Diebold has called "a free market for social responsibility," in which the dynamics of the marketplace will cause corporate resources to be brought to bear on social problems.

In addition, many executives have begun to recognize the inadequacy of past social input in the corporate planning and decision-making process. Corporate executives do have hearts, souls, and consciences in spite of what their critics believe. Because the executive knows he is human, and because his corporation is made up of other humans, the evidence of growing public outrage over "corporate social irresponsibility" and disaffection for American business has forced him to perceive that there has been inadequate provision within the corporate organization of the kind of data he needs to make socially responsible decisions. As this vacuum is identified, corporations are adding professional staff to fill it and restructuring their organizations not only to provide sociological input, but to insure that it will be brought to bear in the decision-making process.

Managements know the futility of corporate social efforts that are regarded by the organization as peripheral and philanthropic, and the need to involve the total organization by integrating social objectives into the operating structure of the company. It is with this aspect of the problem that the remainder of this article will deal.

Several generations of corporate history have demonstrated that any significant corporate activity must be locked into the mainstream of corporate operations or it doesn't get done. Social policies will remain placebos for the tortured executive conscience until they are implemented with the same iron-fisted management tools that are routinely employed in other areas of activity to measure performance, secure accountability, and distribute penalties and rewards.

Arjay Miller stressed this need earlier this year in an address before the White House Conference on the Industrial World Ahead:[2]

> I urge you to integrate social objectives into the basic fabric of your company, treating them just as you would any of your regular corporate activities. Although there is a role for a staff Director of Public Affairs or whatever else you might want to call him, the task of responding to new social needs must be accepted by all layers of management in all components throughout the entire organization. The general manager of a division or a subsidiary, for example, should feel the same responsibility for meeting established social objectives as he does for meeting profit objectives.
>
> This means that "reporting" and "scorekeeping" for both sets of objectives must be subject to the same internal accounting procedures. And of course, to be consistent, the reward system must be structured in such a way as to penalize a manager for failing to meet either kind of objective.

There are a number of reasons why this doctrine is crucial. First, a major roadblock in achieving social goals that are perceived as peripheral rather than integral elements of normal operations arises from the fact that in these days of lean corporate organizations most employees have too much to do. If an employee is held accountable for traditional corporate tasks whose performance will determine his success or failure, and is also urged to undertake social objectives on which his performance is not measured, the result is inevitable. Even the most well-intentioned employee will devote his time and attention to the functions on which his career progress depends.

A second consequence of failure to enforce social policies, although primarily psychological, is even more devastating. Anyone who serves time in

[2]Arjay Miller, an address, "Social Responsibility of Business," Washington, D.C., February 7, 1972.

any form of bureaucracy, including the corporate variety, soon learns that management communicates as much by what it doesn't do or say as by what it says and does. In fact, behavioral forms of communication are apt to have more credibility than spoken or written forms. Consequently, a policy that isn't enforced isn't believed.

Employees are quick to sense what is and is not of serious concern to management, and to arrive at the following syllogism: management enforces the policies about which it is serious; management doesn't enforce its social policies; therefore, management isn't really serious about its social policies. Since most managers are uncomfortable with, and may even be hostile to, many of the social programs advocated by top management, they are apt to grasp eagerly at such a rationale in order to avoid doing things they don't really want to do.

It may also be argued that accountability and performance measurement with respect to social goals are essential because they force management to test its own sincerity. Rhetoric is an inexhaustible resource that the chief executive officer can squander freely without noticeable impact on the bottom line. A great deal of it is dispensed in lieu of costlier action, and most employees know it. But the values change when the rhetoric is translated into action in line operations. Consequently, it is only after line and staff people have tested management's willingness to support social deeds with profit dollars that social policies achieve credibility.

At issue here is a fundamental conflict in the implementation of corporate social policies because of the difference in perception of profit objectives that exists between top management and the line organization. The senior corporate executives justify social policies and their associated costs on the basis of long-range profit potentials. Thus, current social expenditures are perceived as a long-term investment in maintaining or creating an environment in which future profits will be possible.

In practice, however, these long-range profit objectives are rarely reflected in current budgeting and accounting procedures, which remain geared to short-term profit objectives. The operating manager is restricted by annual sales or production goals that he is expected to reach within a predetermined operating budget. If he attains or exceeds the goals within his budget, the company will reach its profit objectives for the year, at least insofar as his segment of the total operation is concerned; his stature will be enhanced and he will be appropriately rewarded. If he fails to reach them, for whatever reason, his career will suffer.

Few companies have yet succeeded in resolving this conflict, or given much evidence that they want to do so. Management may assert, in the interest of long-term objectives, that it wishes to employ and train the hard-core unemployed, or utilize minority suppliers of goods and services, and that, if necessary, it is willing to accept some cost penalties in the process. However, the manager who seeks to implement such policies and misses his annual operating objectives as a consequence, is not apt to be commended for his adherence to the company's social policies. Instead, he more likely will be reprimanded for failing to meet his budgeted goals. It takes no more than one or two such experiences to convince managers that they had better ignore social objectives and concentrate on business as usual if they want to hold their jobs.

In practice, even those managements that are willing to sacrifice a reasonable amount of current profit in order to achieve long-term objectives would rather not do so. They hope that the staff and line organization will accept social objectives and achieve them by working harder and covering costs out of the excess that management suspects exists in every departmental budget. Consequently, management is reluctant to advertise its willingness to accept cost penalties or productivity losses because it believes that to do so would guarantee that such costs or losses would occur.

If management has really convinced the organization that it is serious, it may be possible to implement social policy without acknowledging a willingness to accept some cost penalties. However, in a tightly run organization, the managerial trauma produced by such a policy may be more costly than the benefits gained. Furthermore, the trauma is enhanced because members of the organization are asked to endure the ordeal in order to achieve objectives that violate principles that have been branded on their souls throughout their corporate experience.

In the past, for example, managers have been expected to hire the most qualified individual available for every job at the wage the company was willing to pay. When unemployment rates were high, this has often meant hiring someone who was overqualified for the job—a dangerous practice but an accepted one.

Now, suddenly, the manager is asked to adjust to a new situation in which he is asked to hire the *least* qualified, teach them to read and write, and tolerate tardiness. He is asked, in the name of social responsibility, to accept what he has been trained to consider personal irresponsibility, and to cover the loss in productivity by overworking others and distirbuting the costs within his existing budget. It is hardly surprising that he often resists.

A similar situation exists in the purchasing department, where the buyer has lived by the mandate that he buy the best possible product at the lowest possible cost from a firm with a superior reputation for delivery and service. In all likelihood, if the purchasing agent is white, he perceives minority suppliers as inexperienced, expensive, and unreliable. He is asked to risk abandoning a reliable white supplier in order to utilize one whom he believes may subject him to serious hazards.

The solution to these conflicts must be some sort of compromise that will salvage as much short-term profit as possible, yet get the long-term job done. It can be accomplished by setting firm goals and timetables on which performance will be measured, asking managers to budget the anticipated costs of achieving the goals, evaluating the cost estimates and modifying them as appropriate, and demanding that the goals be achieved within the budget.

It will be discerned that there is nothing innovative about this approach except its application to social objectives. This precise formula has been accepted corporate procedure in the achievement of traditional corporate goals. It has not been generally adopted in the achievement of social goals because top management, despite its uneasy conviction that it must be concerned with social problems, has continued to focus on traditional short-term profit objectives and views social needs with peripheral vision.

Until corporations begin to measure the individual social performance of their employees against stated objectives and within identified costs, there is no prospect that tools will be developed for measuring the adequacy and worth of the total corporate social performance. Without some form of social accounting that makes cost-benefit analysis possible, no company can make its maximum contribution in the social sphere. And unless corporations begin to make their maximum feasible contribution toward improving the environment in which they operate, their very right to operate may be challenged in the years ahead.

Equal employment opportunity (EEO) offers the classic example of a long-standing corporate social policy that progressed from rhetoric to reality only when management realized that it had been divorcing the problem from the corporate structure, rather than using the structure to solve the problem.

The history of EEO performance reveals quite clearly that the social performance of an individual corporation, like that of American business generally, is subject to what has been called "the tyranny of small decisions." A company's *policy* may be stated by the single individual at the top of the organizational pyramid, but its social behavior will be determined by countless subordinates in the individual decisions that they make from day to day. No single decision to discriminate will undermine corporate non-discrimination policy, but the composite of many such decisions will. Moreover, top management tolerance of noncompliance on the part of one manager will encourage it on the part of others. Most employees abhor the rigidity of the corporate bureaucracy and like to break rules if they know they can get away with it.

Many American corporations had formal nondiscrimination policies for as long as half a century before implementation of Executive Order 11246 and the subsequent requirement that federal contractors adopt affirmative action programs for the employment of minorities and women. In few companies, however, was their significant minority employment except at the most menial levels. The failure of companies to eliminate discrimination arose from their failure to enforce this policy with the determined techniques associated with other policies of the company. It was only when the government insisted that they institute goals, timetables, audit procedures, and performance measurement to encourage minority employment that significant progress began to occur.

Yet even with this demonstration that social objectives can be implemented through traditional corporate methodology, there was little effort to apply the principle in other areas of social action. That it can be applied elsewhere has again been demonstrated, however, by a few companies that have instituted the same affirmative action procedures with respect to use of minority suppliers of goods and services.

An example of one such pioneer program is that of American Oil Company, a Standard Oil (Indiana) subsidiary, which has been adopted as the model for a national program administered by the National Minority Purchasing Council, appointed in April by Secretary of Commerce Peter G. Peterson. The man who may be credited with the success of American Oil's Minority Purchasing Program is Blaine J. Yarrington, a shrewd, tough, pragmatic but thoughtful executive—one of the rare variety who not only senses that corporate survival may hinge on the ability of American business and industry to respond to valid public expectations, but that all of the most finely honed organizational and administrative tools must be employed to get the job done. In this he has the support of senior management in the parent company.

Perceiving that process, not friendly persuasion, was the key to implementing social goals, he first turned his attention to corporate performance in providing equal employment opportunity. He did not do so because his company was more laggard than most in its EEO programs, but because he recognized that provision of economic opportunities for minorities was the area in which American Oil could make its most direct and immediate social contribution.

Yarrington knew that he must act to convince the company organization that he was not merely giving lip service to EEO objectives; that he must demonstrate to the line organization that EEO was not solely the responsibility of staff people in the employee relations department, but that line managers would also be held responsible for EEO performance.

The new president achieved both objectives by looking to the company's traditional structure in achieving other goals. He took these specific actions:

—First, he advised his line vice-presidents that they would be held responsible for achieving adequate minority employment objectives in their respective departments.

—Second, he encouraged the inclusion of EEO objectives as a basis for distributing penalties or rewards.

—Third, he encouraged operating departments to establish fixed percentage objectives in hiring minority workers.

—Finally, Yarrington instructed that progress toward achievement of EEO goals be included routinely in the company's monthly control reports. These reports are of extreme importance to line managers, summarizing results in every area of primary concern to management. The inclusion of EEO data in these reports did more than distribute the data to a broad managerial audience: it told the organization that EEO had become a significant goal of top management, and it introduced a competitive element into the equation. Line managers do not like to have any element of their performance publicly judged as inferior to that of their peers.

Yarrington then turned to a second aspect of routine corporate activity in which a change in behavior would assist in developing the economic strength of the minority community—the increased use of minority suppliers of goods and services.

American Oil, for at least a decade, had been attempting to implement a minority purchasing program. However, it had been focused in the general office purchasing department, with no sharing of responsibility by the operating departments. Despite the designation of staff people to seek out minority suppliers, and even the use of an outside black consultant for this purpose, buyers insisted that they could not find qualified minority suppliers, and the program didn't work.

Yarrington turned things around, in his words, "by applying the same principles that made for effective programs in equal employment opportunity." He cites three such principles:[3]

First—It is not enough for top management to adopt a corporate policy. The line and staff organization must understand that management means what it says.

Second—The minority purchasing effort must not be perceived as a kind of extra-curricular social venture. It must be integrated into normal corporate operations.

[3]Blaine J. Yarrington, "Corporate Social Responsibility: Ritual or Reality," address to the International Assembly of Better Business Bureaus, Chicago, Ill., May 27, 1972.

Third—The search cannot be limited to suppliers who are qualified. The word instead is "qualifiable." Firms must be included that would not meet ordinary standards, but that can—with some assistance—become qualified as suppliers of goods and services.

Yarrington sensed that the critical question of the three, which was also supportive of the other two, was the credibility of top management. He notes:[4]

If a minority purchasing program is indeed to be cranked into the system, the men in the executive suite must do more than announce it by memorandum. Without communication—without follow-up—the program dies, and the blame cannot be put on middle management, whose members simply continue to perform as they have in the past—like good, profit-oriented managers. Minority purchasing becomes a front-office program and it doesn't get done.

What we have found to be effective is a form of affirmative action program, in which definite goals are established, together with timetables for their accomplishment—in which, individuals are held accountable for results—and in which performance in finding and developing minority suppliers is measured in the same way as every other aspect of an employee's job.

The ultimate responsibility for success rests with both the purchasing people and the line organization for which they work. Both were involved in the initial goal-setting function. It came as an encouraging surprise that when people in the organization were asked to set their own goals, these turned out to be higher than top management had expected. In addition, a number of locations have actually exceeded their own expectations.

Much of the reason for this, I believe, has been our constant attention to the second principle I mentioned: making the program a part of normal corporate operations. We repeated, again and again, the point that finding more minority suppliers was as much a part of everyone's job as meeting sales quotas or operating expense objectives. More than that, it was not to be accomplished at the expense of those other goals, but in conjunction with them.

As a consequence of this strategy, American Oil in 1971 set a goal of tripling its minority purchases, and far exceeded it. The number of minority suppliers utilized by the company increased from a handful to well over 100, and the number continues to grow. The company has provided substantial amounts of technical assistance to its minority suppliers, but few direct-cost penalties have been involved and most of these are being eliminated as the minority supplier gains experience.

I have emphasized the need for management to acknowledge its willingness to sacrifice some immediate profit in behalf of social action because it is crucial to the credibility within the company of top management's social

[4]*Ibid.*

rhetoric. However, most of the evidence that this author has been able to accumulate suggests that fears that corporate social action must impact adversely on profits are groundless, even in the short term. In fact, such fears may be no more than a rationalization of antisocial behavior by individuals in the company who don't want to do what top management wants them to do.

The social contribution of the American corporation will be proportionate to the ability of corporate society to find ways of making social responsibility profitable, and to use the corporate structure to solve the problem. The time has come to stop trying to rationalize the expenditure of profit dollars on charitable efforts, and turn the corporation to the search for ways to make money through socially responsible behavior.

Corporate management must therefore devote less attention to forecasting what society may do to the American corporation, and more attention to planning what the corporation can do for society and how to do it. As Russell Ackoff has said: "The thing to do with the future is not to forecast it, but to create it. The objective of planning should be to design a desirable future and to invent ways of bringing it about."[5]

[5]Russell Ackoff (Chairman, Department of Management Science, University of Pennsylvania), address for the American Association for the Advancement of Science, Philadelphia, Penn., December 1971.

Organizing for Corporate Social Responsibility

●●

● JOHN L. PALUSZEK

President
Corporate Social Action, Inc.,
New York City

Early in 1972, the Presidents' Association, composed of approximately 1200 chief executive officers and affiliated with the American Management Association, commissioned a study on the subject of organizing for corporate social responsibility. The study was to be focused, understandably, on the needs and interests of those presidents attempting to move their companies toward a greater commitment to social responsibility, and sought to tell these executives what others who had recently trod this path had experienced. The emphasis was internal—what must be done within the company to meet this new challenge.

The study was not conducted in accordance with the disciplines of social science. It was, instead, an informal, yet in-depth investigation of seven companies known to have made organizational commitments to social responsibility. Main sources of information were the chief executive officers and their corporate colleagues who establish and implement social responsibility policy at the companies selected. In most cases, the president provided the basic description of his company's goals, structure, and progress, while his colleagues supplied details. In all, five presidents, two executive vice-presidents, four senior vice-presidents, and six vice-presidents were interviewed.

Several sections of the report contain frame-of-reference material gath-

267

ered from a variety of other sources, including seminars and publications.

The result is a broad-brush survey of the current corporate responsibility landscape—what seven selected companies are doing internally to assign responsibility, to motivate employees, and to evaluate results—the inner workings, and the mechanics of corporate social responsibility.[1]

None of these companies is satisfied with its corporate social responsibility programs. Each one wants to be still more effective, still more successful, in attacking social problems. And, like most companies committed to such programs, each is willing to try all manner of relevant and responsible suggestions.

Chief Executive's Role

Some conclusions on the role of the chief executive officer in the social responsibility area were reached by presidents who have led their companies into aggressive social responsibility programs:

(1) The chief executive's commitment must be personal and total. Although the development and implementation of strategy and tactics must be delegated, the hand of the president must be constantly and conspicuously in the corporate-responsibility effort. As one president told us: "In the final analysis, I'm the 'Director of Corporate Responsibility' in our company."

(2) Corporate philanthropy in the traditional sense will not do the job. There must now be good business reasons for choosing areas of involvement and in developing program approaches. Recognition that such good business reasons for corporate social action do indeed exist is increasing on a number of corporate fronts.

(3) Corporate social responsibility can be viewed in the perspective of long-term profits. Prudent management has traditionally been willing to sacrifice some short-term earnings in order to strengthen the company's profit position a few years down the road. It must now be willing to make corporate social investment on the same basis.

(4) Social responsibility programs do not have to cut into short-term profitability. John R. Bunting, Chairman and Chief Executive Officer of First Pennsylvania Corporation and First Pennsylvania Bank, has noted: "We view these two considerations, profits and

[1]John Paluszek, *Organizing for Corporate Social Responsibility*, Special Study No. 51 (New York: President's Association, American Management Association, 1973).

social responsibility, so often portrayed as 'either/or', as anything but mutually exclusive. The much-touted 'corporate social responsibility' that refers to business's involvement in social issues is now popularly said to have a healthy and favorable effect on corporate profitability in *the long run*. . . . We do not disagree, but we also see the positive results of such policies in a context which is more immediate—*the short run*. And we think our operating results authenticate this belief."

(5) Management communicates more by deeds than words. If social policy is to be believed and implemented it must be enforced—as are traditional business objectives—with specific goals, timetables, accountability, performance measurement, penalties, and rewards.

(6) Social goals must be accorded status comparable to traditional corporate goals. Therefore, social goals must be quantified to the maximum extent possible. Corporate people speak arithmetic even more than they speak English.

In sum, presidents who have trod the corporate social responsibility path in recent years offer this composite map: First, make the personal commitment; then look around you and determine the unique set of circumstances —the environment—in which your company is doing business; assign responsibility to the best talent available, not just available talent; provide the needed resources; set clear policy; insist on accountability—specific goals, timetables, and measurement methods; and finally, communicate the commitment continuously throughout the organization and to other publics as well.

Corporate Structure

There are so many different approaches to structuring the corporation's social responsibility effort that only one generality seems supportable: The overriding, long-term objective is to have social responsibility policy and practice so permeate the line organization that it becomes standard operating procedure.

These executives (whose titles range from director of corporate responsibility to director of urban affairs, public affairs, or environmental affairs) are realistic and candid in appraising their mission. A composite expression of their views would be: "Our departments are simply a resource. We have been charged by management to support it in getting a particular kind of job done. But we don't relieve any line department of its responsibility. The bee is always on purchasing or manufacturing to do better. We can help with special data, with expert staff, and as a link to the rest of society. But in the last analysis, the department heads and their people will make social responsibility programs succeed or fail."

Each of the companies studied has evolved social action lines of authority particularly suited to its nature, its development history, and its current social interfaces. No two companies are exactly alike in this regard—nor should they be. However, I've chosen to include one example of a social responsibility organization chart—that of Standard Oil Company (Indiana) —for several reasons: (1) it is the most recent restructuring of such responsibility that I know of; (2) it reflects many months of analysis of how all corporate social responsibility functions should come together for regular top management review; and (3) it is as comprehensive an organization as any encountered during the study (see figure 1).

Managers of Corporate Social Responsibility Programs

Having made a commitment to move more aggressively on social responsibility programs, the chief executive officer must delegate responsibility to one or several executives. What kind of people are best suited for such responsibility?

The decisions of the presidents who have made such choices fall into no clear pattern, but they do offer insights into the value of several approaches.

At Equitable Life Assurance Society, John W. Riley, Jr., Senior Vice-president of Corporate Affairs, has been the hub around which much of the company's social responsibility activity has centered. Riley joined Equitable as Second Vice-president and Director of Social Research in 1960 after a distinguished career in the social sciences and education.

At Levi Strauss, Thomas E. Harris is Director of Community Affairs. He is another specialist recruited to manage key parts of that company's corporate responsibility program. Harris, who joined Levi Strauss in 1969 after a career in the field of community work, formerly spent 12 years working with Boys Clubs of America in the San Francisco area.

In establishing its Urban Affairs Department, First Pennsylvania Bank also went outside for a director and hired Elmer Young, Jr. as Vice-president, Urban Affairs. Young was formerly Administrative Assistant to Leon Sullivan, founder and chairman of Opportunities Industrialization Center

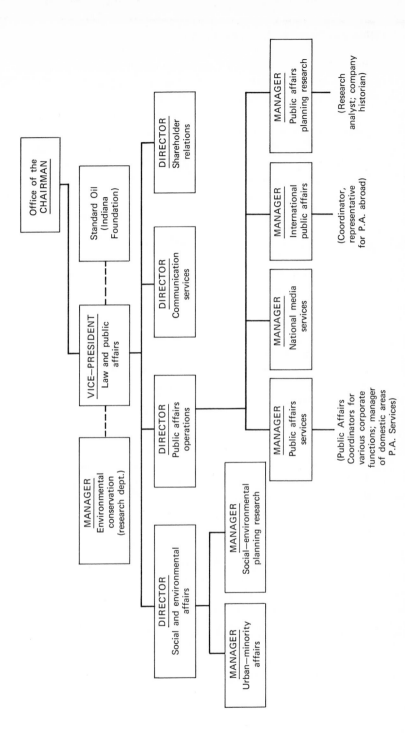

FIGURE 1. Corporate social responsibility at Standard Oil Company (Indiana).

where he developed and managed Progress Plaza Shopping Center in Philadelphia, the first black-owned shopping center in America.

By stark contrast, Bank of America decided to entrust its corporate responsibility department to a ranking member of its line organization. G. Robert Truex, Jr., Bank of America's Executive Vice-president, Social Responsibility, is a career banker who, prior to being named to the position, was Bank of America's senior credit officer in Southern California since 1968. Significantly, he was a member of the bank's managing committee at the time of his appointment to the social policy position.

Budgeting

On the basis of our study, corporations now seem to be getting down to business in handling the corporate social responsibility function. They are beginning to approach it the way they approach most other matters of running business. Within that general summary, there exist many procedural variations.

At Whirlpool Corporation, according to Whirlpool's Vice-president of Corporate & Public Affairs, Juel Ranum, budgeting for urban affairs develops this way: "We budget for this activity exactly the way we budget for other company functions. Our official budgeting procedure begins in September. Based on the experience we've had, we can pretty well identify the projects we want to undertake, develop or complete in the coming year. We identify the costs—in addition to our manpower—and we submit an itemized recommendtaion to the Whirlpool financial committee."

Thomas Harris at Levi Strauss describes his company's approach to budgeting this way: "An effective response by a company to social problems requires a pool of money that is predictable and not dependent on whim. This is essential if sound management practices are to be applied to the area of social responsibility. To this end, we have pledged a minimum of three percent of after-tax income." This pool, of course, is in addition to certain expenses that are absorbed in the normal course of Levi's business operations, *e.g.*, the cost of product integrity and equal opportunity hiring.

First Pennsylvania Bank looks at social responsibility still another way— somewhat like research and development expenditures. Therefore, in many cases, it initiates a corporate responsibility program by funding it out of corporate executive overhead. If the program succeeds and grows, it is absorbed into the operating structure with costs shared by the departments involved.

Corporate Social Accounting

Company presidents told us that they would look for two basic types of information from a social audit:

(1) How well are we doing socially? In relation to our potential, in relation to other companies in our industry, in relation to business generally, and in relation to what is being asked/demanded of us? If a financial audit seeks to establish a company's financial health, it seems reasonable, these presidents say, that a social audit should attempt to provide a parallel analysis in the social area.

(2) What do our social responsibility programs cost and what benefits do the company and society derive from them? Quantifying the costs of social responsibility programs, in general terms, is arduous—but possible. Quantifying the benefits, as Professor Bauer has indicated, is a mighty perilous activity.[2]

Corporate social accounting is still evolving and may continue to evolve for quite some time. But during our study, as we dwelt on the president's social audit needs, several basic steps for social responsibility review emerged. The first three steps can be said to fall under the basic category of, where are we now?:

(1) Introspection. It's worth considering the specific nature and status of the company being analyzed: its products or services, its locations, its specific interfaces with the public, its financial and commercial health.

(2) Inventory of social responsibility programs—a comprehensive list of such programs already in operation in the company.

(3) Cost estimate. Management should be given as accurate an idea as possible of the cost of the program on the social responsibility inventory list. Presidents know that the cost estimate isn't going to be perfect; there are a number of elements in such programs that can't be costed precisely. Generally, they accept Bauer's advice to at least get the out-of-pocket costs and 'do your best' in getting the other costs.[3]

You now know what the company is doing about what it costs. The next fundamental question is, Where should we be going?

---

[2]Raymond A. Bauer and Dan H. Fenn, Jr., *Corporate Social Audit* (New York: Russell Sage Foundation, 1972).

[3]*Ibid.*

Three additional steps should bring you a long way toward answering that question:

(4) Development of the comprehensive program. With your inventory of social programs close at hand, focus on two very fundamental questions: Is the company conducting its business in as socially responsible a manner as possible? Apply that question against the company's major interfaces with the public—stockholder relations, customer relations, community relations, environmental affairs, etc. Obviously, within each of these basic interface zones, there are a number of specific activities to be examined. Can the company's resources and special competencies be applied productively to selected social problems without damage to its basic financial and commercial position? Here a checklist of current social problems should be scrutinized to see whether the company can extend itself further into society productively. Certainly, the company's contributions program is one resource that can be applied in this area. There may well be others.

Now, whether you've added no special responsibility programs or a dozen new programs to the original inventory list, that inventory list must be scanned once again to be sure that each program on the new list has goals, schedules, budgets, and evaluation methods, and that the entire list is arranged in terms of priorities.

(5) Review corporate responsibility structure. There's a slew of points to be covered in this step. Among the most important are these: Who has the responsibility to make each program work? And what is top management doing to motivate employees—especially middle management—to help make these programs successful?

(6) All five of these steps represent the company reflecting on itself. Obviously, that isn't sufficient. So the sixth and final step in the social responsibility review is an outward step—an attempt to get an evaluation of how the company's attempts to fulfill its social obligations are perceived by its major publics.

Most presidents are now aware that "major publics" no longer include only those most directly involved with the company—its investors, employees, and customers. It's most important that the company knows how activist groups feel about it, and legislators and regulators, and minority-group organizations and college students as well.

Obviously, these six steps should be repeated on a regular basis—perhaps annually—to provide a continuous monitoring of the company's social responsibility performance. The first time the effort will be quite substantial; subsequent reevaluations are far less time and resource consuming.

Communications Vehicles

John F. Kennedy is said to have remarked that the one thing a leader cannot afford is to look back over his shoulder and find that no one is following him. On the other hand, I recently saw a worthwhile piece of management philosophy framed and hanging near an executive's desk. It said: "I must hurry. They have gone, and I am their leader."

The employee, of course, is the key to success for many corporate responsibility programs. Recognizing this, companies seeking to move forward aggressively in the social responsibility area have used a wide variety of communications vehicles—some traditional, some highly innovative.

American Oil Company, a subsidiary of Standard Oil Company of Indiana, took a long stride in convincing employees that its equal employment opportunity commitment was genuine by including department EEO analyses in the company's 'monthly control reports.' These reports are the bible for line managers because they summarize results in every area of prime concern for management. The inclusion of EEO data not only distributed the information broadly but also communicated the fact that EEO had become a significant top goal of management. And it introduced an element of healthy competition among line managers.

Whirlpool Corporation has used a variety of employee communications vehicles to indicate quite clearly that employee performance in corporate social responsibility areas is being measured in the same way as all other aspects of job performance.

Employee publications are an example of existing corporate communications vehicles that can be used to convey management commitments and company progress toward social responsibility goals. The subject can be communicated on a continuing basis or in special editions—such as First Pennsylvania Bank's "Enterprise" edition of its house organ last winter.

Top management policy statements on the subject of a company's overall social responsibility commitment or individual aspects of that commitment have been distributed by many companies. Their effectiveness is normally in direct ratio to the clarity of expression of top management's abiding interest in the subject.

Equitable has conducted middle management rap sessions to sensitize supervisors to the need for further progress in equal employment opportunity and to anticipated problems in managing a changing labor force.

In some cases, special employee communications vehicles must be designed. Levi Strauss now publishes a special periodical for its community relations teams around the country, called *Community Affairs Bulletin*, which serves an as effective clearinghouse for community relations ideas and activities as well as providing information on the company and Levi Strauss Foundation activity.

Atlantic Richfield has used a traveling production of a play, "The Man Nobody Saw," to build employee support for its equal employment opportunity affirmative action program. The play, written and produced by the Family Service Association of America's "Plays for Living" Division, has been shown to some 50 Atlantic Richfield management meetings across the country. The company's affirmative action plan has also been effectively communicated to employees via a film of a recent address by Atlantic Richfield President T. F. Bradshaw, outlining his equal employment opportunity objectives for the company, and a mailing of a special brochure on the company's affirmative action plan to the homes of all employees.

Communications with other corporate audiences can hardly be neglected if the company's efforts are to be widely recognized and appreciated. In this regard, the annual report has been used by a large number of companies to convey social responsibility commitment and progress to investors and potential investors. But few have approached Bank of America's 1970 annual report, which devoted its first 15 pages to an analysis of social issues and the bank's role in helping to resolve some of them.

How about effective corporate communications with the minority community? "Point of View," a column written regularly by First Pennsylvania's Vice-president, Elmer Young, Jr., in the *Philadelphia Tribune*, a black biweekly, is an excellent example of creating bridges between the corporation and minorities. Young, who offers readers financial management counsel and broad economic advice makes a real contribution to his audience while representing the bank in admirable fashion.

Data: New Types, New Importance

"We don't like surprises." That's how one president sums up the current corporate emphasis on gathering and analyzing sociological information. In recent years, a number of companies have developed special antennae in order not to be surprised. Similarly, industry associations have set up data clearinghouse for their members.

Basically, these capabilities are designed to inform their sponsors of:

(1) Society's likely overall development in the years and decades immediately ahead.

(2) The emergence of specific significant socioeconomic trends.

(3) Social action taking place within the business community generally and within a specific industry.

(4) And, in larger companies, successful local or regional socially oriented projects that might be applicable to other parts of the organization.

John W. Riley, Jr., of Equitable, now maintain a social research section composed of three professionals to keep him and Equitable management abreast of all such developments. When special in-depth analysis of social data is required, Equitable often contracts for university research.

Beyond the Company: Participation in Industry Associations, Business Consortia; Liaison with Government

Like it or not, there comes a time when the company, acting individually, just can't cope with a social problem. Generally, a company can have great impact on social responsibility problems that are totally within its organization. But when it seeks to grapple with some of the basic social problems of this age—which impact on it—it should consider looking for help.

Many businessmen have, of course, been doing this for years. They've banded together within an industry or across industry lines to attack special social problems. Some of the more outstanding recent accomplishments of industry associations include the channeling of some $2 billion worth of life insurance industry investments into urban development and rehabilitation projects across the country, and the commitment by the nation's commercial banks of $1 billion for financing minority-owned businesses.

Business consortia across industry lines—especially on a local basis—can also be a powerful instrument for progressive social change. Whirlpool Corporation learned this when it led in the establishment of the Benton Harbor (Michigan) Area Resources Improvement Council after the disastrous riots in the Whirlpool headquarters city in the late 1960's. The council, composed of 30 high-level executives from major companies in the community, mounted a successful broad-based program to improve the area's educational system and lower its employment rate significantly.

The urban affairs director of one of the companies expected to participate in another consortium defends such participation this way: "We have a great stake in this city. In it we must find a good number of people willing and able to be our employees and a far greater number ready to buy our products. If as a company we make investments to develop natural resources for our manufacturing operations, shouldn't we make investments in 'growing' good employees and 'growing' good customers?"

Conclusions

Our study goes into considerable detail on how companies have plunged into the deep and often complex day-to-day matters of launching and maintaining a wide variety of social responsibility programs, including equal employment opportunity affirmative action programs, environmental affairs, minority purchasing, support to education and the arts, consumer relations, and urban affairs.

I would conclude as I began by addressing my student readers. Make no mistake. The business world you will be entering is far different than the one I did in the mid-1950's. In terms of social commitment, it's far different from that of even the mid-1960's. Even if you feel that today's business efforts to help solve social problems are incomplete, ineffective—even clumsy—recognize them for what they are: genuine commitments.

If I were finishing by studies and considering a career in business, I would find such commitments encouraging. I would consider quite carefully how my training and my interests might best be applied to improve such efforts, and I would be sure to be ready to play a role in this new era of American business.

An Integrated Communications Model of Corporate Adaptation to Social Uncertainty

●●●

● REBECCA A. GOULD

School of Business Administration
The Pennsylvania State University

● EUGENE J. KELLEY

School of Business Administration
The Pennsylvania State University

How are corporations perceiving and adapting to messages from the social environment? How is the firm communicating its adaptations to the various segments of the social system? What weaknesses exist in current social communications programs? These questions are discussed, and elements of a communications model are presented in this paper.

Such issues as the need for a new concept of corporate responsibility of business are not examined. The area is discussed in current business literature. This paper includes selected references on this subject.[1] Examples refer principally to large corporations, but the material presented is applicable to smaller corporations, particularly those firms in a position of high social visibility.

[1]M. Anshen, "Changing the Social Contract: A Role for Business," *Columbia Journal of World Business* 5 (November-December 1970): 6–14; O. A. Bremer, "Is Business the Source

279

Uncertainty and Adaptation

Sources of Uncertainty

Management traditionally has faced two major sources of uncertainty: product or technological uncertanity, and market uncertainty. A new topic or source of uncertainty, social uncertanity, has emerged in recent business experiences with the external environment. Social uncertanity evolves from the relative success of our economic system, and affects the family, community, government, educational processes, and the corporation. We contend that this social uncertanity will be a powerful and challenging force affecting business policies and decision making in the immediate future.

Social uncertanity has been given many labels in the last decade. It has been called social unrest, changing social values, a rejection of traditional values, concern for the quality of life, or simply a growing social involvement. While social uncertanity may technically be considered a part of market uncertanity, we believe it to be so large and so separate from the traditional concept of market uncertanity that it warrants a separate category.

This is not to suggest that social uncertainty represents revolutionary change for business. Foote presented an interesting perspective when he pointed out that many of the change agents of today—youth, minority, women, and consumers, etc.—"while demanding change in the life style of this country, are not demanding change in value, but are in fact reasserting

---

of New Social Values?" *Harvard Business Review* 49 (November-December 1971): 121–126; M. N. Browne and P. F. Haas, "Social Responsibility and Market Performance," *M.S.U. Business Topics* 19 (Fall 1971): 7–10; A. Z. Carr, "Can an Executive Afford a Conscience?" *Harvard Business Review* 48 (July-August 1970): 58–64; Committee for Economic Development, *Social Responsibilities of Business Corporations* (New York); Daniel Yankelovich, Inc., "Corporate Priorities: A Continuing Study of the New Demands on Business" (Stamford, Conn.: 1972); L. M. Dawson, "The Human Concept: New Philosophy for Business," *Business Horizons* 12 (December 1969): 29–38; A. O. Elbing, Jr., "The Value Issue of Business: The Responsibility of the Businessman," *Academy of Management Journal* 13 (March 1970): 79–89; H. Henderson, "Should Business Tackle Society's Problems?" *Harvard Business Review* 46 (July-August 1968): 77–85; H. Henderson, "Toward Managing Social Conflict," *Harvard Business Review* 49 (May-June, 1971): 82–90; A. Mitchell, "Changing Values and the Marketplace," presented at the American Marketing Association's 54th International Marketing Congress, New York City, April 13, 1971; D. Yankelovich, "The New Odds," presented at the 11th Annual Marketing Strategy Conference of the Sales Executives Club of New York, October 11, 1971.

values traditionally honored in our society—equality, honesty, professional ethics, personal fulfillment."[2]

The significant point is not whether these changes are new or merely reassertions. It is, as Foote and other critics have put it, that the changes will have "profound effects on marketing and the conduct of business generally."[3] Ultimately, these changes will pervade every aspect of current business practice.

One way to conceptualize social uncertainty is to consider the public's acceptance of economic success and an emerging concern for social achievement. This concern for social achievement involves improvements in such areas as: personal and environmental health; public and environmental safety; basic schooling and higher education; skills and jobs; amount, adequacy, and continuity of income; housing; quality of the neighborhood; access to the neighborhood; recreational opportunities; quality of the larger environment; the arts and sciences; nature and beauty; interrelationships between economic growth and the use of discretionary time; concerns with liberty and democratic values; and quality of the social environment. These areas are generally identified as national social goals; they have received much coverage and study in the last few years.[4]

Social uncertainty is communicated to the rest of society, including business firms, through messages from the external environment. These messages may be in the form of civil disturbances, social criticism, legislation, or media criticism. Each firm must decide, either by policy changes or by default, if and how it will adapt to a particular message or series of messages from the environment.

[2] "Join the Activists, Don't Fight Them, Marketers Are Advised," *Industrial Week* 171 (November 1, 1971): 8–10.

[3] *Ibid.*

[4] R. A. Bauer, ed., *Social Indicators* (Cambridge: M.I.T. Press), 1966; H. Henderson, "Value Systems in Conflict: Economists vs. Ecology," presented at the Annual Meeting of the National Association of Business Economists, Pittsburgh, Penn., September 28, 1971; K. C. Land, "On the Definition of Social Indicators," *The American Sociologist* 6 (November 1971): 322–325; H. C. Lipson; E. J. Kelley; and S. Marshak, "Integrating Social Feedback and Social Audits into Corporate Planning," Working Series in Marketing Research, Pennsylvania State University, University Park, Penn., April 12, 1972); R. S. Raymond and E. Richards, "Social Indicators and Business Decision," *M.S.U. Business Topics* 19 (Fall 1971): 42–46; N. E. Terleckyj, "Measuring Possibilities of Social Change," *Looking Ahead* (1970): 1–11; U.S. Department of Health, Education and Welfare, *Toward A Social Report* (Washington, D.C.: Government Printing Office, 1969).

Adaptation

A system oriented to adaptation is concerned with significant changes in three areas: the functions and/or structure of the organization; the relationship between these factors; and the interdependencies between these factors and the total organizational system. An adaptation-oriented system is also concerned with future growth possibilities within the system due to the creation or deletion of new and different parts, relationships, and interdependencies.

There are two major types of adaptation. The first, "symbolic adaptation," concerns the anticipation of problems and the development of solutions to these problems. That is, symbolic adaptation concerns the conceptual understanding of the problem and the design of a plan to meet this problem. The second, "behavioral adaptation," concerns the operational aspects of these solutions within the firm. That is, behavioral adaptation is the active implementation and acceptance of the solution designed in the symbolic adaptation phase.

To illustrate this difference, consider a manager who has come to the conclusion that his subordinates should participate more actively in decision making. His decision and announcement of it could be considered symbolic adaptation. If, however, he either ignores their inputs or does not involve the subordinates in any way, he has not achieved behavioral adaptation.

The essence of corporate adaptation strategy is the development of corporate capabilities and policies to anticipate social uncertainty. To anticipate social uncertainty, the firm must be able effectively to utilize two-way communications channels between the firm and the community, the consumer, other firms, and members of the firm. These channels provide necessary information inputs into corporate decision making. They provide the firm with insights into the second- and third-level consequences of their operations and products, what problems exist in their environment, some of the causes of these problems, what has to be done to solve them, and the corporate relationship to each of these points.

For example, General Motors has been criticized severely on the ground that it did not do any basic thinking about the social impact of GM policies and products. It consistently underestimated social uncertainty communicated through such vehicles as Campaign GM and Ralph Nader. General Motors under its new chairman, Richard C. Gerstenberg, has decided to establish its credentials as a socially concerned company. One recent move encouraged by their broad-level public policy committee is the decision to add more socially oriented issues to their long-range planning group's topics. It will involve the hiring of behavioral scientists, economists, and technologists to anticipate social uncertainty. Research will be conducted not only in transportation fields, "but also in urban planning, bio-medicine, and the behavioral sciences."[5]

Corporate Adaptations: Current Responses

Each firm selects its own pattern of adaptation to messages caused by social uncertainty. By studying the adaptations of various firms, we have identified six major categories of corporate response to messages from the environment. These categories can be considered either as symbolic adaptation or behavioral adaptation responses. The first stage in studying these various forms of adaptation by a firm is to look at what stimulated these changes. Then each type or category of adaptation is evaluated. Following this, the communication of the adaptation back to the environment is considered.

Symbolic Adaptation

One of the first types of messages sent to corporate America during the 1960's was civil disturbances and protests. These disturbances took various forms; student demonstrations, civil rights demonstrations, and war protests were some of the more common. While these messages were not actually directed at the corporation, they were directed at the institutions and practices that the corporate system symbolized or supported. Depending on the proximity of the demonstrations to the corporation, and whether management perceived the disturbance to be directed wholly or in part at it, response took one of two general forms if it occurred at all. Both of these responses aimed at an initial identification of the problem area, and the corporation's relationship to the problem.

Response by Rhetoric. The first type of adaptation is response by rhetoric. In this form, the firm perceives a message from the environment and then transmits its response back to the environment with little, if any, actual programs adopted to combat the cause or source of the communication. The firm's response back to the environment is through speeches, through corporate policy statements, and through public relations releases.

Response by rhetoric is a first step in the firm's recognition of social un-

---

[5]"Better Late than Never," *Forbes* 110 (September 1, 1972), p. 30.

certainty. The rhetoric has the merit of focusing the attention and aware-ness of the organization on the problem area. However, there has been so much of this rhetoric with such limited behavioral response that the term "credibility gap" is often employed to describe this adaptation. It is essen-tial to recognize that this credibility gap does exist particularly among the young, minorities, and intellectuals. Moskowitz cites several examples of this response by rhetoric situation.[6]

Ad Hoc Committees. A second type of adaptation to this first series of messages is the formation of *ad hoc* committees to study the questions raised by the civil disturbances, or to study the larger issue of community or social problems, and the relationship of the corporation to these problems.

Organizational Change. An additional type of symbolic adaptation may be stimulated by changes in the messages. If these messages are aimed more directly at the firm, if they become more frequent or stronger, or if man-agement perceives them to be more important, the firm may adapt by in-stituting organizational changes. These organizational changes may be of two major types.

The first of these is appointment of an executive to direct corporate ac-tions for part or all of the corporate social program. The areas of concern this executive deals with depend in part on the content of the messages from the social environment. To illustrate, if these messages are concerned with consumer issues, an executive or consumer ombudsman may be ap-pointed to deal with these issues, such as the appointment of Esther Peter-son as consumer ombudsman at Giant Foods. This adaptation is generally relayed back to the environment through public relations releases announc-ing the appointment, or through the annual report of the corporation.

The second type of organizational change is the appointment of a com-mittee for social affairs, generally composed of senior level executives or board members, to direct or advise the company's social or public pro-grams. Depending on the authority given these committees to implement their programs, they may or may not be effective. General Motors has re-cently formed a public policy committee consisting of five outside directors. The Bank of America has both a social policy committee composed of senior officers and a board-level public policy committee.

These last two reactions are classified as symbolic adaptation. Announc-ing the appointment of an executive or the formation of a committee does not necessarily mean that attitudes and practice have changed within the

---

[6]M. Moskowitz, "Conscientious Corporations: A Record," *Sloan Management Review* 13 (Fall, 1971): 25–30.

membership of the firm. Top management announcement of certain appointments does not mean members of the firm exhibit the same concern for these problem areas, or that members will become more responsive to social uncertainty, or that consideration of this uncertainty will be present in decision making. It only means that the firm has recognized this uncertainty and is attempting to find a solution, not that it has implemented this solution.

Behavioral Adaptation

Once a firm begins implementing programs to meet the social uncertainty it faces, behavioral adaptation is reached. There are three main types of corporate adaptations in this area. They include corporate programs, cooperative industry programs, and individual contributions by members of the firm.

Corporate Programs. Corporate programs are those programs sponsored by a single corporation. They can be divided into those which are consumer oriented and those which are community oriented.

The first of these subdivisions may technically be considered a part of market uncertainty. However, consumerism and the new consumer demands of this decade are not parts of the traditional market uncertainty a firm faces. Rather, they are an outgrowth of our economic success and relative affluence. Both of these cause the consumer to look for more from the corporation in terms of service, product policies, manufacturing policies, and even who the other customers of the firm are. These programs can thus be considered a reaction to the consumerism facet of social uncertainty.

Message sources stimulating consumer-oriented programs are varied. Four major types of these sources are: individual activity; group activity; government and legal activity; and competition and industry practices. Individual activity is evidenced principally through attacks by consumer advocates. These attacks draw public attention to those actions perceived as injustices by the advocates. Group activity, or collective actions of individual consumers, in its strongest forms consist of consumer boycotts and consumer class suits. Government and legal activities have many sides, including governmental regulation and pressure from governmental agencies and consumer affairs offices. Competitor- and industry-inspired practices are those programs implemented by a firm to maintain its market position.

Consumer-oriented programs are somewhat varied. One of the more common types of programs includes some form of a consumer hotline to corporate headquarters. One of the first to adopt this communications link with its consumers was Whirlpool. Travelers Insurance, Chrysler, Ford, and General Motors have followed Whirlpool's lead and added consumer hotlines. This program varies from a rather simple addition to the corporate structure, as the above, to a reorganization as exemplified by Ford's new customer service division with offices across the country.

The corporation generally communicates its adaptations to these consumerism-related messages by mass media advertising. Caution should be exercised when using mass media advertisements to relay corporate adaptations to the consumer. This is due to the tendency by various publics to mistrust corporate advertisements extolling corporate good that is paid for by corporate money. This problem is similar to that faced by the firm when communicating in a response-by-rhetoric situation.

Community-oriented corporate programs are generally designed to meet specific demands of members of the community against the firm. These demands or messages are generally communicated through civil disturbances such as pickets or boycotts directed against the firm, stock fights at annual meetings as shown by Campaign GM, or charges made through the media. Depending on whether the firm believes the changes are justified, certain programs may be implemented. For example, Levi Strauss would not locate any plants in the South until it was assured that there would be no segregation of employees. Other examples may include special minority hiring programs, job upgrading, or enrichment classes. These adoptations are generally communicated to the social system through press releases, hiring or other internal policies, or annual reports.

Cooperative Industry Programs. A second type of behavioral adaptation response is that of cooperative industry programs. These programs are inherently commendable because of the industry cooperation and pooling of resources and talents. However, this cooperation may subject the participating companies to criticism if the firms are only participating for public relations purposes, or if the programs are poorly planned.

Two principal types of cooperative programs can be identified: inter-industry programs and intra-industry programs. The first subdivision, inter-industry cooperative programs, are those programs in which several firms within a particular region pool resources to provide a service to the community. For example, in Los Angeles in 1968, IBM, Bank of America, and the Greater Los Angeles Urban League began operating a data processing training center for disadvantaged residents.

The second subdivision, intra-industry cooperative programs, are programs in which members of a specific industry cooperate to achieve a particular end. In New Jersey, the insurance industry and the state insurance commissioner's office are jointly sponsoring a minority employment scholarship program. This program, financed by donations from the industry, is designed to provide the necessary education for entry into management-level positions by minority group members.

These programs are communicated to the environment in various ways. Announcement may be made of the programs through public-relations-type messages. The programs could be included in general advertisements of the participating corporations or in specific advertisements sponsored by the participating corporations. Or, these programs could be communicated only to those segments for whom the corporations are providing the programs.

Individual Contributions. The final category of adaptation is that of individual contributions by members of the firm. This could perhaps be considered the pinnacle of achievement or involvement by a firm in the social area. We say this because it signifies that the individual has accepted corporate involvement, and, perhaps, has undergone an attitude change to increase his own participation in this area.

Individual contributions can be employee initiated or firm initiated, and can be during the firm's time or during the individual's free time. To conceptualize these alternatives, we have made a cross-classification in a grid form.

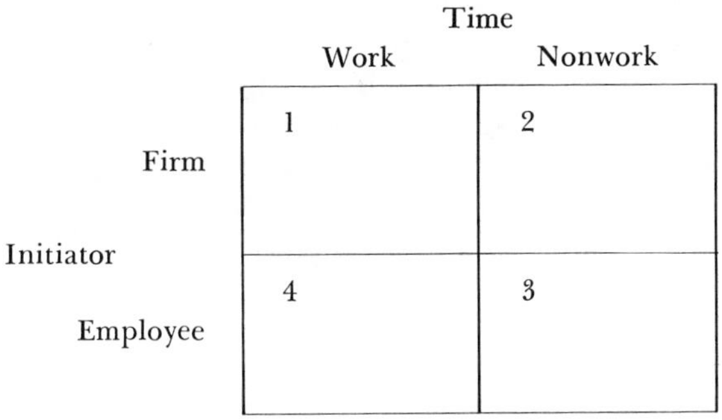

FIGURE 1.

Projects found in area 1 are generally those in which the firm loans personnel for particular projects. These projects are worked on during the firm's time; they may be in response to an unexpected, natural disaster, or simply be a commitment by the firm.

Projects in area 2 are those in which the firm encourages the employee to participate during his free time, such as in local government or service organizations.

Area 3 is perhaps the response that encourages the firm to become involved or more involved. These are the projects that are employee initiated and done during the employee's free time. Projects may include leading teaching or training classes, or working with volunteer agencies.

Area 4 is the one that we consider to be the pinnacle of corporate involvement. These projects are employee initiated and done during the corporation's time. A leading example of this is Xerox's sabbatical program. In this program, employees are eligible to participate in projects of their own choosing for up to 12 months with full pay. Participants' projects must be approved by an evaluation committee, but need not be related to the employee's job specialty.

The most typical way to communicate these contributions by firm members is through announcements of the public relations type or press briefings to explain the concept of the program and what is being done by those participating in the program. These messages are usually picked up by trade journals and may also be covered by the local media.

Weaknesses in the Communications of Present Adaptations

Six types of adaptations by corporations in response to messages of social uncertainty were identified in the previous section of this paper. Each adaptation should, in turn, be communicated back to the environment. The more common means now used include speeches, public relations releases, press conferences, advertisements, and annual reports. Each of these communications methods has various weaknesses. These weaknesses must be recognized by the firm and met in the design of an integrated social communications program.

Corporate Attitudes

One of the first weaknesses in the current communications methods used is the attitude of the firm sending these communications. Many firms still have not accepted the changes in the expectations of the American people: expectations for increased corporate awareness of the second- and third-level consequences of its operations and products, and expectations for assistance in solving or helping to solve the social problems and issues facing the nation. Because of a lack of understanding and acceptance of these changing expectations, some firms believe that any action taken for other than a profit motive, either short or long run, is merely a charitable or optional action on their part. They may also believe that, because of these actions, praise is warranted; they do not understand that these actions are perceived as part of corporate responsibility by many groups, and that the actions may also be considered to be long overdue.

Receiver Mistrust

A second weakness of these messages is mistrust of the communication by the reciever. This mistrust is due to the content of the message, the medium used to transmit the message, or the sender of the message.

Mistrust due to the content of the message is a result of past mistakes or miscommunications the firm has made. These mistakes may include false or inaccurate reporting on the firm's actions or products, reporting on or announcing programs or opportunities with little or no followthrough of the programs, or announcing programs or opportunities with so many restrictions that the people they were designed to help cannot qualify. Receivers may also not believe the message content because of past product messages from firms. Receiver mistrust may also result from the message medium used. The various publics the firm is trying to reach may simply distrust the medium because of messages other firms have sent in it. This mistrust is closely related to mistrust resulting from message content. The third cause of receiver mistrust is rejection of the message sender, the firm. This mistrust or rejection may be due to cynical attitudes toward corporate motives. Or, it may be due to nonsupport of the economic system leading to the desire for different economic or social objectives. Or, it may be due to a difference in values between sender and receiver leading to a lack of common understanding between these two groups.

Lack of Integration

The lack of integration in reporting the adaptations to social uncertainty is a third weakness in current communications efforts. Some adaptations are reported in one or few media, such as press releases or advertisements; others may only be reported in annual reports or not at all. The variety of methods used to report these adaptations typically presents an inaccurate and, at times, incomplete picture of corporate adaptations to the various publics the firm is attempting to reach.

Need for Objectivity

A fourth problem in the area of communications is a lack of objectivity in messages or reports of adaptations currently being sent by the firm. This lack of objectivity may be real or only perceived by the receivers of the message. This perceived lack of objectivity may be present because the firm is the source of the message; receivers may believe that the firm is reluctant to present an unfavorable picture of itself and its social adaptations.

This need for objectivity may also be perceived by the message receivers because current communications generally report only the successes, with little or no mention of failures or program delections, and with little, if any, discussion of the causes or stimulation of the adaptations.

Elements of a Communications Model

The communications model in figure 2 conceptualizes the interchange of communications between the social system and the business subsystem. The first stage in this model is the encoding of messages of social uncertainty by the social system. These messages are then sent to the firm subject to various noise or distortion factors. In the next stage, the firm must decode and evaluate these messages.

During evaluation, the firm decides whether or not to respond to these messages. If the decision is not to respond, no further progress is made in the model. If the firm does decide to respond, some type of adaptive action, either symbolic or behavioral, takes place.

At this point the firm may either stop or continue. If it continues, the firm encodes some form of message to describe what adaptive actions it has taken. These messages then proceed through various noise and distortion factors to the receiver, the social system.

The social system must then decode and evaluate these messages. It, too, has the option of stopping the process here or continuing its messages to the firm.

Action Guidelines

The firm should follow three principal guidelines when designing and transmitting its social communications. The first of these guidelines is an integrated, total social performance report. This total social performance report should include discussion of both the successes and failures of the firm's social adaptations. It should also include a discussion of what problems the firm feels it faces, why these areas are recognized as problems, how the firm identified these problems, and in what manner the firm defines its relationship with these problems. This total social performances report should include this information in order for the social system to under-

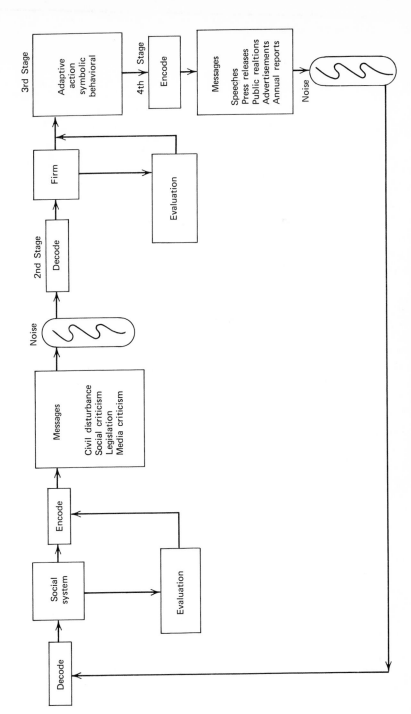

FIGURE 2. A communications model.

stand where and how the firm views itself in relation to the social uncertainty it faces.

A second guideline concerns objectivity in the preparation of this report. To help provide objectivity in the total social performance report, some of the report preparers should be nonaffiliated with the firm. The objectivity desired would only be hurt if this group were all pro or all antibusiness, or all from one special interest group. One way to obtain an independent group would be to have representatives from each of the population segments in the area, or from the various interest groups, or some combination of the two.

A third guideline is the need for honesty on the part of the firm. This honesty is necessary in assessing the problem and the relationship of the firm to it, in determining what adaptive action to take, and in communicating this action to the social system.

In summary, we have presented a model to describe exchanges between the social system and the business subsystem stimulating adaptive actions by the business subsystem. These actions, while not typical of the entire business subsystem, have been taken by certain members of this subsystem in response to a new and growing type of uncertainty, social uncertainty. Six classes of adaptations were presented: response by rhetoric, *ad hoc* committees, organizational change, corporate programs, cooperative industry programs, and individual contributions.

These actions are then, ideally, encoded and communicated to the various segments of the social system in a comprehensive, integrative, objective social communications program.

The Performance Context of Corporate Responsibility

●●●

● GEORGE P. HINCKLEY
Vice-President of Marketing Services
Travelers Insurance Companies

● JAMES E. POST
Graduate School of Management
State University of New York, Buffalo

I

One of the most persistent and critical problems in understanding and explaining relationships between business and other social institutions, both for academicians and managers, has been that of developing an adequate focus. At an academic level, attempts have been made to analyze the historical development and modern status of the business organization from such varied disciplinary foci as economics, sociology, psychology, cultural anthropology, and social psychology. Other avenues of inquiry have included organization theory and political science. Nonacademicians have criticized these approaches for their failure to take into account the illogic of reality. On the managerial level the problem often seems to be one of excessive regard for the illogic of reality and too little recognition of the value of a disciplinary focus. Beset by a bewildering number of specific issues, problems, and pressures, the manager's focus on broad business-society relationships is rarely the outgrowth of academic reasoning. Understandably, it is far more likely to be the product of beliefs and values, truths and untruths, culled from experience and involvement in solving real problems.

The search for an adequate focus to satisfy both academic and managerial interests must address itself to two questions: (1) What is the basis of business-society relationship? (2) What are the dimensions of that relationship? This paper will first concern itself with the second question by making certain assumptions about the first one, namely, that regardless of any historical basis for the relationship, the continuing relationship is singularly based on the concept of performance.

Concern about business performance has an historic quality that has been expressed throughout the reform movements of the past. It is interesting to note that Calvin Coolidge's well-known epigram that the "business of America is business" and Theodore Roosevelt's public vow to attack the "malefactors of great wealth" both refer to the performance of the business community. "Our laws," said Roosevelt, "have failed in enforcing the performance of duty by the man of property toward the man who works for him, but the corporation toward the investor, the wage earner and the general public." The issue that runs throughout the reform movements has not been who possesses the wealth, nor how much they possess, but rather, whether they are properly using that wealth. Performance has been, and continues to be the dominant issue—malefactors abuse wealth, philanthropists ennoble it!

The Coolidge-Roosevelt comparison is also suggestive of the two great sides of the corporate responsibility issue. There are those who argue that business ought to be concerned only with narrowly defined and strictly construed traditional interests and held accountable only for the results produced in that context. Others argue, however, that business responsibilities are broad, if limited, and that it is accountable for all of its activities, the by-products of those activities (to the second and third order of impact), and such other matters as the public wishes to impose. Both sides argue in terms of performance, although they are more the outgrowth of alternative propositions about the social character of business. But the great umbrella-like issue continues to be that of performance. In that regard, it is notable that Milton Friedman notwithstanding, there is an ever-growing acceptance by managers, economists, social critics, and the public of the proposition that the performance of the modern corporation cannot be confined to the simple production and distribution of goods and services at a profit. Neither the substance of production and distribution activity nor the procedures by which it is carried on are without significant effects throughout the rest of society. The greater the interdependence between all social groups, the more unlikely it becomes that the counter proposition of business concentration on production, distribution, and profit maximization will attract supporters. The upshot of these changed performance expectations is that profits, the traditional performance measurement, have become an inadequate measure of the varied performances society now demands.

Beyond the question of profits as a measure of corporate performance is the underlying question of what types of performance the corporation is called upon to render. A favorable economic performance is indeed required. But it involves more than merely making a profit. Also involved are judgments about the quality of the product being sold, the environmental impact of producing the product, the truthfulness of the advertising by which consumers are induced to purchase the product, the comparative price at which it is sold, its availability to consumers, and the service provided by the seller once the sale is consummated. All of these economic performances have some indirect, albeit final relation to profits. Moreover, to the extent that the public has definite anticipations and expectations with respect to these matters, they are potential issues for the business community.

In addition to economic performance there are also public expectations about a company's social performance, that is, its impact on society in general. Unlike economic performance that has relatively definable contours, the dimensions of a company's social performance are difficult to determine. Although such issues as discrimination and minority employment, pollution and environmental control, and product safety and consumer protection are generally regarded as connected with economic performance, beyond a certain point each of these issues becomes so unrelated to the economic activity of a particular firm as to be a social matter with respect to it. In addition, social performance also includes such matters as charitable contributions and support for community development and improvement.

Notwithstanding the specific categorization, there is a wide range of economic and social matters about which business is expected to render minimum acceptable performances. Categorization simply assists us in our thinking about the relationship of a particular business organization to the social environment. It is logical to suggest that those companies that extend the effort to consider seriously their relationship with the environment, will be able to understand better the contours of, and the pressures and issues within that environment.

II

The task of defining the many influences and impacts of the corporation on society is difficult, the activities of corporations being diverse, the society complex, and the relationships multiple. The result is much more a complicated mosaic rather than an orderly structure. In seeking to delineate the various types and degrees of impact an organization has on the public, however, there appears to be a useful general distinction possible between the economic—that is, the direct, profit-related—performances of the organization and the essentially noneconomic or social performances. The former relate to the organization's economic mission format, the latter relate to all of the organization's activities that are not directly related to the economic purpose and mission. This basis of distinction is clearly not the only one on which categorization can proceed, but it has proven especially useful when discussing a wide range of diverse issues.

The Economic Performance Issues

Notions of the market, its competitive activity, and a resulting maximization of social-economic benefit have been prominent in American economic thinking for 150 years. Flowing from this concept of competition in the marketplace are accepted principles of the manner in which the business firm must operate. It must be competitive, seek to maximize profits, pursue close cost control, etc. These notions, among others, are all a part of what can be referred to as the "mythology of capitalism."

Given this mythology and the fact that we have schooled generations of managers on such tenets, it is not surprising that businessmen have favored the conceptual separation of the economic impact of an act from its social impact.

Typically, therefore, only pressure has succeeded in forcing companies to cope with such antisocial by-products of economic activity as pollution, discriminatory employment practices, insensitivity to customer complaints, and hazardous working conditions. This class of issues has a clear and direct relationship to the economic activity of the organization, but it has been the impinging of social values that has forced business to accept the cost of correcting these ills rather than allowing them to be treated as general social costs. In the instances mentioned, legislation has been required. In other instances, matters such as job improvement, purchases from minority vendors, and internal due process have been voluntarily accepted in response to the stimulus of pressure. The uneven manner in which organizations have acted on these matters is largely attributable to the variances in the intensity with which such matters have been pursued by their proponents.

The Social Performance Issues

These issues are unrelated to the day-to-day economic operations of the firm. They involve matters in which claimants are suggesting that the firm either become involved in or change a current involvement in some non-economic activity. The range of issues is wide, extending from all types of conventional philanthropic activities to such unconventional claims as for massive company-supported urban rehabilitation projects or the underwriting of minority businessmen.

Also significant is the fact that various types of social performance have been institutionalized by virtue of their long-standing acceptance by management or through the adoption of formal company policies. Tradition has led to such institutionalized social performances as gifts to educational institutions, support for specific charities, and the lending of manpower to community welfare projects.

The distinction between the economic and social performance of an organization is but a starting point since it is a one-dimensional view of the multifaceted relationship between business and the public. Another dimension of that relationship can be understood by noting the various types of stimuli that can prompt organizational activity.

An organization can be stimulated to act in a desired manner through several means, some of which prompt voluntary action, others involuntary. There are three general types of stimuli that underlie organizational responses to all types of social claims. They are (1) legal mandate, which creates a form of involuntary or compelled acceptance of a social claim, (2) public pressure, which creates a type of "voluntary" acceptance of social claims on an *ad hoc* or individual issue basis, and (3) the initiative of the organization, a genuine voluntary situation in which the organization is acting of its own accord or, at the most, as a result of some general social pressure.

A company can become "responsible" in both its economic and social performances as the result of any or all of these motivating forces. In the economic performance area, such matters as product safety, pollution control, truth-in-lending, and occupational safety standards are examples of compelled responsibility through the enactment of legislation. There are examples of compelled responsibility in the social performance area as well, where, for example, company contributions to social security, some investments in economically undesirable but socially necessary projects, and involvement in affirmative action employment programs have all been compelled by law. The federal no-fault automobile insurance bill that was reported out of the Senate Commerce Committee in the summer of 1972 contained a provision that would force a stipulated percentage of all insurance premiums collected to be paid to a fund for research into medical care systems. That, quite clearly, would have imposed a social performance on the insurance carriers.

Public pressure on the organization is another method of stimulating it to perform in a responsible manner. The organization always responds in some fashion (including the no-answer response) to the stimulus of public pressure. Whether or not that response is predictable, and by what rules, if any, the organizational response mechanism operates is still problematic. But examples of situations in which pressure has had a demonstrable effect on the corporation's performance are legion in number. In the economic performance area alone, various companies have established consumer information hotlines, voluntary pollution controls, directed investments into urban and ghetto rehabilitation projects, expanded the scope of employee pension rights, and developed job enrichment programs as voluntary responses to the stimulation of pressure. Similar examples exist in the social performance area; public pressure has promoted business to become involved in a variety of local, state, and national programs ranging from participation in local educational programs to the participation in national drug rehabilitation projects.

Perhaps the purest form of corporate responsibility occurs when the organization itself recognizes a shortcoming or need for improvement in its economic or social performance or determines that it should become involved in a new form of activity. Independence in decision making is the concomitant of initiative, and primary examples of such independence in economic performance involve choice of market, choice of product mix, choice of warranty and customer service practices, and decisions to deposit funds in minority owned banks. To some extent, the general pressure of public needs may underlie various types of independent activity, such as when the life insurance industry recognized the need for urban rehabilitation following the urban riots of the mid-1960's and embarked on a course of action that eventually underwrote $2 billion of urban housing. Independent initiative is an important stimulus in social performance as well, when, for example, charitable contribution policies, the development of urban affairs units, or the creation of a philanthropic foundation may be the outgrowth of the organization's desire to act. Within this category of performances is the occasional company request for the development of legislation that will enable it to engage in some activity perceived as socially necessary, but which they are prevented from engaging in under present economic or legal disabilities. Thus, requesting a regulatory commission to free investment rules to permit investment in high-risk/low-yield ghetto housing or the request of an antitrust waiver to permit the creation of a consortium of competitors to cooperate in pollution control research are examples of actions that will allow the companies to expand the scope of their responsible performances.

It should be apparent that the willingness of a company to be responsible about one group of issues is not indicative of its willingness to do so about another group. Thus, the type of stimulus necessary to prompt responsible action will have to vary as well.

Table 1 illustrates the framework we have been discussing. It is not intended to be a comprehensive statement of the specific performances rendered by each firm in each industry throughout the country. Rather, it is a framework within which any individual performance of a specific firm in a specific industry can be appropriately placed. It is likely that even among competitive firms in the same industry the same performance item may be the result of different stimuli. Product information practices in the home appliance industry and modification of warranty terms in the automobile industry are examples of situations in which one firm took the initiative to improve its economic performance *vis a vis* consumers, thereby causing public pressure on competitors to upgrade their own performances.

It is also possible for a specific performance issue to move among categories over time. Thus, pollution control efforts that were at one time inspired by public pressure may now be included in the compelled category by virtue of environmental protection legislation. While such movement tends to be within one of the broad categories, it is also possible that an issue that is currently considered a social performance matter may become an economic performance item.

There are several popular issues that are not directly introducible into this framework. For example, the framework would have no specific category into which the issues of concentration of wealth and power or the social dominance of the corporation might be placed. What must be recognized about such broad issues, however, is that they are the product and outgrowth of social evaluations about a number of specific corporate performances involving consumer welfare, the use of wealth, and political initiative, all of which are includable in this format. Business performance persists as the real issue therefore, whether viewed on an individual issue basis or as the producer of broader issues.

III

We had earlier assumed that the continuing business-society relationship was based on corporate performance. We must now restate the question, which the assumption enables us to avoid. Arguments about the basis of the business-society relationship seem to be traceable to a basic conflict over the source of the relationship. There are two alternative propositions. The first holds that business was chartered to fulfill a dynamic function, a function

TABLE 1.   Economic and Social Performances.

Types of Performance	Legal Mandate (Compelled)	Public Pressure[1]	Organizational Initiative
Economic Performance Matters	Fair labor standards EPA pollution standards Truth-in-lending Equal employment opportunities (EEO) requirements Antitrust standards: competitive practice rules Tax payments	Minority "quota" hirings Job training Job enrichment Employee benefits Improved social effect of investment, e.g., placing a plant in a ghetto area Deposit of funds in minority owned bank Purchases from minority vendors	Market choice Product mix choice Customer warranty policies Customer service policies Establishment of daycare centers Consumer information programs Development of new products with high social utility or low social cost, e.g., biodegradable products, recycling processes, etc.
Social Performance Matters	Social security contributions Compelled Investment[2] Compelled subsidization[3] Affirmative action employment programs	Cooperative education programs Support for community drug rehabilitation centers Urban investment rehabilitation program	Internal charitable and philanthropic policies Development of "on the street" urban affairs units Creation of, support for philanthropic foundations Xerox-style "social service leave" program Participation in JOBS and MESBIC programs

[1]The term "public" applies to any of the many publics with which the organization is involved, e.g., employees, customers, shareholders, local community, business groups, etc.
[2]The State of Texas had for many years a statute requiring that, as a condition of selling life insurance in the state, a company had to agree to invest a certain percentage of its reserves in the state.
[3]The federal no-fault insurance bill that reached the Senate floor in 1972 contained a provision that would compel direct payments of a percentage of premiums collected to a fund established for the financing of health care research.

that society would define and continue to redefine over time. The alternative proposition holds that business was chartered by the public to be a free institution, capable of acting as its management wished, pursuant and subject to the general laws of conduct set forth by the political expression of society.

The difference between the propositions is one of deciding who will determine the nature of the continuing function of the business organization and what performances it will be held accountable to render. If the first proposition is adopted, society, through the mechanism of social pressure, will continuously define the performance it wishes business to render. Thus, the principle responsibility of business is that of becoming ever more responsive to those restatements of its purpose. If the alternative proposition is adopted, however, the performances to be rendered are left to the determination of the organization itself or are the result of a political restatement of the laws of conduct. Here, the principle responsibility of business is to act in its own best interest, a course with economic theory specifies will result in a maximum social benefit.

Businessmen have generally adopted the latter proposition while social critics have chosen the former. Indeed, arguments about the legitimacy of the corporation or the existence of the corporate state are invariably linked to the dichotomy of the two propositions. These propositions also suggest the existence of the various stimuli discussed above—law, public pressure, and organizational initiative. The fact that there are significant segments of the population that have adopted each view and have been vigorous in their advocacy accounts for the overwhelming importance of performance. The public has accepted both propositions. Both have been acted upon, casting the dispute in performance terms, and thereby making business responsiveness the overriding practical issue.

Conclusion

This discussion is intended to reemphasize the need for a comprehensive and systematic manner of analyzing the performances of the bsuiness organization. It has recently been suggested that among the dominant interests of the organization are the creation of effective responses to dangerous, threatening environments and the ability to deal rapidly and effectively with environmental complexity and change.[1] The managerial imperative

[1]Roger Harrison, "Understanding Your Organization's Character," *Harvard Business Review*, May-June 1972, p. 119.

is systematically to order the range of issues that are likely to confront the organization, to expand the range of responses available, and to plan coordinated patterns of response. The principal difference between an organization that simply reacts to stimuli and one that consciously and purposively determines its future course rests on the latter's ability and capacity for gathering, synthesizing, and utilizing information about the social environment. However, in order to effectively search the environment and plan the dimensions of a future relationship, one must understand the general dimensions of its present relationship.

The performance model presented here is descriptive, not normative. There are a large number of problems that this paper has not addressed, which are associated with the dimensions of performance outlined. It is hoped that in better undesrtanding and appreciating the scope of the problems, the answers to some of those issues might be slightly easier to derive. Moreover, understanding the scope and dimensions of the business-society relationship is the first step in the development of a performance theory that recognizes the social, as well as the economic performance aspects of the relationship.

Managerial Attitudes Toward Corporate Social Responsibility

●●

● JOHN W. COLLINS
College of Business Administration
Syracuse University

● CHRIS G. GANOTIS
Corporate Staff
The MITRE Corporation, Bedford, Mass.

A dominant contemporary business philosophy holds that a company has a duty to balance and serve the interests of four constituent groups—owners, employees, customers, and the public.[1] Determination of the views of these constituencies is one of the difficult problems confronted by those companies that wish to develop a policy of corporate social responsibility.

Among the competing constituencies, employee attitudes toward social responsibility is of particular importance. The gap between corporate social policy and implementation of that policy has been a recurring problem. Often this difficulty has been attributed to a parallel attitudinal gap between top management, which determines the policy, and the employees who must implement it.

---

[1]Frank W. Abrams, "Management's Responsibilities in a Complex World," *Harvard Business Review*, May 1951, p. 29; David W. Ewing, "Who Wants Corporate Democracy?" *Harvard Business Review*, September-October, 1971, p. 12.

If employee attitudes are determined *prior* to policy decisions, policy makers may choose to pursue social goals that employees perceive as worthwhile, presumably easing the implementation problem. Alternatively, if other factors result in adoption of policy and programs that employees do not presently perceive as socially worthwhile, advance knowledge will help to determine the scope and depth of the need to influence employee attitudes.

This paper reviews an initial effort to survey employee attitudes concerning several aspects of corporate responsibility, sets forth the findings of that survey, and presents an analysis of those findings.

Method

The study is based on a survey of managers[2] employed in a major multi-divisional corporation (over $1 billion in sales) that employs approximately 35,000 personnel in about 150 locations. Questionnaires were distributed to 1135 managers at six major plants and the corporate headquarters. The seven locations are in both the North and South and in rural as well as urban environments.

The questionnaires consisted of a number of statements representing opinions in various ways associated with the subject of corporate responsibility. Each manager was asked to indicate the extent of his agreement with each statement on a seven-response-category, Likert-type scale ranging from "strongly disagree" to "strongly agree." The responses were converted into a numerical scale ranging from one to seven, the weight of four representing "neither agree nor disagree."

The questions fell into three categories:

(1) Personal responsibility and sense of futility. Does the manager feel personally responsible for corporate social policy? Does he believe that he can execute such responsibility within his company?

(2) Business-government-society interrelationship. Does the manager perceive a social role for business? Does he view capitalist idology as preventing a social role for business? What role should government play in the social involvement of business?

(3) Contemporary social responsibility issues. Should business participate in helping to solve the problems of pollution, minority hiring, and

---

[2]More particularly the survey was taken among exempt employees, including some professionals as well as managers. For purposes of this paper, all persons surveyed are referred to as "managers."

female hiring? Will such participation have adverse corporate consequences? Who should pay the cost of corporate social involvement?

The questionnaires were self-administered and respondents were assured of complete anonymity and confidentiality. A total of 531 completed questionnaires were returned that were suitable for analysis, representing a 47-percent-effective rate of return. The demographic breakdown of the respondents is given in table 1.

Findings

The data were analyzed along different dimensions and reported in terms of averages for each category. The response of a particular group of managers on a given question was considered positive or negative depending on whether it was above or below the average response for the total sample. In our reporting of the findings the mean average response rate to a particular proposition is set in parenthesis. Responses from 4.01 to 7.0 repre-

TABLE 1.   Profile of Respondents.

Management Position Level	%		
Fourth level: Foreman, supervisor, sales service	24.5		
Third level: General foreman, superintendent, assistant superintendent, planner, accountant, salesman, administrator.	30.0		
Second level: Production manager, control manager, engineer service manager, industrial relations manager, sales manager.	27.3		
First level: General manager or plant manager.	2.9		
Corporate staff[1]	15.3		

Salary	%	Education	%	Age	%
$5,000–$14,999	52.6[2]	High school or less	23.2	21–30	13.9
$15,000–$19,999	28.9	Some college	28.9	31–40	36.9
$20,000–$24,999	11.8	Four-year college graduate	27.6	41–50	31.0
$25,000 and over	6.7	Post-graduate study	20.3	over 50	18.2[3]

[1]For purposes of analysis within the study, the management position level of "corporate staff" is not included. A review indicated that such a category did not represent a homogenous group. It is believed that a ranking of corporate staff positions is necessary for analytical purposes.
[2]Includes only 13 individuals under $10,000.
[3]Includes only nine individuals older than 60.

sent agreement with the stated proposition—the higher the mean, the greater the agreement. Responses from 3.99 to 1.0 represent disagreement with the stated proposition—the lower the mean the greater the disagreement. More complete statistical information is contained in the appendix to this paper.

Among the most significant findings are:

(1) A sense of futility concerning the ability of lower- and middle-level managers to effect corporate social policy and a perhaps related attitude that social goals can best be achieved by individuals working outside their companies. These attitudes were particularly strong among lower-level managers.

(2) An unexpected lack of "corporate liberalism" among young managers, who evidenced (a) the lowest sense of personal responsibility and (b) the weakest perception of the need for corporate involvement to solve contemporary social problems.

(3) An absence among all managers of ideological beliefs that would serve as barriers to the exercise of corporate social responsibility.

(4) A strong negative reaction to government influence on the social involvement of business, indicating a desire for autonomy.

(5) A preference among managers for having the cost impact of corporate social involvement fall on consumers and stockholders rather than employees.

(6) A wide gap between the positive attitude toward the need for pollution control and the contrasting generally negative attitude toward providing greater job opportunities for minorities and women.

The details of executive responses under various categories are given below.

Personal Responsibility and Sense of Futility

The manager does feel personally responsible to see to it that his company becomes involved in social problem solving.[3] He agrees that if he believes that his company is not doing enough to solve social problems, he has an obligation to try to persuade top management to change their viewpoints. (5.48). When we analyze this attitude in terms of the respondents' education, position, or salary, no relationship appears. However, older managers evidence a stronger sense of personal responsibility than their younger colleagues, a significant attitudinal difference appearing between the over-40 and under-40 manager.

[3]Use of the term "the manager" refers to the mean average response rate of all respondents.

The generally positive attitude toward personal responsibility is offset by some feeling that if top management is not interested in social problem solving, there is little, if anything, that a lower or middle manager can do to change these viewpoints or company practices (4.31). The sense of futility over ability to affect top management viewpoints is strongest at the lowest two managerial positional levels. Unexpected, however, is that older managers, who are the strongest believers in a personal responsibility to influence top management attitudes, are the most skeptical of the chances of success in attempts to carry out that responsibility.

Despite the slight sense of futility, the manager does not believe that expressing his feelings to higher levels of management about practices he feels to be socially questionable is likely to have a detrimental effect on his chances for promotion (2.90).

Business-Government-Society Interrelationship

The manager believes that corporations have a social responsibility. He agrees that many contemporary social problems will not be solved unless corporate managers commit their companies to helping to find solutions (5.49). He also agrees, however, although to a lesser degree, with the proposition that social goals can *best* be accomplished by individuals working outside their companies (4.31).

Older managers more than younger managers, believe that corporate commitment is necessary to solve contemporary social problems. Lower-level managers do not share the attitude of their superiors that corporate commitment is necessary to solve our social problems. Conversely, lower-level managers prefer individual activity for achieving social goals more than do their superiors.

The manager does not see the traditionally cited ideological barriers to corporate responsibility as standing in the way of corporate social involvement. Disregarding the economic gospel according to Adam Smith and Milton Friedman, he disagrees with the idea that business best contributes to social welfare by maximizing profits (3.05). He also disagrees with the arguments that managers should refrain from exercising social responsibility (1) because they are expending funds that belong to stockholders (2.72), (2) because they are not selected in a democratic manner (2.34), or (3) because such action will put their company at a competitive disadvantage (2.96).[4]

---

[4]These opinions may have been biased by the fact that the propositions referred to the specific social issue of pollution control.

Finally, the manager does not believe that it is the responsibility of government rather than industry to formulate social laws for industry to abide by (2.80). He apparently feels that business is responsible for regulating its own activities in the pursuit of social goals.

Interestingly, while responses generally rejected arguments opposing the exercise of social responsibility, the responses are reversed regarding the need for governmental guidelines to achieve social goals through business Here, higher positional-level and higher-salaried managers perceive more than others a need for governmental guidelines. Additionally, younger managers share that attitude more than older managers (see appendix).

Contemporary Social Responsibility Issues

Pollution control. The manager agrees that air and water pollution by industrial corporations are having a harmful effect on people's health (5.26). He also feels strongly that corporations have a definite obligation to clean up air and water pollution (6.37). Of all the survey statements, this was the proposition most agreed upon.

The degree of concern about pollution by industry and the obligation of business to deal with such pollution are both related to age, younger managers having a greater environmental sensitivity than their older colleagues. The only other correlation that appears is between job position and the statement that, "Corporations have a definite obligation to clean up air and water pollution," managers in respectively higher levels of management showing greater agreement with the statement than lower-level managers.

Relationships are also evident between the view that voluntary installation of pollution control equipment will result in a loss of competitive advantage and the demographic factors of position, salary, and age. Generally, older, higher-level and higher-salary managers view voluntary pollution control as competitively dysfunctional.

When questioned about where the cost of pollution control should be borne, the manager prefers that the cost be passed along to the consumer in the form of increased prices. To a lesser extent he would advocate pollution control, even if it meant cutting costs by reducing the number of employees or by reducing dividends to stockholders. He would not, however, favor pollution control if it meant cutting costs by reducing employees' wages.

Finally, the manager is skeptical of the usefulness of the government's role in contributing to the achievement of social goals through business involvement. He does not perceive the primary solution to industrial pollution control to be increased governmental regulation (3.72) and he views current governmental regulations on air and water pollution to be economically unsound (4.83).

Consistent with other findings, older managers are most critical of increased governmental regulation of pollution control and the economic soundness of current regulations. Managers under 30 actually slightly favor increased governmental regulation of pollution control, in contrast to the overall managerial attitude in opposition.

Minority hiring. The manager is ambivalent about whether business in general has an obligation to provide greater job opportunities for minority groups (4.12). He does believe, however, that providing equal employment opportunities for minority groups results in the employment of people who are not best qualified for their positions (5.82). Those managers with more education, higher positions and higher salaries are in greatest agreement that business has an obligation to hire minorities and are least convinced that carrying out that obligation will result in the hiring of less-qualified employees. Those with high school education or less and in the lowest managerial positions, in fact, do not recognize a business obligation to provide job opportunities for minorities.

Belief that minority hiring programs result in failure to hire the most qualified candidates for employment would imply a view that such programs incur a cost to the company. The manager is opposed to imposing that cost on anyone—the employee, through reduced employment or wages; the consumer, through higher prices; or the stockholder, through reduced dividends.

Female hiring. The manager believes that providing equal employment opportunities for women results in the employment of people who are not most qualified for their positions (5.08). Further, although essentially ambivalent, he leans toward disagreeing with the proposition that corporations have an obligation to provide greater job opportunities for women (3.97).

Managers with at least a college degree, those above positional level three, managers making more than $20,000, and those under 40 all perceived there was indeed such an obligation, while the others did not.

Of all the survey statements, the ones most strongly disagreed with concerned whether corporations have a definite obligation to provide greater job opportunities for women, even if it means that costs would be cut by reducing the number of employees or reducing employees' wages. Increasing prices or reducing dividends to accomplish female hiring did not receive much greater support. Consistent with minority hiring questions, although all groups opposed the imposition of costs on anyone, all demographic groups and subgroups were more adverse to the cost impact falling on employees than on stockholders or consumers.

Analysis

Personal Responsibility and Sense of Futility

The authors believe that an effective corporate social policy requires that employees possess a sense of personal responsibility and a perception that they can positively influence such policy. Although the respondents evidenced their personal responsibility, they indicated that they believed that attempts to affect top management viewpoints and company practices would be futile. This sense of futility may have more significance than attitudes concerning particular social issues.

On the other hand, the manager's view that expressing his feelings concerning socially questionable practices is not likely to have a detrimental effect on his chances for promotion indicates that his sense of futility is based on frustration rather than fear, making it an easier attitude to deal with.

It was surprising to discover that the youngest managers, with the least sense of futility, had the lowest sense of personal responsibility. It is difficult to explain this apparent contradiction with the popular conception of youths' values regarding man's relation to institutions with which he is associated, particularly among the under-30 managers. It may be that popular youths' values are in fact not held by young people entering a business management career, or that the unusual finding is restricted to the single corporation surveyed.

As expected, the sense of futility to affect corporate policies was highest at the lowest two levels of management. In contrast, department and general managers were much more of the opinion that viewpoints and company practices could be changed by lower- and middle-level managers. This once again underscores the fact that the lower-level employee does not feel that he has a means of communication with his superiors. Top management must recognize this sense of futility and take action to provide a vehicle for getting ideas to the top.

Employee communication is particularly important in the area of corporate social policy, because the policy can be sabotaged by noncooperative employees who must implement it. A company must take steps to see to it that employee opinion is considered in the development of social policy and that the employees are aware that their voices are being heard.

Business-Government-Society Interrelationship

The manager perceives a social role for business, but not as the sole savior of society. This attitude may be related to the sense of futility in influencing corporate social policy that was discussed above. Again, it is surprising to find the youngest managers as the group least convinced that corporate involvement is necessary for social problem solving. This attitude is particularly interesting since the young managers, as a group, are also least inclined to accept the proposition that social problems can best be solved by individuals working outside their companies.

The opinions of lower-level managers regarding these matters would indicate that a corporation that desires to carry out a policy of social responsibility needs to convince its lower-level managers of the advantages of corporate social involvement.

It does not appear that the manager needs to be convinced that the traditional, capitalistic, ideological arguments do not stand in the way or corporate social responsibility. Their wholesale rejection of profit maximization as a means to achieve social welfare, as well as the other traditional ideological barriers indicates that to whatever extent corporate social responsibility is rejected, the roots of the rejection are based on other, perhaps personal or pragmatic, grounds.

Rejection of social-policy standard setting by government, leaving the setting of standards to business, when compared with the more ambivalent attitude toward the need for governmental regulation of the business sector to best achieve social goals, creates an apparent dilemma. These responses, in addition to the rejection of basic propositions of the capitalistic ethic, would indicate that a primary value of the manager is corporate decision-making autonomy. He desires to be free from the traditional constraints of the shareholder and the market, and to be free also from the growing restraint of governmental regulation.

Top management must make it clear that the road to autonomy is not paved with good intentions, but with results. Only if business can successfully respond to society's demand for corporate social responsibility, will decision-making autonomy be allowed. The alternative to irresponsible use of corporate power is governmental regulation.

Contemporary Social Responsibility Issues

Pollution Control. The youngest managers, in the 21 to 30 group, indicate that they believe the answer to the pollution-control issue to be through increased governmental regulation. This is consistent with findings that younger managers are best prepared for a greater governmental role in solving social problems through business.

On the other hand, high-level managers, who evidenced a more favorable attitude toward the need for governmental regulation to achieve social goals than lower-level managers, are most critical of governmental regulation in the specific instance of pollution control.

Among young, low-salaried, and low-position-level managers there is only minimal agreement for the proposition that voluntary pollution control creates a competitive disadvantage. The view that a competitive disadvantage is created is particularly strong among general managers and plant managers and the over-$20,000 salary levels. These views are especially interesting in light of the Bragdon-Marlin theses that there is a positive correlation between pollution control and profitability and that pollution control efforts may create certain competitive advantages.[5]

Minority and Female Hiring. The manager's enthusiasm for a corporate role in the solving of contemporary problems wanes when the social issue involved changes from pollution control to minority and female hiring. Agreement with the proposition that corporations have a definite responsibility to provide greater job opportunities for minority groups is miniscule, and among low-education and position levels disappears entirely.

Attitudes toward female hiring are even more negative than toward minority hiring. For instance, over-40 managers generally oppose female hiring, although the favor minority hiring. Many "society-watchers" tell us that the growing women's liberation movement will impose ever-increasing pressures on corporations to reform their female hiring and promotion practices. If such predictions are correct, the feminist pressures will be applied to an unreceptive manager, who may very well qualify as a male chauvinist.

Conclusions

The authors believe that employee attitudes are an important factor to be considered in the development of corporate social policy. Inclusion of these attitudes in the decision-making process can reduce the policy-implementation gap, either by bringing company policy into line with employee attitudes or demonstrating the need to influence certain employee attitudes.

[5]Joseph H. Bragdon, Jr. and John Tepper Marlin, "Pollution and Profitability: The Case of the Pulp and Paper Industry," paper presented to the Financial Management Association, Denver, Colorado: October 1971.

This study represents an initial attempt to measure employee attitudes and to present the results in a form that will be useful to decision makers concerned with the development of corporate social policy.

Standing alone, these findings have importance primarily for the company for which the study was conducted. The study, however, also provides a foundation for similar studies by other firms, pointing out the need to deal with the problems raised by requesting extensive demographic information and suggesting the types of attitudinal information that might be sought.

Further inquiry into employee attitudes is needed. Intercompany and interindustry comparisons, hourly paid employee attitudes, and changes in employee attitudes over time are all important areas for future investigation.

APPENDIX

TABLE 1.   Response Summary: Personal Responsibility and Sense of Futility.

(1) If a manager feels that his company is not doing enough to solve pressing social problems, he has an obligation to try to persuade top management to change its viewpoints.

Mean Average: 5.48

Education	Positional Level	Salary	Age*
5.61	5.55	5.51	5.29
5.49	5.36	5.43	5.34
5.26	5.62	5.44	5.63
5.63	5.80	5.43	5.62

(2) If top management is not interested in devoting resource efforts and pressures to solve social problems, there is little, if anything, that a lower- or middle-level manager can do to change either its viewpoints or company practices.

Mean Average: 4.31

Education	Positional Level*	Salary	Age*
4.45	4.54	4.32	4.10
4.11	4.52	4.45	4.18
4.57	3.95	3.86	4.22
4.12	4.00	4.09	4.76

*Demographic factors discussed in text of paper. Mean averages for subcategories follow same order as set out in table 1 in text.

(3) If a manager feels that his company is engaged in some practices that are socially questionable, it would be foolhardy for him to express his feelings to higher levels of management, since it is likely to have a detrimental effect on his chances for promotion.

Mean Average: 2.90

Education	Positional Level	Salary	Age
2.97	2.79	2.92	3.21
2.88	2.94	2.87	2.71
3.15	3.06	2.67	2.98
2.56	2.00	2.98	2.97

TABLE 2. Response Summary: Business-Government-Society Interrelationship.

(1) Many contemporary social problems will not be solved unless corporate managers commit their companies to helping to find solutions.

Mean Average: 5.49

Education	Positional Level*	Salary	Age*
5.25	5.40	5.36	5.21
5.64	5.44	5.63	5.49
5.35	5.55	5.33	5.51
5.73	6.20	6.03	5.64

(2) Social goals can best be accomplished by individuals working outside their companies.

Mean Average: 4.31

Education	Positional Level*	Salary	Age
4.48	4.59	4.41	4.25
4.55	4.54	4.53	4.36
4.37	4.24	4.16	4.33
3.90	3.27	3.40	4.44

(3) The welfare of society is best achieved if all businesses concentrate their efforts on maximizing profits.

Mean Average: 3.05

Education	Positional Level	Salary	Age
3.25	3.10	3.00	2.79
3.00	3.01	2.99	3.15
2.97	2.99	3.48	3.15
3.10	3.33	3.23	3.07

(4) It is not proper for a corporate executive to voluntarily spend corporate funds for controlling pollution caused by his company because he would be spending stockholders' money for a general social purpose.

Mean Average: 2.72

Education*	Positional Level*	Salary*	Age
2.91	2.98	2.86	2.68
2.91	2.79	2.57	2.71
2.59	2.50	2.56	2.58
2.36	2.07	2.40	3.10

(5) It is not proper for a corporate executive to voluntarily spend corporate funds for controlling pollution caused by his company because he has not been selected in a democratic manner to carry out social policies.

Mean Average: 2.34

Education*	Positional Level*	Salary*	Age
3.01	2.69	2.63	2.07
2.35	2.52	2.66	2.44
2.16	2.24	2.28	2.43
2.03	1.60	1.71	2.57

(6) It is not proper for a corporate executive to voluntarily spend corporate funds for controlling pollution caused by his company because such action will provide other companies with a competitive advantage.

Mean Average: 2.96

Education*	Positional Level*	Salary*	Age
3.37	3.50	3.09	2.72
3.14	2.99	3.03	3.13
2.80	2.70	2.62	2.88
2.70	3.20	3.23	3.26

(7) It is the responsibility of government and not industry to formulate social laws for industry to abide by.

Mean Average: 2.80

Education	Positional Level	Salary	Age
2.70	2.86	2.87	3.24
2.81	2.59	2.53	2.69
2.84	2.76	3.02	2.48
2.72	2.40	2.66	2.97

(8) The business sector can best achieve social goals only if government makes guidelines that all corporations must follow.

Mean Average: 3.60

Education*	Positional Level*	Salary*	Age*
3.39	3.39	3.51	3.79
3.56	3.43	3.49	3.68
3.57	3.55	3.82	3.45
3.93	4.93	4.23	3.43

TABLE 3. Response Summary: Pollution Control.

(1) Corporations have a definite obligation to clean up air and water pollution.

Mean Average: 6.37

Education	Positional Level*	Salary	Age*
6.19	6.21	6.37	6.47
6.45	6.39	6.45	6.38
6.43	6.48	6.28	6.31
6.39	6.53	6.20	6.38

(2) Air and water pollution by industrial corporations are having a harmful effect on people's health.

Mean Average: 5.26

Education	Positional Level	Salary	Age*
5.11	5.20	5.35	5.57
5.32	5.20	5.16	5.35
5.31	5.33	5.11	5.10
5.28	5.33	5.31	5.15

(3) Air and water pollution by our company are having an increasingly harmful effect on people's health.

Mean Average: 5.10

Education*	Positional Level*	Salary	Age
4.92	4.97	4.98	5.15
5.03	5.11	5.22	5.02
5.19	5.15	5.36	5.16
5.34	5.60	5.15	5.07

(4) Companies who voluntarily install pollution control devices are at a competitive disadvantage with other companies in the same industry that do not.

Mean Average: 4.78

Education	Positional Level*	Salary*	Age*
4.62	4.53	4.52	4.46
4.64	4.75	4.92	4.82
5.23	4.87	5.21	4.79
4.64	6.07	5.60	5.10

(5) Corporations have a definite obligation to clean up air and water pollution, even if it means that costs must be cut by reducing the number of employees.

Mean Average: 4.66

Education	Positional Level*	Salary	Age
4.34	4.50	4.52	5.07
4.39	4.64	4.79	4.52
5.01	4.75	4.90	4.58
4.97	5.73	5.00	4.77

(6) Corporations have a definite obligation to clean up air and water pollution, even if it means that costs must be cut by reducing employees' wages.

Mean Average: 3.78

Education	Positional Level	Salary	Age
3.82	3.90	3.80	3.76
3.76	3.66	3.87	3.59
4.02	3.89	3.67	3.86
3.53	4.13	3.66	4.12

(7) Corporations have a definite obligation to clean up air and water pollution, even if it means reducing dividends to stockholders.

Mean Average: 4.80

Education	Positional Level	Salary	Age
4.69	4.65	4.89	5.00
4.12	4.83	4.86	4.68
4.94	4.84	4.20	4.87
4.66	4.67	4.74	4.74

(8) The primary solution to industrial pollution control is to increase governmental regulation.

Mean Average: 3.72

Education	Positional Level*	Salary	Age*
3.77	3.86	3.85	4.25
3.66	3.62	3.44	3.69
3.70	3.50	3.54	3.53
3.78	3.53	3.97	3.63

(9) Many of the governmental regulations on air and water pollution are economically unsound.

Mean Average: 4.83

Education	Positional Level*	Salary	Age*
4.82	4.74	4.66	4.29
4.79	4.85	4.85	4.81
4.94	5.01	5.34	4.89
4.67	5.13	4.66	4.97

TABLE 4.   Response Summary: Minority Hiring.

(1) Corporations have a definite responsibility to provide greater job opportunities for minority groups.

Mean Average: 4.12

Education*	Positional Level*	Salary*	Age
3.71	3.79	4.07	4.21
4.07	3.92	4.03	4.01
4.30	4.16	4.28	4.18
4.49	4.60	4.74	4.28*

(2) Attempts to achieve equal employment opportunities for minority groups have led to the employment of people who are not really the best qualified for the position.

Mean Average: 5.82

Education*	Positional Level*	Salary*	Age
6.06	5.98	5.89	5.64
5.82	6.04	5.88	5.86
5.74	5.91	5.70	5.81
5.67	5.20	4.17	5.89*

(3) Corporations have a definite obligation to provide greater job opportunities for minority groups, even if it means that costs must be cut by reducing the number of employees.

Mean Average: 2.32

Education	Positional Level	Salary	Age
2.21	2.04	2.33	2.32
2.14	2.32	2.37	2.33
2.40	2.35	2.26	2.24
2.73	3.27	2.60	2.65

(4) Corporations have a definite obligation to provide greater job opportunities for minority groups, even if it means that costs must be cut by reducing employees' wages.

Mean Average: 2.41

Education	Positional Level	Salary	Age
2.31	2.23	2.33	2.47
2.20	2.34	2.39	2.20
2.60	2.36	2.59	2.41
2.57	3.60	2.66	2.75

(5) Corporations have a definite obligation to provide greater job opportunities for minority groups, even if it means reduced dividends for stockholders.

Mean Average: 2.90

Education	Positional Level	Salary	Age
2.60	2.60	2.91	3.18
2.76	2.60	2.66	2.68
2.89	2.87	2.75	2.80
3.11	3.60	3.09	2.95

(6) Corporations have a definite obligation to provide greater job opportunities for minority groups, even if it means increased prices for consumers.

Mean Average: 2.82

Education	Positional Level	Salary	Age
2.35	2.40	2.73	2.92
2.63	2.78	3.01	2.86
3.20	3.04	3.07	2.81
3.48	3.93	3.37	3.12

TABLE 5.   Response Summary: Female Hiring.

(1) Corporations have a definite obligation to provide greater job opportunities for women.

Mean Average: 3.97

Education*	Positional Level*	Salary*	Age*
3.47	3.46	3.88	4.03
3.91	3.90	3.90	4.00
4.10	4.03	4.05	3.91
4.41	4.93	4.49	3.93

(2) Attempts to achieve equal employment opportunities for women have led to the employment of people who are not really the best qualified for the position.

Mean Average: 5.08

Education*	Positional Level*	Salary*	Age
5.38	5.52	5.23	5.21
5.28	5.32	4.99	5.20
4.74	4.96	4.70	4.79
4.90	5.27	5.06	5.23

(3) Corporations have a definite obligation to provide greater job opportunities for women, even if it means that costs must be cut by reducing the number of employees.

Mean Average: 2.16

Education	Positional Level	Salary	Age
2.02	2.08	2.19	2.44
2.01	2.13	2.10	1.93
2.18	2.04	2.08	2.12
2.63	3.33	2.63	2.57

(4) Corporations have a definite obligation to provide greater job opportunities for women, even if it means that costs must be cut by reducing employee's wages.

Mean Average: 2.19

Education	Positional Level	Salary	Age
1.94	1.98	2.09	2.18
2.12	2.06	2.15	2.05
2.21	2.18	2.34	2.14
2.55	3.87	2.74	2.57

(5) Corporations have a definite responsibility to provide greater job opportunities for women even if it means reduced dividends for stockholders.

Mean Average: 2.62

Education	Positional Level	Salary	Age
2.27	2.28	2.70	2.90
2.55	2.59	2.51	2.57
2.85	2.66	2.51	2.48
2.92	3.80	3.00	2.86

(6) Corporations have a definite obligation to provide greater job opportunities for women, even if it means increased prices for consumers.

Mean Average: 2.56

Education	Positional Level	Salary	Age
2.24	2.16	2.52	2.68
2.32	2.52	2.45	2.50
2.71	2.59	2.72	2.50
3.10	3.80	3.09	2.74

PART VI
Some Dimensions of Business-Society Conflict

••

PART VI. A

Business and
the Physical Environment

●●

> Why these corporations are so shortsighted on this important public relations
> field I cannot understand, but instead of volunteering to join in smoke abate-
> ment they are resisting it. I have about reached the conclusion that, while large
> industry is important, fresh air and clean water are more important, and the
> day may well come when we have to lay that kind of a hand on the table and
> see who is bluffing.
>
> —Senator Barry M. Goldwater

Hardly anyone would disagree that there has been a deterioration in our
physical environment. The phenomenon is not new, nor is public concern
about it. Furthermore, it is not uniquely an American problem, but is
present to a greater or lesser degree in every nation. What is different
about the current concern for the physical environment is the intensity
with which the issues are being argued; the seriousness with which the
advocacy groups are fighting business corporations and other economic
and social institutions whose activities generate some kind of pollution;
the magnitude of potential economic effect on the operation of industry
and other institutions affected by the imposition of more rigid standards
of pollution control; and the major, radical changes that higher standards
of pollution control and the time and method of their enforcement will
bring in our living standards.

In a manner of speaking, every activity performed by human beings—
including breathing—pollutes the environment. What we are concerned
about is not pollution per se, but what kind of pollution and how much
pollution society must endure to enjoy the goods and services that industry provides as a concomitant of creating such pollution. Further, if
pollution is to be reduced, what is the most efficient way of doing it, taking into consideration the interests, economic and other, of the parties
involved.

Pollution sources, measurements, and controls are so diverse and so loaded with technological, economic, social, and political considerations that it is impossible to cover even a few of them in a volume of this size. We have, therefore, confined ourselves to providing three illustrative cases of pollution to show the types of issues involved and the nature of problems that confront their resolution by industry, the general public, and government agencies.

Ernest S. Starkman acknowledges that our environment has paid a huge price in terms of degradation of land, air, water, and other resources for the development of the conveniences that we enjoy today. He points out that the auto industry has realized this and has set new goals for itself to decrease that burden. It is General Motors' position that mandatory regulations have decreased auto emissions considerably, but that the technology for meeting future standards on a reliable mass production basis is not available. Irresponsible behavior by some government agencies—the National Highway Traffic Safety Administration, for example, in developing auto safety features—has resulted in the present situation, which Starkman thinks is a species of overkill. He points out that the industry has tried hard to be more socially responsible, but that compliance with the Clean Air Act standards for auto emissions is almost impossible.

John T. Marlin reviews the history of government and business self-regulation in the area of pollution control and shows that the concept of regulatory agencies as protectors of both the public and of industry must be abandoned. He points out that regulatory agencies are, at best, good for arbitration purposes in a two-sided conflict. Under such imperfect conditions, public advocates or publicly supported research institutions could shed light on the wrongdoings or irresponsible behavior of corporations by devising socially acceptable standards and measurements, which would enable the public to discriminate against socially irresponsible corporations while supporting socially responsible ones.

John E. Logan and Arthur B. Moore, Jr. point to the inefficiency, complexity, and inadequacy of federal and state air, water, and land pollution standards by referring to an actual case: BASF's plant dispute in South Carolina, which involved state and federal governments as well as other authorities. They review the evolutionary history of antipollution legislation and note that this legislation is still inadequate. They emphasize that in any dispute all sides must be well informed and aware of the consequencies of their actions. On the corporate side, the authors advocate more disclosure of corporate motives and purposes, and ask for much more positive action in making ecological decisions. They argue that, because of the enormous effect of any governmental decision on the public, the government must behave in a much more responsive and responsible way than in the past.

SELECTED BIBLIOGRAPHY

Alberts, David S., and Davis, John Marshall. "Decision-making Criteria for Environmental Protection and Control." Paper written for the 12th American Meeting of the Institute of Management Sciences, Detroit, September 29-October 2, 1971.

Baldwin, William. "The Motives of Managers, Environmental Restraints, and the Theory of Managerial Enterprise." *Quarterly Journal of Economics*, May 1964, pp. 238–256.

*Barkley, Paul W., and Seckler, David W. *Economic Growth and Environmental Decay: The Solution Becomes the Problem.* New York: Harcourt Brace Jovanovich, 1972.

Bradt, William R. *Organizing for Effective Public Affairs: How Companies Structure the Corporate Unit.* Studies in Public Affairs no. 5. New York: The Conference Board, 1969.

*Beams, Floyd A., and Fertig, Paul E. "Pollution Control Through Social Cost Conversion." In *The Accounting Sampler,* edited by Thomas J. Burns, and Harvey S. Hendrickson. New York and San Francisco: McGraw-Hill Book Co., 1972.

Bowerman, Frank R. "Managing Solid Waste Disposal." *California Management Review* 14, no. 3 (Spring 1972): 104–106.

Cain, Stanley A. "Environment—An All-encompassing Phenomenon." Remarks at the 12th American Meeting of the Institute of Management Sciences, Detroit, September 29-October 2, 1971.

Cannon, James, and Halloran, Jean. "Steel and the Environment: A Long Way to Go." *Business and Society Review/Innovation,* Winter 1972-1973, pp. 56–61.

Cassell, Eric L. "The Health Effects of Air Pollution and Their Implications for Control." *Law and Contemporary Problems* 33, no. 2 (Spring 1968): 197–216.

Chass, Robert L. "Air Pollution Control: The Case of Los Angeles County." *California Management Review* 14, no. 3 (Spring 1972): 92–103.

Council on Economic Priorities. "Paper Profits: Pollution Audit 1972." *Economic Priorities Report,* July-August 1971.

*Davies, J. Clarence, III. *The Politics of Pollution.* Indianapolis: Bobbs-Merrill Co., Pegasus, 1971.

*Downs, Anthony. "Up and Down With Ecology—the 'Issue-Attention Cycle'." *The Public Interest,* Summer 1972, pp. 38–50.

*Downs, Anthony et al. *The Political Economy of Environmental Control.* Berkeley: Institute of Business and Economic Research, University of California, 1972.

Drucker, Peter. *Technology, Management and Society.* New York: Harper & Row, 1970.

DuPont Corporation. "The Environment: A Special Report." *Context,* February 1972.

*Ehrlich, Paul R.; Ehrlich, Anne H.; and Holdren, John P. *Human Ecology: Problems and Solutions.* San Francisco: W. H. Freeman & Co., 1973.

Enke, Stephen. "Population Growth and Economic Growth." *The Public Interest,* Summer 1973, pp. 86–96.

*Especially recommended for an overall view and for authoritative viewpoints on different perspectives of the issues covered.

*Esposito, John C. *Vanishing Air, The Nader Report*. New York: Grossman, 1970.

Faltermayer, Edmund K. "We Can Afford Clean Air." *Fortune* 72, no. 5: 159–163.

*Freeman, A. Myrick, III, and Haveman, Robert H. "Clean Rhetoric and Dirty Water." *The Public Interest*, Summer 1972, pp. 51–65.

*General Motors Corporation. *1973 Report on Progress in Areas of Public Concern*. Warren, Mich.: GM Technical Center, February 8, 1973.

*Goldman, Marshall, ed. *Controlling Pollution: The Economics of a Cleaner America*. Englewood Cliffs, N.J.: Prenctice-Hall, 1967.

*_____, ed. *Ecology and Economics*. Englewood Cliffs, N.J.: Prentice-Hall, 1972.

Haynes, Robert. "The Environmental Scene: Just How Bad is the View?" *Business and Society Review/Innovation*, Winter 1972–1973, pp. 73–80.

*Heller, Walter W. "Coming to Terms with Growth and the Environment." Paper prepared for the Forum on Energy, Economic Growth and the Environment, Resources for the Future, Washington, D.C., April 1971.

*Henderson, Hazel. "Ecologists versus Economists." *Harvard Business Review*, July-August 1973, pp. 28–40.

Herfindahl, Orris C., and Kneese, Allen V. *Quality of the Environment: An Economic Approach to Some Problems in Using Land, Water, and Air*. Washington, D.C.: Resources for the Future, 1965.

Hills, Gerald E., and Cravens, David W. "A Conceptual Approach for Analyzing Environmental Systems." Presented at the 19th International Meeting of the Institute of Management Sciences, Houstin, April 5, 1972.

Holden, Matthew, Jr. *Pollution Control as a Bargaining Process*. Ithaca, N.Y.: Water Resources, Center, Cornell University, 1966.

*Jacoby, Neil H. "Organization for Environmental Management—National and Transnational." *Management Science*, June 1973, pp. 1138–1150.

Kangun, Norman. "Environmental Problems and Marketing: Saint or Sinner?" Prepared for the National Conference on Social Marketing, University of Illinois, Champaign-Urbana, December 2–5, 1972. p. 31.

Kefalas, Asterios G. "The Management of Environment Information: A Machine for Adapting a System to Its Environment." Presented at the 12th American Meeting of the Institute of Management Sciences, Detroit, September 29-October 2, 1971.

*Kneese, Allen V. "Why Water Pollution Is Economically Unavoidable." *Transaction*, April 1968, pp. 31–36.

_____. "Management Science, Economics and Environmental Science." *Management Science*, June 1973, pp. 1122–1137.

_____. *See also* Herfindahl, Orris C.

Lawrence, Paul R., and Lorsch, Jay W. *Organization and Environment*. Boston: Graduate School of Business Administration, Harvard University, 1967.

"Less Noise, More Action." Editorial, *Fortune*, April 1971, p. 57.

*Lessing, Lawrence. "The Revolt Against the Internal Combustion Engine." *Fortune* 76, no. 1 (July 1967): 78–83.

Marlin, John Tepper. "Accounting for Pollution." *The Journal of Accountancy*, February 1973.

McDonald, John. "Oil and the Environment: The View from Maine." *Fortune*, April 1971, p. 84.

McKee, Jack Edward. "Water Pollution Control: A Task for Technology." *California Management Review* 14, no. 3 (Spring 1972): 88–91.

*Meadows, Donella H., and Randers, Jorgen. "The Carrying Capacity of the Globe." *Sloan Management Review*, Winter 1972, pp. 11–28.

*Mishan, E. J. "On Making the Future Safe for Mankind." *The Public Interest*, Summer 1971, pp. 33–61.

*Moynihan, Daniel P. "The War Against the Automobile." *The Public Interest*, Spring 1966, pp. 10–26.

*Murdoch, William, and Connell, Joseph. "All About Ecology." *Center Magazine* 3, no. 1 (January-February 1970): 56–63.

Perloff, Harvey S., ed. *The Quality of the Urban Environment*. Baltimore: Johns Hopkins Press, 1969.

Petter, F. M. "Pollution and the Public." *Center Magazine*, May-June 1970, pp. 18–24.

*Potter, Frank M., Jr. "Everyone Wants To Save the Environment But No One Knows Quite What To Do." *Center Magazine*, March-April 1970, pp. 34–40.

Ridgeway, James. *The Last Play*. New York: E. P. Dutton & Co., 1973.

Ritchie-Calder, Lord. "Polluting the Environment." *Center Magazine*, May 1969, pp. 7–12.

*Ruff, Larry E. "The Economic Common Sense of Pollution." *The Public Interest*, undated, pp. 69–85.

*Sethi, S. Prakash. *Up Against the Corporate Wall: Modern Corporations and Social Issues of the Seventies*. 2d ed. Englewood Cliffs, N.J.: Prentice-Hall, 1974.

*Simon, Herbert A. "Technology and the Environment." *Management Science*, June 1973, pp. 1110–1121.

*"Society and Its Physical Environment." *Annals of the American Political and Social Sciences* 389 (May 1970): entire issue.

The Conference Board. *Business Amid Urban Crisis: Private-Sector Approaches to City Problems*. Studies in Public Affairs no. 3 New York: The Conference Board, 1968.

*_____. *Corporate Organization for Pollution Control*. New York: The Conference Board, 1970.

"The Politics of Environmental Disruption." Editorial, *Fortune*, January 1971, p. 69.

*Ways, Max. "How To Think About the Environment." *Fortune*, February 1970, pp. 98–101.

*White, Lawrence J. "The Auto Pollution Muddle." *The Public Interest*, Summer 1973, 97–112.

Imposed Constraints on the Auto Industry: A View from Two Perspectives

●●●

● ERNEST S. STARKMAN
Vice-President
Environmental Activities, General Motors Corporation

During the decade of the 1960's it would appear that much of America turned sour on itself. Every major public opinion poll shows this. But I doubt that any pollster would be so bold as to identify with any assurance a single reason—it could be Vietnam, the population explosion, the urban crisis, domestic social concerns, the degradation of the environment, consumerism, or the so-called youth movement.

As part of this trend, the American public has become increasingly critical of the profits, prices, and policies of the country's largest corporations and, indeed, of the entire economic structure. A recent published poll indicated that two-thirds of the public believes Washington should set ceilings on prices, and one-third thinks the same about profits. Some of the populace would break up larger corporations. And the views of intellectual leaders tend to be more critical than those of most others.

Coming on even stronger than economic factors in recent years has been the public concern over the environment. In the area of pollution control, a considerable portion of the public has felt and still feels that business is not doing its share in the cleanup. While it must be recognized that some of the critics are responsible only to themselves and have little technical knowledge on the subject, still, some of the criticism has been well taken.

The public and business itself have been redefining corporate social responsibility. And I hope that the gap between the two opinions is narrowing as industry accepts a larger share of this responsibility. The degree of social responsibility varies from one company to another, but the direction has been obvious. Most companies' annual reports now even devote a special section to a discussion of their efforts and expenditures to solve social and environmental problems. And these are among the major points of discussion at the annual meetings.

The environmental movement continues to be alive and kicking, far more vigorously than most realists expected amid all the words and banners of the first Earth Day in 1970. In the two intervening years, the movement has passed through the fad stage, through the stage of discussing just what the problems are, and has progressed well into the painfully costly job of cleaning up the mess. In place of antics, hard work is under way.

Environmental Concerns in the Auto Industry

At General Motors we have been deeply concerned about public opinion, particularly among intellectual leaders, of which this group might be representative. We have contracted for our own public opinion polls to determine just what the public thinks about the job we've been doing with our product quality and our performance in social areas, and to disclose the issues to major concern.

While these polls indicate that criticism of the auto industry has been leveling off, and that product- and customer-related factors continue to be the most important considerations in judging a manufacturer, there is still considerable concern over the auto industry's performance on a number of social issues. At the top of this list is automative pollution, followed closely by industrial pollution. These happen to be two of the areas to which GM is giving its concerted attention and investing huge sums of manpower and money.

Indeed, that's how I happen to be with GM. I left academia to accept my current position because I became convinced that the company was sincere in its expression of wishing to solve the environmental problems facing it. Prior to seeking my services, GM has observed that environmental concerns were taking increasingly more and more time, resources, and expenditures. To manage these efforts effectively, it was decided to revise the administration within GM and create a new entity—the Environmental Activities Staff—which would combine and coordinate the environmental and safety assignments already in existence elsewhere in the organization.

These staffs had been doing the job, but their message wasn't coming across. There had been criticism of "footdragging." In reality, in some instances, this was the consequence of an attempt to obtain the lead time for a rational and reasonable approach and/or solution to environmental and safety problems. The apparent footdragging, additionally, was also a real reflection of the economic system under which we operate. It is a truism that manufacturing will be done where it can be done most efficiently. It will flow to the lowest-cost producer, all other conditions being comparable—quality, delivery of the product, etc. Those companies that might lead the way environmentally would naturally suffer in the marketplace as their costs increase over those of competitors who are not so socially conscious. So, certainly, legislation was inevitable, and even welcomed by industry.

Environmental Legislation

Much of the environmental legislation that has been passed was adopted without rational conception and essentially programs technological breakthroughs in the auto industry. In a way, it's a compliment that the legislators felt that engineers could develop the expertise to do about anything—perhaps a product of the space age. But in perspective, the passage of legislation as stringent as, for example, the Clean Air Act Amendments of 1970 creates the kind of dilemma we currently face in the vehicle emissions area. Such legislation is capable of being extremely wasteful of resources, while at the same time accomplishing little toward solving the problems. When regulation is unwarranted or ill-considered, and not based on an understanding of technology, costs, and benefits, then it is a severe limitation on the free-enterprise system.

The question has not been whether or not there should be controls, but rather at what level controls should be set. Perhaps the best way to approach this subject of constraints imposed on the auto industry is to bring you up to date on what we've been doing and the problems we're facing, to give you our perspective on the state of the art in environmental areas.

Automotive Emissions

Meeting the requirements of the clean air amendments of 1970 is perhaps the toughest technical challenge that the auto industry has ever faced. This act requires a 90-percent reduction by 1975–1976 in the three main auto pollutants—carbon monoxide (CO), hydrocarbons (HC), and oxides of nitrogen (NO_x)—as measured against the 1970–1971 levels.

Existing legislation (1970) already required that cars and light trucks be reduced in the first two of these pollutants. Consequently, to meet the new law, our vehicles by 1975–1976 must have reductions of 97 percent in hydrocarbons; 96 percent in carbon monoxide; and 92 percent in oxides of nitrogen, as measured from the uncontrolled levels of a 1960 vehicle (table 1).

TABLE 1.   Automobile Exhaust Emission Reduction from Uncontrolled Levels.

	1975–1976 Requirements	Current Emission Reductions
Hydrocarbons	97%	80%*
Carbon Monoxide	96%	70%*
Oxides of Nitrogen	92%	25%†

*May 1972 field performance tests.
†Based on 1971 California tests.

Tests of field performance of our 1972-model cars indicate an 80-percent hydrocarbon reduction, a 70-percent carbon monoxide reduction, and about a 25-percent reduction in oxides of nitrogen (Table 1). As we have added a new control device on the 1973 cars to further control NO_x, we expect to come up to about a 40-percent reduction in this third pollutant in the field. But whether we will be able to meet the 1975–1976 standards in the time available is a developing question.

Now, how has this been accomplished? Shown on figure 1 is our 1973 emission control system. While I will not discuss details of the functions, these devices not only reduce emissions from evaporation and the crankcase, but also minimize the formation of exhaust emissions through better control of the combustion process, more accurate metering of the fuel, timing of the spark, controlling of air temperature, and internal engine design.

Since enactment of the clean air amendments, we have been striving to develop hardware that will meet the emission levels prescribed for 1975 and subsequent model years. You have undoubtedly heard of various experimental control systems that have met the required emission levels of all three pollutants on a laboratory basis. As you may know, some of these systems have been developed by GM.

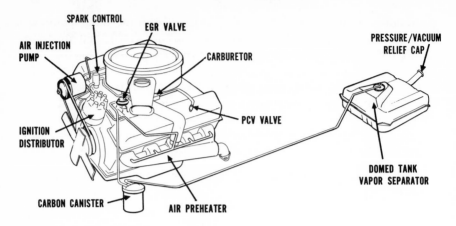

FIGURE 1.   1973 emission control system.

1975–1976 Emission Reduction Levels

In an atempt to meet the standards as written, we currently plan to install all of the hardware shown on figure 2. An air ejection pump will provide additional air for effective operation of a catalytic converter that may be located in the exhaust line or on the exhaust manifold. Also featured will probably be an improved carburetor, a quick-heat manifold for early fuel evaporation, and an electronic high-energy ignition system to improve ignition performance and reliability. Exhaust gas recirculation, which was

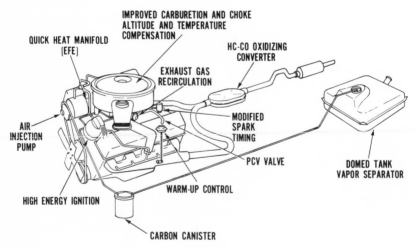

FIGURE 2.   1975 emission control system.

just added in 1973, will be continued through 1975, as will the existing crankcase and evaporative control systems. The system will require contaminant-free fuels. I'd like to emphasize that, as yet, no final decision has been made on any of the precise components to be incorporated in this control system, and many questions remain unanswered.

To give you some perspective on the role of the automobile in the emission concentrations in typical urban areas, figures 3, 4, and 5 show where we are today, and the expected emission reductions from now until 1985, based on the government's own data. For HC, we passed the peak in 1967 or 1968 (figure 3). A similar curve exists for CO—we passed the peak in 1967–1968, with a progressive decline to date (figure 4).

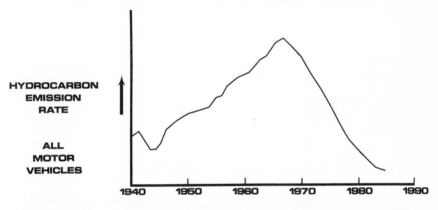

FIGURE 3. Motor vehicle hydrocarbon emissions (typical U.S. urban areas). (U.S. Government data, April 1971.)

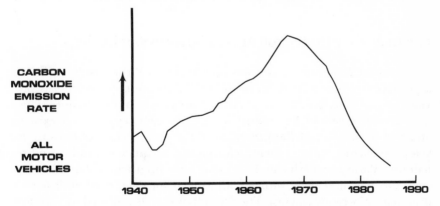

FIGURE 4. Motor vehicle carbon monoxide emissions (typical U.S. urban areas). (U.S. Government data, April 1971.)

Due to the fact that controls for NO_x have only recently been installed on new cars nationwide, a similar downward trend in that pollutant is just now taking place (figure 5). The reported downtrend in air pollution alerts experienced by Los Angeles in 1971 is additional indication that the situation there has been improved. It is reasonable to expect that the same trend is similarly taking place across the nation. This is encouraging, but we do not wish to leave the impression that the air pollution problem has been completely resolved—either in Los Angeles or in other cities of the nation. We do, however, wish to call your attention to the fact that significant progress is being made in cleaning up the motor vehicle—and thus the atmosphere.

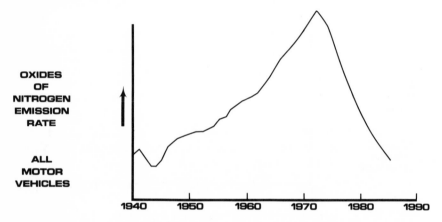

FIGURE 5.   Motor vehicle oxides of nitrogen emissions (typical U.S. urban areas). (U.S. Government data, April 1971.)

Environmental Protection Agency Suspension Hearings

In the recent Environmental Protection Agency (EPA) hearings regarding a possible one-year suspension in the 1975 emission requirements as provided in the congressional act, GM and the other auto companies stated that the delay should be granted since technology does not yet exist to allow us to meet *all* of the provisions of the act, and to enable us to develop, test, and produce systems with proven adequate durability and reliability. Various experimental cars that have been tested showed actual emissions measurements, with no adjustment for deterioration, below or near the 1975 requirements. These results were all achieved at very low mileages, and too recently for adequate follow-up testing for durability and reliability, which requires several months. Further, the fuels used had lead, phosphorus, and sulfur levels below those proposed by EPA.

The GM request also stated that while we were highly optimistic that current problems can be solved and existing uncertainties resolved, it seems virtually impossible that all this can be done quickly enough to permit completion of design, tests, and tooling, as well as running certification tests required for 1975 production.

Problems in Meeting All Requirements

The principal problems related to meeting all the requirements of the Clean Air Act for 1975-model vehicles are not associated with the capability of attaining emission numbers established by the regulations on experimental vehicles or systems run under carefully controlled conditions. Rather, the difficulties are in providing a system capable of mass production, which is sufficiently durable and reliable that it will perform satisfactorily under the widely varied conditions to which it will be subjected by our millions of customers in the field. This was also the basic conclusion of the report made to the EPA by the National Academy of Sciences. It was noted that the incremental improvement lost through the one-year delay is very minor—the effect on the environment is small—compared to the total improvement already achieved and projected.

As you know, EPA Administrator Ruckelshaus rejected all five applicants in his decision in May, with the statement that there was no proof that presently available control technology would not be adequate to achieve compliance with the standards by the statutory deadline. It is noted that Ruckelshaus did not address the point as to whether he considered "the public interest" in his decision, although this is required by the Clean Air Act! Obviously, then, the attempt to meet the 1975 standards is the highest priority item within the company—and has been for some time. Otherwise, in less than two years, we may not be able to sell cars. Be assured that we are going all out.

Before leaving the discussion on automotive emissions, I'd like to add that we realize the atmospheric improvements resulting from the levels of control already applied to the automobile have not been without penalty. Many who have purchased recent-model cars have experienced a decrease in the driving response and, sometimes, difficulty in starting. This adverse effect on driveability is an unfortunate consequence of modifications made in order to decrease the pollutants from the exhaust pipe.

While the individual vehicle owner usually does not measure precisely the fuel consumption of his vehicle, I can confirm what is perhaps your own experience—that the public is paying a penalty in increased fuel usage for the same vehicle applications. This result is not pleasing to any manufacturer—and certainly not to the car buyer. Indeed, GM has had to discontinue some of its engine-vehicle combinations after making modifications to emissions control systems; in our opinion, the driveability and fuel economy of these combinations would not have been acceptable to the public.

Energy Consumption

Increased fuel consumption due to the required emission controls is just the opposite of what we desire in the face of the apparently developing energy crisis. Actually, this might better be called a "clean energy shortage." Last June, in the President's message to Congress, the energy supply was officially recognized for the first time in our history as a major national problem. GM is a major fuel user. We consume one-quarter of one percent of the total U.S. energy output in our manufacturing processes; the transportation industry consumes nearly one-quarter of the total U.S. output.

According to the National Petroleum Council, automobiles account for approximately 38 percent of the petroleum demand. And, as I said, unfortunately they may consume even more as we attempt to further reduce emissions by trading engine efficiency for cleaner air.

Domestic oil production from established reserves is nearing its peak (see figure 6). Except for Alaskan oil, future domestic finds will be devoted to maintaining existing production rates. Growth must come from somewhere else—imports or synthetics from coil or shale. By 1980, imports will comprise nearly half of our oil supply. Concern centers not only on the vast drain this imposes on balance of payments, but the uncertainty of the supply line. Other areas, such as Europe and Japan, will want their share.

Demand for natural gas is high and will continue to rise for two reasons. It is clean and cheap. At the same time, existing reserves are depleting to the point that production rates face a rapid decline. You can't get it out of the ground any faster than the rate shown in figure 7.

Exploration, which is quite limited at present due to price regulation, is not expected to be able to make up the loss. To do so would require additional finds each year, equal to the amount of gas in Alaska's northern slope. The so-called gas gap appears rather permanent. GM plants, at this time, rely on natural gas for about 39 percent of their energy supply.

The continuing operation of U.S. industry is dependent on a viable energy base, and this base is rapidly eroding. To meet these challenges, in

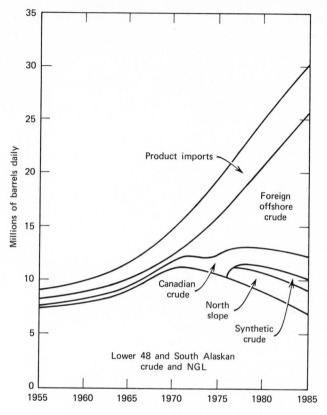

FIGURE 6.   U.S. petroleum supply.

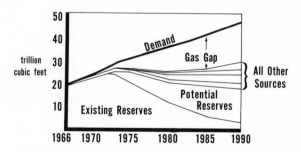

FIGURE 7.   U.S. gas supply-demand.

GM we have formed our own in-house energy planning group to help fore-see how energy trends will affect us. This group will (1) monitor supply and demand, (2) keep track of political and regulatory changes, (3) provide the staffs and divisions with guidance in fuel purchasing, research, investment and planning decisions, and (4) coordinate a corporate energy conserva-tion program.

Automotive Safety

All of our talk about vehicles so far has been of the power plant, particu-larly as it relates to exhaust emissions. Another dynamic area in vehicle design, in which our relationship with the federal government has been equally close, is safety.

For the most part conventional design practices and manufacturing tech-niques have been adequate to allow the product changes instituted for safety. But one innovation now in the process of development is presenting extraordinary problems.

In preparing the standard for occupant protection, the government agency that controls safety, the National Highway Traffic Safety Adminis-tration (NHTSA), paid little regard to the necessities of lead time, cost, and level of technology. This standard calls for front-seat-occupant passive re-straints or a belt system with ignition interlock in 1974 cars, and for all-seat passive restraints in 1976. In a 1972 or 1973 car (see figure 8) you have the warning buzzer and light to remind you to wear your seat belt. With the ignition interlock system next year, you won't be able to start the car until you buckle up. That is the option we are choosing for 1974. In 1976 cars, there is no option; a completely passive system is required. For most people, "passive restraint" means the air bag or, as we call it, the air cushion.

The NHTSA does not specifically require the air cushion. Either interior padding or a passive belt system is acceptable to the government if it pro-tects adequately in all frontal impacts and rollovers up to 30 mph, and side impacts up to 20 mph. A car with the extra padding would not have as much interior room as we are used to, but the potential is good at lower speeds. The requirement of 30 mph seems close to the limit of effective-ness for the padded interior.

Passive Restraint Systems

The system that gets most of the publicity is the air cushion, which has the initial advantage of not changing the appearance of the car's interior

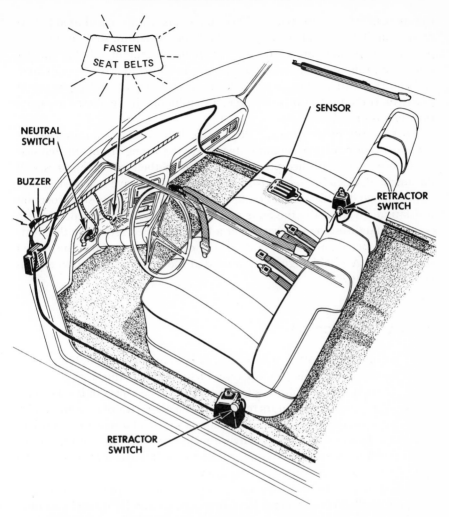

FIGURE 8.   1972 belt restraint system, effective January 1, 1972.

to any marked degree. An advantage over seat belts is that the air cushion distributes the force over a larger area of the body than the belt. It also is calculated to prevent the head from rotating downward to the point where it might strike a harder part of the interior structure. Although for the direct frontal impact the air cushion may be superior to other systems, seat belts give protection in angular and side impacts and in rollovers.

General Motors is in the process of building 1000 Chevrolet Impalas with the air cushion restraint system; 500 of these cars will be distributed to GM fleets, and 500 in commercial fleets. We hope to acquire some needed experience in production, including the establishment of reliable quality control techniques. Diagnostic equipment in the field will be evaluated, and the cars will enable us to establish effective repair and replacement practices. If the project proceeds well, air cushions will be offered as an option on certain 1974 vehicles.

Work is still progressing on the passive belt system as an alternative. Proponents of passive occupant systems have the strong argument that seat belts never have won acceptance, even though their effectiveness is well documented. Coercion methods in the United States have not worked thus far, although the Department of Transportation is proposing coercion legislation. In Australia the State of Victoria had a 17 percent decrease in occupant fatalities the first year after a law was passed requiring the wearing of seat belts, and a year later all the other states in Australia passed similar laws. Available figures indicate that the improvement in safety has continued in 1972.

Vehicle Noise Control

Noise pollution is another subject that is becoming increasingly popular. This concern about noise, in our case, includes our plants and all of our products, from home appliances to locomotives. One aspect of it—the automotive noise problem—is an increasingly immediate area of concern. Noise from motor vehicles is being singled out as a source of annoyance in urban situations. As a result, both the environmentalists and those in regulatory agencies of the government are beginning to take interest and action in the noise abatement of transportation equipment.

Legislation has been passed in 11 states, which requires increasingly stringent decibel requirements for passenger cars and light trucks, as indicated:

—the decibel level limit has been 86 db. since the late 1960's.
—Drops to 84 db. on the 1973 models.
—Down to 80 db. in 1975.
—Down to 75 db. in 1978.
—And eventually to 70 db. by 1988.

Somewhat similar requirements exist for heavy trucks, not quite as tough currently, but they will eventually be as stringent.

Technology exists to a certain extent in the vehicle noise area, although it does not allow us to meet all of the state legislation already on the books. One of our major goals is to acquaint lawmakers with the principles of sound and noise so that they will promote legislation based on scientific principles. We did not act quickly enough to assure reasonableness in much of the legislation on safety and exhaust emissions.

Industrial Air and Water Pollution Control

Regarding a final area of concern, industrial air pollution, the dust and particulate emissions from a foundry operation in the past were so dense that the sun was obscured. While the silhouette in figure 9 may have had some photographic appeal, the tons of dust did not. It should be noted that control devices then available were being used when this picture was taken. However, the wet-caps used were not sufficient enough; only about 50 percent of the dust was removed.

GM worked with suppliers on the application of high-energy scrubbers to control cupola emissions, with the result that a skyline can be converted to one that looks like that of figure 10. The high-energy scrubber used by Chevrolet's nodular iron foundry at Saginaw, Michigan achieves an effi-

FIGURE 9.   Typical foundry of the 1960's.

FIGURE 10.   Chevrolet nodular iron foundry in Saginaw, Michigan.

ciency of better than 98 percent, and all that is visible is a barely discernible plume of water vapor.

One of the tougher problems industry is facing in this area is to clean the sulfur dioxide from stack gases. Since coal is our most plentiful energy source in this country (but low-sulfur coal is scarce), we must figure out a way to eliminate this corrosive gas. For the last four or five years, a number of concerned companies have explored ways to burn coal more cleanly. We have investigated many approaches; our latest is a demonstration project at our Chevrolet-Cleveland operation (figure 11). It uses an alkaline scrubbing solution. The water-cleansing system is completely self-contained and recycled. The only residue is an inert harmless cake material that looks as if it will make acceptable landfill. If this is successful in reducing the sulfur dioxide emissions to required levels, the technology could be applied elsewhere throughout the country to allow us to burn coal, of which this country has, as I said, a plentiful supply.

For water pollution control, the concept of batch treatment is used where potentially toxic wastes such as chrome or cyanide are generated. A batch system simply means that through dual tank storage the wastes are treated, checked, and released only after we are certain they have been detoxified.

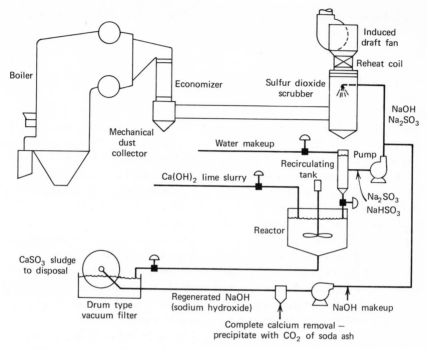

FIGURE 11. Sulfur dioxide control; GM industrial flue gas scrubbing process.

One of the most sophisticated water pollution control facilities in the country is at our Harrison Radiator operation in Lockport, New York. This has 13 outdoor water treatment tanks, with a 10-million gallon capacity. It can treat 6000 gallons of waste water in a minute. This is among the over 100 water pollution control facilities we have installed in the last 25 years in the U.S.

GM's Water Conservation Projects

I might mention at this point that GM is planning a new and major water conservation project. Using all known technology, GM plans to build an effective closed-loop or "totally conserved" water system for a major plant. The purpose is to treat industrial waste water discharges so effectively that the treated water may be used continuously in the manufacturing process. Our goal is to have a pilot installation next year.

The challenges associated with industrial environmental control are complicated, but we feel that we have identified our environmental problems, have established our objectives and priorities, and are well on our way to finding solutions.

Conclusions

One of the things that led the United States to its present position as a world leader has been its impatience. We see immediate problems and want immediate solutions. This, however, often leads to the kind of legislative overkill we have in the clean air amendments requirements for 1975–1976. But in many cases, there is no immediate solution, even if the law has been passed that says there must be. Real progress depends on reasonable public goals and the dedication and creativity of technical people. The environment so far has paid too large a price for the development of civilization that has taken place—in terms of pollution—in terms of degradation of the land itself and the biosphere. From now on, we have to operate under the assumption that, through technological development, we can maintain a sophisticated, industrial type of civilization and at the same time protect the environment. We believe there are solutions to environmental problems, and we expect to make substantial progress.

To buy adequate lead time to do the job, we in industry, and in the government, must anticipate the trends, look beyond the current environmental headlines or the current regulatory requirements, and make a needed investment in the quality of life, with full consideration of cost benefit to the consumer. To thoughtful observers of the contemporary scene, it is increasingly evident that the American free enterprise system is no longer an *economic* system only. It is a *social* system. Corporations are obligated to the total social system. They must be relevant to its culture and concerned with the quality of its life as well as the strength of its economy.

Just as the survival of individual companies is dependent on profits, so the survival of our free-enterprise system is dependent on the reclamation and preservation of a healthful natural environment.

Pollution Control: Let's Stop Waiting for Government*

●●

● JOHN TEPPER MARLIN

Baruch College
City University of New York

The pollution control record of Congress, the executive branch, and the states is not an encouraging one. Recent signs of life among the regulatory agencies, apparently generated by public outrage and consumer activism, should not obscure the fact that their history is one of deference to the industries that they were established to regulate.

Environmentalists must face questions that are inherent in any business-government interface: How, if at all, can regulatory agencies serve the public interest effectively? What alternative methods are there for bringing public pressure to bear on irresponsible businesses? Should the public stop waiting for the government, and confront irresponsible citizens in the business community directly?

This paper reviews the defects in the American regulatory system and concludes that the regulatory agencies are best confined to arbitrative functions. The main problem is providing adequate funding for public advocates. The system is seen as being workable only if agencies have to consider a relatively small number of cases and issues. Business as a whole

*The author would like to thank Alice Tepper Marlin, James Turner, R. Maximilian Geopp III, and Arthur Leff for helpful comments.

345

must be asked to cooperate in the solution of social problems, such as pollution, on a voluntary basis. More information must be made available by companies on their social performance, and centers for the evaluation of this performance must be supported. The public can in turn support socially responsible businesses in the marketplace by taking into account social performance in its buying, investing, working, and voting decisions. But when a business fails to respond voluntarily to appeals and marketplace pressures, consumer advocates are needed to bring irresponsibility before an administrative court for arbitration and compensation.

Governmental Regulation

The spearhead for the attack on regulation has been the efficiency argument propounded by the Chicago School of Economists,[1] especially Milton Friedman. Friedman argues that the government's natural function is that of making uniformly applicable rules within which markets can operate, and serving as umpire for violation of these rules. Its only three other legitimate domestic functions, he says, are to regulate natural or "technical" monopolies (monopolies that aren't actually created by government and that would be eliminated if government withdrew its support of them); compensate victims of "neighborhood effects" such as pollution, while taxing the source of these effects; and protect madmen and children.[2]

While consumer advocates start with a concern for equity rather than efficiency, they are as suspicious of regulatory agencies as efficiency-oriented economists. They, too, have accumulated mountains of data to show that the regulatory agencies are not serving the public and that instead they raise prices, reduce output, and create bureaucratic and unresponsive in-

---

[1]Milton Friedman, *Capitalism and Freedom* (Chicago: University of Chicago Press, 1962), pp. 25–32. Some examples of attacks on the ICC, CAB, and FCC, are: George W. Hilton, "The Consistency of the Interstate Commerce Act," *Journal of Law and Economics* 9 (1966): 87–113; Christopher D. Stone, "ICC: Some Reminiscences on the Future of American Transportation," *New Individualist Review* 2, no. 4 (1963): 3–15; Michael E. Levine, "Landing Fees and the Airport Congestion Problem," *Journal of Law and Economics* 12 (1969): 79–108; Sam Peltzman, "CAB: Freedom from Competition," *New Individualist Review* 2, no. 4 (1963): 16–23; R. H. Coase, "The Federal Communications Commission," *Journal of Law and Economics* 2 (1959): 1–40; Harvey J. Levin, "Federal Control of Entry in the Broadcast Industry," *Journal of Law and Economics* 5 (1962): 49–67, and Harvey J. Levin, "The Radio Spectrum Resource," *Journal of Law and Economics* 11 (October 1968): 433–501.

[2]Friedman, *Capitalism and Freedom*, pp. 25–34.

dustries.[3] Some critics from the left go even further and argue that the regulatory agencies were created as part of a conspiracy to defraud and subjugate the consumer. The degree to which the custodians of free-market theory and consumer advocates are in agreement may be seen by a recent booklet published by the industry-financed American Enterprise Institute, entitled *The Consumer Advocate versus the Consumer*. While it purports to show that consumer advocates are antagonistic to the free market, a careful reading shows just the opposite. The author, Yale Law Professor Ralph Winter, allows that some of the goals of the consumer movement are legitimate and may be classified as rule-making functions of government.. The government should establish uniform standards, suppress false advertising, protect third parties from danger, and even require sellers to identify potentially harmful and inadequately labeled products.[4] Yet these "allowable goals" for consumer advocates encompass the great majority of their demands!

Most economists today would support the view that, when it is desirable for the government to intervene in the marketplace, for example, to protect the environment, it should do so with a minimum of disturbance to price relationships. This means, for example, imposing taxes rather than quotas or outright bans, and making the taxes payable across the board rather than by one sector of the economy, unless the taxes are related to use of public goods.

This view is derived from economist's appreciation of the efficiency of the market as an allocator of goods. Intervention in the market often reduces efficiency. Most economists therefore endorse the charge that the government intervenes in a lot of areas that it should stay out of. The regulatory agencies in particular are pointed to as inefficient forms of governmental intervention.

The confluence of views on the proper role of government makes this a good time in our history to strip the regulatory agencies of their price-setting, advocacy, and entry-barring roles. Their emphasis should be shifted to referee functions such as increased reporting (accurate labeling, more comprehensive annual reports, fair advertising), opening up administrative

[3]The best-known recent consumer attacks on regulatory agencies are perhaps Edward F. Cox et al., *The Nader Report on the Federal Trade Commission* (New York: Grove Press, 1969); Robert Fellmeth, *The Interstate Commerce Omission* (New York: Grossman, 1970); and James S. Turner, *The Chemical Feast: Report on the Food and Drug Administration* (New York: Grossman, 1970). The conspiracy theory of regulatory agencies is expounded in Gabriel Kolko, *The Triumph of Conservatism* (Cleveland: Quadrangle Books, 1963).

[4]Ralph Winter, *The Consumer Advocate versus the Consumer* (Washington, D.C.: American Enterprise Institute, 1972), pp. 4–5.

courts to public advocates, and making public representation mandatory in any case involving judgments about (and therefore possibly concessions to) business. The concept of the agency itself as the representative of the public should in most cases be buried without further ceremony. The exception would be agencies that either regulate monopolies, such as the Antitrust Division of the Justice Department, or could be involved in compensation, such as the Environmental Protection Agency.

Efficient businesses should welcome regulatory reform. Many are hurt by regulation because they are users of regulated services. Businesses are the first to suffer from overregulated railroad, trucking, and airline services, which Interstate Commerce Commission (ICC) and Civil Aeronautics Board (CAB) rules have made overpriced and difficult to deal with. Businesses are also the first to be hurt by the regulatory agencies acting as both advocate and judge, because they have to deal with an arbitrary decision maker whose judgments are difficult to forecast. Even the regulated industry itself, although it benefits for a time by the guaranteed markets it enjoys, often finds itself losing its more competent executives to more dynamic industries and heads into decline.

Self-Regulation of Business

The history of American corporations goes back to the mercantilist system in England, under which the British Crown chartered companies to undertake projects for His/Her Majesty, in return for their undertaking clearly defined obligations to the Crown—which was the repository, according to the era's myths, of the public interest. While Sir Walter Raleigh planned on making money from his project to colonize America, his appeal to the Crown didn't mention profit as an argument.[5] The Crown attempted to protect stockholders, creditors, and the general public from possible malfeasance of management.

The problem with the mercantilist system was that corporations were given special privileges such as free land, reduced taxes, trade or traffic monoplies, and absolution from debts. Adam Smith in 1776 attacked the system because of its restrictions on competition, which kept prices high, supply of goods down, and generally hurt the consumer. He also warned the public that established businesses could and did use the state to restrict competition. His procompetition stance was not based on a faith in business responsibility, but rather on his deep-seated skepticism of it.

Smith's call for free competition was used by a new breed of American

[5]David Finn, *The Corporate Oligarch* (New York: Simon & Schuster, 1969), pp. 48–52.

mercantilists to pursue a weakening of governmental regulation. Smith's warning about business-government ties was all but forgotten. Alexander Hamilton, for example, is credited with having introduced the New Jersey bill for the first incorporation in the United States, along British lines, arguing on the basis of benefits to the public (the corporation was to pursue certain social goals and limit its profits to 15 percent) and requesting in return tax and other concessions. But as more corporations were chartered, the state governments began to give up their requirement that a business pursue social goals. As competition for corporate location stiffened, New York in 1811 and Connecticut in 1837 both broke new ground in making incorporation easier. Finally, Delaware won the potlatch in 1896.[6]

Freedom of incorporation, while it did limit the liability of shareholders and managers and thereby facilitated rapid buildup of capital, was not accompanied by effective restrictions on the activities of the corporations. Business managers had the incentive to hire lobbyists and support political candidates in whatever ways would increase their profits, and they had as a rationale a bastardized form of Smith's free-market model, which justified everything in the name of profit. What was neglected was that the "invisible hand" was not effective against damage to consumer interests by business-government collusion.

In the twentieth century, however, three waves of public unrest have washed over business (the muckrakers, the New Dealers, and the current Nader-inspired consumer advocates), and each one seems to be stronger than the last.[7] These waves may have resulted from the expectations that have been built up by the power and wealth business has accumulated. When society's problems are not solved, the public blames those who seem to have the power to solve them, and this reasoning leads them to look accusingly into corporate boardrooms and executive suites. What has outraged the public most intensely is the discovery of the extent to which business actually lobbies against attempts to solve problems when its own interests are threatened, then absolves itself from responsibility by claiming it's the government's job.

[6]Morton Mintz and Jerry S. Cohen, *America, Inc.* (New York: Dial Press, 1971), p. 435.

[7]Five references can be provided on the "old wine in new bottles" theme: Thomas C. Cochran, *The American Business System: A Historical Perspective, 1900–1955* (Cambridge: Harvard University Press, 1960); Louis Filler, *Crusades for American Liberalism: The Story of the Muckrakers* (New York: Harcourt, Brace & Co., 1939); Ellis Hawley, *The New Deal and the Problem of Monopoly* (Princeton, N.J.: Princeton University Press, 1966); Robert O. Herrman, "Consumerism: Its Goals, Organization and Future," *Journal of Marketing* 34 (October 1970): 55–60; Arthur and Lila Weinberg, *The Muckrakers* (New York: Capricorn Books, 1964). I am indebted to David Vogel for suggesting sources in this area.

What could a "responsible" businessman do under these conditions? For one thing, he should find out what his trade association and other lobbyists are doing in his name, and object to activities that do not make sense from a long-term viewpoint. It does not make sense for paper companies to lobby against pollution control if the industry would be better off in the long run with cleaner mills and if the leaders in pollution control operate at a disadvantage under prevailing competitive conditions.

A simple way for a businessman to start to be a better citizen is for him to attempt to make his corporation more open about its activities. More detailed (and honest) financial statements represent a step in this direction. Beyond this, the annual report could provide the public with both data and relevant standards for evaluation of the company's pollution control status. Some types of information on pollution control are impossible to evaluate by themselves—total expenditures on equipment, for example, or compliance with state environmental regulations (see table 1). Expenditures can be inflated by including costs not directly related to pollution control. Similarly, compliance with state laws may simply reflect relatively lenient state laws and enforcement practices. Wisconsin and North Carolina are significantly less stringent than, for example, Washington and Minnesota, and federal laws will not remove differences in state pollution control enforcement.[8]

There are two feasible and useful ways of reporting and evaluating pollution control performance. One is the state-of-the-art approach pioneered by the Council on Economic Priorities and shown for four sample paper companies in table 2.[9] The other is the acceptable emissions approach used as the basis for evaluating U.S. Army Corps of Engineers' water discharge permits and shown for three sample paper mills in table 3.[10]

Ideally one would like to be able to evaluate a corporation's social impact in doller terms, so that a combined financial and social impact statement could be presented. A company's pollution impact might be measured in terms of the increased medical bills of local residents, increased repainting costs, and so forth. However, the problems of identifying, isolating, and attributing costs—quite apart from the difficulties inherent in any attempt to quantify intangibles such as ugliness—are enormous, and tech-

[8]Information on state laws from Elizabeth Haskell and Victoria Price, *State Environmental Management: Nine Case Studies* (New York: Praeger, in press).

[9]Fuller discussion of standards and auditing proposals may be found in John Tepper Marlin, "Accounting for Pollution," *Journal of Accountancy* 135, no. 2 (1973): 41–46.

[10]John and Alice Tepper Marlin, "The International Paper 1970 Annual Report," *Business and Society Review*, Spring 1972, pp. 118–120.

TABLE 1.   Inadequate Standards for Pollution Control Performance

Company*	Standard	Data	Claim
Diamond International (1970)	None	None	"We will continue to do our share" in environmental protection
International Paper (1970)	Total expenditures on pollution control	$23 million 1965–1970, $100 million 1970-1974, (planned)	"We have been concerned with pollution for years"
St. Regis (1970)	Total expenditures on pollution control	$2.5 million 1970, $65 million more 1971–1976 (planned)	Company has placed "great emphasis" on pollution control
Kimberly-Clark (1971)	Compliance with state laws	16 out of 24 plants using large amounts of water meet legal standards for water pollution control	(No information given on air pollution control)
Great Northern Nekoosa (1971)	Compliance with state laws	None	Company "fully complies" with environmental regulations

*Source: Annual Report Year.

niques for converting social costs into dollars are a long way from the point at which one could describe a "social audit" as feasible. A brave but inadequate attempt in this direction by Abt Associates is excerpted in table 4. The Abt audit is intriguing in that it adds social debts to liabilities but does not deduct social costs from income, so that the net effect is always to raise return on equity! The approach described above for pollution control reporting could be extended to other areas of social concern, such as employment and consumer practices, government contracting, and corporate contributions.

TABLE 2. Adequate Standard I: State-of-the-Art Controls—Four Sets of 1972 Company Ratings, by Plant

Georgia-Pacific Pulp Mill Pollution Control					
	Water			Air	
Mill pulp output	Pri.	Sec.	Ter.	Part.	Gas & Odor
Ketchican, Alaska 630 tons/day	(√)	X	X	X	√
Crossett, Ark. 1250 tons/day	√	√	√	√	√
Samoa, Calif. 550 tons/day	X	X	X	√	√
Pt. Hudson, La. 600 tons/day	(√)	(√)	X	(√)	(√)
Woodland, Me. 800 tons/day	√	X	√	√	√
Lyons-Falls, N.Y. 70 tons/day	'73	'73	X	(√)	—
Plattsburgh, N.Y. 70 tons/day	'73	'73	X	√	—
Toledo, Ore. 1000 tons/day	X	X	X	(√)	√
Bellingham, Wash. 500 tons/day	(√)	X	X	X	√

Scott Paper Pulp Mill Pollution Control					
	Water			Air	
Mill pulp output	Pri.	Sec.	Ter.	Part.	Gas & Odor
Mobile, Ala. 1400 tons/day	√	√	X	'73	X
Brunswick, Ga. 1500 tons/day	√	(√)	X	(√)	(√)
Westbrook, Me. 300 tons/day	√	X	X	√	(√)
Winslow, Me. 430 tons/day	'74	X	X	(√)	—
Menominee, Mich.	Closed				
Muskegon, Mich. 225 tons/day	√	(√)	X	X	√
Anacortes, Wash. 135 tons/day	√	X	X	√	√
Everett, Wash. 850 tons/day	√	X	X	(√)	√
Marinette, Wis.	Closed				
Oconto Falls, Wis. 115 tons/day	√	'73	X	√	X

TABLE 2. (continued)

| | International Paper Pulp Mill Pollution Control | | | | |
| | Water | | | Air | |
Mill pulp output	Pri.	Sec.	Ter.	Part.	Gas & Odor
Mobile, Ala. 1350 tons/day	√	(√)	X	(√)	√
Camden, Ark. 750 tons/day	√	(√)	X	√	(√)
Pine Bluff, Ark. 1550 tons/day	√	(√)	X	√	'73
Panama City, Fla. 1375 tons/day	√	X	X	(√)	(√)
Bastrop, La. 1700 tons/day	√	(√)	X	√	√
Springhill, La. 1725 tons/day	√	(√)	X	√	X
Jay, Maine 675 tons/day	(√)	(√)	X	√	(√)
Moss Point, Miss. 700 tons/day	√	(√)	X	√	(√)
Natchez, Miss. 950 tons/day	(√)	'74	X	'73	X
Vicksburg, Miss. 1200 tons/day	√	√	X	√	√
Corinth, New York 255 tons/day	(√)	(√)	X	√	—
N. Tonawanda, N.Y. 140 tons/day	(√)	(√)	X	(√)	—
Ticonderoga, N.Y. 550 tons/day	√	√	X	√	√
Gardiner, Ore. 640 tons/day	'73	X	X	'75	√
Georgetown, S.C. 2230 tons/day	√	(√)	X	'73	(√)
Texarkana, Texas to open 1973 60,000 tons/year	√	√	X	√	√

TABLE 2.   Adequate Standard I: State-of-the-Art Controls—Four Sets of 1972 Company Ratings, by Plant (continued)

| | Great Northern Nekoosa Pulp Mill Pollution Control | | | | |
| | Water | | | Air | |
Mill pulp output	Pri.	Sec.	Ter.	Part.	Gas & Odor
Ashdown, Ark. 550 tons/day	√	(√)	X	√	X
Cedar Springs, Ga. 2100 tons/day	√	√	X	X	X
E. Millinocket, Me. 800 tons/day	X	X	X	√	—
Millinocket, Me. 1100 tons/day	(√)	X	X	X	√
Nekoosa, Wis. 340 tons/day	'73	'74	X	X	X
Port Edwards, Wis. 230 tons/day	'74	'73	X	X	—

Note: Facilities are rated adequate (√) or inadequate (X) according to criteria explained in the source. A change in status between 1970 and 1972 is circled. When a date appears it indicates that the facility will be adequately controlled in the year listed. Council on Economic Priorities, "Pollution Audit 1972," *Economic Priorities Report* 3 no. 3 (July-August 1972): 11, 22, 25, 28, 39.

What limited information is available shows that companies who have cleaned up their mills have been much more profitable than companies that have not, even under the unfair conditions that already prevailed. Perhaps smart management is good at both earning profits and being a good citizen.[11] More interesting still, in a consumer-minded climate of opinion, there may be incentives for companies not to wait for the government to make them good citizens. In view of this situation, it is surprising that some companies continue to lobby against pollution control regulations. It could be that business sees itself as a foe of environmentalists even when it would be the first to benefit from a reduction in the level of pollution.

Public Support and Use of Special Performance Research

What is often not appreciated by business today is that the consumer movement is not attempting to use the government as its major weapon to promote corporate responsibility. Instead it is attempting to shed light on

[11]Joseph H. Bragdon, Jr. and John Tepper Marlin, "Is Pollution Profitable?" *Risk Management,* April 1972, pp. 9–18.

instances of business irresponsibility (such as environmental damage) to marshall consumer opinion in the marketplace of ideas and the courts. The concept of consumer has been broadened to include groups such as investors, employees, and communities, *i.e.*, any public interest groups.

The first step in any effort to promote business responsibility through the marketplace is to find out who is doing a good job and who isn't. The Council on Economic Priorities (CEP) was the first group dedicated to this effort and is still unique. It generates most of its funds by the sale of its research on the social performance of corporations to its subscribers, including over 150 businesses.

Some groups attempt to bridge the gap between evaluation and advocacy, by releasing recommendations along with analysis. Among church groups, the Corporate Information Center and NARMIC (National Action/Research on the Military Industrial Complex) combine research with activist stands to promote either the divestment by church endowment funds of stocks of companies doing business with the military or in South Africa (the American Committee on Africa also has this as one of its goals) or protests to management. Among student groups the Committee on Corporate Responsibility at Stanford and the National Affiliation of Concerned Business Students are probably the most durable and prominant of those focusing on corporate social performance. They have evaluated companies as potential employers and offered companies their help in preparing social audits.

Although sometimes not accepted as fully fledged members of the consumer movement because of their profit orientation, the "clean" mutual funds that restrict their investments to responsible companies deserve mention. The largest is Dreyfus' Third Century Fund; others include Pax World Fund ("peace portfolio"), First Spectrum Fund, and Social Dimensions Fund. A major problem with all of the funds is that they do not have significant research staffs and do not disclose their data and standards (if they have any) for making their social performance decisions. What is important is that new centers for evaluation of business responsibility are springing up, along with newsletters, reporting services, and a journal, (*Business and Society Review*). They constitute a vitally important link in the development of a society that does not depend solely on government for remedies to consumer dissatisfaction.

Public Legal Action as Consumers

If government agencies and courts are to act as referees, there must be two sides to the debate: Business *and* the public. Environmentalists should be

TABLE 3. Adequate Standard II: Acceptable Emissions—Sample Net Pollution Emissions and Federal Standards[a] of Three New York Plants, by Type of Pollutant

| | Georgia-Pacific, Plattsburgh, N.Y. (NSSC plup) | International Paper, Ticonderoga, N.Y. (kraft pulp) | Scott Paper Co., Fort Edward, N.Y. (tissue manufacture)[b] | | | Federal drinking water standards[c] | |
			#1 White water tank	#1 Sewer	Pulping area, floor drain	Desirable	Permissible
Production (tons/day)	70	550	170	170	170	—	—
Flow ('000 gals./day)	5,000	19,000	127	410	23	—	—
A. BOD	344	18	93?	156?	234?	?(8)[d]	?(14)[d]
Chemical Oxygen Demand	1,742	110	46	254	573	?	?
Solids, Dissolved	1,454	478	3	114	28	200	500
Solids, Suspended	264	21	16	170	399	?(6)[d]	?(10)[d]
B. Color	40	220	0	12	7	10	75
Coliform Bacteria	760,000	20	0?	0?	1,900	100	10,000
Phenols	45	0?	2	5	4	0	.001
Sulfate	9	186	—0.8	0.2	3	50	250
Chloride	15	388	0.7	0.5	3	25	250
Copper	15	0?	35?	30	25	0	1
Lead	0	0?	—12?	—9?	2?	0	0.05
Zinc	—50	0.02	1498	20	22	0	5

^aPollution data are obtained by subtracting concentrations in untreated intake water from those in discharged water; all information from Permit Applications 534, 2, and 432, respectively, filed with U.S. Army Corps of Engineers, New York City. Question marks indicate source figures missing or approximated. Of 16 specific pollutants applicable to the paper industry, the 8 for which federal standards have been established are shown. Excluded are bromide, chromium, mercury, nickel, organic carbon, sodium, specific conductance, and sulfite, on the grounds that this table is for illustrative purposes only. A corporate report should show them all. See *Permits for Work and Structures in, and for Discharges and Deposits into Navigable Waters 3* (Washington, D.C.: Department of the Army, Corps of Engineers, 1972): p. 46. Measurement of pollutants is described on pp. 20-A, 33–38.

^bThere are 11 discharge outlets for Scott's plant; a sample of three was selected. The other outlets are for another tank, four other sewers, and three other drains.

^cWater quality standards are from Federal Water Quality Control Administration (now part of the Environmental Protection Agency). National Technical Advisory Committee to the Secretary of the Interior, *Water Quality Criteria* (Washington, D.C.: Government Printing Office, 1968), p. 20. Question marks indicate no standards.

^dEPA 1972 guidelines (memorandum, April 18) specify that BOD not exceed 14 lbs./ton pulp and 8 lbs./ton tissue. They also limited suspended solids to 10 lbs./ton pulp and 6 lbs./ton tissue. EPA's earlier and similar guidelines are reported in its *Industrial Waste Survey*, p. 245, and in *Air and Water News*, January 24, 1972, p. 5.

TABLE 4.   Desirable but Not Yet Feasible Standard: Indirect Costs, Pollution Accounts (Liabilities) in ABT Social Audit, 1972[a]

	1971 ($)	1970 ($)
Pollution from paper production[b]	1,770	770
Pollution from electric power production[c]	2,200	1,080
Pollution from automobile commuting[d]	10,493	4,333
Total	14,463	6,183

[a]Abt Associates, Inc., *Annual Report & Social Audit* (Cambridge: 1972), pp. 28, 31. Reprinted in "The First Attempts at a Corporate Social Audit," *Business Week*, September 23, 1972, p. 89.
[b]26 tons of paper used in 1971 (22 in 1970) x water pollution abatement cost of $35/ton.
[c]56,000 KWH of electric power used in 1971 (54,000 in 1970) x air pollution abatement cost of 2¢ KWH.
[d]615,960 commuting miles in 1971 (433,260 in 1970) x "obligation to society" for air pollution of 1¢ mile.

represented opposite polluting businesses before the EPA. Similarly, the passenger and home mover should be represented opposite railroads and truckers before the ICC, the private phone user opposite telephone companies before public service commissions, community groups opposite employers before the Equal Employment Opportunity Commission, rail commuters opposite the American Automobile Association before the Department of Transportation, employees opposite employers before the Occupational Health and Safety Division of the Department of Labor, bank users and loan applicants opposite bank officers before the Comptroller of the Currency, Federal Reserve Board, and Federal Deposit Insurance Corporation, the television viewer opposite broadcasters before the Federal Communications Commission.

Effective public representation of consumers would require full-time public advocates specializing in each industry and rewarded with salaries on a par with lawyers doing similar work in government or business. Funding for such representation could come from a real consumers' union (not just a testing and publishing organization); from government; from a consumer tax, a business tax, or a tax on attorneys earning above a certain income. The Consumer Protection Agency bill was a proposal for a forum for such representation, within tightly defined limits. Its defeat in Congress, despite support of business leaders such as Senator Charles Percy, provides further indication that those who are waiting for government to act will be waiting for a long time.

Class actions by consumers are one of the most important mechanisms to which consumer advocates look to balance the scales that are presently weighted in favor of business interests. The idea behind class actions is that court cases will be reduced because many cases will be tried at once, but business lobbyists have argued that the reverse will happen and that the courts will become clogged with cases if class actions are made easier.[12] That this is a danger testifies to the great number of consumer injustices for which the present legal system does not offer realistic aid because of the high cost of counsel. Other opponents are concerned that a tidal wave of unscrupulous lawyers will be unleashed by a broadened class action bill,[13] but some consumer advocates are willing to allay this fear by including in the bill a limit on attorney's fees.[14] A special problem with pollution class actions is that it is difficult to establish a scientific link between an ailment and a pollution source, even though the circumstantial evidence seems overwhelming. In addition, one must claim personal damage in order to have standing for the suit.

In order to broaden their targets and raise the caliber of their weaponry, some consumer advocates have attempted to implicate directors, officers, and shareholders personally. Directors and officers have been sued personally for violation of dumping and pollution laws, and jail terms have occasionally been handed out for such violations. Large shareholders are already vulnerable to suits in cases in which employee wages have not been paid,[15] depositors in a national bank are owed money, or the corporation seems to have been established to avoid responsibility.[16] They could be made liable for their company's pollution by a change in the business corporation laws of their states. In New York State, all that would be needed would be a sentence to the effect that the limited liability provisions do not protect major stockholders from damage suits involving gross environmental degradation or loss of life.

[12]Comparing the "number of consumer class suites likely to be filed under the new law against the very few consumer cases now brought in the federal courts . . . it is clear that the burden will increase." Two witnesses from the judiciary are cited to this effect: American Enterprise Institute, *Consumer Class Action Legislation* (Washington, D.C.: American Enterprise Institute, 1972), p. 25.

[13]The "consumer class action gives the consumers' attorney as unusual opportunity and incentive to control the lawsuit in order to promote his own interest at the consumers' expense": *Ibid.*, p. 17.

[14]Proposal advanced in speeches by James S. Turner, author of *The Chemical Feast*.

[15]Mass. Gen. Laws Ann. c. 156:35; Mich. Const. art. XII: 4 (1909); Tenn. Code Ann. 48:710 (1955); New York BCL 630.

[16]The court may "pierce the corporate veil" in instances of fraud. "When the notion of legal entity is used to defeat public convenience, justify wrong and protect fraud or defend crime, the law will regard the corporation as an association of persons": Justice J. Sanborn in *United States* v. *Milwaukee Refrigerator Transit Co.*, 142 F. 247, 255 (C.C.E.D. Wis. 1905). Justice Holmes commented: "The trick must fail," *Line & Lane Timber Co.* v. *United States*, 236 U.S. 574, 35s Ct. 440, 59 L. Ed. 725 (1915).

Public Action as Stockholders or Employees

In recent years proxy proposals have been used as a device for social action. In 1972, there were at least 13 different groups undertaking shareholder proposals or protect at the annual meetings of 35 U.S. corporations.[17] A leader in this area has been the Project for Corporate Responsibility, which has attempted to elect public directors, increase disclosure, change corporate policies, and (its current focus of attention) revamp corporate structure through proxy resolutions.

Stockholder resolutions have brought to light interesting information on control of corporate shareholdings and the decision-making process in nonprofit corporations. The five-man Harvard Corporation voted with management in the first round of Campaign GM, despite alumni, student, and faculty votes of support for the resolutions of the Project for Corporate Responsibility.

The proxy battles have achieved some of their objectives even though support has never reached as much as ten percent of stockholders, even on resolutions calling for increased disclosure. So far at least 16 universities, seven pension funds, five foundations (including Ford and Rockefeller), two mutual funds, and one bank have voted for socially oriented resolutions that were opposed by management.[18]

Stockholder derivative suits against companies that appear to be acting against the interests of stockholders have also been initiated. For example, in Martindell v. ITT the stockholders are suing International Telephone and Telegraph for acting beyond its power and for wasting corporate assets in its political activities. The federal district court action, now in the discovery phase, cites ITT's gifts to congressmen of golf club and airplane usage and it alleged political activities abroad, especially in Chile.

Another suggestion for attacking a socially irresponsible firm is to have it declared socially bankrupt.[19] Many firms that produce dividends for shareholders are causing tremendous social damage at the same time. If this damage outweighs the company's financial return, it could be declared a "net loss" to society and its assets placed in receivership. A community downstream from a polluter might pursue such a suit and ask to be included with financial creditors on the board of trustees of the bankrupt firm.

[17]Council on Economic Priorities, "Minding the Corporate Conscience: The 1972 Movement for Corporate Responsibility," *Economic Priorities Report* 3, no. 1 (1972).

[18]"Demise of the Wall Street Rule," *Business and Society Review* 2 (Summer 1972): 102.

[19]Ralph Nader, Introduction to Mintz and Cohen, *America, Inc.*

Employees should be given First Amendment protection if they speak up against their company and face reprisals. Often they may be acting in the public interest. Labor unions should file suits on their behalf, and personnel directors should make clear to employees both their rights and the procedures for insuring that they are respected. Unions have been held jointly responsible with companies for violation of equal employment laws, and they might also be held jointly responsible for violation of health and safety laws. When unions are slow to defend their members or other employees, they should themselves be subject to suit. Union members could ask their leadership to include health and safety conditions and First Amendment rights in labor negotiations.

Conclusions

Regulatory agencies have failed to serve the public interest when they have undertaken advocacy functions and should be restricted to arbitration. Arbitration, however, can only be relied on in an environment where most of business is attempting to operate responsibly—whether voluntarily or as a result of a hard-headed appraisal of long-term profit prospects.

This voluntary-arbitrative approach to working for a better society asks business to make a conscious effort at being a better citizen. It asks for more information on company performance, presented in a way that permits public comparison with valid standards. It asks government for the restriction of regulatory agencies to arbitrative functions and for an adequate forum for public advocates. Finally, it asks the public for greater moral and financial support for independent evaluation centers and advocates. Without broad-based public advocates financed by their constituents, no regulatory framework will be effective for long.

Better Decision Making in Ecological Disputes

●●

● JOHN E. LOGAN

College of Business Administration
University of South Carolina

● ARTHUR B. MOORE, JR.

Timberlands Property Accountant
Westvaco Corporation, Summerville, S.C.

The late 1960's were years of considerable turmoil in the United States. Many complex problems that were not easily resolvable, such as race relations and the Vietnam war, faced the nation. Among the serious problems facing the nation was a host of disputes involving the potential location of industrial plants in areas with "unspoiled" natural environments. One such dispute, which occurred in South Carolina, received national attention for several months and was "resolved" in a manner that was unsatisfactory to virtually all the parties involved in the dispute. This dispute would probably have been much more readily resolved had there been clear air and water pollution standards in effect at the time and had the public been confident that these standards were adequate and would be rigorously enforced.

Because of the complexity of the subject and space limitations, we will concentrate our analysis on certain aspects of federal water and air pollution standards. We feel that this limitation does little, if anything, to weaken the relevance of their analysis, since in recent years the federal government has assumed primacy in the areas.

362

There have been drastic changes in federal air and water pollution control policies and enforcement machinery since 1970. However, several problems still exist in federal pollution policy in regard to equity, comprehensiveness, and efficiency. If our society is to make better decisions in ecological disputes in the future than it has in the past, all major parties in these disputes—business officials, government official at all levels, residents of local communities where industrial plants are located, and in some cases the public in general—will have to become more concerned, more involved, and more responsive to the needs of society as a whole than they have been in the past.

We will analyze a dispute about the proposed location of a petrochemical complex in an area of South Carolina with substantial poverty, an unspoiled estuarial system, and a $100-million resort community. The inadequacies of federal pollution laws in effect at this time in terms of aiding in the rational resolution of this dispute will be illustrated. Next, we review major changes in federal aid and water pollution laws since the South Carolina dispute occurred, and analyze how these laws would affect the resolution of a similar dispute today. We conclude with several unanswered questions about ecological decision making and with recommendations for changes.

The BASF Dispute

The dispute in Beaufort County, South Carolina, was a classic one in that it involved the potential location of a large pertochemical complex, which could have provided as many as 7000 jobs in an area with low per capita incomes and an almost total economic dependence on military installations.[1] This area also possesses one of the last unspoiled estuarial systems on the East Coast of the United States and has a burgeoning resort industry—with property values in excess of $100 million—catering almost entirely to wealthy, retired people who want to live in unspoiled surroundings.

The dispute over the proposed location of the chemical plants in Beaufort County raged at the local, state, and even national levels for over a year

---

[1] In 1968, per capital income in three of the four counties in southeastern South Carolina was below $2000, compared to $3412 for the United States as a whole. In 1968, federal government expenditures, mostly military, accounted for 68 percent of personal income in Beaufort County. Oliver G. Wood, Jr., John E. Logan, et al., *The BASF Controversy: Employment vs. Environment* (Columbia: Bureau of Business and Economic Research, University of South Carolina, 1969), pp. 32, 51.

and was finally resolved in a manner that was at least somewhat unsatisfactory to all the parties involved in the dispute.

By June 1969, after examining potential sites in about 20 states, the management of Badische-Analin and Soda Fabrik Co. (BASF), a German chemical firm with sales of $2.4 billion in 1969, decided that they wanted to build a chemical complex in Beaufort County. To lure the firm to the state, South Carolina governmental officials promised to build a railroad spur line, construct a four-lane highway, dredge a river, and exempt the firm from state corporate income taxes for five years.[2] In addition, the state sold BASF the land it needed to build the chemical complex. Estimates of the value of the plants to be built ranged from $100 million to $400 million. The company promised that it would abide by state pollution laws, and state officials stated that the plant would help relieve the employment problems, and spur economic growth, of the area.

In December 1969, Fred Hack and Charles Fraser, developers of the nearby Hilton Head Island resort area, announced their opposition to the location of BASF in the area because the company was not going to spend enough to control pollution and because South Carolina's pollution control laws were full of loopholes and inadequately enforced.

To support their position, Fraser and Hack, as well as various ecologically oriented citizens' groups, undertook a campaign to ensure that BASF would not locate in Beaufort County. They placed advertisements in every major newspaper in South Carolina and several out-of-state newspapers opposing the complex. They sponsored an ecological conference at Hilton Head Island in January 1970, at which several ecologists pointed out the value of the area's pristine estuarial system and enumerated the many dangers the chemical plants posed. They filed suits, along with the fishing interests in the area, attempting to enjoin the building of the plants and engaged in extensive lobbying activities both in Columbia, S.C. and in Washington, D.C. They also paid for a Washington, D.C. consulting firm to study the economic development potential of the area. (The firm, to almost no one's surprise, recommended that the best course of action involved developing industries, such as light manufacturing and agricultural cooperatives, which were compatible with the resort industry.) The island's developers also stated that if BASF did not locate in the area they would develop an amusement park along the lines of Six Flags over Georgia, but this was not done.

Support for the location of the BASF plant in Beaufort County came from some groups; over 7000 citizens of Beaufort County—out of a popula-

[2]*Ibid.*, pp. 1–22.

tion of a little over 50,000—signed a petition supporting BASF. Also supporting BASF were a local group, the Committee for the Advancement of Poor People, and the state National Association for the Advancement of Colored People, whose local field secretary stated that further development of the recreation industry would mean little for blacks, over 40 percent of the population, because none of the traditional jobs in the resort industry offered chances for advancement.

The role of the state government in the dispute was complex and somewhat contradictory. The Governor of South Carolina consistently and actively supported BASF. The State Development Board's key officials supported BASF and repeatedly pointed out the favorable effects the plant would have on the area's economy. The board went so far in their support as to hire a local consulting firm to study the impact of the plant on the Beaufort area; their study estimated 38,000 jobs in Beaufort County in 1980 without the plant and 58,000 jobs with the plant. Officials of the South Carolina Pollution Control Authority used the dispute to indicate that the agency was undermanned and underfinanced and that it needed additional support if it were to do its job adequately. The state legislature, after much debate, substantially tightened South Carolina's pollution control laws and delayed the completion of the BASF project by banning the issuance of any new waste dumping permits in Beaufort County for a one-year period, during which the South Carolina Water Resources Commission as well as other state and federal agencies were to study water resources in the area and the effect of industrial development on those resources.

The federal government was not very active during the initial part of the dispute and at no time were federal standards or requirements explicitly stated for the public. In late March 1971, Secretary of the Interior Walter Hickel wrote a letter to BASF officials warning them not to violate federal law or change the composition of the estuarial waters. Many observers felt that this marked a radical change in federal environmental policy and was a dangerous intervention by the federal government into state and local affairs. Governor McNair was particularly vexed by this action and wondered whether South Carolina was to become "the guinea pig for a new federal policy on . . . pollution." Many felt that Hickel's letter was the last straw in BASF's subsequent decision not to build the plant in South Carolina.

Throughout the dispute, BASF officials attempted to combat the charges leveled against them by emphasizing that they would obey the law and that the chemical complex would have a very favorable effect on the area's economy. However, the firm was constantly on the defensive and let state government officials undertake most efforts against the opposition. In addition, BASF officials never revealed to the public exactly what kind of plant they planned to build and what their specific plans were to prevent pollution. (According to Secretary Hickel, the technology for preventing water pollution in chemical plants was available.)[3] In April 1970, after BASF began losing money, acquired Wyandotte Chemical Co., and after receiving Hickel's letter, they stopped construction at the plant sites and in January 1971 sold the land back to the state.

We feel that the resolution of the BASF dispute was inadequate in many ways and reveals many of the weaknesses in the ways of dealing with pollution problems. The right kinds of information for an informed decision were not available; it was never clear exactly what body, at which level of government, had the right to resolve the dispute; the public did not know what kind of plant BASF planned to build or how they planned to prevent pollution; it was never determined what effects the proposed plant would have had on the ecology; there were not meaningful public hearings on the matter; and the standards that BASF had to meet were never made clear.

Federal Air and Water Pollution Laws

The first federal water pollution control legislation, the Water Pollution Control Act of 1948, was passed as temporary legislation. In 1956, amendments to this act provided that conferences on water pollution problems could be called at the request of the states and that hearings and court suits could follow if individual firms did not follow conference recommendations. Amendments between 1956 and 1969 provided that the states must set water pollution standards that were approved by the Federal Water Pollution Control Administration; streamlined the conference hearing process, although hearings and court suits were still the primary enforcement mechanisms; allowed the federal government to call conferences at their own initiative in interstate cases; and steadily increased the amount of money granted municipalities to improve their sewage treatment facilities. Between 1956 and 1970, 45 enforcement conferences were held.[4]

Air pollution control legislation developed even more slowly than water pollution control legislation. The first federal act dealing with this subject was passed in 1955 and did little but provide temporary authority and funds for research projects dealing with air pollution. The 1963 Clean Air

---

[3]Walter J. Hickel, *Who Owns America?* (Englewood Cliffs, N.J.: Prentice-Hall, 1971), p. 102.

[4]J. Clarence Davies III, *The Politics of Pollution* (New York: Pegasus, 1970), pp. 39, 188.

Act set up a hearings and suit procedure similar to water pollution control procedures and provided for grants for state and local air pollution control agencies. In 1965, the Motor Vehicle Air Pollution Control Act provided for research on automobiles. The Air Quality Act of 1967 streamlined the enforcement procedures and provided for joint federal-state standards for air quality control regions. By 1970, eight enforcement conferences dealing with air pollution had been held.[5]

The federal government did not play a very active part in the BASF dispute because of the laws in force at that time: They could have called for an enforcement conference only if the plant would create an interstate water pollution problem. The Colleton River, which flows by the proposed plant site, flows only in South Carolina, so, unless the state had requested a conference, the federal government could not have called for one. Secretary Hickel's intervention, which may mark the beginning of the use of the 1899 Refuse Act for pollution prevention purposes, may have been merely a bargaining ploy saying in effect: "If you pollute and ruin the estuary, the federal government will prosecute you to the full extent of the law,"[6] but this was never tested.

Between 1969 and 1972 substantial changes were made in federal laws and policies on air and water pollution. Some of the more substantial changes were in the administrative area. In 1969, the Council on Environmental Quality, an advisory body reporting to the President of the United States on environmental matters, was established. In 1970, the Environmental Protection Agency, which took charge over the control of pollution and the administration of federal pollution control laws, was formed. EPA is charged with overseeing all matters pertaining to the environment and with seeing that federal pollution laws are obeyed; by early 1972, it had about 9000 employees and a buget in excess of $2 billion.[7]

Among the major changes in federal water pollution policy between 1969 and 1972 were the following: (1) the requirement, under the terms of the 1899 Refuse Act, that firms must apply for permits to discharge wastes into navigable waterways or streams that flow into navigable waterways; (2) the

---

[5]*Ibid.*, pp. 50, 190.

[6]For a discussion of the bargaining aspects of pollution control, see Matthew Holden, Jr., *Pollution Control as a Bargaining Process* (Ithaca, N.Y.: Water Resources Center, Cornell University, 1966).

[7]Gordon MacDonald, "What Is Government Doing About Pollution?" in *Contemporary Challenges in the Business Society Relationship*, edited by George A. Steiner, (Los Angeles: Graduate School of Management, University of California, 1972), chap. 12, pp. 1–2.

prosecution of firms illegally polluting navigable waterways; (3) the provision for stiff penalties when oil pollution is the result of negligence; (4) stringent regulations regarding the control of sewage waste on ships;[8] and (5) a law in late 1972 that provides $25 billion over a three-year period to fight water pollution, places limitations on the amount of effluents industrial plants can discharge, and requires plants to use the best practicable water pollution control technology by July 1, 1977, and the best available technology by July 1, 1983.[9]

The Clean Air Act of 1970 radically altered federal policy regarding air pollution. Among the major changes promulgated in this act are the following: (1) it tightened exhaust emission standards on automobiles; (2) it gave the administrator of EPA the authority to set nationwide ambient air standards for certain gases; and (3) it gave EPA the power to require that plants in certain industries must install the best available air pollution control equipment.[10]

Several bills have been proposed to Congress that would have further augmented the primary role of the federal government in controlling pollution. President Nixon has proposed that the natural resources departments be brought together into a department of resources. Taxes based on the use of lead in gasoline and sulphur dioxide emissions have been proposed. In the area of water pollution control, administration-sponsored bills have called for providing the authority for EPA to: (1) set effluent emission standards for industrial plants; (2) require new plants in specific industries to install the best-known water pollution control technology; and (3) set stringent limitations on the amounts of certain toxic materials that may be discharged into water.[11]

If BASF attempted to build a chemical plant in South Carolina today, it would be forced to approach the locational problem quite differently. Today there are joint federal-state water standards in South Carolina, and the South Carolina Pollution Control Authority's duties and staff have been greatly augmented. The firm would have to file a statement with EPA stating exactly what effluents the plant would produce and what the firm planned to do to prevent pollution. Also, if the administration-sponsored

[8]*Ibid.*, pp. 6–7.

[9]For an analysis that is strongly critical of fderal water pollution control laws and policies, see Allen V. Kneese, "The Political Economy of Water Quality Management," in Anthony Downs et al., *The Political Economy of Environmental Control* (Berkeley: Institute of of Business and Economic Research, University of California, 1972), pp. 35–66.

[10]MacDonald, "What Is Government Doing About Pollution?" p. 10.

[11]*Ibid.*, pp. 4, 7, 11.

pollution control legislation mentioned earlier is passed into law, the firm would probably have to meet federal standards on effluent discharges and on water pollution prevention equipment; at any rate, they would have to install the best practicable water pollution control equipment by 1977 and the best available equipment by 1983.

Problem Areas

In spite of the remarkable changes in pollution control laws in the United States in recent years, there has been a rash of problems involving the location of many kinds of industrial plants and disputes over pollution emanating from existing plants.[12] Many questions remain concerning the equity, comprehensiveness, the efficiency of federal air and water pollution control policies.

One problem involves the concept of property rights.[13] An area that needs much further study is the extent to which societies should further restrict the traditional rights of private property owners because they are reducing others' amenities and therefore the value of their property rights. Clearly, industrial plants polluting an unspoiled area might reduce the value of much nearby property. The sheer number and density of people in urban areas will eventually have to affect our concepts of property usage.[14] Quite obviously, an economic activity that may not be bothersome or harmful in an area that is uncrowded or where complementary activities are undertaken would distress many people when it is undertaken in a very crowded area or in an area where it is incompatible with other activities. If the value of property rights is to be retained, such disturbing acts will have to be limited.

Questions of equity frequently arise in ecological disputes because of the fact that some gain economically while others lose economically. In the

[12]For analyses of the problems two electric power companies have had in building new facilities, see Roger Starr, "Power and the People—The Case of Con Edison," *The Public Interest*, Winter 1972, pp. 75–99; and Sherman F. Buese, "Locating a Power Plant: A Case Study of Southern California Edison's Siting Problems," in *Contemporary Challenges*, edited by Steiner, chap. 19.

[13]For a brief discussion of the intellectual and legal development and extension of the concept of property rights, see James W. Kuhn and Ivar Berg, *Values in a Business Society* (New York: Harcourt, Brace, and World, 1968), pp. 30–33.

[14]For well-developed arguments along these lines, see Neil W. Chamberlain, *Beyond Malthus: Population and Power* (New York: Basic Books, 1970), pp. 125–127.

BASF dispute, for example, the property owners and developers of Hilton Head Island gained economically because the value of their investments was not diminished by industrial pollution, while potential jobholders and merchants in the Beaufort area lost economically. Two questions should be raised in this connection: How can society determine whose "rights" or interests should prevail in particular ecological disputes? And, should some form of transfer payments be awarded to "losers" in ecological disputes?

A third issue that must receive attention in the next few years is zoning. The lack of zoning leads to inadequate, wasteful land use and the dimunition of the amenities of many peoples' property rights. The BASF dispute raised the question of whether the national interest would best be served by saving the estuary for biological and recreational reasons. If so, why should residents of the Beaufort area suffer because of national or statewide zoning of an area? Either special efforts should be made to provide other economic opportunities for residents of a restricted area or some form of equitable transfer payments should be arranged.

A fourth problem that is present in many ecological disputes is the lack of adequate and reliable information on which to base decisions. Often, decision makers take actions based on little information or on information that is later found to be incomplete. One has only to look to the news that lead substitutes in gasoline may turn out to be more harmful than the lead itself and the recent charge that toxic materials in the catalytic converters planned for automobiles may be more harmful than gasoline fumes to see the validity of these considerations.

In many cases, adequate information would allow disputes to be resolved more readily and rationally. For example, analysis of the BASF dispute reveals that there was not really enough information available to settle the dispute scientifically. About two years after the dispute had ended, the South Carolina Water Resource Commission issued the results of a $200,000 study that revealed that effluents discharged at the proposed plant site would diffuse into the ocean extremely slowly. If such information had been available at the time of the dispute, the dispute might have been resolved by scientific rather than political means. If society is to better resolve ecological disputes in the future, it needs better information on which to base its decisions.

A related problem area in ecological disputes is the lack of full public disclosure and discussions of the issues. In the BASF dispute, for instance, there was never a public hearing on the dispute with all parties to the dispute involved and represented equitably. Even today, while BASF would have had to apply to the federal government for an effluent discharge permit and the firm may have had to meet federally set effluent standards, there is no assurance that a full, public hearing would be held on the location of a chemical plant. The public and members of various interest groups are entitled to know the facts about ecological disputes and have the right to state their positions and question others' positions. Full disclosure of the facts would enhance public confidence in pollution control regulatory procedures and might lead to less opposition to the decisions of regulatory bodies.

Society needs to be concerned not only with the effectiveness of pollution control mechanisms, but also with the efficiency of such mechanisms. Society needs to evaluate heavier use of user charges on pollution as a potentially cheaper way of preventing pollution and as a more equitable way of allowing firms to make economic decisions.[15] Such a system might present monitoring problems, but the information gathered by the government in the water pollution area could offer a good base for it. However, user charges might be more difficult to implement in the air pollution area.

An issue that is just beginning to be discussed is the international control of pollution.[16] Although an international conference on this matter was held in Stockholm in June 1972 under United Nations sponsorship, little in the way of establishing meaningful policies was accomplished.[17] International pollution control problems will be particularly difficult to resolve because of the increasing per capita income gap between the rich and the poor nations. It would be foolish to expect the developing nations to forego industrial development while their people continue to live in abject poverty so that wealthy nations can continue to pollute and live in affluence. If a program of international pollution control or pollution control agreements is to begin to work, it will take very substantial foreign aid programs in the areas of equipment and technology and a tremendous investment in research.

[15]For positions supporting the wider use of user charges to control pollution, see William J. Baumol, "Environmental Protection at Minimum Cost," *American Journal of Economics and Sociology* 30 (October 1971): 337–343; Allen V. Kneese, "Environmental Pollution: Economics and Policy," *Proceedings of the American Economics Association*, May 1971, pp. 153–166; and Larry E. Ruff, "The Economic Common Sense of Pollution," *The Public Interest*, Spring 1970, pp. 69–85.

[16]For discussion of pollution control in an international context, see the May-June 1972 issue of the *Columbia Journal of World Business*; of particular interest is Philip W. Quigg, "Organizing for Global Environmental Management," pp. 26–30.

[17]One positive output of United Nations interest in ecology is the book by Barbara Ward and René Dubos, *Only One Earth* (New York: W. W. Norton & Co., 1972).

Responsibilities in Ecological Disputes

If a society is to make better ecological decisions and reach a greater consensus on the adequacy and reasonableness of these decisions, the parties involved in disputes will have to more fully meet their responsibilities.

Business

In general, industry's position in ecological disputes has been one that is not apt to solicit a great deal of sympathy. Quite often, industry takes a defensive position, pleading that the proposed pollution control measures are to extreme, unworkable, or too costly.[18] Generally, after pressure is applied, the necessary technological changes are made and the new pollution standards met, but such a defensive posture does little, if anything, to enhance business' public image and credibility.

Business executives have concerns about ecological controls for many good reasons. Industry frequently has to absorb part of the cost of technical changes necessitated by pollution control legislation; changes in pollution control standards disrupt production processes and sometimes place in jeopardy the continued existence of plants whose effluent discharges were within legal limits when the plants were built.

Specifically, business executives are concerned with who sets pollution standards and what standards are set. Business wants pollution control administrators to be familiar with the problems of business, to be sympathetic toward those problems, to interpret standards reasonably, and to allow the necessary time and options for technological changes that have to be made. They want uniform standards so that competitive positions within industries are not unduly upset. Impractical standards are too expensive to achieve and/or involve using technology that has not yet been developed or tested. Finally, business wants standards that do not require extremely rapid changes and that do not discriminate economically against existing plants.

Many industry leaders have considerable doubts about the wisdom of current ecological decision making, but many government regulators and a substantial portion of the public have considerable doubts about the extent of business concern about ecological matters and its adaptability in

---

[18]For an article criticizing business's approaches to social problems and recommending corrective postures and mechanisms, see Dow Votaw and S. Prakash Sethi, "Do We Need a New Corporate Response to a Changing Environment?" *California Management Review* 12 (Fall 1969): 3–32.

meeting ecological demands. If business is to fare better in ecological disputes in the future, it must meet its responsibilities.

Business leaders need to take much more positive action in ecological matters than they have in the past. Business will have to be willing to undertake more actions on its own to help solve ecological problems before they become matters of emotional public concern. Cooperative activities among firms to help solve technical pollution problems would be extremely helpful. (It is regrettable that federal officials recently prohibited the cooperative efforts of automobile manufacturers on the ground that it would tend to lessen competition.) A defensive strategy by business firms in ecological matters will become increasingly less appropriate as time passes.

Government

Governmental units at all levels, and particularly the federal government, affect the quality of ecological decision making in many ways. For example, governmental units affect pollution as producers of goods, and pollution laws and policies affect the following problem areas: efficiency, equity, the setting of standards, and the enforcement process.[19] The federal government's major concerns in the area of pollution controls appear to be to keep environmental problems at the lowest level that is economically feasible and to protect areas of natural beauty and interest that are currently unspoiled.

One of the areas in which substantial improvements are necessary is in municipal waste treatment facilities. For many years, many municipal governments have polluted streams but have been relatively free from prosecution, compared to business firms. The recent $24.6-billion federal water pollution control law may aid municipalities in solving water pollution problems, since most of the monies appropriated are directed to the improvement of municipal facilities. In order to reduce water pollution levels and provide for credibility in enforcement, the EPA must enforce standards uniformly, whether the institution involved is public or private.

The questions of efficiency and equity are issues that have not yet been satisfactorily dealt with, in our opinion. We feel that ways need to be developed to measure who loses economically as a result of ecological decisions and that those who are seriously injured should be compensated by some means of transfer payments. More effort should be made to tax

[19]Another area in which improvements must be effected is in international pollution control. For a study that predicts rapidly rising world pollution levels if present trends continue, see Donnella H. Meadows, et al., *The Limits to Growth* (New York: Universe Books, 1972), especially pp. 89–128.

effluent discharges by the use of rate-setting regulatory authorities, who would regulate rates and apply the taxes collected to control pollution in the most efficient way, that is, remove the most pollution possible with a given sum of money. Such a system has been used in the Ruhr River region in Germany for over 40 years with great apparent success.[20] In addition, the federal government should, as it apparently has generally done in the past, be sure the pollution control technology that is required is workable and reasonably economical.

Governmental responsibilities include the setting of standards and the choice of enforcement mechanisms. Not much can be said about standards, except that they should reflect economic costs when feasible and should allow for minimal environmental damage. Unfortunately, this is not always possible. Perhaps a further governmental function in this area should be to find out what the consensus of experts are in a given problem area and to find out what the public wants and what the public is willing to pay. To date, this has rarely, if ever, been done.

Changes could be made in enforcement mechanisms. Generally, serious ecological disputes have been resolved in the courts, not, in our opinion, the best place to resolve these disputes, because of the technical evidence involved and the delays in decisions because of crowded court dockets and appeals. We feel that it is the responsibility of governmental units at all levels to provide for simplified, clear-cut decision-making mechanisms in ecological disputes, so that they can be more readily and efficiently resolved. The concept of regional ecological decision-making bodies is one that should be fully explored.

Experts

Experts are constantly involved in ecological disputes. Their usual role is to investigate the impact of proposed industrial plants or to testify for or against a plant location or a regulatory proposal. Problems frequently arise in ecological disputes because some disputes involve virgin territory from a research standpoint and because experts' value systems differ. When opinions differ significantly in testimony in a particular dispute, the public and governmental decision makers are apt to be confused and the public image of the scientific fraternity is apt to be substantially lessened.

Members of the scientific fraternity dealing with ecological disputes

---

[20]For a description and analysis of this system, see Allen V. Kneese, "Water Quality Management by Regional Authorities in the Ruhr Area," in *Ecology and Economics*, 2d ed., ed. Marshall Goldman (Englewood Cliffs, N.J.: Prentice-Hall, 1972), pp. 172–190.

should be sure that they have considered all aspects and viewpoints of the dispute before they take a stand. They should also be sure to state the assumptions on which they base their premises and to indicate the data and research on which they base their conclusions. More careful and less partial analysis by those with technical expertise is needed in ecological disputes if society is to improve its decision-making record.

The Public

Although the number of active conservation-ecology groups and the opposition to many plans for industrial expansion have increased, it is difficult to know the real extent of the public's concern over pollution and whether that concern is increasing or decreasing. Polls of public attitudes toward pollution and public willingness to pay for the costs of reducing pollution have been conducted. In general, they show that, between 1965 and 1971, the extent of public concern about pollution increased; that concerns varied substantially in different sectors of the United States, with the greatest concern shown in the industrialized Northeast and the least concern shown in the less industrialized Southeast; and that most people were willing to pay little to reduce the cost of pollution.[21] Recently, opinions have been expressed that concern for the environment has declined as a social issue or that interest in it soon will decline.[22]

The responsibility of the public in ecological disputes is very difficult to state except in very general terms. We feel that the public would be more responsive if interest groups were to take a more balanced approach to problem solving instead of stating their demands in all-or-nothing terms, and if the public's willingness to pay the cost of solving pollution problems was more in line with its apparent concern over the problem. Solving pollution problems will be a long-term process, and substantial numbers of the public will have to exhibit constructive concern over their resolution if they are to be solved. It is also quite probable that resolving these problems will involve some rather drastic changes in our life styles. Thus, it will be necessary for the public to bear most of the costs and the inconveniences of these changes.

---

[21]For some recent articles analyzing the results of these polls, see Hazel Erskine, "The Polls: Pollution and Its Costs," *Public Opinion Quarterly* 36 (Spring 1972): 120–135; Arvin W. Murch, "Public Concern for Environmental Pollution," *Public Opinion Quarterly* 35 (Spring 1971): 100–106; and Rita James Simon, "Public Attitudes Toward Population and Pollution," *Public Opinion Quarterly* 35 (Spring 1971): 93–99.

[22]See Anthony Downs, "Up and Down With Ecology—The Issue-Attention Cycle," *The Public Interest*, Summer 1972, pp. 38–50.

Conclusions

If ecological decision making is to improve in the future, we believe that the parties involved need to be more concerned about the public interest and the public welfare than they have been in the past. Business executives will need to undertake more positive action and be more candid. Governmental units will have to make improvements in several areas, such as: municipal water treatment facilities, the setting of pollution standards, enforcement mechanisms and decision making bodies, efficiency in lowering pollution levels, and equity in ecological decision making. Experts testifying in ecological disputes will have to be more impartial in their analysis of ecological problems and impacts and will have to base their conclusion on more concrete evidence. The public will have to show continued, constructive interest in ecological problems, be willing to pay for necessary changes, and be willing to make life-style changes for the sake of the government.

The authors believe that pollution control issues are among the most difficult that man has ever had to face, given his propensity not to deal effectively with problems until they reach the crisis stage. It is hoped that interest in ecological issues does not wane, as has happened in the past with so many other social issues, for the results of neglect and the lack of planning and resources devoted to ecological issues will effect all life on earth.

PART VI. B
Business and
the Minority Groups

●●

We have seen too many patterns of deception: In political life, impossible dreams; in advertising, extravagant claims; in business, shoddy deals . . . pay more heed to one of the great cries of the young today . . . their demand for honesty—intellectual honesty, personal honesty, public honesty.
                                                              —President Richard M. Nixon

By now volumes have been written on the plight of the blacks and other minority groups in American society. All responsible elements of society have recognized the existence of both overt and indirect discrimination against minority groups in education, housing, jobs, social relationships, and political processes. The discrimination has been pervasive and widespread.

In the last few years there have been some genuine efforts by industry to provide better jobs and training to the minority groups to hasten their upward mobility and provide an equality of opportunity with other segments of society. There is no denying the fact that blacks have made significant progress in gaining better jobs and in narrowing the areas of discrimination. However, there is considerable disagreement about whether industry is doing all it can to remove areas of discrimination and also whether some of these efforts have been mere tokens.

Minority groups have been pressing for special consideration, e.g., establishment of special quotas and relaxation of entry requirements, in order to accelerate upward mobility and the process of integration. They argue that once the black community has achieved its rightful place in the American economy, its members will no longer need special consideration because the problem of the black community will no longer be a special problem. "Unfortunately, the business community has not shown any enthusiasm for such a course of action. . . . Much of the effort of the private sector has so far been directed toward training and hiring minority group members for entry-level positions."[1]

There is a great deal that industry must do to prove to the black community that its efforts are sincere and its programs are intended to bring about permanent, long-term improvement in job opportunities for minority groups. Otherwise it will increase the cynicism and distrust in the black community and widen the schism between blacks and whites. "Business corporations have a golden opportunity to utilize their immense resources in helping the country to alleviate the misery of her black citizens. . . . We have seen that on moral, social and economic grounds the black man is only asking what is his due and what his white brothers have, that is, an equal chance to prove that he is a man. How can we do less and still call ourselves decent men?"[2]

The articles in this section are primarily aimed at evaluating the effectiveness of the policies and programs undertaken by industry and government to increase the number and participation level of minority group members in the economy. Theodore Purcell and Frank J. Toner open their paper with the shocking projection that it will take 55 years for blacks to gain their fair share of jobs if everything goes as will as between 1966 and 1969, the base period for their study. Even that projection, they warn, will be far from reality unless all sectors of American Society cooperate fully and sincerely in achieving a minority participation parity program. They acknowledge that the complexity of the problem demands an attack on the entire minority manpower planning program rather than on isolated problem areas.

Purcell and Toner suggest that a systems approach to the development of minority manpower planning is necessary, encompassing all job levels from entry to top management. For practical implementation purposes, an effective measurement-audit-sanction system, rewarding or sanctioning responsible individuals for achieving or not achieving target goals, is indispensable. They give a lengthy review of such measurement-audit-sanctions as well as other techniques for implementing minority parity programs. The paper makes it quite clear that the full cooperation of business, government, educational institutions, and other social organizations is of absolute necessity in developing such a program.

Gerald F. Cavanagh and Johnny Stewart review the advantages and disadvantages associated with the introduction of blacks into the organization. They argue that, despite short-run disruptions and costs, they

---

[1] S. Prakash Sethi, *Business Corporations and the Black Man: An Analysis of Social Conflict, the Kodak-Fight Controversy* (Scranton, Pa.: Chandler Publishing Co., 1970), p. 135.
[2] *Ibid.*, p. 137.

bring many long-run advantages to the firm that could not have been gained otherwise. They refer to the value system of blacks as distinct from that of whites, resulting from differences in their social and cultural backgrounds. These differences, they argue, can introduce many unexpected symptoms—high rates of turnover, absenteeism, and tardiness—into the work environment. However, this should work as an early warning system to the management of the firm to bring about adequate changes to deal with the real problems behind these symptoms. Understanding and trying to solve these problems at different levels of management will mean long-run advantages—a better communications system and a more flexible and innovative organization, among others. These in turn result in a better organization, a more efficient use of manpower, and finally in a direct effect on the success of the firm as well as an indirect effect on its public image.

Jules Cohn presents some of the problems that he encountered in the acceptance of affirmative action programs (AAP) during his 18 months of observation or participation. He indicates that the adoption of AAP introduces a redefinition of the personnel function, tensions and strains among employees, necessary changes in the organizational structure, and a possible reduction in productivity. In his detailed examination of each of these issues, he notes, for example, that the redefinition of the corporate personnel function is inevitable, because the central function of personnel—to find potentially capable people for prospective positions on the basis of merit—is no longer the prime objective. Tensions naturally arise from following new AAP measures rather than the familiar old ones. He argues that in some instances the employer and the government have to negotiate their AAP goals. He ends his paper on the happy note that the issue at hand is to achieve social justice—a consideration well beyond personnel matters and their associated problems.

SELECTED BIBLIOGRAPHY

America, Richard F., Jr. "What Do You People Want?", *Harvard Business Review*, March-April 1969, pp. 103–112.

Bastide, Roger. "Color Racism and Christianity." *Daedalus* 96, no. 2 (Spring 1967): 312–327.

Bender, Marilyn. "Women at Avon: No Room at the Top." *Business and Society Review/Innovation*, Winter 1972–1973, pp. 19–24.

*Especially recommended for an overall view and for authoritative viewpoints on different perspectives of the issues covered.

Bunke, Harvey. "Negro Must Be Full Partner in Market." *Business and Society* 5, no. 2 (Spring 1965): 3–9.

Campbell, Angus. *White Attitudes Toward Black People.* Ann Arbor, Mich.: Institute for Social Research, 1971.

Cordtz, Dan. "The Negro Middle Class Is Right in the Middle," *Fortune* 74, no. 6 (November 1966): 174–180.

*Cross, Theodore L. *Black Capitalism.* New York: Atheneum, 1969.

Davis, John P., ed. *The American Negro Reference Book.* Englewood Cliffs, N.J.: Prentice-Hall, 1966.

Doeringer, Peter B., ed. *Programs to Employ the Disadvantaged.* Englewood Cliffs, N.J.: Prentice-Hall, 1969.

Domm, Donald R., and Stafford, James E. "Assimilating Blacks into the Organization." *California Management Review* 15, no. 1 (Fall 1972): 46–51.

Downs, Anthony. "Alternative Futures for the American Ghetto." *Daedalus* 97 (Fall 1968): 1331–1378.

Fichter, Joseph H. "American Religion and the Negro." *Daedalus* 94 (Fall 1965): 1085–1106.

Fletcher, Arthur. "Whatever Happened to the Philadelphia Plan?" *Business and Society Review/Innovation*, Spring, 1973, pp. 24–28.

Folgelson, Robert M. "From Resentment to Confrontation: The Police, the Negroes, and the Outbreak of the Nineteen-Sixties Riots." *Political Science Quarterly* 83, no. 2 (June 1968): 217–247.

Gassler, Lee S. "How Companies Are Helping the Undereducated Worker." *Personnel*, July-August 1967, pp. 47–55.

Goode, Kenneth G. "Query: Can the Afro-American be an Effective Executive?" *California Management Review* 13, no. 1 (Fall 1970): 22–26.

Goodman, Richard A. "Hidden Issues in Minority Employment." *California Management Review*, Summer 1969, pp. 27–30.

Hanrahan, George D. "Why Social Programs Fail." *Economic and Business Bulletin*, Spring-Summer 1972, pp. 51–59.

Holsendolph, Ernest. "Middle-class Blacks Are Moving Off the Middle." *Fortune* 80, no. 7 (December 1969): 90–95.

*Janger, Allen R., and Shaeffer, Ruth G. *Managing Programs for the Disadvantaged.* New York: The Conference Board, 1970.

*Jones, Edward W., Jr. "What It's Like To Be a Black Manager." *Harvard Business Review*, July-August 1973, pp. 108–116.

Kain, John H., and Persky, Joseph J. "Alternative to Guilded Ghetto." *The Public Interest*, Winter 1969, 74–87.

Lyford, Joseph P. "Business and the Negro Community." In *The Negro Challenge to the Business Community*, edited by Eli Ginzberg. New York: McGraw-Hill Book Co., 1964, pp. 96–100.

Maggard, John P. "Negro Market—Fact or Fiction?" *California Management Review* 14, no. 1 (Fall 1971): 71–80.

*Moskowitz, Milton. "The Black Directors: Tokenism or a Big Leap Forward?" *Business and Society Review/Innovation*, Fall 1972, pp. 73–80.

Moynihan, Daniel P. "Employment, Income and the Ordeal of the Negro Family." *Daedalus* 94 (Fall 1965), 745–770.

Orth, Charles D., III, and Jacobs, Frederic. "Women in Management." *Harvard Business Review*, July-August 1972, pp. 139–147.

Palmeri, Richard A. "Business and the Black Revolt." *California Management Review*, Summer 1969, pp. 31-36.

*Pascal, Anthony H. "Black Gold and Black Capitalism." *The Public Interest*, Spring 1970, pp. 111-119.

Purcell, Theodore V. "Break Down Your Employment Barriers." *Harvard Business Review*, July-August 1968, pp. 65-76.

_____. "The Case of the Borderline Black." *Harvard Business Review*, November-December 1971, pp. 128-133, 142-150.

Purcell, Theodore V., and Webster, Rosalind. "Window on the Hardcore World." *Harvard Business Review*, July-August 1969, pp. 118-129.

*Purcell, Theodore V., and Cavanagh, Gerald F. *Blacks in the Industrial World: Issues for the Manager.* New York: Free Press, 1972.

Purcell, Theodore V., Rodgers, Irene W. "Young Black Workers Speak Their Minds." *California Management Review* 14, no. 4 (Summer 1972): 45-51.

Rose, Arnold M. "The Negro Protest," *Annals of the American Academy of Political and Social Sciences* 357 (January 1965): 1-126.

*Scheibla, Shirley. "Fairness by Fiat: Some Employees These Days Are More Equal than Others." *Barron's*, January 20, 1969, pp. 5-27.

*Sethi, S. Prakash. *Business Corporations and the Black Man: An Analysis of Social Conflict, the Kodak-Fight Controversy.* Scranton, Pa.: Chandler, 1970.

*_____. *Up Against the Corporate Wall: Modern Corporations and Social Issues of the Seventies.* 2d ed. Englewood, N.J.: Prentice-Hall, 1974.

Sleeper, C. Freeman. *Black Power and Christian Responsibility.* Nashville: Abingdon Press, 1969.

Spratlen, Thaddeus H. "A Black Perspective on 'Black Business Development'." *Journal of Marketing* 34, no. 4 (October 1970): 72-73.

Sturdivant, Frederick O. "Limits of Black Capitalism." *Harvard Business Review*, January-February 1969, pp. 122-128.

The Conference Board. Company Experience with Negro Employment. New York: The Conference Board, 1966, pp. 1-55.

*_____. *Education, Training, and Employment of the Disadvantaged.* Studies in Public Affairs No. 4. New York: The Conference Board, 1969.

*The Twentieth Century Fund. *The Job Crisis for Black Youth.* New York: Praeger, 1971.

Tobin, James. "On Improving the Economic Status of the Negro." *Daedalus* 94 (Fall 1965): 878-898.

*U.S. Departments of Labor and Commerce. *The Social and Economic Status of Negroes in the United States, 1969.* BLS Report No. 375, Current Population Reports, Series P-23, no. 29.

Weaver, Charles N. "Job Performance Comparisons: Mexican-American and Anglo Employees." *California Management Review* 13, no. 1 (Fall 1970): 27-30.

Weiss, Nancy J. "The Negro and the New Freedom: Fighting Wilsonian Segregation." *Political Science Quarterly* 84 no. 1 (March 1969): 61-79.

Two Major Corporate Strategies Toward Full Minority Participation in Business*

●●

● **THEODORE V. PURCELL**

Jesuit Center for Social Studies
Georgetown University

● **FRANK J. TONER**

Manager
Employee Relations Management and Practices
General Electric Company

This paper is written within the context of the new theories of corporate social responsibility, although we are not so much concerned with responsibility theory as we are with its practice, assuming a commitment by management to go beyond the requirements of federal law. Managers are being asked to hire and promote black workers at all levels, not only for the sake of more efficient business operations but also as a deliberate effort to change the forces that are splitting this country along racial lines. There is develop-

*This paper owes much to the expert assistance of James I. Nixon, Manager, GE Corporate Equal Opportunity—Minority Relations Operation, and Jacqueline Pinckney, Manager, EO/MR Program Development and Communications.

ing a new unwritten charter of expectations about the corporation, asking it to confront such complex urban problems as full minority participation.

We treat only two very important management strategies or techniques. For economy of thought and space we concentrate on blacks, though the participation of other minority groups and especially women is also urgent.

The American racial climate of 1972 is different from that of the 1960's, especially from that of 1967 to 1970. The summer ghetto riots have passed. Black leaders such as Arthur Fletcher, Jesse Jackson, Julian Bond, and Vernon Jordan, although not of one mind, take the positive stance of working within the system through political activism, with stress on economic participation. However, we observe a deepening alienation and frustration with life in America, especially among white, lower-middle-class, blue-collar, and ethnic workers. This alienation is expressed in support for Governor Wallace and antibussing and antiwelfare sentiments as symbols of white discontent. Not all of this alienation is racial, although some of it certainly is. Further, concern for black participation must now compete with the newer claims of the Spanish-speaking and women. The enthusiasm of the 1960's for black civil rights seems to be less evident in the 1970's.

Basic Problems of Black Participation

But the basic problems of black participation in American business, the problems manifested so bluntly in the 1960's, are still with us. Many of these issues remain unsolved. There has been some progress, but it has been very slow. For example, in the decade of the 1960's blacks made important income gains, but they did not obtain the level of their white counterparts. Census reports show that, outside of the South, black husband-wife families, in which the husband is 35 or younger, are earning as much as comparable white families. But, as the Urban League's Robert Hill points out, this income parity exists only for black families in which both husband and wife work, compared to white families in which only the husband works. When both parties work, we have attendant problems of child care and possible delinquency. While black family income grew faster than that of whites, the dollar gap between the two actually widened over the decade of the 1960's from $3250 in 1960 to about $3600 in 1970.[1]

Second, while black unemployment dropped during the 1960's, it remains today nearly twice that of whites. Unemployment for young black men in our cities between the ages of 20 and 24 in 1971 was about 19 per-

[1]U.S. Census studies reported by *Business Week*, January 22, 1972, p. 80.

cent, and for black teenagers nearly 35 percent.[2] This has been called "social dynamite."

It is true that during the 1960's blacks made significant gains by moving into higher-paying white-collar positions. But, nevertheless, their share of white-collar occupations still falls far short of their proportion in the total work force. At this point, let us look more carefully at the prediction statistics for black participation developed by Purcell and Cavanagh.[3]

Projected Changes in Black Participation

How many years will it take before blacks hold a fair proportion of jobs at every step of the industrial and office ladder? We base our projections on changes in black participation in the electrical manufacturing industry between 1966 and 1969. The electrical-electronic industry is both so diversified, producing everything from glass and chemicals to jet engines as well as electrical equipment, and also so extensive that it can speak well for American industry generally, at least at the white-collar level. While blacks are about 11 percent of our population, they are close to ten percent of our working population. Let us take a conservative norm of ten percent as a desirable proportion of blacks in the American work force. We recognize, of course, that in many cities blacks will be a much higher percentage than ten percent. However, let us set up a target, an ideal, that blacks should comprise (if they so desire) at least ten percent of the employees at every level of the business ladder. Then let us see what their actual number is at each level. Extracting index numbers from this data, we can see what percentage the attainment is of the ideal. This is shown in Table 1.

We see from Table 1 that in 1966 blacks participated at the officials and managers level at 4.3 percent of the ideal of ten percent. This improved by 4.9 to 9.2 percent in 1969. If this improvement rate were continued, it would take 55.5 years for blacks to achieve parity (parity being only 10 percent) at the officials and managers level. The blue-collar jobs, with the exception of craftsmen, are already well over-achieved, which anyone can see by going into a factory. But for white-collar jobs, especially those of the professional and technical level, blacks are far below. At our 1966–1969 growth rate, it would take 14 years for blacks to hold 10 percent of craftsmen jobs. Clerical should be integrated in 9 years, technical positions in 22,

[2]*The Job Crisis for Black Youth*, Report of the Twentieth Century Fund (New York: Praeger, 1971), p. 3.

[3]Theodore V. Purcell and Gerald F. Cavanagh, *Blacks in the Industrial World: Issues for the Manager* (New York: Free Press, 1972).

TABLE 1. Predicting Black Employment in the Electrical Manufacturing Industry (Base: 1966–1969)

	Participation index numbers		Three-year change in index numbers	Deficit (or excess) of 1969 index number from 100%	Years to achieve 100% integration at 1966–1969 change rate[a]
	1966	1969			
Officials and managers	4.3	9.2	+ 4.9	−90.8	55.5
Professionals	7.3	10.4	+ 3.1	−89.6	86.7
Technicians	22.2	31.5	+ 9.3	−68.5	22.2
Sales workers	2.5	6.5	+ 4.0	−93.5	70.2
Office and clerical	19.5	39.0	+19.5	−61.0	9.3
Craftsmen	29.7	42.0	+12.3	−58.0	14.1
Operatives	83.6	115.2	+31.6	+15.2	achieved
Laborers	99.3	127.5	+28.2	+27.5	achieved
Service workers	175.3	191.6	+16.3	+91.6	achieved

[a]1969 deficit from 100 percent parity divided by the preceding three-year improvement. The quotient is then multiplied by three. For example, to overcome a 90.8 deficit with improvement of 4.9 every three years, it would take (90.8/4.9 = 18.5 × 3) 55.5 years.

sales not until 70, professionals in 86, and officials and managers in 55 years. The white-collar picture is hardly encouraging.

We use these projections only as illustrations of what could very well happen. We do not propose them as holding a high degree of precision. Three factors could either raise or lower the years required for blacks to achieve parity: first, factors regarding the business cycle and its requirements. The period from 1966 to 1969 was the culmination of the most prosperous decade in the history of America. Unemployment during that decade steadily declined and in 1966 was 3.8 percent or 2.2 percent for the insured unemployed, and in 1969, 3.5 and 2.1 percent, respectively. A growth rate based on a three-year period within this decade would be very optimistic. Recessions during the 1970's or 1980's would lower the growth rate, although wars, of course, would raise it.

Second, the constant American trend toward a greater proportion of technical jobs as opposed to semiskilled jobs will make it doubly difficult for blacks. Many service, laborer, and operative jobs are being automated out of existence. These were the jobs traditionally open to blacks.

Third, we must propose a caution regarding the status of blacks and their attitudes. During the 1960's, blacks participated a little more in apprenticeship training programs, vocational schools, and engineering colleges—the main routes to craft jobs and management positions. But they are also competing with whites who are anxious to get into these schools and into these positions. Recall the statement of the Red Queen in *Alice in Wonderland*, "Now here you see it takes all the running you can do to keep in the same place. If you want to get somewhere else you must run twice as fast as that!" True it is that blacks are running faster, but so are whites.

Housing, neighborhood, and family conditions also affect the preparation of a young man or woman for a business position, especially in a managerial or professional job. Another caution is the matter of civil rights laws and white reactions. No doubt the pressures of laws, courts, and compliance agencies will increase black participation, but if these pressures are greatly extended, they might develop into expensive legalisms that could slow down the process. White backlash and polarization of the two races remain a possibility during the 1970's.

All of these factors, especially that of the business cycle, will affect the time predicted in table 1. Full black participation in American business life could easily take much longer, perhaps twice as long. Unless drastic improvements are made and creative management strategies developed, black people will not be adequately represnted in white-collar jobs in American industry for years and years.

A self-made vice-president of a major agricultural chemical firm in Houston on reading this said: "My father was born an immigrant from central Europe in 1890. He was on relief. I was born in 1932, one of seven children. In 1956 I graduated from the University of Texas. It took 66 years (from 1890 to 1956) for my *white* family to become 'professional'." However, the forefathers of the blacks now working for this man's company were unwilling immigrants to this country 200 or 300 years ago, and not one black employee is near to becoming vice-president of the company today. Will black people have the patience; does American industry have the time; can our society assume the right to wait so long?

Implications for Management

Obviously the government and other private groups are involved, but what are the implications for the businessman? Management, of course, will have to deal with the demands of the federal government, with the U.S. Department of Labor Office of Federal Contract Compliance, the Equal Employment Opportunity Commission with its 1972, enhanced enforcement powers, and with other governmental compliance agencies. But because the corporation is an integral part of the society in which it operates, it also makes sense for the businessman to help society attain its goals.

It makes good business sense for the corporation to utilize 100 percent of the human resources available for its labor pool. No segment of these resources—whether minority or female—can be underutilized without a concurrent loss in efficiency. Indeed, although the labor force has increased in size over recent years and will continue to increase, certain skilled people are not in plentiful supply. When these qualified professional, managerial, and technical people are scarce, the businessman must not overlook or underutilize the nontraditional sources of supply.

The corporation whose offices and plants are in urban centers has an additional burden placed on it—the need to protect its corporate investment. One effective way to do so is to create a climate in which its facilities can operate effectively—a climate of mutual cooperation and support. Companies who operate in the big cities can rarely, if ever, escape from the problems of the city, because there is literally nowhere to hide. With manufacturing plants in big cities in which a high percentage of employees are black, companies have found that black representation in management jobs enhances the pride and self-confidence of the black community.

Most businessmen are aware that minority groups represent a very large and ever-growing market for their products. They realize that minority customers are proud to know that the products they buy are made by minority workers in the factory, are designed and marketed by minority technical people, and that minorities are managing those businesses. Minority annual income, which is projected to be about $52 billion by 1975, thus becomes an important economic factor to businessmen. Additionally, when people become employed, the welfare rolls and accompanying tax burden decrease and there is a concommitant increase in the nation's economic growth. A few years ago someone calculated that every person who is taken off welfare and put into a job will add $10,000 to the GNP, gain $3400 in purchasing power, and cut welfare costs by $1300 annually. That is significant.

One aspect of management's response involves measuring the effectiveness of its affirmative action practices.

Successful corporate change toward the full participation of minority people within the corporate structure will call, of course, for a strong top management policy and for a systems approach toward the implementation of that policy, at least for the large corporation. Management will need to consider minority manpower objectives in its financial planning, research and development, facilities planning, economic and social forecasting, etc. This systems approach will involve the location of responsibility, the communication of policy, the identifying of problem areas, and the development of innovative programs to meet targets. But, more than anything, it will involve an effective system of measurement and sanctions with goals and time tables for minority programs, although not for quotas imposed from the outside. Every manager knows the importance of having a goal or target for next year's sales or cost reduction plans. Without a target, or with only a vague target, policy is rarely implemented. Part of the problem is that measurement inevitably involves some qualitative practices. But even the quantitative practices require value judgments for their interpretations.

An Effective Measurement-Audit-Sanction System

Let us look at an example of one comprehensive measurement system used by a large, decentralized company, General Electric. General Electric has had in operation for three years now an "EO/MR Measurement Format."[4] This is a rather lengthy questionnaire that must be filled our regularly by every key GE manager. The important point here is that this activity is now a required part of the general, regular, annual, business review process, so that, from the smallest component to the company as a whole, the performance of every manager and every component within the corporation is subject to in-line review.

The first part of the format concerns itself with a report on recent past and present minority and female goals as estimated, and then as achieved or partially achieved, with the addition of a five-year goal:

(1) Present and projected population growth in labor market areas: the percentage of blacks, Spanish, and other minorities in the plant as related to the total population of the labor market area. These data are simply to give the minority profile for the Standard Metropolitan Statistical Area in which the plant or component is located.

(2) Total minority and female work force—five-year results and estimates: the minority and female percentages of the total work force in the plant for the current year, also the current year as estimated in the last year, and then with a five-year goal.

(3) The number of persons hired in the current year: the minority and female percentages of exempt, nonexempt, and hourly employees to the total work force hired in the given year.

[4]Copies of the complete "Format" can be obtained from the authors.

(4) Recruiting goals for minority college graduates (excluding corporate training programs): the current goal as projected from last year, the actual achievement, and the goal for this year for minority college graduates. There is no five-year target in this case.

(5) Number of removals from payroll: the minority and female percentage of all persons laid off, on leave of absence, or permanently removed from the company's payrolls during the current year.

(6) Minority participation index:[5] an index number constructed from the percentage of the minorities in the plant work force as related to the percentage of minorities in the local Standard Metropolitan Statistical Area. The past and current year and a five-year projection are given. A ratio or index of 1.0 indicates the same percentage of minorities in the plant work force as in the local community.

The second part of the format concerns itself with upward distribution in job categories and penetration into salary levels.

(1) The first report gives the minority and female percentages for managers, for sales persons in exempt jobs, and for all other exempt positions. These data are the recent past, present, and five-year goals.

(2) Then a further breakdown is given with the measurement of exempt minority and female distribution percentages through the various salary levels used at General Electric. There are five groupings of these salary levels, and data are presented for each grouping.

(3) Data on training activity is presented. First, for cooperative programs, that is, work-school programs for the minority and female percentages for both the exempt and the nonexempt people who are in training. Second, for those in exempt training programs. Third, for those in apprentice training programs. These occupational-level and training-program data give the operating manager and top management a fairly clear picture, at least for the short term, of what the likelihood is for improving minority participation in white-collar and management positions.

---

[5]We might ask this question: Would it also be helpful and advisable to set up the additional statistic of parity participation goals? The "ideal" minority participation might be computed for each of the nine job categories or steps of the ladder. This ideal could be based on the minority percentage for the company as a whole. For example, if the company as a whole is ten percent black, then the ideal target for top managers would be ten percent black. The same ten percent target would hold for professionals and so forth. An index number of what approximation to the ideal target is actually achieved at each level could be computed.

The third part of the format is qualitative and deals with program development and evaluation of major opportunities, problems, management commitment, and affirmative action plans in the plant or component.

(1) The manager is to report on significant equal employment programs and activities that have produced results.

(2) The manager is to report on the status of affirmative action plans established in his department's plants, service shops, sales offices, credit offices, field offices, etc., in accordance with the Office of Federal Contract Compliance's Revised Order No. 4.

(3) The manager is to describe any potential problems of significance that might arise in job relationships and job assignments.

(4) A report is made on any productivity problems that might have arisen in implementing equal employment opportunity programs.

The fourth part of the format concerns programs and opportunities in the local plant communities. Here the manager is to describe any actions taken in the past year to demonstrate management involvement in his local community. These are contributions to minority organizations; working with educational leaders to develop curricula and work-study programs oriented to business needs; working with key minority organizations; supporting low- or middle-income housing and making efforts toward increased open housing opportunities for minorities.

The manager is also to report the relationship of his companies to minority business enterprises. Has a manager with responsibility for liaison been appointed to deal with minority business enterprises in the local community? Has a vendors' list been developed for use by the company's purchasing department for purchasing from minority companies? Contracts and purchase orders by dollar value and contracts awarded to minority vendors and suppliers are to be reported. A description is to be given of the local component or company's support to minority business enterprises in terms of financial aid, technical assistance, loans of equipment, etc. Finally, the manager is asked whether or not he has established a total contract dollar goal to minority businesses as suppliers and sellers, and what his plans are in this for the next year.

Some of the data reported on in this fourth section of the format are qualitative. Some are simple quantitative material, such as the listing of contracts that have been maintained with local minority businesses and the amount of these contracts.

The fifth part of the format deals with government reviews and complaint cases. The manager is to describe any significant problems or cases in litigation or conciliation with a government agency, along with any unusual requests made by review officers. Generally, this section presents no surprises since any unusual situations would already be known to divisional and corporate equal employment officers.

Quantitative data need to be interpreted in line with other variables. Quantitative data may seem simple but we all know the dangers of the "numbers game." If we were to compare the simple quantitative percentages of minority at any level in a plant with those in another plant, we would need to know the plant's type of operation. The plant might have a large amount of engineering or highly technical personnel, for example, as opposed to the other personnel. We would want to know if the plant is north or south and the racial climate of its neighborhood. Along with statistics about the local minority labor markets, factors such as these are needed in order to interpret the statistics intelligently.

It is not easy to establish five-year targets that are balanced neither too low nor too high. Value judgments will be involved in such targets. Past experience of undershooting or overshooting will give clues toward more accurate target setting for the limited five-year period. A company may wish to set targets for itself that are higher than those immediately demanded by compliance review agencies.

When we look at sections two, three, and four of the EO/MR measurement format, we find many qualitative descriptions of programs and relationships of the company with employees and with the local community. The immediate question, of course, is: How valid are these descriptions; are they comparable from one plant to another, one division to another, one department to another, or one group to another? Presumably, they are not perfectly comparable, but as experience is developed and as EO/MR officers interpret and probe these data, better degrees of comparability will be developed. We cannot expect, however, to make this kind of data quantitative in the perfect sense of the word. It is very important data, and the best measurement system in the world can simply try to make it as objective as possible.

Reports like this might indicate that the corporate headquarters would be deluged with documents and data; this is offset by the value of many innovative and creative programs that are described. In the case of GE, these reports are combined into a document entitled the "EO/MR Best Buy" report and distributed throughout the company as a handbook of workable affirmative action plans and programs that can be adapted by the various components according to their business needs.

An important question often arises with regard to any measurement system: Does it affect management compensation and status? Managers in major industries are generally rewarded first in terms of basic salary; second, by a bonus based on performance; and third, by stock options. These rewards are tied into the annual performance appraisal review with a higher manager. Factors affecting incentive compensation are usually the profitability of the local operation, its market position (or share of the market), and the growth of the business. Other considerations, such as man-power development and especially minority manpower participation and planning, are factored into the manager's appraisal, but lack the precision of profit and market-share quantitative evaluations against goals. It would seem necessary to make a direct connection between Economic Employment Opportunity progress reports and a given manager's performance bonus. There are instances in which this has been done, but the practice has yet to become general. We judge that it should become general if realistic change is to be achieved.

One obstacle is this inevitable complaint:

> You equal-employment people want us to work on the problems of the environment. You want us to work with the so-called new work force. You want us to work with blacks and other minorities and to hire veterans. Now you want us to hire and promote more women. Why do you hit us so hard? Why don't you leave us alone so we can make some money? Moreover, among all these issues, what gets priority? Would you, for example, give us some allowance on our profitability picture if we make extra efforts in the equal employment area, even though they may affect profits?

The reply from corporate headquarters would probably be, "No, you must try to do all of these." Inevitably there is a value judgment in balancing these various goals so that priorities can be made clear. However, unless the concept of measuring managers on EEO progress is seriously tied to executive compensation and status, little will be achieved.

One constructive aspect of the measurement of management in the area of minority participation is that, thanks to the Civil Rights Act's reporting requirement in form EEO-1 (for which all these categories are computed), management is taking a closer look at the entire area of manpower development and planning to insure that there are no discriminatory barriers to the effective utilization of all employees with ability, interest, and willingness to progress—key criteria. The measurement system we have discussed here could perhaps be applied to other areas besides minority participation and so be a very important instrument for securing progressive management and organizational change. In any case, it is an important strategy for achieving full minority participation.

The Development of Faster Upward Mobility for Blacks

While entry-level hiring of blacks remains an urgent need, a new challenge to management for the 1970's is upgrading blacks at every level of the corporate structure. There are many reasons for such upgrading: the sheer need for more people in white-collar and management jobs; the need to correct the credibility gap with blacks regarding their futures for higher positions in the corporation; the need for role models for younger black employees; and the need for white managers to have black managers at their own level who can advise them regarding black employees at lower levels.

Analyzing and Planning Upward Mobility

In reviewing the status of its equal opportunity and affirmative action programs last year, GE found that the company had pretty much learned how to hire and retain minority employees in the aggregate through the systems approach discussed earlier. The new dimension, the new thrust of company effort, would be to develop a structured and orderly system of upward mobility—minority participation at all levels of the organization. The company found that a dual approach was necessary. First, GE addressed the question of providing additional promotional opportunities for the minority men and women who were already employees. Second, they looked at the supply side of the equation to ascertain how to enlarge the number of entry-level employees with the skills and educational background that a technically oriented company demands.

The first time around, GE's analysis was aimed at finding out how, if all things were equal, a given number of minorities would attain the general-manager level, positions of responsibility that pay more than $30,000 a year. They found that, of the present minority professionals and managers in the pipeline, only a small number would be on that rung of the corporate ladder a dozen years hence.

Taking another look and factoring in certain variables—for example, age, education, and relevant work experience—they found that the problem was a much larger one. One of the critical variables was the question of education: Is a college degree required for certain kinds of jobs? What kind of degree—technical or nontechnical? An analysis of all the exempt employees and their education revealed that at the lower levels of the organizational ladder most of the incumbents had nontechnical degrees or in some cases no college degrees. Higher up the ladder, in the exempt jobs paying $20,000 a year and up, more than 60 percent of the employees had four-year technical degrees. These people work in the technical-critical functions of the business—manufacturing, engineering, marketing—and they are the top managers. Incidentally, it was interesting to note that the fact that there are exempt employees with no degree proves that there are some opportunities to use human resources even if they do not have the paper qualifications.

The next step in the upward mobility model analysis was to make an assessment of the promotional opportunities available for employees. Because GE's organizational structure, like most other corporations, resembles a pyramid, the higher up one goes the fewer positions there are. What they found was that in general there are between five and ten times as many candidates for promotion as there are available openings on the next rung of the ladder. Obviously, this makes for a highly competitive situation for everybody, regardless of race or sex.

The result of this rather comprehensive analysis led to some conclusions that have special significance for employers such as GE who have set challenging goals for themselves for the employment or promotion of minority professionals to achieve and better distribute them up through the ranks of management. First, it was noted that an average well-qualified individual, regardless of race or sex, takes about 13 years to progress from an entry-level, professional position up through lower management ranks. Even a "high potential" or "fast-track" individual consumes 20 to 22 years to progress from entry level to upper-level management.

Thus, the *best* that can be reasonably expected in minority participation in middle management 10 to 15 years out, is that percentage that minorities were of the entry-level group this year. Similarly, this percentage also represents the best reasonable expectation for minority participation in upper management 20 to 25 years out. These projections, incidentally, assume that the company will be able to continue to recruit higher-level minority professionals in at least sufficient numbers to make up for turnover loss.

The second observation made, based on review of the computer model analysis, is that upward mobility in a large organization such as GE is not a particularly fast process for all employees, even the most talented and capable, regardless of race or sex. This is due in large measure to the fact that lower-level management in this type of organization often has responsibility (and associated pay levels) comparable to middle and upper management in proportionately smaller companies. Still, this has an impact on frustration levels of minority professional employees (as well as on nonminority professionals) who perceive that their peers in smaller outfits are "progressing" faster.

The third observation of special importance here is that holding a technical degree—a major in engineering, science, accounting, or law—is of major significance in assessing advancement opportunities in a technologically oriented company. These degree programs, incidentally, are still the ones *least likely* to be pursued by minority students, even though these days minorities make up a significantly higher percentage of college enrollments than a decade ago.

Two approaches can be taken to translate the upward mobility concept into reality. One is the approach of so-called accelerated promotion practices. The other is General Electric's program to broaden the base of the pyramid by significantly enlarging the supply of qualified, technically trained minorities to be hired at the professional entry level.

Accelerated Promotion Practices[6]

Acceleration practice inevitably involves giving a certain amount of preference. Preference at first sight seems too un-American. But what is the real American climate in this area? When we look at the myths of equality or rewards for merit in American society, we are reminded that "all men are equal, but some are more equal than others."

The American economy, although based on competition, is replete with instances of governmental intervention to favor one group at the expense of other groups. To name a few, there are land grants to railroads, depletion allowances to extractive industries, subsidies to farmers, tariffs favoring certain industries, the social security program with weighted benefits, and civil service preference to war veterans.

Also, in the private sector preferential practice has often been the rule. Consider, for instance, law firms that prefer Harvard or Chicago law school graduates, craft unions that favor sons or nephews of union members, WASP company managements that choose their associates because of family ties or name, and non-WASP companies that exclude WASPS. Favoritism is very common.

The Civil Rights Act of 1964 neither requires an employer or labor organization to give preferential treatment nor does it exclude it, except insofar as the tenor of the law is equal treatment with respect to race:

> *Nothing* contained in this title shall be interpreted to *require* any employer, employment agency, labor organization, or joint labor-management committee

[6]Proposed in Purcell and Cavanagh, *Blacks in the Industrial World; see also* Theodore V. Purcell, "The Case of the Borderline Black," *Harvard Business Review*, November-December 1971, pp. 128–133, 142–150; and Timothy B. Blodgett, "Borderline Black Revisited," *Harvard Business Review*, March-April 1972, pp. 132–137.

subject to this title to grant *preferential treatment* to any individual or to any group because of the race, color, religion, sex, or national origin of such individual or group *on account of an imbalance* which may exist with respect to the total number or percentage of persons of any race, color, religion, sex, or national origin employed by any employer, referred or classified for employment by any employment agency or labor organization, admitted to membership or classified by any labor organization, or admitted to, or employed in, any apprenticeship or other training program, in comparison with the total number or percentage of persons of such race, color, religion, sex, or national origin in any community, state, section, or other area, or in the available work force in any community, state, section, or other area.[7]

However, the Office of Federal Contract Compliance goes far beyond the Civil Rights Act. Its Order No. 4 requires that a government contractor remedy any underutilization of minority people in his company. Underutilization means having fewer minority workers in a given job category "than would be reasonably expected by their availability."

Expectations are formulated by looking at the minority population, the minority unemployment, and the minority work force in the area, including the degrees of skill that could be reasonably recruited, and finally by looking at the promotability of minority people already employed. The contractor is also expected to deal with outside training institutions and consider what training he could reasonably provide to build up his minority work force, guided implicity by percentages of available persons in the area.

Order No. 4 makes no mention of preferential practice. It does not set inflexible quotas, but rather uses "targets" as one measurement of the "good faith effort" applied to an affirmative action plan. The directive also asserts that it is "not to be used to discriminate against any applicant or employee (presumably white) because of race, color, religion, sex, or national origin." But the order implicitly calls for a certain amount of preferential practice.

What do we mean by acceleration practices regarding blacks? By acceleration practice we mean giving a qualified black, precisely because of his race, specific hiring or especially promotion or upgrading preference over one white person or over a group of white persons so that of two qualified people, one black and one white, management will choose the black for the promotion. Now this acceleration practice is clearly preferential and it requires two careful provisos.

First, the black person who receives such a promotion is either qualified now for the new position, or can become qualified after a reasonable

[7]The Civil Rights Act of 1964, Section 703(j). Emphasis added.

amount of time according to a single standard of *minimum* qualifications applicable to *all* employees. To help someone advance merely because of his identity with a certain race, with no respect to his ability, robs him of his self-respect. It is actually a kind of paternalistic racism in disguise. Surely a black man, or any person, wants to be hired and promoted eventually because he is valued as a person who can do the job.

The second proviso calls for an *ad hoc* decision in each case. Since acceleration practice gives a specific preference to a black person over a white, the needs of both parties, along with the circumstances of the case should be carefully investigated and balanced. Remember, we assume both black and white are adequately qualified or qualifiable. If, in addition, the black were clearly superior to the white, there would be no problem about preferring him. If the white were superior to the (qualified) black, the specific circumstances of the case must be examined. It might still be justifiable to pick the black. But if there were some special urgency about the job, then passing up the black could be justified. Now suppose there was a big gap, and the white was far superior to the (qualified) black, here the black would rarely be picked, although again the circumstances would give the clue. For example, if an astronaut were sought to do a difficult mission and a black and white were both qualified, yet the white had super qualifications, it would seem reasonable to pick the white, that is, to pick the best possible person for the difficult job. This does not mean, however, that circumstances would *always* dictate picking "the best possible person."

A final point of caution is that we do not propose the need for acceleration practices for black Americans at work as something necessary forever. In time, we should not even have to notice a man's race in looking at his promotional chances. GE, for instance, has set as a long-range goal in this area the "elimination of any consideration of race or sex in any facet of the employees' spectrum." Yet it is very doubtful that this ideal will be realized in our lifetime. By the year 2000 a management strategy like this one should be an anachronism. In the 1970's it is vitally needed. Furthermore, we are not forgetting the need for *individual* concern for any person to work, especially regarding promotion. Apart from race, sex, age, and length of service, the employee is an individual person, and ideally management will look at him as an individual and will deal with him in that way.

Can we really justify acceleration practice regarding blacks? We can, for two reasons. First, discrimination and segregation have separated blacks as a group from the rest of American society, leading to lower per capita income, often inferior education, and a constellation of sociological and psychic disabilities for many, though, of course, not for all blacks. Collectively, blacks have been alienated from the rest of American society, not by any innate inferiority but by white racism, both personal and institutional, and the rights of groups as well.

Because man is a social being, inevitably shaped by the social and economic structures within which he lives, justice is not achieved simply by ensuring the rights of persons as individuals. Justice also requires just socioeconomic institutions. Since most whites, no matter how well meaning, have extremely limited capabilities for the recognition of talent and qualifications among blacks in those qualities that are not quantifiable, acceleration practice can be seen as simply a tool we must use to assure equal consideration of minorities when important employment decisions are being made. When encrusted patterns of education, employment, and housing put one group at a disadvantage, we are obligated to change those institutions. Whites have a moral obligation to help reform those institutions and make them open to all Americans.

Our second reason is the need for order in American life. The choice before us may be rapid integration and upgrading of Negroes or an escalation of the turmoil and polarization of the 1960's and early 1970's. Unless radical change takes place, blacks and whites may grow further apart, rending the very fabric of American life.

Such reasoning is not intended to be a "law and order" argument. It is more important to have a just social order than to have a peaceful one. Life in the plantation days of slavery was tranquil enough, but it also represented a shocking violation of the human dignity of almost half its citizens. Peace under justice involves not only Negroes but all Americans; our entire community, our cities and our suburbs are entitled to the peace and order necessary for a stable and happy society.

People who say that acceleration practice as preferential is discrimination in reverse have not carefully read our two provisos. For example, the "crutch of blackness" argument: "If you give acceleration preference to someone, you impede his motivation or you deprive him of dignity by treating him as a child instead of as a man." This objection ignores our first proviso. Blackness is not a crutch but a wedge. Blacks may need that wedge for many years.

Second, the "white man's burden" argument: "Acceleration practice assumes that blacks are inherently inferior. They, their children, and maybe even their children's children, must be given special treatment and carried on the white man's back just as the Africans and Asians once were carried by the European colonials." Preference means no such thing. Go back again to our first proviso. Qualifying time, neither forever nor unreasonably long, must be factored into any intelligent planning for affirmative action and upgrading.

The "tokenism" argument: "Acceleration practice implies that management simply wants the house black. They want a man's blackness, not his skills." Once again go back to proviso number one.

Fourth, the "white rights" argument: "What about the rights of the white employee who is passed over?" We are assuming here that the white and black employees are about the same in their qualifications. If so, this overrides no particular rights of the white person to a given promotion. He has no more rights than the black person if we have fulfilled proviso number two. There is no discrimination in reverse here whatsoever.

Note that in this argument we are not presupposing the Jackie Robinson syndrome. Management need not wait until it gets the superblack. Acceleration practices can apply to superblacks and to superwhites, to average blacks and average whites, and to borderline blacks and borderline whites. Rightly understood, acceleration practice is a dignified phrase and a necessary management strategy.

Will acceleration practice cause white resentment and backlash? This fear can be exaggerated. As Reverened Leon Sullivan, founder of the Opportunities Industrialization Centers, puts it, "White backlash? Wait until paycheck time comes; when management holds on to black fellows, white backlash lasts for a couple of paychecks."

In the field studies for *Blacks in the Industrial World*,[8] integration was accepted much better than expected in two plants in Virginia and Tennessee. Preferential hiring of a small number of disadvantaged blacks in two northern plants and very rapid, although nonpreferential, black hiring at a plant in Chicago were also achieved with little significant resentment.

One key to acceptance is a firm management stand. Part of a manager's affirmative action responsibility is helping to create a climate in which employees can learn to understand the need for special efforts on behalf of blacks.

The manager of the 1970's will need to think through both policy and implementation of policy on acceleration practice for black employees, especially at the white-collar and management levels. Management may wish to develop its own cases requiring the careful exploration and thought necessary to develop and refine its implementation of acceleration policy. But there is no need to apologize for this policy or sweep it under the rug. Acclereation practice, as we present it, is by no means discrimination in reverse. It does not deny the merit system, although at times it may deny the super-merit system. There may be some resistance by those who are not preferred or accelerated, although, hopefully, they will see the justice and

[8]Purcell and Cavanagh, *Blacks in the Industrial World*.

wisdom of this management strategy. In any case, management needs the courage to carry out this strategy if we are to have the development of faster upward mobility for blacks in American business.

GE's "Base-Building" Approach

An indicated earlier, General Electric has adopted the approach of broadening the base of the pyramid by increasing the supply of technically trained minorities and women.

In assessing minority representation in the professional and managerial ranks today, GE found not a problem of demand, but a problem of supply. No one will argue that it takes special education and special training to qualify for the top jobs in our complex industrial society. It does not matter how hard an individual works or how bright he is, he cannot do a competent technical job unless he has expertise in engineering, science, finance, or other technically oriented disciplines. Industry as a whole needs many technically skilled employees because industry is based on technology. Consequently, if industry does not help develop a supply of qualified black engineers, scientists, financial experts, etc., we are not going to see many blacks in the top jobs. Engineering is a good example; of over 43,000 engineers who graduated this year, less than 500 were black and only a handful were other minorities (around 1 percent).

Given the fact that it takes anywhere from 13 to 25 years to penetrate the upper levels of the corporation, this means that if industry is getting only 1-percent minority engineers today, there will be only 1-percent minority representation in the leadership positions in 1990. A Howard University study of minorities in engineering over the past ten years indicates that the number of black youngsters signing up for engineering courses has increased slightly. But if the number of blacks graduating from engineering schools is increased by 15 percent a year, it would still take 50 years to achieve proportionate representation in America's engineering community. The challenge is clear. Unless a way is found to multiply the present supply of minorities in engineering and other technically oriented disciplines, such as business administration, by a factor of 15 within this decade, full minority participation will still be an elusive dream.

What is needed are bold, creative, all-out programs to dramatically increase the supply of minority technical graduates. Most black students have chosen education, sociology, the ministry, and other disciplines in which they believed there were opportunities for success or the return to the minority community to help deal with the problems of their own people.

Additionally, their "success images" are teachers, ministers, doctors, and lawyers, not engineers, MBA's, and computer experts. A second obstacle is the lack of quality education that, unfortunately, is the plight of the black youngster who has attended a ghetto school and is poorly prepared in mathematics and science. Both obstacles point to the need for motivating minority students to study technical subjects and for providing remedial education so that they can keep pace in college. Obviously, this will take a lot of time and dollars.

One of the more promising solutions offered is a combination work-study program in which minority youngsters would study technical subjects during part of the college year and work in industry on a related job during the rest of the year. The student-employee would gain both money to defray the expenses of his education and experience in an industrial environment. This cooperative educational or technical internship program needs the support of the entire business community, not a single corporation. Government support will be needed and the colleges and universities, professional and technical societies, foundations, and minority organizations all need to join the effort.

Fortunately, forecasts of the demand side of the supply-demand equation are favorable in spite of the present, temporary employment crisis for engineers. In this decade there will be 50 percent more professional and technical jobs in 1980, as reported by Andrew Brimmer of the Federal Reserve Board in an authoritative study, "The Economic Outlook and the Demand for College Graduates."[9] It looks as if the nation will have 36,000 fewer engineers and scientists than it will need in the years ahead unless enrollments in the disciplines increase. Thus, minority students who can be sold on technical courses should indeed find the door wide open.

Before identifying the technical internship program as one of the ways to build the minority supply and broaden the technical base, GE examined a number of other concepts. For example, making scholarship funds available to minority students was suggested, or providing scholarships for the children of minority employees who wanted to take technical college courses. GE entertained the notion of operating the engineering school at a black college, buying an existing college, or establishing a GE institute along the lines of the General Motors Institute. But the company discovered that aside from the millions of dollars involved in pursuing any of these approaches, there would still be no guarantee that these efforts would

[9]An address by Governor Andrew Brimmer for the Cooperative Education Institute, sponsored by Tuskegee Institute, Atlanta, Georgia, May 30, 1972.

directly increase the absolute numbers of minority technical graduates, especially not in sufficient quantity to provide for GE's needed input to meet its long-term minority employment goals. The General Electric studies also showed that a number of other approaches are available, and some of them are already being tried; for example, educational grants and awards from the GE Foundation, participation in minority recruiting seminars, relationships with secondary schools, and liaison with the United Negro College Fund. The company will continue to pursue these approaches, and their commitment is described in recent talks by Fred Borch, Chairman of the Board, and J. Stanford Smith, Senior Vice-president. However, these approaches will not alone solve the enormous problem of building the minority supply manyfold.

Building a broader minority supply base will require government funds, industry commitment on jobs, curriculum changes by educators, motivational work with minorities through more effective counseling at the high school level, participation and support from minority organizations, and involvement of minorities in the development of these programs.

Similar joint efforts were developed by government, industry, minority organizations, unions, and educators through the National Alliance of Businessmen, which combined funds and training to bring disadvantaged people into the world of work. This was treating a symptom and not getting at the fundamental problem of why people were dropping out of society.

Now we need to combine motivational encouragement of minorities to pursue technical careers with a commitment of industry to provide the jobs that lead to upward mobility and to the placement of minorities in key professional and managerial positions.

GE is working to bring the involved institutions together and has already met with the deans from the major engineering schools (including the predominately black schools); leaders from minority organizations, such as the NAACP, Urban League, Opportunities Industrialization Center; the U.S. Labor Department and other government agencies; high school guidance counselors; business organizations such as National Chamber of Commerce; and the National Association of Manufacturers and independent groups, such as the Conference Board. Results of these efforts can have a pronounced effect on reducing the 55 years now projected to achieve a 10-percent minority participation at the managerial and professional levels.

In addition to all this effort, black students must be persuaded that engineering, mathematics, finance, and the physical sciences are the pathways to improved minority participation.

Summary and Conclusions

The grim prediction statistics given at the beginning of this paper will be proved accurate unless every segment of our American society cooperates towards creative and massive programs to secure full minority participation in American industry. The corporation has its own central role to play in such programs.

One necessary corporate program is the development of a systems approach toward minority manpower planning, including primarily an effective measurement-audit-sanctions system. Unless plant top managers, middle managers, and first-line supervisors are rewarded and sanctioned for their efforts in building up and developing minority people in their work force, little change will occur in most organizations. Effective measurement-sanction systems are practical, as demonstrated by GE's EO/MR Measurement Format.

Second, entry-level jobs for minorities will continue to be an urgent problem along with vestibule and on-the-job programs in aid of the disadvantaged. But the main thrust of the 1970's will be the development of faster upward mobility tracks for blacks at white-collar and management levels.

This paper presents three techniques for speeding advancement: careful analysis of a firm's actual promotional patterns; policy and implementation for acceleration practices; and fast construction of a much broader base of technically prepared minority employees, especially through work-study programs.

Clearly, business cannot perform its significant role in promotion full minority participation without the cooperation of the government, unions, and educational and community organizations. Fast construction of a broader base of technically prepared minority people will require extensive federal money. Business can do much to help make such financing politically viable.

As the Committee for Economic Development put it in 1971: "Responsible management must have the vision and exert the leadership to develop a broader social role for the corporation if business is to continue to receive public confidence and support. . . . We believe that business will respond constructively to this new challenge."[10]

---

[10]*Social Responsibility of Business Corporations*, A Statement on National Policy by the Research and Policy Committee of the Committee for Economic Development, New York City, June 1971, p. 61.

Short-versus Long-run Effects of the Introduction of Black Workers into the Firm

●●

● GERALD F. CAVANAGH

Department of Management and Organization Sciences
Wayne State University

● JOHNNY STEWART

Department of Management and Organization Sciences
Wayne State University

When blacks enter a firm, they bring with them different attitudes, aspirations, hopes, and cultural values than whites have. They don't settle into the programmed life of the industrial plant easily. Initial reaction of white workers is often misunderstanding and friction. Whites are told not to complain, to be quiet. Blacks, who protest at what seems to be discrimination and blacklash, are told to be patient. What is the long-run effect of the juxtaposition of these two sets of values on communications, plant atmosphere, and corporate structure? The major proposition of this paper is that, although the differences in these two value systems can cause disruption in the short run, the long-run benefits outweigh the disadvantages.

In the late 1960's corporations increased their efforts to hire and train

404

blacks. These new activities were precipitated by social pressures: riots; activities of civil rights and other organizations; pressures from government agencies such as the Equal Employment Opportunity Commission (EEOC) and Office of Federal Contract Compliance (OFCC); and corporate executives who exerted leadership in the area of corporate responsibility.

Minority Workers Cause Disruption

The new black employees brought along quite different values and hence new problems for the firm. Although there are differences in the attitudes of middle-class salaried blacks and lower-class unskilled black workers, both groups bring previously unconfronted fears, hopes, and demands to their new jobs.

The unskilled, disadvantaged black worker is fearful and often withdrawn when he comes to his job. He is sometimes less verbal in expressing his fears and anxieties but speaks through his body language (gestures and walk) and behavior.[1] Many disadvantaged people have a greater need for satisfactory and warm personal relations than do other employees. This is to some extent because they have not been successful in previous jobs, so

---

[1]Nonverbal communication is well exemplified in an unpublished incident from the field work that was done for the book, *Blacks in the Industrial World: Issues for the Manager* by Theodore V. Purcell and Gerald F. Cavanagh (New York: Free Press, 1972). At one of the plants, a black man had a reputation as a militant with the plant manager and most of the plant supervision. At one point, he began to wear an elaborate cowboy hat to work. His foreman and others took this as a sign of militancy and defiance of plant rules. They were afraid even to raise the question with him. One of the superintendents in the plant was more open and sensitive to blacks. Here is how he described their encounter:

Well, he came into work with a cowboy hat on and nobody said anything to him. It was the second time that I noticed he had it on. . . . I asked someone, "Why's he have a hat on?" He said he didn't know. I said, "Why don't you ask him?" He said he wasn't sure it would accomplish anything if he did ask him. So, I flagged the guy down and said, "Hey, that's a hell of a fine hat you've got on!" And he smiled. And I said, "Gee, I wish I could wear a hat like that." And we got into quite a conversation about this, and this was a status symbol to have. He was told that . . . certain things would be frowned upon, and that if you did something like this you couldn't get your work done by some of his fellow workers. So, he was just proving that he could get his work done. And by our ignoring it, we were ignoring the fact that he was accomplishing his work and he was real happy to talk to me about it, that I had got it figured out. The next day, he had his hat off. I didn't ask him to take it off, but he had accomplished something. He had got to me.

they come to the plant with distrust and fear.[2] The plant environment is a noisy and unknown labyrinth and, therefore, threatening.

This ambivalent young black is often met on the plant floor by a hard-driving, production-oriented foreman. The supervisor, usually an old-timer who is more familiar with the work ethic common to the white ethnic, is likely to be ill at ease with this young black with his afro and outward coolness. Not knowing how to deal with him, the supervisor keeps at a distance and does not adequately explain the job.

The young worker, who will want to see some value in the work he is doing and to be treated as a person, may be disappointed. He then becomes even more aloof and uncommunicative, as a defense. This leads to a further lessening of interest in work, increasing alienation and frustration, the sequence of events forming a vicious circle.

Foremen as well as higher levels of management are concerned about the blacks will have on the internal behavior of the group. For example, will white workers accept, reject, or be indifferent to the new black employee? A statement by Goodman summarizes the clash of values:

> Turning to the specific problem of minority employment, an initial axiomatic statement would be as follows: As the influx of minority group employees grows in number, more and more members of the organization will have value systems which are at variance with that of the organization.[3]

These contrasting value systems cause conflict, which is manifested in a wide variety of ways, from subtle tardiness to open hostility. If the organization is rigid and tends to be highly bureaucratized, it will exhibit a low tolerance for conflict.[4] In this instance and to the extent to which it is true, blacks will not be integrated into the plant social system. They will be isolated and put off to one side. The system is threatened by these new elements and, nonverbally and even unconsciously, it tries to reject them.

The young black worker's resultant lack of involvement, his disinterest, is most quickly and easily seen in his higher rates of turnover, absenteeism, and tardiness (TAT). While almost all supervisors of disadvantaged black

---

[2]Theodore V. Purcell and Gerald F. Cavanagh, "Alternate Routes to Employing the Disadvantaged Within the Enterprise," 22nd Annual Meeting of the Industrial Relations Research Association, New York, 1969, p. 72.

[3]Richard Alan Goodman, "A Hidden Issue in Minority Employment," *California Management Review*, Summer 1969, p. 28.

[4]See, *e.g.*, Paul R. Lawrence and Jay W. Lorsch, *Organization and Environment* (Boston: Graduate School of Business Administration, Harvard University, 1967). The authors found that high-performing organizations were characterized by open confrontation as a form of conflict resolution (pp. 149–151).

workers say that they do average or better work when they are present, they also point out that the disadvantaged have a higher rate of turnover, absenteeism, and tardiness,[5] and plant documents support this fact. This high level of TAT is disruptive to the organization and costly to the firm.

High turnover, absenteeism, and tardiness among disadvantaged black workers are not only serious problems in their own right, but also are symptoms of more serious underlying difficulties. But the symptoms shout loudly, and can easily divert all of management's attention to short-run solutions that do not get to the roots. The fact that increased TAT characterize younger workers in general[6] supports the hypothesis that it makes a serious and deep-rooted problem that must eventually be addressed by the firm. Black disadvantaged workers have provided management with an early warning system.

Discrimination at Professional Levels

Salaried and professional blacks have faced parallel problems of coping with new value systems when they move into industrial jobs. It is a new world, and the measures of success must be learned. To make the situation even more acute, many salaried blacks were faced with more rigorous selection and promotion criteria until quite recently, and it has left its scars.

In a recent research study,[7] most of the plants reported several instances of able black persons who were qualified and wanted a promotion—most often to first-line supervisor. They never received the promotion. These capable blacks, who are now in their forties and fifties felt discrimination keenly. Sometimes they even spoke out, and when they did they quickly got the reputation of being "trouble makers." In spite of their own efforts and abilities, they did not get the jobs they fought for.

Given the internal pressure these older blacks provided, plus the external pressures on the firm, younger black men did eventually get those managerial jobs. In sum, younger black men stood on the shoulders of their older brothers. The younger blacks received the promotions that were denied the older blacks, even though the older blacks are the ones who fought the hardest for those chances.

[5]Purcell and Cavanagh, *Blacks in the Industrial World*, p. 248. Foremen find higher rates of turnover, absenteeism, and tardiness to be true of black hourly workers generally, although to a lesser extent (see table B-1, p. 321).

[6]*Ibid.*, pp. 61, 67, 165–167.

[7]A four-year research project investigating the employment of blacks, reported in Purcell and Cavanagh, *Blacks in the Industrial World*. The situation described in the text was especially true of, though not exclusive to, southern plants.

In addition to the above bias and resulting lack of fairness, work loads and working conditions are often more demanding for the black. An informed observer of the black experience notes that the black employee is often expected to: (1) have academic credentials and experience for positions that offer limited, if any, growth; (2) be able to adjust instantly to obscure and unwritten corporate mores, prescriptions, and proscriptions; (3) have an ability to ignore provocations from so-called well-meaning coworkers; (4) show willingness to speak favorably for or to represent the corporation at "race functions"; (5) generate enthusiasm over BBD (Black by the Door) positions that inflate the company's equal opportunity image while contributing very little to his/her professional development.[8]

After meeting the above selection criteria, black professional candidates are then frequently placed in staff jobs with the "relations" suffix or "special" prefix.[9] These include personnel relations, administrative relations, public relations, community relations, education relations, special projects, special markets, etc. This trend began in the early 1960's when the first efforts were made to hire and integrate blacks into firms. Then it was more justifiable because blacks had been systematically excluded from the business world and consequently had little, if any, experience. Today, black graduates react negatively to offers for such positions, because the positions with the most growth potential are in marketing and sales, management, manufacturing operations, accounting and finance, engineering, and long-range planning.

These heightened job expectations, coupled with the marginal role the black is asked to play, do not tend to reinforce his sense of confidence. He sees his career, which means so much to him, as being at stake, and, as a result, he may become suspicious and fearful. He may be reluctant to change jobs or even to accept a promotion. He has some assurance of how to perform his present job assignment; a new position would mean he would have to begin all over again.

A black worker often has a greater sensitivity to injustice, due to the long-standing discrimination his people have endured, in addition to the discrimination he personally has experienced. When Martin Luther King very early criticized American bombing and killing in Vietnam, it surprised most Americans; we found it difficult to see any connection between domestic racism and an Asian war. This greater sensitivity to the value of

[8]Lewis M. Rambo, "So You've Hired A Black American," *Personnel Administration*, May 10, 1970, pp. 6–7.
[9]William Pickens III, "The Interview—The Black Viewpoint," *Business Horizons*, October 1970, pp. 13–22.

the human person, regardless of color or class, can be a short-run burden but a long-run asset to both the person and the firm.

The foreign and unsympathetic environment that many blacks meet, whether they be professionals or unskilled, coupled with this sensitivity often ultimately result in their leaving the firm.[10] The company loses qualified and potentially qualified blacks due to frustration with the company, their supervisor, and their coworkers. The firm then suffers, since high black turnover is costly, and the firm may then encounter increased pressure from civil rights and other organizations. Also detrimental to the firm will be the negative image to the black community that will be presented by blacks who have left the company.

Attitude of White Workers

The average white worker is sympathetic and does want the black worker to get a fair chance at a job and promotions.[11] Studies by Goeke and Weymar[12] and by Campbell[13] indicate such a trend toward a more open and liberal attitude. Nevertheless, there does remain a minority, and often a quite vocal minority, who resent close association with blacks.[14] A larger number of whites resent any hint of preferential treatment for blacks for entry jobs or promotion.

The firm cannot wait for all whites to become more open minded. It has pressures on it from all sides to bring blacks into the organization. As a result, the firm has to serve as a catalyst for expediting the change in attitudes by whites and concurrently demonstrate to blacks that their employment is not merely for affirmative action purposes or to improve the company's image in the eyes of the public and civil rights organizations. This situation is delicate and difficult for the company in the short run, because, if whites think blacks are getting preferential treatment, they will react negatively. While, on the other hand, if whites are permitted to display open resentment, blacks will become discouraged and aliented. In any case, if the firm does not perform the balancing act well, poor morale, disruption, and perhaps open hostility will ensue. This will hinder the per-

---

[10]See Purcell and Cavanagh, *Blacks in the Industrial World*, p. 71.

[11]*Ibid.*, pp. 18, 19, 172–173, 257–258.

[12]Joseph R. Goeke and Caroline S. Weymar, "Barriers to Hiring the Blacks," *Harvard Business Review*, September-October 1969, pp. 144–149.

[13]Angus Campbell, *White Attitudes Toward Black People* (Ann Arbor: Institute for Social Research, 1971).

[14]Purcell and Cavanagh, *Blacks in the Industrial World*, pp. 161–163.

formance of the firm, surely in the short run and perhaps even in the long run.

Long-run Effects

The industrial firm that hires and promotes blacks will find that it must face new problems, some subtle and others obvious, measurable, and costly. Nonetheless, it is the thesis of this paper that the effects of introducing blacks into the firm are of considerable long-run benefit to the organization in a wide variety of ways.

When blacks are introduced into the firm, the major long-term values to the organization are in the realm of: (1) better use of its human resources, and (2) encouraging a more flexible organizational structure. Other, more easily measurable benefits also accrue to the organization through the introduction of blacks into the firm.

When business conditions are poor, layoffs are sometimes necessary. As business picks up, the plant recalls those workers. The larger the number that returns the better off the plant is, since it is then saved training costs, break-in time, and orientation. Blacks usually respond to a recall in greater numbers than do whites. After a 1968 recall at a large General Electric plant, of the hourly semiskilled workers, 68 percent of the whites returned, while 87 percent of the blacks returned.[15] The blacks brought a considerable saving to the firm by their higher rate of return.

Selection criteria and instruments for determining job competence have been and still remain quite primitive. Until recently, many firms required a high school diploma and successful completion of some form of written examination to work in a shop on unskilled or semiskilled work. The federal government now requires employers to validate these examinations, to make sure that passing the tests actually provides a good prediction of successful job performance. The fact that a person has finished high school or can pass a written examination may have little relation to his ability to perform a job in a plant. Many blacks who had not finished high school criticized the educational criteria that had been used. Further they maintained and demonstrated that the written examinations were culturally biased, that is, that it was easier for a white to pass them than for a black of equal ability to do so.

Given these pressures from the federal government and from blacks,

---

[15]*Ibid.*, p. 105.

selection instruments and promotional criteria were reexamined for their ability to predict successful job performance, and they were found wanting. This means that many men and women had been turned away from the plant gates and turned down for promotion in the past who could have done the job just as well or better than many of those who were hired or promoted. This reexamination of selection and promotion criteria means that many talents, which would have been wasted using past criteria, will be put to better use in the future. This is clearly an advantage to both the individual and the firm.

When roles and relations are stable in a large organization, communications can become stylized, predictable, and even minimal. A crisis opens the system up, because new information is needed; the accepted truths and networks are not working. When large numbers of blacks, with their varying values, were introduced into the firm, a series of misunderstandings and even confrontations often followed. Supervisors, especially, realized that they were not well equipped to deal with these new values, and they became more open to new methods of managing and upward communications from their own men. This was encouraged by various foremen training programs, which often included some sort of sensitivity training.[16] So, because of the introduction of blacks into the firm, communications have often been improved, both among salaried personnel and in the hourly ranks.

As was shown earlier, the principal and surely most easily measurable and costly problems that generally accompany the introduction of disadvantaged black workers are that famous triumvirate: turnover, absenteeism, and tardiness (TAT). A temptation faces management when the turnover rates begin to rise—to treat only the symptoms. Often management will treat these problems with a patchwork of wishful solutions. Plant superintendents, threatened by these new values, have attempted to tighten up on discipline. They, and personnel people faced with a growing number of grievances, sometimes try to enforce the rules more exactly, rather than to treat each complaint on its own merits. Each of these techniques generally results in increased, rather than lowered TAT.

Other attempts to meet with these problems take the form of contests and prizes for those with the best attendance records. Open house for families sometimes help to increase interest in work and to temporarily reduce turnover, absenteeism, and tardiness. But none of these solutions get to the roots of the problem.

[16]*Ibid.*, pp. 210, 231, 246.

Early Warning System

When blacks entered the plant and increased the rates of TAT, they provided plant management with an on-the-spot early warning system of coming problems. Just about all of the studies of disadvantaged workers[17] have focused on these problems and the importance of long-range solutions. These solutions indicate the importance of: sensitive, knowledgeable, and flexible foremen; orientation to the job so that the worker realizes the importance of what he is doing; and even job redesign, if possible, to enable the worker to see and appreciate the product of his own labor.[18] These insights are now new; they were suggested long ago by organization researchers such as McGregor, Likert, and Maslow.[19] But when disadvantaged workers came into the firm in large numbers a few years ago, the need to reassess jobs and relations to supervisors and coworkers moved from being a matter of theory and exhortation, however well founded. These new, young, disadvantaged workers, many of whom were asking for a new work environment, were a matter of present fact; they had to be dealt with.

Listen to one plant superintendent, a man who had more than 1200 men working for him, a quarter of whom were black, and who had faced some serious racial confrontation problems. When asked why he was having so much trouble in the plant, he said:

> If I knew that, I could probably settle a lot of the problems in the United States today. I don't know what the answer is. You know, you keep batting your head against that wall. And that's what I'm going to continue to do, and one of these days I may not find it, but somebody will find it. And boy, I'm all ears to anybody that has any suggestions on what to do with not only the minority race, what to do with people today.[20]

He recognizes and underscores the fact that the new values that blacks have brought to the firm are only a preview of the values of younger workers in general.

Although the early warning system of black disadvantaged workers pro-

---

[17] See, for example, the nine studies compiled in *Programs to Employ the Disadvantaged*, ed. Peter B. Doeringer (Englewood Cliffs: Prentice-Hall, 1969).

[18] Purcell and Cavanagh, "Alternate Routes to Employing the Disadvantaged," p. 77.

[19] See, *e.g.*, Douglas M. McGregor, *The Human Side of Enterprise* (New York: McGraw-Hill Book Co., 1960); Rensis Likert, *The Human Organization* (New York: McGraw-Hill Book Co., 1967); Abraham A. Maslow, *Motivation and Personality* (New York: Harper & Row, 1964).

[20] Interviewed as part of the research reported in Purcell and Cavanagh, *Blacks in the Industrial World*.

vided this information to management a number of years ago, it has only recently been generally acknowledged as one of the most important problems facing the firm.[21] Firms who hired disadvantaged blacks were forced to face this issue earlier. It became a current, real, pressing problem, which called out for probing the deeper causes, if even for only a minority of the employees. For those firms who faced the issue straightforwardly, it brought a new emphasis on human resources. Moreover there is considerable evidence that this new sensitivity to the worker was repaid with success: more interested workers and better work.[22]

More Efficient Use of Human Resources

All of the above are clearly long-run advantages that come to the firm when they hire and promote black workers. But we have yet to treat the two major benefits: (1) a better treatment and use of human resources, and (2) a more open and flexible organizational structure.

Better use of human resources is a value to the individual supervisor and to the firm as a whole. In the face of these new challenges, the individual supervisor, from first-line foreman to plant manager, is encouraged or even forced to think through his role more clearly, and deal more effectively and sensitively with his people. When a foreman's role is no longer taken for granted, when he is questioned about various of his directives, he is forced to investigate his own knowledge and understanding of the function of a supervisor. Some old-timers find this very difficult; they look on it as harassment. They are therefore not only unable to respond to even casual and worthwhile questioning, but they become irritated and feel threatened when such questions arise. The supervisors who rise to the occasion, who embrace the situation as an opportunity to reexamine their own role, usually find that this is a unique opportunity to learn and to grow. They are often helped in this reexamination by a wide variety of company-sponsored foreman training programs. These range all the way from those in-plant programs specifically focused on working with younger workers and with blacks (sensitivity training, role playing, the Bell and Howell foreman training program) to university-sponsored management training programs.

These foreman training programs generally have a large component directed to making the supervisor more sensitive to the different life styles, values, and interests of the young and the black worker. This greater per-

---

[21]E.g., "Job Monotony Becomes Critical," *Business Week*, September 9, 1972, p. 108.

[22]Cf., *e.g.*, Purcell and Cavanagh, *Blacks in the Industrial World*, pp. 255–261.

sonal openness can make the individual a far better supervisor, who is able to handle the young black worker and is not threatened by him. When left to their own devices, foremen are tempted to enforce the rules and discipline more strictly or to employ watchdog tactics (to continually keep their eye on their employees).[23] When these tactics have been employed to meet the immediate problem, they seldom do much to solve it, and most often lay open and make worse the underlying and more important problems.

This is not to say that discipline is not required for the young black worker. It is; perhaps even more than for the average worker. But what is important are the attitudes of the person doing the disciplining. Illustrating the delicate balance are the insightful comments of a young black foreman at a Chicago electrical machinery plant:

> I would like to see supervision, people in management, working a little bit closer with these people. . . .
>
> This is what I would like to see: more on-the-spot corrections. Don't be afraid of getting slugged in the jaw. This is what I would like to see. And I think if we did this, there is a possibility that we would have less termination of these kids, hard kids, poor kids, kids that we have here. Because no one has been big enough, and brave enough to stand up to this kid and say, "now look, you've got to get in here on time. And when I tell you to do this, I intend for you to do it."[24]

Precisely because he was sensitive and open to these young blacks, he also require discipline. He realized that lessening discipline tells the young black that neither the supervisor nor the company really cares enough about him to help him.

Challenge Aids Management

The supervisor, the line manager, is in a crucial position when it comes to integrating new minority workers into the work force. Without a sensitive, knowledgeable, and flexible foreman, the task is probably impossible. Responding to the early demands of young blacks made many of these supervisors better able to handle the huge number of younger people who are now coming into the plant with many of the same attitudes and demands.

---

[23]Chris Argyris found the same tension between traditional management values and the atmosphere of a more open organization. See his *Management and Organizational Development* (New York: McGraw-Hill Book Co., 1971), p. 191.

[24]Purcell and Cavanagh, *Blacks in the Industrial World*, p. 266.

There is evidence that the presence of minority workers in the firm has influenced top-line managers more than it has staff personnel in changing their attitudes and broadening their perspective. In autumn 1971, Theodore V. Purcell published a difficult case of a marginal black engineer who was threatened with layoff.[25] He and the editors of the journal invited comment from readers on the case. While the replies do not constitute a random sample of top managers, their content does contribute to our discussion. Coding the letters on the subject matter we are concerned with here revealed that 83 percent of the 12 top managers who responded thought that there was a need for a change in the attitudes of top managers toward blacks; the same number felt that, because of the new challenges presented by the black community, there was a need for fundamental change in the organizational structure itself. On the other hand, of the six staff specialists, *e.g.*, engineers and finance men, who responded, only 33 percent felt that the attitudes of top management were wanting and that the organizational structure was too rigid and inflexible.

This evidence appears to support the hypothesis that when blacks bring new attitudes and values to the firm, which cause pressure in the organization, a long-range benefit of this pressure can be a reexamination of attitudes and of the organization itself. While the immediate impulse is to meet the pressing need, line management generally will look deeper; will recognize a need for change in hiring and promotion criteria; and will also see a need for greater openness and flexibility for the organization itself.

Focusing on the better use of human resources not only helps the individual supervisor, but quite clearly can help the organization as a whole. Trying to determine the best strategy for successfully bringing blacks into the firm has forced companies to rethink their entire selection and orientation processes. I have already dealt with the fact that most traditional selection criteria have failed to predict successful job performance; when examined, they were found to be inadequate and not just for minorities.

In introducing black workers to the firm, it became clear that it was not sufficient to merely hire them and juxtapose them with other workers in the company. In past decades the socialization process would have been sufficient to change the new employee's attitudes, but mere contact with older workers does not change younger workers' attitudes. Orientation programs,

---

[25]Theodore V. Purcell, "Case of the Borderline Black," *Harvard Business Review*, November-December 1971, pp. 128-135. The letters were interesting enough to prompt a second article containing reader comment: Timothy B. Blodgett, "Bordrline Black Revisited," *Harvard Business Review*, March-April, 1972, pp. 132-137.

beyond the traditional slide lecture on the plant, its product, and benefits, were seen to be necessary. Moreover, good orientation programs provided an opportunity for some two-way communication. It gave the new employee a chance to see some importance in the work he was doing. He wanted to see and understand the product, and to understand exactly what he was contributing by his work to bring it about. Some of these programs were government funded; many others were designed by the firm itself, and they were found to be a profitable expenditure if they were able to lessen turnover at all.

In general, the firm found that it was more successful in dealing with black workers if it did so honestly, without dissimulation or trying to "sell" them. In describing the work environment, turnover was found to be less when all of the difficulties of the work situation were not skirted, but were treated straightforwardly.[26] Supervisors, too, learned that the more honest they were in dealing with their subordinates, the more satisfied they were. Black workers again forced management to deal more factually and honestly with their employees.

The most significant advantage to the firm, and one that is widely recognized, is that the organization can now more fully use all of the human talent that it has available. Abilities will be less apt to be underutilized because of cultural expectations or prejudice. An example of underutilization of personnel was found in an electrical plant in Memphis that was desegregated in the early 1960's. Fully one-third of the plant workers, most of whom were women, had some college education.[27] The repetitive factory job hardly tapped the abilities and the education of many of these very bright, capable women; they were underemployed.

A southern-born superintendent of a manufacturing unit at the General Electric plant in Lynchburg, Virginia, feels strongly that any bias against minorities hurts everyone in the long run: "These vast resources that are not getting a chance to develop, to help the community, themselves, this type of thing. You see that something's not right. So, I feel that I can be reasonably fair."[28]

When faced with the waste of talent and education that prejudice against minorities bring, top managers see the inequity. Efficiency and avoiding

[26]John P. Wanous, "Matching Individual and Organization: The Effect of Job Previews," presented at annual meeting of Academy of Management, Minneapolis, Minn., August 14–16, 1972.

[27]Purcell and Cavanagh, *Blacks in the Industrial World*, p. 185.

[28]Interviewed as part of the research reported in Purcell and Cavanagh, *Blacks in the Industrial World*.

waste is a traditional value with managers, and wasting human abilities is doubly bad, since there is a person involved. A lessening of prejudice has enabled firms to better use the human talents that are working for them, and this is a considerable advantage to every-one involved.

Creativity in the Organization

Flexibility and innovation are essential elements for any organization operating in a changing society. My goal in this section of the paper is to show that the introduction of black workers into a firm helps to bring about and to sustain an organizational climate that encourages innovation and creativity.[29] New attitudes introduced by young black workers demand that management consider these new values and goals. The organization thus becomes more of an open system,[30] and hence more flexible and creative.

Those already in organizations can be blind to new information, strategies, and opportunities. Festinger[31] shows how individuals tend to interpret events around them consonant with their own opinions, filtering out what is in disagreement with them and their needs and accepting only what is in agreement with them. On the other hand, Lewis Coser[32] suggested that, when an organization is subjected to criticism and conflict, it is better able to adapt to the new, and to innovate. As has been pointed out above, blacks come into the organization, asking for greater sensitivity on the part of their supervisors and coworkers and also asking to see some value in the work that they are doing. These are two of the most important "people problems" that face industry today, and the fact that they were raised early and strongly by blacks is to the long-run advantage of the firm. As we have seen, blacks are more sensitive to injustice. Ethnic whites and older workers have lived with lower expectations for many years.

It is an advantage to the firm to have present in the work force people of varying values. This is confirmed in small group research. In one experi-

---

[29]Gary Steiner, in summarizing the results of a conference in *The Creative Organization* (Chicago: University of Chicago Press, 1965), says that among the elements of an organization that encourage creativity are heterogeneous personnel—even marginal and unusual types (pp. 16–18).

[30]For a discussion of what makes the organization more of an open system, see John G. Maurer, *Readings in Organization Theory: Open-System Approaches* (New York: Random House, 1971), especially pp. 3–11.

[31]Leon Festinger, *A Theory of Cognitive Dissonance* (Evanston, Ill.: Row, Patterson, 1957).

[32]*The Functions of Social Conflict* (New York: Free Press, 1956). Coser suggests that, when an organization is subjected to criticism and conflict, it is better able to adapt to the new, to innovate.

mental setting, a problem was presented to each of several groups. In some of these groups a "deviant" was placed, one who had some basic values differing from those of the group, and in the other groups there were no deviants:

> In every case, the group containing a deviant came out with a richer analysis of the problem and a more elegant solution. The next step was to request each group to throw out one member. The deviant was thrown out every time! As long as the group had to work with him, the results were creative, but faced with a choice, the group found it easier to continue minus the person who forced them to confront conflicting views and to integrate them.[33]

In short, it is not to the organization's benefit to hire and promote "more of the same." Men and women of varying backgrounds and attitudes bring a broader perspective to the organization. As the organization is urged to face these new attitudes and the deeper problems they often manifest, it becomes more flexible, adaptive, and creative at the same time. The conflict leads to greater flexibility and creativity.[34]

In an unprecedented move, General Motors voted a black, Reverend Leon Sullivan, onto their board of directors in spring 1971. This move was partially the result of the pressure of outside groups, such as the Campaign GM, partly to placate the large number of blacks in semiskilled jobs, and also partly to bring new dimensions and new attitudes to the board. In rapid succession, GM announced two new vice-presidents, one with responsibility over environmental questions and the other with responsibility over salaried personnel and educational efforts. In both areas, GM had been severely criticized, and in both cases the firm looked outside the corporation for men for these positions. GM has always been notorious for promoting from within, almost never turning to the outside for managerial talent. But significantly, in these problem areas where they very much needed new ideas, they looked outside the corporation.

The introduction of blacks into its various plants has been treated by General Electric in a serious and responsible manner.[35] The GE approach

---

[33]Recounted by Elise Boulding, *Conflict: Management in Organizations* (Ann Arbor: Foundation for Research on Human Behavior, 1964), p. 54.

[34]Crises generally precede any new period of organizational growth and development, according to Larry E. Greiner, "Evolution and Revolution as Organizations Grow," *Harvard Business Review*, July-August 1972, pp. 37–46. The conflict and resultant reexamination are necessary if the organization is to survive and grow.

[35]*General Electric's Commitment to Progress in Equal Opportunity and Minority Relations: A Case Study of a Systems Analysis Approach to Social Responsibility Programs* (New York: General Electric, 1970).

is treated in more detail in a paper by Theodore V. Purcell and Frank J. Toner in this volume, but suffice it to say that the very introduction of blacks brought on a reexamination of the entire corporation, from recruiting to management rewards. This reexamination has brought in new talent and ideas for the benefit of management and the corporation as a whole.

Along with all of the above long-run[36] advantages to the firm resulting from the introduction of black employees, it is obvious that the firm will also be meeting and helping to solve a serious national social problem. The social image of the firm in the community will improve following the reality of its actions. Image is obviously important to the corporation, judging from the variety of self-acclamations we view daily on TV and in magazine ads. But we are well aware that image without substance can backfire. Providing blacks with significant job opportunities supports the image with substance.

Summary and Conclusions

Although the introduction of minority workers into a firm often brings short-run disruptions and costs, their presence is a distinct advantage to the firm in the long run. Better communications both vertically and horizontally are stimulated in the firm. New values and demands open people up to new information and new solutions. When the firm hires and promotes blacks, it bolsters its public image by its actions and policies. Public relations efforts are not only not enough to convince the public of the good conscience of the corporation, but when unsupported they can be counterproductive.

The elimination of discriminatory selection and promotion instruments and criteria enable the firm to make more efficient use of its own resources. Black men and women, whose talents would have been largely wasted a few years ago, are able to contribute more of their talents. Furthermore, there is pressure to use more of a person's talents than just his mechanical machinelike movements. Young black workers look for the value of the work they do, and they expect to be treated honestly and as individuals by their foremen. As a result of these demands, more complete employee orientation programs and also foreman training have been instituted. These pressures from blacks came several years ago, before the widespread

[36]These long-run effects could also be described by the sociologist as latent functions of the introduction of blacks into the firm. See Robert K. Merton, *Social Theory and Social Structure* (New York: Free Press, 1957), pp. 61–69.

identical demands of youth in general. Thus, even through their costly turnover, absenteeism, and tardiness, disadvantaged black workers provided management with an early warning system of future planning needs.

Varying values introduced into an organization can make that organization more flexible and innovative. Incumbents are more likely to be blind to new information and opportunities. New outside talent can open the organization up to new ideas, strategies, and opportunities. Blacks in the recent past have done precisely this for many firms.

Affirmative Action Programs: Their Organizational Impact in the Corporate World

● JULES COHN
City University of New York

The federal affirmative action (AA) program for hiring and upgrading blacks, Puerto Ricans, other minorities, and women in accordance with number goals and timetables, will have some important, albeit unintended, organizational consequences. To critics of the corporate world, the potential gains from the general thrust of the AA approach are clear; quantitative goals encourage renewed efforts by employers, and timetables serve as yardsticks for the measurement and evaluation of these efforts. To female and minority job applicants, the AA program assures that employer practices will be scrutinized by government agencies and that government pressure can be brought to bear to insure that job applications receive nondiscriminatory consideration.

In addition to the above contributions, however, AA programs may produce negative consequences that were not anticipated by their proponents. And, because they have been busily occupied with negotiating goals and establishing timetables, many corporate executives have not yet had time to consider these negative consequences. However, as company AA programs get underway, these negative aspects will become evident to employers, job applicants, and corporate critics. For the past 18 months, I have been able to study the negotiation and development of AA programs by several major corporations. Accordingly, the comments and speculations that follow are based in part on firsthand observation.

Affirmative action programs, once the process for setting them up has begun, may have some of the following effects on corporate organization: (1) a redefinition of the personnel function; (2) tensions and strains among employees, and between employees and managers; (3) reduced productivity; and (4) changes in corporate organization and structure.

Redefinition of the Personnel Function

Quite plainly, the AA concept makes inevitable a redefinition of the corporate personnel function. Until now, personnel work has centered on the need to find, screen, and test able candidates, determine where to place them, and develop practices that will help retain them. Salary scales, fringe benefits, and procedures for advancement have also been the charge of personnel officers. In recent years, a new issue has received the attention of personnel departments: nonmaterial ways to motivate or to "humanize" (the word now in vogue) work. AA also represents an expansion of function, because it introduces a new emphasis—doing all of the above, while paying special attention to women and other minority groups.

A new dimension is thereby added to personnel work. The personnel officer is asked to identify employees and potential employees by the racial and sexual groups into which they fit. Policy must be formulated in accordance with these classifications. Personnel officers are, in effect, asked to be agents of society's newest priorities as well as of their companies.

Personnel executives who are sensitive about their responsibilities and thoughtful about their tasks could well be troubled by this new dimension of their work. How, for example, will they relate individual merit to racial and sexual factors when it comes to filling a vacancy? Their problems will be complex, their decisions controversial. Therefore, their work can no longer be dismissed as it was in the past as passive and clerical in nature; on the contrary, it will be discretionary, and more a focal point of public attention under the pressures brought by AA programs.

Tension and Strain Among Employees

Employee relations with a company will be affected by the new AA programs. In some companies, negative effects are already being felt. As the new goals and timetables are announced, employees wonder how their hopes and plans for advancement will be affected by a corporate commitment to allot a specified number of jobs to women, blacks, and Spanish-surnamed Americans. The employee who doesn't fit into the new "protected" groups may feel, on the one hand, that it is about time, that the company should do more to provide the opportunities to people hitherto left out in the cold. But, on the other hand, he may also very naturally feel concern about his own ability to advance or to get a fair hearing when he wants to transfer.

Companies that added new jobs to their organizational charts a few years ago so that minority group members who felt they were being discirminated against would have a department to take their grievances to will probably have to consider creating still another new post to receive and mediate complaints from nonminority group members. The racial and ethnic conflicts among employees that occupied personnel executives in recent years, when minority group members, particularly the disadvantaged, were being hired, will resume. The techniques that were applied to deal with them, such as special training programs for supervisors, orientation sessions, and incentive programs, may once again be needed as new problems arise between white and black, or male and female employees. Personnel executives will have to explain the nuances of the new programs to employees and be prepared to answer tough questions about them.

Reduced Productivity

The new AA programs may have other unintended and unwelcome effects: They may, albeit indirectly, reduce productivity. Employers will have to take on a lot of new paperwork. Supervisors, for example, will have to fill out forms and file reports on recruiting, hiring, and advancement of employees. More paperwork means more time, and more man (or woman) power. Master files have to be augumented, computers newly programmed, and new sets of instructions for recordkeeping devised and disseminated.

The added paperwork is only one aspect of the problem, however. Productivity may also be affected, particularly at the outset, by the array of attitudes with which employees greet the announcement of AA programs. Large companies, in particular, where news of changes or new direction in personnel practices must be transmitted through layers of management and through regional and local offices, may find considerable amounts of confusion among their employees. Therefore, time will have to be set aside for explanations, orientations, and interpretations. Confusion may be a minor attutudinal problem. Some employees will protest; others will scrutinize the AA program and discern ambiguities that demand clarification. "What are *my* rights?" they will ask. "How does this affect me?"

Moreover, their supervisors may feel torn between alternatives: recruiting, hiring, and advancing employees on racial or sexual grounds, on the one hand, or on grounds of ability, on the other. It will not always be easy to find the right resolution of these alternatives.

Will AA goals and timetables be given first priority in filling, say, a key slot on the assembly line? Or will production goals come first? How can the two priorities be balanced? At what level will these questions be answered —in headquarters, in the offices of personnel executives, or by the assembly line foreman? How these questions are answered will surely affect productivity, along with the time- and manpower-consuming process of finding the answers.

Changes in Organization and Structure

The poverty programs of the 1960's and many of the social welfare programs launched during the New Deal often had as their major beneficiaries the social welfare professionals assigned to implement them, rather than their official clientele groups. Similarly, AA programs could potentially be more helpful to the careers of personnel officials than to minority group members or women. Because of the AA program, a new corporate title has already been created in some organizations: every large company's personnel department has designated at least one manager as the person in charge of developing and administering the new programs. His (her) task usually involves negotiating the details of the AA program with federal officials and interpreting the program to line managers.

Although the AA program job is not an easy one, it will provide a career opportunity for personnel executives by offering "exposure" to a man (or woman) who wants to be noticed by top management, as well as the prospect of introductions to federal officials.

The problems that go with affirmative action, however, are many. Negotiations over AA goals and timetables are usually complicated and delicate and may seem to continue endlessly as corporate and government officials haggle over numbers and dates. Job titles and work assignments throughout the country usually need to be defined in minute details in order to complete an AA program. Some jobs need to be redefined or created. Goals for women in jobs formerly filled exclusively by men need to be developed. The government's notions about what these goals should be are often different from the ideas of the AA officer's superiors, or his (her) colleagues. Thus, the government may ask that ten percent of all outside repair jobs be set aside for women in a utilities company, but colleagues on the line may (perhaps mistakenly) feel that ten percent is too high a number—unrealistic and unattainable.

In short, the AA manager will have to negotiate between the company's notions and needs, on the one hand, and those of the government, on the other. In one large company that I have been observing, these negotiations have already taken ten full months and have involved an AA group of six personnel executives and a government team of the same number. In addition, other executives and bureaucrats have dropped in and out of the negotiations, from time to time, as advisers.

The new job of AA officer will not be fun. One newly appointed AA officer said:

> My children are egging me on to press for more blacks in our southern departments. At the same time, my boss is pressuring me to develop conservative projections, for he's concerned about keeping smooth relationships with the field organizations. But the government bureaucrats are on the same side as my kids. As to my own conscience, I waver between feeling guilty in the office with my colleagues. I guess you could say that I'm not going to be able to satisfy anybody in this job, least of all myself. No matter what I do, I'm wrong.

The AA officer's job resembles that of the urban affairs officer. Each is paid to be an in-house gadfly, but such gadflies function under obvious constraints. They can lobby within the company, up to a point, and can try to persuade, push, convince, and cajole. But, unless they are granted sufficient power by employers, they cannot alone decide what the company's position will be, what goals and timetables it will seek to establish. If anything, the AA officer is destined to be even more uncomfortable than his urban affairs counterpart, whose job was created in an atmosphere of similar social pressures only a few years ago. He or she is the link between the company and the government (usually represented by the General Services Administration or the Office of Federal Contract Compliance in the Labor Department). Even if the AA officer is able to keep his (her) cool, he (she) may be seated across the bargaining table from ideologists. Even if he (she) has made every effort to push the company forward toward a progressive program, there is always the risk of being attacked by outside adversaries as a "front man" or "puppet."

Conclusions

Some steps can be taken to lessen the seriousness of the above problems. Although the AA program concept will inevitably raise the issues, the alert corporate management will have opportunities to resolve some of these issues. Probably the most important requirement is *planning*.

The sad fact is that many companies add the AA job to the organizational chart too quickly. The pressure to develop AA programs was steady and strong, and action had to be taken before an organizational plan could be developed. But now there is time to think through the implications of the new job, its responsibilities, and the problems that are associated with it. What kind of person seems best for it? To whom should this person report? What kind of support will he (she) require in order to do an effective job?

Developing appropriate and effective means for communicating the details of the new AAP to employees will also be useful. Orientation programs that are thorough and that allow ample time for employee questions should be scheduled. As open an atmosphere as possible for these meetings will also help; if employees are encouraged to express their anxieties and raise their questions, personnel executives will be able to provide assurances and clarify confusion.

Some problems will not be cleared up by orientation sessions, however, or by putting the AA job in the right spot on the organizational chart. But these problems flow from the basic issue of social policy raised by the affirmative action approach. Now that government agencies have the right to scrutinize the decision-making process with regard to hiring, refusing to hire, promoting or refusing to promote, or, as in the case of the universities, reappointing or refusing to reappoint personnel, the issue goes beyond personnel matters. How to achieve social justice is the issue. Everybody wants justice, but there are disagreements about how to assure it, or even what it is. Years of discrimination against blacks, women, Jews, and other minority group members were in part the result of an unspoken (even sometimes, unwitting) gentlemen's agreement about what constituted fairness, and where and when it was applicable: Fairness simply didn't apply to these groups according to the gentlemen's agreement. Otherwise—within the boundaries drawn by prejudice—issues were decided on the merits: For example, which white Anglo male is most competent?

The question now is whether or not the merits or a potential new unfairness will prevail. In other words, there is the risk that a new kind of gentlemen's agreement will be implemented by corporate personnel,, who, under pressure to meet AA goals and timetables, will—with good intentions—make their choices on the basis of racial, ethnic, and sexual biases, just as they were doing a few years ago.

PART VI. C
Business and the Consumer

●●

> The biggest big business in America is not steel, automobiles or television. It is the manufacture, refinement and distribution of anxiety. . . .
>
> Logically extended, this process can only terminate in a mass nervous breakdown or in a collective condition of resentment. . . .
>
> —Eric Sevareid

Among the variety of conflicts between business and other social institutions, none is perhaps more widespread and evokes more emotional reactions from the largest segments of the populace than consumerism. Broadly defined, consumerism is generally understood to include those "activities of government, business and independent organizations that are designed to protect individuals from practices that infringe upon their rights as consumers. This view of consumerism emphasizes the direct relationship between the individual consumer and the business firm."[1]

Considerable controversy exists on the nature and scope of abuses suffered by the consumer in the marketplace, the extent of protection that should be afforded the consumer against such real or alleged abuses when weighed against the potential costs of providing such protection, and through what channels and in what form such protection should be provided.

The advocates of consumer protection argue that business has been by and large deliberately, or simply in the nature of things, fleecing the consumer by misleading and fraudulent advertising; unsafe, potentially dangerous, shoddy, or even useless goods; and, through effective lobbying, making enforcement of existing laws relatively ineffective and the passage of new laws with teeth relatively difficult.

[1]David A. Aaker and George S. Day, *Consumerism: Search for the Consumer Interest* (New York: Free Press, 1971), p. 3.

427

The critics of current consumer movements counter by saying that the claims of consumer abuse are grossly exaggerated, self-serving, and not founded in fact; that the consumer advocates tend to impose their own values on those of the consumers; that by and large corporations are responsive to consumer needs—they have to be if they want to survive as businesses—but where there are abuses, industry self-regulation or government regulation works, and when government regulation does not work it is because the regulatory bodies do not understand the market system.[2]

Consumer protection as an issue and consumerism as a movement are not likely to fade away in the near future, and the businessmen who ignore them do so at their own peril. There is every probability that they will be increasingly integrated as part of the overall social concern about the quality of life. What is called for, therefore, is not name calling or more rhetoric, but serious thought and dialogue about distinctions between substantial issues and trivia and ways in which the often conflicting approaches of business, consumer advocates, and public agencies can be harmonized to improve the quality of products, services, and information offered to the consumer to protect him from the unscrupulous businessman and to assist him in making intelligent choices from among the available alternatives.

The articles included in this section present a broad discussion of the multifaceted nature of consumerism and a serious discussion about the various approaches advocated by academicians, businessmen, consumer advocates, and public officials to attack the problems.

Jagdish N. Sheth and Nicholas J. Mammana attempt to find the root causes of several recent failures in consumer protection, arguing that, without the elimination of these problems, consumer protection will be confronted with a "Catch-22" phenomenon. They investigate the roles of the legislative-regulatory process, competition and the free-enterprise process, and consumer advocates in minimizing or eradicating consumer problems. Although they do not view any of these processes in a particularly optimistic light, they suggest several improvements: (1) selective concentration of resources on various aspects of the problem; (2) a "national crash program" of research on consumer behavior; (3) changes in professional training and higher education; and (4) changes in childrearing practices and secondary education to incorporate the realities of a mass-consumption society.

---

[2]A host of references following this discussion concern various points. The reader may particularly wish to consult Aaker and Day 1974, Nader 1973, Nicosia 1974, Posner 1970, Schrag 1972, and Winter 1972.

Donald L. Kanter argues that the nature and extent of advertising regulation should be considered in the context of other factors, such.as society's view of itself and its future, the vulnerability of its consumers, and empirical assessments of advertising effectiveness. He suggests that the first step in developing a system of regulation should be an evaluation of the actual social role of today's advertising practices.

Lee Richardson categorizes the types of contacts between consumers and various government agencies. The response of the agencies to these contacts is still in its infancy, but agencies are developing a greater responsiveness to consumer needs and interests. The most promising of these developments, he feels, is the concept of a governmental consumer advocate.

It is Mervin Field's view that consumerism is a natural outgrowth of the many recent changes in various sectors of American society. Advertising, which until recently has made one-sided presentations, has attracted increasing attention from the public and from governmental regulatory bodies. Consumerism is forcing upon advertising an adversary system that holds the promise of creating a better business climate.

Howard H. Bell describes the formation of the National Advertising Review Board and other self-regulatory organizations within the American Advertising Federation, with the objective of assuring and maintaining high standards of truth and accuracy in advertising. The functions of this program and its results are outlined, and Bell expresses optimism that public confidence in advertising and the free competitive process will be restored through the actions of these groups.

Channing Lushbough emphasizes the dissemination of information to the consumer as the chief function of advertising. The conflict between the informational and persuasional functions and their varying emphasis by advertisers with differing senses of responsibility to consumers means that honest and fair advertising can only be assured by integrating the efforts of consumers and responsible advertisers.

The history of the consumerist movement in this century is outlined in William J. Wilson's paper. He sees consumer skepticism as a growing reality that will continue unabated, and suggests that businessmen must be concerned with the effect of this attitude on their operations. He describes the results of a recent personal interview study of 18,000 individuals and their attitudes toward advertising. He concludes that growing skepticism and demands for responsibility and accountability by business will inevitably lead to greater corporate concern with image.

Guenther Baumgart focuses on cooperative industry programs that work to benefit consumers. He describes programs in his own industry— consumer-durable goods manufacturing—and suggests that mutual interest is the essential relationship between producers and consumers. He makes several suggestions for those involved in the formation of voluntary industrywide programs and urges that all such programs be designed with the end in view of exposing the consumer to the widest possible choices.

SELECTED BIBLIOGRAPHY

Aaker, David A. *Directory of Government Agencies Safeguarding Consumer and Environment.* Alexandria, Va.: Serina Press, 1971.

*Aaker, David A., and Day, George S., eds. *Consumerism: Search for the Consumer Interest.* Rev. ed. New York: Free Press, 1974.

Alexander, Tom. "The Packaging Problem Is a Can of Worms." *Fortune,* June 1972, p. 105.

Bowen, William. "Auto Safety Needs a New Road Map." *Fortune,* April 1972, p. 98.

Caplovita, David. *The Poor Pay More.* New York: Free Press, 1967.

Cordty, Dan. "Autos: A Hazardous Stretch Ahead." *Fortune,* April 1971, p. 64.

Cravens, David W., and Hills, Gerald E. "Consumerism: A Perspective for Business." *Business Horizons* 13, no. 4 (August 1970): 21–28.

Duggan, Michael A. "Management Science, Ecology, and The Quality of Life: The Law and the Legal Process." *Management Science,* June 1973, pp. 1162–1171.

*Eovaldi, Thomas L., and Gestrin, Joan E. "Justice for Consumers: The Mechanism of Redress." *Northwestern University Law Review* 66, no. 3 (July-August 1971): 281–325.

Estes, Robert. "Consumerism and Business." *California Management Review* 14, no. 2 (Winter 1971): 5–12.

*"Extrajudicial Consumer Pressure: An Effective Impediment to Unethical Business Practices." *Duke Law Journal,* October 1969, p. 1011.

Faltermayer, Edmund K. "The Energy 'Joyride' Is Over." *Fortune,* September 1972, p. 99.

Fellmeth, Robert. *The Interstate Commerce Omission.* New York: Grossman, 1970.

*Greer, Carl C. "Measuring the Value of Information in Consumer Credit Screening." *Management Services,* May-June 1967, pp. 44–54.

Gross, Edwin J. "Needed: Consumer Ombudsmen." *Business and Society* 9, no. 1 (Fall 1968): 22–27.

*Gross, Jennifer. *The Super Market Trap.* Bloomington: Indiana University Press, 1970.

*Hopkinson, Tom M. "New Battleground—Consumer Interest." *Harvard Business Review,* September-October, 1964, pp. 97–104.

Hunter, Beatrice Trum. *Consumer Beware.* New York: Bantam Books, 1971.

_____. *Beware of the Food You Eat.* New York: New American Library, Signet Books, 1972.

Jacobson, Michael F. *Eater's Digest, the Consumer's Fact Book of Food Additives.* Garden City, N.Y.: Doubleday & Co., Anchor Books, 1972.

*Jones, Mary Gardiner, and Boyer, Barry B. "Improving the Quality of Justice in the

*Especially recommended for an overall view and for authoritative viewpoints on different perspectives of the issues covered.

Marketplace: The Need for Better Consumer Remedies." *The George Washington Law Review* 40, no. 3 (March 1972): 357–415.

*Kotler, Philip. "What Consumerism Means for Marketers." *Harvard Business Review* 50, no. 3 (May 1972): 48–57.

Lernwand, Gerald. *The Consumer*. New York: Simon & Schuster, Pocket Books 1970.

*Magnuson, W. F., and Carper, J. *The Dark Side of the Marketplace*. Englewood Cliffs, N.J.: Prentice-Hall, 1968.

Mancke, Richard B. "An Alternative Approach to Auto Emission Control." *California Management Review* 14, no. 4 (Summer 1972): 82–86.

Margolius, Sidney. *The Great American Food Hoax*. New York: Dell Publishing Co., 1971.

Mather, L. L., ed. *Economics of Consumer Protection*. Danville, Ill.: Interstate, 1971.

McQuade, Walter. "Why Nobody's Happy About Appliances." *Fortune*, May 1972, p. 181.

*Myers, John G. *Social Issues in Advertising*. New York: AAAA, Educational Foundation, 1971.

*Nader, Ralph, ed. *The Consumer and Corporate Accountability*. New York: Harcourt Brace Jovanovich, 1973.

*Posner, Richard A. "Antitrust Policy and the Consumer Movement." *Antitrust Bulletin*, Summer 1970, pp. 361–366.

Radoes, David L. "Product Liability: Tougher Ground Rules." *Harvard Business Review* 47, no. 4 (July-August 1969): 144–152.

Ross, Ivan. "Consumer Information." Paper prepared for the National Conference on Social Marketing, University of Illinois, Champaign-Urbana, Ill., December 2–5, 1972. p. 68.

Rukeyser, William Simon. "Fact and Foam in the Row Over Phosphates." *Fortune*, January 1972, p. 71.

Scher, Irving. "Anti-Trust and Consumerism." *Case & Western Reserve Law Review* 22, no. 1: 11–34.

Schmalensee, Richard L. "Regulation and the Durability of Goods." *The Bell Journal of Economics and Management Science*, Spring 1970, pp. 54–65.

*Schrag, Philip G. *Counsel for the Deceived: Case Studies in Consumer Fraud*. N.Y.: Pantheon Books, 1972.

*Sethi, S. Prakash, *Up Against the Corporate Wall: Modern Corporations and Social Issues of the Seventies*. 2d. ed. Englewood Cliffs, N.J.: Prentice-Hall, 1974.

Sherman, Howard, and Hunt, E. K. "Pollution in Radical Perspective. *Business and Society Review/Innovation*, Fall 1972, pp. 48–53.

*Thorelli, Hans. "Concentration of Information Power Among Consumer." *Journal of Marketing Research* 8 (November 1971): 427–432.

*Turner, James S. *The Chemical Feast: Report on the Food and Drug Administration*. New York: Grossman, 1970.

Tyboat, Richard A. "Pricing Pollution and Other Negative Externalities." *The Bell Journal of Economics and Management Science* 3 no. 1 (Spring 1972): 252–266.

Warne, C. E. "Impact of Consumerism on the Market." *San Diego Law Review* 8, no. 1 (February 1971): 30–37.

White, Lawrence J. "Quality Variation when Prices are Regulated." *The Bell Journal of Economics and Management Science*, Fall 1972, pp. 425–436.

*Winter, Ralph. *The Consumer Advocate versus the Consumer*. Washington, D.C.: American Enterprise Institute, 1972.

Winter, Ruth. *A Consumer's Dictionary of Food Additives*. New York: Crown, 1972.

*Wood, Roberta A. "The Consumer Credit Protection Act: An Analysis of Public Policy Formulation." *Journal of Consumer Affairs* 5, no. 2 (Winter 1971): 196–211.

How Have the Current Approaches to Consumer Protection Failed?

●●●

● JAGDISH N. SHETH

College of Commerce and Business Administration
University of Illinois, Urbana-Champaign

● NICHOLAS J. MAMMANA

Director of Marketing Research
American Telephone and Telegraph Company

Our primary objective in preparing this paper is to investigate and expose some fundamental causes underlying the actual failures of several recent efforts in consumer protection. We strongly believe that, unless these root problems are eliminated or minimized, there is very little hope that consumers in the marketplace can be sufficiently or effectively protected from threats to rational, safe buyer behavior and consumption behavior. Indeed, we clearly see the presence of a "Catch-22" phenomenon in the present state of consumerism efforts.

Review of Consumerism

Not surprisingly, but unfortunately, consumerism means different things to different groups and entities. For example, to the new militant activists in the area, it is simply *caveat venditor* or let the seller beware. To the busi-

432

ness entity, it has meant, at least in some quarters, a threat to free enterprise and capitalism. Peter Drucker defines it as follows: "Consumerism means that the consumer looks upon the manufacturer as somebody who is interested but who really does not know what the consumer's realities are. He regards the manufacturer as somebody who has not made the effort to find out, who does not understand the world in which the consumer lives, and who expects the consumer to be able to make distinctions which the consumer is neither willing nor able to make."[1] Accordingly, if we consider marketing as the process of identifying and satisfying customer needs, wants, and desire for a profit, consumerism can exist only if the marketing concepts have either not worked or (more probably) not been fully utilized by management. The industry has, therefore, often considered modern marketing practice as an alternative to the consumerism movement.[2] Finally, according to the Consumer Advisory Council, consumerism has meant the provision and enforcement of a bill of rights of consumers, consisting of the right to safety, the right to be informed, the right to choose, and the right to be heard.[3]

Despite the differences of opinions among various groups and entities, consumerism is generally considered to include some form of protection to people against (1) physical threat to life, health, and property; (2) economic threat to rational and satisfying consumption benefit as a result of market imperfections, abuses, fraud, and deception; and (3) threat from other consumers in the process of collective consumption in the modern technological mass consumption society.[4] Similarly, most researchers and practitioners in consumerism believe that there are three distinct processes with identifiable entities that should safeguard consumer interest.[5] They are: (1) the government through the process of legislation and regulation; (2) the business through the process of free competition and industrywide

[1]Peter Drucker, "The Shame of Marketing," *Marketing Communication* 297 (August 19, 1969): 61.

[2]W. Christopherson, comments made as President, Jewel Companies, Inc. to the National Workshop on Social Marketing, University of Illinois, Urbana, December 1972.

[3]*Consumer Advisory Council* (Washington, D.C.: Government Printing Office, 1963), pp. 23–27.

[4]David A. Aaker and George S. Day, *Consumerism: Search for the Consumer Interest* (New York: Free Press, 1971); Ralph M. Gaedeke and Warren Etcheson, eds., *Consumerism: Viewpoints from Business, Government and the Public Interest* (New York: Canfield Press, 1972).

[5]J. N. Uhl, "Consumer Education and Protection: A Synergistic Relationship," in *Economics of Consumer Protection*, ed. Loys L. Mather (Danville, Ill.: Interstate Printers & Publishers, 1971).

self-regulation, and (3) the consumer activists through the process of consumer education and consumer consciousness of their rights in the marketplace. The following diagram, adapted from J. N. Uhl[6] pretty much summarizes these three entities and processes:

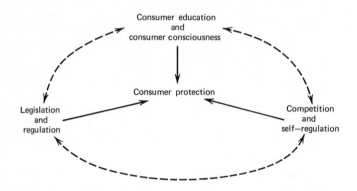

There is, however, virtually no agreement among practitioners of consumerism about which process or entity is more desirable for realistic protection of consumer interests. If anything, partisan lines have been so strongly etched that we fear it often leads to "negative-sum" gameplaying among the three entities. Furthermore, the fact that the three processes interact and influence one another in their efforts to provide consumer protection is often forgotten. For example, greater consumer education and consciousness often leads to better legislation and regulation as well as greater self-regulation. Greater regulation is likely to generate more self-regulation and competition, and intense competition often produces additional legislation and regulation.

We define consumerism as the organized efforts by or for consumers to maintain on enhance consumption welfare in a mass-consumption technological society. Tacitly, we think that consumerism as a concept or ideology is less relevant to agrarian and other less developed economies. Accordingly, the three types of threats from which consumers need protection are presumed to be largely a function of mass production and mass consumption possible in an industrial state.

[6]*Ibid.*

Physical Safety and Hazards of Mass Consumption

Physical safety is probably the most obvious and relevant area of consumer protection. As stated above, physical safety is presumed to be largely a phenomenon and consequence of high technology. We believe that the safety consequences of man-made technology are the least known to us and, therefore, present a much greater threat to human life than the natural hazards. For example, we know very little about the consequences of consuming preservatives and other chemicals in our food.

The physical safety typology can be divided into two types: (1) safety in the voluntary consumption of products and services, such as consumer durables and nondurables, and (2) safety in the involuntary consumption of a polluted environment. The latter includes collective consumption of polluted natural resources essential to human survival, such as water and air. Most of the involuntary consumption activities are collective and therefore possess the inherent danger of mass effects of photochemical smog in highly industralized, metropolitan cities, such as Tokyo and Los Angeles.

Economic Rationality

This type of consumer protection refers to economic loss, sacrifice, or disutility, which the consumer often encounters in the market place. It is further stratified into four categories: (1) protection against what Senator Magnuson calls the dark side of the marketplace.[7] This includes fraud, deception, and intentional misrepresentation, as well as coercive and high-pressure tactics of marketers, such as bait-and-switch advertising, chain-referral selling, free gimmicks, and fear-sell. (2) The right to choose, which includes concern related to monopoly powers, price collusions among oligopolists, and other activities presumed to inhibit competition. (3) The right to be informed, which concerns questions about unfounded claims, exaggerations, and misresentations of product attributes and also questions of partial or incomplete information or disclosure. (4) The right to be heard, which is primarily concerned with the question of consumer redress.

Environmental Imbalance and Threats to Humanity

This type of consumerism is best described as the marco, long-term effects of mass consumption. We can divide it further into three subcategories;

---

[7]Warren G. Magnuson and Jean Carper, *The Dark Side of the Marketplace* (Englewood Cliffs, N.J.: Prentice-Hall, 1972).

(1) excessive resource depletion and exploitation. In their industrial dynamics simulation of demand and supply of world resources, Meadows et al. suggest that limits to growth are finite and much closer than realized because of the heavy depletion of natural resources like metals, energy, and chemicals.[8] (2) Pollution of the environment in the process of mass consumption. Solid waste, air pollution, and water pollution are major aspects of this category, including the economics of recycling. (3) Standardization of the human species. Major concern has been recently raised about the homogeneity of human biology due to mass consumption of identical nutrients, chemicals, and other life-support entities and the lack of immunity such standardization is likely to generate. While very little is known and researched, recent experiences with standardized agricultural crops also cause concern in this area.

Social Safety and Social Inequities

Along with the physical safety considerations in the personal consumption of products and services, the psychological and physical safety considerations in mass consumption societies are equally critical. It is argued that we live in an "other-directed society" where the social pressures of conspicuous consumption and conspicuous nonconsumption are equally important. Under this typology, we distinguish five subcategories of concern in consumerism: (1) safety and protection from other consumers. This includes the effects of smoking on nonsmokers, discarding potentially dangerous containers and the like; (2) the problem of low-income families who cannot meet the social expectations of minimum mass consumption behavior; (3) safeguard of minority interests from exploitation by marketers of products and services, e.g., recent mass efforts to segment blacks in numerous industries; (4) the negative side effects of mass communication and consumption, such as the effects of television programming on children; and (5) dehumanization in mass consumption society, such as the lack of concern, interest, or even shock in witnessing crimes, poverty, and wars.

As can be seen from the above typology, the issues of consumerism are diverse and far reaching. Some of them are more immediate, for example, physical safety considerations, and others are far removed from the daily immediate activities of consumers, such as dehumanization and standardization of species. Some of the issues are pragmatic and others are ideological and therefore more abstract.

[8]Donella H. Meadows et al., *The Limits to Growth* (New York: Universe Books, 1972).

The Role of the Legislative-Regulatory Process

Perhaps the single most commonly recommended process to solve consumer problems is governmental legislation and regulation.[9] Based on our review of a number of books and articles, we find that the following major weaknesses and limitations make governmental legislation or regulation ineffective in solving problems of consumerism:

(1) Lack of technical know-how. It is no exaggeration when we state that regulatory agencies know very little about the market realities they are asked to regulate and certainly they know much less than the managers of the regulated industry.[10] While there are a number of explanations possible for this ironic reality, the most interesting to us is the singular lack of interest among professionals in the civil service. Until very recently, the best graduating students in any applied discipline have consistently shunned governmental employment opportunities.

It also seems that a number of technological advancements have been transformed into product realities without a full comprehension of all their manifest or latent hazards. For example, very few people, including the regulatory agencies, know the physical effects of cyclamates, hexachlorophene, and enzymes, let alone their more subtle psychological effects.

(2) The starvation budgets of the regulatory agencies. Ralph Nader dramatically points out this limitation by some statistics: The combined annual budget of the Federal Trade Commission and the Antitrust Division of the Justice Department in 1968 was $23 million, with which they were supposed to collect data, initiate investigations, and enforce the laws dealing with deceptive and anticompetitive practices of a $350-billion economy.[11] If we examine the annual budget of the FTC alone, it is at least 40 times less than the annual advertising and promotion budget of Proctor & Gamble. The

[9]R. J. Barber. "Government and the Consumer," *Michigan Law Review* 64 (May 1966): 1203–1217; Richard H. Holton, "Government Consumer Interest: Conflicts and Prospects," *Changing Marketing Systems*, 1967 Proceedings of the American Marketing Association (Chicago: American Marketing Association, 1967), pp. 15–17.

[10]J. R. Withrow, "The Inadequacies of Consumer Protection," in *1967 New York State Bar Association Antitrust Law Symposium* (Chicago: Commerce Clearing House, 1967), pp. 58–73; D. Cohen, "The Federal Trade Commission and the Regulation of Advertising in the Consumer Interest," *Journal of Marketing* 33 (January 1969): 40–44.

[11]Ralph Nader, "The Great American Gyp," *New York Review of Books* 11 (November 21, 1968): 27–34.

starvation budgets make the regulatory agencies virtually ineffective in their efforts to detect and legally support evidence pointing toward deception, misrepresentation, or fraud. Thus, even if the regulatory agencies were technically competent, they don't have the means to enforce laws.

(3) Lack of uniformity in enforcement. Surprisingly, the process of enforcement, even in the limited number of cases in which it exists, is haphazard and almost random. Most enforcement activities are initiated by complaints from competitors or by letters from consumers.[12] In other words, the regulatory agencies have been practicing on the principle of management by exception rather than on the principle of management by objectives.

(4) Enforcement limited to trivia. A stronger indictment of the regulatory agencies has been their singular efforts to limit enforcement to trivial aspects. For example, according to the American Bar Association Commission Report, the FTC has ignored fundamental aspects such as ghetto frauds, monitoring advertising practices, and securing effective compliance with orders, and at the same time has concentrated on the failure to disclose that "Navy Shoes" were not made by the navy, that flies were imported, that Indian trinkets were not manufactured by American Indians, and that Havana cigars were not made entirely of Cuban tobacco.[13] Case histories of the regaling in trivia prevalent in other agencies, such as the Antitrust Division and Food and Drug Administration (FDA), can be found in Withrow and Dunkelberger.[14]

(5) Antiquated organizational structures. Even in the enforcement of trivia on a haphazard basis with limited funds and technical competence, we find that bureaucracy par excellence has often mitigated its impact. There are simply too many agencies in too many places to deal with a single problem.[15] The problem is even worse at the state and local levels where the doctrine of political patronage tends to dominate any enforcement activity.

---

[12]American Bar Association, *Report of the ABA Commission to Study the Federal Trade Commission* (Chicago: September 15, 1969).

[13]*Ibid.*

[14]Withrow, "Inadequacies of Consumer Protection"; H. E. Dunkelberger, "The Fair Packaging and Labeling Act—Some Unanswered Questions," *Food, Drug and Cosmetic Law Journal* 24 (January 1969): 17–36.

[15]Louis M. Kohlmeier, *The Regulators: Watchdog Agencies and the Public Interest* (New York: Harper & Row, 1969).

(6) Lack of realistic theories of buyer behavior. Perhaps the single most critical problem in both legislative and enforcement activities is the lack of any theory of buyer behavior. Unfortunately, many of the laws enacted to protect the consumer are based on value judgments, on partial knowledge of the realities of consumer behavior, or, worse yet, on classical enonomic concepts of utility that no longer hold true in the marketplace. Withrow very clearly points out this problem as it relates to the antitrust policy.[16] Another example is the recent proposal to enact unit-pricing laws in grocery stores based on the presumptions that the housewife is neither aware nor capable of calculating unit prices and that unit-price information can, at best, have a positive effect on rational choice and at worst no effect. Just as the marketing practitioner has chosen to ignore the negative impacts of advertising, so also it seems that proponents of unit pricing have chosen to ignore its negative consequences, such as overstocking and overconsumption.

The problem created by the lack of a theory of buyer behavior is further compounded when existing laws are interpreted and enforced by regulatory agencies. McGhee demonstrated this in the enforcement of the Robinson-Patman Act; Dunkelberger finds this problem inherent in the enforcement of truth-in-packaging laws; and Cohen pleads for more behavioral theories in FTC thinking.[17] Indeed, the recent case of the boomerang effect of the "corrective advertising" concept in bread industry is a direct testimonal to the lack of theory of buyer behavior in federal enforcement activities.

(7) The economic might of the industry. Some have bitterly complained about the strong lobby efforts that industry can and often does use to block the passage of certain laws, such as truth-in-packaging and truth-in-lending bills. The economic might of the industry is felt even greater because of a direct contrast in the lobbying efforts of the consumer advocates.[18] A second and only indirectly related aspect of the economic might vested in industry is the systematic hiring of regulatory agency officials after they resign or retire from their duties. It is alleged that often regulatory officials remain softhearted

---

[16]Withrow, "Inadequacies of Consumer Protection."

[17]J. McGhee, "Some Economic Issues in Robinson-Patman Land," *Law and Contemporary Problems* 30 (1965): 531–551; Dunkelberger, "Fair Packaging and Labeling Act"; Cohen, "Federal Trade Commission."

[18]Nader, "Great American Gyp."

in expectation of the economic windfall they will receive from such employment.

It should be evident from the above discussion that the prospects of consumer protection by the process of government regulation, intervention, and legislation are rather small.

The Role of Competition and the Free-Enterprise Process

Although we are not as pessimistic about the role of competition and the free-enterprise process of the business world as about that of the regulatory-legislative process, we are concerned about some factors that seem to inhibit the free-enterprise process from providing consumer protection.

(1) The lack of customer-oriented marketing. Perhaps the single most critical reason why business may fail to play "positive sum" games with the consumers and therefore fail to safeguard consumer interests is the lack of consumer-oriented marketing. Unfortunately, there is a strong technology orientation among business decision makers that leads them to focus myopically on products instead of customer needs, to believe that marketing is selling, and to define corporate objective as profits from sales instead of profits from satisfied customers.[19] To this end, Drucker flatly explains the presence of consumerism as the shame of the total marketing concept.[20] It can also be shown that product-oriented marketing practice leading to an innovate-or-perish policy is not only incapable of providing consumer protection, but it may be the heart of our current problems in multinational marketing.[21]

Fortunately, there seem to have been enough unpleasant experiences with the innovate-or-perish policy to encourage managment to plan business activities by working backward from the needs of customers in the marketplace. To this extent, we think there is at least some hope that the problems of consumerism may be mitigated by a customer-oriented marketing concept.[22]

[19]Philip Kotler, *Marketing Management: Analysis, Planning, and Control*, 2d ed. (New York: Prentice-Hall, 1972).

[20]Drucker, "Shame of Marketing."

[21]Jagdish N. Sheth, "A Conceptual Model of Long-Range Multinational Marketing," *Management International Review* 12 (1972): 3–15.

[22]Christopherson, at Workshop on Social Marketing.

(2) Problems in the self-regulation of industry. The most common alternative suggested to prevent and cure the ills of marketing malpractices by a minority of business firms is the concept of self-regulation. Unfortunately, the track record of self-regulation as a potential alternative to protect consumer interests is not good. Overwhelmingly, empirical evidence and thinking of scholars and practitioners suggest that self-regulation is unlikely to solve the problems of consumer protection because it is not a workable proposition.[23] A number of reasons have been cited for the actual and potential failure of self-regulation to protect consumer interests. The first and foremost is the fear, and sometimes the actual reality, that any collective activity such as self-regulation may be in violation of the Sherman Act or some other antitrust legislation. This fear often leads some members of an industry to give up on any self-regulatory activities by resigning themselves to the view that "you will be damned if you don't, but doubly damned if you do." In short, the fear of legal complications and problems often short-circuits any initiative or desire toward self-regulation. We consider this an another example of the Catch-22 phenomenon in the realm of consumer protection.

A second common reason for the failure of self-regulation is that there are too many parties involved, each with differences in goals and perceptions. Accordingly, it is inevitable that group conflict will be present and persistent, and this often entails an inefficient resolution by the process of bargaining and politicizing.[24]

Finally, it is difficult and sometimes impossible to provide adequate internal safeguards to monitor and police some self-serving members of industry. In this regard, there seems to be a parallel between the governmental regulatory agencies and the industry.

(3) Lack of interest and commitment. A third major factor that is likely to limit the role of a business entity in providing consumer protection is a total commitment to achieving day-to-day profit maximiza-

---

[23]H. W. Boyd and H. J. Claycamp, "Industrial Self-Regulation and the Public Interest," *Michigan Law Review* 64 (May 1966): 1239–1254; L. Stern, "Consumer Protection via Self-Regulation," *Journal of Marketing* 35 (July 1971): 47–53; H. J. Levin, "The Limits of Self Regulation," *Columbia Law Review* 67 (March 1967): 603–642; J. G. Van Cise, "Regulation—By Business or Government?" *Harvard Business Review* 44 (March-April 1966): 53–63; D. F. Turner, "Consumer Protection by Private Joint Action," in *1967 New York State Bar Association Antitrust Law Symposium*, pp. 36–46.

[24]James C. March and Herbert A. Simon, *Organizations* (New York: John Wiley & Sons, 1958), chap. 5; Jagdish N. Sheth, "A Theory of Industrial Buying Decisions," in Proceedings of AIDS Annual Conference, November 1972.

tion.[25] It seems that even an enlightened management suffers from lack of time to envision the long-term consequences of a sense of social responsibility is partly encouraged by the pressures of competition. This is further compounded by a strong belief that the doctrines of *caveat emptor* and free enterprise should and do provide enough incentives and safeguards to minimize consumer problems. In fact, it is relatively easy to trace the reason for the typical defensive reactions of industry to any legislative, advocacy, or regulatory challenges to these beliefs.

The Role of the Consumer Advocates

We think the role of the consumer advocates is even more limited than the government or the business entity. This may seem paradoxical at first blush, but there is enough evidence and reasoning to support our position. What are the underlying factors that minimize the potential of consumer advocates to solve consumer problems?

The first and the most serious factor relates to a total lack of the consumer's own viewpoint on the matter. Most consumer advocates thrive on normative models of ideal consumers and consider themselves evangelists in pointing out what is good for the consumer. Often such normative models are too far removed from the realities of buyer behavior to be useful; a case in point is the recent effort to legislate unit pricing without any systematic research into the psychology of buyers and their information processing and decisions in a supermarket situation. A related factor is the typical neglect of any negative consequences that could ensue from proposed legislative or regulatory changes, because most such proposals are based on the normative thinking that such changes will be all for the good of the consumer. In other words, often only one side of the coin is examined and researched by the consumer advocates.

A second factor detrimental to the efforts of consumer advocates is that they tend to be issue oriented rather than problem oriented. Often there is no conceptualization of the totality of a consumer problem area; therefore, the efforts often resemble the proverbial blind men and the elephant. Most efforts and even research on specific problem areas tend to be symptomatic instead of explanatory and casual. We strongly believe that the myopic issue-oriented viewpoint simply generates unnecessary and irrelevant con-

[25]T. Levitt, "Why Business Always Loses," *Harvard Business Review*, March-April 1968, pp. 81–89.

troversies and debates on how to solve the problem, rather than providing its actual solution. Therefore, we must also note the Catch-22 phenomenon in the efforts of consumer advocates.

The third factor that limits the role of consumer advocates is their starvation budgets for research and lobbying efforts and the absence of professional credibility in most of their fundamental research on products.[26] In addition, whatever labeling and testing information is diffused to consumers tends to be so complex and technical as to be of little interest. Related to the problem of credibility, we find that problems of consumerism are often handled in an emotional manner rather than in rational manner. While there is nothing wrong in emotional reasoning and expression of the dire need for consumer protection, it often leads to a general disbelief among interested parties, especially industry.

Finally, there is the tragedy of the realities of consumer education and information: Those consumers who need the information most are the least concerned about educating themselves or actively searching for relevant information. The classic example of this tragedy is the fact that the *Consumer Reports* is primarily read by college-educated professional people and not by ghetto consumers; the latter probably need that type of information most and, as we understand, *Consumer Reports* was published primarily for them in its humble beginning. We think this is a tragedy, not because less-educated consumers are irrational decision makers, but because consumer advocates have grossly failed to incorporate the customer-oriented approach into their marketing efforts of providing consumer education and information.

What About the Team Effort?

The suggestion is often made that what we need is a joint cooperative effort among all the three entities and processes to minimize or even to eradicate consumer problems.

Our viewpoint on the possibility and success of team effort is also pessimistic. In regard to the cooperative efforts between the government and industry, our pessimism is simply an echo of an elegant analysis by Bauer and Greyser in what they call "the dialogue that never happens."[27] What

[26]H. B. Thorelli, "Consumer Information Policy in Sweden—What Can be Learned?" *Journal of Marketing* 35 (January 1971): 50–55.

[27]Raymond A. Bauer and Stephen A. Greyser, "The Dialogue that Never Happens," *Harvard Business Review*, January-February 1969, pp. 122–128.

are some of the reasons for this pessimistic attitude prevalent among many scholars and researchers?

First, it is argued that there are some fundamental differences between the regulatory agencies and the industry in their models of buyer behavior. Each one is looking into the world of consumer behavior with a different pair of glasses. At the heart of this difference is the prevalence of a normative model (how consumers should behave) among the regulatory agencies and a descriptive model (how consumers do behave) among the marketing practitioners. Furthermore, the structure of the two models and reliance on specific disciplines differ significantly. For example, the regulatory agencies typically presume the greater importance of price and promotion in manipulating consumers, while industry typically relies on product innovation and distribution as more important adaptive mechanisms to meet the changing needs of consumers. Similarly, regulatory agencies often examine the market performance in terms of aggregate market behavior, but the industry invariably looks at market performance in terms of market segments.

A second major factor that has limited the team effort is the blindly defensive attitudes and reactions of industry to any governmental legislation or regulation. *Business Week* neatly describes this defensive reaction as consisting of the following sequential stages of reactions to any proposed legislation: (1) deny everything, (2) blame wrongdoing on the small marginal companies in the industry, (3) discredit the critics, (4) hire a public relations man, (5) defang the legislation, (6) launch a fact-finding committee or even a research institute, and (7) actually do something about the consumer problems.[28]

Unfortunately, the defensive attitudes and reactions are sufficiently widespread as to qualify as a mass phenomenon. We think they have arisen from two casual factors: (1) the lack of modern-day realities of market structure and consumer behavior in professional education in economics and business. For example, we still get educated in the principles of classical theory of the firm and perfect competition, despite the fact that it is so rarely present in today's market structure and competitive behavior as to be almost mythical. (2) The past experience—the "track record"—of legislating and regulating the free play of market behavior is dismal to say the least.[29]

[28]"How Business Responds to Consumerism," *Business Week*, September 6, 1969, pp. 94–108.
[29]Barber, "Government and the Consumer"; Withrow, "Inadequacies of Consumer Protection."

A third factor that limits the role of team effort in protecting consumers is the fact that both suffer from the same limitations: myopic views of consumers, organizational bureaucracy, and technical inability to assess the effects of technology. Thus, rather than pulling together each other's strengths, a team effort often results in examining each other's weaknesses. Furthermore, the fat is added to the fire by basic mistrust and value differences among professionals in the regulatory agencies and industry.

Are There Any Solutions?

If the reader by now feels that this paper is a strong indictment of all the entities and processes engaged in consumer protection, we have fulfilled one of our objectives. We may have ignored or minimized the positive efforts of some of the processes; however, our review of the literature reveals more fervors and failures than favorable actions and results.

The reader may also feel that this paper is a reflection of the pessimism of the authors. This feeling is partly a true reflection of pessimism and partly our deep-seated belief that fundamental long-term changes are mandatory if we are to succeed in providing appropriate protection to consumer welfare. What are some of these fundamental changes?

The first recommendation is to adopt a strategy of selectivity and segmentation among the three entities and their processes. (See Sheth for some general segmentation propositions.)[30] The problem of consumerism is complex, multidimensional, and diverse, as can be judged from the typology of areas of consumer protection. No single entity can therefore fully tackle the totality of consumerism, especially when each entity seems to suffer from economic and expertise resources. We recommend that the total problem area of consumer protection be segmented and that each entity selectively concentrate on a segmented problem area. Below is a grid of problem-entity interaction that capitalizes on the potential strengths of each entity and its process.

In the above grid, we think it is best to motivate industry to provide physical safety in consumption; to encourage the consumer himself to become a more rational buyer; to rechannel the energies of consumer advocates toward problems of social safety and social inequities; and to mandate the government to forestall environmental imbalance.

---

[30]Jagdish N. Sheth, "Relevance of Segmentation for Marketing Planning," presented at the ESOMAR Seminar on Segmentation and Typology, May 1972.

	Govern- ment	Industry	Consumer advocates	Consumer himself
Physical safety	2	1	4	3
Economic rationality	3	4	2	1
Social safety and inequities	2	4	1	3
Environmental imbalance	1	4	3	2

A second recommendation is a national crash program to understand the complexity and realities of consumer behavior. Despite living in an industrial state and in a mass consumption society, we know very little from a policy viewpoint about buyer behavior. What we need is a national research council, endorsed and financed by both government and industry, that will engage in the compilation and analysis of data on consumption behavior at a psychological microlevel. Furthermore, it should have national recognition and a status comparable to that of the National Science Foundation.

From this research effort, we expect the emergence of realistic, comprehensive theories of buyer behavior that should then guide the thinking and policy decisions of all the entities engaged in consumer protection. Such comprehensive theories of buyer behavior should prove useful as a vista of consumer behavior, as a common frame of reference and vocabulary among all the entities, and as a guide to fundamental research in consumer behavior. Fortunately, there is a good deal of hope that such an endeavor is realistic and feasible.[31]

A third recommendation is introducing some fundamental changes in our professional training and education at the higher level. Unfortunately, most schools, explicitly or implicitly, seem to encourage the attitude that business ends justify any means. There is too great an emphasis on winning the game and too little on sportsmanship in our professional education and training. These attitudes are reinforced by basic job insecurity and a reward system based on competitive aggressive behavior. The net result is the common occurrence of a professional individual in a big company stooping to deceptive and sometimes fraudulent activities "for the sake of the corporation," despite consistent parental insistence on a religious following of the ten commandments. We hope that both the corporate entity

---

[31]Jagdish N. Sheth, "The Future of Buyer Behavior Theory," in M. Venkatesan (Ed.), Proceedings of the Third Annual Conference of Consumer Research (Chicago, November 1972), pp. 562–575.

and professional individuals working in the corporation can temper the spirit of competition with business ethics and personal values.

The last recommendation is the most radical and probably very difficult to implement. We strongly believe that childrearing practices and secondary school education do not teach the new generation to cope with the realities of a complex mass consumption society. It is surprising to reflect on the very few changes in educational processes, both in content and format, and contrast them to the enormous, rapid changes in the socioeconomic base of our society. Therefore, we recommend a mass education of children and young adults, especially in the public school systems, to develop an awareness and competence of the following aspects of realities of mass consumption:

(1) Formal knowledge about the criteria with which to evaluate complex technical products and services and choose rationally among them.
(2) Managerial and decision-making skills as consumers, comparable to the type of skills we inculcate in people to become professional workers in industry or government.
(3) Increased consumer knowledge of the workings of business, government, and the marketplace.
(4) Values and consciousness that will encourage respect and concern for other consumers in their pursuit of collective consumption.

We think it is highly desirable, even mandatory, in the not too distant future to replace abstract subjects such as mathematics, physics, chemistry, and languages with more applied courses in managerial consumer behavior, market analysis, business organization, and applied technology. Unless there is a major change in our present mass consumption habits brought about by the above revisions in mass education, the negative side effects of mass consumption may endanger our very existence.

Psychological Considerations in Advertising Regulation

●●

● DONALD L. KANTER

School of Business Administration
University of Southern California

In one sense, regulation in most areas represents an accommodation among adversaries. In the advertising area, this is certainly true. What is generally missing, however, from the regulatory thrust is an exploration of key assumptions on both sides: A case in point is the dialogue surrounding advertising regulation. Stephen A. Greyser begins this task in his important paper, "Advertising: Attacks and Counters,"[1] based on testimony before the Federal Trade Commission (FTC), in which he tries to sort out the most verbalized issues and allegations about the social effects of advertising.

There are some questions, assumptions, and concepts that should be identified before the process of advertising regulation can be discussed or approached meaningfully. That is the aim of this paper—to look at some of the questions that should be answered before arguing one way or another about the nature and extent of advertising regulation.

My thesis is that advertising regulation, at the very least, depends on these factors:

—A vision of society in terms of its goals, its values, its beliefs, and its future.

---

[1]*Harvard Business Review*, March-April 1972, p. 22.

—A conception of human nature—How vulnerable are consumers?
—A fact-based empirical assessment of advertising effectiveness.
—An attitude toward regulation and regulators.

I believe that these issues should form the basis for any significant discussion of advertising regulation. Moreover, these issues—taken as a whole—have been roundly ignored or benignly neglected in the conflicts surrounding advertising regulation.

A Vision of Society

Each of us in his role as citizen is concerned about the directions his society is taking or should be taking. Nevertheless, in the area of advertising regulation there seems to be very little agreement about what the role of advertising should be in our conceptualizing of the future.

For example, how commercial should American society be? It is interesting to note that of all the postindustrial Western societies, the United States has much more sheer advertising volume than any other country. American radio, television, and newspapers devote more time and space to advertising than do any other Western nation's.

In the words of Adam Raphael, for several years the United States correspondent for the *Manchester Guardian*:

> Never has a more beautiful country been so badly and systematically scarred by commercial development. . . . The American passion for guns and the acceptance of their toll in lives is hard for any foreigner to understand. So too is the continuing acceptance of the fodder put out by American commercial television networks. . . .[2]

Raphael's comments may be somewhat harsh, but they seem to reflect the same tragic disappointment in the American potential for "the good life" that Arthur Miller did in his "Death of a Salesman." Both of these social commentators place part of the blame for the difference between the myth and reality of the American quality of life on the society's tolerance for rampant commercialism.

What about some of the possible by-products of this massive advertising bombardment? Does the omnipresence of advertising in all media create

[2]Reprinted in part from the *Manchester Guardian* by the *Los Angeles Times*, February 11, 1973.

an environment that has to be selectively ignored and therefore, to some extent, psychologically discountd as unreal? Said in another way, most consumers must somehow ignore or discount most advertisements, which compete for their attention. Does this very process of selectivity somehow cheapen the currency, as it were, and help to foster the impression that most advertising is irrelevant and foolish, something to be tolerated but not listened to very carefully? Point: Are we, as a society, so tolerant and accepting of all commercial effort, factless, ineffective, or not, that we treat it as Muzak—a sore of meaningless background hum—simply because it represents a commercial effort? If so, this is a telling commentary upon and revealing view of the American value system.

From a social point of view, if the foregoing is true, this might not be the healthiest or most rational climate for youngsters who are taught and are able to observe for themselves early on that most advertising is somewhere between hogwash and irrelevance.

A particularly poignant example follows, based on a research project about Mexican-American perceptions of advertising:

> *When asked whether they talk about advertising,* all of the respondents said that *their children talked about it more than they did.* All the mothers said that their children regularly memorized many of the commercials—both Anglo and Spanish—because they sounded so different from their everyday lives. . . .
>
> Moreover, mothers said that . . . they did not mind very much that their children listened to all the commercials because it taught them to be aware of phoniness and silliness. . . .
>
> In short, commercials—to the children of the Barrios—are not only an entertainment (as they are in Italy), but they are used by mothers (and Mexican mothers are in control of their younger children) to teach them about the untruths and chicaneries of the commercial world in general and the Anglo world in particular. . . .
>
> Advertising, then, is part, used as a teaching device to show the perils of commercial blandishments to the children of the Barrios. Advertising is viewed by many Mexican-Americans as not painting a totally truthful picture of products and lends itself to parental wishes to teach skepticism, cynicism, and caution to their children. . . .
>
> Mothers themselves seem to talk a bit more about advertising than do their Anglo counterparts. The talk, however, seems to be cautionary—rather than laudatory. . . .
>
> Most of the women feel they have been taken by false advertising—both Spanish-speaking and Anglo media—and feel it is a duty to converse with their friends about the pitfall of untruthful advertising. This is to be expected in a community where the family incomes are at a minimal level—and where market-

ing mistakes are economically and psychologically more costly than in the higher-income Anglo community. . . .[3]

The effects of advertising on minority groups notwithstanding, what do we as Americans think of television and radio commercialization, with their concomitant interruptions? What is the rationale for tolerating massive doses of advertising far in excess of even the legally allotted advertising time? Is this overall media devotion to commercial things simply reinforcing the American approval of material things; or is it in fact helping to create it?

Is it because "the business of America is business," as one post-World War I president said? Or is it because tune-out is so successful that few people think of advertisments as intrusions? Or is it because of a deepseated American conviction that advertising is so impotent it really doesn't matter?

Another point: We should take account of what must be called comparatively excessive commercialization of the media in any meaningful discussion of regulation. What is being suggested is that the values and goals of a society are somehow reflected or perhaps even partially determined by its attitudes toward commercialization. Is the American commercial toleration in the culture so strong that its acceptance should be unquestioned? I don't believe so.

Is overcommercialization stifling, so to speak, other cultural thrusts? Is it getting in the way of more salutory social aspirations? This concept of the commercialization of the total media environment and its possible consequences has been argued, but not studied, philosophyically or emperically. It is worth doing.

A Conception of Human Nature— How Vulnerable Are Consumers?

What are the defenses that consumers have against the blandishments of advertising? My own research and that of others[4] has led me to believe that the consumer has many: He is obstinate, skeptical and quite cautious.

---

[3]Donald L. Kanter, "Advertising and the Mexican-American Consumer," presented to the FCC Anti-Defamation Hearings, Washington, D.C., November 18, 1971. Emphasis added.

[4]Raymond A. Bauer and Stephen A. Greyser, *Advertising in America—The Consumer View* (Boston: Division of Research, Harvard Business School, 1968); and Raymond A. Bauer, "The Obstinate Audience," *American Psychologist*, May 1964, pp. 319-328.

Obviously, this varies by age and market segments. Nevertheless, I believe that the conception of the "defenseless consumer" is incorrect:

> One more hard fact seems germane to this discussion of criticism and advertising in the name of the need for consumer protection. To me, it is a core finding and one of the most reassuring bits of data on human response to mass stimuli I know. The major reason why people found advertisements to be either annoying or offensive is that they contradicted experience with, or knowledge of, the product. This one reason superseded any other in the negative evaluation of the 9325 advertisements we studied. . . .
>
> It is important to remember that consumers are reality oriented. The world of products is part of their everyday life, and when advertising has irrelevant fantasy and absurd selling propositions, the consumer knows this. The consumer relates the contents of advertising to his experience. He is strongly and knowledgeably product oriented in his evaluation of advertisements. . . .
>
> In addition to having built-in resistances to being sold by advertising or in person, he views sales messages through a filter of doubt, prior experience—and not a little boredom and disinterest. He "protects" himself from the blind acceptance of advertising as he does from other promises and panaceas he is proferred. In the judgment of the research team, the myth of the long-suffering consumer can be laid to rest. . . .
>
> On the evidence, then, what we see is that consumers look at advertising as they do politics, with skepticism and restraint. This healthy stance is the caveat by which the consumer, literally and figuratively, protects himself. He has the protective mechanisms of cynicism, tune-out, and reality testing at his disposal to accomplish this. . . .[5]

The implications of the above quotation are many. It certainly raises the question of how far government and other bodies have to go in order to protect an unwary, yielding consumer. Moreover, it suggests that there may be certain kinds of blandishments that even the most skeptical and obstinate consumer will not consciously want to resist.

Most importantly, it suggests that ignorance of the product and its secondary effects might be as proper an area for consumer protection as, say, protection from advertisements per se. One of the major obstacles to completely rational buying (should that cherished but ill-conceived goal be desired) might be the information gaps the consumer has. This calls, it would seem, for more, not less, information. It is interesting to speculate how current advertising campaign practices would stack up against a

---

[5]Donald L. Kanter, "The Myth of the Long-Suffering Consumer," in *Marketing for Tomorrow . . . Today*, ed. M. S. Moyer and R. E. Vosburgh, 1967 June Conference of the American Marketing Association, Series No. 25 (Chicago: American Marketing Association, 1967), pp. 132–133.

separate consumer information campaign. One can imagine that some product categories would be more affected than others.

A case in point is the recent evidence from the National Institute of Mental Health's study of over-the-counter drugs, which reveals information gaps not entirely generated by advertising.[6] This would seem to be a case in which regulation might well take the form of more information of a relevant public service nature than any impositions placed on advertising itself.

At any rate, a working conception of consumers' strengths and vulnerabilities in all the product categories advertised should be a prerequisite to any sensible advertising regulation. This assessment of consumer vulnerability and strength, ignorance and information, can only be done by appropriate consumer research. The data base generated from this research might and should provide the foundation for meaningful discussions about advertising regulation.

It may be, for example, that in some product categories consumers have a serious information gap and appear to be behaving counterproductively in terms of their ostensible self-interest. In other product categories this may prove not to be the case. The point is, without an appropriate data base, the dialogue between adversaries regarding regulation becomes persiflage.

An Empirical Assessment of Advertising Effectiveness

How powerful—in terms of persuasion—is advertising and under what conditions? Clearly this varies by product category, market segment, and personal need. Nevertheless, one must take into account opposing conceptions of advertising's effectiveness: same believe that it is a pernicious, hidden, sinister, powerful force; others believe that it is simply part of the landscape and consumers use it selectively in making their buying decisions. My own view is that we really do not have the data base to handle the discussion in an intelligent way.

Moreover, some people believe advertising, as distinct from other media inputs, is a meretricious taste maker, a creator of false wants and needs by, among other devices, the use of reference groups to create conformity. These people, at least tacitly, imply that advertising has implanted all the

---

[6]"Study Cities Overuse of OTC Drugs," *Advertising Age*, October 16, 1972, p. 2.

status cravings and buying urges found in the American consumer. This seems to me to be a patently false and uninformed point of view.

What we really need to know, or at least come to some decision about, is how advertising operates in consumer decisions involving different product categories with different consumer segments, for example, one suspects that the toy-category advertising has a different influence with children than cereal or snack-food advertising. Generalizations are, perhaps, less valuable in assessment than particulars, even in the discussions concerning advertising to children.

Advertising's psychological influence may be different in terms of the role it plays in purchase decisions. It is plausible that, in some situations, advertising acts to reduce cognitive dissidence or conflict in terms of purchase versus no purchase. A case in point is developed in my monograph, "Pharmaceutical Advertising and Youth."

> Even though advertising, per se, may not be considered uniquely responsible for attitudes towards legal and illegal drugs, the students, nevertheless, feel that it is potentially an influencing agent, particularly on the youngest students. . . .
>
> Moreover, given the fact that many students feel that advertising for some pharmaceuticals might lead to misuse of the product, it is a reasonable hypothesis that some pharmaceutical advertising functions as a reinforcing element in the entire complex of drug attitudes among the young. Further, the finding that users of illegal drugs tend to be more receptive to pharmaceutical advertisements than non-users also suggests that pharmaceutical advertising may be reducing cognitive dissonance (personal conflicts) by implying, symbolically to the users that . . . "Everyone turns on in his own way." This might be an important rationalization for the furtive user. . . .
>
> The presence, then, of pharmaceutical advertising may be a reminder, so to speak, to its beholder that . . . "Everybody takes some kind of drug for something some of the time." . . .
>
> The trends in the study concerning the various age groups suggest forcefully that it is the elementary school children who tend to be most receptive and least critical of advertisements. It is in this younger group of students that the influences of pharmaceutical advertising—as a reinforcing agency—may be most pronounced. . . .
>
> This suggests that the industry codes for the content and timing of mass media campaigns be thoroughly reviewed with the understanding that pharmaceutical campaigns about the ingestion of over-the-counter drugs seem to have a potential influence on younger people by presenting a symbolic, cultural approval by their very presence in mass media.[7]

In other kinds of purchasing decisions or product categories, advertising,

---

[7]Monograph No. 91–94 (Washington, D.C.: Government Printing Office, 1971), p. 104.

obviously, might function in a different way. It may even create some wants and desires that were not there (it is fair to say that this may not necessarily be evil or even undesirable).

The point is that advertising may work in different ways with different segments in different product categories. We have generalized models, but we do not have the data to decide the important questions surrounding regulation.[8] This is something that seems obtainable and desirable to have. Again, a data-based agreement on what role advertising plays in the buying decisions of various products becomes crucial in arriving at a cogent and reasonable view of advertising regulation.

Another implication of assessing the nature of advertising's potency in various categories is that we must come to realize that advertising probably doesn't work in a uniform way in all situations. Some of the spokesmen who doubt any undesirable ramifications from advertising usually do it by the logically questionable way of explaining and demonstrating that advertising is not casual (in this instance, drug abuse) and from there proceed to argue that advertising in no way has been proven responsible for any ill effects it may somehow have engendered.[9]

The problem is to decide what the nature of advertising's contribution is to buying decisions—along with all other influences—before we can determine its total vindication or total culpability. One suspects, however, that all but the most zealous ideologues would agree that advertising is neither an unmixed blessing nor an unmixed evil. In passing, it is worth observing that many of the controversies between advertising agencies and their clients are related to the comparative inability of researchers to parse out the role of advertising from other elements in the marketing mixture in terms of judging its cost effectiveness. It is clear to most students of advertising that effects in the marketplace are multicausal; hence, to try to heap all blame or praise on advertising would seem to be inconsistent.

An Attitude Toward Regulation

Who is to protect whom from what? Most thoughtful Western students of political systems would argue that the more individual freedom a society can tolerate, the more mature and less represssive that society is. The ideal

---

[8]Francesco M. Nicosia, *Consumer Decision Processes* (Englewood Cliffs, N.J.: Prentice-Hall, 1966).

[9]"Statement Before the National Commission on Marijuana and Drug Abuse," American Association of Advertising Agencies, Bulletin No. 3049–F, New York, July 27, 1972.

way of achieving this is, of course, through individual regulation, or, in the case of government and industry, self-regulation. It has not had a glorious history in the advertising field. This does not mean, however, that the new machinery of the National Advertising Review Board might not change this. Still, many existing codes appear to be frequently violated. Those concerning the advertising of nonprescription drugs are a case to ponder.

It is difficult, however, to judge whether self-regulation works, as indeed we must hope it will, without some sort of criteria. These criteria are contained, in my judgment, in the questions concerning what a relevant conception of human nature is and what an appropriate vision of society should be.

It is also difficult to understand how these questions can be resolved without developing an appropriate data base. In other words, a research approach to the psycho-logic of advertising regulation must be made if we are to have a sensible and satisfying approach to advertising regulation. This is not to discourage legal, moral, and philosophical approaches also. Empiricism and philosophy are all of a piece.

In this connection, dialogue is usually strained between the regulated and the regulators. The reason is not always substantive; sometimes it is, as it were, stylistic.

Attorneys in the regulator positions often, through academic training, think in modes that are different from marketing and advertising executives. Lawyers tend to be linear, sequential, Aristotelian, and analogical, while their adversaries tend to think in terms of psychological, less precise categories, and approach problems from a "field theoretical" point of view.

These stylistic differences in cognitive approaches to problems of regulation should be recognized and, insofar as possible, overcome. One step in this direction is the ongoing dialogue with lawyers that members of Division 23 of the American Psychological Association are having. It may go a long way toward developing a "meta-language" by which individuals with different cognitive styles and approaches may deal with their common problems more effectively.

It is even more difficult to know how to set up government, industry, and academic machinery to do a regulatory job. Senator Frank Moss's proposal to set up an institute to study the effects of mass marketing on society seems to have merit and may yet serve as a blueprint for the future:

> The plan, outlined by Senator Frank Moss (D. Utah), visualizes a National Institute of Marketing and Society, as part of the U.S. Public Health Service or the National Science Foundation. The senator said his efforts to get behavior

testimony on marketing issues in recent years convince him that too little is being done, and too much of what is being done is locked in the files of individual companies.

As he visualizes it, the institute could be given a broad mandate to consider the social impact of the consumer culture. . . . "It could be encouraged to engage in the analysis of specific marketing themes and techniques and behavioral problems, such as drug abuses, as well as broad studies illuminating fundamental conflicts between the consumer culture and national goals and ideals," he said. . . .

He suggested that the institute, by providing broader financing for research, will enable academicians to engage in broader investigation "of advertising and marketing as a socializing and educational force in our society." . . . "Put in another way, we are approaching the end of the 20th century knee-deep in a marketing economy and a consumer culture which we barely comprehend. To the child growing up in America, marketing measures are as pervasive as the air he breathes." . . .

"For more than 50 years, through the FTC, we have sought to regulate the economic impact of marketing practices, but we have never thought, on a systematic basis, even to seek an accounting of the social costs of marketing and advertising," he said. "Yet we are beset with profound and unsettling questions concerning the social role of advertising."[10]

No matter what the machinery is to evaluate the effects of marketing and advertising practices on society, it must be developed in order to judge what the nature and degree of regulation might be. Evaluating the actual social role of advertising ought to be the first step[11] in the total process of deciding how American society *should* be affected by advertising. Legal regulations which then take account of the philosophical imperatives as well as the psychological realities may then be consistently developed.

It should almost go without saying that advertising is only part of the total media environment and there seems to be little question that the rest of the media environment might well stand the logical and psychological scrutiny usually give to advertising per se.

---

[10]*Advertising Age*, February 15, 1971.

[11]For a solid discussion of some aspects of this problem, see John G. Myers, *Social Issues in Advertising* (New York: AAAA, Educational Foundation, 1971).

Consumers in the Federal Decision-Making Process

●●●

● **LEE RICHARDSON**
Director of Consumer Education
Office of Consumer Affairs
Executive Office of the President

That consumers are seeking solutions to problems they perceive as primarily caused by the business system is a characteristic of modern consumerism. These consumers, individually and collectively, are looking to government to fulfill wants that corporate policy doesn't: goods, services, information, and so on. The development of the consumer movement to this point has generated much divergent opinion on the validity of its specific complaints, but its efforts reflect frustration and skepticism regarding the ability of the business system to deliver efficiently the standard of living to which many of the 210 million American consumers feel entitled. More specifically these consumers feel they could obtain this higher standard of living with their available buying power. This differs from the traditional way of raising one's standard of living by increasing earnings.

Their frustration and skepticism are difficult to analyze because there is little evidence to suggest that the business system's efficiency has declined sharply. Regardless of the varieties of causes, whether real or imagined, the consumerists' behavior patterns stemming from these new attitudes are significant subjects for study.

A review of consumers' modes of contact and communication with federal agencies should lead to answers to these basic questions about the consumer movement:

458

—What are the reasons behind the contacts?

—How much contact is there and what does that indicate about the seriousness of consumer unrest?

—How do federal agencies cope with the contacts from consumers?

—What are the current methods used by consumers to influence federal decisions affecting them?

—What are some of the new developments in current federal decision making that will involve the consumer interest?

Since complete answers to these questions are not possible, conceptualizations of some of the answers will be the goals of this article through a synthesis of some of the legal, administrative, and consumer perspectives on these five problems.

Current Varieties of Consumer-Federal Contact

Most of the measures of consumer contacts of various agencies (exclusive of political action) are seriously limited indicators of consumer problems and needs. They tend to fall into three categories:

(1) Individual requests for information or general assistance. These range from selecting automobile tires to regulating an industry's safety procedures.

(2) Individual complaints. Consumers increasingly write federal agencies to solve problems they have with automobiles, appliances, delivery, advertising, consumer credit, retailers, and manufacturers.

(3) Consumer advice. Consumers, amazingly, offer considerable advice to their public servants both in formal proceedings and informally. Agencies and administrators receive unsolicited consumer inputs, sometimes critical of their past actions or inactions and sometimes merely for information. Some consumers participate, individually or through organizations, in regulatory proceedings, advisory committees, and other formal mechanisms.

The common limitations of all three of these contacts is that knowledge of them is shallow and irregularly distributed among various strata of the population.

The Consumer Product Information Coordinating Center launched by President Nixon is a partial solution to the distribution and promotion problem for consumer information available in government. However, there remain needs for improved data gathering, analyses, editorial work, and general publishing efforts to supply the public with more useful information from federal sources. Outstanding but uncoordinated efforts of individual departments and agencies exist, notably in the forms of pamphlets, extension or outreach workers, and technical information to the mass media for rewrite and further dissemination. There is far too much information in existence, however, that is not yet being systematically produced and distributed for consumer use in spite of a seemingly impressive list of federal activities. Food and Drug Administration consumer specialists, Department of Agriculture subsidized cooperative extension specialists, Office of Economic Opportunity community action agencies neighborhood workers, and other personnel on a full- or part-time basis disseminate consumer information through speeches, counseling, and other means.

The individual complaint, according to the *Guide to Federal Consumer Services*, can be sent to the Office of Consumer Affairs (OCA). OCA can mediate in a limited manner or refer complaints; it processes 3000 to 5000 complaints per month. Some contacts are phoned in, but most are mailed. These represent an extremely small sample of nationwide consumer complaints. The Federal Trade Commission receives complaints but may not take legal action on behalf of individual consumers. Virtually all analyses of consumer complaints going to federal agencies are summaries by non-standardized categories that represent a mixture of industry and functional activities of business. Only limited analyses have been performed on them to attempt to determine the state of individual consumers' unrest.

The third major variety of contact is consumers' efforts to influence policy through nonpolitical means. This includes delicate matters involving democratic procedures, citizen participation, and federal sensitivity to the public. It raises questions of the balance of influence between opposing interests and points of view. These issues are to be touched on in the subsequent evaluation.

Quantities of Consumer Federal Contact

The quantity of contacts reflects the major problem referred to earlier—the lack of knowledge of consumer opportunities to make the contacts. However, some observations still pertain:

(1) The Consumer Product Information Center reports that circulation of its basic index pamphlet exceeds ten million and that it has increased sales of consumer pamphlets several fold in less than two years. This implies that a vast untapped market for federal consumer information has existed and is still relatively uncharted.

(2) The complaint data, while extremely small, reflects the fact that a

nationwide consumer complaint handling mechanism doesn't exist. Washington is the letter writer's last resort when business has failed, trade groups have failed, or state and local government has failed. All of these failures are reflected in letters written to many federal agencies in Washington. It would be quite a curious statistic on the other hand to report the number of consumers who might write to Washington if they were truly encouraged to do so.

(3) Quantitative measures of complaints will not reveal the relative seriousness of individual complaints either in social or economic terms. The complaints against mail order firms are less serious on the average as a social indicator than complaints against hazardous glass doors. There is a need for better measurement here.

(4) Since any reporting agency's measure of consumer complaints is a sample from a population of problems of unknown number, efforts to compare numbers of complaints by categories of industries or business functions are generally invalid. Few consumers complain about the schemes that bilk them, the complex problems of life insurance, or the problems associated with emotional subjects such as funerals. A consumer is often a good judge of an advertising annoyance or deceptive sales practice, but will be unaware of a failure of a doctor or that funds are due him as a result of an insurance policy cancellation.

(5) Evaluation of the extent of serious efforts of consumers to influence federal decision making shows disappointing results. However, the trend is upward and there have been some recent developments to try to stimulate more of it. The *Consumer Register,* published as part of the OCA newsletter, *Consumer News,* is a condensed version of the parts of the *Federal Register* pertinent to consumer affairs. Some simplification of regulatory hearing procedures to allow consumer participation has occurred. There are several functioning consumer advisory boards, the most prominent of which is the President's Consumer Advisory Council. The Product Safety Bill signed by the President in October 1972 provides for a board of safety advisors.

Federal Efforts to Cope with Consumers' Problems

Efforts of agencies to deal with consumer information requests and complaints is making painful progress. The information problem is a question of increasing the commitment in view of the other priorities of government. Analysis of the complaint problem suggests that the desired federal role is not well defined in view of the alternatives of potential improvements in business firm, trade association (including the Better Business Bureau), state and local government, and private action methods of remedying the problems.

Efforts to supply information and handle individual complaints must not be restricted to consumers who exhibit a great deal of initiative and search behavior. Informational campaigns will be required to reach consumers who are unaware of services in these areas. The problems of alerting millions of people to the availability of services that they will need only on occasion require not only good communications systems, but also a simplified organization of these services so that the public will have easy access. Both the government and large corporations tend to frustrate an individual trying to locate an answer or satisfy a problem.

It may be presumptuous for a federal employee to judge the responsiveness of federal agencies to consumer advice. Unsolicited and unexpected correspondence from a concerned letter writer sometimes unveils a whole area of problems or opportunities that an agency was unaware of. Some government reactions may be to ignore even potentially useful advice, whereas other personnel may decide to investigate the issue, develop a program to deal with it, and spend money to execute the program. In any event, the decisions to act remain with the government in cases of these types.

The possibilities of agency action increase to the extent that consumer advice is parallel to the motives of the agency. Some of those motives include:

(1) Personal motives of the administrators, whether idealistic or to advance a career. The possibilities here are as varied as the people and this is an important reason for agencies to seek progressive, professional, policy-making personnel.

(2) The agency's organizational motive to provide a public service of the type to which the consumer is referring. A consumer who reveals a lead poisoning problem relevant to an aggressive agency's assigned mission is likely to see some action taken.

(3) Motives related to public controversies. Agencies seek to appear positive and credible when they are connected with publicly debated issues. This means they want to do a good job, but logically, they wish to get proper credit for it too. For instance, a consumer should expect an agency to offer support for rights of women, since this seems to be an issue whose time has come.

(4) Political motives. Admittedly there are politics in government, but far less than many people assume. This is true especially in the established departments that remain intact from one presidential administration to another. Career administrators are, in fact, often quite negative toward attempted political pressures.

This list of motives reflects the good and bad of government. Public opinions toward federal agency motives tend to range from one extreme to another—mostly negative or at best cautious in any praise.

The motivations are important for any consumer to know. This should enable consumers to influence their public servants' decisions. Not only should consumers seek out memberships on the formal advisory boards or participation in regulatory proceedings, but they need the informal contacts in the agencies to be able to assess the directions and potential directions government is taking. Although the Federal Trade Commission is approximately the same agency today according to law that it was in 1968, it is now much more likely to heed the public clamor for reform of, say, an allegedly deceptive advertising practice because its mission and the motives of its personnel were thoroughly revamped by Executive decisions in 1969–1970.

Consumer Influences on Federal Decisions

Consumer advice, of course, does influence federal decision making. The effective lobbyist has no power in the legal sense, but instead supplies information and help to the government in an effort to reveal the wisdom of his client's position in view of the government's mission and motives. Consumers will have to learn to present their views in similar ways, but they haven't yet done so.

Consumers' influence on decision making today is a special case of the unspecial interest. The consumer interest lacks the unity of purpose that unites producer organizations or labor. As a result, the few organizations devoted to the national-level interests of consumers have unimpressive size, staff, and funding. Their voices collectively are weak. Sometimes, opposition to consumers' interests is quite effective.

Consumers are further unable to address government at the appropriate points because of the fractionalized consumer responsibilities of so many different agencies. Unorganized consumers trying to influence an amorphous government on thousands of problems results in very little direct effect on federal decisions.

The consumer movement has some unique assets, however. The weight of mass media editorial opinion rests clearly with the general consumer interest. The congressional and presidential candidates must heed some of the consumer issues of the day because individuals sometimes vote in accordance with their views on critical consumer issues such as food prices. With consumerism commanding fairly prominent public attention, the political impact is heightened despite the lack of strong organized consumer groups.

Direct consumer participation in federal decisions does not exist, per se, for reasons outlined later. Consumer influence has consisted of indirect public pressure through the media, a little effort in regulatory proceedings, some scattered advisory boards, and an occasional good suggestion or other communication that is consistent with the motives of particular agencies and agency personnel.

New Federal Decision-Making Modes for Consumers

The oldest form of federal decision making affecting consumers is the representative system of government through elections. As complex and diverse as consumer concerns are, it is difficult for voters, with their fractionalized interests as consumers, to pay much attention to anything less than the extremely important consumer problems. Elected officials perhaps could be encouraged to exercise greater concern for administrators' actions on consumer issues, as a recent newspaper editorial mentioned, and if they had, the U.S. might not have had the outcry of consumerism that it has been experiencing. As government functions have multiplied and thus divided the interests of Congress into so many consumer issues (not to overlook the manyfold more important nonconsumer problems such as defense, welfare, taxes, and so on), it has become evident that the consumer interest needs reinforcement in the federal administration. There are several new developments to fill the gaps that merit attention.

One potential method of greater consumer involvement is direct consumer participation in the decisions affecting them. Actually, this is better posed as a model of democracy rather than as a realistic alternative, because decision-making power cannot be delegated directly to *ad hoc* citizens or groups of consumers. These citizens must be accountable in some way as would employees of the government. Someone or somebody would have to select them in an approved fashion.

The realization that direct consumer participation is impossible leads to consideration of the greatest area of innovation—assignments of consumer responsibilities to new forms of federal bodies. Of special interest are the concepts of the consumer advocate, the ombudsman, and the hiring of consumer-oriented personnel.

The consumer advocate role in the federal government is now assigned by executive order to the Office of Consumer Affairs. This office is the focal point for consumers trying to deal with the federal government. It should take the consumers' interests to many agencies and levels, including advisory services to the President, through its director, Virginia Knauer, who is also the Special Assistant to the President for Consumer Affairs. As a consequence of the fact that the office has no statutory authority, OCA does not undertake any legal actions on behalf of consumers, disburse grant money for any consumer projects, or have specified rights of intervention in the affairs of the various federal agencies. By virtue of its status in the Executive Office, however, it does indeed have potential power as spokesman to the federal agencies as well as to business and other nongovernmental groups. It is noted for the voluntary programs it has induced in business in areas such as cosmetic labeling, life insurance price disclosures, unit pricing, and other programs. Due to its limited scope, OCA also has only limited capacity as the federal government's complaint-handling agency or as a producer of major consumer education and informational campaigns and programs.

The OCA probably will be superseded some day, since the 91st and 92nd Congresses both were generally inclined to favor the concept of a Consumer Protection Agency (CPA). They couldn't agree, however, on all of the features of such an agency. It is difficult to predict what the 93rd Congress will do. Nevertheless, the central idea of all versions of CPA considered to date has been that of the consumer advocate. No one is arguing for regulatory authority for the consumer protection agency. The advocate will be assigned the heretofore difficult ask of prodding agencies into movement toward the solution of diverse consumer problems, which neither consumers nor Congress have been able to achieve under the existing structure for the reasons outlined earlier. Thus, consumer advice should be better heeded, consumer complaints more efficiently resolved, and consumer information and even educational programs more effectively developed through the urgings of the consumer advocate. It is a new idea in consumer affairs at the federal level that has the support in principle of the executive and legislative branches, but which has not yet taken its final statutory shape.

A CPA will be the most important development in federal efforts to assist consumers for another reason, often overlooked. The historical rise and fall of interest in consumer issues at the federal level during this century will be less likely to occur because of the existence of an agency whose responsibility is consumer advocacy. The advocate will not let the government forget, and, equally important, it will be much easier for concerned consumers to know where to look in case they feel that something in the consumer interest is being ignored.

The concept of advocate has gained ground at the agency level as well as at the pinnacle of the Executive Office. At Health, Education and Welfare, for example, a small staff functions as consumer advocates in the Office of Consumer Services in the secretary's office. In some other agencies, a lone individual has become the appointed consumer voice, sometimes informally.

The ombudsman is a limited form of consumer advocate. Intended basically as a person or office concerned with helping individuals whose serious problems don't quite fit the specific requirements or thrusts of government agency programs, an ombudsman is given certain powers to see that these individuals are considered and helped if at all possible. They are more than referral agencies because they have subpoena and other powers beyond those of mediator or advisor. The ombudsman could be useful in handling complaints of consumers in some instances when federal agencies were involved, but consumer complaints usually involve businesses over which ombudsmen would need additional powers to assist consumers.

Another area of innovation is the increasing concern with the fact that the federal agencies need consumer-oriented employees at policy-making levels. Recognition of this need is growing commensurate with the acknowledgment that the consumer interest is a separate, recognizable interest apart from the other economic and social perspectives. It is hoped, then, that high-level civil service personnel, key staff persons whose influence in policy decisions is critical, and appointees to boards and commissions will include significant numbers of persons attuned to the consumer interest.

Summary

The consumer interest in the federal government can be identified in terms of the three major forms of nonpolitical contacts that are made with federal agencies—requests for information, requests for assistance on complaints, and consumer advice. The significance of these contacts has gone largely unmeasured because standards of measure are not easily developed. The federal response to the varieties of consumer contacts suffers from several shortcomings, including a lack of well-directed consumer inputs and the diverse nature of federal agencies and their motives for action. Consumer efforts to influence federal decisions will soon face stiff obstacles. New modes of federal decision making, however, have been developing and will tend to overcome some of the deficiencies in the federal administration of consumer affairs. Most notable among the new developments is the concept of the consumer advocate within government.

Reading the Fine Print in the Social Contract

●●●

● **MERVIN D. FIELD**
President
Field Research Corporation, San Francisco

The rise of consumerism is an outgrowth of the multitude of changes in recent years occurring in many sectors of our society. Business use of opinion and market research techniques have been a factor in democratizing the marketplace.

The increased attention being paid to advertising by the public and governmental regulatory bodies is part of a larger change going on in our society. Until recently, advertising has been one-sided in its presentation—constituting mostly praise, encomium, and flattery. The consumerism movement is leading to a return to John Stuart Mill's idea that truth will only emerge from the free and open conflict of ideas. The adversary system is being brought to the advertising arena and it is not without promise as a way of creating a better business climate.

Whenever an industry gets in trouble and is assailed by its critics, it is interesting to note how its leaders respond to the challenge. One of the comforting things about observing human behavior is that no matter how homogeneous, specialized, or narrowly based a group may be, there is always a refreshing diversity of human response.

A recent issue of *Advertising Age* reports that at a meeting of the American Association of Advertising Agencies and the American Business Press, "speakers seemed bent on warning that the final day of judgment was close at hand for the advertising business unless the industry rises up to smite the evil forces that surround it." One speaker, Ralph K. Winter, Jr., Professor of Law at Yale University, called consumer advocacy as practiced today a "public relations gimmick" and a "threat to the consumer interest." Some time ago, Howard Bell, President of the American Advertising Federation, is reported as saying, "The consumer movement is a fad that will soon pass. Throughout history, consumerism has had a tremendous influence on business and government. The only thing new is the label."

This kind of response to current challenges to the advertising industry reminds me of the story of the boy with a younger brother who often embroidered his account of an event. This tendency to enlarge the truth would invariably infuriate the older brother and quite often in his anger he would upbraid his younger brother with: "Stop exaggerating, I've told you at least *ten million times*—stop exaggerating."

I don't think the present concern about advertising and social values, which is a component of a larger concern about our basic business system, is an exaggerated phenomenon by any means. In the last decade, there have been hundreds of major pieces of federal legislation enacted to protect the consumer in one way or another. This is apart from hundreds or so of additional pieces of legislation in Congress—some of which are still pending—and numerous pieces of legislation either enacted or introduced in the 50 state legislatures. A recent study estimates that there are now something over 400 consumer protection activities scattered over some 40 federal agencies. This study calculates that these agencies employ more than 32,000 persons and have a combined budget of well over a billion dollars annually.

Some might argue that these statistics could just as well exemplify a swollen federal bureaucracy, spending money and causing discomfiture to business whether the public needs or wants it. In fact, it has been suggested that if these statistics were better publicized, the result could start a counter trend—the spawning of an *anti*consumerism movement by the public.

When you are in the midst of social and business changes, it is easy to misperceive the full range of its effects. I think that what is happening to us when we view the growing concern of the role of business in our present-day society as similar to the experience of two shipwrecked sailors when they first viewed a giant Coca-Cola bottle as it washed up on the beach of the deserted island where they were marooned. They were shipwrecked on the island before Coca-Cola and other bottlers had introduced a bottle size as large as the king size. So here were our two castaways gazing at this very familiarly shaped bottle, but wide-eyed in wonderment because it was so large. Finally, one looked at the other and said: "My God, Walter, we've shrunk."

Robert Estes of General Electric summarizes the businessman's dilemma very well:

In any discussion of consumerism, a businessman—even a nonparanoid type—tends to come on somewhat like a later-day Harry Houdini: wrapped in chains, handcuffed, nailed in a coffin, under 30 feet of water.

There are some interesting parallels: he has only himself to blame; he did it to himself in the process of trying to make a living; he is supremely confident he can get out of the mess by himself. Despite this confidence, a certain amount of suspense is generated among the on-lookers. Finally, no one is supposed to offer help . . . until it is too late.

How did the businessman get to this perilous point? Actually, the consumer and the businessman are not natural enemies: To the contrary—business was under the impression that it got ahead by seeking out and filling people's needs and tended to be rather proud of how well the job was done. However, at least two developments intervened to put the businessman into a Houdini syndrome: There was a sudden and dramatic shift in values—but not by everybody, not all in the same direction, and not all at the same pace. Priorities became infinitely more complex as needs changed. Consumer segments split off and became sharply polarized to the point at which to serve one was automatically to antagonize others. To meet one area of man's needs meant penalizing him in another.

A simple example is the pharmaceutical house that comes up with a cure for one malady, but in curing this malady diminishes a person's ability to resist others. Another more relevant example, perhaps, is the dilemma we face in meeting the energy crisis. Do we push pell-mell ahead in attmpting to meet our insatiable demands for power by building more power plants that use nuclear fuel, without really knowing whether we can build them fast and safe enough to meet the ever-increasing need? Or do we take an entirely different look, gambling on other untried sources of power generation?

From a broad historical perspective, the current wave of public concern about corporate social policy is the result of a society that has always had a strong, continuing expansionistic thrust—a society that has created an incredibly complicated materialistic economy. However, like any other dynamic, long-driving force, it has created excesses that have to be corrected. It has caused fissures in our social fabric that have to be healed. Its motive power has to be overhauled and its direction recalibrated.

Business has moved from the production concept to a marketing concept—almost in one generation. It has developed large consumer franchises, and these have become much bigger assets than plants and machinery. To maintain these consumer franchises, business has had to assume a posture of responding more and more in its public. In the process it has become more democratic. Too many marketing companies have learned the bitter lesson that a consumer franchise once built will not always be there. They know that the public is deciding and choosing each day, quickly changing its tastes, continually altering its hierarchy of the values it wants in goods and services. It is not bound by any means to yesterday's habit patterns.

The phenomenon of consumerism, of which the present concern about advertising is a component, is an umbrella for several kinds of consumer concerns and resentments, which have evolved from fundamental changes in American business over the past half-century. These changes have occurred as competitive emphasis has moved from production to marketing, and as private enterprise has moved to managerial enterprise.

Managerial enterprise emphasizes optimizing on lucrative segments of the market and ignoring others; emphasizing the average situation instead of the total market; appealing to some segments, ignoring, or even discriminating against others. The competitive pressure on marketing emphasizes making the sale instead of making the product. This emphasis on making the sale, if carried beyond bounds, causes the excesses we are talking about.

Curiously, a strong, contributory current, feeding and shaping this wave of consumerism, is the enlightment displayed by business and government institutions during the past 30 years. Business has made heavy use of marketing and social research; it has created and maintained extensive marketing and social feedback informational systems. While most of these have had the narrow original objective of gaining a competitive edge, their collateral effect has been to democratize the marketplace. Consumers now know very well how to communicate with business, often to the distress of business managers.

Recent government administrations, both Republican and Democratic, may have been unresponsive and unheeding of the public's will in such matters as what wars it wants to fight, but very responsive in other areas. We have a government with a unique system of legal justice that in many ways, during the last 20 years in particular, has been responsive to a variety of social needs. Indeed it has been so responsive at times that it has been charged with going beyond its proscribed limits and indulging in excesses of its own—becoming too much the cutting edge—and being too far in the vanguard of social change.

Advertising Values

The rise of consumerism and the increased, sometimes painful scrutiny of advertising by the public, by governmental regulatory bodies, and by the advertising industry itself are parts of a much larger change occurring within our social, business, and government institutions. I think it will help if we recognize that the current storm about advertising values is just one storm within a larger storm.

Twenty-five years ago, business, political, and academic interest in public opinion as an area of study was at an all-time high. But 25 years before that, in 1922, many of the problems that emerged in later attempts to study public opinion were anticipated by Walter Lippmann in his distinguished book *Public Opinion*. Today we accept the fact of public opinion, but exactly what we intend to convey when we talk about public opinion or consumer opinion is perhaps less clear today than it was 25 years ago. A return to Walter Lippmann might be helpful. Lippmann suggested that, "the analysis of public opinion must begin by recognizing the triangular relationship between the scene of action, the human picture of that scene and the human response to that picture working itself out upon the real scene of action."[1]

This triangular relationship occurs because the scene of action or the "real environment is altogether too big, too complex, and too fleeting for direct acquaintance. We are not equipped to deal with so much subtlety, so much variety, or so many permutations and combinations. Although we have to act on the environment in the scene of action, we have to reconstruct it on a simpler model before we can manage it."[2] To traverse the consumer world of products, men need maps of it. But their persistent difficulty is to get maps on which some manufacturer's or advertiser's needs have not sketched in the shores of the promised land.

The world we have to deal with politically and "consumeristically" is then actually out of reach and out of sight. It has to be explored and reported and imagined. While man is no Olympian who can see all existence at one glance, he has invented ways of seeing with his mind vast portions of the world that he could never see with his eyes. These maps, or pictures, inside human heads, these pictures of themselves, of others, of their needs and purposes and relationships, are their public opinions—with small letters.

However, when these pictures are acted on by groups such as manufacturers or advertisers, they become Public Opinion, in capital letters. Lippmann asks us why the picture inside so often misleads men in their dealing with the world outside. He suggests primarily that men are misled by those factors that limit access to the facts. These are first, deliberate censorship, that is, when the advertiser censors all negative information about his products or ideas; or when the politician censors all praise for his opponent

---

[1]Walter Lippmann, *Public Opinion* (New York: Harcourt Brace and Co., 1922).
[2]*Ibid.*

from his remarks. There are other factors. For example, the meager time available in each day for paying attention to consumer and public information. Or the understandable distortion arising because products and events have to be compressed into very short messages, or the difficulty of making a small vocabulary express a complicated world, and finally Lippmann says there is the fear of facing those facts that seem to threaten the established routine of men's lives.

But it is the first and primary factor that concerns us here, that is, self-imposed censorship by politicians and advertisers. It is interesting to note that, except for a handful of recent exceptions, when all advertising across all products is added up, nothing is found but praise, encomium, and flattery. But when all political appeals on both sides are added up, they mostly contain criticism, aspersion, and slander. Perhaps there is some insight to this in that both product and political communications may be trying to provide information that they believe harmonize with the mood of the public, or Public Opinion.

The recent consumer movement, however, seems to me to suggest a changing Public Opinion. The constant censoring of criticism by advertisers has led to a vacuum on the negative side, which is now being filled by legislative leaders, government bureaucrats, Ralph Nader, and others. Certainly our adversary system and the competitive traditions stemming from John Stuart Mill's ideas that the truth will only emerge from the free and open conflict of ideas have applications to marketing and advertising.

To make the adversary system work, I believe that self-regulation is as unrealistic in product promotion as it is in our court system. That is, we do not expect our own lawyer to surface the weaknesses of our case in open court simply because it meets an abstract canon of objectivity. We do expect opposing counsel to do this, however, and feel he is remiss when he does not vigorously pursue all valid lines of attack. The court enforces only the rules of admissability, it does not offer its own evidence.

What I am suggesting is that the maps to the product that world advertisers give to the public consumer are misleading, not so much because of deliberate misrepresentation—a legitimate concern of the Federal Trade Commission and consumer groups—but more because of the one-sidedness of their disclosures. If our adversary system works at all, it should work in the advertising arena.

Self-Regulation by the Advertising Industry

● ●

● **HOWARD H. BELL**

President
American Advertising Federation,
Washington, D.C.

It is always risky to generalize on complex questions, especially those involving human behavior patterns and attitudes. But I shall do so in suggesting that corporate social policy has reached its present level of management priority because of increasing demands for public accountability. In the past the prime concern as with economic policy and its relation to stockholder accountability. Times have changed, however, and a characteristic of the present social revolution is a questioning of all our institutions—private and public.

Public opinion polls seek to measure change, and the accuracy of their most recent political predictions may reflect a desire by the public to slow down the rapid rate of changes taking place in the past decade.

During this period of social revolution there has been a decline in the level of public confidence in business and advertising. In one public opinion poll, only politicians received a lower ranking from the public, which says something about the severity of the problem. Space does not permit a probing of the reasons behind this erosion process, except for one or two generalizations: Consumer expectations have risen because of their higher levels of educational and economic attainment; the youth market and the youth culture have had an enormous impact on attitudes, culture, and buying habits; and consumerism has sparked the frustrations of the individual and the aspirations of the politician. Flaws in the marketing process are identified and given focus, thus assuring credibility and permanence to the consumer movement.

The result of all this has been a barrage of negatives overshadowing the good but less newsworthy side of American life. This has helped to generate and fan feelings of suspicion and unrest. In the case of business and advertising, the impression is created that *caveat emptor* is still the rule and high profits are the only corporate goal.

This is not the case, but I suspect that such reports as the one on "Corporate Policies and Procedures on Advertising and Promotion," recently released by the National Business Council for Consumer Affairs through the U.S. Department of Commerce will receive little public attention. It reflects the increasing commitment of top management to voluntary standards of responsibility for advertising practices. The public should be more aware of such attitudes and policies.

Advertising is the most visible communications area of business, which is why it has absorbed much of the public criticism of business generally. Today that criticim goes far beyond traditional concerns with taste and honesty into the more elusive areas of social impact and the implications of advertising. The proposal of Senator Moss (D-Utah) for an institute of advertising, marketing, and society reflects this concern.[1] So do the controversies over cigarette advertising, drug advertising, and the advertising of products for children. The debate over counteradvertising and the so-called Federal Communications Commission Fairness Doctrine is another example.

Some of the concern and criticism results from a lack of understanding of the role and function of advertising and the misguided notion that deep-seated social ills can be solved by such a simplistic approach as simply banning certain types of advertising. The broadcast ban on cigarette advertising did not solve the smoking and health problem in this country, as smoking statistics clearly indicate. But it did open the door to similar moves in other areas.

The tide of public opinion is not running in favor of reason and fact on such measures. If the tide is to be reversed, it will require more than lofty words and objectives by business. More positive programs that reflect industry's concern for public sensitivities are needed, and a way must be found to bring such programs to the attention of the public.

Even Ralph Nader has conceded that there is merit in talking about the good things business is doing to protect the consumer, and he has

---

[1]*Advertising Age*, February 15, 1971, p. 14.

undertaken such a project. I suspect it will be one of his least publicized reports by the very nature of what it is and because it is not considered newsworthy by today's standards.

Self-regulation can present a positive response to the public's need for high standards of performance in a highly competitive marketing environment. Our federation has long advocated such programs, and our advertising clubs have had traditional ties with local better business bureaus over the years. At the American Advertising Federation convention in 1970, we urged that a meaningful program be undertaken, and the chairman of our advertising standards committee, Fred Baker of Ayer/Baker, Seattle, and the then-chairman of the American Advertising Federation, Victor Elting of Quaker Oats, Chicago, unveiled recommendations for such a program. A pro-and-con industry dialogue followed, which was joined by other major advertising interests and organizations. The result was the adoption of the first industrywide program in 1971, the most significant step in advertising self-regulation ever undertaken. As one who has had considerable experience with the general field of self-regulation and recognizes its strengths and weaknesses, I do not make that statement lightly.

This is a program whose performance could well equal, if not exceed, its promise, and I would like to tell you why and briefly describe its operation. Most industrial codes and statements of high principle simply express good intentions; there are no mechanisms for carrying them out and no enforcement procedures to assure adherence, or, if there are, they rely only on the power of persuasion and the goodwill of the people involved. We recognized that something more was needed to be effective for industry and responsive to public interest.

Our objective was to assure and maintain high standards of truth and accuracy in national advertising. The key ingredients would be machinery to implement the objective, effective sanctions, and public involvement in the program. It was essential that it be a program that met legal standards and requirements for reasonableness and due process and that would have industry's acceptance and support.

Months of study and negotiation resulted in the adoption of a two-tiered program, consisting of a new, independent national advertising review board (NARB) and a new national advertising division (NAD) within the reorganized and revitalized Council of Better Business Bureaus (CBBB). A separate corporation was formed to administer the project; it was composed of the American Advertising Federation (AAF), the Association of National Advertisers, the American Association of Advertising Agencies, and the CBBB. The presidents and chairmen of the respective organizations serve on the corporation board, which performs the housekeeping chores for the new apparatus: recommended budgets, procedures, and NARB appointments. This body is known as the National Advertising Review Council. Extracts from its bylaws are an appendix to this paper.

Complaints about national advertising from any source are referred first to the NAD, which performs the staff function of reviewing, evaluating, and negotiating charges in advertising as required. This involves substantiating claims material from an advertiser to determine if the claims are supportable on the basis of reasonable data collected under acceptable research procedures.

If the complainant's position is upheld and the advertiser makes the necessary changes in the specific advertising, the case is closed at the NAD level. However, a complainant who is not satisfied with a staff decision is entitled to appeal to the NARB. If the advertiser does not agree with a staff decision, he also may appeal to the NARB.

The review board performs an appellate function through a five-member panel appointed by the chairman to hear the case and arrive at a final judgment. There is no appeal to the full NARB.

Former United Nations Ambassador Charles W. Yost is chairman of NARB, and he is a working chairman. In addition, there are 50 members of the Board—30 representing national advertisers, ten representing advertising agencies, and ten nonindustry members representing the public, many of whom are identified with consumer interests.

When a complaint cannot be resolved with the advertiser, public disclosure of the case is made, and it is referred to the appropriate government agency. During the first year of operation, no cases required invoking this ultimate remedy.

During the first year of operation, the NAD received or initiated from its own monitoring 337 complaints against national advertising: 112 complaints were dismissed as being without merit; 72 complaints were found to be justified, and in all cases the advertiser agreed either to withdraw the ad or modify it; and 153 complaints were still under investigation.

Six cases dismissed by NAD were appealed by the complainant to NARB for panel adjudication with the following results: four complaints were not sustained, and two complaints were upheld. In the latter cases, no further action was required, since the advertisers agreed that the challenged ads would not be used in the future.

The time required to process complaints ranged up to several months. Although some feel that it should move more quickly and the expeditious handling of complaints is a basic provision of the procedures, this time span is one of the advantages of self-regulation over governmental action. The latter often takes years of litigation to resolve an issue.

Commenting on the first year of operation, Ambassador Yost noted that "the self-regulatory machinery isn't perfect but it is flexible, and changes are being made as they are needed." He also pointed out that "neither NARB nor its investigative staff can be considered an apologist for questionable advertising practices or a 'defender' of the advertising industry. They act judiciously and fairly on all matters that come before them."

The new program has experienced some growing pains: Its procedures have been put to the test by certain consumer groups, with pressures for modifications in the apparatus and its policies. The NARC and NARB have been cognizant for these pressures and have sought to deal with them constructively. For example, early in the operation of the program there was pressure to expand NARB jurisdiction to deal with questions over and above factual representations, such as matters of taste and social responsibility. Since there is no government agency to which such cases could be referred, it is a difficult area to cover and involves subjective judgments and evaluations. However, the procedures were amended to provide for consultative panels of NARB to consider such questions, determine problem areas, and sponsor policy papers to alert the industry to practices that should be avoided.

Standards against which advertising could be measured were needed. So as not to encroach on existing standards of other industry groups, the NARB adopted a general advertising evaluation statement. The NAD draws on the existing codes of CBBB, the NAB, and others. When a case reaches an NARB panel, the question is whether, to the reasonable man, the ad in question misleads the public or has the capacity to mislead.

There has been pressure to open NARB and NAD decisions to public view and scrutiny—in some cases confidential action was subsequently released by complainants to the press. It was felt that confidentiality was desirable to secure industry's cooperation. It was also realized that the public should know as much about the work of this body as possible. The result was that changes in procedures have been developed to provide for greater public visibility and accountability.

The AAF and the CBBB have developed a plan to extend the national program to local communities by establishing local review boards. These are being developed jointly by local ad clubs and better business bureaus. More than a dozen cities have already launched such efforts.

As one who has been involved in this program from the beginning, I am gratified by the progress that has been made in such a short time. At the outset I suggested certain cautions. The program is not a panacea: It will not solve all of advertising's problems, and it will not silence all our critics. It is not intended to do either nor is it a substitute for proper governmental jurisdiction and action. However, if it does its job well, it may earn the respect of government and even relieve it of some existing burdens and pressures.

I would hope that it will help to restore public confidence in the free competitive process, because I believe it is in the public's interest to preserve that process. In a society of growing skepticism about most things, including the ability of industry to regulate itself, there is some reason to believe that this program can work. It deserves that chance.

APPENDIX I
Advertising Self-Regulation
Proposal and Outline

Preface

A new program of industry self-regulation pertaining to national consumer advertising was announced jointly on September 28, 1971 by the American Advertising Federation (AAF), the American Association of Advertising Agencies (AAA), the Association of National Advertisers (ANA), and the Council of Better Business Bureaus, Inc. (CBBB). This major industry step is designed to improve advertising standards, enhance public confidence, and correct such abuses as may exist before governmental action becomes necessary.

There are two distinguishing features to this new self-regulatory apparatus that are essential to its long-range success—meaningful enforcement procedures and public representation.

Recognizing the need to develop an effective local effort, the guidelines presented herein are designed to extend the national program to local communities through the cooperative effort of advertising clubs and better business bureaus. The development of effective local machinery will be an important additional step in assuring high standards of performance in all advertising.

The Proposal

Local advertising clubs and better business bureaus jointly establish local advertising review boards to review and decide appeals affecting truth and accuracy in local and regional consumer advertising.

It is recommended that the local program be modeled after the national effort, which comprises a new national advertising division (NAD) within the CBBB and an independent national advertising review board (NARB) to handle complaints that cannot be resolved by the staff of the NAD.

In essence, the local better business bureaus would perform the same function locally that the NAD does nationally in receiving, evaluating, and acting on consumer complaints. Unresolved complaints would be referred by the local BBB to the Review Board for final consideration and appropriate action.

The Organizational Structure

Initial Review of Complaints

Local better business bureaus traditionally have handled complaints about local and regional consumer advertising. The plan contained herein is designed to continue and strengthen that program when necessary.

The Appeals Process

When the local better business bureau is unable to negotiate a satisfactory resolution of a specific complaint with respect to local advertising, the entire file should be turned over to the advertising review board and the local or regional advertiser notified of this procedure.

Recommendations for Formation and Composition of Advertising Review Boards in Local Communities

(1) A committee of the local advertising club and the local better business bureau be formed for the purpose of implementing the project, including the selection and appointment of the local advertising review board.

(2) The composition of the board be as follows: local advertisers, 60 percent; local advertising agencies, 20 percent; and local public members, 20 percent.

The actual size of the review board may vary depending on size of the city, volume of complaints and workload and availability of people in the several categories.

(3) The chairman of the local advertising review board be selected from among prominent persons in advertising or public life within the local community.

(4) Board members serve for at least two years on a rotating basis, with the chairman eligible for reelection.

(5) Continuing liaison between the review board and the better business bureaus is important to the overall operation and to the preparation of material for review board consideration. In those cases in which the advertising club has an executive director who is in a position to handle this function, this would be one way to provide for such staff assistance separate from the better business bureau function relating to initial complaint, review, and negotiation.

(6) A separate local corporation under the laws of the individual state might be desirable for the purpose of administering the review board function.

(7) The review board chairman will serve as the overall coordinator and administrator of the activities of the review board and will serve as its public spokesman.

(8) Advertising review board panels. (a) Appointment to facilitate and encourage speed in the decision-making process, it is desirable that the review board be divided into panels by the chairman of the board for the purpose of reviewing individual appeals that come before it. (b) Eligibility of Panelists. An advertiser or agency member of the review board should be considered as not qualified to serve on an individual panel if his employing company manufacturers or sells a product or service, or represents a company, that directly competes with the product or service sold by the advertiser involved in the proceeding. A review board member, including a nonindustry member, should consider himself as disqualified in case of bias due to current or past associations.

(9) The review board should report annually to the public on the activities of the board during the year. The board may direct the preparation and publication of such interim reports as it deems necessary.

(10) In the review and disposition of all cases coming before it, the advertising review board must be completely autonomous and independent of any and all other persons and organizations, including sponsoring groups.

Enforcement Procedures

When the panel reaches a decision that an advertisement is misleading or deceptive and is thereby in violation of review board standards, it should notify the advertiser in writing of its decision and request that the specific advertisement(s) be modified or withdrawn within a time period appropriate to the circumstances in the case. The advertiser should have ten days to respond. If he fails to respond or indicates his unwillingness to accept or comply with the decision, the panel will notify him that the matter will be publicly referred to an appropriate government agency.

The panel, through the advertising review board chairman or staff executive, should maintain a complete file and record of its proceedings. All deliberations, meetings, proceedings, and writings of the panel should be confidential.

When the panel has obtained voluntary compliance from the advertiser or has reached a decision that the questioned advertising is not misleading for any reason, it should prepare a report of its findings and decision and transmit the file to the advertising review board chairman or staff executive. The advertising review board chairman or staff executive should inform the advertiser, the local better business bureau, and the complainant of the review board's decision, the reasons therefore, and that the matter has been closed.

Advertising Standards

The advertising review board should adopt general standards dealing with truth and accuracy of local consumer advertising. The Advertising Code of American Business, developed by the AAF in cooperation with the better business bureaus and other organizations, is one appropriate standard to apply (see Appendix II).

However, it is not recommended that the review board deal with matters beyond truth and accuracy, such as taste, advertising volume, etc., since objective standards are difficult to develop and administer in those areas.

APPENDIX II
The Advertising Code
of American Business

    I.   TRUTH. Advertising shall tell the truth, and shall reveal significant facts, the concealment of which would mislead the public.

   II. RESPONSIBILITY. Advertising agencies and advertisers shall be willing to provide substantiation of claims made.

  III. TASTE AND DECENCY. Advertising shall be free of statements, illustrations or implications which are offensive to good taste or public decency.

  IV. DISPARAGEMENT. Advertising shall offer merchandise or service on its merits, and refrain from attacking competitors unfairly or disparaging their products, services or methods of doing business.

   V. BAIT ADVERTISING. Advertising shall offer only merchandise or services which are readily available for purchase at the advertised price.

  VI. GUARANTEES AND WARRANTIES. Advertising of guarantees and warranties shall be explicit. Advertising of any guarantee or warranty shall clearly and conspicuously disclose its nature and extent, the manner in which the guarantor and warrantor will perform and the identity of the guarantor or warrantor.

  VII. PRICE CLAIMS. Advertising shall avoid price or savings claims which are false or misleading, or which do not offer provable bargains or savings.

 VIII. UNPROVABLE CLAIMS. Advertising shall avoid the use of exaggerated or unprovable claims.

  IX. TESTIMONIALS. Advertising containing testimonials shall be limited to those of competent witnesses who are reflecting a real and honest choice.

Advertising: Consumer Information and Consumer Deception

●●

● CHANNING H. LUSHBOUGH

Associate Director
Consumers Union of the United States,
Mount Vernon, N.Y.

In the simplest of economic systems, mass production and the necessary transportation of mass-produced products from a factory to the consumer do not exist. Under these circumstances, modern marketing and advertising assuredly could not exist. Such a marketplace would involve the direct presentation of products and related consumer information by the maker of the product to his customer at the point of purchase: the classic shoemaker.

But Adam Smith correctly foresaw that the division of labor and mass production would lead to such great productive efficiencies that completely new elements and concepts would necessarily enter the marketplace where goods are bought and sold. The expense of developing marketing plans and advertising for a product seldom exceeds ten percent, and probably averages approximately five percent of the wholesale prices received for consumer products. Compared to a likely average of ten percent for transportation costs today, the effort to locate willing purchasers by manufacturers' advertising probably comprises no more than two or three percent of the retail price paid.

The following comments are made to suggest a viewpoint consonant with the attitudes and ideals of those active in the consumer movement in this country today. A most important feature of advertising is to provide all needed consumer information regarding the product or service advertised. This is especially important for new products and products made with new materials, for which, in the early marketing stages at least, there is very little information available.

The Sears and Ward's mail-order catalog may, for example, be thought of as a nearly ideal form of advertising. Each product is presented briefly and with pertinent details regarding its design and function. But by looking a bit deeper comes the discovery that two things have happened:

(1) In presenting several hundred thousand different items for possible purchase, most of the advertising effort of the mail-order catalog is necessarily wasted on each particular potential customer.

(2) With the very substantial recent increases in distribution costs for individual parcels and retail shipments, the economy and efficiency of mail-order purchasing has suffered.

It is widely alleged that the public is exposed to vast numbers of advertisements each day—as many as 500 to 1500. If so, there is surely a direct parallel with the mail-order catalog. Most consumers pay no attention to advertisements for products and services that are of neither direct and immediate nor eventual interest to them as potential customers. This is probably true whether the advertisement appears on television, is heard on the radio, or is seen in magazines and newspapers—*unless* the advertisement is entertaining as such.

We must therefore conclude that, by whatever medium, the ultimate efficiency of advertising is low when one measures the number of actual and potential advertising exposures against actual product sales.

And so we come directly to the issue: How can an inherently inefficient operation—advertising—efficiently provide the consumer with all the information he needs to reach an informed decision to purchase or not to purchase? From the very nature and purpose of the media, no particular advertisement can be expected to do this job competently. The only advertising legally required to provide full disclosure is print advertising for prescription drugs. Even here, reminder ads are an exception. But prescription drug advertising is directed only to the medical and ancillary health professions, all of whom have, and are expected to continue to have, a degree of expertise substantially greater than that of the lay consumer to whom most advertising is directed.

Thus, the essential task for advertising—to provide all needed information to the consumer—is a basic problem of careful design and programming. And what a single, brief advertisement cannot do, a series of advertisements can do very well.

The attractiveness of this concept of advertising is that it can be used both to inform the potential purchaser about specific qualities and attributes of the advertised product or service, and to educate him on the basic values of those particular qualities. For example, suppose a breakfast cereal manufacturer were to initiate a series of advertisements designed to tell why he fortifies his product with the specific vitamins and minerals he uses. He might include some very basic and useful information on the importance of particular vitamins and minerals in maintaining vigorous good health.

The author has chosen as an example a "food for special dietary use" for the last 30 years or more. Nutritional labeling is now, however, coming into being for all foods on a voluntary basis under regulations proposed by the U.S. Food and Drug Administration. One of the first companies to take full advantage of this opportunity is Del Monte; and they are to be commended for assuming a leadership position and putting it into prompt practice for the fuller education of their customers.

In addition to providing information with which consumers may decide for or against a specific purchase, advertising is commonly designed to *persuade* its readers, listeners, and viewers to buy a specific product or service. Most advertising men would doubtless agree that this is its primary and most important purpose. When the persuasion is based on a fair and honest presentation of the exceptional features and basic qualities of the product, we as consumers cannot object. But when it assumes a more irrational tone (for example, using sex appeal to sell copper plumbing in new homes), we can at best be bemused—for in our ideal world, every consumer would be the economist's hypothetical "rational man."

And if he were, of course, such irrational appeals would get the advertiser nowhere. But they do get him somewhere; for most consumers like to be flattered, want to be persuaded, and enjoy the special attention that carefully devised advertising messages can lead him to believe he will receive. For example, glamorous images in pictures and language used to advertise fragrances and cosmetics persuade the purchaser that she can be as attractive as a the model shown in the advertisement if she uses the product. And we would take no exception to this kind of decision by the purchaser if she really knew that it is a *fantasy*, and not merely a particular product, for which she is paying. Yet we doubt that there is often clear recognition of this distinction in the mind of the customer at the moment the transaction occurs.

We would conclude with a comment that there remains today entirely too much deceptive advertising—deceptive in that what appears to be promised could not possibly be delivered; that, compared to other substantially equivalent products, the one advertised is essentially identical except for extravagant claims; and that the advertisement leads immature youngsters to believe a message that is essentially false and misleading when fully understood by their more mature parents.

One need not look far to find examples of such advertising. Furthermore, the reputable advertiser and his agency must compete with less reputable, inherently unethical advertisers. Consumers and responsible manufacturers must join hands to help assure that fair, honest and informative ads play their proper part in stimulating development of a marketplace in which honesty and fair dealing are the rule, and where a fully competitive free-enterprise system can flourish.

Consumer Reality and Corporate Image

●●

● WILLIAM J. WILSON

President
Daniel Starch & Staff, Inc.,
Mamaroneck, N.Y.

America has experienced three distinct periods of consumerism, or consumer movements, in this century. The first occurred in the early 1900's
when it was recognized that existing market mechanisms did not always
serve the valid interests of the consumer. *Caveat venditor* (let the seller
beware) began to replace *caveat emptor* as the guiding criterion in court
decisions. The first movement is epitomized in Upton Sinclair's *The
Jungle*, which provided the impetus for the Food and Drug Act of 1906.

The second era of consumerism occurred during the depression years of
the 1930's. Issues such as misleading advertising and brand proliferation
began to be examined. The first legal federal recognition of consumer
interest came with labor and consumer advisory boards established by the
short-lived National Recovery Act of 1933.

The third period of consumerism in this century—the one we are experiencing now—began in the late 1950's or early 1960's. In a special message to Congress in March 1962, President Kennedy focused public attention on the fact that consumers are "the only important group in the
economy who are not effectively organized, whose views are often not
heard." During the past decade, a number of special groups, committees
and executive offices have been created to represent, highlight and defend
the interests of the consumer, and Congress has passed numerous bills deal-

487

ing with various aspects of consumer protection. In all three periods, remedial actions have been taken only as a result of increased public pressure. Most of this pressure has been directed against state and federal governments at both the legislative and executive levels. Until recently, relatively little attention has been focused on the private or corporate sector.

In spite of these three distinct periods of consumerism, the movement has been continuous. Nevertheless, the movement has experienced its peaks and valleys, with each peak lasting about 15 years. If the historian Bemis were right—that the study of the past provides a key to the future—then we are about to enter one of the valleys; I think we are not.

The belief that the current consumer movement will continue and grow stronger, that a new phase will follow the old, without pause or valley, rests on two assmptions:

(1) that public attention will increasingly focus on the private sector; and
(2) that business will become increasingly responsive to a public that is rapidly becoming more and more skeptical of the private sector and its efforts to protect and truly serve the consumer.

The "report of the National Goals Research Staff," submitted to the President in July 1970, highlights one of the key factors distinguishing the current movement from the two that preceded it:

> In recent years the emphasis of American business has shifted from production to marketing, with the latter occupying an increasing role in the total job of producing and delivering goods and services. The change reflects the fact that ability to produce goods was mastered earlier than was the ability to detect new needs and then to design, distribute, and promote new products. But many people see production as an honest activity while marketing is considered a nonproductive activity—virtually by definition. This is not the place to analyze this assumption, but rather to record its persistence into an era in which marketing has assumed enormous importance. This negative evaluation of marketing represents an essential ideological difference between much of today's consumerism movement and current business practices.

> To the modern businessman the detection and serving of new and subtle needs is a legitimate and challenging activity. The businessman sees himself as improving the quality of American life, but to his critics, many of these activities are suspect. To the critic, these subtle needs are nonexistent until the marketer creates them. A characteristic reaction is that of Dorothy Sayers: "A society in which consumption has to be artificially stimulated in order to keep production going is a society founded on trash and waste, and such a society is a house built upon sand."[1]

[1]National Goals Research Staff, "Consumerism," *Toward Balanced Growth: Quantity with Quality*. Washington, D.C.: U.S. Government Printing Office, 1970, pp. 138–139.

While Ms. Sayers' attitude may be extreme, it does reflect growing public disillusionment with, and cynicism toward, business and its role in our economic system. The whole marketing "process," the basis for the livelihoods of many of us, is increasingly suspect in the minds of our consumers, our customers.

If growing consumer skepticism is a reality, and I believe it is, then businessmen must be concerned about the effect these attitudes are having on their companies, since the attitudinal environment in which corporate countenance is seen will have some effect on the success of a company's marketing and communication efforts. But *to what extent* is the reality of growing consumer skepticism influencing corporate image?

At my company, Daniel Starch & Staff, our business is marketing and opinion research. So we are deeply involved in the detection and analysis of consumer attitudes, behavior, and needs. We recently completed a personal interview study of 18,000 individuals based on a national probability sample. This annual study is designed primarily to determine the characteristics of the readers of some 75 major publications. To learn more about consumer attitudes and reactions to business practices, a battery of questions on consumerism was included in this year's study. A discussion of some of these findings will follow.

The Consumer Profile

Respondents were exposed to a list of statements about consumer issues and were asked whether they agreed, disagreed, or had no opinion about each statement. The overall results for each statement are shown in Table 1. Reactions to many of these issues—in particular the need for government information, warnings on labels, and advertising and manufacturing quality standards—indicate that substantial skepticism exists today among American consumers, both men and women.

In most cases, responses to the statements can be grouped into two categories: believers and nonbelievers or skeptics. A believer, for the purposes of this exercise, is one who is generally optimistic and trusting in his view of our economic system. For example, one who agrees with the statement, "If a manufacturer deceives the public, the people will find out soon enough," can be classified as a believer.

The skeptic is defined as one who tends to be less truthful and less sanguine about the system and those who operate it. Those who agree with the statement that "Most advertising nowadays tries to deceive people rather than inform them," for example, are skeptics.

TABLE 1.

		Agree	Percentage[a] who Disagree	Have no opinion
(a)	Advertising is more informative nowadays than it was a few years ago.	M[b] 61	23	16
		W 65	19	17
(b)	Consumers need information about products from the government because they cannot depend on producers and distributors to give them all the essential information.	M 70	14	16
		W 67	12	21
(c)	You get a better value for your money by buying private store brands than by buying nationally advertised brands.	M 28	53	19
		W 26	55	18
(d)	You can expect a big company to be readier to stand behind its products than a small company.	M 43	42	16
		W 41	41	18
(e)	If a manufacturer deceives the public, the people will find out soon enough.	M 48	39	14
		W 51	33	16
(f)	Manufacturers nowadays are more concerned about the safety of the public than they were a few years ago.	M 54	32	14
		W 55	28	17
(g)	Advertising causes people to buy things they don't need.	M 68	20	12
		W 66	20	14
(h)	Warnings on labels are sufficient for informing most consumers about the possible dangers of products.	M 42	44	13
		W 41	42	17

[a]Percentage figures in many cases do not add up to 100 due to rounding of numbers.
[b]M = Men; W = Women.

TABLE 1. (Continued)

		Agree	Percentage[a] who Disagree	Have no opinion
(i)	For most products there are really no differences among brands.	M 30 W 26	54 58	16 17
(j)	Most advertising nowadays tries to deceive people rather than inform them.	M 47 W 43	32 32	21 25
(k)	Big companies do a better job than small companies in supplying the kinds of products people need.	M 41 W 36	36 37	23 26
(l)	Manufacturers are using higher quality standards nowadays than they did a few years ago.	M 35 W 35	46 40	19 26

While differences by sex are marked, reactions to their statements differ significantly according to other demographic criteria such as age, income, education, race, and so on. Applying our definitions of the believer and skeptic to these statements, the following demographic profiles emerge:

—The Believer: Generally middle aged or older (frequently over 50); tends to be lower income (under $10,000/year) with a high school education at best; incidence is highest among blacks (particularly men), Southerners, and people residing in nonmetropolitan areas.

—The Skeptic: He (or she) tends to be under 35 and frequently between 18 and 24. Incidence is highest among middle- and upper-income groups ($10,000/year+), the college-educated, people residing in metropolitan areas in the Northeast and West, and whites. This group is also the most knowledgeable about the issues, at least in terms of their willingness to express an opinion.

While these profiles are based on broad generalizations from the data, the generalizations apply with remarkable consistency to each consumer issue. It is impossible within the scope of this paper to examine in detail each of these issues. Two examples should suffice to illustrate the extent and pattern of current consumer attitudes.

Attitudes Toward Advertising Among Men

Consumer protection organizations and the federal government have, over the past few years, given substantial attention to the subject of false or misleading advertising. Indeed, some companies have been forced to spend valuable advertising dollars to retract previous claims, thereby creating an atmosphere of consumer doubt about future claims or promises made. Moreover, the credibility of advertising in general is affected as the consumer is increasingly exposed to the publicity that has attended these events.

While 61 percent of all men feel that advertising is more *informative* today than it was a few years ago, nearly half of them (47 percent) believe that advertising nowadays is basically deceptive rather than informative.

The percentages shown in the following tabulations and in table 2 represent skeptics among those men who agree with the statements in table 1. The following figures are based specifically on those men who agree with the statement (j in table 1): "Most advertising nowadays tries to deceive people rather than inform them." This attitude exists with approximately equal intensity all across the country, although skepticism is highest in the Northeast:

Northeast	50 percent
North Central	46 percent
South	46 percent
West	47 percent

Possibly reflecting a general tendency toward rejection of the "establishment," younger men (under 25) are particularly strong in this point of view:

18–24	55 percent
25–34	47 percent
35–49	45 percent
50–64	47 percent
65 or more	42 percent

Skepticism on this issue seems to be marginally stronger among upper-income groups:

Under $5,000	45 percent
$5,000–$6,999	47 percent
$7,000–$9,999	47 percent
$10,000–$14,999	48 percent
$15,000–$24,999	49 percent
$25,000 and over	45 percent

There are marginally stronger negative attitudes toward advertising among men in larger cities and metropolitan areas:

Central cities	47 percent
Suburbs	49 percent
Total metropolitan areas	48 percent
Total nonmetropolitan areas	45 percent

Blacks are substantially less skeptical than whites:

White	48 percent
Black	36 percent

The more skeptical tend to be less mobile, particularly in terms of air travel and car rental:

No air travel in past 12 months	54 percent
Any air travel in past 12 months	45 percent
One trip	53 percent
Two trips	45 percent
Three-four trips	43 percent
Five or more	42 percent
Rented a car in past 12 months	41 percent
Did not rent a car in past 12 months	48 percent
Rented once in year	47 percent
Rented twice in year	41 percent
Rented three or more times	32 percent

The data suggest the possibility that the traveling businessman is the least skeptical of advertising. This is supported by data on traveler's checks and credit cards; heavy use of traveler's checks is related to lower skepticism. A review of the types of credit cards held also reveals that holders of "prestige cards" tend to be less skeptical of advertising:

Bought traveler's checks	49 percent
Did not buy traveler's checks	47 percent

Amount bought:

Under $100	63 percent
$100–$499	52 percent
$500 or more	39 percent
Have a credit card	48 percent
Do not have a credit card	46 percent

Type of card held:

Any gasoline credit card	46 percent
Master Charge	45 percent
Carte Blanche	43 percent
Bank Americard	43 percent
Car rental card	42 percent
Bell Telephone	40 percent
Any air travel card	34 percent
Diners Club	33 percent
American Express	32 percent

Those who are skeptical about advertising tend to have reservations about other aspects of American business, and tend to be more liberal in attitudes toward social problems.

Table 2 is a series of other statements with which respondents were asked to agree or disagree. The percentages shown represent skeptics among those who agree with each statement in table 1.

TABLE 2.

For most products, there are no differences between brands.	59 percent
Everyone should try drugs at least once to find out what they're like.	57 percent
Advertising causes people to buy things they don't need.	54 percent
The government should provide information about products because they cannot depend on manufacturers and distributors to give them all of the essential information.	53 percent
You can get better value by buying private store brands than by buying nationally advertised brands.	50 percent
Education is the best way of preventing drug abuse.	49 percent
Drug addicts should be treated as sick people, not as criminals.	49 percent
Manufacturers are more concerned about the safety of the public than they were a few years ago.	41 percent
Advertising is more informative now than it was a few years ago.	41 percent
Manufacturers are using higher quality standards now than they did a few years ago.	34 percent

Thus, it seems evident that attitudes toward advertising integrity may be but a part of broader attitudes toward business in general.

Women's Attitudes Toward the Government as a Supplier of Product Information

An indication of "protectionist" sentiment can be obtained from responses to the statement: "Consumers need information about products from the government because they cannot depend on producers and distributors to give them all the essential information." The skeptical female protectionist agrees with the statement, the "believer" disagrees.

Sixty-seven percent of all women interviewed favor government participation in the dissemination of information about products. While the predominant opinion is centered in the East and West coasts and in metropolitan areas and suburbs, there is substantial support in other areas of the country:

Northeast	73 percent	Central cities	68 percent
West	69 percent	Suburbs	71 percent
North Central	67 percent	Total metropolitan areas	70 percent
South	62 percent	Total nonmetropolitan	62 percent

Greatest approval of government participation is evident among younger age groups.

18–24	70 percent
25–34	75 percent
35–49	65 percent
50–64	67 percent
65 and over	60 percent

As income increases, the tendency to support consumer protection by the government increases.

Under $5,000	62 percent
$5,000–$6,999	64 percent
$7,000–$9,999	70 percent
$10,000–$14,999	70 percent
$15,000–$24,999	70 percent
$25,000 and over	69 percent

Probably as a corollary to the income pattern, those in the higher educational levels are more willing to invite government participation.

Grade school or less	60 percent
Some high school	67 percent
High school graduates	66 percent
Some college	69 percent
College graduate	72 percent
Post graduate	77 percent

White females are more agreeable to government advice on products than are blacks:

| White | 69 percent |
| Black | 54 percent |

In general, those who are more skeptical toward other aspects of American business tend to favor governmental information about products. The following table shows the percentage agreeing with governmental participation among those who agree with the various statements shown.

Among Women Who Agree That:	Percent Who Favor Governmental Information
Most advertising tries to deceive people rather than inform them.	75 percent
Advertising causes people to buy things they don't need.	75 percent
Private store brands are a better value than nationally advertised brands.	76 percent
Big companies do a better job than small companies in supplying the kinds of products people need.	72 percent
For most products there are really no differences among brands.	74 percent

Three conclusions are obvious:

—Those who distrust advertising are strongly in favor of governmental information on products.

—Those who see essentially no difference in brands (and therefore equate large and small manufacturers) are highly in favor of governmental participation.

—Those who tend to favor large companies also highly favor a government information program. This suggests that bigness alone, even when perceived as providing more service to the consumer, is not sufficent to counter the desire for more information from the government.

Women with the heaviest exposure to television and magazines have the highest level of agreement that more information about products should be forthcoming from the government. Note, too, that this phenomenon is slightly more closely associated with TV than with magazines.

Level of Exposure		Percent Favoring Governmental Participation
TV	Magazine	
None	none	46 percent
Low TV,	low magazine	63 percent
Low TV,	high magazine	66 percent
High TV,	low magazine	67 percent
High TV,	high magazine	73 percent

Conclusion

The current era of consumerism in this century shows every sign of continuing into the foreseeable future. A relatively dormant period similar to those that followed the two earlier eras is unlikely to occur.

It is the younger, more affluent, more discriminating members of society who are the most consumer oriented; and it is this group that will provide the continuing impetus behind the movement in the future.

The present movement is probably entering a new phase, however, in which responsibility for remedial action will rest to a much larger extent in the corporate or private sector. The newly established National Advertising Review Board is one indication of the industry's recognition of its self-regulatory obligations.

Growing consumer skepticism of the marketing process, coupled with increasing focus of the movement's attention on business and its social responsibilities, must inevitably lead to greater corporate concern with image.

Industrywide Cooperation for Consumer Affairs

●●

President
The Association of Home Appliance Manufacturers,
Chicago

Questions relative to consumer interest and welfare are often discussed within the framework of individual corporations on the one hand or the governmental level on the other hand. This paper focuses at a level between individual corporations and government in which several companies working together develop programs in the interest of consumers (whom I would rather identify as individual people or homemakers than as a category!).

Many such consumer programs are possible. Many kinds of industries can and do engage in them. There are so-called cooperative efforts among retailers, banks, and finance companies. Advertising agencies try to ameliorate the image they have created for themselves. Utility and other service industries are also having their try at it. There are even community consumer activities conducted by chambers of commerce, better business bureaus, and others.

It would be difficult to cover them all or to evaluate their effectiveness in a meaningful way in a paper of this length. Therefore, I will discuss only that industry with which I am most familiar: consumer durable goods manufacturing. This industry manufacturers major household appliances, such as refrigerators, ranges, washers, dryers, freezers, and room air conditioners; and portable appliances, such as mixers, toasters, blenders, irons, hair dryers, and others of this sort. A billion of these products are in use;

498

a million are sold annually. The companies involved account for nearly 100 percent of the production of home appliances in the United States and include such well-known names as General Electric, Frigidaire, Whirlpool, Maytag, Sunbeam, Kelvinator, Magic Chef, and Tappan, totaling some 60 corporations.

These companies have been successful in developing an extensive consumer affairs program of many parts based on close, legally proper cooperation. Their programs have been developed by top management executives from all companies in the industry—directed by the policies of their boards of directors; supported by about a thousand members of some 50 or 60 committees of professional and management people; and served by an association staff of specialists in engineering, marketing, public relations, and consumer affairs.

Available evidence indicates that our consumer concern programs genuinely benefit consumers. They are attracting commendation from some of the most caustic critics of business. Additionally, we have found that we have been one or two steps ahead of government in trying to remedy situations as they develop.

Types of Consumer Affairs Programs

The basic principle underlying these efforts is that the essential relationship between producers and consumers is one of mutual interest. It is *not* a relationship of conflict of interest as some consumers wrongly assume. Every business decision should be tested to make certain it serves this mutual interest and, in good faith, works to eliminate the possibility of conflict.

Two major areas of consumer concern activities are derived from the basic relationship. The first includes programs that precede the sale of the product to the consumer; the second is in the somewhat newer area of postsale concerns.

The consumer may not be aware of some of the activities conducted by an industry for his benefit, nor is it necessary that he be aware of them. They aid in the design, production, and distribution of good products and benefit him in his purchase and use of the product. They include market data analysis, development of product evaluation standards, and government relations.

Presale consumer affairs also include many programs directly related to homemakers as they approach their purchase decisions. Among these are industrywide self-disciplines for advertising and other practices that affect consumers, consumer education and information programs, and certification of product characteristics.

Recently postsale consumer concerns have expanded substantially in importance. Included are such cooperative efforts as assuring the availability of good repair services; providing an effective complaint handling procedure; and continuing consumer education on use, care, safety, and replacement decisions.

Presale Consumer Activities

Underlying all presale activity is the function of providing market data, which complements individual company market research programs. This provides the opportunity for an industry group to know more about its consumers than anyone else can possibly know, helps the individual company to design products and develop market strategy, and provides a basis in sound fact for industry action.

Collection and Reporting of Market Information

Working through its trade association, the appliance industry has an elaborate program for gathering reports from members, consolidating the information, and reporting industry totals without revealing individual company information. Participants get weekly, monthly, and quarterly data on total sales, geographic breakdowns, product characteristic trends, seasonal and secular movements at various levels of distribution, and some information on service experience. Serving the committees that develop the data are staff experts in marketing and the computing section of one of the nation's outstanding public accounting firms.

Development of Product Standards

A second activity in the presale area is the development of industrywide product evaluation standards. These help producers and others measure product performance so that accurate and directly comparable information can be conveyed to consumers about a product's most important characteristics. For example, in the refrigeration field measurement methods are now available to assure that a 14.4 cubic foot refrigerator means the same thing for all brands, including most imports.

Standards for safety prescribe electrical properties, thermostats and cutout switches, and mechanical precautions. Products are submitted to independent testing laboratories, such as Underwriters' Laboratories, to verify that safety standards are met.

Standards provide two benefits to the consumer: (1) better products result; (2) dependable information about the products becomes available to aid the consumer in comparing brands and making sound buying decisions.

Industry-Government Relations

Governmental relations is a third area of presale activity. In my judgment, this is one of the most important consumer affairs any industry has. Through a special government committee and five major subcommittees of the Association of Home Appliance Manufacturers, a consensus of opinion on current legislation is reached and conveyed to senators, congressmen, and the numerous administrative agencies by AHAM as the spokesman for the appliance industry.

In our experience over the last six or more years, there have been about a dozen bills which we have followed and on which we have given frequent testimony. AHAM seeks to protect industry interests in the usual sense, but also to aid as constructively as possible in providing consumer benefits as well. No one company can possibly be as effective as all companies are in joining to advocate an industry position, e.g., that the Product Safety Act of 1972 be written to include imports as well as domestic products.

Advertising Practices and Guidelines

Many industrywide cooperative activities in the presale area are directly related to the consumer himself, aiding his personal planning and purchase decisions. These activities are advertising, marketing, and selling procedures.

One of the most important of these is industrywide self-discipline in voluntary recommended advertising practices and guidelines, which the appliance industry has established for itself. The opening paragraph of these recommendations reads: "The keystone of fair advertising is HONESTY—any advertisement which is misleading or creates a false impression is not an honest advertisement." These recommendations have been accepted not only by the manufacturers but also by the owners of most of the widely distributed private brands. The home laundry industry issued the first such recommendations in 1960, and the refrigerator-freezer industry issued theirs in 1969.

To give effectiveness to these voluntary recommendations, the industry has hit upon an interesting and successful device. With the brand owners' written permission, we list the endorsing brands in pamphlets that are distributed to dealers, the trade press, consumer organizations, and anyone else who is interested. Anyone seeing an ad that appears to violate the recommendations sends it to me, and I relay the complaint to a designated officer of the company owning the brand involved. It goes without identifying the complainant and with a very clear statement that the association is officially neutral.

Over the 12 years we have been doing this, most of the recipients have agreed with the complaint and have taken corrective action. We are, however, reappraising this 12-year-old program with a view to providing more checks and balances, more input from consumer advocates, and a much broader base of coverage, especially at the local retail advertising level.

Other industry voluntary codes and guidelines include recommendations for the form of warranties and the advertising of them, the placement of nameplates on major appliances so they can be found easily, guidelines to define terms, and guidelines for establishing what is "authorized service."

Guidelines for the Consumer

In addition to voluntary guidelines for the industry, guidelines for the consumer are also developed. One, on the safe use of appliances, has resulted in a special publication, "AHAM Consumer Recommendations on the Safe Use of Appliances."

In the presale area also, the appliance industry's third party certification programs have benefited both consumer and industry by providing technical verification of facts about appliances that cannot readily be determined by examining the product on a dealer's display floor. We have three certification programs in operation and one being developed.

The association publishes a directory that lists all brands and the names of the companies—members and nonmembers—that have by contract accepted the certification program discipline. Copies are sent to dealers, libraries, the press, and consumer organizations. Buyers can check the claims made by vendors—so vendors are careful to be accurate. This is a program that needs constant review and updating and several tens of thousands of dollars budgeted each year, but it certainly has been accepted by and beneficial to everyone concerned.

One of the fascinating aspects of this work is the challenge of bringing into the programs those companies that have been skirting the edges of propriety all along. Imported products, especially, seem to present this problem. When they are converted, the producers of these imported products are usually most ardent advocates.

Consumer information and educational efforts in the presale area are of a comprehensive nature and provide authoritative information for the many people who communicate to consumers—college professors, high school teachers, women's page editors in newspapers, magazine editors, extension specialists in adult education, and so on.

In consumer education, it is fortunate for the home appliance industry that over 50 years ago the leaders of the industry recognized the genuine mutual interest between themselves and the homemakers who were their customers. Through their trade association they instituted our present consumer education program in 1921 with a booklet entitled "Laundering at Home." Since then, the program has grown. Twenty-six years ago, the industry held its first educational seminar for teachers, magazine and newspaper editors, and others who communicate directly with consumers. Called the National Home Appliance Conference, this event has become an annual affair attended by over a thousand guests of the industry. For the past three years, universities have offered graduate credit for people who attend the conference and meet specific requirements.

From these conferences and from other materials developed by the industry, we have accumulated an extensive library of informational publications, audio-visual materials, slide sets, and cassette tapes. Our current bibliography has over 140 titles, which are widely distributed on request.

As a part of our efforts, we have strongly advocated that homemaking education be included at junior high and earlier levels when children are receptive, adept, and not yet caught up in the college entrance game or in innovative movements in other directions.

There is one area of presale consumer concern that still needs attention—the training of retail sales personnel. The person selling stoves should know how to cook—and actually do it regularly; the person selling washers should be able to teach laundering. This is a fertile field in which very little work has been done.

Postsale Consumer Concerns

The second general area of industrywide consumer-oriented programs—postsale concerns—is not new for most industries, but the burgeoning of its importance has given it an entirely new perspective. Effective, meaningful and far-reaching consumer education in the postsale area is as important as in the presale. The emphasis, of course, is different. It deals with use, care, safety, and replacement decisions.

There are two other activities that are especially important: making good repair service available when it is needed, and providing effective compliant-handling procedures.

Good Repair Service

Every brand has its own design, its own distribution channels, and its own policy with regard to warranties and service contracts. Each company must develop its own structure for providing service. The association's function is to perform certain supporting functions. Accordingly, we have devised a curriculum for vocational schools to train appliance repairmen, and we have produced a movie to explain the nature of a career in this field. We have distributed these and provided lists of schools from which candidates may select. We have also held seminars on service and have formed a speakers' bureau, which uses member company executives and our own staff as speakers. The AHAM Service Committee has prepared and published a booklet entitled, "Your Career as an Appliance Service Technician."

The service problem may never be totally solved, but, after working on it for nearly 15 years, we believe that the structure is better than it would have been without our efforts.

Effective Complaint Handling

The other postsale consumer activity—providing an effective complaint-handling procedure—is an extremely important one. It is probably the most responsible consumer activity we in the appliance industry have undertaken.

About three years ago the chairman of our consumer Affairs Committee proposed the formation of a panel of consumer-oriented people, entirely independent of the industry or any part of its distribution structure. Perfecting the plan involved persuading various members of the industry to participate and getting cosponsorship from two other industry groups—the gas range industry association and an association of retail merchants who buy appliances from manufacturers and sell them to homemakers. The result was the creation of the Major Appliance Consumer Action Panel (MACAP). Panel members are academic and consumer-organization people, who serve without personal compensation (except travel expenses). In some two-and-a-half years they have received over 6500 of the industry's toughest problems and brought over 70 percent of them to a satisfactory conclusion. Most of the remainder are still in process and will probably be satisfactorily resolved too. Our Consumer Affairs Board and similar groups in the other sponsoring associations provide industry liaison with MACAP. Our Consumer Affairs Department provides staff services for MACAP.

In the careful study the panel gives each complaint, each consumer receives personal attention. This is a unique feature of MACAP, since consumer problems are most commonly considered in classes and groups. Not only does the panel offer this personal concern, but when the complaint reaches the company involved, it goes to the top executive and he, himself, reviews that specific problem and follows through to solution.

Member companies take great pride in responding quickly and correctly to MACAP requests. Companies reserve the right not to be bound by MACAP's recommendations. Sometimes, although rarely, they refuse, but usually they are in complete agreement.

MACAP has earned the respect of the industry and the gratitude of the consumers with whom they have dealt. It has made several recommdations to industry, and industry, almost without exception, has welcomed the input and acted favorably on the recommendations. MACAP has attracted national recognition, as evidenced by such comments as those of Virginia Knauer, Special Assistant to the President for Consumer Affairs. She said:

> Of great significance in the appliance industry outlook is MACAP, the Major Appliance Consumer Action Panel. There is more to MACAP than the figures of complaints resolved. For the first time, a number of major industry organizations undertook a very real risk. The industry organizations undertook these risks and it paid off. MACAP did differ with the industry on legislation, but in differing, it demonstrated its creditiblity. And in demonstrating its credibility, it showed the public it was a true consumer representative. Moreover, not only did it help resolve complaints, but it gave industry some very sophisticated suggestions as to how service and warranties could be improved for the consumer. I have been so pleased with MACAP's performances that I have recommended that other industries study it for possible adaptation."[1]

The companies we work with are competitors. They vie with one another to capture sales. In most situations consumers benefit from these efforts as one company seeks to develop a better product or to offer it at a lower price, or to create an innovative approach. Vigorous competition is basically good, socially desirable, and should be encouraged. Vigorous competition, however, makes it all the more challenging to accomplish proper and legal cooperation. At the outset of any project, there are always as many views as people. Communications are difficult and emotions tend to clash. As one of the corporate officers in our industry put it: "Cooperative

[1] Virginia Knauer, address at the Appliance Suppliers' Exhibit and Conference, Chicago, June 19, 1972.

industry activity is a fragile thing, held together only by the ability of the leading personalities to find their way tactfully and patiently through the maze of alternatives which face the group."[2]

You will note that I have made no mention of advertising or public relations campaigns to "create a good image" or explain "our side of the story." We use the tools of the publicity trades copiously, but do not depend on them to substitute for sound principles at the foundation.

Juel Ranum, Vice-president, Corporate and Public Affairs of the Whirlpool Corporation, said the same thing this way in a recent talk: "The first tenet of our social responsibiilty is insuring that our products and services give fair value and live up to their expectations."[3]

Conclusions

If your work leads you into industrywide efforts in the interest of consumers, and I hope it does, let me offer you these very important considerations.

—First, welcome all the comments and criticism and input you can get from those who are set up to represent consumers. They are helpful and have a great ability to point up key issues. However, remember that in those ranks there are as many self-interests as in business and each must be evaluated accordingly. Remember also that business has an opportunity, if it uses it, to know more about consumers than all the consumer representatives put together. I am referring not only to market research information, but also to acceptance or rejection in the market place, and the opportunity to analyze complaints and repair and service records.

—Second, remember that each industry is inherently different from all the others. I have described for you today a number of programs and activities developed by the appliance industry. They are specifically applied in depth to that industry. These cannot be copied by another industry and result in effective programs for the consumer. Variations must be developed and adapted to the industry.

—Third, remember that industry cooperation requires an advanced de-

---

[2]Michael S. Hunt, "Note on the Major Home Appliance Industry," Harvard University, Graduate School of Business Administration, November 1972, sec. 2, p. 3.

[3]Juel Ranum, address at the Business and Society Conference on Corporate Responsibility, New York, October 1972.

gree of sophistication and high-level policy backing from each company.

—Finally, avoid any action that tends to make decisions for consumers or to restrict the range of choice. Both inside and outside of government and even in industry circles, there are proposals for dictating which product or service characteristics should be permitted and which should be prohibited in the marketplace. There are advocates of prescribing which facts should be given consumers and in what forms—and which claims, even if accurate and true, should not be presented.

In voluntary industrywide programs it is easy to approach these things wthout fully being aware of it. Be sure you have capable and thorough legal counsel, because certain collective actions are illegal. Sometimes the line is subtle or obscure.

I would urge that, even within the legal bounds, you base your decisions on the philosophy presented at one of our conferences by David Schoenfeld, author of *The Consumer and His Dollar* and former Educational Director of the staff of The Special Assistant to the President for Consumer Affairs. He said:

> Let it be clearly understood that the objective is not the direction of consumer choices. Rather it is to expose the individual to all of the alternatives and the opportunities that are available to him and thus enable him to make a more rational choice predicted on his own individual needs. If that same individual, after considering the alternatives, makes what seems to another to be a bizarre decision, that is his prerogative.[4]

[4]David Schoenfeld, address at the National Home Appliance Conference, Denver, October 26, 1968.

PART VI. D

Interaction Between Business and Other Social Institutions

●●●

> I think the corporation today is the basic source of generic power and has the greatest ability either for ill or for good to turn this country around.
>
> —Ralph Nader

The current discontent with corporate performance or lack of social responsiveness has caused certain established groups to join forces with a host of new groups to battle with the corporations and their managements in order to modify their behavior. While it is understandable that new causes create new groups and leaders to fight for them, the change of direction of hitherto established groups in particularly disturbing from the viewpoint of the corporation. On the one hand, it is an indication of the loss of support within the system, which raises the question of legitimacy of power. On the other hand, it makes the conflict broader and that much more difficult to resolve in terms considered reasonable by the corporations.

The most notable of the established groups who have added their voices for corporate reform are the church[1] and the university. To these have been added a whole new set of groups drawn from various professions who operate under the rubric of "public interest," e.g., public interest law firms. The nature of these groups' involvement in social problems in the advocacy position is still in the evolutionary stage. It is

---

[1] For an analysis of the involvement of the church in social confrontation with large corporations, see S. Prakash Sethi, "The Corporation and the Church: Institutional Conflict and Social Responsibility in a Period of Transition," in Dow Votaw and S. Prakash Sethi, *The Corporate Dilemma: Traditional Values versus Contemporary Problems* (Englewood Cliffs, N.J.: Prentice-Hall, 1973), pp. 118–141.

509

not clear what form these groups will ultimately take and what, if any, its side effects will be on the performance of the social system as a whole. However, the phenomenon is rapidly expanding and therefore deserves serious attention.

In the first article in this section, Frank White and Tim Smith talk about the role of the church vis-a-vis corporate responsibility. They realize that institutional investors hold 40 percent of outstanding shares of the nation's major corporate stock. Of these institutional investors, churches with their holdings of $3 billion (book value, not market price) are among the largest ones. They question whether the institutional investor gets involved in the recent wave of social responsibility, divorcing the old, well-known economic criterion of investment in favor of a new one based on social responsibility of business. Describing the recent evolutionary processes in church investment policy, they note there are many practical obstacles. For example, the fact that most of the church's wealth managers are corporate executives, and even the selling of the new investment idea may be a hard task. This is due to legal responsibilities and restrictions as well as moral obligations or convictions. Then, this means that the church has to do a lot of rethinking and reexamining about the management makeup for their funds; whether they need an independent manager or other options. At any rate, they note that the question of criteria in itself is a rather important and complicated one, once economic criteria are abandoned. Regarding the means of measuring a corporation's social responsibility for investment purposes, nothing has been developed yet; it could take a long time to develop such measures. However, the authors indicate that, once the policy procedures and the investment criteria are developed, six strategy alternatives for the implementation of goals or targets are available: petition, divestiture, incentive investment, the proxy machinery, stockholder's class action suits, and combined option.

Marshall Patner's paper, in fact, is a progress report of Business for the Public Interest (BPI). He indicates that, although business supports BPI's action by financing its expenses as a nonprofit organization, BPI's prime concern is attacking business' socially irresponsible actions. BPI, despite its limited staff, has recently brought many of the wrongdoings of business to public attention. In many instances, BPI has entered into court action or legislation for true public interest. The Sears Tower project, opposition to election fraud, the case of legislators and horse racing, and air pollution in Gary are just a few in the long list of their actions. Patner ends the paper with the significant note that BPI is working within the system and is interested in working with government agency officials to inform them or to be informed, to be able to act as an outside conscience of the business community in favor of public interest.

SELECTED BIBLIOGRAPHY

Bachrach, Peter. "Corporate Authority and Democratic Theory." *In Political Theory and Social Change*, edited by David Spitz. New York: Atherton Press, 1967, pp. 257–273.

*Barnett, Rosalind C., and Tagiuri, Renato. "What Young People Think About Managers." *Harvard Business Review*, May-June 1973, pp. 106–118.

*Bunke, Harvey. "Priests Without Cossacks." *Harvard Business Review*, May-June 1965, 103–109.

Fichter, Joseph H. "American Religion and the Negro." *Daedalus* 94 (Fall 1965), 1085–1106.

*Hickel, Walter J. *Who Owns America?* Englewood Cliffs, N.J.: Prenctice-Hall, 1971.

Mace, Myles. *Directors: Myth and Reality*. Cambridge: Harvard Business School, 1971.

*McDonald, D. "The Church and Society." *Center Magazine*, July 1968, 28–35.

Malkiel, B. G., and Quandt, R. E. "Moral Issues in Investment Policy." *Harvard Business Review*, March-April 1971, pp. 37–47.

Monsen, R. Joseph. "The Unrecognized Social Revolution: The Rise of the New Business Elite in America." *California Management Review* 14, no. 2 (Winter 1971): 13–17.

Mowry, Charles E. *The Church and the New Generation*. Nashville: Abingdon Press, 1969.

Nader, Ralph, and Ross, Donald. *Action for a Change: A Student's Manual for Public Interest Organizing*. New York: Grossman, 1971.

New York Stock Exchange. *The Corporate Director and the Investing Public*. New York: New York Stock Exchange, 1965.

Niebuhr, R. H. *Christian Realism and Political Problems*. New York: Charles Scribner's, Sons, 1953.

O'Dea, Thomas F. "The Crisis of the Contemporary Religious Consciousness." *Daedalus* 96, no. 1 (Winter 1967): 116–134.

Rahner, Karl. "Christians in the Modern World." In *Mission and Grace* 1, edited by Karl Rahner. London: Sheed & Ward, Stag Books, 1963.

Schulze, Robert J. "The Role of Economic Dominants in Community Power Structure." *American Sociological Review* 23 (February 1958): 3–9.

Selekman, Sylvia K., and Selekman, Benjamin M. *Power and Morality in a Business Society*. New York: McGraw-Hill Book Co., 1956.

*Sethi, S. Prakash. *Business Corporations and the Black Man: An Analysis of Social Conflict, the Kodak-Fight Controversy*. Scranton, Pa.: Chandler, 1970.

_____. "The Corporation and the Church: Institutional Conflict and Social Responsibility." *California Management Review* 15, no. 1 (Fall 1972): 63–74.

*_____. *Up Against the Corporate Wall: Modern Corporations and Social Issues of the Seventies*. 2d ed. Englewood Cliffs, N. J.: Prentice-Hall, 1974.

*Especially recommended for an overall view and for authoritative viewpoints on different perspectives of the issues covered.

_____. *See also* Votaw, Dow.

*Simon, John G.; Powers, Charles W.; and Gunneman, Jon P. *The Ethical Investor*. New Haven, Conn.: Yale University Press, 1972.

Sleeper, C. Freeman. *Black Power and Christian Responsibility*. Nashville: Abingdon Press, 1969.

*Tannenbaum, Frank. "Institutional Rivalry in Society." *Political Science Quarterly*, December 1946, pp. 481–504.

Vanderwicken, Peter. "Change Invades the Board Room." *Fortune*, May 1957, p. 156.

*Votaw, Dow, and Sethi, S. Prakash. *The Corporate Dilemma: Traditional Values versus Contemporary Problems*. Englewood Cliffs, N.J.: Prentice-Hall, 1973.

Zeigler, Harmon. *Interest Groups in American Society*. Englewood Cliffs, N.J.: Prentice-Hall, 1964.

Corporate Responsibility and the Church

●●

● FRANK WHITE

Director
Corporate Information Center
National Council of Churches, New York City

● TIM SMITH

Executive Secretary
Interfaith Committee on Social Responsibility
in Investments
National Council of Churches, New York City

America is now in the midst of its second revolution, a revolution borne on the shoulders of a "movement" that seeks a radically altered view of life, liberty, and the pursuit of happiness. It is most visible in the struggles for justice, peace, and a more humane community.

Sparked by growing public concern over the rape of our environment, a new part of this movement is spreading to include those not previously committed. Today, ordinary people are becoming conscious of the fact that a great deal of economic power, in the hands of a relatively small number of people, is influencing and making major decisions that affect their lives negatively.

Minority groups have known about this power for decades, because it has determined through imposed restrictions where they must live and work and play—even what kind of work they must do. Antiwar groups have tried to warn the American public for years that inordinate amounts of this

513

power, which could be used for the betterment of life, are used for the research and development of the implements of death.

But now our air and water and food are being affected. Finally, the public is beginning to smell and feel and taste the results of corporate decision making. Restlessness is causing us to raise fundamental questions about our economic and political systems.

As James Reston wrote recently in *The New York Times*, many are beginning to see the "environmental crisis" as raising "fundamental political, economic, and philosophical questions," such as "who should pay" for eliminating pollution, or "what personal and corporate uses of private property are considered to be in conflict with the public interest and a healthy environment. . . ." Reston touches on sacred ground by asking how the implicit need for national planning in the environment area will challenge "not only the private interests of powerful forces in the United States" but also "long established concepts of the rights of private property in capitalist society."[1]

This new part of the movement is called the movement for corporate responsibility. It means that corporate decision makers should begin to consider the social implications of their decisions as carefully and with as much weight as they do the economic. It says that life and death are more important than profit and loss.

Will the Corporate Responsibility Movement Succeed?

Many factors, some perhaps as yet unseen, will answer this question. At least three are important: the mind set of future corporate managers, the degree of local or community interest and action, and the degree of willingness of large institutional investors to become involved.

Although the first two above are extremely important, our concern here is with the third factor: support for advocates of corporate responsibility by the economic power of large institutional investors. Today, institutional investors hold nearly 40 percent of the outstanding shares of the nation's major corporate stock, as reported in The *Institutional Investor*.[2] Commenting on the growing public concern for corporate responsibility, the article said, "If the forces of public concern go against a company which

---

[1]Cited in *Corporate Responsibility and Religious Institutions: Information and Action Documents*, 2d ed. (New York: Corporate Information Center, National Council of Churches, 1971), p. 1.

[2]*Ibid.*, pp. 1–2.

places a great premium on growth but has little concern about how that growth is achieved, for instance, it will be in all probability reflected in the value the market sets on that company."

Following the student demonstration and fire at the Isla Vista branch of the Bank of America in February 1971, Bank of America Executive Vice-president Robert Truex had this to say:

> Until society's institutions are willing to bring to the problems of our society the same fervor and concern reflected by our young people, the best we can hope for is some kind of uneasy and very temporary stalemate. It is strikingly apparent that profitability in and of itself is no longer adequate as the sole determinant of corporate success.[3]

J. Richardson Dilforth, Chairman of Yale's Finance Committee, stated, "It is increasingly clear that there is going to be more concern with social conscience in the investment decision—unless we go back to the cave age."[4] A professor of investment at Harvard Business School, Colyer Crum, argued that it will no longer be a viable possibility for investment managers to use the traditional argument, "I am a money manager and damn the public consequences." Crum continued, "You are going to have to build some kind of credibility, you are going to have to vote against the managers, you are going to have to do some arm twisting in the public interest. An institutional investment manager who chooses not to get involved at this time is going to have a tough row to hoe."[5]

The question remains: Will institutional investors get involved? We will deal with one—the church.

For almost three years, the Corporate Information Center at the National Council of Churches (NCC) has been researching the extent and composition of church investments at national and local levels and has begun to learn, through trial and error, a new science—researching the social impact of American corporate power at home and abroad. During the past year, eight major Protestant denominations formed the Interfaith Committee on Social Responsibility in Investments. The purpose of this group, consisting of treasurers and mission executives, is to plan church action in the corporate responsibility field. The goal of both groups has been and continues to be to work with those in the church who believe that our institution's money (investments) should be where its mouth (teachings, proclamations, and policies) is. Today it is not. Can it be?

[3]*Ibid.*, p. 2.
[4]*Ibid.*
[5]*Ibid.*

The church is important in the battle for corporate responsibility for two reasons. First, of all the potential institutional participants in that battle, such as foundations and universities, the church sees itself in society as a locus of moral and ethical initiative. On this basis, the church is vulnerable to raising the issue. Second, the church has clout. Church wealth has recently been estimated at over $160 billion, more than the combined wealth of AT&T plus the five leading U.S. oil companies. It is second only to the federal government in monies received and distributed yearly—over $22 billion. In New York City alone, church assets exceed $700 million in value. One church—Trinity Episcopal on Wall Street—owns 18 major business buildings plus the Standard and Poor Building, $50 million worth of commercial assets, plus its own building and graveyard valued at over $40 million.

There is a history of church involvement in the use of its invested wealth as an expression of stated moral or ethical policy. For years, many church finance committees have refused to purchase stock in the tobacco and liquor industries. Internationally, the church did take seriously the challenge in 1966 of a campaign against South African investments. The First National City Bank of New York lost a $10 million Methodist church account. Several other church organizations also removed accounts from the banks involved.

In 1967, the Eastman Kodak Company was involved in a labor dispute that centered around its hiring practices of unskilled minority workers in Rochester. The church became involved on the minority side by withholding proxies from management and speaking out at the stockholders' meeting. This proxy fight showed that the holdings in that one company of the church groups involved (United Presbyterian USA, Reformed Church in America, Episcopal Church, United Church of Christ, United Methodist Church) amounted to $2.7 million.

The issue of church investments is emerging as a key test of the moral and ethical dimensions of investment. Most major denominations and the NCC now have developed and issued statements on social investment guidelines. These guidelines deal with five basic areas of corporate policy:

(1) minority group employment policies of a company;
(2) amount of production of military goods and types of weapons;
(3) amount of environmental pollution caused by a company and its products;
(4) effect on the lives of people in underdeveloped lands of a company's investment policies; and
(5) consumer health and safety issues.

On the military-defense issue, a background paper to the NCC policy statement, "Defense and Disarmament: New Requirements for Security," states:

> The vast use of our money, manpower, natural resources, expertise, and energy for defense related purposes removes these resources from work in mainly constructive uses, and perpetuates the long-standing, neglective, increasingly dangerous domestic problems—the power and influence that inevitably accompany the control of such a large portion of our natural resources mean military considerations now influence virtually all other national decisions . . . there is a need for a new establishment of priorities between the claims of military defense and the claims of human rights and values.[6]

Seven of the major denominations represented in the NCC have investments of nearly $150 million in 13 of the major corporations included in the Department of Defense's list of the 50 top defense contractors.

Second, the race issues: "Churches and their agencies should examine their investment portfolios to determine if funds are invested in enterprises which practice racial discrimination, and to remove such investments from enterprises which cannot be persuaded to cease and desist from practicing racial discrimination." This was one of the 1963 National Council of Churches' General Assembly resolutions, entitled "A Call for Action to Meet the Crisis in Race Relations."

Finally, another NCC policy statement, "World Poverty and the Demands of Justice," speaks directly to the foreign investment question:

> Careful studies have shown that many interests have, in fact, controlled the operation of the United States and other Western nations in providing development aid. Military security, the maintenance or extension of power and prestige, and economic advantage have been the chief ones. . . . Any preoccupation merely with dollars given, with quick profits and with "American know-how" should give way to the long range nurturing of economic institutions and leadership conducive to the economic prosperity of the country or region involved. . . .[7]

The tasks ahead for the new committees and other groups tackling the issue of church involvement in corporate responsibility will not be easy. These tasks will fall into three basic categories. Proponents of the use of invested church wealth as a new instrument of mission and church action must (1) sell the concept, (2) determine criteria for selecting companies to

[6]*Ibid.*, pp. 23–24.
[7]*Ibid.*, p. 24.

examine, and (3) choose between varying strategies for action. The first issue is probably the most difficult to accomplish.

Task 1: Selling the Concept

Unfortunately, there has developed over the years a sizable organizational split between church policy makers and those who actually control the invested wealth of major church agencies. Most policy makers and executives are clergymen. However, a recent study of the investment committees of the boards and agencies of seven major denominations showed a different picture in the area of church investment policy.[8] The total number of finance committee members of the boards and agencies studied was 123. The estimated amount of securities controlled by these men was close to $3 million (actual figure, $2,847,986,921), and this figure was actually low as several of the totals reflected book or original value, not market value.

Of the 123 finance committee members, 87 percent (106) were men from the general world of business and finance. The breakdown was as follows: businessmen, 47 percent; bankers, 20 percent; corporate lawyers, 13 percent; church employees, 13 percent; and business school faculty, 5 percent. Of the 13 percent (17) employed by the church, only 8 were clergymen. Most of the businessmen managing this church wealth are top corporate executives. Following is a partial list of job titles taken from the study:

> Board Chairman, Price Waterhouse (retired)
> Treasurer, Eastman Kodak
> Vice-president, Dun and Bradstreet (retired)
> Executive Vice-president, Chemical Bank New York Trust Company (retired)
> President, First Federal Savings and Loan Association
> Vice-president, Manufacturers Hanover Trust Company
> Board Chairman, Bank of New York (retired)
> First Vice-president, Federal Reserve Bank of New York
> Treasurer, Provident Mutual Life Insurance Company
> President, National Life and Accident Insurance Company

The attitude of these men is vitally important in terms of assessing church involvement in the corporate responsibility movement. They will have to be convinced of the legitimacy of using social criteria in portfolio selection. They will raise or be confronted with many legal questions re-

---

[8]*Ibid.*, p. 25.

lated to their assigned tasks as investment stewards. Nonetheless, if the churches are to bridge the gap between their stated moral positions and their investment policies, these issues of social responsibility must be faced, and church investment committees must be expanded to include people who are not white male Americans over 50. At present, such committees are blatantly unrepresentative.

Aggressive Fund Management and Legal Hurdles

The financial investment policies of money managers in the church and other institutions, as they relate to growth potential and use restrictions, provide important background to the new movement for social criteria in investment. An investment committee that worked for the growth of income and principal would make available more money for effective programs. Some of the traditional assumptions held by institutional trustees and investment committee members included under the heading of "the prudent man rule" are now being questioned. It is interesting to note that, in the previously mentioned study, the average rate of return on 12 of the fifteen portfolios studied was 4.21 percent.

A recent Ford Foundation study (1969) dealing with the management of educational endowment funds, but which can be even more strongly applied to the church funds, opens by describing the typical fund trustee or manager:

> As a group they are conservative, and some of them have insisted that their only duty is to safeguard the original dollar value of the funds entrusted to their care. Like the cautious servant in the parable of the talents, they have been well pleased to bury their funds, complacent in the belief that if their talents cannot multiply under their supervision at least they will not be lost. But their talents have been lost, a little each year, as surely as if they were squandered or thrown away.[9]

Aggressive fiscal policies have traditionally been considered "irresponsible" by most finance committee members. If these men have been less than receptive to more aggressive fund management, they have reacted even more strongly against suggestions that the funds under their control be used for social purposes. They have many answers for those who ask why. The answers have often overwhelmed those who cannot claim any special knowledge of such matters; they are impressively framed in "legal" basis and "good business" rules.

A second book in the Ford Foundation series subjects many of these im-

[9]*Ibid.*, p. 27.

portant "truths" to the light of research and analysis. For example, many student groups, when demanding that trustees of their educational institutions use endowment funds for social purposes, have been blocked with the claim that the funds are untouchable because the original donor restricted their use. Again after much study, the authors conclude:

> . . . that in the case of endowment funds which have in the past been classified as restricted as to principal it will frequently be found after careful re-examination that the classification was imposed by the Board of Trustees itself or by an unduly conservative interpretation of the instrument of gift.[10]

This study also contains some revealing and challenging discussions on other commonly held and practiced views of sound portfolio management, such as the impropriety of turnover, the sanctity of "blue chips," the importance of portfolio diversity, and democratic or committee management versus the single professional manager.

Although the second Ford study deals with educational institutions, it is important to note that the church is legally in a stronger position to use its unrestricted funds for social purposes than an educational or any other institution. For example, because the mission of the church includes "caring for the poor," it has the inherent power to use, even to give away, non-restricted funds on behalf of the poor.

The Ford studies support this view. One statement deals with intent and, while specifically directed at the controllers of educational institutions, applies even more to the church: "It is our impression that any educational institution that is *willing* to make the effort may well find a substantial portion of its endowment unencumbered by such restrictions."

One of the most often heard "legal" arguments presented to those who request new uses of endowment funds for social programs is that trustees are prohibited by law from spending any principal. It is commonly known that the law does indeed state that only income from an endowment fund can be spent. The principal must remain inviolate. The question remains, however, whether capital gains or realized appreciation constitute income or principal. The 1969 Ford study, prepared by two lawyers from a New York firm and backed by an advisory committee of "lawyers distinguished for their understanding of the field of charitable corporations," deals specifically with this question. After thorough research and documentation, they conclude:

> . . . there is no substantial authority under existing law to support the widely held view that the realized gains of endowment funds of educational institu-

[10]*Ibid.*

tions must be treated as principal. No case has been found that holds that such an institution does not have the legal right to determine for itself whether to retain all such gains or to expend a prudent part. We submit that there is no reason why the law should deny educational institutions that flexibility.[11]

This study challenges many other supposedly "legal" restrictions such as "past inviability of principal," which holds that any funds previously available for use but which were instead placed in endowments by the institution that received them "can never be removed." The study claims that this rule is:

> an exercise in sophistry because accumulations of gains in endowment cannot realistically be said to be a conscious commitment by an institution which is unaware of its right to spend them. Even if it were, it would be unreasonable for the law to use the choice of one generation of directors in an internal manner such as this to tie the hands of all future directors through all enternity.[12]

Other questions such as the doctrine of "absolute ownership," the donor's intent, and "the prudent man rule" itself are challenged.

In considering church involvement in corporate responsibility, one conclusion of this study of endowment funds is very important: Legal impediments that have been thought to deprive managers of their freedom of action appear on analysis to be more legendary than real.

Other Hurdles

Aside from the difficulty of obtaining acceptance of new ideas from already existing finance committee members, another problem will be in dealing with the investment advisors. While the finance committees have over-all control, day-to-day investment decisions are made, in most cases, by such prestigious institutions as the Chase Manhattan Bank, Brown Brothers, Harriman & Company, U.S. Trust Company, or Morgan Guaranty Trust Company.

Involvement of these institutions presents additional problems for the advocates of change as well as for the institutions themselves. Such institutions may refuse to be limited in their decision-making processes by social criteria, or to be placed in the embarrassing position of blackballing a large customer. Conflicts such as these could necessitate the hiring of an independent investment manager by a church committee.

Churches will have to rethink and reexamine the financial policies of

[11]*Ibid.*, p. 28.
[12]*Ibid.*, p. 29.

their present investment committees. New committees or members may be needed who are willing to pursue more aggressive fund management and to broaden the scope of the church's investment task. Readiness to use the funds under their control in new ways and for new purposes will have to replace the overemphasis on security.

Finally, the church will have to solidify these changes with a new and effective educational process for its constituency. The use of church funds in the corporate responsibility struggle provides vast moral educational possibilities. Mass constituency support is an important criterion for the success of the effort.

Task 2: Determining Criteria

An article in *The Institutional Investor* stated that many of the people interviewed (money managers and fund officers) argued that they had "neither the tools nor the guidelines to make anything other than economically based judgments."[13] The same questions about competence in making social judgments apply to those who now control the church's wealth. This lack of ability is partly a result of the newness of the issue. Until recently there has been very little research done on the social impact of U.S. business. Today that picture is changing.

Information that is needed to establish guidelines and criteria is rapidly becoming available, and there is an immense amount needed for such decisions. There are many thousands of companies, all of which are investment opportunities, on which information must be obtained. This information must be readily available so that criteria levels can be raised and/or lowered and companies moved from unacceptable to acceptable investment options, or vice versa. The use of computers is almost a certainty and could stimulate a new type of social-information industry. At present, the church is just beginning to work out basic rating systems. The Corporate Information Center at NCC is attempting to develop test models for such criteria. Ten years from now, these Dun and Bradstreet type operations will be able to give clients instant social ratings.

It will be necessary to work out methods of criteria application that include all five areas of social concern. For example: Is a company acceptable that institutes a commendable minority hiring and training program, has

[13]*Ibid.*, p. 30.

only minimal Department of Defense contracts, but continues to pollute its surrounding air and waterways?

Task 3: Choosing Strategy Options

When the decision has been made to set up new investment policy procedures and criteria have been developed six strategy options are then available: petition, divestiture, incentive investment, proxy options, stockholder class action suits, or a combination of options.

(1) Petition. Church officials might confront specific corporation managements by letter or in person on questions of social or moral policy. Last year Gulf and Mobil Oil, after consultation with church officials, agreed to publish detailed information on their operations in South Africa.

(2) Divestiture. This is basically the approach used by the church in relation to investments in tobacco and liquor. It is a refusal to buy stock of any company that falls below established criteria levels. Divestiture is generally seen by churches as a last resort.

(3) Incentive investment. Here the results may be similar to divestiture, but the thrust is more positive and involves seeking out established or new companies whose policies and products are above the institution's criteria levels. This might be called "creative capital investment"; it rewards corporate responsibility.

(4) The proxy option. It is obvious that any institution that holds shares of stock in a company has the right to file stockholder resolutions, attend stockholder meetings, and express points of view. A question often raised today is: Are points of view concerning political or social decisions of management appropriate in stockholder meetings? In 1935 the Securities and Exchange Act was passed by Congress. Section 14a of that law dealt with the protection of the stockholders' right to petition companies in which they held stocks. In 1951 a civil rights group of Greyhound Bus Company stockholders petitioned that company to allow its stockholders to vote on the question of segregated seating within Greyhound buses. The company refused. The group then petitioned the Securities Exchange Commission (SEC) under section 14a and was again refused permission on the grounds that moral and political questions were not intended within the context of 14a. That SEC decision was only recently tested in the courts. In July 1970, Justice Tamm of the U.S. Circuit Court of Appeals in Washington, D.C., handed down a potentially important

decision, which could affect stockholders' rights. The case was brought by the Medical Commission on Human Rights, who had petitioned the SEC to allow stockholders of the Dow Chemical Corporation to vote on continued production of napalm. The SEC turned down their request, and the medical group brought their case to the courts. Justice Tamm's decision, in effect, sided with the prosecutors and implied that the SEC should have been an ally of the stockholders under section 14a (when, in fact, it had sided with the company) and that the SEC should review its administrative policies in this area and, in light of that review, reconsider the Medical Commission's case.

Even prior to that decision, Campaign GM (the Project on Corporate Responsibility) began a new action strategy. Although the General Motors Corporation spent considerable amounts of money in a successful drive to defeat the specific aims of this project, reliable sources within GM have admitted privately that the repercussions from that challenge caused significant internal struggles within management circles. The corporation's announcement that four of its board members would review issues in the public interest and the appointment of the Reverend Leon Sullivan, a black job-training specialist, to the Board of Directors show a new concern over public interest.

Although more study and legal interpretation seem inevitable, today the proxy option is a viable strategy for use by church institutions that wish to act independently or in concert with other groups to make their views known and to influence corporate decisions.

(5) Stockholder class action suits. This new, growing form of legal action is a strong possible option for church groups. A class action simply means that any stockholder may bring suit against a corporation for violation of the law in the area of the "human rights" of "life, liberty, and the pursuit of happiness." The implications for such suits in the fields of pollution and consumer interests are obvious, but other areas, such as production of certain weapons and their use, are not excluded.

(6) Combined options. An institutional investor could participate in a proxy confrontation calling for some specific change in corporate policy with the added threat of public divestiture to help make his point. A new investment policy could utilize all five options, thus having great flexibility to encourage and reward corporate responsibility while, at the same time, retaining its ability to speak out against human and/or environmental exploitation.

Conclusions

Those who hope for or even expect the church to assume a leadership role in this new form of social action may be disappointed. And yet, if the church doesn't, who will? If other institutions do and the church does not, the church will have effectively abdicated its role in society as protector and standard bearer of morality.

In the days ahead, the churches will continue to be called upon to act. As one looks at the growing number of churches, nationally and locally, that are actively involved in the corporate responsibility movement, it is clear that the snowball has started to roll and will not be stopped. The future will see more church action and protest in the major areas of corporate responsibility—ecology, South Africa, minority empowerment, the war, and discrimination against women. New forms of pressure will be exerted. The assessment in Christiandom will grow that change no longer comes through individual acts of charity, but as we change systems. Corporations naturally fall under the miscroscope of church scrutiny and will continue to do so as churches try to change systems around them.

The future will see more vigorous interaction between church and corporation, not less.

Business and the Public Interest Law Firm

●●

● MARSHALL PATNER
General Counsel
Businessmen for the Public Interest, Chicago

I work with an unusual group—Businessmen for the Public Interest (BPI).[1] The name of our group contains the word "businessmen" because a good part of our support comes from business, yet a good part of our work is devoted to exposing questionable business practices. In fact, we often tangle with companies that might otherwise support us. We are, therefore, in an unusual position in the community, and I want to tell you something about that, about who we are, who supports us, and about what we do, and how we go about doing it.

BPI was formed in early 1969. Gordon Sherman (then with Midas International), who was our first president and a special inspiration, created a fine Latin motto for us, *Age Aliquid,* "Do Something." We are a Chicago-based nonprofit organization, combining research and legal action to right environmental wrongs and corruptive political and legal practices.

BPI has a full-time, professional staff of three lawyers and a scientist. The staff has a continuing working relationship with students in professional schools, in law and business, and from colleges and universities, in journalism and various fields. We now have a somewhat unique relationship with the Law School of Northwestern Universtiy: Six students work with

---

[1]Presently entitled "Business and Professional People for the Public Interest"; still known as "BPI."

us full time for law school credit, and a member of the faculty joins our staff for the period of the school semester.

BPI is a not-for-profit corporation and tax-exempt under IRS section 501(c) (3). We are supported by contributions from some 30 businesses and a number of foundations, all from the greater Chicago area. We are seeking wider support and would like to see other communities with a BPI operation.

We develop issues, some from referrals from agencies, some on behalf of citizen groups, some from the supporting business community and our own perceptions. We carefully research and analyze each issue, using business, law, and management techniques before we act. We consider and employ negotiation, exposure, and litigation alternatives. I will summarize some of BPI's achievements and continuing projects in our first three years.

The Sears Tower Project

When it appeared that the proposed Sears Tower in Chicago would cause significant "ghosting" of thousands of television sets in the Chicago area, and no one else would take action, BPI and the Illinois Citizens for Better Broadcasting issued a series of public reports on the situation and filed a formal complaint with the Federal Communications Commission.

> The Commission declined jurisdiction on the ground that it lacked power to deal with interference to TV reception caused by tall buildings, a position the courts upheld. Nonetheless, the reports led to a public furor that ultimately forced Sears Roebuck Company to reverse its position and agree to provide antennas atop its building for the stations that desired to move, thereby avoiding the ghosting problem for those stations.[2]

Also, on the Sears Tower project, after careful research we exposed the fact that Sears had been able to acquire the land for the building by using a "front man"—a Chicago manipulator who obtained an alley from the city for the company at a "knockdown" price. After that publicity, other companies, including IBM, had to renegotiate and pay fair prices for city land.

Opposing Election Fraud

In the primary election in Chicago in spring 1972, a pattern of misconduct by election officials became apparent. BPI lawyers filed emergency suits on behalf of the Independent Voters of Illinois and others to obtain voting

²BPI, *Third Report, 1971–1972* (Chicago: BPI, 1972), p. 17.

records, for access by poll watchers and challengers to polling places, and for a balanced system of appointment of election judges.

> Relief was obtained in several of the suits, notably an unprecedented federal court order permitting inspection of thousands of registration cards. As a result of the inspection, carried out by scores of volunteers, we were able to demonstrate massive fraud in the circulation of nominating petitions. Subsequent federal indictments for vote fraud were based in part on these and other citizen litigation efforts. Project LEAP (Legal Elections in All Precincts), a broadly based citizen group for fair electoral practices, has now been organized to perform a watchdog function over the electoral process.[3]

Legislators and Horse Racing

The racetrack case also involves litigation, but this time against public officials personally—to ask that the profit that they made while serving the state be returned to the state, which is not a very popular approach to insiders.

We filed a citizens' suit against a group of state legislators who purchased stock in a newly formed horse-racing association in the early 1960's. This stock was sold several years later at substantial profits. Our suit asserts that the stock was offered to the legislators with the expectation that they would be influenced to favor the racing association in their legislative activities, that by purchasing it under such circumstances they knowingly placed themselves in a conflict-of-interest position, and that the profits on the subsequent sales should therefore be recovered for the state treasury.

Racial Segregation in Public Housing

We are assisting the ACLU in suits against the Chicago Housing Authority and the federal Department of Housing and Urban Development. These suits have already established the proposition that building public housing exclusively in black neighborhoods violates equal protection rights. Within Chicago a long but so far unsuccessful effort is in progress to require the construction of low-rise scattered-site public housing throughout the city.

Public School Segregation

In the Jones High School case, we exposed the racial imbalance in this public school and how that had been arranged. We placed an ad in the

[3]*Ibid.*, p. 12.

paper and asked for radio support to refer minority applicants to Jones. Now, after some confrontation on the facts, Jones High School is representative of the racial balance in Chicago, particularly important in this case because of the job training that it offers.

Air Pollution in Gary

United States Steel Company's 829 coke ovens are the major source of the polluted brown haze that has dominated the Gary, Indiana scene for many years.

> We were asked to represent the City of Gary in hearings before the Gary Air Pollution Appeal Board, and we succeeded in obtaining an order requiring U.S. Steel to eliminate or substantially reduce the pollution. The order was later affirmed by the Indiana Superior Court. Following the affirmance, U.S. Steel announced it would comply with the order and undertake a major compliance program costing tens of millions of dollars.[4]

In consultation with the city, we are monitoring U.S. Steel's activities to insure that the Appeal Board's order is obeyed. There is now hope for a visible Gary, Indiana.

The Lawyers' Role

BPI has worked in the lawyer's field, too. In one particularly unpopular case before the Bar, we attacked the practice of "forwarding fees," a practice condemned by the Canons of Ethics, but accepted by the courts. Such fees are kickbacks to lawyers who refer the case but do no work for the trial laywer who tries it.

We have raised questions about the discipline of lawyers. In Chicago, the practice has been for the Bar Association to "settle" with any lawyer who repays a complaining client, and any possible criminal charges are foregone. As a result of our exposure of manipulation by the chairman of the Ethics Committee of the local Bar, he was removed, a new system was subsequently recommended and will be put into effect by the Chief Judge of the Illinois Supreme Court.

BPI disclosed that hundreds of lawyers who had volunteered to represent indigent defendants in looting and riot cases had performed no service whatsoever, but had merely joined an illegal bail and preliminary hearing

[4]*Ibid.,* p. 11.

system, a "Chicago special." This issue was hotly debated and eventually made its way into the Illinois constitutional convention. There is now a constitutional provision in Illinois requring prompt preliminary hearing.

The Airport in Lake Michigan

Although all of our work is based on careful, factual analysis, not everything is oriented toward the courts. BPI joined a large coalition of community groups to oppose a lake airport that was heavily favored by the mayor. It was felt that this airport would contribute to water pollution, endanger air safety, and precipitate overwhelming congestion of lakefront communities. We publicized the fact that, although the city was spending thousands of dollars on engineernig feasibility studies, it had refused to undertake any studies of the effect of such an airport on the environment. We operated under the acronym SAIL (Stop the Airport in the Lake), with the slogan, "Don't Do It In The Lake." We distributed posters, buttons, bumper stickers, and printed ads in the newspapers. We received a tremendous response from the public and the press. About six weeks after our campaign began, the mayor, at least temporarily, abandoned plans for the airport in the lake and appointed what has turned out to be an excellent, responsible Air Pollution Control Board.

Government, at least local government, is accountable when the public is aroused. Corporate officials are accountable when their names are shown to the public, and when it is shown they are not what they would like to appear to be.

Accountability for the Environment

Next, dealing again with the problem of accountability for the environment, Commonwealth Edison, our local electrical utility, had been placing full-page newspaper ads to tell all that they had been doing to fight pollution. On careful study we found five particularly outrageous distortions, and published a series of ads. The first one read: "Hey, Commonwealth Edison: We have read your many advertisements, brochures, and public relations releases attempting to explain why you are not the pollution villian we and others have been calling you. And all we can say is HOGWASH! ! !" The five "Hogwashes" were then set out with the name of the Company official responsible for each. Among other assertions, Commonwealth Edison had claimed that they were doing all that could be done to fight pollution in the Chicago area, but they had already applied (with no publicity) to the Air Pollution Control Board for an exemption from the law so that they could continue to burn high sulphur coal. Following our ad campaign, the company reversed its policy, and the company president acknowledged that action such as our efforts helped bring about the changes.

The Mayor's Air Pollution Control Board

With rapidly increasing pollution in Chicago, the occasion of the city's annual "Cleaner Air Week," proclaimed by the mayor, seemed a good time to point out the conflicts of interest of most members of the Air Pollution Control Board, who appeared to serve the major polluters of the city rather than its people. BPI ran a full-page newspaper ad to dramatize the inadequacies of Mayor Daley's board. Shortly after the ad appeared, the mayor dissolved the board and made new appointments, with a promise of more independent action by the board.

BPI's Continuing Efforts

The BPI docket continues to be wide and varied. We are presently involved in a suit against the Chicago City Council for withholding financial records, public by statute, of cable TV applicants. We have a similar case against the Police Board, as the meetings of that august organization have been secret, again contrary to statute. And in a case that we lost only a couple of years ago, we are trying again to strike down a particularly obnoxious statute that permits the forfeiture of private homes to a speculator for a deficiency in real property taxes. In this case, the law is the oppressor, and there is no lobby for reform.

Oddly, it can be said that BPI works within the system. We are interested in working with companies, government agencies, and officials if we can, to inform them and to be informed, to inform the public and to negotiate. But we are loners because we want to be free to continue to expose, to bring litigation that may cause some sort of change, and to be a kind of outside conscience for one part of the business community in the city. We try to fulfill, in the most constructive ways, the second half of Gordon Sherman's slogan for BPI—"*Agito, ergo sum*"—I agitate, therefore I am.

About the Contributors

••

RAYMOND A. BAUER. Professor of Business Administration, Harvard University. He is a consultant to Arthur D. Little, Inc.; a member of the Advisory Committee of the Corporate Information Center and the Council on Economic Priorities; and served in 1970 as senior consultant for the National Goals Research Staff, The White House. His publications include *The Corporate Social Audit*, with Dan H. Fenn, Jr. (Russell Sage Foundation, 1972), *Advertising in America: The Consumer View*, with Stephen A. Greyser (Division of Research, Harvard Business School), and editor of *Social Indicators* (M.I.T. Press), as well as numerous articles in academic and professional journals. He received his Ph.D. degree from Harvard University.

GUENTHER BAUMGART. President, Association of Home Appliance Manufacturers, Chicago. He has been active for many years as a trade association executive, and has worked as a market analyst. He is coeditor of *Your Business and Post war Readjustment*. He received his M.B.A. degree from the University of Chicago.

HOWARD H. BELL. President and Chief Executive, American Advertising Federation, Washington, D.C., an organization providing national representation for all segments of advertising on matters of common concern. He previously served as vice-president, National Association of Broadcasters; was appointed director of the Code Authority, NAB, in 1963; proposed establishment of an effective program of self-regulation in 1970 affecting all advertising in all media and developed policies and procedures that led to the creation in 1971 of the independent National Advertising Review Board. He received his B.A. in advertising from the University of Missouri and a J.D. degree from Catholic University Law School.

533

PHILLIP I. BLUMBERG. Professor of Law, Boston University School of Law, and Chairman of Finance Committee, Federated Development Company. Was previously president of Federated Mortgage Investors, president of United Ventures, Inc., and partner and associate in Szold, Brandwen, Meyers & Blumberg. His publications include "Corporate Responsibility and the Environment" *(Conference Board Record)*, "The Politicalization of the Corporation" *(Business Lawyer)*, and "Corporate Responsibility and the Employee's Duty of Loyalty and Obedience: A Preliminary Inquiry" *(Oklahoma Law Review)*. He received his LL.B. magna cum laude from Harvard Law School.

T. F. BRADSHAW. President, Atlantic Richfield Company; formerly professor, Harvard Business School, and partner in a management consulting firm. He is on the board of directors of, among others, Diebold Venture Capital Corporation, RCA, Champion International, and Aspen Institute for Humanistic Studies, as well as a member of the Executive Council of Harvard Business School Association. He received his D.C.S. from Harvard University.

BERNARD L. BUTCHER. Assistant Vice-president to G. Robert Truex, Executive Vice-president for Social Policy, Bank of America. Served two years in the Peace Corps (Uruguay) and a year as a teacher at Deerfield Academy. He graduated from Stanford University and the Columbia Graduate School of Business.

GERALD F. CAVANAGH. Assistant Professor, Department of Management and Organization Sciences, Wayne State University, and Distinguished Lecturer on Corporate Management and Society, Michigan State University. He is a consultant to Manpower Assistance Project, Inc., which designs and provides training for the disadvantaged. His publications include *Blacks in the Industrial World: Issues for the Manager*, with Theodore V. Purcell (Free Press, 1972) and "Alternative Routes to Employing the Disadvantaged Within the Enterprise," with Theodore V. Purcell, in *Proceedings of the 22nd Annual Meeting of the Industrial Relations Research Association* (1969). He received his D.B.A. degree from Michigan State University.

JULES COHN. Professor of Political Science and Chairman, Department of Urban Affairs, City University of New York, Manhattan Community College. He is senior consultant for Employment Opportunity Research, Department of Human Resources Development, American Telephone & Telegraph Company, Inc.; principal investigator for a project on organizational experiences and their effects on employee attitudes toward work, U.S. Department of Labor; and consultant to Human Interaction Research Institute, Los Angeles. His publications include *The Conscience of the Corporations: Business and Urban Affairs (Johns Hopkins*

Press); The Urban Affairs of Business (special issue of *Urban Affairs Quarterly);* coeditor of *Man, Culture, and Society* (Brooklyn College Press); and numerous articles dealing primarily with business and its urban problems. He received his Ph.D. from Rutgers—The State University, New Brunswick, New Jersey.

JOHN W. COLLINS. Assistant Professor of Law and Public Policy, School of Management, Syracuse University. His primary academic interest is the interaction of business and society. He has written and done considerable consulting on the subject of implementing policies of social responsibility, and he previously practiced corporate law. He received his J.D. degree from Harvard University.

PHILLIP T. DROTNING. Director of Urban Affairs, Standard Oil Company (Indiana). He has been cited by President Nixon, Chicago's Coalition for United Community Action, and *Engineering News-Record* for contributions in the field of minority enterprise and employment; has been named vice-chairman of the National Minority Purchasing Council, sponsored by the Department of Commerce. He has authored *Black Heroes in Our Nation's History, Up from the Ghetto, A Guide to Negro History in America,* and *A Job With a Future in the Petroleum Industry;* he is currently under contract for other books, one of which deals with the role of business in urban problem solving. He is a graduate of the University of Wisconsin.

MELVIN A. EISENBERG. Professor in the School of Law, University of California, Berkeley. Previously served as assistant counsel on the Warren Commission and as assistant corporation counsel in New York City, where he was also active on several task forces appointed by Mayor Lindsay. He was a visiting professor of law at Harvard Law School in 1969-1970 and a Guggenheim fellow in 1971-1972. He is the author of a series of articles on the legal roles of shareholders and management in the modern corporation and is currently writing a book on that subject.

DAN H. FENN, Jr. Director of the John F. Kennedy Library; Professor of Business Administration, Harvard University; and Senior Associate of the Harvard-M.I.T. Joint Center on Urban Studies. In 1961 he served as staff assistant to President Kennedy in the development of a continuing talent search for top presidential appointees; was appointed by President Kennedy in 1963 as commissioner on the United States Tariff Commission; and was appointed vice-chairman of the Tariff Commission by President Johnson in 1964. He was also the first director of the World Affairs Council of Boston. He is the editor of a seven-volume management series published by McGraw-Hill Book Co., coauthor of *Business Decision Making and Government Policy,* and coauthor of a book on the social audit published by the Russell Sage Foundation. He has also published articles in several journals, including *Harvard Business Review.* He received his

M.A. degree from Harvard University and an honorary LL.D. from Nasson College.

MERVIN D. FIELD. Founder and President of Field Research Corporation, San Francisco and Los Angeles, which conducts consumer market research for a wide array of clients, including several large corporations, government agencies, and nonprofit institutions. He inaugurated the *California Poll*, which has published more than 700 reports on public preferences for candidates, candidate images, public opinion on election issues, and public response to a variety of concerns.

CHRIS G. GANOTIS. Member of the corporate staff of The MITRE Corporation. He is presently involved in evaluating resource recovery grants proposals submitted by cities to the Environmental Protection Agency. While in the M.B.A. program at Syracuse University, he developed a graduate course syllabus, "The Managerial Role in Environmental Issues." This was later included in an education research proposal that resulted in a Sloan Foundation grant to the Syracuse University School of Management. He received his B.B.A. from Syracuse University.

REBECCA A. GOULD. Doctoral student and Research Assistant in the field of marketing and quantitative business analysis, Pennsylvania State University. Served as executive trainee at Bloomingdale Brothers Department Store, New York, and as sales manager, Bambergers, Menlo Park. She received her B.S. degree from Ohio State University.

DANIEL H. GRAY. Senior Staff Consultant in the Management Counseling Division, Arthur D. Little, Inc., heading a project to develop that company's competence in corporate social responsibility and social accounting. He previously taught economics in a number of universities. He received his Ph.D. in economics and law from Massachusetts Institute of Technology.

JERROLD M. GROCHOW. Management Consultant for American Management Systems, Inc., Arlington, Virginia. While a student at M.I.T. he was president and founder of ECIS, a student consulting firm specializing in seminars with executives on youth, values, and the future of corporations in society. He holds degrees in electrical engineering and computer science from M.I.T. and received his Ph.D. in Management Science from the Sloan School of Management, M.I.T.

GEORGE P. HINCKLEY. Vice-president of the Marketing Services Department of Travelers Insurance Companies and a Director of Broadcast-Plaza, Inc.; Carribbean Atlantic Life Insurance Co. Ltd. (Kingston, Jamaica); and Travelers

Equities Sales, Inc. He has also served as vice-president of the Life, Health, and Financial Services Department of the company. He is a graduate of Queens College, New York.

NEIL H. JACOBY. Professor of Business Economics and Policy and Dean, Graduate School of Business Administration, University of California, Los Angeles. Served as chairman, Task Force on Economic Growth, 1969, and head of the U.S. Aid Evaluation Mission to Taiwan, 1965. His consultancies include the Board of Governors of the Federal Reserve System, U.S. Treasury Department, RAND Corporation, General Motors Corporation, Bank of America, Transamerica Corporation, and Standard Oil of California. He received his Ph.D. degree from the University of Chicago.

MARY GARDINER JONES. Federal Trade Commissioner, nominated by President Johnson in 1964 to fill an unexpired term and was reappointed for a full seven-year term in 1966. She has worked in New York City with Donovan, Leisure, Newton & Irvine in general law practice; as special assistant to General William J. Donovan of the Department of Justice, Antitrust Division; and with the law firm of Webster, Sheffield, Fleischmann, Hitchcock & Chrystie in trial and antitrust work. She has served as vice-president of Yale Law School Association in the District of Columbia; is currently a member of the Committee on Scientific and Technical Information of the Federal Council for Science and Technology. Her publications include articles in various legal, business, and financial periodicals, such as *Law and Computer Technology, Nation's Business*, and the *Yale Law Journal*. She received her J.D. degree from Yale University Law School.

DONALD L. KANTER. Professor of Marketing and Chairman of the Department of Marketing and Communications at the University of Southern California. He is marketing services consultant to and director of Tinker, Dodge and Delano, Inc. of the Interpublic group of companies; formerly served as vice-president, Marketing Services, at Carson/Roberts/Inc., Los Angeles; director of Marketing Services for Smith-Warden, Ltd., London; and international vice-president of SSC&B/ LINTAS International, New York. He was also vice-president and director of research for Tatham-Laird & Kudner, Chicago, for ten years. He is the collaborating author of *Advertising in America: The Consumer View*. He is a graduate of Antioch College.

ROBERT N. KATZ. Member of the faculty, University of California, Berkeley, teaching Legal, Political, and Social Environment of Business; and Editor of *California Management Review*. He was formerly solicitor, Federal Maritime Commission, and previously practiced law. He is coauthor of *Business Decision*

Making and Government Policy, and the author of articles on government regulation of business. He has a J.D. degree from the University of Texas and an M.B.A. degree from Harvard University.

EUGENE J. KELLEY. Research Professor of Business Administration, Pennsylvania State University, Editor of the *Journal of Marketing,* and Prentice-Hall's Foundations of Marketing Series. He was named "Marketing Educator of the Year" in 1969 by Sales and Marketing Executives-International. His publications include *Marketing Planning and Competitive Strategy, Managerial Marketing: Perspectives and Viewpoints,* and *Business Administration: Problems and Functions.* His current research is concerned with marketing planning, social marketing, the integration of technology, and interdisciplinary approaches to marketing management. He received his Ph.D. degree from New York University.

LOUIS M. KOHLMEIER, Jr. Washington, D.C., Correspondent for the *Wall Street Journal.* Won the Pulitzer Prize and the Sigma Delta Chi award (1965) for articles concerning the growth of the Lyndon Johnson family fortune through the ownership of broadcast properties regulated by an agency of the federal government. Is the author of *The Regulators: Watchdog Agencies and Public Interest* (Harper & Row, 1969). He received the degree of Bachelor of Journalism from the University of Missouri.

JOHN E. LOGAN. Assistant Professor of Management, University of South Carolina and member of the Board of Directors of the Southern Management Association. His publications include *An Analysis of Workmen's Compensation: South Carolina and the Nation* (University of South Carolina, 1972), "State and Local Government Expenditures: South Carolina and the Region" *(Business and Economic Review),* and "Teachers' Salaries and Unrest: The Nation and South Carolina" *(ibid.).* He received his Ph.D. degree from Columbia University.

CHANNING H. LUSHBOUGH. Associate Director of Consummers Union of the United States, publisher of *Consumer Reports;* serves as leader of the *ad hoc* Consumer Advisory Group, U.S. Food and Drug Administration; served as vice-president, Planning & Development for Associated Hospital Service of New York. He has published *Life Insurance* (2nd ed.), *The Injury Industry and the Remedy of No-Fault Auto Insurance, The Great American Motor Sickness,* and *Defending the Environment.* He received his Ph.D. from the University of Chicago.

NICHOLAS J. MAMMANA. Director of Marketing Research for American Telephone and Telegraph Company. Was previously assistant vice-president of revenue for American Telephone and Telegraph, and was lecturer at St. John's University. He received his M.B.A. from St. John's University.

JOHN TEPPER MARLIN. Professor of Finance, School of Business Administration, Baruch College, City University of New York. He served for five years in Washington as program analyst and economist for the federal government; was economic consultant for the Nader study, *The Interstate Commerce Omission.* His publications include "Is Pollution Profitable?: The Case of the Pulp and Paper Industry," coauthored with Joseph Bragdon, Jr. *(Risk Management),* and a review of corporate annual reporting for *Business and Society Review* coauthored with his wife, Alice Tepper Marlin. He is editor of his own journal, *Financial Education.* He is a graduate of Harvard, Oxford, and George Washington Universities.

ARTHUR B. MOORE, Jr. Timberlands Property Accountant, Westvaco Corporation. Served as junior labor market analyst for the South Carolina Employment Security Commission. He is currently enrolled in the M.B.A. program at the University of South Carolina.

PHILIP W. MOORE. Executive Director of the Project on Corporate Responsibility, Washington, D.C. He previously served as attorney with Devoe, Shadur, Mikva and Plotkin, a Chicago firm, and as executive director of the ACLU Convention Litigation Project. He received his LL.B. degree from the University of Chicago Law School.

JOHN L. PALUSZEK. President of Corporate Social Action, Inc., and its parent company, John Paluszek and Associates. Served as executive vice-president of Basford Public Relations, Inc.; is chairman of the Public Service Committee of the New York Chapter of the Public Relations Society of America; and is a member of PRSA's National Task Forces on Environment and State and Local Governments and the Urban Task Force of the Black Heritage Association. He is a graduate of Manhattan College.

MARSHALL PATNER. General Counsel, Businessmen and the Public Interest Law Firm, and Visiting Associate Professor at the University of Illinois Circle Campus. His publications include *Appointed Counsel's Guide for Criminal Appeals* (Callaghan and Co., 1968) and *Trial and Appeal Criminal Cases* (Institute for Continuing Legal Education, 1972). He received his J.D. degree from the University of Chicago Law School.

LEO M. PELLERZI. Assistant Attorney General for Administration, Justice Department, Washington, D.C., responsible for the department's business management. He served as a legislative attorney with the Economic Stabilization Agency; assistant general counsel of Subversive Activities Control Board; and trial examiner with the Interstate Commerce Commission. He received the Federal Bar

Association Award as outstanding career lawyer in government in 1967; the Commissioners' Award of the Civil Service Commission in 1968; and the Charles J. Bonaparte Award of the Italian Executives of America, for outstanding public service in the administration of justice. He holds a J.D. and LL.M. degree from George Washington University.

JAMES E. POST. Research Assistant and Ph.D. candidate, State University of New York at Buffalo. Has held faculty positions at St. Bonaventure University and S.U.N.Y. at Buffalo. His publications deal with cable television regulation, business and society relations, and corporate responsibility. He received his J.D. degree at the School of Law, Villanova University, and his M.B.A. from the State University of New York at Buffalo.

THEODORE V. PURCELL. Research Professor, Jesuit Center for Social Studies at Georgetown University. His publications include *Cases in Business Ethics* (Appleton-Century-Crofts, 1968), *The Negro in the Electrical Industry* (University of Pennsylvania Press, 1971), and *Blacks in the Industrial World: Issues for the Manager*, with Gerald F. Cavanagh (Free Press, 1972). His articles include "Work Psycology and Business Values" *(Personnel Psychology)*, "Break Down Your Employment Barriers" *(Harvard Business Review)*, "Case of the Borderline Black" *(ibid.)*, and "Young Black Workers Speak Their Minds" *(California Management Review)*. He received his Ph.D. in Social and Industrial Psychology at Harvard University as a Wertheim Fellow.

LEE RICHARDSON. Director, Consumer Education, Office of Consumer Affairs, Washington, D.C.; on leave from Louisiana State University. Member, President Nixon's Consumer Advisory Council, 1970-1972; vice-chairman, FTC Regional Consumer Advisory Board (New Orleans), 1971-1972. His publications include *Readings in Finance* (1966), *Readings in Marketing: The Qualitative and Quantitative Areas* (1967), and *Dimensions of Communication* (1969), all published by Appleton-Century Crofts. He received his D.B.A. degree from the University of Colorado.

DONALD E. SCHWARTZ. Professor of Law, Georgetown University Law Center; Director, Project on Corporate Responsibilities, and Counsel to Campaign GM; a member of the Committee on Federal Regulation of Securities of the American Bar Association and of the Advisory Board of the *Securities Law and Regulation Reporter* published by the Bureau of National Affairs. He is co-author of the *Manual for Corporation Officers* (Roland Press, 1967) and has lectured and written extensively in the fields of securities regulation and business organization. He received his LL.B. degree from Harvard Law School.

S. PRAKASH SETHI. Associate Professor of Business Administration, University of California, Berkeley. Author of *Business Corporations and the Black Man: An Analysis of Social Conflict, the Kodak-Fight Controversy* (Chandler, 1970); *Up Against the Corporate Wall* (Prentice-Hall, 1971); and with Dow Votaw, *The Corporate Dilemma* (Prentice-Hall, 1973). He is contributing editor to *Business and Society Review*, a frequent contributor to professional and academic journals, and consultant to various American and European corporations. He received his Ph.D. degree from Columbia University.

JAGDISH N. SHETH. Professor of Business and Research at University of Illinois, Urbana-Champaign, and was previously on the faculty of Columbia University and M.I.T. His main areas of interest and research are consumer psychology, multivariate statistics, and international marketing. He is coauthor, with J. A. Howard, of *The Theory of Buyer Behavior* and has published widely in professional and academic journals. He received his Ph.D. degree from the University of Pittsburgh.

ALLAN D. SHOCKER. Lecturer, Graduate School of Business Administration, University of California, Berkeley. Has served as assistant to the Dean, Graduate School of Industrial Administration, Carnegie-Mellon University, and as visiting professor at the University of Pittsburgh. His publications include "An Analytic Methodology for the Generation of Product Ideas," in *Proceedings of the Fall Conference of the American Marketing Association,* "A Methodological Approach to the Identification of Mass Transit Configurations Providing Maximal Satisfaction to Users," in *Proceedings of the Second Annual Meeting of the American Institute for Decision Sciences,* and, forthcoming, "Linear Programming Techniques for the Multidimensional Analysis of Preferences" *(Psychometrika),* and "Development of a Composite Criterion of Managerial Success" *(Organizational Behavior and Human Performance).* He received his Ph.D. from Carnegie-Mellon University.

TIM SMITH. Executive Secretary, Interfaith Committee on Social Responsibility in Investments, a coalition of ten Protestant denominations concerned about various questions of corporate responsibility, such as equal opportunity employment practices, ecology, and advertising practices. He formerly worked as assistant for African Affairs, Council for Christian Social Action, United Church of Christ, and has been concerned with issues of corporate responsibility for the past five years.

ERNEST S. STARKMAN. Vice-president of General Motors for the Environment Activities Staff, concentrating on the performance of GM products in the environment. He served as professor of mechanical engineering at University of California, Berkeley; chairman of Technical Advisory Committee to State of California Air Resources Board; chairman of Advisory Committee on Advanced Power Systems to the Council on Environmental Quality; member of Technical Advisory Board, U.S. Department of Commerce; and recently as a member of the White House Task Force on Air Pollution. He is the recipient of Society of Automotive Engineers' Horning Award and Medal and the Colwell Award for presentations relating to engine combustion. He received his M.S. degree from the University of California, Berkeley.

JOHNNY STEWART. M.B.A. student in personnel management and industrial relations at Wayne State University, Detroit. Has served as admissions counselor, University of Michigan; personnel representative, Vickers Division, Sperry Rand Corporation; and coorganizer of Association of Black Business Students, Wayne State University.

FRANK J. TONER. Manager, Employee Relations Management and Practices, General Electric Company, where he is responsible for corporate direction of policy and practices throughout the company in such areas as equal opportunity, minority relations, and management employee relations. He has served with General Electric in a variety of union and employee relations management positions, including manager of Relations and Utilities for Power Transmission Division, generalist consultant in Employee Relations, and manager of Equal Opportunity and Minority Relations. He is a graduate of Columbia University.

DOW VOTAW. Professor of Business Administration, University of California, Berkeley, and member of the State Bar of California and the American Bar Association, including the antitrust, corporation, banking, and business law sections. He has authored several books, including *Legal Aspects of Business Administration* (Prentice-Hall, 1966), *The Six-Legged Dog: A Study in Power* (University of California Press, 1964), *Modern Corporations* (Prentice- Hall, 1965), and, with S. Prakash Sethi, *The Corporate Dilemma* (Prentice-Hall, 1973). He has written many articles for professional journals on such subjects as corporations, social responsibility, antitrust policy, and legal history. He received his M.B.A. and J.D. degrees from Harvard University.

FRANK WHITE. Director, Corporate Information Center, National Council of Churches, New York City. He has been involved in business sales and management for several years. He is a graduate of Boston University and received his B.D. degree from Yale Divinity School.

IAN H. WILSON. Consultant, Business Environment and Planning for General Electric Company, responsible for research and analysis of future environmental trends affecting corporate planning. Worked with General Electric's Management Institute at Crotonville, New York, planning management education and development activities. He is coauthor, with Earl B. Dunckel and William K. Reed (both of General Electric), of *The Business Environment of the Seventies* (McGraw-Hill Book Co., 1970). He received his M.A. degree from St. John's College, Oxford University.

WILLIAM J. WILSON. President and Chief Executive Officer of Daniel Starch & Staff, Inc. Formerly served as executive vice-president of International Research Associates, in charge of business development; was previously employed by *Reader's Digest*, in charge of advertising in the United States, and for several years with the Reader's Digest Association in Europe as international advertising development manager. He is a graduate of Yale University and holds an M.A. degree equivalent in historical studies from Corpus Christi College, Cambridge, England.

Index

545